31   In 1940, it took 12 weeks to produce a full-grown chicken

32   In 1991, it took 6 weeks to produce a full-grown chicken

33   50% of all solar energy equipment manufactured in the U.S. in 1989 was exported

3 THE HUMAN RESOURCE

34   4% of Fortune 500 companies' personnel departments have used genetic screening or monitoring

35   Since 1989, the size of the average corporate vice president's office has decreased 25%

36   In 1984, 72% of companies with fewer than 100 employees paid all employee health insurance premiums

37   In 1990, 48% did

38   9% of employed Americans work in a shopping center or mall

39   The travel and tourism industry employs approximately 1 person in every 15 worldwide

40   The average ratio of a CEO's salary to that of a blue-collar worker at major Japanese car manufacturers is 20 to 1

41   The average ratio of a CEO's salary to that of a blue-collar worker at major U.S. car manufacturers is 192 to 1

42   White residents are the majority in 3 of the 10 largest U.S. cities today

43   In 1980, whites were the majority in 6 of the 10 largest cities

44   Approximately 284,600 Americans work for Japanese companies in the U.S.

45   50% of two-income families would drop below the poverty line if the wife did not work

46   The 4 managers of the Moscow McDonald's attended the Canadian Institute of Hamburgerology for 9 months

47   Approximately 50% of all MBAs ever awarded were given in the 1980s

4 MARKETING

48   In the U.S., approximately 17 square feet per capita of the total landmass is devoted to shopping malls

49   An item of food consumed in the U.S. has traveled an average of 1,200 miles before being eaten

50   The Campbell Soup Company estimates that 25% of all cars in the year 2000 will be equipped with microwave ovens

51   Asian-Americans are most likely to buy a Ford

52   U.S. telemarketers make approximately 200 unsolicited calls per second

53   In 1990, Levi Strauss received 802,000 calls from people describing what they do in their Levis 501 jeans

54   95% of the food advertising on Saturday morning TV is for junk food

55   The cost of the can in which Coca-Cola is packaged is twice the cost of the beverage in the can

56   Since 1980, the amount of junk mail an American receives each year has increased by 17 pounds

57   In the first two months after the release of Teenage Mutant Ninja Turtles, $500,000,000 was made on sales of merchandise

58   Approximately 200,000,000 M&Ms are sold each day in the U.S.

59   33% of American college students say they use a microwave oven every day

60   Since 1980, the number of American families composed of a housewife, an employed husband, and 2 children has dropped 21%

61   Since 1990, the number of new "gourmet" products introduced in U.S. stores has increased 66%

BUSINESS

FOURTH EDITION

BUSINESS

FOURTH EDITION

William M. Pride

Texas A & M University

Robert J. Hughes

Dallas County Community College

Jack R. Kapoor

College of DuPage

Houghton Mifflin Company   **Boston**   **Toronto**

Dallas   Geneva, Illinois   Palo Alto

Princeton, New Jersey

To Nancy, Allen, and Michael Pride

To Peggy Hughes

*To My parents, Ram and Sheela; My wife, Theresa;
and My children, Karen, Kathy, and Dave*

Credits

Box Credits
Chapter 1
10 Based on information fron Stephanie Anderson Forest, "PC Slump? What PC Slump?" *Business Week*, July 1, 1991, pp. 66–67;

Photo Credits
Pages ii–iii Tom Van Sant/The Stock Market/Ametek.
Chapter 1
Part 1 opener Herbert Lanks/Superstock. **4** ©Masterson, Inc. **6** courtesy Blockbuster Entertainment **7** Globe Staff Photo/John Blanding. **10** Fortune is a registered trademark of the Time Inc. Magazine Co., cover reproduced by permission. **14** The Bancroft Library. **16** Kevin Vesel/Adventure Photo. **22** ©L. Ka Tai. **28** ©M. Abramson. **32** ©Dwight Carter. **(Credits continued on p. C1)**

Sponsoring Editor: *Diane L. McOscar*
Managing Development Editor: *Patricia L. Menard*
Project Editor: *Susan Westendorf*
Production/Design Coordinator: *Renee LeVerrier*
Manufacturing Coordinator: *Holly Schuster*
Cover Design: *Linda Manley Wade*

Printed in the U.S.A.

Library of Congress Catalog Card Number 92-72397

Student ISBN: 0-395-63340-0

Instructor's Annotated Edition ISBN: 0-395-64012-1

3456789-DW-96 95 9 4 93

Brief Contents

v

Contents

Preface

Just in the past two years, we have seen an unprecedented number of important changes in the political, social, technological, and economic fabric of the world. The Soviet Union has collapsed. New countries are being created in Eastern Europe. Full-function computers fit in the palm of your hand. Major U.S. banks have failed and business bankruptcies have become commonplace. Meanwhile, new industries, such as biotechnology, and new businesses, such as Dell Computer, are growing quickly. The impact these changes have on the way we do business today means that we must be more prepared than ever to tackle these challenges and meet these opportunities.

Challenges and opportunities are not only to be found within the borders of the United States. Today, the world of business is indeed the entire world. People from many countries have opened new businesses or branch offices here and business people from the United States have done the same abroad. This exchange of talent and expertise has brought greater and greater cultural diversity into the work force, from the shop floor to the board room.

The fourth edition of *Business* provides professors and students with the most current, dynamic, and interesting text available—one that mirrors the excitement of business itself. We present new topics such as sexual harassment, total quality management, and equity financing, and expand on others, including business ethics, concept testing, and deregulation. These issues as well as many others are integrated into the basic text and are also featured in the vignettes that open each chapter, in boxed inserts, and in cases.

BUILDING GLOBAL AWARENESS AND CULTURAL SENSITIVITY

Today's students will soon be entering a competitive business environment, and the need to build awareness of this new environment is greater than ever before. One of the major themes we have built into this revision is the importance of expanding one's global awareness and sensitivity to cultural differences. Tomorrow's work force will be competing in a world-wide arena. Success will depend on how well students develop a broader, more global perspective on business. Success will also depend on how well students adapt to cultural differences among business people.

To follow this theme, we have introduced some brand new features: a new box feature entitled "Global Perspectives" that brings students in touch with business developments around the world and marginal notes entitled "At a Glance" that give some startling details on our changing, more diverse business environment. In addition, we have woven global and cultural topics into the text itself as often as we could. We also continue to offer a complete chapter dedicated to the international aspects of business, and we have used international examples in many of the chapter-ending cases.

SKILL BUILDING FOR CAREER DEVELOPMENT

Students entering the business world need to know more than just facts about business. They also need to know the skills that will help them succeed. A second major theme of this revision has been to highlight many of the important skills that will help students pursue their chosen careers. A new box feature entitled "Getting Ahead in Business" gives students practical advice on the skills most valued in business. Another new box feature, "Ethical Challenges," focuses on helping students make the right decisions and developing their abilities to think critically about thorny issues. We have also expanded our coverage of career development, with particular emphasis on the skills needed to find the right career. This special attention to career development is also evident in our part-ending "Career Profile" series, which lists requisite skills for many different career paths.

NEW AND EXPANDED SPECIAL BOX PROGRAM

To help us highlight our themes and to help keep the book as current and lively as possible, we have introduced an all-new format of boxes in each chapter. There are five types of boxes throughout the book: "Global Perspectives," "Ethical Challenges," "Focus on Small Business," "Getting Ahead in Business," and "Business Journal."

Global Perspective

As mentioned above, this series of boxes is designed to enhance students' awareness of the globalization and diversity of the business world. Examples include:

- International Business Ethics
- Chinese Entrepreneurship
- Price Shock for Russian Consumers
- Managing Operations in Russian Factories

- MTV Goes Global
- Labor Management Relations in Korea

Ethical Challenges

Also mentioned above, the "Ethical Challenges" special feature is designed to build students' ability to think critically about typical ethical situations that can arise in the business arena. Examples of topics discussed are:

- Sexual Harassment
- Buyer Beware: Scams That Target Consumers
- Problems at TRW Credit Bureau
- Ethics, U.S. Senators, and Lincoln Savings
- Volvo's Unethical Advertising
- Sex in Advertising

Focus on Small Business

Because small companies in the United States outnumber large ones by about nine to one, it follows that many students will either work at small businesses or start their own businesses during their careers. Not only do we devote an entire chapter to small business in Part 1 and include many in-text examples, we discuss numerous aspects of small business in this special feature. Examples include:

- Michael Dell: A Small-Business Owner Who Had a Vision
- Fireworks by Grucci: Bombs Bursting in Air and a Whole Lot More
- Should You Computerize Your Accounting Records?
- Small Businesses Sell Stock to Raise Equity Capital
- Performance Bicycle Shop
- Small Businesses Can Sell to Uncle Sam

Getting Ahead in Business

"Getting Ahead in Business" presents students with practical advice that they can use now. Students are employed in a variety of businesses while going to school. This special feature provides students with skills that can help them on the job today, next week, next year, and throughout their business careers. A sample of topics includes:

- Respect Cultural Differences
- Getting Along with Your Boss
- Romance in the Workplace: Should You Get Involved?
- What It Takes to Be an Entrepreneur
- Asking for a Raise
- Packaging Yourself in Business Attire

Business Journal

The "Business Journal" series explores a wide range of organizations and contemporary business topics that include business trends, technology, social issues, and success stories. Selected topics include:

- The Malcolm A. Baldrige National Quality Award
- Merger Trends for the 1990s
- Computers: The Next Generation
- Humor in the Workplace
- Does the United States Have Too Many Lawyers?
- Cultural Diversity
- Long-Term Care Insurance

IMPORTANT NEW TOPICS

In addition to the five-part box program, we have updated every chapter in the book with significant new topics of special importance today. Examples include:

- Major business challenges (Chapter 1)
- Business ethics (Chapter 2)
- Global perspectives on small business (Chapter 4)
- Total quality management (Chapter 5)
- Managing cultural diversity (Chapter 9)
- Sexual harassment (Chapter 9)

EFFECTIVE PEDAGOGICAL AIDS

We have worked to make *Business, Fourth Edition,* the most interesting and most pedagogically effective of any introductory business text available. Many of the following pedagogical features in the text have been evaluated and recommended by reviewers with years of teaching experience.

Part Introductions

Each of the text's seven parts begins with a concise description of the materials to follow. From the outset of each part, a student not only is made aware of what's in each part but also has a better understanding of how the chapters in that part fit with the chapters in the rest of the text.

Learning Objectives

A student with a purpose will learn more effectively than a student wandering aimlessly through the text. Therefore, each chapter of *Business* contains clearly stated learning objectives that signal important concepts to be mastered. Together, the chapter previews and learning objectives enable the student to see where each chapter is going. To aid instructors, questions in the *Test Bank* are keyed to the learning objectives.

Chapter Previews

Each chapter is introduced with a preview—a capsule summary of what to expect in the chapter. The student can grasp quickly the major topics in the chapter and the sequence in which they are covered. Each chapter preview also serves as a useful reminder of that chapter's contents when the student is ready to review.

Inside Business

Chapter opening vignettes, entitled "Inside Business," bring business concepts alive for students. With Inside Business we introduce the theme of each chapter focusing on pertinent activities of a real organization, including Blockbuster Video, Charles Schwab, Borden's, the Los Angeles Dodgers, and J.C. Penney. The decisions and activities of these and other familiar organizations not only demonstrate what companies are actually doing but also make the materials in each chapter relevant and absorbing for students. When students become involved in the chapter material, critical thinking and active participation replace passive acceptance, and real learning takes place.

Margin Notes

Two types of margin notes help students understand and retain important concepts. First, to aid the student in building a basic business vocabulary, the definition of each key term (in contrasting color) is placed in the margin near the introduction of the term in the text. Second, each learning objective is positioned near the beginning of the section in which that objective is emphasized. This easy reference to terms and objectives reinforces the learning of business fundamentals.

Stimulating Writing Style

One of our major objectives in *Business, Fourth Edition,* is to communicate to students our enthusiasm for business in a direct, engaging manner. Throughout the book we have used a lucid writing style that builds interest and facilitates students' understanding of the concepts discussed. To ensure that the text is stimulating and easy for students to use, we have given special attention to word choice, sentence structure, and the presentation of business language.

Real-World Examples and Illustrations

Numerous real-world examples drawn from familiar organizations and recognizable products are used in each chapter. How did 7 UP avoid competing directly with Coke and Pepsi? How did Tiffany's change its image and become profitable again? Why has Motorola increased spending for training from $7 million a decade ago to $120 million today? What are the fastest-growing industries in the small business sector? Examples such as these from today's business world catch students' attention and enable them to apply the concepts and issues of each chapter.

Complete End-of-Chapter Materials

Each end-of-chapter summary brings important ideas together for the student. A list of key terms and complete set of review questions reinforces the learning of definitions and concepts. Discussion questions and exercises encourage independent thinking about the issues presented in the chapter.

Cases

Each chapter ends with two cases, based on recognizable organizations. These descriptions of current business issues and activities allow students to make real-world applications of the concepts they've covered in the chapter. Questions suitable for class discussion or individual assignments are provided for each case. Sample case titles include:

- Walt Disney Company: The Magic Is Back
- Rubbermaid: Managing to Succeed
- DEC's AIDS Program
- Saturn's New Age Labor-Management Relations
- Crayola Responds to Its Customers' Needs
- The Good News and Bad News at Microsoft Corporation
- RJR Nabisco's Refinancing Plan
- Employment Agency Scams
- Reacting to Rising Health-Care Costs

Glossary

A glossary containing 700 fundamental business terms appears at the end of our text. The glossary serves as a convenient reference tool to reinforce students' learning of basic business vocabulary. *The glossary is also available in Spanish.*

COMPLETE PACKAGE OF SUPPORT MATERIALS

Accompanying the fourth edition of *Business* is a full array of supplementary materials—instructional tools that both augment learning for students and increase the effectiveness of instructors.

Instructor's Annotated Edition

New to the fourth edition, the Instructor's Annotated Edition provides professors with additional teaching material to facilitate class presentation. Marginal annotations in red type include additional examples, business facts, and quotes from business leaders that help make the text material come alive. Each two-page spread also contains a cross reference to the Test Bank, listing the true/false, multiple-choice, and essay questions that are covered by material on those pages. Finally, references to the transparencies that are not figures from the book are keyed to the appropriate place in the text for discussion purposes.

Business Video File

The *Business Video File* (which is free to adopters) contains twenty-four videotapes—one for each chapter. These videos, many developed by business organizations, provide unique insights into real-world companies and products. Examples of organizations featured in the *Business Video File* include the Malcolm Baldrige National Quality Awards, Union Carbide, the American Small Business Development Centers, and the International Management Group's sports management program. Through these videos, students can see ideas in action in today's business world.

Customized Course Management System

In an effort to address the reality of different teaching styles and needs, we have developed a new course management system that allows instructors to prepare more easily for their classes. With this system, instructors can choose to have the Instructor's Annotated Edition, the Instructor's Resource Manual, and the Transparencies in any one of three ways.

First, for instructors who prefer to carry only a chapter or so to class, we will package unbound sets of the Instructor's Annotated Edition, the Instructor's Resource Manual, and the Transparencies chapter-by-chapter in hanging folders in a wire rack. The rack is also spacious enough to hold the rest of the instructional package.

Second, for those who wish to have access to all three items in class, you can choose to have the Instructor's Annotated Edition, Instructor's Resource Manual, and Transparencies punched and packaged, chapter-by-chapter, in a three-ring binder.

Finally, all components of the Pride/Hughes/Kapoor teaching package will be available in the printed and bound formats you are all familiar with. Those professors who prefer to have the complete set with them in class can simply stack up the bound versions of the books they want and carry them to class. For details concerning the course management system, contact your local Houghton Mifflin representative.

Video-Resource Manual

This manual is designed to help instructors integrate the content of the chapters in the text with the videos in the *Business Video File*. For each chapter video, the title, topic, organization, and length are given. Suggested

- Completion questions
- Answer key

Entrepreneur: A Business Simulation

This business simulation, written by Jerald R. Smith and Peggy Golden of the University of Louisville, allows student players to make business decisions through simulated real-world experiences. *Entrepreneur* involves the planning, start-up, and continuing operation of a retail store. Acting as management teams, students encounter many factors as they make decisions for each phase of the business. Additional support materials are provided for instructors.

Student Enrichment Project Manuals

Written by Kathryn Hegar of Mountain View College, the three project manuals are entitled *Toward a Career in Business, Investing in Business,* and *Opening a Business.*

Toward a Career in Business guides students through the four stages of getting a job: self-assessment, occupational search, employment tools, and success techniques.

Investing in Business helps students learn how to invest money and how to maximize returns on their investments. Students who use *Investing in Business* become familiar with the advantages and disadvantages of various investment instruments and develop skills in acquiring financial information.

Opening a Business introduces students to the details of starting a company. Part One guides students through the process of gathering and analyzing essential information about business ownership. Part Two contains worksheets for students to complete based on their findings in Part One. After completing this project, students should be able to evaluate their skills as entrepreneurs and managers, calculate the capital needed to start a business, determine applicable state and federal regulations, and begin the planning process.

Business Careers

Business Careers, by Robert Luke, compiles information about salary, career ladders, and getting ahead in the fields of marketing, management, accounting, entrepreneurship, and finance in an informal style that students will find enjoyable.

William M. Pride
Robert J. Hughes
Jack R. Kapoor

Acknowledgments

We wish to express a great deal of appreciation to Kathryn Hegar, Mountain View College, for developing the **Study Guide** and the three student-involvement projects. For creating **Entrepreneur: A Business Simulation,** we wish to thank Jerald R. Smith and Peggy Golden, University of Louisville. For her assistance in editing and manuscript development, we are indebted to Pam Swartz. Finally we wish to thank the following people for technical assistance: Kathryn Kapoor, Dave Kapoor, Jennifer Maloney, Jose Mireles, Marissa Salinas, and Zed Eric Stephens.

We appreciate the assistance and suggestions of numerous individuals who have helped improve and refine this text and instructional package. For the generous giving of their time and their thoughtful and useful comments and suggestions, we are indebted to the following reviewers of the fourth edition:

David V. Aiken
Hocking College

Phyllis C. Alderdice
Jefferson Community College

Harold Amsbaugh
North Central Technical College

Ed Atzenhoefer
Clark State Community College

Mary Jo Boehms
Jackson State Community College

James Boyle
Glendale Community College

Steve Bradley
Austin Community College

Tom Brinkman
Cincinnati Technical College

Janice Bryan
Jacksonville College

Howard R. Budner
Manhattan Community College

C. Alan Burns
Lee College

Frank Busch
Louisiana Technical University

Joseph E. Cantrell
DeAnza College

Don Cappa
Chabot College

Lawrence Chase
Tompkins Cortland Community College

Robert J. Cox
Salt Lake Community College

Andrew Curran
Antonelli Institute of Art and Photography

Rex R. Cutshall
Vincennes University

Helen M. Davis
Jefferson Community College

Sam Dunbar
Delgado Community College

Pat Ellebracht
Northeast Missouri State University

John H. Espey
Cecil Community College

Janice M. Feldbauer
Austin Community College

Gregory F. Fox
Erie Community College—City

Michael Fritz
Portland Comm. College at Rock Creek

Fred Fry
Bradley University

Carmine Paul Gibaldi
St. John's University

W. Michael Gough
DeAnza College

Cheryl Davisson Gracie
Washtenaw Community College

Roy Grundy
College of DuPage

Aristotle Haretos
Flagler College

Richard Hartley
Solano Community College

Ronald L. Hensell
Mendocino College

Townsend Hopper

Jenna Johannpeter
Belleville Area College

Gene E. A. Johnson
Clark College

Pat Jones
Eastern New Mexico University

Robert Kegel
Cypress College

Isaac W. J. Keim, III
Delta College

George Kelley
Erie Community College

Kenneth Lacho
University of New Orleans

John Lathrop
New Mexico Junior College

Marvin Levine
Orange County Community College

Carl H. Lippold
Embry-Riddle Aeronautical University

Thomas Lloyd
Westmoreland County Community College

Paul James Londrigan
Mott Community College

Anthony Lucas
Community College of Allegheny County—Allegheny

Gayle J. Marco
Robert Morris College

Irving Mason
Herkimer County Community College

Catherine McElroy
Bucks County Community College

Ina Midkiff-Kennedy
Austin Community College—Northridge

Edwin Miner
Phoenix College

Linda Morable
Richland College

Patricia Murray
Virginia Union University

Robert Nay
Stark Technical College

Gerald O'Bryan
Danville Area Community College

Larry Olanrewaju
Virginia Union University

David G. Oliver
Edison Community College

Constantine Petrides
Manhattan Community College

Joseph Platts
Miami-Dade Community College

Fred D. Pragasam
SUNY at Cobleskill

Rick Rowray
Ball State University

Jill Russell
Camden County College

Martin S. St. John
Westmoreland County Community College

Eddie Sanders, Jr.
Chicago State University

Dennis Shannon
Belleville Area College

Raymond Shea
Monroe Community College

Lynette Shishido
Santa Monica College

Carl Sonntag
Pikes Peak Community College

Jeffrey Stauffer
Ventura College

E. George Stook
Anne Arundel Community College

Lynn Suksdorf
Salt Lake Community College

Richard L. Sutton
University of Nevada—Las Vegas

William A. Syvertsen
Fresno City College

William C. Thompson
Foothill Community College

Karen Thoms
St. Cloud University

James B. Thurman
George Washington University

Patric S. Tillman
Grayson County College

Jay Todes
North Lake College

Charles E. Tychsen
Northern Virginia Community College—Annandale

Ted Valvoda
Lakeland Community College

Robert H. Vaughn
Lakeland Community College

John Warner
The University of New Mexico—Albuquerque

W.J. Waters, Jr.
Central Piedmont Community College

Philip A. Weatherford
Embry-Riddle Aeronautical University

Benjamin Wieder
Queensborough Community College

Paul Williams
Mott Community College

Wallace Wirth
South Suburban College

Nathaniel Woods
Columbus State Community College

Marilyn Young
Tulsa Junior College

Individuals who helped shape the development of previous editions of the text are the following reviewers:

Harold Amsbaugh
North Central Technical College

Carole Anderson
Clarion University

James O. Armstrong, II
John Tyler Community College

Xenia P. Balabkins
Middlesex County College

Charles Bennett
Tyler Junior College

Robert W. Bitter
Southwest Missouri State University

Stewart Bonem
Cincinnati Technical College

James Boyle
Glendale Community College

Lyle V. Brenna
Pikes Peak Community College

Tom Brinkman
Cincinnati Technical College

Harvey S. Bronstein
Oakland Community College

Edward Brown
Franklin University

Joseph Brum
Fayetteville Technical Institute

Clara Buitenbos
Pan American University

Robert Carrel
Vincennes University

Richard M. Chamberlain
Lorain County Community College

Bruce H. Charnov
Hofstra University

William Clarey
Bradley University

J. Michael Cicero
Highline Community College

Robert Coiro
LaGuardia Community College

Don Coppa
Chabot College

Rex Cutshall
Vincennes University

John Daily
St. Edward's University

Harris D. Dean
Lansing Community College

Wayne H. Decker
Memphis State University

William M. Dickson
Green River Community College

M. Dougherty
Madison Area Technical College

Robert Elk
Seminole Community College

Carleton S. Everett
Des Moines Area Community College

Frank M. Falcetta
Middlesex County College

Thomas Falcone
Indiana University of Pennsylvania

Coe Fields
Tarrant County Junior College

Eduardo F. Garcia
Laredo Junior College

Arlen Gastineau
Valencia Community College

Edwin Giermak
College of DuPage

R. Gillingham
Vincennes University

Robert Googins
Shasta College

Joseph Gray
Nassau Community College

Ricky W. Griffin
Texas A & M University

Stephen W. Griffin
Tarrant County Junior College

Roy Grundy
College of DuPage

John Gubbay
Moraine Valley Community College

Rick Guidicessi
Des Moines Area Community College

Ronald Hadley
St. Petersburg Junior College

Carnella Hardin
Glendale Community College

Richard D. Hartley
Solano Community College

Sanford Helman
Middlesex County College

Victor B. Heltzer
Middlesex County College

Leonard Herzstein
Skyline College

Donald Hiebert
Northern Oklahoma College

Nathan Himelstein
Essex Community College

L. Duke Hobbs
Texas A & M University

Marie R. Hodge
Bowling Green State University

Joseph Hrebenak
Community College of Allegheny County, Allegheny Campus

James L. Hyek
Los Angeles Valley College

Sally Jefferson
Western Illinois University

Marshall Keyser
Moorpark College

Betty Ann Kirk
Tallahassee Community College

Edward Kirk
Vincennes University

Patrick Kroll
University of Minnesota, General College

Clyde Kobberdahl
Cincinnati Technical College

Robert Kreitner
Arizona State University

R. Michael Lebda
DeVry Institute of Technology

George Leonard
St. Petersburg Junior College

Melvin Levine
Orange County Community College

Chad Lewis
Everett Community College

William M. Lindsay
Northern Kentucky University

James Londrigan
Mott Community College

Fritz Lotz
Southwestern College

Robert C. Lowery
Brookdale Community College

Sheldon A. Mador
Los Angeles Trade and Technical College

John Martin
Mt. San Antonio Community College

John F. McDonough
Menlo College

L. J. McGlamory
North Harris County College

Charles Meiser
Lake Superior State University

Edwin Miner
Phoenix College

Charles Morrow
Cuyahoga Community College

W. Gale Mueller
Spokane Community College

C. Mullery
Humboldt State University

Robert J. Mullin
Orange County Community College

James Nead
Vincennes University

Jerry Novak
Alaska Pacific University

Jerry O'Bryan
Danville Area Community College

Dennis Pappas
Columbus Technical Institute

Roberta F. Passenant
Berkshire Community College

Clarissa M. H. Patterson
Bryant College

Donald Pettit
Suffolk County Community College

Norman Petty
Central Piedmont Community College

Gloria D. Poplawsky
University of Toledo

Kenneth Robinson
Wesley College

John Roisch
Clark County Community College

Karl C. Rutkowski
Pierce Junior College

P. L. Sandlin
East Los Angeles College

Jon E. Seely
Tulsa Junior College

John E. Seitz
Oakton Community College

J. Gregory Service
Broward Community College, North Campus

Richard Shapiro
Cuyahoga Community College

Anne Smevog
Cleveland Technical College

John Spence
University of Southwestern Louisiana

Nancy Z. Spillman
President, Economic Education Enterprises

Richard J. Stanish
Tulsa Junior College

J. Stauffer
Ventura College

W. Sidney Sugg
Lakeland Community College

Robert E. Swindle
Glendale Community College

Raymond D. Tewell
American River College

George Thomas
Johnston Technical College

Judy Thompson
Briar Cliff College

Jay Todes
North Lake College

Theodore F. Valvoda
Lakeland Community College

Frederick A. Viohl
Troy State University

C. Thomas Vogt
Allan Hancock College

Loren K. Waldman
Franklin University

Stephen R. Walsh
Providence College

Jerry E. Wheat
Indiana University, Southeast Campus

Larry Williams
Palomar College

Gregory J. Worosz
Schoolcraft College

For sharing their pedagogical suggestions in the Teaching Idea Exchange section of the *Instructor's Resource Manual,* we thank the following contributors:

Stephen R. Ahrens
L. A. Pierce College

Dave Aiken
Hocking Technical College

Frederick J. Bartelheim
Truckee Meadow Community College

Catherine Ann Beegan
Winona State University

Mary Jo Boehms
Jackson State Community College

Sanford Boswell
Coastal Carolina Community College

Roy K. Boutwell
Midwestern State University

Sallie Branscom
Virginia Western Community College

John Buckley
Orange County Community College

Michael Cicero
Highline Community College

Thomas F. Collins
Central Florida Community College

Allen Commander
University of Houston, Downtown

Bruce L. Conners
Kaskaskia College

Nancy Copeland
Eastern Michigan University

Robert J. Cox
Salt Lake Community College

Rex R. Cutshall
Vincennes University

John DeNisco
Buffalo State College

James Eason
Coastal Carolina College

Pat Ellebracht
Northeast Missouri State University

Elinor Garely
Rus Hotels

Martin Gerber
Kalamazoo Valley Community College

Wynell Goddard
Tyler Junior College

Patricia A. Green
Nassau Community College

Donald Gren
Salt Lake Community College

Gene E. A. Johnson
Clark College

Ted Johnson
Tarrant County Junior College, NE

Jim Kennedy
Angelina College

Edward J. Kirk
Vincennes University

Chad Lewis
Everett Community College

Ann Maddox
Angelo State University

Normand Martin
Oklahoma State University

T. D. McConnell
Manchester Community College

D. Dwain McInnis
Palo Alto College

John Q. McMillian
Walters State Community College

Robert R. Meyer
Brookhaven College

Sylvia Meyer
Scottsdale Community College

Rebecca W. Mihelcic
Howard Community College

James Miles
Anoka-Ramsey Community College

Charles A. Miller
L. A. Southwest College

Craig Miller
Normandale Community College

Robert A. Moore
South Utah State College

Lewis J. Neisner
SUNY College at Buffalo

Fred D. Pragasam
State University of New York

Larry J. Seibert
Purdue University, North Central

Dennis G. Shine
Fresno City College

Lee Sutherland
Suffolk University

Laura Turano
Mohegan Community College

H. R. Werrell
Rose State College

Diane Williams
Baker College

Blaine R. Wilson
Central Washington University

Lance Wrzesinski
South Puget Sound Community College

Nancy Zeliff
Northwest Missouri State University

BUSINESS

FOURTH EDITION

PART 1

American Business Today

This introductory part of *Business* is an overview of American business. We begin with an examination of the American business system, its basis, and its function within our society. Then we discuss the responsibilities of business as part of that society. Next we move to an important and very practical aspect of business: how businesses are owned and by whom. Finally, because the vast majority of businesses are small, we look at American small business in some detail. Included in this part are:

CHAPTER 1 Foundations of Business

CHAPTER 2 Ethics and Social Responsibility

CHAPTER 3 The Forms of Business Ownership

CHAPTER 4 Small Business, Entrepreneurship, and Franchises

Foundations of Business

CHAPTER PREVIEW

In this chapter, we look briefly at what business is and how it got that way. First we define *business,* noting how business systems satisfy needs and earn profits. Then we look back into American history to see how events have shaped today's business system. Next we examine how the three basic economic questions—what, how, and for whom—are answered in both free-market and planned economies. Then our focus shifts to the four degrees of business competition—pure competition, monopolistic competition, oligopoly, and monopoly. We also describe the role of supply and demand in competition. We conclude this chapter with a discussion of America's mixed economy and the challenges it faces in the future.

Blockbuster Video Scores a Hit with Rental Movies

Wow! What a difference. Those four words describe the 1,934 Blockbuster Video stores located in forty-six states, the District of Columbia, Guam, Puerto Rico, Australia, Chile, Mexico, Venezuela, Canada, and the United Kingdom. Each store is big and well-lighted, and each carries a comprehensive selection of more than five thousand different titles. That's twice as many as most independent—sometimes called mom-and-pop—video stores carry. Blockbuster's comprehensive selection, coupled with an aggressive management team, has made the Florida-based Blockbuster Entertainment Corp.—the parent company of Blockbuster Video—extremely successful in a short period of time. In 1991, the company earned over $93 million, which was 36 percent more than it earned in 1990. Not bad for a company that had only twenty stores in 1987.

The driving force behind Blockbuster's success is H. Wayne Huizenga (pronounced *Hy-zing-uh*). This 53-year-old entrepreneur began his career in the bottled-water business. In the early days, he sold the water, but he made his real money renting refrigerated water coolers. Once he had paid for the water coolers, they became "cash machines." Now, he uses the same basic principle, except that he rents videotapes instead of water coolers. Using its size to full advantage, Blockbuster buys videocassettes for an average of $40 directly from the major movie studios and rents them to customers for $3 for three nights. After a videotape has been rented an average of thirteen times, it's paid for.

Size has also enabled Blockbuster to develop a computer network that tracks the number of times each movie title has been rented. As a result, the firm has more information about its customers' video habits than any of its smaller competitors have on theirs. This information can be used not only to stock the shelves with current titles but also to predict the type of movies people will rent in the

future. Using this information, along with movie reviews and the history of box office success, Blockbuster can choose its new releases. By the way, the firm doesn't carry X-rated movies. Because X-rated videos go against Blockbuster's emphasis on family entertainment, it leaves those movies for the independent video stores.

Although revenue growth and overall profits are expected to slow down in the video-rental industry between now and the year 2000, Blockbuster is taking steps to ensure that its own sales revenues and profits continue to increase for at least the next decade. Blockbuster executives are even planning to increase market share by continuing to open new stores. The firm opened 160 new stores in 1991 and hopes to have 3,000 stores by the year 2000. And Blockbuster just entered the Japanese market. This is an especially important development because Japan is the second-largest video market in the world. (The United States is still the number-one video market in the world.) According to Huizenga, "As the years go on, our biggest problem will be how to invest our excess cash."[1] Too bad all firms don't have this problem![2]

Perhaps the most important characteristic of American business is the freedom of individuals to start a business, to work for a business, to buy or sell ownership shares in a business, and to sell a business outright. Within certain limits imposed mainly to ensure public safety, the owners of a business can produce any legal product or service they choose and sell it at any price they set. This system of business, in which individuals decide what to produce, how to produce it, and at what price to sell it, is called **free enterprise.** It is rooted in our traditional and constitutional right to own property.

free enterprise the system of business in which individuals are free to decide what to produce, how to produce it, and at what price to sell it

Our free enterprise system ensures, for example, that Blockbuster Video can open new stores, rent movies, and even operate in Japan, Guam, Puerto Rico, Australia, and other foreign countries. Our system also gives Blockbuster executives like H. Wayne Huizenga the right to manage the company, compete with hundreds of other video-rental businesses, and distribute earnings to stockholders who share in the success of the company. Finally, our system allows customers the right to choose between Blockbuster Video's product—rental movies—and similar products from other firms.

Conch and passion fruit, anyone? Entrepreneurs Yves Michel and Therese Brisson satisfy patrons' hunger for Creole cooking, not in New Orleans but in Cambridge, Massachusetts. Not everyone cares for a meal of goat, passion fruit, and conch, but Chez-Vous will survive as a business as long as it draws enough customers to make a profit for its owners.

Competition like that between Blockbuster Video and hundreds of smaller video stores is a necessary and an extremely important by-product of free enterprise. Because many individuals and groups can open businesses, there are sure to be a number of firms offering similar products. But a potential customer may want only one such product—say, a Jeep Cherokee or an Isuzu Rodeo—and not be interested in purchasing both. Each of the firms offering similar products must therefore try to convince the potential customer to buy its product rather than a similar item made by someone else. In other words, these firms must compete with each other for sales. Business **competition,** then, is essentially a rivalry among businesses for sales to potential customers. In free enterprise, competition works to ensure the efficient and effective operation of American business. Competition also ensures that a firm will survive only if it serves its customers well.

In the next section we begin with a definition of business. We also discuss why a business must be organized, satisfy needs, and earn a profit. Finally, we examine three specific reasons why people study business.

BUSINESS: A DEFINITION

LEARNING OBJECTIVE 1
Define *business* and identify potential risks and rewards.

Business is the organized effort of individuals to produce and sell, for a profit, the goods and services that satisfy society's needs. The general term *business* refers to all such efforts within a society (as in "American business") or within an industry (as in "the steel business"). However, *a business* is a particular organization, such as American Airlines, Inc., or Sunnyside Country Store & Gas Pumps, Inc. To be successful, a business must be organized and satisfy needs.

The Organized Effort of Individuals

No person or group of people actually organized American business as we know it today. Rather, over the years individuals have organized their own particular businesses for their own particular reasons. All these individual businesses have given rise to what we call American business.

A person who risks his or her time, effort, and money to start and operate a business is called an **entrepreneur.** To organize a business, an entrepreneur must combine four kinds of resources: material, human, financial, and informational. *Material* resources include the raw materials used in manufacturing processes, as well as buildings and machinery. *Human* resources are the people who furnish their labor to the business in return for wages. The *financial* resource is the money required to pay employees, purchase materials, and generally keep the business operating. And *information* is the resource that tells the managers of the business how effectively the other resources are being combined and used (see Figure 1.1).

Today, businesses are usually classified as one of three specific types. *Manufacturing businesses* are organized to process various materials into

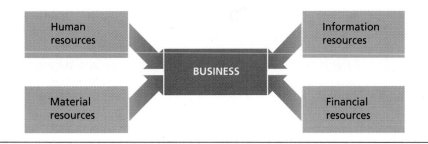

FIGURE 1.1
Combining Resources
All four resources must be combined effectively for a business to be successful.

tangible goods, such as delivery trucks or towels. *Service businesses* produce services, such as haircuts or legal advice. And some firms—called *marketing middlemen*—are organized to buy the goods produced by manufacturers and then resell them. For example, the General Electric Co. is a manufacturer that produces clock radios and stereo "boxes," among other things. These products may be sold to a marketing middleman such as K mart Corp., which then resells them to consumers in its retail stores. **Consumers** are individuals who purchase goods or services for their own personal use rather than to resell them.

consumers individuals who purchase goods or services for their own personal use rather than to resell them

Satisfying Needs

The ultimate objective of every firm must be to satisfy the needs of its customers. People generally don't buy goods and services simply to own them; they buy products to satisfy particular needs. People rarely buy an automobile solely to store it in a garage; they do, however, buy automobiles to satisfy their need for transportation. Some of us may feel that this need is best satisfied by an air-conditioned BMW with stereo compact-disc player, automatic transmission, power seats and windows, and remote-control side mirrors. Others may believe that a Ford Motor Co. Escort with a stick shift and an AM radio will do just fine. Both products are available to those who want them, along with a wide variety of other products that satisfy the need for transportation.

When firms lose sight of their customers' needs, they are likely to find the going rough. This is especially true for firms involved in international trade when they are not sure who their customer is or what their customer wants. But when the businesses that produce and sell goods and services understand their customers' needs and work to satisfy those needs, they are usually successful. Arkansas-based Wal-Mart Stores, Inc. provides the products its customers want and offers excellent prices. This highly successful discount-store organization is expanding throughout the United States.

Business Profit

In the course of normal operations, a business receives money (sales revenue) from its customers in exchange for goods or services. It must also pay out money to cover the various expenses involved in doing business. If the firm's sales revenue is greater than its expenses, it has earned a profit.

FOCUS ON SMALL BUSINESS

Michael Dell: A Small-Business Owner Who Had a Vision

According to *Fortune* magazine, a business must do two things if it really wants to be successful. First, it must put the customer first—listening, understanding, and serving. Second, a firm's management must act with speed and flexibility.* Using those two standards, Michael Dell—the twenty-six-year-old chairman of the board of Austin-based Dell Computer Corporation—achieves a perfect score on both counts. In just eight years, Dell Computer has made its mark in the computer industry because of Michael Dell's ability to see an opportunity that larger competitors like International Business Machines Corp. and Apple Computer, Inc. ignored.

For Michael Dell, this success story started in high school when he became a computer whiz kid. Later, while attending the University of Texas, he began buying personal computers from local retailers who had excess inventory. He supercharged them with new disk drives, enlarged memories, and improved monitors. Then he sold them at a discount through ads in local newspapers and computer magazines. Dell's souped-up computers handled more data faster than machines manufactured by the so-called leaders in the computer industry. As an added bonus, they could be tailored to the needs of Dell's customers. During its first nine months of operation, Dell Computer generated $6 million in revenues—a staggering amount for a firm that began as a one-man show on a part-time basis operating out of a college dorm room.

Early success enabled Dell Computer to concentrate on what it does best—selling computers over the telephone. According to Michael Dell, "Customers tell us what they want and we build computers to meet their needs and ship them out, usually within three working days."** And in many cases, customers can purchase Dell's "customized" computers for 30 to 50 percent less than store brands. In addition to lower prices, direct selling has enabled Dell Computer to stay in touch with its customers. By constantly talking with customers over toll-free phone lines, Dell Computer can find out what customers like and dislike. As a result, the company has incorporated into its new product lines numerous small improvements that give Dell Computer's products an edge over those of its competitors.

According to most industry analysts, the reason Dell Computer is so successful is that it offers service that larger competitors can't match. Just recently, Dell's personal computers were ranked number one for customer satisfaction in a survey conducted by J. D. Power & Associates. And Michael Dell—now worth an estimated $200 million—plans to stay on top. When asked about his goals for Dell Computer, he said, "We want to be the leading supplier of computers to the end user. We don't want to be number two."

* Alan Deutschman, "America's Fastest Risers," *Fortune*, October 7, 1991, p. 48.

** Banning Kent Lary, "An Instinct for Computer Success," *Nation's Business*, April 1991, p. 47.

TOP MUTUAL FUNDS • ASIA'S GROWING POWER • STRESS ON THE JOB

FORTUNE

AMERICA'S
100
FASTEST-
GROWING
COMPANIES

At 26,
Michael Dell
heads a
$679-million-a-year
computer firm

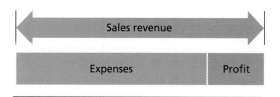

FIGURE 1.2
The Relationship Between Sales Revenue and Profit
Profit is what remains after all business expenses have been deducted from sales revenue.

profit what remains after all business expenses have been deducted from sales revenue

More specifically, as shown in Figure 1.2, **profit** is what remains after all business expenses have been deducted from sales revenue. (A negative profit, which results when a firm's expenses are greater than its sales revenue, is called a *loss*.)

The profit earned by a business becomes the property of its owners. So in one sense profit is the return, or reward, that business owners receive for producing goods and services that consumers want.

Profit is also the payment that business owners receive for assuming the considerable risks of ownership. One of these is the risk of not being paid. Everyone else—employees, suppliers, and lenders—must be paid before the owners. And if there is no profit, there can be *no* payments to owners. A second risk that owners run is the risk of losing whatever they have put into the business. A business that cannot earn a profit is very likely to fail, in which case the owners lose whatever money, effort, and time they have invested.

Why Study Business?

Most people take American business for granted. And yet, there are at least three reasons why you should study business.

You Can Become a More-Informed Consumer and Investor The world of business surrounds you. You cannot buy a home from a building contractor, a new Trans Am from the local Pontiac dealer, or a Black & Decker electric sander at the Home Depot without entering a business transaction. These and thousands of similar transactions describe the true nature of our American business system. (Remember, satisfying society's needs is one part of the definition of business presented earlier in this chapter.) By studying our business system, you become a more-informed consumer, which means that you will be able to make more intelligent buying decisions and spend your money more wisely. This same basic understanding of business will also make you a more-informed investor.

You Can Be a Better Employee Most consumers and investors are also workers. Today, people are looking for a rewarding career that will provide personal satisfaction and the opportunity to be self-sufficient. The information contained in this text will help you select that "ideal" career. Most workers in the United States work for private enterprise, but there are also employment opportunities with the government and not-for-profit organizations. Each of these areas is discussed in more detail in the remaining chapters of this text.

After you select your career, you must obtain the skills required to be successful. Today's employers are looking for job applicants who can *do something,* not just fill a spot on an organizational chart. Employers expect you to have both the technical skills needed to accomplish a specific task and the ability to get along with people. These skills, plus a working knowledge of our business system, can give you an inside edge when you compete against other job applicants.

You Can Start Your Own Business   Some people prefer to work for themselves, and they open their own businesses. To be successful, business owners must possess many of the same skills that successful employees have. And they must be willing to work hard for long hours. Unfortunately, many small-business firms fail. Seventy percent of new businesses fail within the first five years. The material in Chapter 4 and selected topics and examples included throughout this text will help you decide whether you want to open a small business.

To understand our free-enterprise system as it exists today, you must first trace the history of American business back to its roots. In the next section, we begin by taking a look at business during the colonial period of the United States.

THE DEVELOPMENT OF AMERICAN BUSINESS

American business and the free-enterprise system developed together with the nation itself. All three have their roots in the knowledge, skills, and values that were brought to this country by the earliest settlers. Refer to Figure 1.3 for an overall view of the relationship between our history, the development of our business system, and some major inventions that influenced them both.

The Colonial Period

LEARNING OBJECTIVE 2
Summarize the development of our business system.

The first settlers in the New World were concerned mainly with providing themselves with basic necessities—food, clothing, and shelter. Almost all families lived on farms, and the entire family worked at the business of surviving.

The colonists did indeed survive, and eventually they were able to produce more than they consumed. They used their surplus for trading, mainly by barter, among themselves and with the English trading ships that called at the colonies. **Barter** is a system of exchange in which goods or services are traded directly for other goods and/or services—without using money. As this trade increased, small-scale business enterprises began to appear. Most of these businesses produced farm products, primarily rice and tobacco for export. Other industries that had been founded by 1700 were shipbuilding, lumbering, fur trading, rum manufacturing, and fishing. These industries also produced mainly for export. Interna-

barter   a system of exchange in which goods or services are traded directly for other goods and/or services—without using money

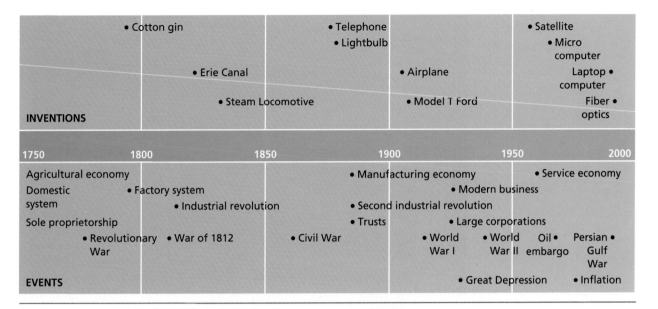

FIGURE 1.3   Time Line of American Business
Notice how invention and innovation naturally led to changes in transportation. This in turn caused a shift to more of a manufacturing economy.

tional trade with England grew, but British trade policies heavily favored British merchants.

As late as the Revolutionary War period, 90 percent of the population lived on farms and were engaged primarily in activities to meet their own needs. Some were able to use their skills and their excess time to work under the domestic system of production. The **domestic system** was a method of manufacturing in which an entrepreneur distributed raw materials to various homes, where families would process them into finished goods. The goods were then offered for sale by the merchant entrepreneur.

During and after the Revolutionary War, Americans began to produce a wider variety of goods, including gunpowder, tools, hats, and cutlery. Later, after the War of 1812, domestic manufacturing and trade became much more important as trade with England and other nations declined.

domestic system a method of manufacturing in which an entrepreneur distributed raw materials to various homes, where families would process them into finished goods to be offered for sale by the merchant entrepreneur

The Industrial Revolution

In 1790 a young English apprentice mechanic named Samuel Slater decided to sail to America. At this time, to protect the English textile industry, British law forbade the export of machinery, technology, and skilled workers. To get around the law, Slater painstakingly memorized the plans for Arkwright's water-powered spinning machine and left England disguised as a farmer. A year later he set up a textile factory in Pawtucket, Rhode Island, to spin raw cotton into thread. Slater's ingenuity resulted in America's first use of the **factory system** of manufacturing, in which all

factory system a system of manufacturing in which all the materials, machinery, and workers required to manufacture a product are assembled in one place

The backbone of the industrial revolution. These somber gentlemen have a reason to look serious and proud. Their railroad, and others like it around the country, carried vital raw materials and finished goods to and from the centers of the industrial revolution. For 150 years, railroads have been essential to America's industrial growth.

the materials, machinery, and workers required to manufacture a product are assembled in one place.

By 1814 Francis Cabot Lowell had established a factory in Waltham, Massachusetts, to spin, weave, and bleach cotton all under one roof. He organized the various manufacturing steps into one uninterrupted sequence, hired professional managers, and was able to produce 30 miles of cloth each day! In doing so, Lowell seems to have used a manufacturing technique called *specialization*. **Specialization** is the separation of a manufacturing process into distinct tasks and the assignment of different tasks to different individuals. Its purpose is to increase the efficiency of industrial workers.

specialization   the separation of a manufacturing process into distinct tasks and the assignment of different tasks to different individuals

The three decades from 1820 to 1850 were the golden age of invention and innovation in machinery. The cotton gin of Eli Whitney greatly increased the supply of cotton for the textile industry. Elias Howe's sewing machine became available to convert materials into clothing. The agricultural machinery of John Deere and Cyrus McCormick revolutionized farm production.

At the same time, new means of transportation greatly expanded the domestic markets for American products. The Erie Canal was opened in the 1820s. Soon, thanks to Robert Fulton's engine, steamboats could move upstream against the current and use the rivers as highways for hauling bulk goods. During the 1830s and 1840s, the railroads began to extend the existing transportation system to the West, carrying goods and people much farther than was possible by waterways alone. Between 1860 and 1880 the number of miles of railroad track tripled; by 1900 it had doubled again.[3]

A SECOND REVOLUTION

Many business historians view the period from 1870 to 1900 as the second industrial revolution; certainly, many characteristics of our modern business system took form during these three decades. In this period, for example, the nation shifted from a farm economy to a manufacturing economy. The developing oil industry provided fuel for light, heat, and energy. Greatly increased immigration furnished labor for expanded production. New means of communication brought sophistication to banking and finance. During this time, the United States became not only an industrial giant but a leading world power as well.

Industrial growth and prosperity continued well into the twentieth century. Henry Ford's moving assembly line, which brought the work to the worker, refined the concept of specialization and spawned the mass production of consumer goods. By the 1920s the automobile industry had begun to influence the entire economy. The steel industry, which supplies materials to the auto industry, grew along with it. The oil and chemical industries grew just as fast and provided countless new synthetic products—new ways to satisfy society's wants. And the emerging airplane and airline industries promised better and faster transportation.

Fundamental changes occurred in business ownership and management as well. The largest businesses were no longer owned by one individual; instead, ownership was in the hands of thousands of corporate shareholders who were willing to invest in—but not to operate—a business.

Certain modern marketing techniques are products of this era, too. Large corporations developed new methods of advertising and selling. Time payment plans made it possible for the average consumer to purchase costly durable goods, such as automobiles, appliances, and furnishings. Advertisements counseled the public to "buy now and pay later." A higher standard of living was created for most people—but it was not to last.

The Great Depression

The "roaring twenties" ended with the sudden crash of the stock market in 1929 and the near collapse of the economy. The Great Depression that followed in the 1930s was a time of misery and human suffering. The unemployment rate varied between 16 and 25 percent in the years 1931 through 1939, and the value of goods and services produced in America fell by almost half. People lost their faith in business and its ability to satisfy the needs of society without government interference.

After the election of President Franklin D. Roosevelt, the federal government devised a number of programs to get the economy moving again. In implementing these programs, the government got deeply involved in business for the first time. Many business people opposed this government intervention, but they reluctantly accepted the new government regulations.

Recovery and Beyond

The economy was on the road to recovery when World War II broke out in Europe in 1939. The need for vast quantities of war materials—first for our allies and then for the American military as well—spurred business activity and technological development. This rapid economic pace continued after the war, and the 1950s and 1960s witnessed both increasing production and a rising standard of living. **Standard of living** is a loose, subjective measure of how well off an individual or a society is, mainly in terms of want satisfaction through goods and services.

In the mid-1970s, however, a shortage of crude oil led to a new set of problems for business. Petroleum products supply most of the energy required to produce goods and services and to transport goods around the world. As the cost of petroleum products increased, a corresponding increase took place in the cost of energy and the cost of goods and services. The result was **inflation,** a general rise in the level of prices, at a rate well over 10 percent per year during the first part of the 1980s. Interest rates

\standard of living   a loose, subjective measure of how well off an individual or a society is, mainly in terms of want satisfaction through goods and services

inflation   a general rise in the level of prices

Jumping for profit. For the most adventuresome—or crazy—Americans of the 1990s, bungee-jumping has become a popular way to liven up the weekend. And when people want a service, someone will supply it. The owners of this balloon and those crucial rubber cords may bear little resemblance to local fast-food franchisees, but they too are part of the growing service economy.

also increased dramatically, so borrowing by both businesses and consumers was reduced. Business profits fell as the consumer's purchasing power was eroded by inflation and high interest rates, and unemployment reached alarming levels. By the mid-1980s, many of these problem areas showed signs of improvement. Unfortunately, many managers now had something else to worry about—corporate mergers and takeovers. Also, a large number of bank failures, coupled with an increasing number of bankruptcies, again made people uneasy about our business system.

The decade of the 1990s began with the United States in what most authorities would call a recession. Although annual inflation rates and overall interest rates have now declined, unemployment has risen. Consumers seem reluctant to borrow money, even at lower interest rates. And banks and other financial institutions—still recovering from the large number of failures in the last part of the 1980s—seem reluctant to lend money unless the loan applicant has excellent credit. As further evidence of recession, the number of business failures was too high and the number of new business ventures was too low.

At the time of this writing, the U.S. economy does show some signs of improvement. Service businesses have become a dominant part of our economy, and we now devote more effort to the production of services than to the production of goods. Because well over half of the American work force is involved in service industries, ours is called a **service economy.** And American businesses are beginning to realize that to be successful, they must enter the global marketplace. In short, American firms must meet the needs not only of American consumers but also of foreign consumers. (Both our service economy and our place in the global marketplace are discussed more fully later in the text.) Finally, politicians say that economic recovery is just around the corner. Only time will tell if their predictions will come true.

service economy an economy in which the majority of the work force is involved in service industries; one in which more effort is devoted to the production of services than to the production of goods

THE ECONOMICS OF BUSINESS

economics the study of how wealth is created and distributed

Economics is the study of how wealth is created and distributed. By *wealth* we mean anything of value, including the products produced and sold by business. "How wealth is distributed" simply means "who gets what." The way in which people deal with the two issues determines the kind of economic system, or **economy,** that a society has. In the United States, our particular answers have provided us with an economy that is based on capitalism, or private enterprise.

economy the system through which a society answers the two economic questions—how wealth is created and distributed

Capitalism

capitalism an economic system in which individuals own and operate the majority of businesses that provide goods and services

Capitalism is an economic system in which individuals own and operate the majority of businesses that provide goods and services. Capitalism—our economic system—stems from the theories of Adam Smith, a Scot. In

1776, in his book *The Wealth of Nations,* Smith argued that a society's interests are best served when the individuals within that society are allowed to pursue their own self-interest.

> Every individual endeavors to employ his capital so that its produce may be of greatest value. . . . And he is in this led by an INVISIBLE HAND to promote an end which was no part of his intention. By pursuing his own interest he frequently promotes that of Society more effectually than when he really intends to promote it.

In other words, Smith believed that each person should be allowed to work toward his or her *own* economic gain, without interference from government. And, according to Smith, society would benefit most when there was the least interference with the individual's pursuit of economic self-interest. Government should therefore leave the economy to its citizens. The French term *laissez faire* describes Smith's capitalistic system and implies that there shall be no interference in the economy. Loosely translated, it means "let them do" (as they see fit). The features of laissez-faire capitalism are summarized in Figure 1.4.

LEARNING OBJECTIVE 3
State the four main ingredients of laissez-faire capitalism.

factors of production   three categories of resources: land, labor, capital

capital   all the financial resources, buildings, machinery, tools, and equipment that are used in an organization's operations

Private Ownership of Property   Smith argued that the creation of wealth (including products) is properly the concern of private individuals, not of government. Hence the resources that are used to create wealth must be owned by private individuals. Economists recognize three categories of resources: land, labor, and capital, also known as the **factors of production.** Land includes the land and the natural resources on and in the land. Labor is the work performed by people. **Capital** includes financial resources, buildings, machinery, tools, and equipment that are used in an organization's operations. We have referred to these resources as material, human, and financial resources, and we shall continue to do so throughout the text. The private ownership of these resources gives us the names *capitalism* and *private enterprise* for our economic system.

Smith argued further that the owners of the factors of production should be free to determine how these resources are used. They should also be free to enjoy the income and other benefits they might derive from the ownership of these resources.

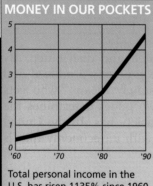

AT A GLANCE

MONEY IN OUR POCKETS

Total personal income in the U.S. has risen 1135% since 1960, while our population has increased 139%.
(In trillions of dollars; not adjusted for inflation)

SOURCE: *Bureau of Economic Analysis, U.S. Dept. of Commerce; Bureau of the Census*

Economic Freedom   Smith's economic freedom extends to all those involved in the economy. For the owners of land and capital, this freedom includes the right to rent, sell, or invest their resources and the right to use their resources to produce any product and offer it for sale at the price they choose. For workers, this economic freedom means the right to accept or reject any job they are offered. For all individuals, economic freedom includes the right to purchase any good or service that is offered for sale by producers. These rights, however, do not include a guarantee of economic success. Nor do they include the right to harm others during the pursuit of one's own self-interest.

Competitive Markets   A crucial part of Smith's theory is the competitive market, composed of large numbers of buyers and sellers. (For now, think

FIGURE 1.4
The Features of
Laissez-Faire Capitalism
Laissez faire ("let them do")
implies that there shall be no
interference in the economy.

LAISSEZ-FAIRE CAPITALISM

| Private ownership of property | Economic freedom | Competitive markets | Limited role of government |

of a market as the interaction of the buyers and sellers of a particular type of product or resource, such as shoes or managerial skills. We discuss a more limited concept of market in Chapter 11.) Economic freedom ensures the existence of competitive markets because sellers and buyers can enter markets as they choose. Sellers enter a market to earn profit, rent, or wages; buyers enter a market to purchase resources and want-satisfying products. This freedom to enter or leave a market at will has given rise to the name **free-market economy** for the capitalism that Smith described.

free-market economy an
economic system in which individuals and firms are free to
enter and leave markets at will

Limited Role of Government In Smith's view, the role of government should be limited to providing defense against foreign enemies, ensuring internal order, and furnishing public works and education. With regard to the economy, government should act only as rule maker and umpire. As rule maker, government should provide laws that ensure economic free-dom and promote competition. As umpire, it should act to settle disputes arising from conflicting interpretations of its laws. Government, according to Adam Smith, should have no economic responsibilities beyond these.

What, How, and for Whom in a Capitalistic Economy

LEARNING OBJECTIVE 4
Know how the three basic economic questions—what, how,
and for whom—are answered in
free-market and planned
economies.

Smith's laissez-faire capitalism sounds as though it should lead to chaos. How can millions of individuals and firms, all intent only on their own self-interest, produce an orderly economic system? One response might be sim-ply, "They can and they do." Most of the industrialized nations of the world exhibit some form of modified capitalist economy, and these economies do work. A better response, however, is that these millions of individuals and firms actually provide very concrete and detailed answers to the following three basic economic questions:

1. What goods and services—and how much of each—will be produced?
2. How will these goods and services be produced?
3. For whom will these goods and services be produced?

Because the answers to these questions have such a dramatic effect on a nation's economy, we examine these questions in more detail in the follow-ing three sections.

What to Produce? Consumers answer this question continually as they spend their dollars in the various markets for goods and services. When consumers buy Nintendo games, they are casting "dollar votes" for these products. Conversely, when consumers refuse to buy a product at its going price, they are voting against the product, telling producers to either reduce the price or ease off on production. In each case, consumers are giving a very specific answer concerning a very specific product.

How to Produce?   This question is answered by producers as they enter various markets and compete for sales and profits. When producing goods and services, business owners must decide which resources will be used. To compete as effectively as possible in the product markets, producers try to use the most efficient (least-cost) combination of resources. When a particular resource can be used to produce two or more different products, then producers must also compete with each other in the market for that resource. And, if the price of one needed resource becomes too high, producers will look for substitute resources—say, plastics in place of metals. The resources that will be used to produce are those that best perform their function at the least cost.

For Whom to Produce?   In a free market economy, goods and services are distributed to those who have the money to purchase them. This money is earned by individuals as wages, rents, profit, and interest—that is, as payment for the use of their economic resources of land, labor, and capital. Money is therefore a medium of exchange, an artificial device that aids in the exchange of resources for goods and services (see Figure 1.5). The dis-

FIGURE 1.5
The Circular Flow in Smith's Laissez-Faire Economy
The use of money enhances the exchange of goods and services for resources, gives rise to the resource and product markets, and helps answer the question, "For whom to produce?"

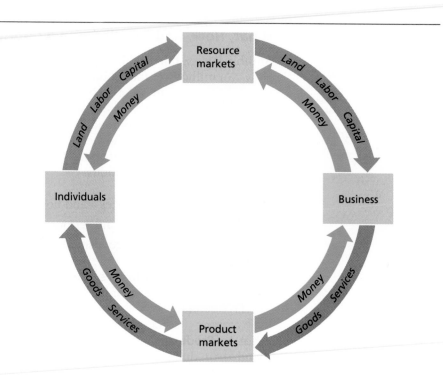

tribution of goods and services ("who gets what") therefore depends on the *current prices* of economic resources and of the various goods and services and who can afford to purchase them.

Planned Economies

Before we discuss how to measure any nation's economic performance, we look quickly at two other economic systems that contrast sharply with capitalism. These systems are sometimes called **planned economies,** because the answers to the three basic economic questions are determined, at least to some degree, through centralized government planning.

planned economy an economy in which the answers to the three basic economic questions (what, how, and for whom) are determined, to some degree, through centralized government planning

Socialism In a *socialist* economy, the key industries are owned and controlled by the government. Such industries usually include transportation, utilities, communications, and those producing important materials such as steel. (Banking, too, is considered extremely important to a nation's economy. In France, the major banks are *nationalized,* or transferred to government control.) Land and raw materials may also be the property of the state in a socialist economy. Depending on the country, private ownership of real property (such as land and buildings) and smaller or less vital businesses is permitted to varying degrees. People usually may choose their own occupations, but many work in state-owned industries.

What to produce and how to produce it are determined in accordance with national goals, which are based on projected needs and the availability of resources—at least for government-owned industries. The distribution of goods and services—who gets what—is also controlled by the state to the extent that it controls rents and wages. Among the professed aims of socialist countries are the equitable distribution of income, the elimination of poverty, the distribution of social services (such as medical care) to all who need them, smooth economic growth, and elimination of the economic waste that supposedly accompanies capitalist competition.

Britain, France, Sweden, and India are democratic countries whose economies include a very visible degree of socialism. Other, more authoritarian countries may actually have socialist economies; however, we tend to think of them as communist because of their almost total lack of freedom.

Communism If Adam Smith was the father of capitalism, Karl Marx was the father of communism. In his writings (during the mid-nineteenth century), Marx advocated a classless society whose citizens together owned all economic resources. He believed that such a society would come about as the result of a class struggle between the owners of capital and the workers they had exploited. All workers would then contribute to this *communist* society according to their ability and would receive benefits according to their need.

The People's Republic of China and Cuba are generally considered to have communist economies. Almost all economic resources are owned by the government in these countries. The basic economic questions are answered through centralized state planning, which sets prices and wages as

"Volunteers" in a planned economy. These students are among 100,000 recruited by the Chinese government to spruce up the city of Beijing for the 11th Asian games. Though called "volunteers," the students probably had little choice, and the banners and overseers give the sense that the government is watching. Other volunteers focused on eradicating the "four pests": mosquitoes, flies, rats, and roaches.

well. In this planning, the needs of the state generally outweigh the needs of individual citizens. Emphasis is placed on the production of goods the government needs rather than on the products that consumers might want, so there are frequent shortages of consumer goods. Workers have little choice of jobs, but special skills or talents seem to be rewarded with special privileges. Various groups of professionals (bureaucrats, university professors, and athletes, for example) fare much better than, say, factory workers.

Today, the so-called communist economies thus seem to be far from Marx's vision of communism. Rather they seem to practice a strictly controlled kind of socialism. There is also a bit of free enterprise here and there. Like all real economies, these economies are neither pure nor static. Every operating economy is a constantly changing mixture of various idealized economic systems. Some, like ours, evolve slowly. Others change more quickly, through either evolution or revolution. And, over many years, a nation, such as Great Britain or Russia, may move first in one direction and then in the opposite direction. It is impossible to say whether any real economy will ever closely resemble Marx's communism.

Measuring Economic Performance

productivity   the average level of output per worker per hour

One way to measure a nation's economic performance is to assess its productivity. **Productivity** is the average level of output per worker per hour. It is a measure of the efficiency of production for an economic system. An increase in productivity results in economic growth because a larger number of goods and services are produced by a given labor force. Although U.S. workers produce more than many workers in other countries, the rate of growth in productivity has declined in the United States and has been exceeded in recent years by workers in Japan and the United Kingdom. Productivity is discussed in detail in Chapter 7.

gross national product (GNP)
the total dollar value of all
goods and services produced by
all citizens of a country for a
given time period

A general measure of a country's national economic output is called its gross national product. **Gross national product (GNP)** is the total dollar value of all goods and services produced by *all* citizens of a country for a given time period. In 1990, the U.S. gross national product was $5.6 trillion. Comparing the GNP for several different time periods allows one to determine the extent to which a country is experiencing economic growth.

To make accurate comparisons of GNP figures for two different years, one must adjust the figures for inflation, that is, higher price levels. By using inflation-adjusted figures, one is able to measure real gross national product. **Real gross national product** is the total dollar value, adjusted for price increases, of all goods and services produced by all citizens of a country during a given time period. Comparisons of real gross national product information allow one to accurately measure differences in output from one time period to another. Figure 1.6 depicts the gross national product of the United States in current dollars and in constant 1982 dollars. The real gross national product figures are represented in the adjusted figures. Note that between 1978 and 1990 our real gross national product grew from $3.1 trillion to $4.2 trillion.

real gross national product
the total dollar value, adjusted
for price increases, of all goods
and services produced by all
citizens of a country during a
given time period

gross domestic product   the
total dollar value of all goods
and services produced by citizens physically located within a
country

Economists also often refer to another popular economic measure—gross domestic product. **Gross domestic product (GDP)** is the total dollar value of all goods and services produced by citizens physically located within a country. The definition of GDP is very similar to the definition of gross national product, but with one exception. GDP excludes production

FIGURE 1.6   Gross National Product in Current Dollars and in Inflation-Adjusted Dollars
The changes in real gross national product from one time period to another can be used to measure economic performance.   *(Source:* Survey of Current Business, *April 1991 and July 1991;* Economic Indicators, *December 1991, U.S. Government Printing Office, Washington, D.C.)*

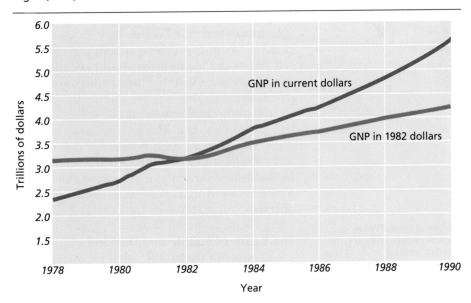

amounts for U.S. citizens working abroad in foreign nations. For 1990, the gross *domestic* product for the United States was $5.5 trillion, which is slightly lower than the GNP ($5.6 trillion) for the same year.

TYPES OF ECONOMIC COMPETITION

LEARNING OBJECTIVE 5
Summarize the four different types of economic competition.

As we have noted, a free-market system implies competition among sellers of products and resources. Economists recognize four different degrees of competition, ranging from ideal complete competition to no competition at all. These are pure competition, monopolistic competition, oligopoly, and monopoly.

Pure Competition

pure competition the market situation in which there are many buyers and sellers of a product, and no single buyer or seller is powerful enough to affect the price of that product

Pure (or perfect) competition is the complete form of competition. **Pure competition** is the market situation in which there are many buyers and sellers of a product, and no single buyer or seller is powerful enough to affect the price of that product. Note that this definition includes several important ideas. First, we are discussing the market for a single product—say, bushels of wheat. (The definition also applies to markets for resources, but we'll limit our discussion here to products.) Second, all sellers offer essentially the same product for sale; a buyer would be just as satisfied with seller *A*'s wheat as with that offered by seller *B* or seller *Z*. Third, all buyers and sellers know everything there is to know about the market (including, in our example, the prices that all sellers are asking for their wheat). And fourth, the market is not affected by the actions of any one buyer or seller.

When pure competition exists, every seller should ask the same price that every other seller is asking. Why? Because if one seller wanted 50 cents more than all the others per bushel of wheat, that seller would not be able to sell a single bushel. Buyers could—and would—do better by purchasing wheat from the competition. On the other hand, a firm willing to sell below the going price would sell all its wheat quickly. But that seller would lose sales revenue (and profit), because buyers are actually willing to pay more.

In pure competition, then, sellers—and buyers as well—must accept the going price. But who or what determines this price? Actually, everyone does. The price of each product is determined by the actions of *all buyers and all sellers together,* through the forces of supply and demand. It is this interaction of buyers and sellers, working for their best interest, that Adam Smith referred to as the "invisible hand" of competition. Let us see how it operates.

LEARNING OBJECTIVE 6
Describe how supply and demand determine price in competitive markets.

supply the quantity of a product that producers are willing to sell at each of various prices

The Basics of Supply and Demand   The **supply** of a particular product is the quantity of the product that producers are willing to sell at each of various prices. Producers are rational people, so we would expect them to offer more of a product for sale at higher prices and to offer less of the product at lower prices, as illustrated in Figure 1.7.

FIGURE 1.7
Supply Curve and Demand Curve
The intersection of a supply curve and a demand curve indicates a single price and quantity at which suppliers will sell products and buyers will purchase them.

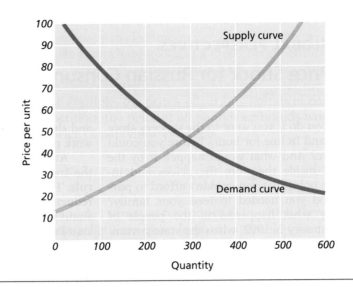

demand   the quantity of a product that buyers are willing to purchase at each of various prices

   The **demand** for a particular product is the quantity that buyers are willing to purchase at each of various prices. Buyers, too, are usually rational, so we would expect them—as a group—to buy more of a product when its price is low and to buy less of the product when its price is high, as depicted in Figure 1.7. This is exactly what happens when the price of wheat rises dramatically. People buy other grains or do without and reduce their purchases of wheat. They buy more wheat only when prices drop.

The Equilibrium, or Market, Price   There is always one certain price at which the demanded quantity of a product is exactly equal to the produced quantity of that product. Suppose producers are willing to *supply* two million bushels of wheat at a price of $5 per bushel, and buyers are willing to *purchase* two million bushels at a price of $5 per bushel. In other words, supply and demand are in balance, or *in equilibrium,* at the price of $5. Economists call this price the *equilibrium price* or *market price.* Under pure competition, the **market price** of any product is the price at which the quantity demanded is exactly equal to the quantity supplied. If suppliers produce two million bushels, then no one who is willing to pay $5 per bushel will have to go without wheat, and no producer who is willing to sell at $5 per bushel will be stuck with unsold wheat.

market price   in pure competition, the price at which the quantity demanded is exactly equal to the quantity supplied

   In theory and in the real world, market prices are affected by anything that affects supply and demand. The *demand* for wheat, for example, might change if researchers suddenly discovered that it had very beneficial effects on users' health. Then more wheat would be demanded at every price. The *supply* of wheat might change if new technology permitted the production of greater quantities of wheat from the same amount of acreage. In that case, producers would be willing to supply more wheat at each price. Either of these changes would result in a new market price. Other changes that can affect competitive prices are shifts in buyer tastes, the development of new products that satisfy old needs, and fluctuations in income due to inflation or recession.

The sweet monopoly ends. During the 1980s, NutraSweet Co. profited by selling aspartame, the world's most popular artificial sweetener. But NutraSweet's patent on aspartame ran out in 1992, forcing the company to look for other sweet and profitable products, like the no-fat ice cream being tested here by NutraSweet's CEO. The end of the monopoly may mean lower prices for some aspartame-flavored products.

and can be used to protect the owners of written materials, ideas, or product brands from unauthorized use by competitors that have not shared in the time, effort, and expense required for development of these items.

Except for natural monopolies and monopolies created by copyrights, patents, and trademarks, federal laws prohibit both monopolies and attempts to form monopolies. A recent amendment to the Sherman Antitrust Act of 1890 made any such attempt a criminal offense, and the Clayton Antitrust Act of 1914 prohibited a number of specific actions that could lead to monopoly. The goal of these and other antitrust laws is to ensure the competitive environment of American business, and protect American consumers.

OUR BUSINESS SYSTEM TODAY

LEARNING OBJECTIVE 7
Identify the roles that households, businesses, and governments play in our business system.

mixed economy an economy that exhibits elements of both capitalism and socialism

So far we have looked at several different aspects of our business system. Its theoretical basis is the laissez-faire economic system of Adam Smith. However, our real-world economy is not as "laissez faire" as Smith would have liked, because government participates as more than umpire and rule maker. Ours is, in fact, a **mixed economy,** one that exhibits elements of both capitalism and socialism.

In today's economy, then, the three basic economic questions (what, how, and for whom) are answered by three groups:

1. *Households,* made up of consumers who seek the best value for their money and the best prices for the economic resources they own
2. *Businesses,* which seek to maximize their profits
3. *Federal, state, and local governments,* which seek to promote public safety and welfare and to serve the public interest

The interactions among these three groups are shown in Figure 1.8, which is similar to Figure 1.5 with government included.

Households

Households are both consumers of goods and owners of the productive resources of land, labor, and capital. As *resource owners,* the members of households provide businesses with the means of production. In return, businesses pay wages, rent, and interest, which households receive as income.

consumer goods   products purchased by individuals for personal consumption

As *consumers,* household members use their income to purchase the goods and services produced by business. Today almost two-thirds of our nation's GDP consists of **consumer goods:** products purchased by individuals for personal consumption. (The remaining one-third is purchased by business and government.) This means that consumers, as a group, are the biggest customer of American business.

Businesses

Like households, businesses are engaged in two exchanges. They exchange money for resources, and they use these resources to produce goods and services. Then they exchange their products for sales revenue. This sales

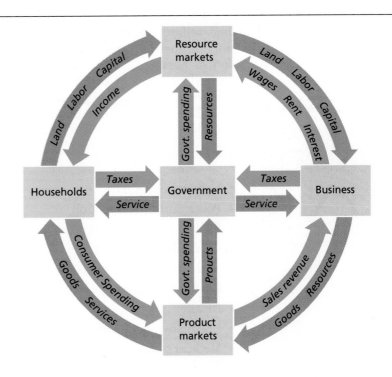

FIGURE 1.8
The Circular Flow in Our Modified Capitalist System Today
Our business system is guided by the interplay of buyers and sellers, but the role of government is taken into account.

revenue, in turn, is exchanged for additional resources, which are used to produce and sell more products. So the circular flow of Figure 1.8 is continuous: Business pays *wages, rent, and interest* which become *household income* which becomes *consumer spending* which becomes *sales revenue* which again becomes *wages, rent, and interest*. And so on.

Along the way, of course, business owners would like to remove something from the circular flow in the form of profits. And households try to retain some income as savings. But are profits and savings really removed from the flow? Usually not! When the economy is running smoothly, households are willing to invest their savings in business. They can do so directly, by buying ownership shares in business or lending money to business. They can also invest indirectly, by placing their savings in bank accounts; banks then invest these savings as part of their normal business operations. In either case, savings usually find their way back into the circular flow.

When business profits are distributed to business owners, these profits become household income. (Business owners are, after all, members of households.) And, as we saw, household income is retained in the circular flow as either consumer spending or invested savings. So business profits, too, are retained in the business system, and the circular flow is complete. How, then, does government fit in?

Governments

The framers of our Constitution desired as little government interference with business as possible. At the same time, the Preamble to the Constitution set forth the responsibility of government to protect and promote the public welfare. Local, state, and federal governments discharge this responsibility through regulation and the provision of services. Government regulation of business has already been mentioned; specific regulations are discussed in detail in various chapters of this book. In addition, government provides a variety of services that are considered important but either (1) would not be produced by private firms in a free-enterprise system or (2) would be produced only for those who could afford them. Among these services are

- National defense
- Police and fire protection
- Welfare payments and retirement income
- Education
- National and state parks, forests, and wilderness areas
- Roads and highways
- Disaster relief
- Unemployment insurance programs
- Medical research
- Development of purity standards for foods and drugs

AT A GLANCE
GROWTH OF THE GDP

The Gross Domestic Product is an indicator of the economy in general.
('92 and '93 estimated)

SOURCE: © FORTUNE, *January 13, 1992*

ETHICAL CHALLENGES
Buyer Beware: Scams That Target Consumers

Borrow up to $100,000 interest free to finance all of your personal and business needs. Put down $300 for "character insurance" and the money will be yours. To begin processing your loan application, make your check payable to Church of God—Houston.

Sound too good to be true? You're right, it *is* too good to be true. This loan scam was used by the Church of God—Houston (also known as Our Father's Congregation). Supposedly, loans were funded on a "funds-available" basis, with a one-year waiting period. In reality, very few people actually got money after paying their $300 for character insurance. Eventually, Melvin White, the church's leader, was imprisoned by the state of Texas for violating court injunctions prohibiting the church's loan scams. Legal action against White is also pending in California, Georgia, Kansas, Louisiana, Missouri, Nebraska, Ohio, Oklahoma, and South Carolina.

Currently, there are 17 million businesses in the United States. Most are ethical, but a growing number are dishonest, intentionally committing fraud or, in some cases, outright theft. Although it is hard to determine the actual dollar amount taken through scams like the one described above, John Perkins, the Missouri securities commissioner, estimates that con artists steal approximately $40 billion a year from unsuspecting individuals. Unfortunately, the people who can least afford a loss—the unemployed, elderly, or poor—are the ones who are most often victimized.

It is often hard to determine if a firm is legitimate or not, but the following guidelines may help evaluate a business or investment opportunity.

1. Guard against all high-pressure sales presentations.

2. Take enough time to make a quality decision when making a purchase.

3. Deal only with firms that you know or with firms that you have checked out with the Better Business Bureau, local authorities, or state authorities.

4. Beware of merchandise or investments offered over the phone. Ask for written information about the product or investment.

5. Don't give your credit card number or bank account number to anyone unless you have dealt with the business before or unless you have initiated the contact.

Today, hundreds of different schemes can be used by con artists to take your money. The most typical schemes include the following areas: (1) home-improvements; (2) worthless investment opportunities; (3) work-at-home employment; (4) credit repair for a fee; (5) fraudulent employment agencies; and (6) unethical charities.

Issues to Consider

1. "Congratulations, you've just won one of three major prizes. All you have to do to claim your prize is to send in a $49.95 processing fee." If you received this statement in the mail, what would you do to check out the offer?

2. A number of government agencies have tried to devise regulations to protect the public from unethical business firms. Are these regulations needed, or are they just another example of too much government control?

This list could go on and on, but the point is clear: Governments are deeply involved in business life. To pay for all these services, governments collect a variety of taxes from households (such as personal income taxes and sales taxes) and from businesses (corporate income taxes).

Figure 1.8 shows this exchange of taxes for government services. It also shows government spending of tax dollars for resources and products

Smiles for the mixed economy. In a purely capitalistic economy, these members of the Dance Theater of Harlem, led by artistic director Arthur Mitchell, would find it harder to smile. The Theater would survive only if it could turn a profit, probably by selling expensive tickets to its performances. But with the support of the government, corporations, and individual patrons, the Theater can bring smiles to rich and poor alike.

required to provide these services. In other words, governments, too, return their incomes to the business system through the resource and product markets.

Actually, with government included, our so-called circular flow looks more like a combination of several flows. And in reality it is. The important point is that, together, the various flows make up a single unit—a complete economic system that effectively provides answers to the basic economic questions. Simply put, the system works.

THE CHALLENGES AHEAD

LEARNING OBJECTIVE 8
Discuss the challenges that American businesses will encounter in the future.

There it is—the American business system in brief. When it works well, it provides jobs for those who are willing to work, a standard of living that few countries can match, and almost unlimited opportunity for personal advancement. But, like every other system devised by humans, it is far from perfect. Our business system may give us prosperity, but it also gave us the Great Depression of the 1930s and the economic problems of the 1970s and early 1990s.

The system obviously can be improved. It may need no more than a bit of fine tuning, or it may require something more extensive. Certainly there are plenty of people who are willing to tell us exactly what *they* think it needs. But these people provide us only with conflicting opinions. Who is right and who is wrong? Even the experts cannot agree.

The experts do agree, however, that several key issues will challenge our business system over the next decade or two. Some of the questions to be resolved are:

- How much government involvement in our economy is necessary for its continued well-being? In what areas should there be less involvement? In what areas, more?
- How can we balance national growth with the conservation of natural resources and the protection of our environment?
- How can we evaluate the long-term economic costs and benefits of existing and proposed government programs?
- How can we hold down inflation and yet stimulate the economy to provide jobs for all who want to work?
- How can we preserve the benefits of competition in our American economic system and still meet the needs of the less fortunate?
- How can we make American manufacturers more productive and more competitive with foreign producers who have lower labor costs?
- How can we market American-made products in foreign nations and thus reduce our trade deficit?

The answers to the problems described in this section are anything but simple. In the past, Americans have always been able to solve their economic problems through ingenuity and creativity. Now, as we approach the year 2000, we need that same ingenuity and creativity not only to solve our current problems but also to compete in the global marketplace.

According to economic experts, if we as a nation can become more competitive, we may solve many of our current domestic problems. As an added bonus, increased competitiveness will also enable us to meet the challenges posed by the European Community, Japan, and the other industrialized nations of the world. The way we solve these problems will affect our own future, our children's future, and that of our nation. Within the American economic and political system, the answers are ours to provide.

The American business system is not perfect by any means, but it does work reasonably well. We shall discuss some of its problems in Chapter 2, wherein we examine the role of business as part of American society.

CHAPTER REVIEW

Summary

Business is the organized effort of individuals to produce and sell, for a profit, the goods and services that satisfy society's needs. Four kinds of resources—material, human, financial, and informational—must be combined to start and operate a business. The three general types of businesses are manufacturers, service businesses, and marketing middlemen.

Profit is what remains after all business expenses are deducted from sales revenue. It is thus the payment that business owners receive for assuming the risks of business: primarily the risks of not receiving payment and of losing whatever has been invested in the firm. Most often, a business that is operated to satisfy its customers earns a reasonable profit.

By studying business, you can become a more informed consumer and investor and be a better employee. And with a working knowledge of business, you may decide to open your own business.

Since its beginnings in the seventeenth century, American business has been based on private ownership of property and freedom of enterprise. And from this beginning, through the Industrial Revolution of the early nineteenth century, to the phenomenal expansion of American industry in the nineteenth and early twentieth centuries, our government maintained an essentially laissez-faire attitude toward business. However, during the Great Depression of the 1930s, the federal government began to provide a number of social services to its citizens. Government's role in business has expanded continually since that time.

Economics is the study of how wealth is created and distributed. An economy is a system through which a society decides those two issues. Capitalism—our economic system—stems from the theories of Adam Smith. Smith's pure laissez-faire capitalism is an economic system in which these decisions are made by individuals and businesses as they pursue their own self-interest. Any economic system must answer three questions: What goods and services will be produced? How will they be produced? For whom will they be produced? In a laissez-faire capitalist system, the factors of production are owned by private individuals, and all individuals are free to use (or not to use) their resources as they see fit; prices are determined by the workings of supply and demand in competitive markets; and the economic role of government is limited to protecting competition.

In planned economies, government, rather than individuals, owns the factors of production and provides the answers to the three basic economic questions. Socialist and communist economies are—at least in theory—planned economies. In the real world, however, no economy attains "theoretical perfection."

One criterion for evaluating the performance of an economic system is to assess changes in productivity, which is the average level of output per worker per hour. A general economic performance measure is gross national product (GNP), which is the total dollar value of all goods and services produced by all the citizens of a country for a given period of time. Although similar to the GNP, the gross domestic product (GDP) is the total dollar value of all goods and services produced by citizens physically located within a country.

Economists recognize four degrees of competition among sellers. Ranging from most to least competitive, the four degrees are: pure competition, monopolistic competition, oligopoly, and monopoly. The factors of supply and demand generally influence the price that consumers pay producers for goods and services.

Our economic system is thus a mixed economy—capitalism cut with some socialism. Although our present business system is essentially capitalist in nature, government takes part in it, along with households and businesses. In the circular flow that characterizes our business system, households and businesses exchange resources for goods and services, using money as the medium of exchange. Government collects taxes from businesses and households and uses tax revenues to purchase the resources and products with which to provide its services.

Today, there are a number of significant challenges for American business. If we as a nation can become more competitive, we may solve our domestic problems. As an added bonus, increased competitiveness will enable us to meet the challenges posed by foreign nations.

Key Terms

You should now be able to define and give an example relevant to each of the following terms:

free enterprise	capital
competition	free-market economy
business	planned economy
entrepreneur	productivity
consumers	gross national product (GNP)
profit	real gross national product
barter	gross domestic product (GDP)
domestic system	pure competition
factory system	supply
specialization	demand
standard of living	market price
inflation	monopolistic competition
service economy	oligopoly
economics	monopoly
economy	natural monopoly
capitalism	mixed economy
factors of production	consumer goods

Questions and Exercises

Review Questions

1. What basic rights are accorded to individuals and businesses in our free enterprise system?
2. What is meant by free enterprise? Why does free enterprise naturally lead to competition among sellers of products?
3. Describe the four resources that one must combine to organize and operate a business. How do they differ from the economist's factors of production?
4. What distinguishes consumers from other buyers of goods and services?
5. Describe the relationship among profit, business risk, and the satisfaction of customers' needs.
6. Trace the steps that led from farming for survival in the American colonial period to today's mass production.
7. Describe the four main ingredients of a laissez-faire capitalist economy.
8. What are the three basic economic questions? How are they answered in a capitalist economy? In a planned economy?
9. What is the difference between gross national product and gross domestic product? Why are these economic measures significant?
10. Identify and compare the four forms of competition that are recognized by economists.
11. Explain how the market price of a product is determined under pure competition.
12. Why is the American economy called a mixed economy?
13. Outline the economic interactions between government and business in our business system. Outline those between government and households.

Discussion Questions

1. In 1987, there were twenty Blockbuster Video stores. In 1991, just four years later, there were 1,934 stores. What factors led to the success that Blockbuster has experienced?
2. Approximately half of the Blockbuster Video stores are franchise operations. Why would a firm like Blockbuster Entertainment Corporation sell franchises? Why would someone purchase a Blockbuster Video franchise?
3. Three specific reasons for studying business were included in this chapter. How does each of these reasons affect your life?

4. What factors caused American business to develop into a mixed economic system rather than some other type of system?
5. Does one individual consumer really have a voice in answering the three basic economic questions?
6. Is gross national product really a reliable indicator of a nation's standard of living? What might be a better indicator?
7. Discuss this statement: "Business competition encourages efficiency of production and leads to improved product quality."
8. In our business system, how is government involved in answering the three basic economic questions? Does government participate in the system or interfere with it?

Exercises

1. Choose a type of business that you are familiar with or interested in. Then list the *specific* material, human, financial, and informational resources you would need to start such a business.
2. Cite four methods (other than pricing) that American auto manufacturers use to differentiate their products. (The best way to do this is to scan their magazine and newspaper ads.) Rate these methods from least effective to most effective, using your own judgment and experience.
3. A marketing middleman like K mart does not process goods in any way, yet it helps satisfy consumer wants. List and explain several ways in which it does so.

CASE 1.1

Walt Disney Company: The Magic Is Back

The stories of Bambi, Cinderella, and Snow White are familiar to all of us and—thanks to the animation genius of Walt Disney—they remain a wonderful and vivid piece of childhood that stays with us as we grow older. But the era during which these films were produced ended with the death of Walt Disney in 1966, and The Walt Disney Company lost much of its sparkle. The creative drive behind Disney seemed to fizzle out. The company produced only three or four new movies a year, and these were not highly successful. Had it not been for Disney's theme parks and real estate holdings, the entertainment giant might have encountered serious financial difficulties.

Then, in 1984, Michael D. Eisner accepted the position of chairman and chief executive officer of The

Walt Disney Company. Through dedication, imagination, and intelligence, Eisner and his team of top executives have successfully put the magic back into Disney. Eisner's strategy was simple: Maximize profits for existing assets while developing new assets for future growth.

Since Eisner became chairman and CEO, the volume of visitors to Disney's theme parks has increased as a result of his decision to advertise them more actively. In addition, the parks have been exported: Both the Tokyo Disneyland and Euro Disney attract millions of people a year. And Disney officials have announced plans for a multibillion-dollar expansion for its theme parks in Florida and California. According to management, it's important to keep investing in theme parks and resorts because these assets provide 52 percent of Disney's revenues. Theme parks and resorts also draw increased interest in Disney motion pictures and videos.

Currently, motion pictures and videos provide 38 percent of Disney's revenues. Much of Disney's success in this segment is the result of the company's appeal to the family market. Animated features, like *Beauty and the Beast*, have been among industry leaders in box-office share. Through its Touchstone Pictures Division, Disney has also been turning out successful films, such as *Father of the Bride*, which attract adult viewers. And Disney's decision to release or re-release videos like *Robin Hood*, *Jungle Book*, and *101 Dalmations* for the home-video market has also increased both sales and profits for this segment of its business.

In keeping with Eisner's goal of maximizing profits, Disney is beginning to license Disney characters—Mickey Mouse and Donald Duck, for example—to other high-quality companies. Licensed products (clothes, toys, watches, stuffed animals, and school supplies displaying Disney characters) now account for 10 percent of the firm's revenues.

The rejuvenation of Disney is indeed a real-life story with a happy ending. Eisner and his associates have transformed Disney from a lifeless giant into a strong and growing company, with average profits of $450 million a year since 1984. And with the exception of 1991, profits have increased every year since Eisner took over in 1984. (According to management, the downturn in profits for 1991 was caused by the economic recession in the United States, which kept would-be tourists at home.)*

Questions

1. Why has The Walt Disney Company become successful after having been in a slump?

2. Who are Disney's customers? How does Disney meet the needs of its customers?

3. What effect would an economic recession or an economic upturn have on a firm like The Walt Disney Company?

*Based on information from *Moody's Handbook of Common Stocks*, Winter 1991–92, Moody's Investors Service, 99 Church Street, New York, NY 10007; "Mickey's Mini-Profits," *Time*, October 14, 1991, p. 56; Christopher Knowlton, "How Disney Keeps the Magic Going," *Fortune*, December 4, 1989, pp. 111–112+; Susan Spillman, "Animation Draws on Its Storied Past," *USA Today*, November 15, 1989, pp. 1D+; and Richard Turner, "Kermit the Frog Jumps to Walt Disney as Company Buys Henson Associates," *Wall Street Journal*, August 29, 1989, p. 1B.

CASE 1.2

Business Philosophy at the J. M. Smucker Company

"With a name like *Smucker's*, it has to be good." Based on the J. M. Smucker Company's recent success and growth in the jam and jelly industry, it would be hard for anyone to doubt that statement. Smucker's total jam and jelly sales are approximately $500 million a year, with annual profits just over $30 million. By first chasing and then surpassing jelly giants Kraft General Foods, Inc., and Welch's, Smucker's now has about 35 percent of the total jam and jelly market and is the leading manufacturer in the industry.

Paul Smucker (the chief executive and grandson of the founder) and his sons Tim (the chairman) and Richard (the president) are not taking their number-one position in the jam and jelly market for granted. The Smuckers know they must fend off foreign jam companies as well as a variety of domestic competitors. Smucker's must also respond to the new waves of health awareness and calorie consciousness in the United States as well as changes in consumers' tastes.

To maintain their number-one position, the Smuckers have concentrated on developing and marketing new products. Recently, Smucker's has introduced a number of successful new entries in the market. Simply Fruit, a spreadable fruit with no preservatives or artificial flavors and no extra sugar, has been well received. And Smucker's is happy with sales for its Fresh Pack Strawberry Preserves, available for only a few weeks each year. Smucker's has also done well with a product named *Goober*—peanut butter already mixed with either grape or strawberry jelly. And the firm's ice-cream toppings (available in microwaveable containers) and a new line of upscale jams and jellies sold under the Dickinson brand name have increased sales revenues.

Besides introducing new products, Smucker's has initiated a number of innovations that have changed the jam and jelly industry. Sensing the coming of a trend, Smucker's was the first company in the jam and jelly industry to print nutritional information on individual product labels. It was the first company to use resealable lids on its jars. Smucker's was also the first to offer single-portion jam and syrup packets to fast-food restaurants and airlines.

The J. M. Smucker Company, based in Orrville, Ohio, has always been and probably always will be a family-run business. The firm started back in 1897 when Jerome Monroe Smucker decided to bring in extra income by making apple cider and apple butter from old family recipes. On the same property where today's modern factory now stands, Jerome carefully monitored the quality of his products, personally signing the paper tied over each container of apple butter. Now, at all of Smucker's ten plants around the country, that same devotion to quality still remains a key element of Smucker's business. If you visit the Orrville plant today, you will receive a card on which is printed: "Quality is the key word and shall apply to our people, our products, our manufacturing methods, and our marketing efforts. . . . Quality comes first; earnings and sales growth will follow."**

Questions

1. The J. M. Smucker Company has been a family-run business since 1897. What are the advantages and disadvantages of family management for this company?
2. Why has Smucker's been able to compete against jelly giants such as Kraft's and Welch's?
3. Economists recognize four different degrees of competition. In which type of competitive situation does Smucker's participate?

**Based on information from Richard Phalon, "Closely Guarded Honey Pot," *Forbes*, November 25, 1991, pp. 48+; Julianne Slovak, "J. M. Smucker Co.," *Fortune*, January 16, 1989, p. 80; "The Corporate Elite," *Business Week*, October 21, 1988, p. 276; Robert McMath, "Jelly Companies Unveil Preserves at Jam Session," *Adweek's Marketing Week*, July 25, 1988, p. 8; and Andrew N. Malcolm, "Of Jams and a Family," *New York Times Magazine*, November 15, 1987, pp. 83+.

Ethics and Social Responsibility

LEARNING OBJECTIVES

After studying this chapter, you should be able to:

1 Identify the types of ethical concerns that arise in the business world.

2 Discuss the ethical pressures placed on decision makers.

3 Explain how ethical decision making can be encouraged.

4 Describe how our current views on the social responsibility of business have evolved.

5 Discuss the factors that led to the consumer movement and list some of its results.

6 Analyze how present employment practices are being used to counteract past abuses.

7 Describe the major types of pollution, their causes, and their cures.

8 Identify the steps a business must take to implement a program of social responsibility.

CHAPTER PREVIEW

We begin by defining business ethics and examining ethical issues confronting business people. Next, we look at the pressures that influence ethical decision making and how it can be encouraged. Then we initiate our discussion of social responsibility by reviewing questionable business practices common before the 1930s and describe how public pressure brought about changes in the business environment after the Great Depression. We define and contrast two present-day models of social responsibility, the economic model and the socioeconomic model. Next, we present the major tenets of the consumer movement, which include consumers' rights to safety, to information, to choice, and to a full hearing of complaints. We discuss how ideas of social responsibility in business have affected employment practices and environmental concerns. Finally, we consider the commitment, planning, and funding that go into a firm's program of social responsibility.

Borden's Commitment to Social Responsibility

Borden, Inc. founded in 1857, is a worldwide producer of foods, nonfood consumer products, and packaging and industrial products. The company recognizes its responsibility to protect the environment and has programs and practices in place worldwide to avoid pollution from its operations and products.

To reinforce this long-standing commitment and to spur employees on to higher standards of excellence, the company developed the Borden Principles of Environmental Policies in 1990, with the full support of top management and the endorsement of the company's board of directors.

Borden has taken several steps to minimize its use of raw materials and to reduce waste. For example, the company's forest products adhesive plants discharge no hazardous liquid wastes. Through a series of sophisticated process engineering developments, potential waste streams are reused within the plants. Similarly, the Borden vinyl film operations regrind virtually all the edge material that is trimmed off when film is cut to uniform roll width; a portion of the trimmings from its wallcovering operations are also reclaimed to reduce waste.

The company also has taken steps to reduce the impact of its product packaging on the environment *after* it leaves the consumer's hands. For example, in an attempt to reduce the disposal load on landfills, Borden tries to use lighter weight but equally strong packages. Furthermore, the company encourages consumers to recycle Borden packaging and makes recycling easier for processors. During 1990, Borden's accomplishments in this area included:

- Introduction of mandatory coding of rigid plastic containers, using a system developed by the Society of the Plastics Industry, to help recyclers identify and sort plastic materials.
- Launching of a program to mark glass, steel, aluminum, and paper packages with symbols that remind consumers that the materials are recyclable in areas where collection facilities exist.
- Initiation of a phased reduction of heavy metals in package printing inks, adhesives, and labels, toward a goal of reducing the amount of hazardous metals that can escape to the atmosphere when packages are incinerated, or that could reach groundwater when they are deposited in landfills.

Borden itself uses recycled packaging materials if the materials pose no risk of contaminating the product. Most paperboard in Borden's U.S. pasta boxes is 100 percent recycled material; the company's glass, steel, and aluminum packages also contain an increasingly larger amount of recycled material.

Borden actively participates in many industry groups working on environmental issues. Among them are the Council for Solid Waste Solutions, the packaging/solid waste committee of the International Life Sciences Institute, the World Environmental Center, and the Council on Plastic Packaging in the Environment.[1]

Obviously, organizations such as Borden want to be recognized as responsible corporate citizens. Socially responsible companies recognize the need to harmonize their operations with increasingly strict environmental requirements. Such firms take a serious view of their environmental responsibilities in handling and using raw materials, manufacturing their products, and packaging and distributing what they make. For example, to ensure that corporate citizenship receives top-level attention, in 1990 Borden created the position of vice president, social responsibility, reporting directly to the chairman and chief executive officer.

Not all firms have taken these steps. Some managers still regard ethical and socially responsible business practices as a poor investment, in which the cost is not worth the return. Other managers—indeed, most managers—view the cost of these practices as a necessary business expense, similar to wages or rent. An increasing number of firms are making the sort of commitment Borden has made—they are making ethics and social responsibility an essential part of their business operations.

BUSINESS ETHICS DEFINED

ethics the study of right and wrong and of the morality of choices made by individuals

business ethics the application of moral standards to business situations

Ethics is the study of right and wrong and of the morality of choices that individuals make. An ethical decision or action is one that is "right" according to some standard of behavior. **Business ethics** is the application of moral standards to business situations. Recent court cases of unethical behavior such as the Wall Street insider-trading scandals of Salomon Brothers Inc. and the questionable pricing tactics of federal defense contractor General Dynamics Corp. and others have helped to make business ethics a matter of public concern.

ETHICAL ISSUES

LEARNING OBJECTIVE 1
Identify the types of ethical concerns that arise in the business world.

Ethical issues are not confined to court cases. All business people face them daily, and they stem from a variety of sources. Although some types

41

Social Responsibility Before the 1930s

During the first quarter of the twentieth century, businesses were free to operate pretty much as they chose. Government protection of workers and consumers was minimal. This was indeed a period of laissez-faire business conditions. (Remember, *laissez-faire* is a French term that implies there shall be no government interference in the economy.) As a result, people either accepted what business had to offer or they did without.

Working Conditions   Before 1930, working conditions were often deplorable by today's standards. The average workweek in most industries exceeded sixty hours, and no minimum-wage law existed. Employee benefits such as paid vacations, medical insurance, and paid overtime were also almost nonexistent. Work areas were crowded and unsafe, and industrial accidents were the rule rather than the exception.

In an effort to improve working conditions, employees organized and joined labor unions. But during the early 1900s, businesses—with the help of government—were able to use such weapons as court orders, force, and even the few existing antitrust laws to defeat the union attempts to improve working conditions.

Consumer Rights   Then as now, most people in business were honest people who produced and sold acceptable products. However, some business owners, eager for even greater profits, engaged in misleading advertising and sold shoddy and unsafe merchandise.

During this period, consumers were generally subject to the doctrine of **caveat emptor,** a Latin phrase meaning "let the buyer beware." In other

caveat emptor   a Latin phrase meaning "let the buyer beware"

Profit 1, Walruses 0. Few people thought about social responsibility in 1596, when these walruses were slaughtered in Canada's Gulf of St. Lawrence. The area had a higher concentration of walruses than anywhere on earth, and Europeans killed thousands of them for their hides, tusks, and blubber. Because the Europeans thought only of profit, you won't find any walruses in the St. Lawrence today.

words, "what you see is what you get," and too bad if it's not what you expected. Although victims of unscrupulous business practices could take legal action, going to court was very expensive and consumers rarely won their cases. Moreover, there were no consumer groups or government agencies to publicize their discoveries and hold sellers accountable for their actions.

In such an atmosphere, government intervention to curb abuses by business would seem almost inevitable. But in the early 1900s, there was as yet no great public outcry for such intervention.

Government Regulation   Prior to the 1930s, most people believed that competition and the action of the marketplace would correct abuses in time. Government became involved in day-to-day business activities only when there was an obvious abuse of the free-market system.

Six of the more important federal laws passed between 1887 and 1914 are described in Table 2.1. As you can see, these laws were aimed more at encouraging competition than at correcting business abuses, although two of them did deal with the purity of food and drug products. Such laws did little to curb abuses that occurred on a regular basis.

Social Responsibility After the 1930s

The collapse of the stock market on October 29, 1929, triggered the Great Depression and years of economic problems for the United States. As we noted in Chapter 1, U.S. production fell by almost one-half, and up to

TABLE 2.1   Early Government Regulations That Affected American Business

Government Regulation	Major Provisions
Interstate Commerce Act (1887)	First federal act to regulate business practices; provided regulation of railroads and shipping rates
Sherman Antitrust Act (1890)	Prevented monopolies or mergers where competition was endangered
Pure Food and Drug Act (1906)	Established limited supervision of interstate sale of food and drugs
Meat Inspection Act (1906)	Provided for limited supervision of interstate sale of meat and meat products
Federal Trade Commission Act (1914)	Created the Federal Trade Commission to investigate illegal trade practices
Clayton Act (1914)	Eliminated many forms of price discrimination that gave large businesses a competitive advantage over smaller firms

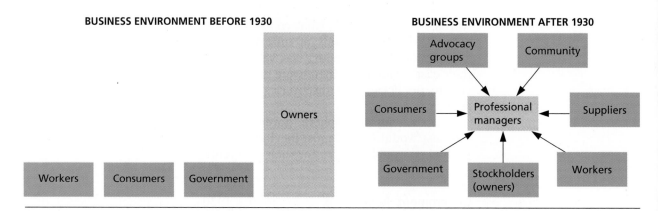

FIGURE 2.1 **The Business Environment Before and After 1930**
Prior to 1930, the owners of businesses were very powerful and government, consumers, and workers had little or no influence. After 1930, this power was more limited, and many groups were able to affect the way businesses were managed.

25 percent of the nation's work force was unemployed. At last public pressure mounted for government to "do something" about the economy and about worsening social conditions.

When Franklin Roosevelt was inaugurated as president in 1933, he instituted programs to restore the economy and to improve social conditions. Laws were passed to correct what many viewed as the monopolistic abuses of big business, and various social services were provided for individuals. These massive federal programs became the foundation for increased government involvement in the dealings between business and society.

As government involvement has increased, so has everyone's awareness of the social responsibility of business. Today business owners are concerned about the return on their investment, but at the same time most of them demand ethical behavior from professional business managers. In addition, employees demand better working conditions, and consumers want safe, reliable products. Various advocacy groups echo these concerns and also call for careful consideration of our delicate ecological balance. Managers must therefore operate in a complex business environment—one in which they are just as responsible for their managerial actions as for their actions as individual citizens. Figure 2.1 illustrates the change in emphasis in the business environment before and after the 1930s.

TWO VIEWS OF SOCIAL RESPONSIBILITY

Government regulation and public awareness are *external* forces that have increased the social responsibility of business. But business decisions are made *within* the firm—and there, social responsibility begins with the attitude of management. Two contrasting philosophies, or models, define the range of management attitudes toward social responsibility.

The Economic Model

According to the traditional concept of business, a firm exists to produce quality goods and services, earn a reasonable profit, and provide jobs. In line with this concept, the **economic model of social responsibility** holds that society will benefit most when business is left alone to produce and market profitable products that society needs. The economic model has its origins in the eighteenth century when businesses were owned primarily by entrepreneurs or owner-managers. Competition was vigorous among small firms, and short-run profits and survival were primary concerns.

economic model of social responsibility   the view that society will benefit most when business is left alone to produce and market profitable products that are needed by society

To the manager who adopts this traditional attitude, social responsibility is someone else's job. After all, stockholders invest in a corporation to earn a return on their investment, not because the firm is socially responsible, and the firm is legally obligated to act in the economic interest of its stockholders. Moreover, profitable firms pay federal, state, and local taxes that are used to meet the needs of society. Thus, managers who concentrate on profit believe they fulfill their social responsibility indirectly, through the taxes paid by their firms. As a result, social responsibility becomes the problem of government, various environmental groups, charitable foundations, and similar organizations.

The Socioeconomic Model

In contrast, some managers believe they have a responsibility not only to stockholders but also to customers, employees, suppliers, and the general public. This broader view is referred to as the **socioeconomic model of social responsibility.** It places emphasis not only on profits, but also on the impact of business decisions on society.

socioeconomic model of social responsibility   the concept that business should emphasize not only profits, but the impact of its decisions on society

Recently, increasing numbers of managers and firms have adopted the socioeconomic model, and they have done so for at least three reasons: First, business is dominated by the corporate form of ownership, and the corporation is a creation of society. If a corporation doesn't perform as a good citizen, society can and will demand changes. Second, many firms are beginning to take pride in their social responsibility records. IBM, Arco, John Hancock, and Johnson & Johnson are very proud of their commitment to social responsibility. And, of course, there are many other corporations that are more socially responsible today than they were ten years ago. Third, many business people believe it is in their best interest to take the initiative in this area. The alternative may be legal action brought against the firm by some special-interest group; in such a situation, the firm may lose control of its activities.

The Pros and Cons of Social Responsibility

The merits of the economic and socioeconomic models have been debated for years by business owners, managers, consumers, and government officials. Each side seems to have four major arguments to reinforce its viewpoint.

Arguments for Increased Social Responsibility   Proponents of the socioeconomic model maintain that a business must do more than simply seek profits. To support their position, they offer the following arguments:

1. Business cannot ignore social issues because business is a part of our society.
2. Business has the technical, financial, and managerial resources that are needed to tackle today's complex social issues.
3. By helping resolve social issues, business can create a more stable environment for long-term profitability.
4. Socially responsible decision making by business firms can prevent increased government intervention, which would force businesses to do what they fail to do voluntarily.

These arguments are based on the assumption that a business has a responsibility not only to stockholders but also to customers, employees, suppliers, and the general public.

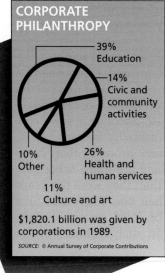

AT A GLANCE

CORPORATE PHILANTHROPY

- 39% Education
- 14% Civic and community activities
- 10% Other
- 26% Health and human services
- 11% Culture and art

$1,820.1 billion was given by corporations in 1989.

SOURCE: © Annual Survey of Corporate Contributions

Arguments Against Increased Social Responsibility   Opponents of the socioeconomic model argue that business should do what it does best: earn a profit by manufacturing and marketing products that people want. Those who support their position argue as follows:

1. Business managers are primarily responsible to stockholders, so management must be concerned with providing a return on owners' investments.
2. Corporate time, money, and talent should be used to maximize profits, not to solve society's problems.
3. Social problems affect society in general, so individual businesses should not be expected to solve these problems.
4. Social issues are the responsibility of government officials who are elected for that purpose and who are accountable to the voters for their decisions.

These arguments are obviously based on the assumption that the primary objective of business is to earn profits, whereas government and social institutions should deal with social problems.

TABLE 2.2   A Comparison of the Economic and Socioeconomic Models as Implemented in Business

Economic Model			Socioeconomic Model
Primary emphasis is on			**Primary emphasis is on**
1. Production	M	G	1. Quality of life
2. Exploitation of natural resources	I	R	2. Conservation of natural resources
3. Internal, market-based decisions	D	O	3. Market-based decisions, with some community controls
4. Economic return (profit)	D	U	4. Balance of economic return and social return
5. Firm's or manager's interest	L	N	5. Firm's and community's interest
6. Minor role for government	E	D	6. Active government involvement

Source: Adapted from Keith Davis, William C. Frederick, and Robert L. Blomstrom, *Business and Society: Concepts and Policy Issues* (New York: McGraw-Hill, 1980), p. 9. Used by permission of McGraw-Hill Book Company.

Table 2.2 compares the economic and socioeconomic viewpoints in terms of business emphasis. Today, few firms are either purely economic or purely socioeconomic in outlook; most have chosen some middle ground between the two. However, our society generally seems to want—and even to expect—some degree of social responsibility from business. Thus, within this middle ground between the two extremes, businesses are leaning toward the socioeconomic view. In the next several sections, we shall look at some results of this movement in four specific areas: consumerism, employment practices, concern for the environment, and implementing a social responsibility program.

CONSUMERISM

consumerism   all those activities intended to protect the rights of consumers in their dealings with business

Consumerism consists of all those activities that are undertaken to protect the rights of consumers in their dealings with business. Consumerism has been with us to some extent since the early nineteenth century, but the movement came to life only in the 1960s. It was then that President John F. Kennedy declared that the consumer was entitled to a new "bill of rights."

The Four Basic Rights of Consumers

LEARNING OBJECTIVE 5
Discuss the factors that led to the consumer movement and list some of its results.

President Kennedy's consumer bill of rights asserted that consumers have a right to safety, to be informed, to choose, and to be heard. These four rights are the basis of much of the consumer-oriented legislation that has been passed during the last thirty years. These rights also provide an effective outline of the objectives and accomplishments of the consumer movement.

For consumers who care. These three labels show various corporate responses to consumers' desires for socially responsible products. Some cosmetics users want to be sure their cosmetics are not tested on animals; health- and weight-conscious consumers want to know that Bread & Circus's Apple Cider will be good for them; and tuna eaters are comforted knowing that no dolphins died to make their lunches.

The Right to Safety   The right to safety means that products purchased by consumers must

- Be safe for their intended use.
- Include thorough and explicit directions for proper use.
- Have been tested by the manufacturer to ensure product quality and reliability.

There are several reasons why American business firms must be concerned about product safety. Federal agencies such as the Food and Drug Administration and the Consumer Product Safety Commission have the power to force businesses that make or sell defective products to take corrective actions. Such actions include offering refunds, recalling defective products, issuing public warnings, and reimbursing consumers—all of which can be expensive. Business firms should also be aware that consumers and the government have been winning an increasing number of product-liability lawsuits against sellers of defective products. Moreover, the amount of the awards in these suits has been steadily increasing. In 1991, for example, a state jury in Texas awarded $33.8 million in damages to the parents of a girl born with birth defects allegedly because her mother took Benedectin while she was pregnant. Merrell-Dow Pharmaceuticals Inc., manufacturer of the anti-nausea prescription drug, planned to seek a new trial or to appeal the verdict. (Benedectin was taken off the market in 1983, even though the drug is still approved by U.S. and foreign regulatory agencies.)[6] Yet another major reason for improving product safety is the consumer's demand for safe products. People will simply stop buying a product they believe is unsafe or unreliable.

The Right to Be Informed   The right to be informed means that consumers must have access to complete information about a product before they buy it. Detailed information about ingredients must be provided on food containers, information about fabrics and laundering methods must be attached to clothing, and lenders must disclose the true cost of borrowing the money that they make available to customers who purchase merchandise on credit.

In addition, manufacturers must inform consumers about the potential dangers of using their products. Manufacturers who fail to provide such information can be held responsible for personal injuries suffered because of their products. For example, General Electric provides customers with a twenty-page booklet that describes how they should use an automatic clothes washer. Sometimes such warnings seem excessive, but they are necessary if user injuries (and resulting lawsuits) are to be avoided.

The Right to Choose   The right to choose means that consumers have a choice of products, offered by different manufacturers and sellers, to satisfy a particular need. The government has done its part by encouraging competition through antitrust legislation. The more competition there is, the greater the choice available to consumers.

Competition and the resulting freedom of choice provide an additional benefit for consumers: They work to reduce the price of goods and services. Consider the electronic calculators that are so popular today. The Bowmar Brain, one of the first calculators introduced, carried a retail price tag in excess of $150. The product was so profitable that Texas Instruments Incorporated, Rockwell International Corp., and many other firms began to compete with Bowmar Instrument Corp. As a result, calculators can now be purchased for less than $10.

The Right to Be Heard   This fourth right means that someone will listen and take appropriate action when consumers complain. Actually, management began to listen to consumers after World War II, when competition between businesses that manufactured and sold consumer goods increased. One way firms got a competitive edge was to listen to consumers and provide the products they said they wanted and needed. Today, businesses are listening even more attentively, and many larger firms have consumer relations departments that the buying public can easily contact via toll-free phone numbers. Other groups listen, too. Most large cities and some states have consumer affairs offices to act on citizens' complaints.

Recent Developments in Consumerism

The greatest advances in consumerism have come through federal legislation. Some laws that have been passed in the last thirty-three years to protect your rights as a consumer are listed and described in Table 2.3. In addition to federal legislation, most business people now realize that they ignore consumer issues only at their own peril. Managers know that improper handling of consumer complaints can mean lost sales, bad publicity, and lawsuits.

TABLE 2.3   Major Federal Legislation Protecting Consumers Since 1960

Legislation	Main Provisions
Federal Hazardous Substances Labeling Act (1960)	Requires warning labels on household chemicals if they are highly toxic.
Color Additives Amendment (1960)	Requires manufacturers to disclose when colorings are added to foods.
Kefauver-Harris Drug Amendments (1962)	Established testing practices for drugs and requires manufacturers to label drugs with generic names in addition to trade names.
Cigarette Labeling Act (1965)	Requires manufacturers to place standard warning labels on all cigarette packages and advertising.
Fair Packaging and Labeling Act (1966)	Calls for all products sold across state lines to be labeled with net weight, ingredients, and manufacturer's name and address.
Motor Vehicle Safety Act (1966)	Established standards for safer cars.
Wholesome Meat Act (1967)	Requires states to inspect meat (but not poultry) sold within the state.
Flammable Fabrics Act (1967)	Strengthened flammability standards for clothing, to include children's sleepwear in sizes 0 to 6X.
Truth in Lending Act (1968)	Requires lenders and credit merchants to disclose the full cost of finance charges in both dollars and annual percentage rates.
Land Sales Disclosure Act (1968)	Provides protection for consumers from unscrupulous practices in interstate land sales.
Child Protection and Toy Act (1969)	Bans from interstate commerce toys with mechanical or electrical defects.
Credit Card Liability Act (1970)	Limits credit-card holder's liability to $50 per card and stops credit-card companies from issuing unsolicited cards.
Fair Credit Reporting Act (1971)	Requires credit bureaus to provide credit reports to consumers regarding their own credit files; also provides for correction of incorrect information.
Consumer Product Safety Commission Act (1972)	Established the Consumer Product Safety Commission.
Trade Regulation Rule (1972)	Established a "cooling-off" period of 72 hours for door-to-door sales.
Fair Credit Billing Act (1974)	Amended the Truth in Lending Act to enable consumers to challenge billing errors.
Equal Credit Opportunity Act (1974)	Provides equal credit opportunities for males and females and for married and single individuals.
Magnuson-Moss Warranty-Federal Trade Commission Act (1975)	Provides for minimum disclosure standards for written consumer product warranties for products that cost more than $15.
Amendment to Equal Credit Opportunity Act (1976)	Prevents discrimination based on race, creed, color, religion, age, and income when granting credit.
Fair Debt Collection Practices Act (1977)	Outlaws abusive collection practices by third parties.
Drug Price Competition and Patent Restoration Act (1984)	Established an abbreviated procedure for registering certain generic drugs.
Orphan Drug Act (1985)	Amended the original 1983 Orphan Drug Act and extends tax incentives to encourage the development of drugs for rare diseases.
Nutrition Labeling and Education Act (1990)	Requires the FDA to review current food labeling and packaging focusing on nutrition label content, label format, ingredient labeling, food descriptors and standards, and health messages.

EMPLOYMENT PRACTICES

LEARNING OBJECTIVE 6
Analyze how present employment practices are being used to
counteract past abuses.

We have seen that a combination of managers who subscribe to the socioeconomic view of business's social responsibility and significant government legislation enacted to protect the buying public has broadened the
rights of consumers. The last two decades have seen similar progress in af-
firming the rights of employees to equal treatment in the workplace.

Everyone who works for a living should have the opportunity to land a
job for which he or she is qualified and to be rewarded on the basis of
ability and performance. This is an important issue for society, and it also
makes good business sense. Yet, over the years, this opportunity has been
denied to members of various minority groups. A **minority** is a racial, religious, political, national, or other group regarded as different from the
larger group of which it is a part, often singled out for unfavorable treatment.

minority a racial, religious,
political, national, or other
group regarded as different
from the larger group of which
it is a part, often singled out for
unfavorable treatment

The federal government responded to the outcry of minority groups
during the 1960s and 1970s by passing a number of laws forbidding discrimination in the workplace. (These laws are discussed in Chapter 9 in the
context of human resources management.) Now, almost thirty years after
passage of the first of these (the Civil Rights Act of 1964), abuses still exist.
An example is the disparity in income levels for whites, blacks, and Hispanics, as illustrated in Figure 2.2. Lower incomes and higher unemployment
rates also affect Native Americans, handicapped persons, and women. Responsible managers have instituted a number of programs to counteract
the results of discrimination.

Affirmative Action Programs

affirmative action program
a plan designed to increase the
number of minority employees
at all levels within an organization

An **affirmative action program** is a plan designed to increase the number
of minority employees at all levels within an organization. Employers with
federal contracts of more than $50,000 per year must have written affirma-
tive action plans. The objective of such programs is to ensure that minorities are represented within the organization in approximately the same

FIGURE 2.2
Comparative Income Levels
Figure represents the median
household incomes of the
total population and of white,
black, and Hispanic workers in
1988. (Hispanic persons may
be of any race.) *(Source:* Statistical Abstract of the United
States, *1990, U.S. Bureau of
the Census, p. 420.)*

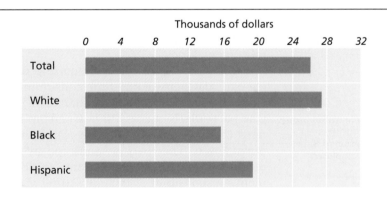

proportion as in the surrounding community. If 25 percent of the electricians in a geographic area in which a company is located are black, then approximately 25 percent of the electricians it employs should also be black. Affirmative action plans encompass all areas of human resources management: recruiting, hiring, training, promotion, and pay.

Unfortunately, affirmative action programs have been plagued by two problems. The first involves quotas. In the beginning, many firms pledged to recruit and hire a certain number of minority members by a specific date. To achieve this goal, they were forced to consider only minority applicants for job openings; if they hired nonminority workers, they would be defeating their own purpose. But the courts have ruled that such quotas are unconstitutional even though their purpose is commendable. They are, in fact, a form of discrimination called reverse discrimination.

The second problem is that although most such programs have been reasonably successful, not all business people are in favor of affirmative action programs. Managers not committed to these programs can "play the game" and still discriminate against workers. To help solve this problem, Congress created (and later strengthened) the **Equal Employment Opportunity Commission (EEOC),** a government agency with power to investigate complaints of employment discrimination and power to sue firms that practice it. In one case, a jury in Los Angeles awarded $15 million in punitive damages to Janella Sue Martin, who filed a sex discrimination case in 1986 against Texaco Inc. The 48-year-old woman sued the company, claiming that on two occasions she had been passed over for promotion in favor of men, even though she was equally qualified. Martin still works for Texaco as western region credit supervisor.[7]

The threat of legal action has persuaded some corporations to amend their hiring and promotional policies, but the discrepancy between men's and women's salaries has not really been affected, as illustrated in Figure 2.3. For more than thirty years, women have consistently earned only about 60 cents for each dollar earned by men.

Equal Employment Opportunity Commission (EEOC) a government agency with the power to investigate complaints of employment discrimination and the power to sue firms that practice it

Training Programs for the Hard-Core Unemployed

For some firms, social responsibility extends far beyond placing a help-wanted ad in the local newspaper. These firms have assumed the task of helping the **hard-core unemployed:** workers with little education or vocational training and a long history of unemployment. In the past, such workers were often routinely turned down by personnel managers, even for the most menial jobs.

hard-core unemployed workers with little education or vocational training and a long history of unemployment

Obviously, such workers require training; just as obviously, this training can be expensive and time-consuming. To share the costs, business and government have joined together in a number of cooperative programs. One particularly successful partnership is the **National Alliance of Business (NAB),** a joint business-government program to train the hard-core unemployed. The NAB is sponsored by participating corporations, whose executives contribute their talents to do the actual training. The government's responsibilities include setting objectives, establishing priorities, offering the right incentives, and providing limited financing.

National Alliance of Business (NAB) a joint business-government program to train the hard-core unemployed

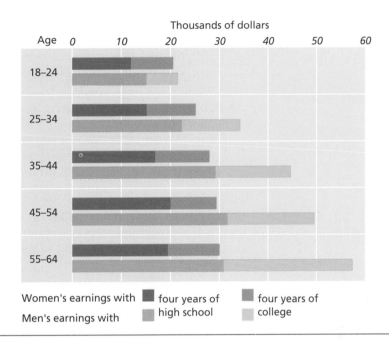

FIGURE 2.3   The Relative Earnings of Male and Female Workers
For more than three decades, the ratio of women's to men's annual full-time earnings has remained fixed at about the 60 percent level. (Indeed, some observers claim this ratio goes back to biblical times, citing that for purposes of tithing an adult woman was valued at 30 shekels of silver, compared with a man's 50 shekels.) *(Source: Statistical Abstract of the United States, 1990, U.S. Bureau of the Census, p. 420.)*

CONCERN FOR THE ENVIRONMENT

The social consciousness of responsible managers and the encouragement of a concerned government have also made the public and the business community partners in a major effort to reduce environmental pollution, conserve natural resources, and reverse some of the worst effects of past negligence in this area.

pollution the contamination of water, air, or land through the actions of people in an industrialized society

Pollution is the contamination of water, air, or land through the actions of people in an industrialized society. For several decades, environmentalists have been warning us about the dangers of industrial pollution. Unfortunately, business and government leaders either ignored the problem or weren't concerned about it until pollution became a threat to life and health in America. Consider the following list.

LEARNING OBJECTIVE 7
Describe the major types of pollution, their causes, and their cures.

• According to the Environmental Protection Agency (EPA), gasoline vapors from motor vehicles contribute to smog and can aggravate respiratory problems for millions of Americans. In 1987, the EPA proposed a regulation requiring that motor vehicles be equipped with systems to control about 90 percent of refueling vapors.[8]

- Billions of dollars will be needed to clean up America's worst hazardous waste sites, which now number almost 1,200. In fiscal year 1990, the EPA obtained settlements with the responsible parties to perform $731 million worth of cleanup and to repay EPA $87 million in costs.[9]

- People who change their own car oil produce as much as 400 million gallons of waste oil each year, which is the equivalent of *thirty-six Exxon Valdez* spills. Almost 90 percent of the waste oil ends up in the ground, streams, and sewers, instead of at service stations or recyclers, where it can be disposed of properly.[10]

These are not isolated cases. Such situations, occurring throughout the United States, have made pollution a matter of national concern. Today Americans expect business and government leaders to take swift action to clean up our environment—and to keep it clean.

Effects of Environmental Legislation

As in other areas of concern to our society, legislation and regulations play a crucial role in pollution control. The laws outlined in Table 2.4 reflect the scope of current environmental legislation. Of major importance was the creation of the Environmental Protection Agency (EPA), the federal agency charged with enforcing laws designed to protect the environment.

When they are aware of a pollution problem, most firms respond to it rather than wait to be cited by the EPA. But other owners and managers take the position that environmental standards are too strict. (Loosely translated, this means that compliance with present standards is too expensive.) Consequently, it has often been necessary for the EPA to take legal action to force firms to install antipollution equipment and clean up waste storage areas.

Experience has shown that the combination of environmental legislation, voluntary compliance, and EPA action can succeed in cleaning up the environment and keeping it clean. However, much still remains to be done.

Water Pollution   Although the quality of our nation's rivers, lakes, and streams has improved significantly in recent years, many of these surface waters remain severely polluted. Currently, one of the most serious water-quality problems results from the high level of toxic pollutants found in these waters. The EPA estimates that 554.7 million pounds of toxic materials were discharged to surface waters in 1987 alone.[11]

Among the serious threats to people posed by these pollutants are respiratory irritation, cancer, kidney and liver damage, anemia, and heart failure. Toxic pollutants also damage fish and other forms of wildlife. In fish, they cause tumors or reproductive problems; shellfish and wildlife living in or drinking from toxin-infested waters have also suffered genetic defects.

In addition to its adverse impacts on human health and aquatic life, toxic water pollution inflicts significant economic damages. According to the EPA, toxic discharges to surface waters cause losses of approximately

TABLE 2.4   Summary of Major Environmental Laws

Legislation	Major Provisions
National Environmental Policy Act of 1970	Established the Environmental Protection Agency (EPA) to enforce federal laws that involve the environment.
Clean Air Amendment of 1970	Provides stringent automotive, aircraft, and factory emission standards.
Water Quality Improvement Act of 1970	Strengthened existing water pollution regulations and provides for large monetary fines against violators.
Resource Recovery Act of 1970	Enlarged the solid-waste disposal program and provides for enforcement by the EPA.
Water Pollution Control Act Amendment of 1972	Established standards for cleaning navigable streams and lakes and eliminating all harmful waste disposal by 1985.
Noise Control Act of 1972	Established standards for major sources of noise and required the EPA to advise the Federal Aviation Administration on standards for airplanes.
Clean Air Act Amendment of 1977	Established new deadlines for cleaning up polluted areas; also required review of existing air-quality standards.
Resource Conservation and Recovery Act of 1984	Amended the original 1976 act and required federal regulation of potentially dangerous solid-waste disposal.
Clean Air Act Amendment of 1987	Established a national air-quality standard for ozone.
Oil Pollution Act of 1990	Expanded the nation's oil spill prevention and response activities; also established the Oil Spill Liability Trust Fund.
Clean Air Act Amendments of 1990	Required that motor vehicles be equipped with onboard systems to control about 90 percent of refueling vapors.

$800 million per year in recreational fishing, swimming, and boating opportunities.[12]

The task of water cleanup has proved to be extremely complicated and costly because of pollution run-off and toxic contamination. And yet, improved water quality is not only necessary; it is also achievable. Consider Cleveland's Cuyahoga River. A few years ago the river was so contaminated by industrial wastes that it burst into flames one hot summer day! Now, after a sustained community cleanup effort, the river is pure enough for fish to live in.

Another serious issue is acid rain, which is contributing significantly to the deterioration of coastal waters, lakes, and marine life in the eastern United States.[13] It forms when sulfur is emitted by smokestacks in industrialized areas. The sulfur combines with moisture in the atmosphere to form acids that are spread by winds. The acids then fall to the earth in rain, which finds its way into streams, rivers, and lakes. The acid-rain problem has spread rapidly in recent years, and experts fear the situation will worsen if the nation begins to burn more coal to generate electricity. To solve the problem, investigators must first determine where the sulfur is being emitted. The expenses that this vital investigation and cleanup entail are going to be high. The human costs of having ignored the problem so long may be higher still.

Air Pollution   Usually two or three factors combine to form air pollution in any given location. The first factor is large amounts of carbon monoxide and hydrocarbons emitted by motor vehicles concentrated in a relatively small area. The second is the smoke and other pollutants emitted by manufacturing facilities. These two factors can be partially eliminated through pollution-control devices on cars, trucks, and smokestacks.

The third factor that contributes to air pollution—one that cannot be changed—is the combination of weather and geography. The Los Angeles basin, for example, combines just the right weather and geographic conditions for creating dense smog. Los Angeles has strict regulations regarding air pollution. If other U.S. cities adopted such strict regulations, they would be able to meet the national air-quality standards.[14] Even with these strict regulations, however, Los Angeles still struggles with air pollution problems because of uncontrollable conditions.

How effective is air pollution control? Most authorities agree that there has been progress since the mid-1970s. (Read the accompanying *Business Journal* to learn what efforts are being made to make our automobiles more fuel-efficient.) A number of cities have cleaner air today than they did twenty years ago. Numerous chemical companies have recognized that they must take responsibility for operating their plants in an environmentally safe manner. Some of them now devote as much as 20 percent of their capital expenditures to purchasing antipollution devices.[15] However, air levels of sulfur dioxide and nitrogen dioxide—the main elements that cause acid rain—as well as of soot continue to increase.

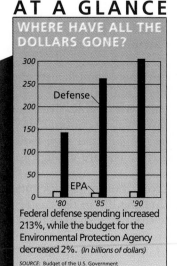

AT A GLANCE

WHERE HAVE ALL THE DOLLARS GONE?

Defense

EPA

Federal defense spending increased 213%, while the budget for the Environmental Protection Agency decreased 2%. *(In billions of dollars)*

SOURCE: Budget of the U.S. Government

Land Pollution   Air and water quality may be improving, but land pollution is still a serious problem in many areas. The fundamental issues are (1) how to restore damaged or contaminated land at a reasonable cost and (2) how to protect unpolluted land from future damage.

The land pollution problem has been worsening over the past few years, as modern technology has continued to produce increasing amounts of chemical and radioactive waste. U.S. manufacturers produce an estimated 40 to 60 million tons of contaminated oil, solvents, acids, and sludges each year. Service businesses, utility companies, hospitals, and other industries dump vast amounts of wastes into the environment.

Individuals in the United States also contribute to the waste disposal problem. On the average, each of us accounts for approximately 1,547 pounds of garbage each year.[16] A nationwide shortage of landfills makes garbage disposal an especially serious predicament. Incinerators are a possible solution to the problem of a landfill shortage, but they bring with them their own problems. They reduce the amounts of garbage but also leave tons of ash to be buried—ash that often has a higher concentration of

BUSINESS JOURNAL

Should Our Automobiles Be More Fuel Efficient?

"Increasing the fuel efficiency of our automobiles will put this country on the road to a rational energy future based on efficiency," says Melanie Griffin, the Sierra Club's Washington D.C. Director, Energy and Climate Policy. However, Thomas H. Hanna, president and chief executive officer of the Motor Vehicle Manufacturers Association of the United States, Inc. counters: "Manufacturers support better fuel economy, but not at the expense of safety, transportation efficiency, and consumers' mobility needs."

Senator Richard R. Bryan and Representative Barbara Boxer have introduced legislation that would require automakers to increase the average fuel efficiency of automobiles in model year 2001 by 40 percent and 60 percent, respectively (as compared with 1991 automobiles).

The Sierra Club strongly supports the Motor Vehicle Fuel Efficiency acts introduced by Senator Bryan and Representative Boxer. The Sierra Club envisions numerous benefits through improved Corporate Average Fuel Economy (CAFE). Griffin contends that reduced gasoline consumption would:

- Cut our dependence on foreign oil and avoid future oil wars.

- Reduce half of our huge trade deficit.

- Save more than $650 million in the next twenty years, which could then be invested elsewhere in our economy.

- Protect our environment by slowing the build-up of the greenhouse gases that cause global warming.

- Reduce demands for oil drilling in sensitive areas like Alaska's pristine Arctic National Wildlife Refuge, and help reduce dangerous oil spills.

Supporters of new legislation claim that even if car manufacturers decide to reach these levels of efficiency by building smaller cars, they could do so safely. Large cars are not inherently safer than small cars; the small Volkswagen Jetta, for example, has a lower passenger death rate than many gas-guzzling larger cars, such as the Mercury Grand Marquis, Chevy Caprice, and Oldsmobile Ninety-Eight. And the Nissan Stanza and Mazda 626 have lower rates of serious injuries than the Chevy Impala and Buick Electra. Of the ten 1985–86 models with the lowest passenger death rate, only three were in the "large" class. Six were midsize cars and one was in the "small" class.

Furthermore, supporters claim that the technology to produce fuel-efficient cars already exists. In just one example of this technology, Japanese automakers have developed an engine that provides a more efficient mix of air and fuel, which increases engine efficiency up to 20 percent. Volkswagen has developed a "stop-start" engine that stops operating while idling, thereby improving efficiency 30 percent on the highway. Both General Motors and Ford are scheduled to begin production of a "two-stroke" engine in 1993, which will be 20 to 30 percent more efficient than conventional engines.

Nevertheless, Hanna contends that there simply are no "magic" technologies that can increase fuel efficiency to the level required by the Bryan and Boxer acts. He also questions the safety implications of further downsizing to achieve higher CAFE standards. Projections of potential fuel savings by the U.S. Department of Energy are considerably less than estimated by the Sierra Club, Hanna notes. Contrary to claims by proponents of higher CAFE, history provides evidence that CAFE standards are no guarantee that the level of oil imports will be reduced.

Opponents of the proposed legislation dispute the statement that raising CAFE by 40 percent will reduce heat-trapping carbon dioxide and thus help prevent global warming. Hanna concludes, "CAFE is bad public policy. Not only does it fail its objectives, it places manufacturers at war with their customers by depriving them of the vehicles to meet their personal and business needs."

What stand do you take on this important environmental issue of the twenty-first century? Do you believe that consumers and the environment will benefit from stronger fuel efficiency legislation, or that "CAFE is bad public policy"?

toxicity than the original garbage.[17] Other causes of land pollution include strip-mining of coal, nonselective cutting of forests, and the development of agricultural land for housing and industry.

To help pay the enormous costs of cleaning up land polluted with chemicals and industrial wastes, Congress created a $1.6 billion Superfund in 1980. Originally, money was to flow into the Superfund from a tax paid by 800 oil and chemical companies that produce toxic waste. Then the EPA was to use the money in the Superfund to finance the cleanup of hazardous waste sites across the nation. To replenish the Superfund, the EPA had two options: It could sue the companies that were guilty of dumping chemicals at specific waste sites, or it could negotiate with guilty companies and thus completely avoid the legal system. During the 1980s, officials at the EPA came under fire because they preferred negotiated settlements. Critics referred to these settlements as "sweetheart deals" with industry. They felt the EPA should be much more aggressive in reducing land pollution in the United States. Of course, most corporate executives believe that cleanup efficiency and quality might be improved if companies were more involved. A 1986 amendment to the Superfund Act established strict guidelines for cleanups and gives residents the right to know what substances local chemical plants are producing.[18]

Noise Pollution   Excessive noise caused by traffic, aircraft, and machinery can do physical harm to human beings. Research has shown that people who are exposed to loud noises for long periods of time can suffer permanent hearing loss. The Noise Control Act of 1972 established noise emission standards for aircraft and airports, railroads, and interstate motor carriers. The act also provides funding for noise research at state and local levels.

Noise levels can be reduced by two methods. The source of noise pollution can be isolated as much as possible. (Thus, many metropolitan airports are located outside the cities.) And engineers can modify machinery and equipment to reduce noise levels. If it is impossible to reduce industrial noise to acceptable levels, workers should be required to wear earplugs to guard against permanent hearing damage.

Who Should Pay for a Clean Environment?

Governments and businesses are spending billions of dollars annually to reduce pollution—approximately $35 billion to control air pollution, $25 billion to control water pollution, and $12 billion to treat hazardous wastes. Proposed amendments to the 1970 Clean Air Act could add as much as $35 billion yearly to cleanup costs.[19]

To make matters worse, much of the money required to purify the environment is supposed to come from already depressed industries, such as the chemical industry. And a few firms have discovered that it is cheaper to pay a fine than to install expensive pollution control equipment.

Who, then, will pay for the environmental cleanup? Many business leaders offer one answer—tax money should be used to clean up the environment and keep it clean. They reason that business is not the only source of pollution, so business should not be forced to absorb the entire cost of

It's a very precious gift. Don't blow it.

We all know that to make a wish come true you have to blow out the candles. Unfortunately, protecting our planet is going to take a lot more than wishful thinking.

At C. Itoh our purpose in establishing the Department of Global Environment is to address many of the problems that can still be remedied, so that we can help put the environment back in healthy condition. Now

our management policies are looked at for their ecological soundness as well as economic benefit. And that's in addition to our growing involvement in eliminating acid rain, global warming and deforestation.

The way we look at it, this could be our last chance to do something to help the Earth. And we don't plan to blow it.

C. ITOH & CO., LTD.

Helping the world and themselves. With advertisements like this, companies like C. Itoh are betting that their increased sense of corporate responsibility will benefit themselves *and* the world. The ad is not selling a product, but the company hopes that it will give environmentally conscious readers a good feeling about C. Itoh, a feeling that may influence a business transaction in the future.

LEARNING OBJECTIVE 8
Identify the steps a business must take to implement a program of social responsibility.

social audit   a comprehensive report of what an organization has done, and is doing, with regard to social issues that affect it

the cleanup. Environmentalists disagree—they believe that the cost of proper treatment and disposal of industrial wastes is an expense of doing business. In either case, consumers may have to pay a large part of the cost—either as taxes or in the form of higher prices for goods and services.

IMPLEMENTING A SOCIAL RESPONSIBILITY PROGRAM

A firm's decision to be socially responsible is a step in the right direction—but only the first step. The firm must then develop and implement a tangible program to reach this goal. A particular firm's social responsibility program will be affected by its size, financial resources, past record in the area of social responsibility, and competition. But above all, the program must have total commitment or it will fail.

Developing a Social Responsibility Program

An effective program for social responsibility takes time, money, and organization. In most cases, developing and implementing such a program will require four steps: commitment of top executives, planning, appointment of a director, and preparing a social audit.

Commitment of Top Executives   Without the support of top executives, any program will soon falter and become ineffective. As evidence of their commitment to social responsibility, top managers should develop a policy statement that outlines key areas of concern. This statement "sets the tone" (one of positive enthusiasm) and will later serve as a guide for other employees as they become involved in the program.

Planning   Next, a committee of managers should be appointed to plan the program. Whatever the form of their plan, it should deal with each of the issues described in the top management policy statement. If necessary, outside consultants can be hired to help develop the plan.

Appointment of a Director   After the social responsibility plan is established, a top-level executive should be appointed to direct the organization's activities in implementing it. This individual should be charged with recommending specific policies and helping individual departments understand and live up to the social responsibilities the firm has assumed. Depending on the size of the firm, the director may require a staff to handle the program on a day-to-day basis.

The Social Audit   At specified intervals, the program director should prepare a social audit for the firm. A **social audit** is a comprehensive report of what an organization has done, and is doing, with regard to social issues that affect it. This document provides the information the firm needs to evaluate and revise its social responsibility program. Typical subject areas include human resources, community involvement, the quality and safety of products, business practices, and efforts to reduce pollution and improve the environment. The information included in a social audit should be as accurate and as quantitative as possible, and it should reveal both positive and negative aspects of the program.

Funding the Program

We have noted that social responsibility costs money. Thus, just like any other program, a program to improve social responsibility must be funded. Funding can come from three sources: (1) Management can pass the cost on to consumers in the form of higher prices. (2) The corporation may be forced to absorb the cost of the program if, for example, the competitive situation does not permit a price increase. In this case, the cost is treated as a business expense, and profit is reduced. (3) The federal government may pay for all or part of the cost through tax reductions or other incentives.

In this chapter and in Chapter 1, we have used the general term *business owners* and the more specific term *stockholders*. In the next chapter, wherein we discuss the various forms of business and business ownership, you will see who these people are.

CHAPTER REVIEW

Summary

Ethics is the study of right and wrong and of the morality of choices. Business ethics is the application of moral standards to business situations. Because ethical issues arise in business situations every day, the business person should make an effort to be fair, to consider the welfare of customers and others within a firm, to avoid conflicts of interest, and to communicate honestly.

Investors, customers, employees, creditors, and competitors each exert specific pressures on a firm. Business people should not compromise their ethics to either satisfy or mislead any group. Because no international business code of ethics exists and payoffs are sometimes part of international business practices, U.S. firms may directly or indirectly face ethical dilemmas when engaged in foreign business operations.

Any ethical action should be able to withstand open scrutiny. A person's individual values and experiences, the absence of an employer's code of ethics, and coworkers' values and behaviors all influence a person's ethical decision making. The government, trade associations, and individual firms can help establish a more ethical business environment. An ethical employee working in an unethical environment may resort to whistle blowing to bring a particular situation to light.

In a socially responsible business, management realizes that its activities have an impact on society, and that impact is considered in the decision-making process. Before the 1930s, workers, consumers, and government had very little influence on business activities; as a result, business gave little thought to its social responsibility. All this changed with the Great Depression. Government regulation, employee demands, and consumer awareness combined to create a demand that businesses act in a socially responsible manner.

According to the economic model of social responsibility, society benefits most when business is left alone to produce profitable goods and services. According to the socioeconomic model, business has as much responsibility to society as it has to its owners. Most managers adopt a viewpoint somewhere between these two extremes.

Three major areas of social concern to business and society are consumerism, employment practices, and the environment. The consumer movement has generally demanded—and received—attention from business in the areas of product safety, product information, product choices through competition, and the resolution of complaints about products and business practices.

Legislation and public demand have prompted some businesses to correct past abuses in employment practices—mainly with regard to minority groups. Affirmative action and training of the hard-core unemployed are two types of programs that have been used successfully.

Industry has contributed to the pollution of our land and water through the dumping of wastes, and to air pollution through vehicle and smokestack emissions. This contamination can be cleaned up and controlled, but the big question is who will pay for it. Present cleanup efforts are funded partly by government tax revenues, partly by business, and, in the long run, by consumers.

A program to implement social responsibility in a business begins with total commitment by top management. The program should be carefully planned, and a capable director should be appointed to implement it. Social audits should be prepared periodically as a means of evaluating and revising the program. Programs may be funded through federal incentives or through price increases.

Key Terms

You should now be able to define and give an example relevant to each of the following terms:

ethics	minority
business ethics	affirmative action
corporate code of ethics	program
whistle blowing	Equal Employment
social responsibility	Opportunity Commis-
caveat emptor	sion (EEOC)
economic model of social	hard-core unemployed
responsibility	National Alliance of
socioeconomic model of	Business (NAB)
social responsibility	pollution
consumerism	social audit

Questions and Exercises

Review Questions

1. Why might an individual with high ethical standards act less ethically in business than in his or her personal life?

2. How would an organizational code of ethics help ensure ethical business behavior?

3. How and why did the American business environment change after the Great Depression?

4. What are the major differences between the economic model of social responsibility and the socioeconomic model?

5. What are the arguments for and against increased social responsibility for business?

6. Describe and give an example of each of the four basic rights of consumers.

7. There are more women than men in the United States. Why, then, are women considered a minority with regard to employment?

8. What is the goal of affirmative action programs? How is this goal achieved?

9. What is the primary function of the Equal Employment Opportunity Commission?

10. How do businesses contribute to each of the four forms of pollution? How can they avoid polluting the environment?

11. Our environment *can* be cleaned up and kept clean. Why haven't we simply done so?

12. Describe the steps involved in developing a social responsibility program within a large corporation.

Discussion Questions

1. Why is it a sound business policy for Borden, Inc. to be socially responsible?

2. What additional steps, if any, should Borden take to safeguard the environment and be more socially responsible?

3. How can an employee take an ethical stand regarding a business decision when his or her superior has already taken a different position?

4. Overall, would it be more profitable for a business to follow the economic model or the socioeconomic model of social responsibility?

5. Why should business take on the task of training the hard-core unemployed?

6. To what extent should the blame for vehicular air pollution be shared by manufacturers, consumers, and government?

7. Why is there so much government regulation involving social responsibility issues? Should there be less?

Exercises

1. Write out four "guidelines" that can be included as part of the code of ethics that prevails at your school or at a firm where you have worked.

2. Research one case in which the EEOC or the EPA successfully brought suit against one or more

firms. Report on that case, giving your own evaluation of the merits of the case.

3. List some items that should be included in a social audit for a small business that is not a retail store.

CASE 2.1

Companies with Strong Codes of Ethics

Many organizations have established strong codes of ethics or policies related to ethics, and they have also developed strategies for enforcing them. Although codes of ethics will not solve every ethical dilemma, they do provide rules and guidelines for employees to follow in a variety of situations, from internal operations to sales presentations to financial disclosure practices. Three of these organizations with strong codes of ethics and policies for enforcing them are Caterpillar Inc., S. C. Johnson & Son, Inc., and Texas Instruments Incorporated. These companies are not unique in their industries in having adopted ethical codes, but they do represent good examples of best practice.

Caterpillar is a multinational company that makes heavy machinery and engines. In October 1974, its chairman, W. H. Franklin, issued "Caterpillar's Code of Worldwide Business Conduct and Operating Principles." A letter to employees explains that the code is not a prescription for action in every business encounter but rather is an attempt to define ethical conduct and what it means to Caterpillar. The company believes it is important to delineate for employees the standards and rules that make daily operations run smoothly, fairly, and honestly.

Caterpillar's code points out that the ethical performance of the company is the sum of the ethics of all its employees. If employees maintain high personal ethical standards, the company will achieve its desired level of ethical standards. The code also stresses that the company should maintain ethical standards well above the minimum level required by law.

S. C. Johnson & Son is a large, consumer-goods manufacturer whose products include Glade, Raid, and Johnson Wax. The company recognizes that it must abide by the laws and mores of society, and that it must behave in ways that the public perceives as ethical and responsible.

The words by H. F. Johnson, Sr., reflect Johnson's commitment to the guiding principles of its own company policy concerning ethics: "The goodwill of the people is the only enduring thing in any business. It is the sole substance. The rest is shadow." The company policy expresses basic beliefs about employees, consumers, the general public, neighbors and hosts, and the world community.

Texas Instruments (TI) is a large multinational firm that manufactures computers, calculators, and other high technology products. Its code of ethics is similar to those of many other organizations. The code addresses issues relating to policies and procedures; government laws and regulations; relationships with customers, suppliers, and competitors; gifts and entertainment; political contributions; business payments; conflicts of interest; investment in TI stock; handling of proprietary information and trade secrets; relationships with government officials and agencies; and enforcement of the code. TI's code emphasizes that ethical behavior is critical to maintaining a profitable enterprise.

These three organizations have long traditions of ethical and socially responsible behavior that they wish to maintain into the future. By explicitly spelling out what they expect of their employees and what behaviors they consider unacceptable, and by enforcing their codes wholeheartedly, the companies have taken logical steps to safeguard their excellent reputations for ethical and socially responsible behavior.*

Questions

1. Should all companies, large and small, have codes of ethics? Explain your answer.
2. Does having a code of ethics necessarily make a company and its employees more ethical in their behavior? Why or why not?
3. Do you agree with the statement that, "If employees maintain high personal ethical standards, the company will achieve its desired level of ethical standards"? Explain your position.

*Source: Based on O. C. Ferrell and John Fraedrich, *Business Ethics: Ethical Decision Making and Cases* (Boston: Houghton Mifflin Company, 1991), pp. 240–244. Facts are from "A Code of Worldwide Business Conduct and Operating Principles," Caterpillar, Inc., May 1, 1985; Caterpillar, Inc., annual reports, 1987 and 1988; "Cornerstone," TI Ethics Office, Texas Instruments Incorporated, 1988; "Ethics in the Business of TI," Texas Instruments Incorporated, 1987; Ronald Henkoff, "This Cat Is Acting Like a Tiger," *Fortune*, December 19, 1988, pp. 71–76 and Gene R. Laczniak and Patrick E. Murphy, *Marketing Ethics: Guidelines for Managers* (Lexington, Mass.: Lexington Books, 1985), pp. 111–16, 125–27, 133.

CASE 2.2

Bhopal Disaster That Just Won't Go Away

In December 1984, Union Carbide's chemical plant in Bhopal, India, sprang a deadly leak. Methyl isocyanate gas streamed into the air, causing the deaths of 3,700 persons. People are still dying at the rate of one a day. More than 200,000 persons were hospitalized, and nearly 25 percent of the women in the first trimester of pregnancy at the time of the accident miscarried, gave birth prematurely, or gave birth to handicapped children. More than 60,000 Bhopalis cannot do a full day's work. Clearly this is one of the worst industrial accidents in history.

Initially, Warren M. Anderson, then chairman of Union Carbide, said he would devote the rest of his career to resolving the problems caused by the accident. The company immediately donated $1 million to the Bhopal relief effort, and Union Carbide's employees donated an additional $150,000. A year later, Anderson told reporters he had overreacted. His admitting that he felt sorry about the accident increased Union Carbide's liability, thus jeopardizing the stockholders' investment and weakening the insurance carrier's position. Eventually, the Indian government charged Anderson with culpable homicide.

In April 1986, Union Carbide announced it had reached a tentative settlement with U.S. lawyers representing victims of the Bhopal accident. The company agreed to pay $350 million in damages. But after Union Carbide's announcement, the Indian government rejected the offer. Rajiv Gandhi, the late prime minister of India, called the settlement "inadequate." The Indian government insisted that it would agree to a settlement only if it fully and fairly compensated all of the Bhopal victims. Privately, Indian officials suggested that a settlement in the range of $700 million to $1 billion would be more acceptable.

India's highest court ruled that Union Carbide should pay the Bhopal survivors (500,000 claimants in all) $470 million in damages. The Indian government charged that flaws in the chemical plant's design and poor maintenance caused the disaster. Union Carbide insists that an unhappy and vengeful employee (whom they refuse to name) sabotaged the plant. India's Supreme Court, however, did not address the issue of blame and, as part of the settlement, dismissed all criminal charges and civil suits against Union Carbide and its officials.

But, like the earlier settlement, this settlement was short-lived. And, unlike the Gandhi administration that agreed to the settlement offer in 1989, the current government contends that Union Carbide *is* criminally responsible for the leak. By overturning the $470 mil-

lion settlement, the present government will be free to pursue the original claim for $3.3 billion.

Union Carbide's chief executive, Robert Kennedy, is convinced that sabotage caused the disaster, and he charges the Indian government with "virtually ignoring the interests of the victims." Kennedy hopes the Indian Supreme Court will act quickly and again approve the payment. "The money should then be immediately distributed to the victims. Let's get on with it."**

Questions

1. Warren M. Anderson initially said he would devote the rest of his career to resolving the problems caused by the Bhopal accident. A year later he said that he had overreacted. Why do you think he changed his position?

2. Do you think the settlement between the Gandhi administration and Union Carbide was fair to the claimants? Why or why not?

3. Based on feasibility studies, management at Union Carbide was concerned about whether this type of plant could be maintained in India. What could have been done to minimize this concern and to ensure the safety of the Bhopal workers?

**Based on information from David Bergman, "Judges May Free India to Renew Battle Over Bhopal," *New Scientist*, January 12, 1991, p. 24; Jeremy Main, "Where Bhopal's Money Went," *Fortune*, June 3, 1991, p. 17; David Bergman, "Bhopal Polluters Accused of Hypocrisy," *New Scientist*, November 24, 1990, p. 18; David Bergman, "Surviving Bhopal," *New Statesman & Society*, November 16, 1990, p. 5; K. S. Jayaram, "Deal Is Less Than Final," *Nature*, August 9, 1990, p. 503; "Haunted by a Gas Cloud," *Time*, February 5, 1990, p. 53; Gordon Walker, "Bhopal: Five Years On," *Geography*, April 1990, p. 158; Jeffrey P. Koplan, Henry Falk, and Gareth Green, "Public Health Lessons from the Bhopal Chemical Disaster," *The Journal of the American Medical Association*, December 5, 1990, p. 2795; Pushpa S. Mehta, Anant S. Mehta, Sunder J. Mehta, and Arjun B. Makhijani, "Bhopal Tragedy's Health Effects," *The Journal of the American Medical Association*, December 5, 1990, p. 2781; "Appeals Court Denies Bid for Bhopal Fees," *The National Law Journal*, March 11, 1991, p. 6; "State Court Says Union Carbide Can Collect Millions in Insurance," *The National Law Journal*, February 18, 1991, p. 44; Subrata N. Chakravarty, "The Ghost Returns," *Forbes*, December 10, 1990, p. 108; Falguni Sen and William G. Egelhoff, "Six Years and Counting: Learning from Crisis Management at Bhopal," *Public Relations Review*, Spring 1991, p. 69; Steve Dodson, "$470 Million Accord in Bhopal Tragedy," *New York Times*, February 19, 1989, p. 14F; and Sanjoy Hazarika, "Many Details Unsettled on Bhopal Distributions," *New York Times*, February 16, 1989, p. 29.

The Forms of Business Ownership

CHAPTER PREVIEW

Our initial focus in this chapter is on three common forms of business ownership: sole proprietorships, partnerships, and corporations. We discuss how these types of businesses are formed and note the advantages and disadvantages of each. Next, we consider several types of corporations organized for special purposes, including S-corporations, government-owned corporations, and not-for-profit corporations. We also describe corporate patterns of growth, which may result from internal expansion or from mergers with other corporations. We conclude the chapter with a discussion of cooperatives, joint ventures, and syndicates—forms of business ownership that are less common but useful in special situations.

IBM and Apple: Partnership of the Decade

It's official. International Business Machines Corp. and Apple Computer, Inc. have formed a partnership. The contract, which was signed in late 1991, will enable the two computer giants to work on at least three major projects designed to develop state-of-the-art technology that could dramatically change the future of the computer industry. Although the companies refuse to discuss the financial details, this partnership could result in increased profits for both IBM and Apple by 1992 or early 1993.

Under the terms of the agreement, the two firms will develop software programs that will enable Apple's personal computers to communicate with IBM's larger mainframe computers. Today, computers manufactured by the two companies use different operating systems—the software that controls the internal operations of the computer. As a result, IBM and Apple computers cannot directly communicate with each other. This project is especially important for Apple, which in the past has had difficulty selling its personal computers to business firms.

Apple and IBM also plan to develop a new, advanced operating system that should be available by 1994. If successful, this project could establish the industry standard for the next generation of personal computers. The project is code-named *Pink* because of the project members' penchant for pink sneakers and shirts, lounging on pink couches, shooting baskets with pink balls, and taking notes with pink pens. Pink is an important project for IBM because of the company's recent split with Microsoft Corp.—the firm that developed the *MS-DOS* operating system used with IBM personal computers since 1981. It's no secret that IBM would like to end its dependence on Microsoft's *MS-DOS*. For this project, Apple—a firm known for its expertise in software development—was a natural choice.

The third project is just as important as the first two, according to IBM and Apple officials. The

two firms will develop multimedia software that will enable computers to use enhanced video, sound, and animation capabilities. Again, timing is crucial, and the project is important to both IBM and Apple for two reasons. First, they would like to beat the Japanese. (Rumors are already flying that Japan's Sony Corp., NEC, and Fujitsu are working on multimedia software.) And second, multimedia software is the wave of the future. Both firms need this software to accompany the new, more sophisticated personal computers they plan to introduce in the mid-1990s.

Although the three IBM/Apple projects are impressive, industry analysts are quick to point out that there may be problems. Apple—the young, upstart company founded in 1976 by a couple of computer whizzes—is used to playing by its own rules and doing its own thing. And IBM already has a history of high-profile partnerships, joint ventures, and corporate alliances that have failed before they could deliver marketable new products. There may be problems, but a successful partnership between IBM and Apple could revitalize the U.S. computer industry. For the two firms, it could lead to a return of the glory days that each of them experienced in the 1980s.[1]

The fact that IBM and Apple could bury the hatchet and sign a partnership agreement is a sign of the times. Faced with lower profits, stiff competition, and technological changes in the computer industry, these two corporations formed a partnership because it was a logical way to solve the problems of both firms. If successful, this partnership could ensure that the two firms maintain their number-one and number-two rankings in the computer industry for years to come.

Not all businesses choose the corporate or partnership forms of organization. Many choose to organize as sole proprietorships. The type of organization that is right for a particular business depends on a number of factors discussed in this chapter. In reality, some businesses start as a sole proprietorship, change to a partnership, and then change to a corporation. That is exactly what happened in the case of Sears, Roebuck and Co.—the well-known department store chain.

LEARNING OBJECTIVE 1
Describe the basic differences among the three most common forms of business ownership: sole proprietorships, partnerships, and corporations.

SOLE PROPRIETORSHIPS

sole proprietorship a business that is owned (and usually operated) by one person

A **sole proprietorship** is a business that is owned (and usually operated) by one person. Sole proprietorship is the simplest form of business ownership and the easiest to start. In most instances, the owner (the *sole* proprietor) simply decides he or she is in business and begins operations. Some of the largest of today's corporations, including Ford Motor Company, H.J. Heinz Company, and J. C. Penney Company, started out as tiny—and, in many cases, struggling—sole proprietorships.

As you can see in Figure 3.1, there are more than 12.3 million sole proprietorships in the United States. They account for more than two-thirds of the country's business firms. Sole proprietorships are most common in retailing, service, and agriculture. Thus the clothing shop, corner grocery, and television repair shop down the street are likely to be sole proprietorships.

Advantages of Sole Proprietorships

LEARNING OBJECTIVE 2
Explain the advantages and disadvantages of proprietorships, partnerships, and corporations.

Most of the advantages of sole proprietorships arise from the two main characteristics of this form of ownership: simplicity and individual control.

FIGURE 3.1
Relative Percentages of Sole Proprietorships, Partnerships, and Corporations in the United States
Sole proprietorships, the most common form of business ownership, are most common in retailing, agriculture, and the service industries.
(Source: U.S. Department of Commerce, Bureau of the Census, Statistical Abstract of the United States, *1990, p. 521.)*

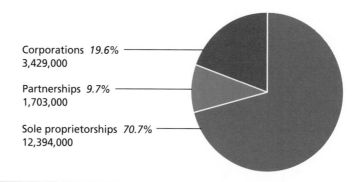

Corporations *19.6%*
3,429,000

Partnerships *9.7%*
1,703,000

Sole proprietorships *70.7%*
12,394,000

Ease and Low Cost of Formation and Dissolution   No contracts, agreements, or other legal documents are required to start a sole proprietorship. Most are established without even an attorney. A state or city license may be required for certain types of businesses, such as restaurants or catering services, that are regulated in the interest of public safety. But beyond that, a sole proprietor pays no special start-up fees or taxes. Nor are there any minimum capital requirements.

If the enterprise does not succeed, or if the owner decides to enter another line of business, the firm can be closed as easily as it was opened. Creditors must be paid, of course. But generally, the owner does not have to go through any legal procedure before hanging up an "Out of Business" sign.

Retention of All Profits   Because all profits earned by a sole proprietorship become the personal earnings of the owner, the owner has a strong—perhaps the strongest—incentive to succeed. This direct financial reward attracts many entrepreneurs to the sole proprietorship form of business and, if the business succeeds, is a source of great satisfaction.

AT A GLANCE

NUMBER OF PARTNERSHIPS, 1988

300

200

100

0

Manufacturing   Construction   Wholesale and retail trade   Services

(In thousands, based on tax returns filed)

SOURCE: U.S. Internal Revenue Service

Flexibility   The sole owner of a business is completely free to make decisions about the firm's operations. Without asking or waiting for anyone's approval, a sole proprietor can switch from retailing to wholesaling, move a shop's location, open a new store, or close an old one.

A sole owner can also respond to changes in market conditions much more quickly than the partnership or corporate forms of business. Suppose the sole owner of an appliance store finds that many customers now prefer to shop on Sunday afternoons. He or she can make an immediate change in business hours to take advantage of that information (provided that state laws allow such stores to open on Sunday). The manager of one store in a large corporate chain may have to seek the approval of numerous managers before making such a change. Furthermore, a sole proprietor can quickly switch suppliers to take advantage of a lower price, whereas such a switch could take weeks in a more complex business.

Possible Tax Advantages   The sole proprietorship's profits are taxed as personal income of the owner. Thus a sole proprietorship does not pay the

GLOBAL PERSPECTIVES
Entrepreneurs: Building a New Capitalistic Economy in Russia

Despite shortages of meat, vegetables, and bread, and the fact that many consumer products, such as Levi jeans and Nike running shoes are too expensive for the average citizen, the wave of capitalism continues to grow in Russia. Most experts seem to agree that entrepreneurs will play a major role in solving the problems in the new Russian economy. To prove their point, they cite an increasing number of privately owned businesses—at least 250,000 by current estimates—that, taken together, employ over six million employees.

Most of these private businesses are either sole proprietorships or partnerships. Typical private businesses include clothing manufacturers, restaurants, garages, repair shops for electronic appliances, or other small service or retail firms. But regardless of the type of business, one thing is common: Russian entrepreneurs are motivated by the lure of profits.

The financial success of some entrepreneurs makes other would-be entrepreneurs eager to start their own private businesses. According to one U.S. embassy official, an average of six to twelve would-be entrepreneurs show up each day to talk with potential partners from the United States. Although these entrepreneurs know the risks and the economic problems they will face, they nevertheless want to be their own boss and own their own business.

But success in Russia does create problems for some entrepreneurs. After decades of communist training, most Russians distrust successful business owners. According to the "old" philosophy, a poor man is an honest man, but a rich man is a thief.* Most government officials also distrust the new breed of entrepreneurs—a particularly perplexing problem, since private business must be licensed by the government. Officials can shut down any business at the drop of a hat. Most of the new breed of entrepreneurs avoid this problem by making "political contributions" to the right people.

Despite all their problems and drawbacks, Russian entrepreneurs are proud of their success. In Moscow, a group of young entrepreneurs have formed the Young Millionaires Club of Russia. To belong, each member must have a net worth of one million rubles—the equivalent of about $30,000 in U.S. currency. In addition to the prestige of belonging to the club, members help each other form new business ventures, which they hope will create even more profits for this select group of entrepreneurs.

*Malcolm Gray, "Capitalism, Soviet-style," *Macleans*, April 29, 1991, pp. 25–26.

special state and federal income taxes that corporations pay. (As you will see later, the result of these special taxes is that a corporation's profits are taxed twice. A sole proprietorship's profits are taxed only once.) Also, recent changes in federal tax laws have resulted in higher tax rates for corporations than for individuals at some income levels.

Secrecy   Sole proprietors are not required by federal or state governments to publicly reveal their business plans, profits, or other vital facts. Therefore, competitors cannot get their hands on this information. Of course, sole proprietorships must report certain financial information on their personal tax forms, but that information is kept secret by taxing authorities.

A corporation with a different look. Many people think of corporations as faceless entities that manufacture anonymous products. But co-owners Marta Gutiérrez and her son Fernando also constitute a corporation, and their "products" are works of art from Latin America and all over the world.

the state, in which the state recognizes the formation of the artificial person that is the corporation. Usually the charter (and thus the articles of incorporation) includes the following information:

- Firm's name and address
- Incorporators' names and addresses
- Purpose of the corporation
- Maximum amount of stock and types of stock to be issued
- Rights and privileges of shareholders
- Length of time the corporation is to exist (usually without limit)

Each of these key details is the result of decisions the incorporators must make as they organize the firm—before they submit the articles of incorporation. Let's look at one such area: stockholders' rights.

common stock stock owned by individuals or firms who may vote on corporate matters, but whose claims on profit and assets are subordinate to the claims of others

preferred stock stock owned by individuals or firms who usually do not have voting rights, but whose claims on profit and assets take precedence over those of common-stock owners

Stockholders' Rights   There are two basic types of stock (some variations on these two types are discussed in Chapters 18 and 19). Each entitles the owner to a different set of rights and privileges. Owners of **common stock** may vote on corporate matters, but their claims on profit and assets are subordinate to the claims of others. Generally, an owner of common stock has one vote for each share owned. The owners of **preferred stock** usually have no voting rights, but their claims on profit and assets take precedence over those of common-stock owners.

Small Business, Entrepreneurship, and Franchises

LEARNING OBJECTIVES

After studying this chapter, you should be able to:

1 Define what a small business is and recognize the fields in which small businesses are concentrated.

2 Identify the people who start small businesses and the reasons why some succeed and many fail.

3 Assess the contributions of small businesses to our economy.

4 Judge the advantages and disadvantages of operating a small business.

5 Explain how the Small Business Administration helps small businesses.

6 Appraise the concept and types of franchising.

7 Analyze the growth of franchising and its advantages and disadvantages.

CHAPTER PREVIEW

In this chapter we do not take small businesses for granted. Instead we look closely at this important business sector—beginning with a definition of small business, a description of industries that often attract small businesses, and a profile of some of the people who start small businesses. Next, we consider the importance of small businesses in our economy. We also present the advantages and disadvantages of smallness in business. Then, we describe services provided by the Small Business Administration, a government agency formed to assist owners and managers of small businesses. We conclude the chapter with a discussion of the pros and cons of franchising, an approach to small business ownership that has become very popular in the last two decades.

Entrepreneurial Rap, Harvard Style

In August 1988, two Harvard seniors, Jon Shecter and David Mays, pooled $200 of their own money to write and publish a one-page rap music newsletter on a Macintosh computer. Neither Shecter nor Mays were business, journalism, or broadcasting majors; Shecter was majoring in English and Mays was taking a degree in government.

During their freshman year in 1986, the duo became friends and discovered that both saw the need for a "serious magazine that took rap music seriously." By early 1987, Shecter and Mays started co-hosting "Street Beat," a weekly show about rap on the Harvard student radio station. Shecter remembers that "we had so many people call us up during the show that we compiled a mailing list. We got the idea to put together the newsletter as a service to our listeners in Boston, but also as an experiment to see just how much interest there might be out there for something more substantive."

Today, Mays is the publisher and Shecter is the editor-in-chief of *The Source*, a magazine they describe as "the voice of the rap music industry." One national executive called *The Source* "the hippest, dopest, freshest thing to happen to the rap community in a long time."

Mays's entrepreneurial spirit dates back to his junior high school days when his lawn-mowing service boasted fifty accounts. In his new venture, Mays handles all business matters and sells 95 percent of the ads for *The Source*. He learned his managerial skills during his sophomore year at Harvard when he managed a local rap group.

Shecter is the creative genious behind *The Source*. During his high school years, he worked at a radio station in Philadelphia and envisioned himself a disk jockey or a performer. During his sophomore year at Harvard, he formed a rap group called "BMOC," and cut a rap single. "We want to make money, sure," he says, "but we don't want to forget what we are doing. We always want to be conscious

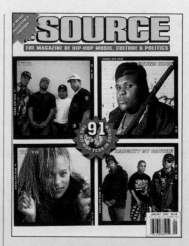

that this is a black art form. We see rap as a major social movement that offers empowerment to African-American people. We want to stay involved in the kind of social activism that goes along with rap."

Of course the $200 initial investment was not enough to run a business. Mays and Shecter borrowed $10,000 from a friend, bought a bigger computer, set up an off-campus office in an apartment, and started publishing 10,000 copies of *The Source*. The bimonthly magazine, which runs 30 to 40 pages an issue, is already well known to the major rap record labels.

After graduating in June 1990, Mays and Shecter moved to New York and rented loft space to produce the magazine. To raise cash, they asked record-label executives for advance payments for ads. After raising $70,000 in cash, *The Source* was in business.

The founders now are talking to such potential backers as Time Warner; producer/composer Quincy Jones; and Russell Simmons, a black entertainment entrepreneur. Their plan is to make *The Source* the next *Rolling Stone*.[1]

The kind of growth enjoyed by Mays and Shecter is unusual. Most businesses start small, and those that survive usually stay small. They provide a solid foundation for our economy—as employers, as suppliers and purchasers of goods and services, and as taxpayers.

SMALL BUSINESS: A PROFILE

LEARNING OBJECTIVE 1
Define what a small business is and name the fields in which small businesses are concentrated.

The Small Business Administration (SBA) defines a **small business** as "one which is independently owned and operated for profit and is not dominant in its field." How small must a firm be not to dominate its field? That depends on the particular industry it is in. The SBA has developed specific "smallness" guidelines for the various industries:[2]

- *Manufacturing:* a maximum number of employees ranging from 500 to 1,500, depending on the products manufactured
- *Wholesaling:* a maximum number of employees not to exceed 500
- *Retailing:* maximum yearly sales or receipts ranging from $10 million to $13.5 million, depending on the industry
- *General construction:* average annual receipts ranging from $9.5 million to $17 million, depending on the industry
- *Special trade construction:* annual sales ranging up to $7 million
- *Agriculture:* maximum annual receipts of $0.5 million to $3.5 million
- *Services:* maximum annual receipts ranging from $2.5 million to $14.5 million, depending on the type of service

A new standard, based only on the number of employees, has been proposed but not yet adopted by the SBA.

Annual sales in the millions of dollars may not seem very small. However, for many firms, profit is only a small percentage of total sales. Thus a firm may earn only $30,000 or $40,000 on yearly sales of $1 million—and that *is* small in comparison to the profits earned by most medium-sized and large firms. Moreover, most small firms have annual sales well below the limits the SBA has used in its definitions.

An entrepreneur's armload.
Many entrepreneurs are
driven by the desire to be their
own bosses, do what they
want to do, and turn passions
into profit-making businesses.
No doubt Jeanette de Goede
loved flowers long before she
started growing tulips like
these at her Skagit Valley Bulb
Farm in Mount Vernon,
Washington.

The Small-Business Sector

A surprising number of Americans take advantage of their freedom to start
a business. There are, in fact, about 20 million businesses in this country.
More than 90 percent are small, and many are new. Over 677,000 new
businesses are incorporated in a typical year.[3]

At the same time that new firms are being created, others are going
out of business. Statistically, over 70 percent of new businesses can be expected to fail within their first five years.[4] The primary reason for these
failures is mismanagement resulting from a lack of business know-how.
The makeup of the small-business sector is thus constantly changing. In
spite of the high failure rate, many small businesses succeed modestly.
Some, like Apple Computer, Inc., are extremely successful—to the point
where they can no longer be considered small. Taken together, small businesses are also responsible for providing a high percentage of the jobs in
the United States. According to some estimates, this figure is well over
50 percent.

Industries That Attract Small Businesses

Some industries, such as auto manufacturing, require huge investments in
machinery and equipment. Businesses in such industries are big from the
day they are started—if an entrepreneur or group of entrepreneurs can
gather the capital required to start one.

By contrast, a number of other industries require only a low initial investment and some special skills or knowledge. It is these industries that
tend to attract new businesses. Growing industries, such as outpatient care
facilities, are attractive because of their profit potential. However, knowl-
edgeable entrepreneurs choose areas with which they are familiar, and
these are most often the more established industries. Consider the example
of Eastern Delivery Services, Inc. of Wilmington, N.C., which specializes in
relatively small, time-sensitive, and fragile shipments. The company was
started in 1977 when Katherine Moore and her former husband received a
$20,000 business loan from the SBA. After two years, the firm had two
trucks and a lot of debt. When Moore and her husband separated in 1979,
she decided to run the company, and her efforts paid off. Today, Eastern
Delivery operates fourteen delivery trucks and records annual sales of
about $500,000.[5]

Small enterprise spans the gamut from corner newspaper vending to
the development of optical fibers. The owners of small businesses sell gasoline, flowers, and coffee to go. They publish magazines, haul freight, teach
languages, and program computers. They make wines, movies, and high-
fashion clothes. They build new homes and restore old ones. They fix appliances, recycle metals, and sell used cars. They drive cabs and fly planes.
They make us well when we are ill, and they sell us the products of corporate giants.

As Figure 4.1 shows, the various kinds of businesses generally fall into
three broad categories of industries: distribution, service, and production.
Within these categories, small businesses tend to cluster in the service in-

FIGURE 4.1
The Relative Proportions of Small Businesses by Industry
Small businesses are found in three major industries; most are in service and distribution. *(Source: Adapted from* The State of Small Business: A Report of the President *[Washington D.C.: GPO, 1989], p. 18.)*

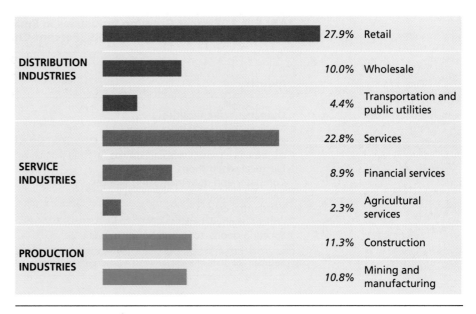

DISTRIBUTION INDUSTRIES	27.9%	Retail
	10.0%	Wholesale
	4.4%	Transportation and public utilities
SERVICE INDUSTRIES	22.8%	Services
	8.9%	Financial services
	2.3%	Agricultural services
PRODUCTION INDUSTRIES	11.3%	Construction
	10.8%	Mining and manufacturing

dustries and in retailing. Table 4.1 shows the fastest growing industries in the small business sector.

Service Industries   This category accounts for about 34 percent of all small businesses. Of these, about three-quarters provide such nonfinancial services as medical and dental care; watch, shoe, and TV repairs; hair-cutting and styling; restaurant meals; and dry cleaning. About 9 percent of the small service firms offer financial services, such as accounting, insurance, and investment counseling.

Distribution Industries   This category includes retailing, wholesaling, transportation, and communications—industries that are concerned with the movement of goods from producers to consumers. Distribution industries account for approximately 42 percent of all small businesses. Of these, almost three-quarters are involved in retailing, the sale of goods directly to consumers. Clothing and jewelry stores, pet shops, bookstores, and grocery stores, for example, are all retailing firms. Slightly less than one-quarter of the small distribution firms are wholesalers. Wholesalers purchase products in quantity from manufacturers and then resell them to retailers.

Production Industries   This last category includes the construction, mining, and manufacturing industries. Only about 22 percent of all small businesses are in this group, mainly because these industries require relatively large initial investments. Small firms that do venture into production generally make parts and subassemblies for larger manufacturing firms or supply special skills to larger construction firms. Consider P Precision Electronic Manufacturing, a small Tulsa, Oklahoma, company headed by Pauline Smith. P Precision manufactured components of three military

TABLE 4.1 Fastest Growing Industries in Small Business: December 1988 to December 1989 (Percent Change in Employment)

Industry	Percent Change in Employment
Outpatient care facilities	20.1
Medical and dental laboratories	14.5
Mailing, reproduction, stenographic	14.2
Automotive rentals without drivers	12.6
Electrical repair shops	11.4
Computer and data processing services	10.9
Railroad equipment	9.8
Residential care	9.3
Offices of physicians	8.7
Sporting goods, toys, and hobby goods	8.5

Source: *The State of Small Business: A Report of the President* (Washington, D.C.: GPO, 1990), p. 25.

weapons used by Desert Storm troops—weapons for a multiple-launch rocket system, the M-87 land mine launcher and the TOW anti-tank missile. Smith's firm also has held contracts connected with the Hawk anti-aircraft missile and the *Challenger* space shuttle.[6]

The People in Small Businesses: The Entrepreneurs

LEARNING OBJECTIVE 2
Identify the people who start small businesses and the reasons why some succeed and many fail.

Small businesses are typically managed by the people who started and own them. Most of these people have held jobs with other firms and could still have such jobs if they wanted them. Yet owners of small businesses would rather take the risk of starting and operating their own firms, even if the money they make is less than the salaries they might otherwise earn.

Researchers have suggested a variety of personal factors as reasons why individuals go into business. One that is often cited is the "entrepreneurial spirit"—the desire to create a new business. Other factors, such as independence, the desire to determine one's own destiny, and the willingness to find and accept a challenge certainly play a part. Background may exert an influence as well. In particular, researchers think that people whose families have been in business (successfully or not) are most apt to start and run their own businesses. Those who start their own businesses also tend to cluster around certain ages—more than 70 percent are between 24 and 44 years old (see Figure 4.2). Women own 4.6 million businesses and are starting new businesses at twice the rate of men.[7]

Finally, there must be some motivation to start a business. A person may decide she has simply "had enough" of working and earning a profit for someone else. Another may lose his job for some reason and decide to start the business he has always wanted rather than seek another job. Still another person may have an idea for a new product or a new way to sell an existing product. Or the opportunity to go into business may arise suddenly, perhaps as a result of a hobby.

GETTING AHEAD IN BUSINESS
What It Takes to Be an Entrepreneur

The following quiz is designed to help you find out if you have what it takes to be an entrepreneur. If you score better than 50 percent, maybe you should start working on your business plan.

1. WAS ONE OF YOUR PARENTS AN ENTREPRENEUR?

An entrepreneur in the family is the single most telling indicator of successful entrepreneurs. In fact, counting such businesses as law practices, farms, or ministerships, fully 80 percent of today's entrepreneurs come from a family heritage of individual businesses.

2. ARE YOU AN IMMIGRANT?

There is a high correlation between immigrants and entrepreneurs. In this sense, "immigrant" includes not only those who were born outside the United States but also those who moved from farm or city or, for example, from the Midwest to the West Coast. A study of 254 technical entrepreneurs on the West Coast reveals that their average residence there was only nine years.

3. DID YOU HAVE A PAPER ROUTE?

Yes? Fine. An entrepreneurial streak shows up early in life. And although rising at 5:30 a.m. undoubtedly builds moral fiber, an even more indicative sign of entrepreneurial tendencies would be that you had subcontracted the deliveries to a younger sibling and dickered with the news company for an adjoining route.

4. WERE YOU A GOOD STUDENT?

The typical entrepreneur was anything but a model student. There is no indication that he or she is less well educated than others, but the entrepreneur often has an expulsion listed on school records.

5. WHAT IS YOUR FAVORITE SPECTATOR SPORT?

The best answer is "none." Entrepreneurs are poor spectators. Not surprisingly, they excel at individual sports such as sailing and skiing—but not golf. Golf is too slow and involves too much walking.

6. WHAT IS THE SIZE OF THE COMPANY WHERE YOU NOW WORK?

Statistics show that a preponderance of entrepreneurs have come from medium-sized companies—those with thirty to five hundred employees.

7. HAVE YOU EVER BEEN FIRED?

Having been fired may not look good on your résumé for a job at General Foods, but it indicates that you may have entrepreneurial timber. Entrepreneurs make poor employees—that's why they become entrepreneurs.

8. IN YOUR NEW BUSINESS, WOULD YOU PLAY YOUR CARDS CLOSE TO THE VEST, OR WOULD YOU BE WILLING TO DISCUSS PROBLEMS WITH YOUR EMPLOYEES?

An open communication policy may be good business, but the typical entrepreneur has a secretive streak. If he or she confides in anyone, it will probably be another entrepreneur.

9. ARE YOU AN INVENTOR? A PH.D.?

These are not positive indicators. Inventors fall in love with their products; Ph.D.s with their research. They are not really interested in sharing the fruits of their labors. Entrepreneurs are less enamored of their products than in pricing them right and getting them into the marketplace.

10. HOW OLD ARE YOU?

Although people of all ages start new businesses, the ideal age seems to be 32–35. It takes a certain number of years of building business self-confidence to carry the entrepreneur beyond the adversity certain to be encountered in a new venture. It also takes time to develop a critical mass of frustration with being an employee. Furthermore, as a person reaches the early 30s, not only finances but family life may stabilize, and those with children are not yet facing college tuition bills. The person who waits much beyond these years may have figured out a way of dealing with the frustration. After age 40, many people feel locked into the corporate pension plan.

11. WHEN DO YOU PLAN TO RETIRE?

It doesn't much matter what you answer. If you're an entrepreneur, you won't retire. The real distinction between the entrepreneur and the nonentrepreneur is that no matter what the stage of life, the entrepreneur is out there starting businesses.

FIGURE 4.2
How Old Is the Average Entrepreneur?
People in all age groups become entrepreneurs, but almost 70 percent are between 24 and 44.   *(Source: Data developed and provided by the NFIB Foundation and sponsored by the American Express Travel Related Services Company, Inc.)*

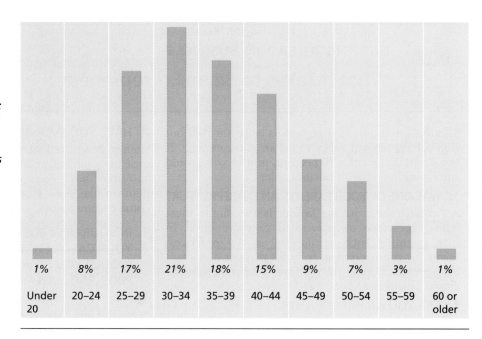

| 1% | 8% | 17% | 21% | 18% | 15% | 9% | 7% | 3% | 1% |
| Under 20 | 20–24 | 25–29 | 30–34 | 35–39 | 40–44 | 45–49 | 50–54 | 55–59 | 60 or older |

When Brett Gibson was 15, he was already known around his home town as a first-rate telephone installer. Carefully concealing his age (when possible), he took over customer contracts of the local telephone company when it closed its offices. Though his grandmother drove him to business appointments and his parents had to lend him money because banks refused to take him seriously, Gibson managed to build his company, Mid American Telephone Supply, into a $700,000-a-year business. Gibson is now in his early twenties, and his firm continues to grow. However, he still runs into occasional credibility problems because of his age.[8]

In some people the motivation develops more slowly, as they gain the knowledge and ability required for success as a business owner. Knowledge and ability—especially management ability—are probably the most important factors involved. A new firm is very much built around the entrepreneur. The owner must be able to manage the firm's finances, its personnel (if there are any employees), and its day-to-day operations. He or she must handle sales, advertising, purchasing, pricing, and a variety of other business functions. The knowledge and ability to do so are most often acquired through experience working for other firms in the same area of business.

Consider a successful small business owner, Pedro Garza, Jr. Garza, a native of Miranda City, Texas, spent his childhood as a migrant worker, traveling with his family to harvest crops in Texas, Florida, Washington, and Oregon. His formal education ended in the tenth grade. After a hitch in the Army, Garza became a cement mason and worked in that trade for twenty-seven years. That occupation ended abruptly in 1975, when Garza lost both kneecaps in an automobile accident.

AT A GLANCE
SMALL GIANTS

The top five companies with high market value and 1990 sales below $100 million are all in drugs and research.
(Market value shown in millions of dollars)
SOURCE: Standard & Poor's Compustat Services, Inc.

No longer able to perform heavy manual labor, Garza drew upon his childhood experiences and started a small tree-thinning and planting company. At the same time, he took part in business training offered by SBA—studying government contracting regulations and pricing. He switched his company's focus from tree work to general building contracting. During the first year, Garza's sales were only $109,000. Today, Garza's firm has up to thirty employees and his gross sales total about $4.5 million a year.[9]

Why Small Businesses Fail

Small businesses are prone to failure. Capital, management, and planning are the key ingredients in the survival of a small business, and also the most common reasons for failure. Businesses can experience a number of money-related problems. It may take several years before a business begins to show a profit. Entrepreneurs need to have not only the capital to open a business but also the money to operate it in its possibly lengthy start-up phase. One cash-flow obstacle often leads to others. And a series of cash-flow predicaments usually leads to a business failure.

Many entrepreneurs lack the management skills required to run a business. Money, time, personnel, and inventory all need to be effectively managed if a small business is to succeed. Starting a small business requires much more than optimism and a good idea.

Success and expansion sometimes lead to problems. Frequently entrepreneurs with successful small businesses make the mistake of overexpansion. But fast growth often results in dramatic changes in a business. Thus the entrepreneur must plan carefully and adjust competently to potentially new and disruptive situations.

Every day, and in every part of the country, people open new businesses. Though many will fail, others represent well-conceived ideas developed by entrepreneurs who have the expertise, resources, and determination to make their businesses succeed. As these well-prepared entrepreneurs pursue their individual goals, our society benefits in many ways from their work and creativity. Billion-dollar companies such as Apple Computer, McDonald's Corporation, and Procter & Gamble are all examples of small businesses that expanded into industry giants.

THE IMPORTANCE OF SMALL BUSINESSES IN OUR ECONOMY

LEARNING OBJECTIVE 3
Assess the contributions of small business to our economy.

This country's economic history is chock full of stories of ambitious men and women who turned their ideas into business dynasties. The Ford Motor Company started as a one-man operation with a new method for industrial production. L.L. Bean, Inc. can trace its beginnings to a basement shop on Maine Street in Freeport, Maine. Both Xerox Corp. and Polaroid Corp. began as small firms with a better way to do a job.

Team Rollerblade Rolls. Occasionally a small business will pioneer a new market even launch a new sport. Rollerblade did both by introducing a skate with narrow wheels arranged in a straight line. Team Rollerblade has been one of the company's most effective promotions, performing dance and stunt routines before millions of viewers at places like the Superbowl. The popularity of in-line skates has spawned a whole new industry.

Providing Technical Innovation

Invention and innovation are among the foundations of our economy. The increases in productivity that have characterized the past two hundred years of our history are all rooted in one principal source: new ways to do a job with less effort, at a lower cost. Studies show that the incidence of innovation among small-business workers is significantly higher than among workers in large businesses. Small firms produce two and a half times as many innovations as large firms, relative to the number of persons employed.[10]

According to the U.S. Office of Management and Budget, more than half the major technological advances of this century originated with individual inventors and small companies. A sampling of those innovations is remarkable:

- Air conditioning
- Automatic transmission
- Ball-point pen
- FM radio
- Helicopter
- Instant camera

- Insulin
- Jet engine
- Penicillin
- Power steering
- Xerography
- Zipper

Perhaps even more remarkable and important is the fact that many of these inventions sparked major new U.S. industries.

Providing Employment

Small businesses employ approximately one-half of the nation's private work force. Small businesses have thus contributed significantly to solving unemployment problems. Historically, small businesses have created the bulk of new jobs. Table 4.2 shows the small-business industries that are generating the most new jobs.

Providing Competition

Small businesses challenge larger, established firms in many ways, causing them to become more efficient and more responsive to consumer needs. A small business cannot, of course, compete with a large firm in all respects. But a number of small firms, each competing in its own particular area and its own particular way, together have the desired competitive effect. Thus, several small janitorial companies together add up to reasonable competition for the no-longer-small ServiceMaster.

Filling Needs of Society and Other Businesses

By their nature, large firms must operate on a large scale. Many may be unwilling or unable to meet the special needs of smaller groups of consumers. Such groups create almost perfect markets for small companies, which can tailor their products to these groups and fill their needs profitably. A prime example is a firm that modifies automobile controls to accommodate handicapped drivers.

Small firms also provide a variety of goods and services to each other and to much larger firms. Sears, Roebuck purchases merchandise from approximately 12,000 suppliers—and most of them are small businesses. General Motors relies on more than 32,000 companies for parts and supplies. And it depends on more than 11,000 independent dealers to sell its

TABLE 4.2   Small Business Industries Generating Most New Jobs Between December 1988 and December 1989

Industry	Employment Increase (Thousands)
Eating and drinking places	107.0
Offices of physicians	100.7
Computer and data processing services	78.8
Nursing and personal care facilities	78.3
Trucking and trucking terminals	69.8
Miscellaneous business services	65.2
Outpatient care facilities	57.8
Machinery, equipment, and supplies	57.1
Residential care	38.0
Mailing, reproduction, stenographic	32.9

Source: *The State of Small Business: A Report of the President* (Washington, D.C.: GPO, 1990), p. 26.

GLOBAL PERSPECTIVES
Chinese Entrepreneurship

A private enterprise in China is defined as a private, profit-seeking business with at least eight employees, but the life of an entrepreneur in the People's Republic of China has never been an easy one. In addition to the general problems faced by entrepreneurs, China's entrepreneurs must cope with the unpredictable political winds.

During the 1980s, the winds were favorable. Deng Xiaoping came to power and declared that "to get rich is glorious." He explained his policy of economic pragmatism with the proverb, "It doesn't matter if the cat is black or white, so long as it catches mice."

Then in June 1989, the winds changed direction. Former Communist Party chief and heir-apparent to Deng Xiaoping, Zhao Ziyang, the main champion of free enterprise, lost his job and was placed under house arrest. Private enterprises *(siying qiye)* and individual businesses *(getihu)* were at-

tacked as the government tried to regain control over the private sector. In August 1989, two months after the Tiananmen Square massacre in Beijing, the State Taxation Bureau began a two-month campaign to detect tax evasion in the private sector. (Private businesses in China are required by law to pay 52 percent of their profit to the state and to put 30 percent back into the business. The remaining 18 percent is often eaten away by local taxes and fees and by the necessity to pay bribes.)

Jiang Zemin, who replaced Zhao Ziyang as General Secretary of the Communist Party, referred to private entrepreneurs as "exploiters" and accused them of profiteering, cheating, and taking advantage of the people.

Entrepreneurs who turn away from the socialist road of state-sponsored security in China come from all walks of life. Some are college educated, others are barely literate. Men and women, representing both the majority Han Chinese group and the minority groups, choose the capitalist road, even with all its associated risks. The crushing of the prodemocracy movement in 1989 and the crackdowns that followed dealt a blow to entrepreneurs and other individuals in the private sector.

Premier Li Peng has stated that China needs to strike a balance between "building socialism with Chinese characteristics" and continuing with market-oriented reforms. Until he and the rest of the Chinese leaders realize that such a balance is ultimately untenable, China's entrepreneurs will remain stuck in the unenviable position of looking toward Beijing to see which way the winds are blowing.

automobiles and trucks. Large firms generally buy parts and assemblies from smaller firms for one very good reason: It is less expensive than manufacturing the parts in their own factories. This lower cost is eventually reflected in the price that consumers pay for their products.

Centennial One, Inc. is a highly successful janitorial company based in Prince George's County, Md. The company's founder and president, Lillian H. Lincoln-Youman proudly counts among her clients Westinghouse, IBM, Comsat, and Dulles International Airport in Washington, D.C. (In 1988,

SBA Management Assistance

Statistics show that most failures in small business are due to poor management. For this reason, the SBA places special emphasis on improving the management ability of the owners and managers of small businesses. The SBA's Management Assistance Program is extensive and diversified. It includes free individual counseling, courses, conferences, workshops, and a wide range of publications. During a recent year the SBA indicated that it counseled or trained more than 500,000 people and answered over 300,000 calls.[15]

Management Courses and Workshops The management courses offered by the SBA cover all the functions, duties, and roles of managers. Instructors may be teachers from local colleges and universities or professionals such as management consultants, bankers, lawyers, and accountants. Fees for these courses are quite low. The most popular such course is a general survey of eight to ten different areas of business management. In follow-up studies, business people may concentrate in depth on one or more of these areas, depending on their own particular strengths and weaknesses. The SBA occasionally offers one-day conferences. These conferences are aimed at keeping owner-managers up to date on new management developments, tax laws, and the like.

The SBA also invites prospective owners of small businesses to workshops, where management problems and good management practices are discussed. A major goal of these sessions is to emphasize the need for sufficient preparation before starting a new venture. Sometimes the sessions convince eager but poorly prepared entrepreneurs to wait until they are ready for the difficulties that lie ahead.

Service Corps of Retired Executives (SCORE) a group of retired business people who volunteer their services to small businesses through the SBA

SCORE and ACE The **Service Corps of Retired Executives (SCORE)** is a group of 13,000 retired business people who volunteer their services to small businesses through the SBA. The collective experience of SCORE volunteers spans the full range of American enterprise.

A small-business owner who has a particular problem can request free counseling from SCORE. An assigned counselor visits the owner in his or her establishment and, through careful observation, analyzes the business situation and the problem. If the problem is complex, the counselor may call on other volunteer experts to assist. Finally, the counselor offers a plan for solving the problem and helping the owner through the critical period.

Active Corps of Executives (ACE) a group of active managers who counsel small-business owners on a volunteer basis

The **Active Corps of Executives (ACE)** is a group of active managers who counsel small-business owners on a volunteer basis. ACE was established to supplement the services available through SCORE and to keep the SBA's management counseling as current as possible. ACE volunteers come from major corporations, trade associations, educational institutions, and professions.

Help for Minority-Owned Small Businesses Americans who are members of minority groups have had difficulty entering the nation's economic mainstream. Raising money is a nagging problem for minority business owners, who may also lack adequate training. Members of minority groups are, of course, eligible for all SBA programs, but the SBA makes a special effort to assist those who want to start small businesses or expand existing ones. For example, the Minority Business Development Agency awards grants to develop and increase business opportunities for members of racial and ethnic minorities.

Helping women become entrepreneurs is also a special goal of the SBA. Women make up more than half of America's population, but they own about one-fourth of its businesses. In 1980 an SBA Assistant Administrator for Women's Business Enterprise was appointed, and programs directed specifically toward this group were expanded.

Small Business Institute (SBI)   a group of senior and graduate students in business administration who provide management counseling to small businesses

Small Business Institutes   A **Small Business Institute (SBI)** is a group of senior and graduate students in business administration who provide management counseling to small businesses. SBIs have been organized on almost 520 college campuses as another way to help business owners. The students, who work in small groups, are guided by faculty advisers and SBA management-assistance experts. Like SCORE volunteers, they analyze and help solve the problems of small-business owners at their business establishments.

Small Business Development Center (SBDC)   university-based group that provides individual counseling and practical training to owners of small businesses

Small Business Development Centers   A **Small Business Development Center (SBDC)** is one of forty-five university-based groups that provide individual counseling and practical training to owners of small businesses. SBDCs draw from the resources of local, state, and federal governments; private business; and universities. These groups can provide managerial and technical help, data from research studies, and other types of specialized assistance that are of value to small businesses.

According to a recent report by the U.S. Senate Committee on Small Business, 69 percent of clients were satisfied overall with the counseling they received. Similarly, 76 percent of the clients indicated they would contact the SBDC for future help and 82 percent would recommend the SBDC program to others.[16]

In a new program started in 1991, SBDCs are helping small businesses in East European economies. For example, the University of Washington's business school has received a $1.2 million federal grant for a joint project with the Washington State University (WSU) Small Business Development Center to help Romanians learn about free market economies. The university's Economics Education Program for Romania offered seminars in 1991 in Bucharest on the fundamentals of the free market system. WSU's SBDC is sending business development specialists to train Romanian faculty in small business assistance counseling.[17]

SBA Publications   The SBA issues management, marketing, and technical publications dealing with hundreds of topics of interest to present and prospective managers of small firms. Most of these publications are available from the SBA free of charge. Others can be obtained for a small fee from the U.S. Government Printing Office.

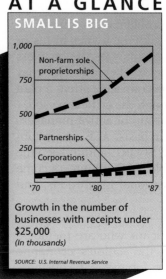

AT A GLANCE

SMALL IS BIG

Non-farm sole proprietorships

Partnerships

Corporations

'70   '80   '87

Growth in the number of businesses with receipts under $25,000
(In thousands)

SOURCE: U.S. Internal Revenue Service

SBA Financial Assistance

Small businesses seem to be constantly in need of money. An owner may have enough capital to start and operate the business. But then he or she may require more money to finance increased operations during peak selling seasons, to pay for required pollution-control equipment, to mop up after a natural disaster such as a flood, or to finance an expansion. The SBA offers special financial-assistance programs that cover all these situations. However, its primary financial function is to guarantee loans to eligible businesses.

Regular Business Loans   Most of the SBA's business loans are actually made by private lenders such as banks, but repayment is partially guaranteed by the agency. That is, the SBA may guarantee that it will repay the lender up to 90 percent of the loan if the borrowing firm cannot repay it. Guaranteed loans may be as large as $750,000. The average size of an SBA-guaranteed business loan is $165,000 and its average duration is about eight years.

venture capital   money that is invested in small (and sometimes struggling) firms that have the potential to become very successful

Small Business Investment Companies   **Venture capital** is money that is invested in small (and sometimes struggling) firms that have the potential to become very successful. In many cases, only a lack of capital keeps these firms from rapid and solid growth. The people who invest in such firms expect that their investments will grow with the firms and become quite profitable.

The popularity of these investments has increased over the past ten years, but most new, small firms still have difficulty in obtaining venture capital. To help such firms, the SBA licenses, regulates, and provides financial assistance to Small Business Investment Companies. A **Small Business Investment Company (SBIC)** is a privately owned firm that provides venture capital to small enterprises that meet its investment standards. SBICs are intended to be profit-making organizations. However, SBA aid allows them to invest in small businesses that would not otherwise attract venture capital.

Small Business Investment Company (SBIC)   privately owned firm that provides venture capital to small enterprises that meet its investment standards

We have discussed the importance of the small-business segment of our economy. We have weighed the advantages and drawbacks of operating a small business as compared with a large one. But is there a way to achieve the best of both worlds? Can one preserve one's independence as a business owner and still enjoy some of the benefits of "bigness"? Let's take a close look at franchising.

FRANCHISING

franchise   a license to operate an individually owned business as though it were part of a chain of outlets or stores

A **franchise** is a license to operate an individually owned business as if it were part of a chain of outlets or stores. Often the business itself is also

BUSINESS JOURNAL
Evaluating a Franchise

How can you protect yourself against making a mistake in buying a franchise? No answer is 100 percent reliable, but there are several important steps you can take before making a commitment to buy a franchise.

EXAMINE THE FRANCHISE OPPORTUNITY ITSELF

1. Did your lawyer approve the franchise contract after he or she studied it, paragraph by paragraph?
2. Does the franchise call upon you to take any steps which are, according to your lawyer, unwise or illegal in your state, county, or city?
3. Does the franchise give you an exclusive territory for the length of the franchise, or can the franchisor sell a second or third franchise in your territory?
4. Is the franchisor connected in any way with any other franchise companies handling similar merchandise or services?
5. If the answer to the last question is yes, what is your protection against this second franchisor organization?
6. Under what circumstances and at what cost can you pull out of the franchise contract?
7. If you sell your franchise, will you be paid for your goodwill, or will the goodwill you have built into the business be lost to you?

TAKE A HARD LOOK AT THE FRANCHISOR

1. For how many years has the franchisor been in business?
2. Does the franchisor have a reputation for honesty and fair dealing among the local entrepreneurs holding its franchise?
3. Has the franchisor shown you any certified figures indicating exact net profits of one or more going franchises, which you yourself checked with the franchisee?
4. Will the franchisor help you with:
   a. A management training program?
   b. An employee training program?
   c. A public relations program?
   d. Merchandising ideas?
   e. Financing?
5. Will the franchisor help you find a good location for your franchise?

6. Is the franchisor adequately financed so that it can carry out its stated plan of financial help and expansion?
7. Is the franchisor a one-person company or a larger company with a trained and experienced management team so that there is always an experienced person as its head?
8. Exactly what can the franchisor offer you that you cannot do for yourself?
9. Has the franchisor investigated you carefully enough to ensure that you can successfully operate one of their franchises at a profit, both to them and to you?

TAKE AN EQUALLY HARD LOOK AT THE FRANCHISEE—YOU AND YOUR EXPECTATIONS

1. How much capital will you need to buy the franchise and operate it until your sales revenues equal your expenses?
2. Where are going to get the capital you need?
3. Are you prepared to give up some independence of action to get the advantages offered by the franchise?
4. Do you really believe you have the ability, training, and experience to work smoothly and profitably with the franchisor, your employees, and your customers?
5. Are you ready to spend much or all of the rest of your business life with this franchisor, offering its product or service to your customers?

IS THERE A MARKET FOR YOUR PRODUCT?

1. Have you made any study to find out whether the product or service you propose to sell under franchise has a market in your territory at the prices you will have to charge?
2. Will the population in your territory increase, remain static, or decrease over the next five years?
3. Will the demand for the product or service you are considering be greater, about the same, or less in five years?
4. What competition exists in your territory for the product or service, either from nonfranchise firms or franchise firms?

called a *franchise*. Among the most familiar franchises are McDonald's, H & R Block, AAMCO Transmissions, Jazzercize, and Pier 1 Imports. Many other franchises carry familiar names; this method of doing business has become very popular in the last twenty-five years or so. It is an attractive means of starting and operating a small business.

What Is Franchising?

franchising   the actual granting of a franchise

franchisor   an individual or organization granting a franchise

franchisee   a person or organization purchasing a franchise

Franchising is the actual granting of a franchise. A **franchisor** is an individual or organization granting a franchise. A **franchisee** is a person or organization purchasing a franchise. The franchisor supplies a known and advertised business name, management skills, the required training and materials, and a method of doing business. The franchisee supplies labor and capital, operates the franchised business, and agrees to abide by the provisions of the franchise agreement. Table 4.4 lists some items that would be covered in a typical franchise agreement.

TABLE 4.4   McDonald's Conventional Franchise as of January 1991

McDonald's (Franchisor) Provides	Individual (Franchisee) Supplies
1. Nationally recognized trademarks and established reputation for quality 2. Designs and color schemes for restaurants, signs, and equipment 3. Formulas and specifications for certain food products 4. Proven methods of inventory and operations control 5. Bookkeeping, accounting, and policies manuals specially geared toward a franchised restaurant 6. A franchise term of up to 20 years 7. Formal training program completed on a part-time basis in approximately 18–24 months in a McDonald's restaurant 8. Five weeks of classroom training, including two weeks at Hamburger University 9. Ongoing regional support services and field service staff 10. Research and development into labor-saving equipment and methods 11. Monthly bulletins, periodicals, and meetings to inform franchisees about management and marketing techniques	1. Total investment of approximately $610,000; includes initial franchise fee of $22,500 and refundable security deposit of $15,000 2. Approximate cash requirement of 40 percent of total investment 3. A minimum of 3.5 percent of gross sales annually for marketing and advertising 4. Payment of 12 percent of gross sales monthly to McDonald Corp. 5. Kitchen equipment, seating, decor, lighting, and signs in conformity with McDonald's standards (included in total investment figure) 6. Willingness to relocate 7. Taxes, insurance, and maintenance costs 8. Commitment to assuring high-quality standards and upholding McDonald's reputation

Source: *McDonald's Franchising;* McDonald Corporation, Oak Brook, Ill., January 1991. Used by permission.

Types of Franchising Arrangements

LEARNING OBJECTIVE 6
Appraise the concept and types of franchising.

Franchising arrangements fall into three general categories. In the first approach, a manufacturer authorizes a number of retail stores to sell a certain brand-name item. This franchising arrangement, one of the oldest, is prevalent in sales of passenger cars and trucks, farm equipment, shoes, paint, earth-moving equipment, and petroleum. About 90 percent of all gasoline is sold through franchised independent retail service stations, and franchised dealers handle virtually all sales of new cars and trucks. In the second type of franchising arrangement, a producer licenses distributors to sell a given product to retailers. This arrangement is common in the soft-drink industry. Most national manufacturers of soft-drink syrups—The Coca-Cola Company, Dr Pepper Co., PepsiCo, The Seven-Up Company, Royal Crown Companies Inc.—franchise independent bottlers who then serve retailers. In a third form of franchising, a franchisor supplies brand names, techniques, or other services, instead of a complete product. Although the franchisor may provide certain production and distribution services, its primary role is the careful development and control of marketing strategies. This approach to franchising, which is the most typical today, is used by Holiday Inns Inc., Howard Johnson Co., AAMCO Transmissions, McDonald's, Dairy Queen, Avis, Inc., The Hertz Corporation, KFC Corporation, and H & R Block, to name a few.

The Growth of Franchising

LEARNING OBJECTIVE 7
Analyze the growth of franchising and its advantages and disadvantages.

Franchising has been used since the early 1900s, primarily for filling stations and car dealerships. However, it has experienced enormous growth since the mid-1960s. This growth has generally paralleled the expansion of the fast-food industry—the industry in which franchising is used to the greatest extent. As Table 4.5 shows, *Entrepreneur* magazine's top-ranked franchises were nearly all in this industry.

Of course, franchising is not limited to fast foods. Hair salons, tanning salons, and professionals such as dentists and lawyers are expected to participate in franchising arrangements in growing numbers. Franchised health clubs, exterminators, and campgrounds are already widespread, as are franchised tax preparers and travel agencies. The real estate industry has also experienced a rapid increase in franchising. In 1988, approximately $716 billion in sales at over 509,000 franchised outlets accounted for about one-third of all retail sales in the United States. The Department of Commerce estimates that by the year 2000, franchising will account for more than half of all sales.[18]

Are Franchises Successful?

Franchising is designed to provide a tested formula for success, along with ongoing advice and training. The success rate for businesses owned and operated by franchisees is significantly higher than the success rate for other independently owned small businesses. Only 5 to 8 percent of franchised businesses fail during the first two years of operation, whereas

TABLE 4.5 Top Ten Franchises (ranked by *Entrepreneur* magazine)

Rank	Name of Franchise	Minimum Start-up Costs
1	McDonald's	Varies ($610,000*)
2	Subway	$34,400
3	Dunkin' Donuts	$120,000–$280,000
4	Jani-King	$1,000–$7,500
5	Baskin-Robbins USA Co.	$134,000–$150,000
6	ServiceMaster	$8,400–$10,200
7	Chem-Dry	$3,480–$7,040
8	Hardee's	$699,000–$1,740,000
9	Arby's	$525,000–$850,000
10	Domino's Pizza	$76,500–$187,500

Source: Reprinted with permission from *Entrepreneur Magazine,* January 1992.
*Figure from McDonald Corp., January 1991.

approximately 54 percent of independent businesses fail during that time period.[19]

Nevertheless, franchising is not a guarantee of success for either franchisees or franchisors. Too rapid expansion, inadequate capital or management skills, and a host of other problems can cause failure for both. Thus, for example, the Dizzy Dean's Beef and Burger franchise is no longer in business, and Gibraltar Transmissions Corp. is in bankruptcy proceedings.[20]

Advantages of Franchising

Franchising plays a vital role in our economy and may soon become the dominant form of retailing. Why? Because franchising offers advantages to both the franchisor and the franchisee.

To the Franchisor The franchisor gains fast and selective distribution of its products without incurring the high cost of constructing and operating its own outlets. The franchisor thus has more capital available to expand production and to use for advertising. At the same time, it can ensure, through the franchise agreement, that outlets are maintained and operated according to its own standards.

The franchisor also benefits from the fact that the franchisee—a sole proprietor in most cases—is likely to be very highly motivated to succeed. The success of the franchise means more sales, which translate into higher royalties for the franchisor.

To the Franchisee The franchisee gets the opportunity to start a business with limited capital and to make use of the business experience of others. Moreover, an outlet with a nationally advertised name, such as Radio Shack,

Wendy's Osaka. Opening a franchise in a foreign country presents particular problems and opportunities. Japanese customers have no doubt heard of Wendy's and are drawn to the franchise by its old-fashioned image and high-quality menu. But individual franchisees may need to adjust the franchise formula to accommodate local tastes. Wendy's Japanese stores, for instance, offer Teriyaki Hamburger and Shrimp Sandwiches.

McDonald's, or Century 21 Real Estate, has guaranteed customers as soon as it opens.

If business problems arise, the franchisor gives the franchisee guidance and advice. This counseling is primarily responsible for the very high degree of success enjoyed by franchises. In most cases, the franchisee does not pay for such help.

The franchisee also receives materials to use in local advertising and can take part in national promotional campaigns sponsored by the franchisor. McDonald's and its franchisees, for example, constitute one of the nation's top twenty purchasers of advertising. Finally, the franchisee may be able to minimize the cost of advertising, of supplies, and of various business necessities by purchasing them in cooperation with other franchisees.

Disadvantages of Franchising

The disadvantages of franchising mainly affect the franchisee because the franchisor retains a great deal of control. The franchisor's contract can dictate every aspect of the business: decor, design of employees' uniforms, types of signs, and all the details of business operations. All Burger King french fries taste the same because all Burger King franchisees have to make them the same way.

Contract disputes are the cause of many lawsuits. Some franchisees claim that contracts are unfairly tilted toward the franchisors. Some franchisees have charged that they lost their franchise and investment because their franchisor would not approve the sale of the business when they found a buyer.[21]

Franchise holders pay for their security, usually with a one-time franchise fee and continuing royalty and advertising fees, collected as a percentage of sales. As shown in Table 4.4, a McDonald's franchisee pays an initial franchise fee of about $22,500, an annual fee of 3.5 percent of gross sales (for advertising), and a monthly fee of 12 percent of gross sales. Table 4.5 shows how much money a franchisee needs to start a new franchise for selected organizations.

Franchise operators work hard. They often put in ten- and twelve-hour days, six days a week. And in some fields, franchise agreements are not uniform: One franchisee may pay more than another for the same services.

Even success can cause problems. Sometimes a franchise is so successful that the franchisor opens its own outlet nearby, in direct competition. A spokesperson for one franchisor says that the company "gives no geographical protection" to its franchise holders and thus is free to move in on them.

The International Franchise Association advises prospective franchise purchasers to investigate before investing and to approach buying a franchise cautiously. Franchises vary widely in approach as well as in products. Some, like Dunkin' Donuts and Baskin-Robbins ice cream stores, demand long hours. Others, like Command Performance hair salons and Uncle John's Family Restaurants, are more appropriate for those who don't want to spend many hours at their stores.

GLOBAL PERSPECTIVES IN SMALL BUSINESS

For American small businesses, the world is becoming smaller. National and international economies are growing more and more interdependent as political leadership and national economic directions change and trade barriers diminish or disappear. Globalization, plus instant worldwide communications, are rapidly shrinking distances at the same time they are expanding business opportunities.

Even the U.S. Small Business Administration is offering to help the nation's small-business owners enter the world markets. The SBA's efforts include counseling small firms on how and where to market overseas, matching U.S. small-business executives with potential overseas customers, and helping exporters secure financing. The agency brings small U.S. firms into direct contact with potential overseas buyers and partners.

International trade will become more important to small-business owners as they face unique challenges in the new century. Small businesses, which are expected to remain the dominant form of organization in this country, must be prepared to adapt to significant international demographic and economic changes in the world marketplace.

This chapter ends our discussion of the foundations of American business. From here on, we shall be looking closely at various aspects of business operations. We begin, in the next chapter, with a discussion of management—what it is, what managers do, and how they work to coordinate the basic economic resources within a business organization.

CHAPTER REVIEW

Summary

A small business is one that is independently owned and operated for profit and is not dominant in its field.

There are about 20 million businesses in this country, and more than 90 percent of them are small businesses. Small businesses employ more than one-half of the nation's private work force, in spite of the fact that about 70 percent of new businesses can be expected to fail within five years. More than half of all small businesses are retailing and service businesses.

Such personal characteristics as independence, desire to create a new enterprise, and willingness to accept a challenge may impel individuals to start small businesses. Various external circumstances, such as special expertise or even the loss of a job, can also supply the motivation to strike out on one's own. Lack of capital and of management experience and poor planning are the major causes of failure.

Small businesses have been responsible for a wide variety of inventions and innovations, some of which have given rise to new industries. Historically, small businesses have created the bulk of the new jobs and have mounted effective competition to larger firms. They have provided things that society needs, acted as suppliers to larger firms, and served as customers of other businesses, both large and small.

The advantages of smallness in business include the opportunity to establish personal relationships with customers and employees, the ability to adapt to changes quickly, independence, and simplified record-keeping. The major disadvantages are the high risk of failure and the limited potential for growth.

A business plan—a carefully constructed guide for a person starting a new business—should be easy to read, uncluttered, and complete. Potential investors will examine the plan to decide whether to assist in financing.

The U.S. Small Business Administration was created in 1953 to assist and counsel the millions of small-business owners. The SBA offers management courses and workshops; managerial help, including one-to-one counseling through SCORE and ACE; various publications; and financial assistance through guaranteed loans and SBICs. It places special emphasis on aid to minority-owned businesses, including those owned by women.

A franchise is a license to operate an individually owned business as though it were part of a chain. The franchisor provides a known business name, management skills, a method of doing business, training, and required materials. The franchisee contributes labor and capital, operates the franchised business, and agrees to abide by the provisions of the franchise agreement. There are three major categories of franchise agreements. Franchising has grown tremendously since the mid-1960s.

The franchisor's major advantage in franchising is fast and well-controlled distribution of products, with minimal capital outlay. In return, the franchisee has the opportunity to open a business with limited capital, to make use of the business experience of others, and to sell to an existing clientele. For this, the franchisee must usually pay both an initial franchise fee and a continuing royalty based on sales. He or she must also follow the dictates of the franchise with regard to operation of the business.

Worldwide business opportunities are expanding for small businesses. Even the U.S. Small Business Administration is assisting small business owners in penetrating foreign markets. The next century will present unique challenges and opportunities for small business owners.

Key Terms

You should now be able to define and give an example relevant to each of the following terms:

small business	Small Business
business plan	Administration (SBA)

Service Corps of Retired
Executives (SCORE)

Active Corps of
Executives (ACE)

Small Business Institute
(SBI)

Small Business
Development Center
(SBDC)

venture capital

Small Business
Investment Company
(SBIC)

franchise

franchising

franchisor

franchisee

Questions and Exercises

Review Questions

1. What information would you need to determine whether a particular business is small according to SBA guidelines?
2. Which two areas of business generally attract the most small businesses? Why are these areas attractive to small business?
3. Distinguish among service industries, distribution industries, and production industries.
4. What kinds of factors impel certain people to start new businesses?
5. What are the major causes of small-business failure? Do these causes also apply to larger businesses?
6. Briefly describe four contributions of small business to the American economy.
7. What are the major advantages and disadvantages of smallness in business?
8. What are the major components of a business plan? Why should an individual develop a business plan?
9. Identify five ways in which the SBA provides management assistance to small businesses.
10. Identify two ways in which the SBA provides financial assistance to small businesses.
11. Why does the SBA concentrate on providing management and financial assistance to small businesses?
12. What is venture capital? How does the SBA help small businesses obtain it?
13. Explain the relationships among a franchise, the franchisor, and the franchisee.
14. What does the franchisor receive in a franchising agreement? What does the franchisee receive? What does each provide?
15. Cite one major benefit of franchising for the franchisor. Cite one major benefit of franchising for the franchisee.

Discussion Questions

1. In what ways are Jon Shecter and David Mays similar to other entrepreneurs?
2. Identify at least three factors that contribute to the success of *The Source* magazine.
3. Most people who start small businesses know of the high failure rate and the reasons for it. Why, then, do they not take steps to protect their firms from failure? What steps should they take?
4. Are the so-called advantages of small business really advantages? Wouldn't every small-business owner like his or her business to grow into a large firm?
5. Do average citizens benefit from the activities of the SBA, or is the SBA just another way to spend our tax money?
6. Would you rather own your own business independently or become a franchisee? Why?

Exercises

1. From a sampling of twenty-five small businesses in your community, calculate the percentage in service industries, distribution industries, and production industries. Explain any major differences between your results and Figure 4.1.
2. Devise a plan for opening a new bicycle sales and repair shop in your community. Consider each of the components described in the business plan. Also give some thought to how you will avoid the major causes of small-business failure.

CASE 4.1

From Insurance Sales to Franchising

Ron Schultz is a life insurance salesman, modestly providing for his wife and two sons. They live in a quiet, urban neighborhood on the tight budget that many families with limited income find necessary.

At 42 years of age, Schultz wants to enter a new field—one that would enable him to increase his income. One opportunity he is considering is a franchise with one of the nation's automatic transmission repair services. Investigation reveals a fast-growing market with little competition:

- New-car dealers are equipped to repair only the one make of transmission they sell. Because of their high overhead, their transmission repair prices run high.

- Neighborhood garages farm out their transmission repair work to small shops that vary sharply in quality and cost.

The potential is clear, but Schultz is bothered by his lack of a mechanical background. The franchisor's intensive training program is designed to overcome just such doubt. Spanning four weeks, the program runs forty-eight hours a week and covers pricing, employee recruiting, advertising, customer service, supervision, and cost controls.

The program's objective is to familiarize the franchisee with all aspects of the transmission repair business—with an emphasis on managing transmission specialists rather than on doing the actual mechanical work.

At the franchisor's suggestion, Schultz picked several names at random from a list of its franchisees, and visited each of them. Each franchisee seemed pleased with his or her business, and each urged Schultz to purchase his own franchise.

Further investigation indicates that the site for the new franchise could be right in Schultz's area. The tentative site boasts 40,000 registered automobiles within a thirty-minute drive.

Schultz's initial cash investment for the franchise would be $110,000. (The franchisor is ready to help him raise the money.) The investment covers the following:

- Initial rental and parts inventory
- Special tools and outdoor signs
- Workbenches and office supplies

Continuing help offered by the franchisor includes monthly conferences for all area franchisees to review sales progress and business proficiency.

The requirements Schultz has to meet—besides his $110,000 investment—are a strong desire to earn money and a knack for communicating with people.[*]

Questions

1. What do you think Schultz should do?
2. What advantages do you see in the franchisor's offer?
3. What disadvantages do you see in the offer?
4. What other information would you advise Schultz to get before he makes a decision?

[*]Source: Adapted from a case prepared by the U.S. Small Business Administration, and Nicholas C. Siropolis, *Small Business Management* (Boston: Houghton Mifflin Company, 1990), pp. 157–158. Used by permission.

CASE 4.2

Bow-Wow Boutique, Inc.

Karla Addington is an entrepreneur in the truest sense. At the age of 18, combining an idea on how to improve a service with a steely determination to succeed, she opened a small business from the basement of her mother's home. In 1988, that business had two locations in Cincinnati, with sales revenues that were expected to top $350,000.

Her business, Bow-Wow Boutique, Inc., is an award-winning grooming and pet supply service for the pampered dogs and cats of Cincinnati. To date, Bow-Wow Boutique's success story has been featured on numerous national trade publications, on seven television news programs, and in five radio interviews.

Entrepreneurial activity is nothing new to Addington. To promote a childhood lemonade stand, "I would ride my bike around the neighborhood with this silly hat with lemons all over it," she said. At the age of 14, she was honing her sales skills by selling Fuller Brush products door-to-door.

Bow-Wow Boutique had its genesis in Addington's work experience at other grooming shops. Disappointed with what she saw at other shops as a "lack of knowledge, courtesy, and cleanliness," and bothered that the "professionals" were not taking the time to educate clients on proper pet care, Addington began thinking about how she could offer better service.

She planned to provide a clean, attractive atmosphere and safe, healthy, and unique gifts for both pets and pet lovers. But the foundation of Addington's business would be superior customer service. "I knew I could do it better," she said.

To finance her business's start-up, Addington worked three jobs until she had saved $1,000. "Things were definitely tight," she said. "I had absolutely no knowledge of projections, key assumptions, or business plans—but I had chutzpah. I knew I could never be happy unless I took the risk."

After opening her first shop, Addington ran headlong into one of the obstacles facing young entrepreneurs today. "Not too many people took me seriously," she said. "I was an 18-year-old female with absolutely no business knowledge. Salesmen would call on the shop, look me over, and ask for the manager."

But Addington was not about to let her lack of knowledge stop her. She took an assertiveness-training course, read management books, attended management seminars, and "even started to read the business section of the *Cincinnati Enquirer*" to sharpen her business skills. Addington said, "I wasn't really sure what cash flow was, but I was going to learn!"

What makes Bow-Wow Boutique special? Besides the superior service that Addington provides, the boutique carries pet gifts you would expect to find only in the most spoiled pet's home. Doggie tuxedos and top hats, hand-finished cherry waterbeds, and white gamma mink coats are just a few of the extravagant pet gifts found at Bow-Wow Boutique.

Do not, however, expect to find Addington resting on her past success. "Actually, I feel I've just touched the tip of what I call personal success. I have not yet achieved my business or financial goals." Her ultimate goal? "To be the Mary Kay of the pet industry," said the now 28-year-old Addington.**

Questions

1. To what do you attribute Addington's success?
2. What role did education play in Addington's success?
3. Comment on Addington's ultimate goal "to be the Mary Kay of the pet industry."

**Source: U.S. Small Business Administration, *Young Entrepreneur Seminars* (Washington, D.C.: U.S. Government Printing Office, 1988), pp. 75–76.

Career Profile

CAREER PLANNING

The future looks bright for individuals who possess the training and skills needed for the technological challenges of the future. The courses that you take in college, your early employment experience, and early career exploration are all important as you plan your own career.

CAREER INFORMATION FOR EACH MAJOR PART OF *BUSINESS*

To help you explore different employment opportunities and plan for your future, we have included specific career information at the end of each major part in your textbook. Most of this career information is from the U.S. Department of Labor's *Occupational Outlook Handbook*. It is presented in an easy-to-use grid format.

CHAPTER 24—CAREERS IN BUSINESS

We also include detailed career coverage in the last chapter. As authors, we chose to place this chapter last so that it will be a capstone activity or completion activity—after you have examined the areas of management, marketing, finance, accounting, and international business. Topics include the importance of career choices, trends in employment, occupational search activities, career planning and preparation, résumé writing, and interviewing techniques. We also provide information on the traits that employees need to be successful.

ADDITIONAL CAREER PUBLICATIONS

Finally, two additional sources of career information are available from Houghton Mifflin—the publisher of your text. *Toward a Career in Business*, by Kathryn Hegar, provides students with job-search techniques. Constructed in a workbook format, this project book provides hands-on experience in these areas: (1) self-assessment; (2) occupational search; (3) employment tools; and, (4) success techniques. *Business Careers*, by Robert Luke, provides specific, detailed information for the areas of accounting, computer infor-

PART 1   Sample Career Table

Job Title	Job Description	Salary Range
Accountant—Corporate	Analyze source documents and journalize accounting entries for a private business; post journal entries to ledger accounts; prepare a trial balance and financial statements for each accounting period; and close the accounting books at the end of each accounting period	3–4
Computer Operator	Use available software programs to process data into information; prepare reports based on original input data; communicate with managers and other personnel who need processed information	1–2
First-line supervisor	Ensure that workers, equipment, and materials are used properly and efficiently; make sure machinery is set up correctly; schedule maintenance of machinery; tell workers what to do and make sure it's done safely, correctly, and on time; keep employee records; enforce safety regulations; recommend wage increases; make sure union rules are followed	3

mation systems, finance, management, marketing, entrepreneurship, and international business.

A FINAL NOTE ON CAREERS

Throughout the fourth edition of *Business* we have made a special effort to emphasize that the business environment is undergoing rapid changes. Your success in career planning will be based to some extent on your ability to adapt to these changes. Good luck!

EXPLANATION OF TABLE

Job Title

This column lists common job titles that correspond to job opportunities in the employment world today. Entries are alphabetized for easy reference.

Job Description

This column lists the elements that an individual in this type of job would perform on a regular basis.

Salary Range

Salary ranges for each job title are included here. Of course, actual salary will be determined by employee qualifications, geographical differences in salary levels, and other factors.

Educational Requirements

Here the general educational level for each job title in column one is shown. In some cases, on-the-job experience is also necessary.

Skills

Typical skills that an employee in this type of job or position would need for success.

Prospects for Growth

Employment prospects for each job title are indicated by a relative scale. In descending order, the scale ranges from greatest growth through average growth to no growth.

The figure in the salary column approximates the expected annual income after two or three years of service.
1 = $12,000–$15,000; 2 = $16,000–$20,000; 3 = $21,000–$27,000; 4 = $28,000–$35,000; 5 = $36,000 and up.

Educational Requirements	Skills Required	Prospects for Growth
Bachelor's degree in accounting; master's degree preferred	Computer; problem solving; quantitative; analytical; diagnostic; conceptual; critical thinking	Greatest
Two years of college in data processing; on-the-job experience	Computer; problem solving; quantitative; technical	Greatest
High school diploma; some college preferred	Organizational; leadership; technical; decision making	Below average

PART

2

Management and Organization

This part of the book deals with the organization—the "thing" that is a business. We begin with a discussion of the functions involved in developing and operating an organization. Then we analyze the organization itself, to see what makes it tick. Next we put the two together, to examine the part of a business that is concerned with the conversion of material resources into products. Included in this part are:

The Management Process

CHAPTER PREVIEW

In this chapter we define the process of management and describe the four basic management functions of goal setting and planning, organizing, leading and motivating, and controlling. Then we focus on the types of managers with respect to levels of responsibility and areas of expertise. Next, we focus on the skills of effective managers and the different roles managers must play. Then, we explore what corporate culture is and what it means to an organization. We examine several styles of leadership and explore the process by which managers make decisions. We conclude this chapter with a look at various sources of managers, both inside and outside an organization and a discussion of total quality management.

Southwest Airlines Manages to Succeed

His admirers call him flamboyant and colorful. His competitors call him offbeat or downright crazy. His employees call him "Uncle Herbie." He's Herb Kelleher, the CEO of Southwest Airlines. In an industry where deregulation, recession, and sky-rocketing fuel costs killed off Eastern Airlines, PanAm, and Braniff, Southwest keeps on growing and making a profit—in fact, the cover of the organization's annual report once simply stated, "We made a profit." Kelleher didn't start a small regional airline and build it into the country's eighth largest—it now serves thirty-two cities in eighteen states and has a fleet of 118 jets—by being lucky. He did it by being a skilled manager who knows how to keep his costs low and his employees happy.

By tightly controlling expenses, Kelleher boasts the lowest operating costs in the industry, 15 percent lower than those of his nearest competitor. He says that he manages the airline for survival, never letting spending get out of control, even in the good times. To keep costs down, all flights are no-food, no-first-class, no-frill affairs. Kelleher always keeps staff to a minimum. Southwest negotiated with the union for more flexible work rules so that flight attendants and even pilots can clean inside the planes between flights.

But Kelleher also gives his employees the same respect and attention he gives Southwest's passengers, and he inspires a loyal and productive workforce. Southwest selectively seeks employees with upbeat attitudes and promotes from within its own ranks 80 percent of the time. It's not high salaries that keep the airline's turnover rate under 10 percent, says its head of human resources, but the family feeling that employees have at Southwest. When it's time for making decisions, everyone who will be

affected is encouraged to get involved, and Kelleher's door is always open. Because he believes people who enjoy their work do a better job, Kelleher injects fun into the workplace whenever and wherever possible. Every Friday is "Fun Day," set aside for wearing casual clothes and holding parties. On a company videotape for new employees, workers don't just explain their jobs, they describe them in rap rhythms. Kelleher himself is known for making unexpected visits, such as the time he surprised the maintenance crew at 2 a.m. by dressing up as Klinger from the TV show "MASH" and showing up at one of the hangars.

When fuel prices rose dramatically during the Persian Gulf War, almost one-third of Southwest's 8,600 employees volunteered to take paycuts to cover the extra expenses. Industry experts believe this kind of loyalty is inspired by Herb Kelleher's charisma. His well-publicized five-pack-a-day cigarette habit has led many analysts to wonder if Southwest could survive without him.[1]

Without a doubt, management is one of the most exciting, challenging, and rewarding professions. The men and women who manage business firms play an important part in shaping the world we live in. Southwest Airlines is successful largely because of its effective management. Through the application of appropriate management skills and techniques, Southwest Airlines is experiencing significant growth and is making a profit when most airlines are not.

Depending on its size, an organization may employ a number of specialized managers who are responsible for particular areas of management. An organization also includes managers at its several operational levels to coordinate resources and activities at those levels. Must every organization employ all these managers in area after area and level upon level? Yes and no. A very large organization may actually field a battalion of managers, each responsible for activities on one particular level of one management area. In contrast, the owner of a sole proprietorship may be the only manager in the organization. He or she is responsible for all levels and areas of management (and probably for getting the mail out on time, as well).

What is important to an organization is not the number of managers it employs but the ability of these managers to achieve the organization's goals, such as those established by the management at Southwest Airlines. As you will see, this task requires the application of a variety of skills to a wide range of functions and roles.

WHAT IS MANAGEMENT?

management the process of coordinating the resources of an organization to achieve the primary goals of the organization

LEARNING OBJECTIVE 1
Define what management is.

Management is the process of coordinating the resources of an organization to achieve the primary goals of the organization. As we saw in Chapter 1, most organizations make use of four kinds of resources: material, human, financial, and informational (see Figure 5.1).

Material resources are the tangible, physical resources an organization uses. For example, General Motors uses steel, glass, and fiber glass to produce cars and trucks on complex machine-driven assembly lines. Both the assembly lines and the buildings that house them are material resources, as are the actual materials from which vehicles are built. A college or university uses books, classroom buildings, desks, and computers to educate

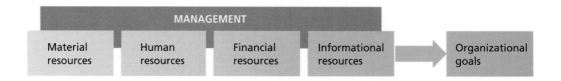

FIGURE 5.1   The Four Main Resources of Management
Managers coordinate an organization's resources to achieve the primary goals of the organization.

students. And the Mayo Clinic uses beds, operating room equipment, and diagnostic machines to provide health care.

Perhaps the most important resources of any organization are its *human resources*—people. In fact, some firms live by the philosophy that their employees are their most important assets. To keep employees content, a variety of incentives are used, including higher-than-average pay, flexible working hours, recreational facilities, day-care centers, lengthy paid vacations, cafeterias offering inexpensive meals, and generous benefit programs. At Southwest Airlines, employees are encouraged to have fun.

Financial resources are the funds the organization uses to meet its obligations to various creditors. A grocery store obtains money from customers at the check-out counters and uses a portion of that money to pay the wholesalers from which it buys food. Citicorp, a large New York bank, borrows and lends money. A college obtains money in the form of tuition, income from its endowments, and state and federal grants. It uses the money to pay utility bills, insurance premiums, and professors' salaries. Each of these transactions involves financial resources.

Finally, many organizations increasingly find they cannot afford to ignore *information*. External environmental conditions—including the economy, consumer markets, technology, politics, and cultural forces—are all changing so rapidly that an organization that does not adapt will probably not survive. And, to adapt to change, the organization must know what is changing and how it is changing. Companies are finding it increasingly important to gather information about their competitors in today's business environment. Companies such as Ford Motor Company and General Electric are known to collect information about their competitors. These companies are technology based, but other types of companies, such as Kraft and J. C. Penney, collect information as well. As we discuss in Part 5, information generated within the organization is just as important as external information.

It is important to realize that these are only general categories of resources. Within each category are hundreds or thousands of more specific resources, from which management must choose those that can best accomplish its goals. When we consider choices from all four categories, we end up with an extremely complex group of specific resources. It is this complex group of specific resources—and not simply "some of each" of the four general categories—that managers must coordinate to produce goods and services.

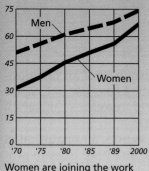

AT A GLANCE
GROWTH OF THE WORK FORCE

Women are joining the work force in higher numbers than men.
(In millions; 2000 projected)
SOURCE: U.S. Bureau of Labor Statistics

Another interesting way to look at management is in terms of the functions managers perform. These functions have been identified as goal setting and planning, organizing, leading and motivating employees, and controlling ongoing activities. We shall explore them in some detail in the next section.

BASIC MANAGEMENT FUNCTIONS

LEARNING OBJECTIVE 2
Describe the four basic management functions: goal setting and planning, organizing, leading and motivating, and controlling.

A number of management functions must be performed if any organization is to succeed. Some seem to be most important when a new enterprise is first formed or when something is obviously wrong. Others appear to be essentially day-to-day activities. In truth, however, all are part of the ongoing process of management.

First, goals must be established for the organization, and plans must be developed to achieve those goals. Next, managers must organize people and other resources into a logical and efficient "well-oiled machine" capable of accomplishing the chosen goals. Then, managers must lead employees in such a way as to motivate them to work effectively to help achieve the goals of the organization. Finally, managers need to maintain adequate control to ensure that the organization is working steadily toward its goals.

When Lee Iacocca took the reins at Chrysler Corp., the firm was on the brink of bankruptcy. One of the first things he did was to establish a series of specific goals for sales growth and a strategy for achieving them. He changed the basic structure of the organization. Then he provided effective leadership by working for $1 a year until he had turned the company around. He also developed an elaborate control system to keep Chrysler on track.

Management functions do not occur according to some rigid, preset timetable. Managers don't plan in January, organize in February, lead and motivate in March, and control in April. At any given time, managers may engage in a number of functions simultaneously. However, each function tends to lead naturally to others. Figure 5.2 provides a visual framework for discussion of these management functions.

FIGURE 5.2   The Management Process
Note that management is not a step-by-step procedure, but a process with a feedback loop that represents a flow.

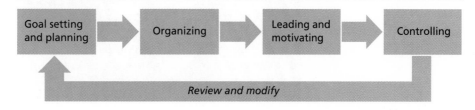

Goal Setting and Planning

As we have noted, management must set goals for the organization. Then the managers must develop plans by which to achieve those goals.

goal an end state that the organization is expected to achieve over a certain or set period of time

goal setting the process of developing and committing an organization to a set of goals

purpose the reason for an organization's existence

mission the means by which an organization is to fulfill its purpose

objective a specific statement detailing what an organization intends to accomplish as it goes about its mission

Goal Setting   A **goal** is an end state that the organization is expected to achieve over a certain or set period of time. **Goal setting,** then, is the process of developing—and committing an organization to—a set of goals. Every organization has goals of several types.

The most fundamental type of goal is the organization's **purpose,** the reason for the organization's existence. Texaco Inc.'s purpose is to earn a profit for its owners. Houston Community College System's purpose is to provide an education for local citizens. The purpose of the Secret Service is to protect the life of the president. The organization's **mission** is the means by which it is to fulfill its purpose. Apple Computer attempts to fulfill its purpose (making a profit) by manufacturing computers, whereas Ford Motor Company fulfills the same purpose by manufacturing cars. Finally, an **objective** is a specific statement detailing what the organization intends to accomplish as it goes about its mission. For McDonald's, one objective might be that all customers will be served within two minutes of their arrival. Sears, Roebuck might adopt the objective that sales will be increased

Procter & Gamble's new image. Changing a company's image is not easy. But Procter & Gamble set a goal of becoming a leader in beauty aids, shedding its no-frills image built by years of selling Tide and Crest. It bought a number of other companies and used its marketing know-how and large advertising budget to produce ads like this one for Navy perfume. Already the planning has paid off.

by 7 percent this year. For IBM, one objective might be to reduce the average delivery time for personal computers to retailers by four days next year.

Goals can deal with a variety of factors, such as sales, company growth, costs, customer satisfaction, and employee morale. They can also span various periods of time. Whereas a small manufacturer may focus primarily on sales objectives for the next six months, Exxon Corporation may be more interested in objectives for the year 2000. Finally, goals are set at every level of the organization. Every member of the organization—the president of the company, the head of a department, and an operating employee at the lowest level—has a set of goals he or she hopes to achieve.

The goals developed for these different levels must be consistent with one another. However, it is likely that some conflict will arise. A production department, for example, may have a goal of minimizing costs. One way to do this is to produce only one type of product and offer no "frills." Marketing, on the other hand, may have a goal of maximizing sales. And one way to implement this goal is to offer prospective customers a wide range of products with many options. As part of his or her own goal setting, the manager who is ultimately responsible for *both* departments must achieve some sort of balance between such competing or conflicting goals. This balancing process is called *optimization*.

The optimization of conflicting goals requires insight and ability. Faced with the marketing-versus-production conflict just described, most managers would probably not adopt either viewpoint completely. Instead, they might decide on a reasonably diverse product line offering only the most widely sought-after options. Such a compromise would seem to be best for the organization as a whole.

Planning   Once goals have been set for the organization, managers must develop plans for achieving them. A **plan** is an outline of the actions by which the organization intends to accomplish its goals. The processes involved in developing plans are referred to as **planning.** Just as it has several goals, the organization should develop several types of plans.

An organization's **strategy** is its broadest set of plans and is developed as a guide for major policy setting and decision making. A firm's strategy defines what business the company is in or wants to be in and the kind of company it is or wants to be. When the Surgeon General issued a report linking smoking and cancer in the 1950s, top management at Philip Morris Companies recognized that the company's very survival was threatened. Action was needed to broaden the company's operations. Major elements in the overall Philip Morris strategy were first to purchase several non-tobacco-related companies (such as Miller Brewing) and then aggressively promote the companies' products. As a result of its strategy, Philip Morris seems to have attained the goal of being less dependent on tobacco sales.

Most organizations also employ several narrower kinds of plans. A **tactical plan** is a smaller-scale (and usually shorter-range) plan developed to implement a strategy. If a strategic plan will take five years to complete, the firm may develop five tactical plans, one covering each year. Tactical plans may be updated periodically as conditions and experience dictate. Their narrower scope permits them to be changed more easily than strategies.

plan   an outline of the actions by which an organization intends to accomplish its goals

planning   the processes involved in developing plans

strategy   an organization's broadest set of plans, developed as a guide for major policy setting and decision making; it defines what business the company is in or wants to be in and the kind of company it is or wants to be

tactical plan   a small-scale, short-range plan developed to implement a strategy

Another category of plans is referred to as *standing plans*. These result from—and implement—decisions that have previously been made by management. A **policy** is a general guide for action in a situation that occurs repeatedly. A **standard operating procedure (SOP)** is a type of standing plan that outlines the steps to be taken in a situation that arises again and again. An SOP is thus more specific than a policy. For example, a department store may have a policy of accepting deliveries only between 9 a.m. and 4 p.m. Its standard operating procedure might require that each accepted delivery be checked, sorted, and stored before closing time on the day of delivery.

policy a general guide for action in a situation that occurs repeatedly

standard operating procedure (SOP) a type of standing plan that outlines the steps to be taken in a situation that arises again and again

Organizing the Enterprise

After goal setting and planning, the second major function of the manager is organization. **Organizing** is the grouping of resources and activities to accomplish some end result in an efficient and effective manner. Consider the case of an inventor who creates a new product and goes into business to sell it. At first, she will probably do everything herself—purchase raw materials, make the product, advertise it, sell it, and keep her business records up to date. Eventually, as business grows, she will find that she needs help. To begin with, she might hire a professional sales representative and a part-time bookkeeper. Later she might need to hire full-time sales personnel, other people to assist with production, and an accountant. As she hires each new person, she must decide what that person will do, to whom that person will report, and generally how that person can best take part in the organization's activities. We shall discuss these and other facets of the organizing function in much more detail in the next chapter.

organizing the grouping of resources and activities to accomplish some end result in an efficient and effective manner

Leading and Motivating

The leading and motivating functions are concerned with the human resources within the organization. **Leading** is the process of influencing people to work toward a common goal. **Motivating** is the process of providing reasons for people to work in the best interests of the organization. Together, leading and motivating are often referred to as **directing.**

We have already noted the importance of an organization's human resources. Because of this importance, leading and motivating are critical activities. Obviously, different people do things for different reasons—that is, they have different *motivations*. Some are primarily interested in earning as much money as they can. Others may be spurred on by opportunities to get ahead in an organization. Part of the manager's job, then, is to determine what things motivate subordinates and to try to provide those things in a way that encourages effective performance.

Quite a bit of research has been done on both motivation and leadership. As you will see in Chapter 8, research on motivation has yielded very useful information. Research on leadership has been less successful. In

leading the process of influencing people to work toward a common goal

motivating the process of providing reasons for people to work in the best interests of the organization

directing the combined processes of leading and motivating

spite of decades of study, no one has discovered a general set of personal traits or characteristics that makes a good leader. Later in this chapter, leadership is discussed in more detail.

Controlling Ongoing Activities

controlling the process of evaluating and regulating ongoing activities to ensure that goals are achieved

Controlling is the process of evaluating and regulating ongoing activities to ensure that goals are achieved. To see how controlling works, consider a rocket launched by NASA to place a satellite in orbit. Do NASA personnel simply fire the rocket and then check back in a few days to find out whether the satellite is in place? Of course not. The rocket is constantly monitored, and its course is regulated and adjusted as needed to get the satellite to its destination. Similarly, managerial control involves both close monitoring of the progress of the organization as it works toward its goals, and the regulating and adjusting required to keep it on course.

For example, suppose that United Air Lines, Inc. establishes a goal of increasing its profit by 12 percent next year. To ensure that this goal is reached, United's management might monitor its profit on a monthly basis. After three months, if profit has increased by 3 percent, management might be able to assume that everything is going according to schedule. Probably no action will be taken. However, if profit has increased by only 1 percent after three months, some corrective action would be needed to get the firm on track. The particular action that is required depends on the reason for the low increase in profit.

The control function includes three steps (see Figure 5.3). The first is *setting standards,* or specific goals to which performance can be compared. (Quantitative goals, such as United's 3 percent profit increase in three months, are perhaps the most useful.) The second step is *measuring actual performance* and comparing it with the standard. And the third step is *taking corrective action* as necessary. The results of this third step may affect the setting of standards. Notice that the control function is circular in nature. The steps in the control function must be repeated periodically until the primary goal is achieved.

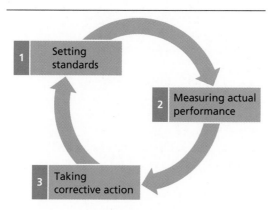

FIGURE 5.3
The Control Function
The control function includes the three steps of setting standards, measuring actual performance, and taking corrective action.

KINDS OF MANAGERS

LEARNING OBJECTIVE 3
Distinguish among the various kinds of managers, in terms of both level and area of management.

Managers can be classified along two dimensions: level within the organization and area of management. We will use these two perspectives to explore the various types of managers.

Levels of Management

For the moment, think of an organization as a three-story structure (as illustrated in Figure 5.4). Each story corresponds to one of the three general levels of management: top managers, middle managers, and first-line managers.

top manager an upper-level executive who guides and controls the overall fortunes of the organization

Top Managers   A **top manager** is an upper-level executive who guides and controls the overall fortunes of the organization. Top managers constitute a small group. In terms of planning, they are generally responsible for interpreting the organization's purpose and developing its mission. They also determine the firm's strategy and define its major policies. It takes years of hard work and determination, as well as talent and no small share of good luck, to reach the ranks of top management in large companies. Common titles associated with top managers are president, vice president, chief executive officer (CEO), and chief operating officer (COO).

middle manager a manager who implements the strategy and major policies developed by top management

Middle Managers   A **middle manager** is a manager who implements the strategy and major policies handed down from the top level of the organization. Middle managers develop tactical plans, policies, and standard operating procedures, and they coordinate and supervise the activities of first-line managers. Titles at the middle-management level include division manager, department head, plant manager, and operations manager.

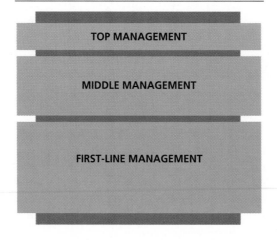

FIGURE 5.4
Management Levels Found in Most Companies
The coordinated effort of all three levels of managers is required to implement the goals of any company.

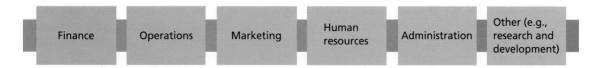

| Finance | Operations | Marketing | Human resources | Administration | Other (e.g., research and development) |

FIGURE 5.5   Areas of Management Specialization
Other areas may have to be added, depending on the nature of the firm and the industry.

First-Line Managers   A **first-line manager** is a manager who coordinates and supervises the activities of operating employees. First-line managers spend most of their time working with and motivating employees, answering questions, and solving day-to-day problems. Most first-line managers are former operating employees who, owing to their hard work and potential, were promoted into management. Many of today's middle and top managers began their careers on this first management level. Common titles for first-line managers include office manager, supervisor, and foreman.

first-line manager   a manager who coordinates and supervises the activities of operating employees

Areas of Management

Our organizational structure can also be divided more or less vertically into areas of management specialization (see Figure 5.5). The most common areas are finance, operations, marketing, human resources, and administration. Depending on its purpose and mission, an organization may include other areas as well—research and development, for example.

Financial Managers   A **financial manager** is primarily responsible for the organization's financial resources. Accounting and investment are specialized areas within financial management. Because financing affects the operation of the entire firm, many of the presidents of this country's largest companies are people who got their "basic training" as financial managers.

financial manager   a manager who is primarily responsible for the organization's financial resources

Operations Managers   An **operations manager** creates and manages the systems that convert resources into goods and services. Traditionally, operations management has been equated with manufacturing—the production of goods. However, in recent years many of the techniques and procedures of operations management have been applied to the production of services and to a variety of nonbusiness activities. Like financial management, operations management has produced a good percentage of today's company presidents.

operations manager   a manager who creates and manages the systems that convert resources into goods and services

Marketing Managers   A **marketing manager** is responsible for facilitating the exchange of products between the organization and its customers or clients. Specific areas within marketing are marketing research, advertising, promotion, sales, and distribution. A sizable number of today's company presidents have risen from the ranks of marketing management.

marketing manager   a manager who is responsible for facilitating the exchange of products between the organization and its customers or clients

human resources manager   a person charged with managing the organization's formal human resources programs

Human Resources Managers   A **human resources manager** is charged with managing the organization's formal human resources programs. He or she engages in human resources planning; designs systems for hiring, training, and appraising the performance of employees; and ensures that the organization follows government regulations concerning employment practices. Because human resources management is a relatively new area of specialization in many organizations, few top managers have this kind of background. However, this situation should change with the passage of time.

administrative manager   a manager who is not associated with any specific functional area but who provides overall administrative guidance and leadership

Administrative Managers   An **administrative manager** (also called a *general manager*) is not associated with any specific functional area but provides overall administrative guidance and leadership. A hospital administrator is a good example of an administrative manager. He or she does not specialize in operations, finance, marketing, or human resources management but instead coordinates the activities of specialized managers in all these areas. In many respects, most top managers are really administrative managers.

Whatever their level in the organization and whatever area they specialize in, successful managers generally exhibit certain key skills and are able to play certain managerial roles. But, as we shall see, some skills may be more critical at one level of management than at another.

WHAT MAKES EFFECTIVE MANAGERS?

In general, effective managers are those who (1) possess certain important skills and (2) are able to use these skills in a number of managerial roles. Probably no manager is called on to use any particular skill *constantly* or to play a particular role all the time. However, these skills and abilities must be available when they are needed.

Key Management Skills

LEARNING OBJECTIVE 4
Identify the key management skills and the management roles in which these skills are used.

technical skill   a specific skill needed to accomplish a specialized activity

The skills that typify effective managers tend to fall into five general categories: technical, conceptual, interpersonal, diagnostic, and analytic.

Technical Skills   A **technical skill** is a specific skill needed to accomplish a specialized activity. For example, the skills engineers and machinists need to do their jobs are technical skills. First-line managers (and, to a lesser extent, middle managers) need the technical skills relevant to the activities they manage. Although these managers may not have to perform the technical tasks themselves, they must be able to train subordinates, answer questions, and otherwise provide guidance and direction. In general, top managers do not rely on technical skills as heavily as do managers at other levels. Still, understanding the technical side of things is an aid to effective management at every level.

 GETTING AHEAD IN BUSINESS
Managing a Scarce Resource: Your Time

More and more American workers feel like the White Rabbit from *Alice and Wonderland*, racing around, frantically glancing at their watches and thinking, "I'm late, I'm late." Product deadlines, technology that demands faster work, managers who are compulsive about getting more done—all these plus intense business competition—combine to produce stressed-out workers who complain that there just aren't enough hours in the day.

Major time muncher: Going to meetings
Why? Often they are run inefficiently.
To cope: Streamline the process by
- Holding fewer meetings.
- Handing out agendas beforehand so that everyone can prepare.
- Opening the meeting with some brief remarks that focus specifically on issues to be addressed.
- Limiting deliberations.

One company's suggestion: Put a huge clock on the wall of every corporate conference room.

Major time muncher: Paperwork (managers typically have ten hours every week to do thirty-five to forty hours of paperwork).
To cope: Prioritize paperwork by
- Attacking paper one piece at a time.
- Acting on it, referring it to someone else, or filing it.
- Using the waste basket liberally.

One company's suggestion: Label individual baskets "To Do," "To Pay," "To File," and "To Read."

Even though there is no perfect time-management formula, experts have some general Do's and Don'ts for spinning your wheels less and moving forward more:

Don't: Let planning overwhelm you.

Do: Make suggestions before you think they're perfect.

Don't: Study and discuss too long.

Do: Trust your own judgment and act quickly on your decisions.

Don't: Always adhere to rigid bureaucratic company rules.

Do: Simplify the system by bending or breaking a few rules.

Don't: Believe you can do everything and do it better than anyone else.

Do: Delegate responsibility and let go.

At Canadian Hunter's Company in Calgary, Canada, there are two clocks in the main lobby. One is set on local time; the other, set five minutes fast, bears a sign underneath that advises "Stay Ahead." That business philosophy will probably become more critical as the competitive twentieth century races toward its close. Those who are able to manage their time more efficiently stand a better chance of winning instead of falling down a hole as Alice and the White Rabbit did.

---

conceptual skill the ability to think in abstract terms

Conceptual Skills Conceptual skill is the ability to think in abstract terms. Conceptual skill allows the manager to see the "big picture" and to understand how the various parts of an organization or an idea can fit together. In 1951 a man named Charles Wilson decided to take his family on a cross-country vacation. All along the way, the family was forced to put up with high-priced but shabby hotel accommodations. Wilson reasoned that most travelers would welcome a chain of moderately priced, good-quality roadside hotels. You are probably familiar with what he conceived: Holiday Inns. Wilson was able to identify a number of isolated factors (existing accommodation patterns, the need for a different kind of hotel, and his own

Man of many skills. Terdema Ussery is a lawyer who has degrees from Princeton, Harvard, and Berkeley. Now he holds not just a basketball but a whole basketball league—Continental Basketball Association—in his hands. As the Association's commissioner, he must use legal, business, and public relations skills as well as deal effectively with people all day. What does he call himself? A facilitator.

investment interests) to "dream up" the new business opportunity and to carry it through to completion.

Conceptual skills are useful in a wide range of situations, including the optimization of goals described earlier. They appear, however, to be more crucial for top managers than for middle or first-line managers.

interpersonal skill the ability to deal effectively with other people

Interpersonal Skills   An **interpersonal skill** is the ability to deal effectively with other people, both inside and outside the organization. Examples of interpersonal skills are the ability to relate to people, understand their needs and motives, and show genuine compassion. When all other things are equal, the manager able to exhibit these skills will be more successful than the arrogant and brash manager who doesn't care about others.

diagnostic skill the ability to assess a particular situation and identify its causes

Diagnostic Skills   **Diagnostic skill** is the ability to assess a particular situation and identify its causes. The diagnostic skills of the successful manager parallel those of the physician, who assesses the patient's symptoms to pinpoint the underlying medical problem. We can take this parallel one step further. In management as in medicine, correct diagnosis is often critical in determining the appropriate action to take. All managers need to make use of diagnostic skills, but these skills are probably used most by top managers.

analytic skill the ability to identify relevant issues or variables in a situation, to determine how they are related, and to assess their relative importance

Analytic Skills   **Analytic skill** is used to identify relevant issues (or variables) in a situation, to determine how they are related, and to assess their relative importance. Regardless of level or area, all managers need analytic skills. Analytic skills often come into play along with diagnostic skills. For example, a manager assigned to a new position may be confronted with a wide variety of problems that all need attention. Diagnostic skills will be needed to identify the causes of each problem. But first the manager must analyze the problem of "too many problems" to determine which problems need immediate attention and which ones can wait.

Managerial Roles

Research suggests that managers must, from time to time, act in ten different roles if they are to be successful.[2] (By *role* we mean a part that someone plays.) These ten roles can be grouped into three categories: decisional, interpersonal, and informational.

decisional role   a role that involves various aspects of management decision making

Decisional Roles   As you might suspect, a **decisional role** is one that involves various aspects of management decision making. In the role of *entrepreneur*, the manager is the voluntary initiator of change. For example, the manager who develops a new strategy or expands the sales force into a new market is playing the entrepreneur's role. A second decisional role is that of *disturbance handler*. A manager who settles a strike, or finds a new supplier of raw materials because there have been inventory shortages, is handling a disturbance. Third, the manager also occasionally plays the role of *resource allocator*. In this role, the manager might have to decide which departmental budgets to cut and which expenditure requests to approve. The fourth and last decisional role is that of *negotiator*. Being a negotiator might involve settling a dispute between a manager and the manager's subordinate or negotiating a new labor contract.

interpersonal role   a role in which the manager deals with people

Interpersonal Roles   Dealing with people is an integral part of the manager's job. An **interpersonal role** is one in which the manager deals with people. The manager may be called on to serve as a *figurehead*, perhaps by attending a ribbon-cutting ceremony or taking an important client to dinner. The manager may also have to play the role of *liaison* by serving as a go-between for two different groups. In this case, one of the two groups is the manager's own company. As a liaison, a manager might represent his or her firm at meetings of an industrywide trade organization. Finally, the manager often has to serve as a *leader*. Playing the role of leader includes being an example for others in the organization as well as developing the skills, abilities, and motivation of subordinates.

informational role   a role in which the manager either gathers or provides information

Informational Roles   An **informational role** is one in which the manager either gathers or provides information. In the role of *monitor*, the manager actively seeks information that may be of value to the organization. For example, a manager who hears about a good business opportunity, or is told by subordinates that employees are contemplating a strike, is engaging in the role of monitor. The second informational role is that of *disseminator*. In this role, the manager transmits key information to those who can use it. As a disseminator, the above-mentioned manager would tip off the appropriate marketing manager about the business opportunity and warn the human resources manager about the possible strike. The third informational role is that of *spokesperson*. In this role, the manager provides information to people outside the organization, such as the press and the public.

ETHICAL CHALLENGES
Alcoa: A Company with a Conscience

At more than 150 sites in the United States, the Aluminum Company of America, better known as Alcoa, mines bauxite ore and produces aluminum for automobiles, canning, aerospace, and construction. In an era when each day seems to deliver news of corporate corruption, executives at Alcoa want their firm to be a place where values are paramount and a code of ethics is more than mere window dressing. Alcoa's "Visions and Values" program not only specifies six core values, but spends millions of dollars and thousands of hours teaching sixty thousand workers, supervisors, and executives to implement them.

Company president Paul H. O'Neill says that the code of ethics is just the Golden Rule, but it's really more precise than that. The six core values—integrity, safety and health, quality of work, treatment of people, accountability, and profitability—are intended to cultivate a unified and productive working environment. Alcoa puts muscle behind an extensive, on-the-job safety policy by telling workers that anyone who doesn't adhere to the standards will be disciplined and possibly fired. With a staff of thirty and a $6 million budget, the new vice president for quality control makes sure that workers get finished products more than "almost right." Workers are testing the aluminum more often during and after manufacture, and prominent customer Anheuser-Busch says the quality of sheet metal it buys from Alcoa is consistently better. Managers pay more attention to the people they manage, cleaning plants to make working environments more pleasant, installing air conditioning and ventilation, and acting on employee suggestions more often.

Despite good intentions, Alcoa is discovering that adhering to its values isn't always easy. Even though employees now lose fewer days because of on-the-job injuries, two workers were killed within ten days at one plant when their coworkers didn't follow safety rules. The Tennessee Department of Labor cited Alcoa with five violations of state laws. Recent charges suggest that one Alcoa plant is endangering the health of nearby residents by releasing above-acceptable amounts of PCBs and other suspended solids in its waste, and another is discharging toxic aluminum oxide into the air.

In addition to troubles from on-the-job accidents and chemical emissions, Alcoa is facing rough economic times. In one year, revenues dropped more than $1 billion. When companies feel the profit pinch, values often play second fiddle to profits, but Alcoa executives insist their ethics program won't go away. Departing CEO C. Fred Fetterolf issued a memo to employees affirming his belief in the "Vision and Values" policy, and O'Neill remains convinced that he won't have to compromise values to succeed economically.

CORPORATE CULTURE

LEARNING OBJECTIVE 5
Describe corporate culture.

corporate culture   the inner rites, rituals, heroes, and values of a firm

Managers do not perform their jobs in a vacuum. Most managers function within a corporate culture. A **corporate culture** is generally defined as the inner rites, rituals, heroes, and values of a firm. Rituals that might seem silly to an outsider can have a powerful influence on how the employees of a particular organization think and act. For example, new employees at Honda Motor Co.'s Marysville, Ohio, manufacturing facility are encouraged to plant a small pine tree on the company's property. Symbolically, the growth of each employee's tree represents his or her personal growth and development at Honda.[3]

Terrence Deal (a Harvard University professor) and Allan Kennedy (a management consultant) have identified several key types of cultures.[4] One

Nurturing Two Cultures.
What's the CEO of a phone company, US West, doing with his very own buffalo pelt? The Lakota Indians presented Richard McCormick with the pelt to honor what US West has done to help Native American cultures. While under McCormick's leadership, the company has given $1.3 million to Indian colleges and has hired as many Indians as possible, bringing America's oldest culture to US West.

is the *tough-guy, macho culture,* in which people act as rugged individuals who like to take chances. Another is the *work hard/play hard culture.* Here the emphasis is on fun and action with few risks. Southwest Airlines has this type of culture. A third major form of corporate culture is the *bet-your-company culture.* In this corporate situation, the emphasis is on big-stakes decisions and gambles that may pay off far in the future. Finally, there is the *process culture,* in which the organization functions mechanically, with much "red tape" and little actual exchange of information.

Corporate culture is generally thought to have a very strong influence on a firm's performance over time. Hence it is useful to be able to assess a firm's corporate culture. Common indicators include the physical setting (building, office layouts, and so on); what the company itself says about its corporate culture (in its advertising and news releases, for example); how the company greets its guests (does it have formal or informal reception areas?); and how employees spend their time (working alone in an office most of the time or spending much of the day working with others).

Deal and Kennedy believe that cultural change is needed when the company's environment is changing, when the industry is becoming more competitive, when the company's performance is mediocre, when the company is growing rapidly, or when the company is about to become a truly large corporation. Moreover, they believe organizations of the future will look quite different from those of today. In particular, they predict that tomorrow's business firms will be made up of small task-oriented work groups, each with control over its own activities. These small groups will be coordinated through an elaborate computer network and held together by a strong corporate culture.

LEADERSHIP

leadership the ability to influence others

LEARNING OBJECTIVE 6
Explain the different types of leadership.

Leadership has been broadly defined as the ability to influence others. A leader has power and can use it to affect the behavior of others.[5] Leadership is different from management in that a leader strives for voluntary cooperation, whereas a manager may depend on coercion to change employee behavior.

Formal and Informal Leadership

Some experts make a distinction between formal leadership and informal leadership. Formal leaders have power of position; that is, they have *authority* within an organization and influence others to work for the organization's objectives. Informal leaders usually have no authority and may or may not exert their influence in support of the organization. Both formal and informal leaders make use of several kinds of power, including the ability to grant rewards or impose punishments, the possession of expert knowledge, and personal attraction or charisma.

Styles of Leadership

For many years leadership was viewed as a combination of personality traits, such as self-confidence, intelligence, and dependability. Achieving a consensus on which traits were most important was difficult, however, and attention turned to styles of leadership behavior. In the last few decades several styles of leadership have been identified: authoritarian, laissez-faire, and democratic.[6] The **authoritarian leader** holds all authority and responsibility, with communication usually moving from top to bottom. This leader assigns workers to specific tasks and expects orderly, precise results. The leaders at United Parcel Service employ authoritarian leadership. At the other extreme is the **laissez-faire leader,** who waives responsibility and allows subordinates to work as they choose with a minimum of interference. Communication flows horizontally among group members. The **democratic leader** holds final responsibility but also delegates authority to others, who participate in determining work assignments. In this leadership style, communication is active both upward and downward.

Each of these styles has its advantages and disadvantages. For example, democratic leadership can motivate employees to work effectively because it is *their* decisions that they are implementing. On the other hand, the decision-making process takes time that subordinates could otherwise be devoting to their tasks. Actually, each of the three leadership styles can be effective. The style that is *most* effective depends on the interaction among the subordinates, the characteristics of the work situation, and the manager's personality.

authoritarian leader one who holds all authority and responsibility, with communication usually moving from top to bottom

laissez-faire leader one who waives responsibility and allows subordinates to work as they choose with a minimum of interference; communication flows horizontally among group members

democratic leader one who holds final responsibility but also delegates authority to others, who help determine work assignments; communication is active upward and downward

MANAGERIAL DECISION MAKING

Decision making is the process of developing a set of possible alternative solutions and choosing one alternative from among that set.[7] In ordinary, everyday situations our decisions are made casually and informally. We encounter a problem, mull it over for a way out, settle on a likely solution, and go on. Managers, however, require a more systematic method for solving complex problems in a variety of situations. As shown in Figure 5.6, managerial decision making involves four steps: (1) identifying the problem or opportunity, (2) generating alternatives, (3) selecting an alternative, and (4) implementing the solution.[8]

decision making the process of developing a set of possible alternative solutions and choosing one alternative from among that set

LEARNING OBJECTIVE 7
Discuss the various stages of the managerial decision-making process.

Identifying the Problem or Opportunity

A problem is the discrepancy between an actual condition and a desired condition—the difference between what is occurring and what one wishes to occur. A "problem" may be negative or positive. A positive problem may be viewed as an "opportunity."

Although accurate identification of a problem is essential for the solving of that problem, this stage of decision making creates many difficulties

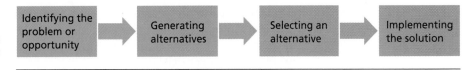

FIGURE 5.6
Major Steps in the Manage-rial Decision-Making Process
Managers require a systematic method for solving problems in a variety of ways.   *(Source: Kreitner, Robert,* Manage-ment, *5th ed. Copyright © 1992 by Houghton Mifflin Company. Adapted with per-mission.)*

for managers. Sometimes managers' preconceptions of the problem prevent them from seeing the situation as it actually is. They produce an answer before the proper question has ever been asked. In other cases, managers overlook truly significant issues by focusing on unimportant matters. Also, managers may analyze problems in terms of symptoms rather than underlying causes.

Effective managers learn to look ahead so that they are prepared when decisions must be made. They clarify situations and examine the causes of problems, asking whether the presence or absence of certain variables alters a given situation. Finally, they consider how individual behaviors and values affect the way problems or opportunities are defined.

Generating Alternatives

After a problem has been suitably defined, the next task is to generate alternatives. Generally, the more important the decision, the more attention is devoted to this stage. Managers should be open to fresh, innovative ideas as well as to more obvious answers.

Certain techniques can aid in the generation of creative alternatives. Brainstorming, commonly used in group discussions, encourages participants to come up with as many new ideas as possible, no matter how outrageous. Other group members are not permitted to criticize or ridicule. Another approach to generating alternatives, developed by the U.S. Navy, is called "Blast! Then Refine." Group members tackle a recurring problem afresh, erasing from their minds all solutions and procedures tried in the past. The group then re-evaluates its original objectives, modifies them if necessary, and devises new solutions to the problem. Other techniques for stimulating new ideas are also useful in this stage of decision making.

Selecting an Alternative

A final decision is influenced by a number of considerations, including financial constraints, finite human and information resources, time limits, legal obstacles, and political factors. Managers must select the alternative that will be most effective and practical under the circumstances. At times two or more alternatives, or some combination of alternatives, will be equally appropriate.

Managers may choose solutions to problems on several levels. The word *satisfice* has been coined to describe solutions that are only adequate, not the best possible. Managers often make decisions that satisfice if they lack time or information, even though this is not the most productive approach in the long run. Managers should try to optimize—that is, to carefully investigate alternatives and select the one that best solves the problem. In a few cases managers may be able to maximize, or achieve all of their goals. Finally, managers may change the basic situation so that the problem no longer exists.

Implementing the Solution

Implementation of a decision requires time, planning, and preparation of personnel. Managers must usually deal with unforeseen consequences as well, even when alternatives have been carefully considered.

If the chosen course of action removes the difference between the actual conditions and the desired conditions, it is judged effective. If the problem persists, however, managers may decide to give the alternative more time to work, adopt a different alternative, or start the problem identification process all over again.

SOURCES OF MANAGERS

LEARNING OBJECTIVE 8
List the major sources of managers.

We have discussed a number of functions managers must perform, skills they must use, and roles they must play. But where do they acquire the ability to do all this? We can best answer this question by turning it around and asking where organizations get management personnel. There are three primary sources of managers: lower levels in the organization, other organizations, and schools and universities (see Figure 5.7).

Inside the Organization

You have probably heard about firms whose policy is to "promote from within." This simply means that when a position needs to be filled, the firm makes a genuine effort to promote someone from a lower level in the firm to that position. This approach has two advantages. First, the person promoted from within is already familiar with how the organization operates, its strategy, its people, and most other facets of the organization. Second, promotion from within may increase job motivation for all employees. If employees recognize that good work can lead to a promotion, they are more likely to work harder and better and to stay with the company rather than seeking advancement elsewhere.

A disadvantage of promoting from within is that it may limit innovation. The new manager may simply continue to do things the way the previous manager did them—the way they have always been done in the organization. Furthermore, at the time a particular position needs to be filled, there might not be anyone in the organization who is truly qualified for that position. Hence, even firms that seek to promote from within may occasionally have to hire someone from another organization.

FIGURE 5.7
Sources of Managers
Potential managers may be promoted from within, hired away from other companies, or hired directly from college.

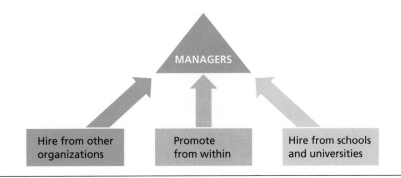

Other Organizations

The practice of hiring managers from other organizations seems to be used particularly to fill top management positions. Specialized executive employment agencies (sometimes unflatteringly called "head-hunters") search out qualified personnel who may be interested in leaving their organizations for better jobs. The agencies then match these people with firms seeking top managers. For example, recently head-hunters were responsible for replacing CEOs at Gerber Products, United Air Lines, Firestone Tire & Rubber Co., Mellon Bank, Datapoint, and Reebok.[9] Of course, many managers are hired by the more direct process of simply applying to the firm that has advertised an opening.

The principal advantages of hiring from the outside are that applicants may be judged objectively, based on their work record in the previous organization, and may bring new ideas and fresh perspectives to the firm. The bad news is that the hiring firm may not be able to learn as much about the applicant as it might like. Also, hiring from outside may cause resentment among present employees.

Schools and Universities

The third important source of managers is school and university campuses. Most large companies—and many smaller ones as well—routinely interview prospective graduates who might be interested in working for them. A number of recruiters look for people who are well trained and who have participated in internship programs and campus organizations. Those who are hired usually go through a management training program before being assigned a position. The program acquaints them with the firm and its products and prepares them for higher-level positions in the firm. Hence, educational institutions provide a pool of management talent that the organization then develops further, with the eventual goal of promotion to higher management levels.

Even after potential managers leave school and begin their working careers, their education is often not finished. Many return to school for an advanced degree, such as an MBA (Master of Business Administration), or to receive specialized training in management development programs and seminars.

MANAGING TOTAL QUALITY

total quality management
the coordination of efforts directed at improving customer satisfaction, increasing employee participation and empowerment, forming and strengthening supplier partnerships, and facilitating an organizational atmosphere of continuous quality improvement.

A high priority in some organizations today is the management of quality. Major reasons for a greater focus on quality include foreign competition, more demanding customers, and poorer profit performance resulting from reduced market shares and higher costs. Over the last few years, several U.S. firms have lost the dominant, competitive positions they had held for decades.

Total quality management is a much broader concept than just controlling the quality of the product itself (which is discussed in Chapter 7). **Total quality management** is the coordination of efforts directed at improving customer satisfaction, increasing employee participation and empowerment, forming and strengthening supplier partnerships, and facilitating an organizational atmosphere of continuous quality improvement. Improving customer satisfaction can occur through higher quality products and through better customer service, such as reduced delivery times, faster responses to customer inquiries, and simply treating customers better by showing them that the company really cares. Increasing employee involvement can mean allowing employees to participate in decisions to a greater extent, developing self-managed work teams, and placing responsibility and accountability on employees for improving the quality of their work. Improved supplier partnerships translates into obtaining the right supplies and materials on time at lower costs. Quality improvement should not be viewed as achievable through one single program that has a target objec-

The feedback expert. No matter how many quality tests a manufacturer performs, the customer is still the final judge of quality and the best source for product change ideas. So Rosetta Riley, Cadillac's director of customer satisfaction, doesn't try to calm customers, she tries to get them to speak up. And she makes the company listen. One result of her efforts: Cadillac won the U.S. Department of Commerce's Malcolm Baldrige National Quality Award in 1990.

BUSINESS JOURNAL
The Malcolm A. Baldrige National Quality Award

U.S. consumers are tired of brand new American cars with factory defects and customer service with service sadly lacking. Critical buyers are increasingly turning to foreign competitors, and corporate America has been losing its battle for market share. To help reverse that downward trend, the U.S. Department of Commerce established the Malcolm Baldrige National Quality Award to be presented to American companies with superior products, excellent service, and exceptional employee and customer relations. Since its creation in 1987, some of the Baldrige's well-known recipients have been Xerox, IBM, Federal Express, and Cadillac, but you don't have to be a corporate giant to win. Unassuming small businesses like the family-owned Wallace Company, Marlow Industries, Zytec, and the Solectron Corporation have been winners, too.

Each year, six firms, two manufacturing firms, two small businesses, and two service organizations, have a chance to win a Baldrige Award. Instead of being nominated by industry experts or government officials, companies nominate themselves through an arduous, time-consuming process. The entry form alone is fifty pages long. Of the 180,000 copies sent to potential applicants, usually only about one hundred are completed and returned. Judges who visit finalists must have the freedom to talk to anyone and have access to everything from assembly lines to company bathrooms.

To win the Baldrige Award, companies must demonstrate excellence in seven quality-related categories: leadership, information and analysis, strategic quality planning, human resource utilization, quality assurance of products and services, quality results, and customer satisfaction. Quality leadership means that senior executives are involved both in outlining specific quality values and goals and in coming up with systems for achieving them. Information and analysis refers to how well a company acquires, manages, and uses available data. To stand out in the human resources category, firms must demonstrate that they work hard to develop and use the full potential of their workforce, including management. "Quality results" refers not only to the quality of the end product but to an organization's ongoing commitment to reduce defects and errors and to improve efficiency and responsiveness to customers.

In the 1990s, customers demand superior goods and services. Is the Baldrige Award helping to provide them? Some analysts believe the award has been instrumental in improving the quality of American industry, citing as evidence reduced defects and customer service response time, increased productivity, customer satisfaction, and product performance, and improved on-the-job safety records. Even the more skeptical industry watchers acknowledge that, at the very least, the Baldrige has made American companies begin to think about continuous improvement.

tive. Instead, a culture based on continuous improvement has proved to be the most effective approach in the long run.

The costs of poor quality—remanufacturing, repairs, and reperformance of service—can range from 25 to 40 percent of sales. Fortunately, there is considerable evidence that the quality of U.S. products is improving. In 1981, for example, over 70 percent of new U.S. cars displayed defects within six months; a decade later, fewer than 40 percent had defects. Today's figure is closer to the 30 percent defects figure achieved by Japanese car makers. An increased interest in quality is also reflected in the number of companies requesting applications for the Malcolm Baldrige National Quality Award. In two years—from 1988 to 1990—that figure rose from 12,000 to 180,000 requests.

Although many factors influence the effectiveness of a total quality management program, two issues are crucial. First, top management must make a strong commitment to a total quality management program by treating quality improvement as a top priority and one that needs frequent attention. Firms that establish a total quality management program but then focus on other priorities will find that their quality improvement initiatives will fail. Second, management must coordinate the specific elements of a total management program so that they work in harmony with each other.

Although only about one-fourth of U.S. companies have total quality management programs, these programs provide many benefits. Overall financial benefits include lower operating costs, higher return on sales and on investment, and an improved ability to use premium pricing rather than competitive pricing. Additional benefits include faster development of innovations, improved access to global markets, higher levels of customer retention, and an enhanced reputation.[10]

In the next chapter we shall examine the organizing function in some detail. We shall look specifically at various forms that organizations take and the management concepts that result in these forms. Like most things in management, the form of an organization depends on the organization's goals, strategies, and personnel.

CHAPTER REVIEW

Summary

Management is the process of coordinating the resources of an organization to achieve the primary goals of the organization. Managers are concerned with four types of resources—material, financial, human, and informational.

Managers perform four basic functions. The amount of time they devote to each depends on the situation of the firm and of the manager within the firm. First, managers engage in goal setting and planning (determining where the firm should be going and how to get there). Three types of plans, from the broadest to the most specific, are strategies, tactical plans, and standing plans. Next, managers organize resources and activities to accomplish results in an efficient and effective manner. Then, managers must lead and motivate others to inspire them to work in the best interest of the organization. Finally, managers must control ongoing activities, through continual evaluation and regulation, to keep the organization on course as it pursues its goals.

Managers—or management positions—may be classified from two different perspectives. From the perspective of level, there are top managers, who control the fortunes of the organization; middle managers, who implement strategies and major policies; and first-line managers, who supervise the activities of operating employees. From the viewpoint of area of management, managers most often deal with the functions of finance, operations, marketing, human resources, and administration.

Effective managers tend to possess a specific set of skills and to fill ten basic managerial roles. Technical, conceptual, interpersonal, diagnostic, and analytic skills are all important, though the relative importance of each varies with the level of management. All the key managerial roles can be classified as decisional, interpersonal, or informational.

Managers function within a corporate culture—a system consisting of a firm's inner rites, rituals, heroes, and values. Managers may find it useful to assess that culture.

Managers' own effectiveness often depends on their styles of leadership—that is, their ability to influence others, either formally or informally. Leadership styles include the authoritarian "do it my way" style, the laissez-faire "do it your way" style, and the democratic "let's do it together" style.

Decision making, an integral part of a manager's work, is the process of developing a set of possible alternative solutions and choosing one alternative from among that set. Managerial decision making involves four steps. Managers must accurately identify problems, come up with several possible solutions, choose the solution that will be most effective under the circumstances, and finally implement the chosen course of action.

Candidates for management positions learn their skills and roles in lower levels within the organization, in other organizations, and in schools and universities.

Total quality management is the coordination of efforts directed at improving customer satisfaction, increasing employee participation and empowerment, forming and strengthening supplier partnerships, and facilitating an organizational atmosphere of continuous quality improvement. To have an effective total quality management program, top management must make a strong, sustained commitment to the program and must be able to coordinate all of the program's elements so that they work in harmony.

Key Terms

You should now be able to define and give an example relevant to each of the following terms:

management	middle manager
goal	first-line manager
goal setting	financial manager
purpose	operations manager
mission	marketing manager
objective	human resources
plan	manager
planning	administrative manager
strategy	technical skill
tactical plan	conceptual skill
policy	interpersonal skill
standard operating	diagnostic skill
procedure (SOP)	analytic skill
organizing	decisional role
leading	interpersonal role
motivating	informational role
directing	corporate culture
controlling	leadership
top manager	authoritarian leader

laissez-faire leader	decision making
democratic leader	total quality management

Questions and Exercises

Review Questions

1. Define the term *manager* without using the word *management* in your definition.
2. What are the purpose and the mission of a neighborhood restaurant? of the Salvation Army? What might be reasonable objectives for these organizations?
3. How do a strategy, a tactical plan, and a policy differ? What do they all have in common?
4. What exactly does a manager organize, and for what reason?
5. Why are leadership and motivation necessary in a business where people are paid for their work?
6. Explain the steps involved in the control function.
7. How are the two perspectives on kinds of managers—that is, level and area—different from each other?
8. In what way are management skills related to the roles managers play? Provide a specific example to support your answer.
9. What is meant by corporate culture?
10. Compare and contrast the major styles of leadership.
11. Discuss what happens during each stage of the managerial decision-making process.
12. What are the advantages and disadvantages of promoting from within, compared with hiring new managers from outside the organization?
13. What are the major benefits of a total quality management program?

Discussion Questions

1. Why is Southwest Airlines successful when many of its competitors are not?
2. What types of management skills are demonstrated by Herb Kelleher?
3. Does a healthy firm (one that is doing well) have to worry about effective management? Explain.
4. Which of the management functions, skills, and roles don't really apply to the owner-operator of a sole proprietorship?
5. Which leadership style might be best suited to each of the three general levels of management?
6. Do you think people are really as important to an organization as this chapter seems to indicate?

CHAPTER

6

Creating the Organization

LEARNING OBJECTIVES

After studying this chapter you should be able to:

1 Understand what organizations are and what their organization charts show.

2 Outline the overall dimensions of organizational structure.

3 Explain why job specialization is important and why some firms are using less of it.

4 Identify the various bases for departmentalization.

5 Explain how decentralization follows from delegation.

6 Understand the span of management and how it describes an organization.

7 Distinguish between line and staff management.

8 Describe the three basic forms of organizational structure: bureaucratic, organic, and matrix.

9 Define what an informal organization is and how it operates through informal groups and the grapevine.

CHAPTER PREVIEW

We begin this chapter by examining the business organization—what it is and how its various positions are structured. Next, we focus one by one on five dimensions of organizational structure. We discuss job specialization within a company; the grouping of jobs into manageable units or departments; the delegation of power from management to subordinates; the span of management; and the differences between line and staff management. Then, we step back for an overall view of three approaches to organizational structure—the bureaucratic structure, the organic structure, and the matrix structure. Finally, we look at the network of social interactions—the informal organization—that operates within the formal business structure.

Bruegger's Bagel Bakery Bakes Up Successful Organization

When an attorney, an accountant, and the owner of a construction company started a bagel business in 1983, they admitted knowing next to nothing about food service. They also wanted freedom from many of the hassles franchise managers cope with daily—the late-night calls, long hours, negotiations with suppliers, and dealings with temperamental customers. They began by discarding the notion that, as founders, they had to make decisions about how to run stores, how to staff them, and even what to sell. Instead, they gave those responsibilities and headaches to the managers at Bruegger's Bagel Bakery and provided incentives to make it all worthwhile.

Bruegger's founders structured their organization so that one manager is responsible for an average of six stores. Cluster managers develop their own management styles and decorate their own shops. They hire and train personnel, determine prices, even invent unique menu items like "pizza bagels" and "bagel dogs." What do managers get in return? In addition to starting salaries of around $30,000, they become "partners," owning 20 percent of the cluster they supervise. As further incentive, they can buy stock and share in pre-tax profits at the end of every year. When a crabby, demanding customer sends a bagel and cream cheese back for the third time, the cluster manager stands to benefit directly from service with a smile.

By offering managers a stake in their own business, Bruegger's attracted take-charge, high-caliber people. The plan seems to work, and growth is the measure of its success. Of course, that growth has brought some changes. Managers have had to give up some of their independence as some decision areas have been centralized. Although managers are still free to set prices, hire and fire employees, and structure their organizations, some operations and decisions are now centrally controlled. Instead of

making their own bagel dough, all stores receive formed, ready-to-bake dough from a Bruegger's commissary. Managers must show a proprietary videotape on bagel-baking to new bakers, as well as prominently display an illustrated poster, "The Official Bagel Baker's Guide to Perfect Bagels," which catalogs twenty common bagel flaws, ranging from malformed holes to wrinkled crusts. Relying on test marketing, executives now dictate a single menu for all shops. Customers who regularly eat at Bruegger's in Boston know just what to expect if they eat at Bruegger's in Cedar Rapids, Iowa.

When the firm's founders applied for a loan to start their business, bankers were skeptical, convinced that bagels were too ethnic to be accepted all over the United States. Bruegger's proved them wrong. Today, it's a $30 million enterprise with eight hundred employees operating fifty shops in eight states. Since the company began, only four of its fifteen managers have left. Evidently, one part autonomy and one part profit sharing is the recipe for success at Bruegger's Bagel Bakeries.[1]

Bruegger's Bagel Bakery, like many companies, is organized in a way that helps it achieve a set of general objectives. When firms are organized, the focus is sometimes on achieving low operating costs. In other cases, the emphasis is on providing high-quality products to ensure customer satisfaction. The way that a firm is organized influences its performance. Thus, the issue of organization is important.

WHAT IS AN ORGANIZATION?

We used the term *organization* throughout Chapter 5 without really defining it, mainly because its everyday meaning is close to its business meaning. Here, however, let us agree that an **organization** is a group of two or more people working together in a predetermined fashion to achieve a common set of goals. A neighborhood dry cleaner owned and operated by a husband-and-wife team is an organization. IBM, which employs hundreds of thousands of workers worldwide, is also an organization in the very same sense. Although IBM's organizational structure is vastly more complex than that of the dry cleaning establishment, each must be organized if it is to achieve its goals.

Organizing

An inventor who goes into business to produce and market a new invention hires people, decides what each will do, determines who will report to whom, and so on. These activities are the essence of organizing, or creating, the organization. *Organizing,* as we saw in Chapter 5, is the process of grouping resources and activities to accomplish some result in an efficient and effective manner. Out of the organizing process comes an **organizational structure,** which is a fixed pattern of (1) positions within the organization and (2) relationships among those positions.

Developing Organization Charts

An **organization chart** is a diagram that represents the positions and relationships within an organization—that is, it reveals the company's

169

Key

——— Chain of command

— — — Staff

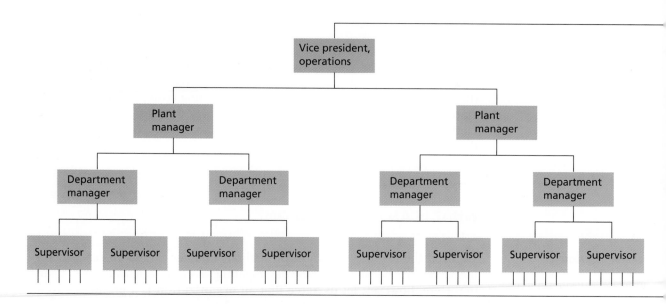

FIGURE 6.1 A Typical Corporate Organization Chart
A company's organization chart represents the positions and relationships within an organization and shows the managerial chains of command.

organizational structure. An example of an organization chart is shown in Figure 6.1. What does it tell us?

Each rectangle in the chart represents a particular position or person in the organization. At the top of the chart is the president; at the next level are the vice presidents. The solid vertical lines connecting the vice presidents to the president indicate that the vice presidents are in the chain of command. The **chain of command** is the line of authority that extends from the highest to the lowest levels of the organization. Moreover, each vice president reports directly to the president. Similarly, the plant managers, regional sales managers, and accounting department manager report directly to the vice presidents.

Notice that the directors of legal services, public affairs, and human resources are shown with a broken line; these people are not part of the direct chain of command. Instead, they hold *advisory,* or *staff,* positions. This difference will be made clear later in the chapter, when we discuss line and staff positions.

Most smaller organizations find organization charts useful. They clarify positions and reporting relationships for everyone in the organization,

chain of command the line of authority that extends from the highest to the lowest levels of an organization

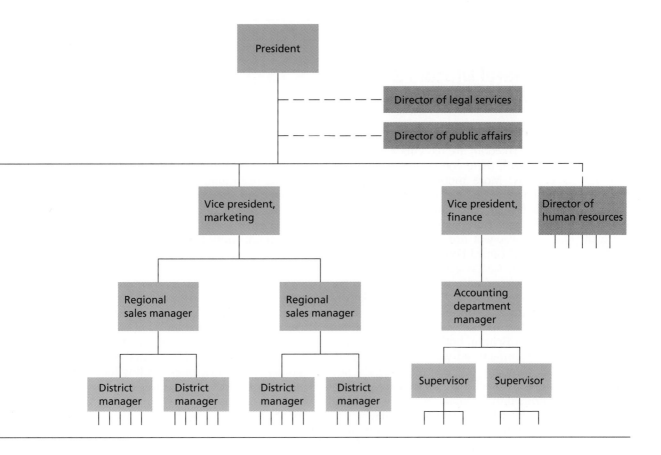

and they help managers track growth and change in the organizational structure. For two reasons, however, many large organizations do not maintain complete, detailed charts. It is difficult to chart accurately even a few dozen positions, much less the thousands that characterize larger firms. And larger organizations are almost always changing one part of their structure or another. An organization chart would probably be outdated before it was completed.

In the next several sections we shall consider five major dimensions of organizational structure, most of which are not immediately apparent on the company's organization chart.

THE DIMENSIONS OF ORGANIZATIONAL STRUCTURE

When a firm is started, management must decide how to organize the firm. These decisions are all part of five major steps that sum up the organizing

GLOBAL PERSPECTIVES
General Motors Reorganizes to Serve Global Markets

Winds of political freedom are blowing across Eastern Europe, and with them comes increased mobility for its citizens. More mobility translates into more demand for cars, and right now, General Motors Corp. is the foreign auto company best meeting those demands. Only European car makers Volkswagen, Fiat, and Peugeot are growing faster, and GM's sales recently topped Ford's in Europe. Industry experts say that GM is conquering Europe because the company reorganized its operations there. In the past, GM segmented its European markets by country, each with a separate management structure. Opel, GM's German subsidiary, ran operations in that country. In Britain, both the GM subsidiary and the car it manufactured were known as Vauxhall. However, company officers, piloted by a new CEO, became convinced that approaching all of Europe as a unified automobile market would lead to increased production of high-quality cars.

To accomplish that goal, the corporation eliminated layers of management, consolidating European operations at a new headquarters in Zurich, Switzerland. GM now ships partially built cars from one factory to another for final assembly. New engine and transmission plants in Hungary and Czechoslovakia reduce the need to pay the high prices often charged by German suppliers. By cultivating consistently better relationships with unions, GM has been able to increase European assembly plants from two-shift days to three-shift days, boosting production so that Europeans clamoring for American cars can get them. In place of the many small units that worked alone, General Motors' European enterprise has been reorganized into a more efficient unified machine.

Being designated by *Fortune* as the "world's largest corporation" doesn't mean General Motors is immune to problems. In the United States, the firm recently recorded losses of $4.6 billion. In contrast to its grim domestic picture, GM has increased its European profits by $1.9 billion. Although the firm's long-standing focus has been its U.S. auto business, executives are now looking toward Europe as the most promising site of future growth. Despite cutbacks in its U.S. operations, the organization expects to expand European automaking by 25 percent over the next few years. Hoping to write a sequel to its European success story, GM announced plans to close six assembly plants as well as fifteen other factories, and is considering shuffling U.S. management to make domestic operations more like international ones.

process. The results of these steps are often called the *dimensions of organizational structure* because they are reflected in the organization and its organization chart. The five steps are as follows:

LEARNING OBJECTIVE 2
Outline the overall dimensions of organizational structure.

1. Divide the work that is to be done by the entire organization into separate parts, and assign those parts to positions within the organization. This step is sometimes called job design. The resulting dimension is the *degree of specialization* within the organization.

2. Group the various positions into manageable units. This step determines the *nature and degree of departmentalization* of the organization.

3. Distribute responsibility and authority within the organization. This step results in a particular *degree of centralization* for the organization.

4. Determine the number of subordinates who will report to each manager. The resulting dimension is called the *span of management*.

5. Distinguish between those positions with direct authority and those that are support positions. This establishes the organization's *chain of command*.

JOB DESIGN

Until recently, the watchword in job design was specialization for worker efficiency. Now, however, the tide has turned. Many jobs are now designed to include more variety.

Job Specialization

LEARNING OBJECTIVE 3
Explain why job specialization is important and why some firms are using less of it.

job specialization the separation of all organizational activities into distinct tasks and the assignment of different tasks to different people

In Chapter 1 we defined *specialization* as the separation of a manufacturing process into distinct tasks and the assignment of different tasks to different people. Here we are extending that concept to *all* the activities that are performed within the organization. **Job specialization** is the separation of all organizational activities into distinct tasks and the assignment of different tasks to different people.

As we noted in Chapter 1, Adam Smith was the first to emphasize the power of specialization in his book *The Wealth of Nations*. According to Smith, the various tasks in a particular pin factory were arranged so that one worker drew the wire for the pins, another straightened the wire, a third cut it, a fourth ground the point, and a fifth attached the head. Using this method, Smith claimed, ten men were able to produce 48,000 pins per day. They could produce only 200 pins per day if each worker had to perform all five tasks!

The Rationale for Specialization

For a number of reasons, at least some specialization is necessary. First and foremost is the simple fact that the "job" of most organizations is simply too large for one person to handle. In a firm that produces goods, several production people may be needed. Others will be needed to sell the product, to control the firm's finances, and so on.

Second, when a worker has to learn only a specific, highly specialized task, that individual should be able to learn to do it very efficiently. Third, the worker who is doing the same job over and over does not lose time changing from one operation to another, as the pin workers probably did when each was producing a complete pin. Fourth, the more specialized the job, the easier it may be to design specialized equipment for those who do it. And finally, the more specialized the job, the easier it is to train new employees when an employee quits or is absent from work.

Unfortunately, specialization can have some negative consequences as well. The most significant drawback is the boredom and dissatisfaction many employees feel when they do the same job over and over. Monotony can be deadening. Bored employees may be absent from work frequently, may not put much effort into their work, and may even sabotage the company. Because of these negative side effects, managers have recently begun to search for alternatives to specialization in the design of jobs.

Alternatives to Job Specialization

The three most common antidotes to the problems that job specialization can breed are job rotation, job enlargement, and job enrichment.

job rotation the systematic shifting of employees from one job to another

Job Rotation   **Job rotation** is the systematic shifting of employees from one job to another. For example, a worker may be assigned to a different job every week for a four-week period and then return to the first job in the fifth week. The idea behind job rotation is to provide a variety of jobs so that workers will be less likely to get bored and dissatisfied. Companies that use job rotation include Ford, Xerox, The Prudential Insurance Co. of America, and the U.S. Nissan subsidiary.

Unfortunately, many firms have had less than total success with job rotation. Often the worker is shifted to one narrow and boring job after another. Therefore, although there may be a short period of revived interest after each new assignment, this interest wears off quickly. Still, job rotation is widely used, and it offers the added advantage of being an excellent tool for teaching employees new skills.

job enlargement   giving a worker more things to do within the same job

Job Enlargement   In job rotation, the employee is shifted from job to job, but the jobs are not changed. In **job enlargement,** the worker is given more things to do within the same job. For example, under job specialization, each worker on an assembly line might connect three wires to the product as it moves down the line. After job enlargement, each worker might connect five wires. Unfortunately, the added tasks are often just as routine as those that the workers performed before the change. In such cases, enlargement may not be effective. AT&T, IBM, and the Maytag Co. have all experimented with job enlargement.

job enrichment   providing workers with both more tasks to do and more control over how they do their work

Job Enrichment   Job enrichment is perhaps the most advanced alternative to job specialization. Whereas job rotation and job enlargement do not really change the routine and monotonous nature of jobs, job enrichment does. **Job enrichment** is, in essence, providing workers with both more tasks to do and more control over how they do their work. In particular, under job enrichment many controls are removed from jobs, workers are given more authority, and work is assigned in complete, natural units. Moreover, employees are frequently given new and challenging job assignments. By blending more planning and decision making into jobs, job enrichment builds more depth and complexity into jobs. These changes tend to increase the employee's sense of responsibility and provide motivating opportunities for growth and advancement.

Job enrichment works best when employees seek more challenging work. Not all workers, however, respond positively to job enrichment programs. Employees must desire personal growth and have the skills and knowledge to perform enriched jobs. Lack of self-confidence, fear of failure, or distrust of management's intentions is likely to lead to ineffective performance of enriched jobs. The company that uses job enrichment as an alternative to specialization also faces extra expenses, such as the costs of retraining. Among the companies that have used job enrichment are General Foods and Texas Instruments.

DEPARTMENTALIZATION

departmentalization   the process of grouping jobs into manageable units according to some reasonable scheme

After jobs are designed, they must be grouped together into "working units" in keeping with the organization's goals. This process is called departmentalization. More specifically, **departmentalization** is the process of grouping jobs into manageable units according to some reasonable scheme. Several departmentalization schemes, or bases, are commonly used. Most firms use more than one of them. The groups of positions that result from the departmentalization process are usually called *departments*, although they are sometimes known as units, groups, or divisions.

Departmentalization Bases

LEARNING OBJECTIVE 4
Identify the various bases for departmentalization.

departmentalization basis
the scheme or criterion by which jobs are grouped into units

departmentalization by function   the grouping together of all jobs that relate to the same organizational activity

A **departmentalization basis** is the scheme or criterion by which jobs are grouped into units. The most common bases are function, product, location, and customer.

By Function   **Departmentalization by function** is the grouping of all jobs that relate to the same organizational activity. Under this scheme, all marketing personnel are grouped together in the marketing department, all production personnel in the production department, and so on.

Most smaller and newer organizations base their departmentalization on function. Such grouping permits each department to be efficiently staffed by experts. Supervision is simplified because everyone is involved in the same kinds of activities, and coordination is fairly easy. The disadvantages of this method of grouping jobs are that it can lead to slow decision making and that it tends to emphasize the department rather than the organization as a whole.

departmentalization by product   the grouping together of all activities related to a particular product or product group

By Product   **Departmentalization by product** is the grouping together of all activities related to a particular product or product group. This scheme is often used by older and larger firms that produce and sell a variety of products. Each product department handles its own marketing, production, financial management, and human resources activities.

Departmentalization by product makes decision making easier and provides for the integration of all activities associated with each product or

ETHICAL CHALLENGES
Organizing to Cope with Unethical Conduct

When the marketing director for a large American manufacturing firm discovered that a loophole in federal regulations was making it possible for his company to offer a below-standard product, he strongly advised cancellation of that product. Was he rewarded for his integrity and ethical recommendation? No. Not only did the company go ahead with the project, but three months later, it fired the marketing director.

From the decisions everyone faces on the job every day, to headline news like insider trading on Wall Street, coping with unethical conduct is a hot topic on American corporate agendas. In a recent survey of corporate employees, 56 percent of those responding believe that American business ethics are steadily declining, and a healthy majority of them said they'd personally observed expense account padding, stealing, favoritism, discrimination, sexual harassment, and lying to employees and clients.

For many firms, the first step in organizing to deal with unethical conduct is to establish a formal code of ethics that captures company values and commitments and outlines expectations and sanctions for unethical conduct. According to a recent study by the Center for Business Ethics, 90 percent of *Fortune 1000* companies have written codes, a 15 percent jump in five years. But it's not enough to have some words on a piece of paper. Instead, firms must use the code, talk about it, print it on company memos and in newsletters, even apply it as one requirement for raises and promotions. In other words, make sure employees know the company's values and incorporate them into the way they do their jobs.

Having a code of ethics is a good start, but companies are also implementing organizational changes that make it easier for employees to do the right thing. The typical American corporation is bound by a hierarchy—if you make a detour around the chain of command to report ethical wrongdoing, you are a threat to that hierarchy. And what happens if it's your immediate superior's actions you want to report, or the person who sits next to you every day? More and more company presidents are initiating open-door policies and inviting employees to write confidential letters with promises of follow-up. The chairman of Colgate-Palmolive Co. encourages workers to come forward by sitting down with them at more than eighty breakfast meetings a year. Some firms designate a particular person—someone inside the company but independent of the corporate hierarchy—with whom employees can confidentially discuss ethical dilemmas. Others set up special telephone lines in their legal and security departments so that employees can call and discuss their complaints. At Nynex Corporation, workers reach the eight-member ethics office by mail, by a toll-free phone call, or by fax, and the board investigates every complaint, even anonymous ones.

The cost to organizations when unethical conduct occurs is measured not only in millions of dollars but often in lost and ruined lives and irreparable environmental damage. American companies are awakening to the reality that requiring an ethical business environment and reorganizing to create one is not a matter of sacrifice—it's a question of survival.

Issues to Consider

1. How would you feel about reporting one of your coworkers for violating the organization's code of ethics?

2. What factors would most influence your decision to report or not report a coworker for an ethics code violation?

product group. However, it causes some duplication of specialized activities—such as finance—from department to department. And the emphasis is placed on the product rather than on the whole organization.

Digital Equipment Corporation, one of the largest computer manufacturers in the world, was originally organized around eighteen separate product groups. Each group competed with the others and became protective rather than cooperative. Instead of working for the common goals of the company, members of each product group worked for the good of that group. As a result, Digital Equipment's efficiency and profits suffered.

By Location **Departmentalization by location** is the grouping together of all activities according to the geographic area in which they are performed. Departmental areas may range from whole countries (for multinational firms) to regions within countries (for national firms) to areas of several city blocks (for police departments organized into precincts). Departmentalization by location allows the organization to respond readily to the unique demands or requirements of different locations. Nevertheless, a large administrative staff and an elaborate control system may be needed to coordinate operations in many locations.

One of the ways that the president of Digital Equipment solved the problem of counterproductive product groups was to combine the twelve U.S. product groups into three regional management centers. This helped to clear up communication problems among different departments and consolidated much of the administrative paperwork, which had been slowing down important decisions.

By Customer **Departmentalization by customer** is the grouping together of all activities according to the needs of various customer groups. A car dealership, for example, may have one sales staff to deal with individual consumers and a different sales staff to work with corporate fleet buyers. The obvious advantage of this approach is that it allows the firm to deal efficiently with unique customers or customer groups. The biggest drawback is that a larger-than-usual administrative staff is needed.

Another part of Digital Equipment's reorganization was the assigning of the sales force to specific customers rather than to specific markets. Before the reorganization, as many as six salespeople, each from a different product group, could call on one large customer. The situation was confusing and frustrating for customers, and not very profitable for Digital Equipment.

Using Combinations of Bases

Few organizations exhibit only one departmentalization basis. In fact, many firms use several different bases within a single organization (see Figure 6.2). An example is General Motors Corp. GM has realigned its divisions into small-vehicle and large-vehicle groups. Each GM division, in turn, is departmentalized by function; each has its own marketing, finance,

departmentalization by location the grouping together of all activities according to the geographic area in which they are performed

departmentalization by customer the grouping together of all activities according to the needs of various customer groups

FIGURE 6.2
Multibase
Departmentalization
Most firms use more than one
basis for departmentalization
to improve efficiency and to
avoid overlapping positions.

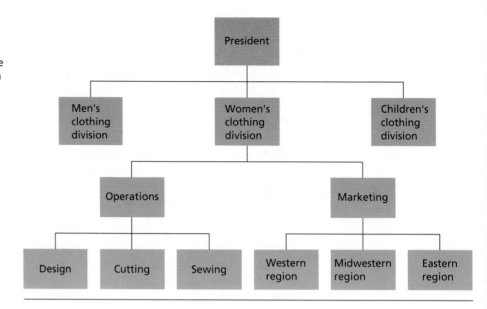

and personnel groups. Production groups might be further departmentalized by plant location, with each plant comprising an individual unit. Similarly, a divisional marketing group might be divided in such a way that one
unit handles consumer sales and another handles fleet and corporate sales.

All this adds up to the fact that multibase departmentalization is the
rule rather than the exception for larger firms. Like every management
tool, departmentalization is used however and wherever it will benefit the
organization most.

DELEGATION, DECENTRALIZATION, AND CENTRALIZATION

LEARNING OBJECTIVE 5
Explain how decentralization
follows from delegation.

The third major step in the organizing process is to distribute power in
the organization. Delegation is the act of distributing power from management to subordinates. The degree of centralization or decentralization of
authority is determined by the overall pattern of delegation within the
organization.

Delegation of Authority

delegation   the assigning of
part of a manager's work and
power to a subordinate

Delegation is the assigning of part of a manager's work and power to a
subordinate. Because no manager can do everything alone, delegation is
vital to the completion of a manager's work. Delegation is also important in
developing the skills and abilities of subordinates. It allows those who are
being groomed for higher-level positions to play increasingly important
roles in decision making.

responsibility the duty to do a job or perform a task

authority the power, within the organization, to accomplish an assigned job or task

accountability the obligation of a subordinate to accomplish an assigned job or task

Steps in Delegation Three steps are generally involved in the delegation process (see Figure 6.3). First, the manager must *assign responsibility*. **Responsibility** is the duty to do a job or perform a task. Along with assigning responsibility, the manager must *grant authority*. **Authority** is the power, within the organization, to accomplish an assigned job or task. This might include the power to obtain specific information, order supplies, authorize relevant expenditures, and make certain decisions. Finally, the manager must *create accountability*. **Accountability** is the obligation of a subordinate to accomplish an assigned job or task.

Note that accountability is created but that it cannot be delegated away. Suppose we are responsible for performing some job. We, in turn, delegate part of the work to a subordinate. We nonetheless remain accountable to our immediate superior for getting the job done properly. If our subordinate fails to complete the assignment, we—not the subordinate—will be called on to account for what has become *our* failure.

Barriers to Delegation For several reasons, managers may be unwilling to delegate work. One reason was just stated—the person who delegates remains accountable for the work. Many managers are reluctant to delegate simply because they want to be sure the work gets done properly. In other words, they just don't trust their subordinates. Another reason for reluctance to delegate stems from the opposite situation. The manager fears the subordinate will do the work so well that he or she will attract the approving notice of higher-level managers and will therefore become a threat to the manager. Finally, some managers don't delegate because they are so disorganized they simply are not able to plan and assign work effectively.

Decentralization of Authority

decentralized organization an organization in which management consciously attempts to spread authority widely in the lower levels of the organization

centralized organization an organization that systematically works to concentrate authority at the upper levels of the organization

The general pattern of delegation throughout an organization determines the extent to which that organization is decentralized or centralized. In a **decentralized organization,** management consciously attempts to spread authority widely in the lower organization levels. A **centralized organization** systematically works to concentrate authority at the upper levels.

A variety of factors can influence the extent to which a firm is decentralized. One is the external environment in which the firm operates. The

FIGURE 6.3
Steps in the Delegation Process
To be successful, a good manager must learn how to delegate. No one can do everything alone.

Same product, different face.
Grace Specialty Chemicals manufactures Cryovac food storage bags and film in eighteen plants around the world, this one in Brazil. Grace is a global company that stays attuned to individual customers and specialized markets by hiring local managers who speak the customers' languages and know the customs and cultures of the region.

span of management (or **span of control**)   the number of subordinates who report directly to one manager

LEARNING OBJECTIVE 6
Understand the span of management and how it describes an organization.

more complex and unpredictable this environment is, the more likely it is that top management will let lower-level managers make important decisions. Another factor is the nature of the decision itself. The riskier the decision, the greater the tendency to centralize decision making. A third factor is the abilities of lower-level managers. If these managers do not have strong decision-making skills, top managers will be reluctant to decentralize. And, in contrast, strong lower-level decision-making skills encourage decentralization. Finally, a firm that has traditionally practiced centralization is likely to maintain that centralization in the future, and vice versa.

In principle, neither decentralization nor centralization is right or wrong. What works for one organization may or may not work for another. K mart Corporation, Toys "Я" Us, Inc., and McDonald's have all been very successful—and they all practice centralization. By the same token, decentralization has worked very well for General Electric, Du Pont, and Sears, Roebuck. Every organization must assess its own situation and then choose the level of centralization or decentralization that it feels will work best in that situation.

THE SPAN OF MANAGEMENT

The fourth major dimension of organizational structure, the **span of management** (or **span of control**) is the number of subordinates who report directly to one manager. For hundreds of years, theorists have searched for an optimal span of management. When it became apparent that there is no perfect number of subordinates for a manager to supervise, they turned their attention to the more general issue of whether the span should be wide or narrow.

Wide and Narrow Spans of Control

A *wide* span of management exists when a manager has a large number of subordinates. A *narrow* span exists when the manager has only a few subordinates. Several factors determine the span that is better for a particular manager (see Figure 6.4). Generally, the span should be narrow (1) when subordinates are physically located far from each other, (2) when the manager has much work to do in addition to supervising subordinates, (3) when a great deal of interaction is required between supervisor and subordinates, and (4) when new problems arise frequently. The span of control may be wide (1) when the manager and the subordinates are very competent, (2) when the organization has a well-established set of standard operating procedures, and (3) when few new problems are expected to arise.

Organizational Height

The span of management has an obvious impact on relations between superiors and subordinates. It has a more subtle but equally important

FIGURE 6.4
The Span of Management
Several criteria determine whether a firm uses a wide span of management, in which several subordinates report to one manager, or a narrow span, in which a manager has only a few subordinates.

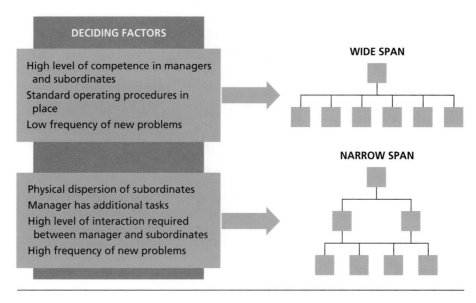

DECIDING FACTORS

High level of competence in managers and subordinates
Standard operating procedures in place
Low frequency of new problems

WIDE SPAN

Physical dispersion of subordinates
Manager has additional tasks
High level of interaction required between manager and subordinates
High frequency of new problems

NARROW SPAN

organizational height the number of layers, or levels, of management in a firm

impact on the height of the organization. **Organizational height** is the number of layers, or levels, of management in a firm. The span of management plays a direct role in determining the height of the organization, as shown in Figure 6.4. If spans of management are generally narrow, more levels are needed and the resulting organization is *tall*. If spans of management are wider, fewer levels are needed and the organization is *flat*.

In a taller organization, administrative costs are higher because more managers are needed. And communication among levels may become distorted because information has to pass up and down through more people. Although flat organizations avoid those problems, their managers may all have to perform more administrative duties simply because there are fewer managers. They may have to spend considerably more time supervising and working with subordinates.

LINE AND STAFF MANAGEMENT

line management position a position that is part of the chain of command and that includes direct responsibility for achieving the goals of the organization

staff management position a position created to provide support, advice, and expertise within an organization

Our last major organizational dimension is the chain of command (or line of authority) that reaches from the uppermost to the lowest levels of management. A **line management position** is part of the chain of command; it's a position in which a person makes decisions and gives orders to subordinates to achieve the goals of the organization. A **staff management position,** by contrast, is a position created to provide support, advice, and expertise to someone in the chain of command. Staff positions are not part of the chain of command but do have authority over their assistants. Staff personnel are not specifically accountable for accomplishing the goals of the firm. A marketing executive is generally a line manager because marketing is directly related to accomplishing the firm's purpose, mission, and

Line meets staff. The traditional division between line and staff functions sometimes creates a barrier between the two groups that can make managing the company difficult. Therefore when a chief executive like McDonald's Mike Quinlan puts on an apron with the staff of a local McDonald's, it's likely to mean something to the staff members and perhaps have an effect throughout the company.

objectives. A legal adviser, however, doesn't actively engage in profit-making activities but rather provides legal support to those who do. Hence the legal adviser occupies a staff position (see Figure 6.5).

Line and Staff Positions Compared

LEARNING OBJECTIVE 7
Distinguish between line and staff management.

Both line and staff managers are needed for effective management, but the two kinds of positions differ in important ways. The basic difference is in terms of authority. Line managers have *line authority*, which means that they can make decisions and issue directives that relate to the organization's goals. Staff managers seldom have this kind of authority. Instead, they usually have either advisory authority or functional authority.

Advisory authority is simply the expectation that line managers will consult the appropriate staff manager when making decisions. (Even so, line managers generally don't have to follow the advice they get from staff managers.) Functional authority is stronger, and in some ways it is like line authority. *Functional authority* is the authority of staff managers to make decisions and issue directives, but only about their own areas of expertise. For example, a legal adviser can decide whether to retain a particular clause in a contract, but not what price to charge for a new product. Contracts are part of the legal adviser's area of expertise; pricing is not.

Line-Staff Conflict

For a variety of reasons, conflict between line managers and staff managers is fairly common in business. Staff managers often have more formal education and are sometimes younger (and perhaps more ambitious) than line managers. Line managers may perceive staff managers as a threat to their own authority, or they may resent them. For their part, staff managers may become resentful if their expert recommendations—in public relations or human resources management, for example—are not adopted by line management.

FIGURE 6.5
Line and Staff Management
A line manager has direct responsibility for achieving the company's goals and is in the direct chain of command. A staff manager supports and advises the line managers.

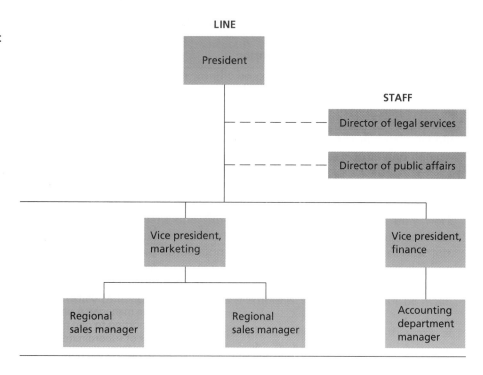

Fortunately, there are several ways to minimize the possibility of such conflict. One way is to integrate line and staff managers into one team working together. Another is to ensure that the areas of responsibility of line and staff managers are clearly defined. Finally, line and staff managers can both be held accountable for the results of their activities.

OTHER ELEMENTS OF ORGANIZATIONAL STRUCTURE

We have now discussed the five major dimensions of organizational structure. In this section we shall look at three other elements of organization: work schedules, committees, and coordination techniques (see Table 6.1).

Work Schedules

To most people, *work schedule* means the standard 9 a.m.-to-5 p.m. forty-hour workweek. In reality, though, many people have work schedules that are quite different from this. Police officers, firefighters, restaurant personnel, airline employees, and medical personnel, for example, usually have work schedules that are far from standard. Some manufacturers also rotate personnel from shift to shift. And many professional people—such as managers, artists, and lawyers—work more than forty hours per week because

GETTING AHEAD IN BUSINESS
Getting Along with Your Boss

You are Dagwood Bumstead, and your boss, Mr. Dithers, screams at you all the time and never gives you a raise. You cringe when you see him coming, hide from him when you can, and do as little work as possible. In the comics, such situations may make us laugh, but in the real world, there's nothing funny about an adversarial relationship with your boss.

If you feel you're being ignored or picked on, or if you're having problems communicating, you need to decide on a strategy to cope with the situation. Correcting bad relations with your boss may be crucial—not only to your career but to your health. According to one recent study, the onset of employee depression can often be traced to conflict with a supervisor. If you have a problem with your boss, you will probably have to take the initiative to solve it.

What won't work:
- Whining
- Complaining
- Accusing
- Insisting you are right and your boss is wrong
- Storming into your superior's office when you are angry or frustrated
- Groveling (probably not an option anyway)

What might work:
- Figuring out what your superiors want and giving it to them

- Acting in ways that show off your talents, rather than irritating your superior
- Following the chain of command
- Scheduling a meeting so you have time to prepare what you want to say
- Phrasing criticism as information-giving—you won't win points by saying, "You're always on my back," but you might get your boss's attention if you say, "I'm the kind of person who values my independence."
- Requesting your superior's guidance about your own strengths and weaknesses and what you can do differently—bosses are usually more receptive to a two-way exchange.

To keep your job, you'll probably have to follow your boss's advice, even when you disagree. If you really don't like your boss, you can't be dedicated to your job and happy at work. If that's the case, it may be time to leave. You should look for a new boss to whom you can be committed, but be sure it's someone who is also committed to you and treats you at least as well as the customers. Good bosses are out there. A recent survey reveals that almost 75 percent of workers interviewed say their superiors listen to their problems and concerns and encourage them to make suggestions and decisions. Hopefully, most of the mean, domineering bosses are only in the comics.

---

managerial hierarchy the arrangement that provides increasing authority at higher levels of management

maximize effectiveness. Several coordination techniques have proved useful. One technique is simply to make use of the **managerial hierarchy,** which is the arrangement that provides increasing authority at higher levels of management. One manager is placed in charge of all the resources that are to be coordinated. That person is able to coordinate them by virtue of the authority accompanying that position.

Resources can also be coordinated through rules and procedures. For example, a rule can govern how a firm's travel budget is to be allocated. This particular resource, then, would be coordinated in terms of that rule.

In complex situations, more sophisticated coordination techniques may be called for. One approach is to establish a liaison. Recall from Chapter 5 that a liaison is a go-between—a person who coordinates the activities of two groups. Suppose Ford Motor Company is negotiating a complicated contract with a supplier of steering wheels. The supplier might appoint a liaison whose primary responsibility is to coordinate the contract negotiations. Finally, for *very* complex coordination needs, a committee (that is, a task force) could be established. Suppose Ford is in the process of purchasing the steering-wheel supplier. In this case a task force might be appointed to integrate the new firm into Ford's larger organizational structure.

FORMS OF ORGANIZATIONAL STRUCTURE

LEARNING OBJECTIVE 8
Describe the three basic forms of organizational structure: bureaucratic, organic, and matrix.

Up to this point, we have focused our attention on the major dimensions of organizational structure. In many ways, this is like discussing the important parts of a jigsaw puzzle one by one. Now it is time to put the puzzle together. In particular, we discuss three basic forms of organizational structure: bureaucratic, organic, and matrix.

The Bureaucratic Structure

The term *bureaucracy* is often used in an unfavorable context, and it tends to suggest rigidity and red tape. This image may be a negative one, but it does capture something of the bureaucratic structure.

bureaucratic structure a management system based on a formal framework of authority that is carefully outlined and precisely followed

A **bureaucratic structure** is a management system based on a formal framework of authority that is carefully outlined and precisely followed. In terms of the major structural dimensions, a bureaucracy is likely to have the following characteristics:

1. A high level of job specialization
2. Departmentalization by function
3. Precise and formal patterns of delegation
4. A high degree of centralization
5. Narrow spans of management, resulting in a tall organization
6. Clearly defined line and staff positions, with formal relationships between the two

Perhaps the best examples of contemporary bureaucracies are government agencies, colleges, and universities. Consider the very rigid and formal college entrance and registration procedures. The reason for such procedures is to ensure that the organization is able to deal with large numbers of people in an equitable and fair manner. We may not enjoy them, but regulations and standard operating procedures pretty much guarantee uniformity.

The biggest drawback to the bureaucratic structure is its lack of flexibility. The bureaucracy has trouble adjusting to change and coping with the unexpected. Because today's business environment is dynamic and

Post-it Notes versus red tape.
The wall next to Bell Atlantic's CEO, Raymond Smith, may look like a collection of kids' graffiti, but it's actually an important weapon in Bell Atlantic's war against bureaucracy. Executives keep the wall full of suggestions, flow charts, and hierarchy diagrams, and everyone who wanders in looks for something to cross out, some way to cut the red tape.

complex, many firms have found that the bureaucratic structure is not an appropriate organizational structure.

The Organic Structure

organic structure   a management system founded on cooperation and knowledge-based authority

An **organic structure** is a management system founded on cooperation and knowledge-based authority. It is much less formal than the bureaucracy and much more flexible. An organic structure tends to have the following structural dimensions:

1. A low level of job specialization
2. Departmentalization by product, location, or customer
3. General and informal patterns of delegation
4. A high degree of decentralization
5. Wide spans of management, resulting in a flat organization
6. Less clearly defined line and staff positions, with less formal relationships between the two

The organic structure tends to be more effective when the environment of the firm is complex and dynamic. This structure allows the organization to monitor the environment and react quickly to changes. Of course, the organic structure requires more cooperation among employees than the bureaucracy does. Employees must be willing and able to work together in an informal atmosphere where lines of authority may shift according to the situation.

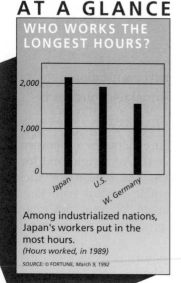

AT A GLANCE

WHO WORKS THE LONGEST HOURS?

Among industrialized nations, Japan's workers put in the most hours.
(Hours worked, in 1989)

SOURCE: © FORTUNE, March 9, 1992

The Matrix Structure

The matrix structure is the newest and most complex organizational structure. Its hallmark is a multiple command system, in which individuals report to more than one superior at the same time. The **matrix structure** combines vertical and horizontal lines of authority. The matrix structure occurs when product departmentalization is superimposed on a functionally departmentalized organization. In a matrix organization, authority flows both down and across.

To see what this is like, first consider the usual functional arrangement, with people working in departments such as marketing and finance. Now suppose we assign people from these departments to a special group that is working on a new project as a team. This special group is really a product department. The manager in charge of the group is usually called a *project manager*. Any individual who is working with the group reports to *both* the project manager and the individual's superior in the functional department (see Figure 6.6).

A matrix structure usually evolves through four stages. At first the firm is organized simply as a functional structure. Then a smaller number of interdepartmental groups are created to work on especially important projects. Next, more groups are created, and they become an integral and important part of the organization. Finally, the firm becomes what is called a *mature matrix*. In the mature matrix, project managers and functional managers have equal authority. Some employees float (or shift) from

matrix structure an organizational structure that combines vertical and horizontal lines of authority by superimposing product departmentalization on a functionally departmentalized organization

FIGURE 6.6
A Matrix Organization
A matrix is usually the result of combining product depart-mentalization with function departmentalization. It is a complex structure in which employees have more than one supervisor. *(Source: Ricky W. Griffin,* Management, *3/e. Copyright © 1990 by Houghton Mifflin Company. Used by permission.)*

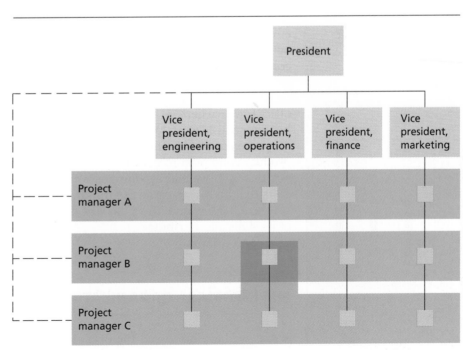

group to group without ever being "tied" to a particular functional department. Eventually the activities of the project teams become the major focus of the organization.

Many firms have experimented with matrix structures. Notable examples include Texas Instruments, Monsanto, and Chase Manhattan Bank. Matrix structures offer several advantages over the conventional organizational forms. Added flexibility is probably the most obvious advantage. Motivation also improves because people become more deeply committed to their special projects. In addition, employees experience personal development through doing a variety of jobs. And people communicate more as they become liaisons between their project groups and their functional departments.

The matrix structure also has some disadvantages. The multiple command system can cause confusion about who has authority in various situations. Like committees, groups may take longer to resolve problems and issues than individuals working alone. And, because more managers and support staff may be needed, a matrix structure may be more expensive to maintain than a conventional structure. All things considered, though, the matrix appears to offer a number of benefits to business. It is likely that in the future more and more firms will begin to explore and experiment with this innovative method of organization.

Intrapreneurship

intrapreneur an employee in an organizational environment who takes responsibility for pushing an innovative idea, product, or process through the organization.

Since innovations are important to companies, and entrepreneurs are among the most innovative people around, it seems almost natural that an entrepreneurial character would prominently surface in many of today's larger organizations. An **intrapreneur** is an employee in an organizational environment who takes responsibility for pushing an innovative idea, product, or process through the organization.[2] An intrapreneur possesses the confidence and drive of an entrepreneur but is allowed to use organizational resources for idea development.

Arthur Fry, inventor of the colorful Post-it Notes that are now seen in offices everywhere, is a devoted advocate of intrapreneurship. Nurturing his note-pad idea at 3M for years, Fry speaks highly of the intrapreneurial commitment at 3M. On being an intrapreneur, Fry says, "First you need a product champion to get that core vision going. Then, you need the facilities that 3M has and a willingness to pull the concept together."[3] Fry suggests that an intrapreneur is an individual who doesn't have all the skills to get the job done, and, thus, has to work within an organization, making use of its skills and attributes.

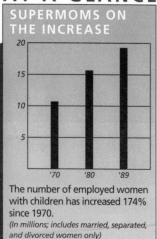

AT A GLANCE

SUPERMOMS ON THE INCREASE

The number of employed women with children has increased 174% since 1970.
(In millions; includes married, separated, and divorced women only)

SOURCE: U.S. Bureau of Labor Statistics

THE INFORMAL ORGANIZATION

So far we have discussed the organization as a more or less formal structure consisting of positions and relationships among those positions. This is the organization that is shown on an organization chart. There is another kind of organization, however, that does not show up on any chart. We shall define this **informal organization** as the pattern of behavior and interaction that stems from personal rather than official relationships. Firmly embedded within every informal organization are informal groups and the notorious grapevine.

informal organization   the pattern of behavior and interaction that stems from personal rather than official relationships

Informal Groups

A formal group is one that is created by the organization to help accomplish the organization's goals. Such groups as departments, task forces, and committees are thus formal groups. In contrast, an **informal group** is created by the group members themselves to accomplish goals that may or may not be relevant to the organization. Workers may create an informal group to go bowling, play softball, form a union, get a particular manager fired or transferred, or have lunch together every day. The group may last for several years or only a few hours.

informal group   a group created by the members themselves to accomplish goals that may or may not be relevant to the organization

Employees join informal groups for a variety of reasons. Perhaps the main reason is that people like to be with others who are similar to themselves. The activities of a particular group may also be appealing. (A person who likes to bowl may be inclined to join a group of Thursday-night bowlers.) Or it may be that the goals of the group appeal to the individual. (If a group has been formed to try to get the company to install a new cafeteria, and if a particular employee happens to think a new cafeteria is needed, he or she will probably join the group.) Others may join informal groups simply because they have a need to be with their associates and be accepted by them.

LEARNING OBJECTIVE 9
Define what an informal organization is and how it operates through informal groups and the grapevine.

Informal groups can be powerful forces in organizations. They can restrict output, or they can help managers through tight spots. They can cause disagreement and conflict, or they can help boost morale and job satisfaction. They can show new people how to contribute to the organization, or they can help people get away with substandard performance. Clearly, managers should be aware of these informal groups. Those who make the mistake of fighting the informal organization have a major obstacle to overcome.

The Grapevine

The **grapevine** is the informal communications network within an organization. It is completely separate from—and sometimes much faster than—the organization's formal channels of communication. Formal communication usually follows a path that parallels the organizational chain of command. By contrast, information can be transmitted through the grapevine in any direction—up, down, diagonally, or horizontally across the organizational structure. Subordinates may pass information to their bosses, an executive may relay something to a maintenance worker, or there may be an exchange of information between people who work in totally unrelated departments.

grapevine   the informal communications network within an organization

Grapevine information may be concerned with topics ranging from the latest management decisions, to the results of today's World Series game, to pure gossip. It can be important or of little interest. And it can be highly accurate or totally distorted.

How should managers treat the grapevine? Certainly they would be making a big mistake if they tried to eliminate it. People working together, day in and day out, are going to communicate. And even if a manager could eliminate informal communication at work, employees would still get together and talk outside the office. A more rational approach is to recognize the existence of the grapevine as a part—though an unofficial part—of the organization. For example, managers should respond promptly and aggressively to inaccurate grapevine information to minimize the damage that such misinformation might do. Moreover, the grapevine can come in handy when managers are on the receiving end of important communications from the informal organization.

In the next chapter, we apply these and other management concepts to an extremely important business function: the production of goods and services.

CHAPTER REVIEW

Summary

Organizing is the process of grouping resources and activities to accomplish some end in an efficient and effective manner. The purpose of this process is to mold an organizational structure, which is a fixed pattern of positions and relationships. An organization chart is a diagram that represents the organizational structure. The five steps in the organizing process result in five basic dimensions of organizational structure. These are degree of job specialization, nature and degree of departmentalization, degree of centralization, the span of management, and the chain of command as determined by line-staff arrangements.

Job specialization is the separation of all the activities within the organization into smaller components and the assignment of different components to different people. Several factors combine to make specialization a useful technique for designing jobs, but high levels of specialization may cause employee dissatisfaction and boredom. Techniques for overcoming these problems include job rotation, job enlargement, and job enrichment.

Departmentalization is the grouping of jobs into manageable units according to some reasonable scheme or basis. These bases include departmentalization by function, product, location, and customer. Because each of these bases provides particular advantages, most firms use different bases in different organizational situations.

Delegation is the assigning of part of a manager's work to a subordinate. It involves the assignment of responsibility, the granting of authority, and the creation of accountability. A decentralized firm is one that delegates as much power as possible to people in the lower management levels. In a centralized firm, on the other hand, power is systematically retained at the upper levels.

The span of management is the number of subordinates who report directly to a manager. Spans are generally characterized as wide (many subordinates per manager) or narrow (few subordinates per manager). Wide spans generally result in flat organizations (few layers of management); narrow spans generally result in tall organizations (many layers of management).

A line position is one that is in the organization's chain of command (line of authority), whereas a staff position is supportive in nature. Staff positions may carry some authority, but it usually applies only within staff areas of expertise.

Additional elements that must be considered in structuring an organization are the establishment of work schedules, use of committees, and development of techniques for achieving coordination among various groups within the organization.

There are three basic forms of organizational structure. The bureaucratic structure is characterized by formality and rigidity. The organic structure is characterized by flexibility. And the newer matrix structure may be visualized as product departmentalization superimposed on functional departmentalization. An intrapreneur is an employee in an organizational environment who takes responsibility for pushing an innovative idea, product, or process through the organization.

The informal organization consists of social and personal interactions within the more formal organizational structure. Key aspects of the informal organization are informal groups created by the group members themselves and the grapevine, which is an informal information network. Managers must recognize the existence of the informal organization and even learn to use the grapevine to their advantage.

Key Terms

You should now be able to define and give an example relevant to each of the following terms:

organization
organizational structure
organization chart
chain of command
job specialization
job rotation
job enlargement
job enrichment
departmentalization
departmentalization basis
departmentalization by function
departmentalization by product
departmentalization by location
departmentalization by customer
delegation
responsibility

authority
accountability
decentralized organization
centralized organization
span of management (or span of control)
organizational height
line management position
staff management position
compressed workweek
flexible workweek
job sharing
ad hoc committee
standing committee
task force
managerial hierarchy
bureaucratic structure
organic structure
matrix structure

intrapreneur
informal organization

informal group
grapevine

Questions and Exercises

Review Questions

1. In what way do organization charts illustrate our definition of organizational structure?
2. What determines the degree of specialization within an organization?
3. Describe and contrast the three alternatives to job specialization.
4. What are the major differences among the four departmentalization bases?
5. Why do most firms employ several departmentalization bases?
6. What three steps are involved in delegation? Explain each.
7. How does a firm's top management influence its degree of centralization?
8. How is organizational height related to the span of management?
9. What are the key differences between line and staff positions and the authority their occupants wield?
10. Describe three alternatives to the standard five-day, forty-hour workweek.
11. How may the managerial hierarchy be used to coordinate the organization's resources?
12. Contrast the bureaucratic and organic forms of organizational structure.
13. Which form of organizational structure would probably lead to the strongest informal organization? Why?

Discussion Questions

1. Why did the founders of Bruegger's Bagel Bakery organize their company using autonomous cluster managers?
2. What major changes have been made in how Bruegger's Bagel Bakery is organized?
3. Explain how the five steps of the organizing process determine the dimensions of the resulting organizational structure. Which steps are most important?
4. Which kinds of firms would probably operate most effectively as centralized firms? as decentralized firms?
5. How do decisions concerning work schedules, the use of committees, and coordination techniques affect organizational structure?

6. How might a manager go about formalizing the informal organization?

Exercises

1. Draw the organization chart for the academic institution that you are attending. State your assumptions if you must make them.

2. Chart your own workweek and determine what type it is (standard, compressed, flexible, job sharing, or working at home).

CASE 6.1

Western Union's Reorganization

Although Western Union Corporation has survived for over 140 years, its future is anything but secure. Created in 1851, the New Jersey-based company pioneered the U.S. telegram industry. Today, however, people are more likely to communicate using state-of-the-art technology such as fax machines or electronic mail rather than by sending a telegram. Two recent reorganizations of the ailing company may prevent losses from forcing Western Union into bankruptcy.

Company president and CEO Robert J. Amman's first move to bring the company back to health was the purchase of ITT Corp. for $178 million, which brought more modern technology to Western Union. To cut company costs, Amman trimmed the work force by 25 percent, laying off about 1,800 workers. The layoffs, which eliminated overlapping jobs, affected almost every job category. Amman also closed Western Union's nationwide microwave network, sold the company's four-satellite network, and unloaded its little-known but expensive-to-operate domestic long-distance service.

Amman's restructuring plan divided Western Union's services into totally separate business units that operated independently. The five units were Business Communications Services, Consumer Communications and Financial Services, Priority Mail Services, Advanced Transmission Systems, and Network Services. Business Communications, the largest group, was responsible for international and domestic telex services and EasyLink electronic mail service. Consumer Communications handled money transfer services, Mailgrams (telegrams delivered by the postal service), and telegrams for the public through Western Union's nationwide network of agents. The company's Priority Mail Service provided commercial Mailgrams, computer letters to businesses, and priority letters. Advanced Transmissions was involved in building and operating fiberoptic telecommunication facilities, and

Network Services marketed Western Union's international transmission services.

Despite major reorganization and cost-cutting efforts, Western Union continues to experience losses in the millions and is undergoing a second major restructuring that involves selling most of its recently created units. For $180 million, AT&T acquired most of Western Union's Business Services Unit, including EasyLink electronic mail, telex operations, voice mail, and computer-to-computer transmission. MCI bought the Advanced Transmission Division. Most recently, the company began considering the sale of its Mailgram business, part of the Priority Services Group. Western Union will continue to operate its money transfer service and deliver about one million mailgrams a year.

Once a seemingly invincible communications giant, Western Union is now a smaller struggling organization with losses in one recent year of $218.8 million. The company's president hopes that a new money-order service and a service that allows customers to obtain cash advances with their credit cards will help the money-transfer business to grow. Pointing to a recent rise in the value of its stock, he expresses optimism that Western Union will remain a viable company.*

Questions

1. How effective do you think Western Union's initial restructuring of its organization has been?

2. Are Western Union's current problems primarily organizational?

*Based on information from Betsy August, "Western Union Says Its Merger Spurred Cuts," *The Record* (Hackensack, NJ), April 14, 1988; Neil Barsky, "The Western Union Wire: Hit the Road, Workers," *New York Daily News*, April 14, 1988; John T. Harding, "Western Union to Cut Workforce by 25%," *Star-Ledger* (Newark, NJ), April 13, 1988; John J. Keller, "Bob Amman Tries to Reinvent the Onion," *Business Week*, June 13, 1988, p. 33; Margie Quimpo, "Western Union Selling Most of Unit," *Washington Post*, July 4, 1990; John J. Keller, "Western Union Agrees to Sell Nearly All of Its Business Services Unit to AT&T," *Wall Street Journal*, July 5, 1990; Keith Bradsher, "AT&T Buying 3 Units of Western Union," *New York Times*, July 4, 1990; Floyd Norris, "Western Union's Reorganization," *New York Times*, July 26, 1990; "MCI Communications Buys Transmission-based Concern," *Wall Street Journal*, March 9, 1990; "Western Union Might Sell Unit," *New York Times*, January 16, 1991.

CASE 6.2

Encouraging Innovation at 3M

Scotch tape and masking tape, software diskettes, Bufpuf skincare products, paint stripper, Scotchguard fabric protector, medical diagnostic equipment, sandpaper, and Post-it Notes—these are merely a sampling of the 60,000 diverse products made by the 3M Company. Headquartered in Minneapolis, Minnesota, the sixty-year-old firm is recognized as a champion of innovation and the world's most prolific new-product producer. On any given day, 3M's researchers are working on forty to fifty product ideas, coming up with about two hundred new products every year. Most of these end up dominating their respective markets.

William L. McKnight knew he was on to something when he originally established company philosophies and policies. He believed that, given enough freedom and flexibility, people are likely to come up with innovative ideas. He believed that failure, rather than being the end, is merely a natural step on the road to innovation. He encouraged innovation by promoting staff who were willing to take risks. Six decades later, McKnight's beliefs continue to underlie 3M's goals and corporate structure, and, ultimately, its phenomenal success.

Innovation isn't planned—it just happens. But it happens more often when employees know it is their firm's top priority—and 3M employees know it. At 3M, management always encourages new ideas, and if a new product line begins to take off, they immediately target it with more resources. When a company scientist devoted energy and hours to an idea for sticky-backed pieces of paper, he wasn't worried that someone would complain that he was wasting time. Company policy states that researchers may use 15 percent of their time on any project they choose. That freedom resulted in the Post-it Notes, without which no modern office can survive.

The organization's forty product divisions operate like small autonomous companies, each with its own mission and personality. These product units are further subdivided into cross-functional teams. Made up of designers, engineers, marketers, accountants, and others, "action teams" have enormous freedom to outline their own goals and to develop products of their own choosing. There's only one catch. One corporate rule applies consistently throughout the organization: Each division must generate 25 percent of its revenues from products introduced within the previous five years.

Creating three levels of research and development allows 3M to keep new products coming while at the same time encouraging long-range projects. Division laboratories do short-term research that generates products destined for specific markets. To come up with technologies and applications needed three to ten years in the future, 3M initiated the sector laboratories. Basic research that may not lead to actual products for ten to twenty years goes on in the corporate laboratories. Sharing technology among the three levels is standard procedure. At 3M, products belong to individual operating units, but technologies belong to everyone. Sharing technology helps 3M turn innovative concepts into new products quickly.

Executives at 3M are also innovative at finding ways to encourage innovation. To keep researchers doing what they do best, the company offers a dual-ladder promotion system. Lab employees who are advancing up the managerial ladder can continue doing research by advancing up the technological ladder at the same time. The "Golden Step Program" honors cross-functional teams when they introduce successful new products, and the "Carleton Society" honors those making long-range contributions.

The 3M flexible organizational structure and its speed at turning ideas into products recently earned it a place on *Industry Week's* elite list of "World Class" organizations. With 175 factories operating in the United States alone, business dealings in 55 countries, and yearly earnings of $3.4 billion, "world class" is no exaggeration.**

Questions

1. What are the major organizational characteristics that facilitate innovation at 3M?
2. Are 3M employees entrepreneurs or intrapreneurs? Explain.
3. In what ways does 3M benefit from innovations?

**Based on information from David Altany, "The New Bottom Line," *Industry Week*, January 22, 1990, pp. 13–14, 16–20; Dan Cordtz, "Corporate R&D," *FW*, October 1, 1991, pp. 32–37; "3M Co. Means Matrix, Matrix and More Matrix," *Computerworld*, June 17, 1991, p. 59; Alan J. Ryan and Michael Sullivan-Trainor, "Sticking with Innovation," *Computerworld Premier 100*, October 8, 1990, pp. 56–57; Ronald A. Mitsch, "Three Roads to Innovation," *The Journal of Business Strategy*, September-October 1990, pp. 18–21; Barbara Burgower, "Sweetening the Lure of the Lab," *Business Month*, August 1990, pp. 76–77.

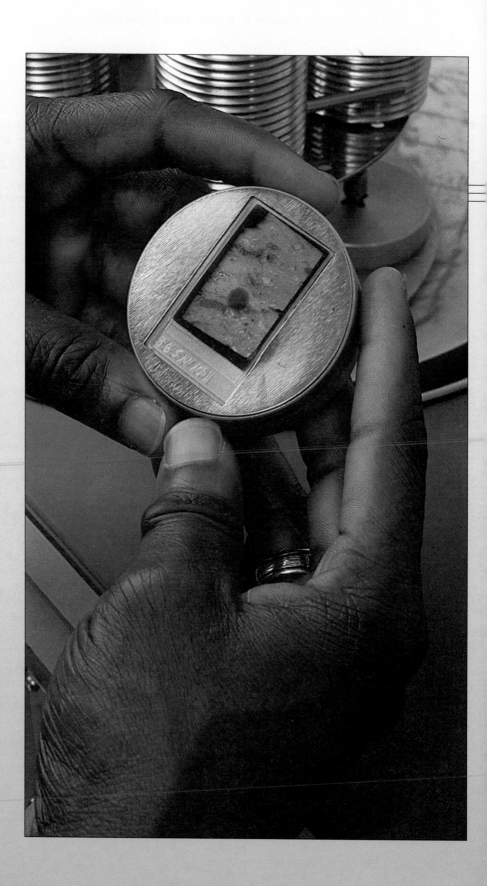

Operations Management

CHAPTER PREVIEW

We begin this chapter with an overview of operations management—the activities involved in the conversion of resources into products. We describe the technology or conversion systems that make production possible and also note the growing role of services in our economy. Then we examine more closely three important aspects of operations management: developing ideas for new products, planning product design and production facilities, and effectively controlling operations after production has begun. Next, we discuss changes in production as a result of automation, robotics, and computer-aided manufacturing. We close the chapter with a look at productivity trends and ways productivity can be improved.

197

Levi Strauss Factories in Eastern Europe

Growing political freedom in Eastern Europe makes it increasingly attractive to Western manufacturers. For Levi Strauss, opening factories there fits in nicely with the company's global manufacturing strategy—to supply customers from nearby factories. Eastern Europeans already know and love Levi's jeans, so making them right there is an efficient way to satisfy a hungry market. When the iron curtain came down, Levi's wasted no time in developing production facilities.

Levi's opened its first Eastern European factory in Budapest, Hungary, right next door to the Texcoop plant, a state-owned sweater factory that had gone out of business. In contrast to the museum-quality sewing and knitting machines collecting dust next door, 350 workers at the Levi factory use state-of-the-art equipment to stitch seams and sew pockets on more than one million jackets and pairs of jeans a year. When asked to compare operations at Texcoop with those at Levi's, employees not only praise technological advances but point out that working conditions are better and that materials are always there when needed. Workers are also amazed that there are only eight supervisors for the whole factory—the government-run Texcoop employed one manager for every three workers.

Many experts believe that the years under the Communist system led to slipshod work habits. Since the Levi's trademark has been synonymous with high-quality denim jeans for over a century, the company wanted to make sure that jeans coming out of the Hungarian factory were worthy of the famous name. Levi's tries to motivate its workers not only to maintain standards of quality but to be as productive as possible. Salaries are high enough to discourage moonlighting, a practice the company believes will adversely affect quality. Plant managers reward workers by taking those with the best work record out to dinner once a month; employees with the best yearly record win one week's paid vacation. Hungarian workers are proud that, in just one year, their plant became as productive as most of Levi's fifty other factories around the world.

Encouraged by the Hungarian plant's success, Levi's recently opened a factory in Poland. Operations started with the rental and conversion of two football field-sized warehouses into a factory and the hiring of six hundred workers. The company's goal is to manufacture jeans good enough to be sold in Paris or New York as well as in Warsaw. It has some stumbling blocks to overcome—poor telecommunications (calls to Warsaw have to go through Geneva, Switzerland) and ensuring an adequate supply of high-quality thread and certain chemicals (these have to be imported). If it clears those hurdles, the company plans to hire an additional six hundred workers, buy the warehouses it currently rents, and make Plock, Poland, famous for manufacturing Levi's jeans.[1]

Whether in Hungary, Poland, the United States, or another country, Levi Strauss seeks high levels of productivity and high-quality products. To achieve these objectives, organizations like Levi Strauss expend considerable resources to ensure that they have effective operations management.

Operations management encompasses numerous activities. Transforming new materials and other resources into goods and services is a part of operations management. The purpose of this transformation of resources into goods and services is to provide utility to customers. **Utility** is the ability of a good or service to satisfy a human need. Although there are four types of utility—form, place, time, and possession—operations management and production focus primarily on the creation of form utility. **Form utility** is created by converting production inputs into finished products. Controlling product quality is another prime responsibility of operations managers. A firm that consistently produces goods or services of poor quality will, at the very least, lose customers in droves. In more extreme cases, faulty goods or services may involve a firm in costly legal battles.

Another key part of operations management is effective use of resources—especially human resources—in the production of goods and services. Detroit automakers have found that their operating employees are a valuable resource in more ways than one. Not only are workers producing cars, but they are also helping to solve quality control problems through such techniques as quality circles.

Inventory management is still another responsibility of operations managers. Every part stored for future use (such as on an auto assembly line) must be financed. These financing costs eventually either find their way into the price of the product or eat away at profit. Scheduling control is closely allied to inventory control. The better the scheduling of incoming parts, the smaller the required inventory. The ideal is to have every part become available just when it is needed—just in time.

Excessive inventory, poor scheduling, less than full use of resources, and even excess management all increase costs and thus raise prices for consumers. These higher prices and the lack of superior quality to make up for it—poor fuel economy in cars, for example—caused American consumers to switch to Japanese products in the 1970s. But, as we have seen, American manufacturers have begun to fight back, primarily through more effective operations management. Operations management is clearly a topic that warrants careful study.

LEARNING OBJECTIVE 1
Explain the nature of operations management.

utility   the ability of a good or service to satisfy a human need

form utility   utility created by converting production inputs into finished products

The *process layout* is used when different sequences of operations are required for creating small batches of different products. The plant is arranged so that each operation is performed in a particular area, and the work is moved from area to area to match its own sequence of operations. An auto repair shop provides an example of a process layout. The various operations might be engine repair, body work, wheel alignment, and safety inspection. Each is performed in a different area. A particular car "visits" only those areas performing the kinds of work it needs.

A *product layout* is used when all products undergo the same operations in the same sequence. Work stations are arranged to match the sequence of operations, and work flows from station to station. An assembly line is the best example of a product layout.

Human Resources   In many ways, human resources are more the concern of human resources managers than of operations managers, but the two must work together at the design-planning stage. Several design-planning activities affect the work of human resources managers. For example, suppose a sophisticated technology requiring special skills is called for. The firm will have to recruit employees with the appropriate skills, develop training programs, or do both. Depending on where facilities are to be located, arrangements may have to be made to transfer skilled workers to the new locations or to train local workers.

Human resources managers can also obtain and provide valuable information on availability of skilled workers in various areas, wage rates, and other factors that may influence choices of technology and location.

Operational Planning

operational planning   the development of plans for using production facilities and resources

Once the production process and facilities have been designed, operations personnel must plan for their use. **Operational planning** is the development of plans for using production facilities and resources. Operational plans are developed and revised periodically for each facility. The objective of operational planning is to decide on a level of output for the facility. Four steps are required: (1) selecting a planning horizon, (2) estimating market demand, (3) comparing demand with capacity, and (4) adjusting output to demand.

planning horizon   the period during which a plan will be in effect

Selecting a Planning Horizon   A **planning horizon** is simply the period during which a plan will be in effect. A common planning horizon for operational plans is one year. That is, operations personnel plan production output one year in advance. Before each year is up, they plan for the next.

A planning horizon of one year is generally long enough to average out seasonal increases and decreases in sales. At the same time, it is short enough for planners to adjust output to accommodate long-range sales trends. Firms that operate in a rapidly changing business environment may find it best to select a shorter horizon to keep their operational planning current.

The figure in the salary column approximates the expected annual income after two or three years of service.
1 = $12,000–$15,000; 2 = $16,000–$20,000; 3 = $21,000–$27,000; 4 = $28,000–$35,000; 5 = $36,000 and up.

Educational Requirements	Skills Required	Prospects for Growth
High school diploma; some college helpful	Organizational; leadership; technical; decision making	Below average
Two years of college or trade school; on-the-job experience	Decision making; interviewing; supervisory; clerical	Above average
Bachelor's degree in business or hospital administration; master's degree preferred	Communication; interpersonal; public speaking; decision making	Greatest
Some college helpful; bachelor's degree preferred; on-the-job experience	Decision making; communication; problem solving	Above average
Bachelor's degree in management; on-the-job experience	Communication; problem solving; interpersonal; analytical	Above average
Bachelor's degree in math; statistics, or computers	Problem solving; math; interpersonal; analytical	Above average
Bachelor's degree in business; on-the-job experience helpful	Decision making; budgeting; interpersonal; inspection	Average
High school diploma; on-the-job experience; some college preferred	Basic office skills; initiative; writing; interpersonal; organizational	Average
Some college; degree helpful	Analytical; decision making; communication	Average

PART
3

The Human Resource

This part of *Business* is concerned with the most important and least predictable of all resources—people. We begin by discussing various ideas about why people behave as they do, paying special attention to the work environment. Then we apply these ideas to the management of a firm's work force. Finally, we look at organized labor in the United States and probe the sometimes controversial relationship between business management and labor unions. Included in this part are:

People and Motivation in Business

LEARNING OBJECTIVES

After studying this chapter you should be able to:

1 Explain what motivation is.

2 Recognize some earlier perspectives on motivation: scientific management, Theory X, and Theory Y.

3 Outline Maslow's hierarchy of needs.

4 Discuss Herzberg's motivation-hygiene theory.

5 Describe four contemporary views of motivation: equity theory, expectancy theory, reinforcement theory, and Theory Z.

6 Identify the characteristics of effective reward systems and describe several relatively new kinds of reward systems.

7 Explain several techniques for increasing employee motivation.

CHAPTER PREVIEW

First, to provide a perspective of current motivational theories, we present several early views of motivation that influenced management practices, including Taylor's ideas of scientific management, Mayo's Hawthorne Studies, and McGregor's Theory X and Theory Y. We also describe two widely known theories of human motivation—Maslow's hierarchy of needs and Herzberg's concepts of satisfaction and dissatisfaction. Then, turning our attention to contemporary ideas, we examine equity theory, expectancy theory, reinforcement theory, and Theory Z, and explain how these motivational theories can be applied in an organization's reward system. Finally, we discuss specific techniques managers can use to improve employee motivation.

Motivating the Los Angeles Dodgers

Celebrated throughout the baseball industry as a master motivator, Los Angeles Dodgers' manager Tommy Lasorda has a knack for turning a potentially explosive group of insecure rookies, seasoned veterans, and temperamental prima donnas into one of baseball's winningest teams. When he steps into the clubhouse and puts on his blue uniform, he radiates so much enthusiasm and confidence that it spills over onto his players. But Lasorda is only the most visible figure in an organization that motivates everyone from million-dollar players to ballpark ushers by treating them like human beings instead of property.

Sixty-one-year-old Lasorda, who has managed the Dodgers for more than fifteen seasons, believes that building togetherness and team spirit and respecting each player as a unique individual creates confident players who try to top what they're already doing. He also maintains that happy players are better players, and he works hard to keep them that way. Talking individually with them as much as possible, he avoids words like *can't, won't,* and *don't,* choosing instead to emphasize the positive and upbeat. He hugs his players and pats them on the back. After games, he often brings celebrities to the clubhouse to meet players. As a way of welcoming newcomers to the club, he gives each one a nickname. He always lets players know he appreciates a base hit or a home run, but he gives them honest criticism when strikeouts and fumbled catches happen too often. Pitching great Orel Hershiser credits his concentration and focus on the mound to Lasorda's incredible talent for motivating him.

Like Lasorda with his players, Dodger management as a whole works hard to make everyone feel appreciated. Sports-industry analysts contend that, as a result, Dodger employees from managers on down are more motivated and loyal than those of any other major-league club. When the team is on the road, travel arrangements and facilities are always top-notch, and there are frequent organized get-togethers for spouses and children. The Dodgers employ baseball's only full-time psychiatrist to work with major- and minor-league players on a confidential basis. Employees at all levels have access to the club's top-level financial officer and can take advantage of profit sharing. When the team won the World Series in 1981, the Dodgers' owner took all department heads and their spouses to Hawaii.

In a recent interview, Tommy Lasorda stated his belief that any corporate executive would benefit by taking a page from his book on motivation. He points out that he knows the names of all the people working for him, and he invites them into his office to ask what he can do to make their jobs better. Many executives and managers cannot make that claim. But if they did make employees feel as though they were a very important part of the organization, they might have the kind of team that produces a corporate league leader.[1]

To effectively achieve organizational goals, employees need more than the right raw materials, adequate facilities, and equipment that works. Whether it's the Los Angeles Dodgers, Apple Computer, or a local convenience store, organizations must also have motivated employees. Although from time to time workers are dissatisfied, other employees are quite satisfied with their jobs and are motivated to meet high performance goals. To some extent, a high level of employee motivation derives from management practices such as job rotation, employee participation, rewarding "job team" performance, and a philosophy of worker equality.

WHAT IS MOTIVATION?

LEARNING OBJECTIVE 1
Explain what motivation is.

We look at various levels of needs and motivation later in this chapter, but first we must ask, what exactly is motivation? Most often, the term is used to explain people's behavior. Successful athletes are said to be highly motivated. A student who avoids work is said to be unmotivated. (From another viewpoint, the student might be thought of as motivated—to avoid work.)

motivation the individual, internal process that energizes, directs, and sustains behavior; the personal "force" that causes one to behave in a particular way

We define **motivation** as the individual, internal process that energizes, directs, and sustains behavior. Motivation is the personal "force" that causes one to behave in a particular way. When we say that job rotation motivates employees, we mean that it activates this force or process within employees.

morale an employee's feelings toward his or her job and superiors and toward the firm itself

An employee's **morale** is his or her feelings toward the job and superiors and toward the firm itself. High morale results mainly from the satisfaction of needs on the job or as a result of the job. One need that might be satisfied on the job is the need for *recognition* as an important contributor to the organization. Another need satisfied as a result of the job is the need for *financial security*. High morale, in turn, leads to the dedication and loyalty that are in evidence at the Japanese auto plants in the United States, as well as to the desire to do the job well. Low morale can lead to shoddy work, absenteeism, and high rates of turnover as employees leave to seek more satisfying jobs with other firms.

Motivation, morale, and the satisfaction of employees' needs are thus intertwined. Along with productivity, they have been the subject of much

BUSINESS JOURNAL
Lightening Up the Workplace: Why Not Have a Little Fun?

Takeovers, mergers, downsizing, automating, intense competitive pressure—from CEOs to factory workers on the line, everyone is being asked to do more, and the results are showing up as stress and job dissatisfaction. Stress-related disabilities make up the fastest growing category of worker compensation claims. A recent survey of 12,000 workers revealed that only 19 percent of lower-level workers honestly enjoyed their work, and 61 percent described their working environment as dull and boring. Twenty-four percent of non-management employees called their workplace a prison.

So, how do you turn workers who can't wait until 5 p.m. on Friday into workers who look forward to 8 a.m. on Monday? Maybe, like Walmart's Sam Walton, they should wear grass skirts and dance a hula down Wall Street, because experts say humor is the answer. Laughter, from little giggles to full-blown knee slapping, improves morale, alleviates stress, diffuses conflicts, builds team spirit, and increases productivity. Psychologists have found a correlation between good feelings and creativity. In one study, subjects who were laughing over TV bloopers before taking problem-solving tests came up with more innovative solutions than those who didn't get to see the show. Humor consulting firms like "The Humor Project," "Playfair," and "Speakeasy, Inc." are springing up, and corporations like AT&T, Kodak, IBM, and DuPont are hiring them to help their managers and employees laugh.

Making work fun requires more than giving an office party every Christmas and a picnic every summer. Companywide humor programs include everything from cartoon bulletin boards to "funny hat day" to attending seminars in superhero costumes. At Nickelodeon TV, floors made of recycled rubber tires put a spring in employees' step, and Friday meetings are held on the floor in the hallways. The "Joy Gang" at Ben and Jerry's Ice Cream organized an Elvis dress-up day to commemorate the anniversary of his death. Everyone at Digital Equipment Corporation learned to juggle bean bags to relieve stress, and its "Grouch Patrol" has the power to tell grumpy workers to take a break. When a group of workers in one high-tech firm was assigned to implement an unpopular new policy, their manager came in at night and changed the last name on all their name plates to read "Dangerfield," predicting that they would be "getting no respect."

For people in the 1990s, quality of life is becoming a maxim. To attract workers whose bottom line is not necessarily salary, companies are lightening up the workplace. Real work may never be like life at the office on the set of "Murphy Brown," but it doesn't have to be a place where you better not crack a smile—or a joke.

study since the end of the nineteenth century. Let us continue our discussion of motivation by outlining some landmarks of that early research.

HISTORICAL PERSPECTIVES ON MOTIVATION

LEARNING OBJECTIVE 2
Recognize some earlier perspectives on motivation: scientific management, Theory X, and Theory Y.

Researchers often begin a study with some fairly narrow goal in mind. But after they develop an understanding of their subject, they realize that both their goal and their research should be broadened. This is exactly what

In the Canadian wilderness, Reflexite pylons guide incoming hospital helicopters to a safe landing, and the U.S. Air Force used it to light runways during the Persian Gulf War. What has made Reflexite a profitable company, a serious competitor to corporate giant 3M, and the 1992 winner of *Inc.* magazine's "Entrepreneur of the Year" award is more than its marketing a great product with lots of uses. At Reflexite, employees own the company, giving each one a personal stake in its success or failure and making them an intensely motivated group of workers.

After brothers Hugh and Bill Rowland invented a new method for producing retroreflective material, they acquired a patent and set up a business to sell it commercially. By the early 1980s, 3M had heard of the product and offered to buy the Rowlands out for about $5 million. Although the money was attractive, the brothers were well aware that 3M wanted only the technology, not the Connecticut factory or the employees depending on it for their livelihood. Instead of selling to 3M, they hired a new president and offered a stock ownership plan to their employees, who bought the company, kept their jobs, and turned Reflexite into a phenomenal success. In 1991, sales rose 37 percent, to total more than $31 million. Although the company's basic material is still manufactured at the original New Britain site, there is now a Reflexite Europa, a Reflexite UK, a Reflexite Deutschland, and distribution centers in Korea, Singapore, and Taiwan.

Together and as individuals, Reflexite employees own 59 percent of the company, and a monthly owner's bonus check is their tangible reminder of how business is faring. Employee shareholders receive 3 percent of the operating profits which, in a good month, can add several hundred dollars to a paycheck. Of course, in a bad month, no one gets a bonus check at all. Because the quality of their own work directly affects the amount of money they take home, Reflexite employees are uncommonly motivated to do their best. One technician reported that he takes extra interest in his work because he knows that if he makes mistakes, it's his own money going out the door.

The longer people remain with the company, the more shares they get, so experienced employees almost never leave. Turnover among those who stay more than one year is almost nonexistent. What this means for Reflexite is an ability to keep almost all of its people with know-how. In addition, employee excitement about research and development keeps Reflexite on the cutting edge of new technology. Putting new products on the market equals more money for the company, which equals more money for each and every employee.

The loyalty of Reflexite's employees was recently demonstrated when many took voluntary leaves of absence without pay, and top managers took 10 percent pay cuts to avoid layoffs and losses during the nationwide economic downturn. The eagerness of others to come to work for Reflexite was demonstrated when 1,700 people responded to an ad for the position of sales and marketing general manager, and 2,100 responded when the job of vice president of finance became available.

From hourly workers to executive officers, feelings of ownership are strong. When the company president gets nibbles from would-be buyers, he enjoys informing them that the company has already been sold—to its employees.**

Questions

1. What benefits accrue to Reflexite as a result of its employee ownership?
2. Are there disadvantages to the company or its employees when employees own a major portion of the firm? Discuss.
3. How would your work behavior and your attitudes toward various aspects of your job be affected if you shared in the ownership of a major portion of the company that you work for?

**Based on information from John Case, "Collective Effort," *Inc.,* January 1992, pp. 32–35, 38, 42–43; Sid De Boer, "Reflexite Glows Bright in Dark Economy," *New Britain (CN) Herald,* June 25, 1991; "Personal Safety Is Reflexite's Premium Concern," *Reflexite Corporation News,* Summer 1990, pp. 1, 4; "Reflexite AP1000 Makes a Safe Landing in Canada," *Reflexite Corporation News,* Summer 1991, pp. 1, 4; "From the President," *Reflexite Corporation News,* Summer 1991, p. 4; Reflexite Corporation, *Annual Report,* 1991.

Human Resources Management

After studying this chapter you should be able to:

1. Describe the major components of human resources management.

2. Identify the steps in human resources planning.

3. Describe cultural diversity and understand some of the challenges and opportunities associated with it.

4. Explain the objectives and uses of job analysis.

5. Describe the processes of recruiting, employee selection, and orientation.

6. Discuss the primary elements of employee compensation and benefits.

7. Explain the purposes and techniques of employee training, development, and performance appraisal.

8. Outline the major legislation affecting human resources management.

CHAPTER PREVIEW

We begin our study of human resources management, or HRM, with an overview of how businesses acquire, maintain, and develop their human resources. After listing the steps by which firms match their human resources needs with the supply of human resources available, we explore several dimensions of cultural diversity. Then we examine the concept of job analysis. Next we focus on a firm's recruiting, selection, and orientation procedures as the means of acquiring employees. We also describe forms of employee compensation that motivate employees to remain with the firm and to work effectively. Then we discuss employee training, management development, and performance appraisal methods. Finally, we consider legislation that affects HRM practices.

Time Warner's Work & Family Program

What is your view of an effective employee benefit? The answer to that question depends a great deal on you as an individual. You might be a part of a two-career family in need of quality day care for your newborn or elder care for your aging father. Some help in setting aside a portion of your weekly paycheck to cover the cost of that care might be your ideal benefit. Maybe you need money for your daughter's college tuition or for a course you want to take to further your own career. Or you might want a short-term, paid, maternity leave, or six months off without pay to take care of your mother after her surgery, or emergency time off with pay to care for your uncle who was in a car accident. Perhaps you're interested in working part time, or at home, or in sharing your job with someone else. Maybe you just need some free counseling to help you get through a rough spot. You would be entitled to some of these benefits and more if you were an employee of Time Warner Inc., whether you worked at *Sports Illustrated*, Cinemax, Atlantic Records, the Book of the Month Club, or on the set of a Time Warner television show.

Despite its decentralized operations and formidable size, Time Warner is sensitive to the growing number of its employees who are juggling the demands of career and family. The company came up with its trend-setting "Work and Family Program" to provide not only benefits but a whole range of resources that help its 33,000 United States' employees cope. The program also furnishes the corporation's far-flung units with guidance in dealing with critical issues related to work and family.

Time Warner's strategy for creating a comprehensive program began with a survey of its various divisions to discover the programs that were already in place and then to identify additional needs that weren't being met. Combining the results of the Work and Family survey with management goals and community resources resulted in the creation

of Work and Family Program Models. An individual Time Warner unit can mold corporate models to fit its own needs. The program includes the following:

- A plan for a Work and Family Resource Area that will provide a comfortable at-work setting where employees can go to read or watch videotapes dealing with family-related topics.

- A model for an annual Work/Family/Community Resources Fair with raffles, door prizes, and exhibits on parenting, child care, elder care, health issues, and other related topics.

- A plan for effectively communicating the company's Work and Family benefits, including a sample *Work and Family Resources Booklet*, which fully explains the impressive corporate policies and procedures regarding family issues.

The last ingredient in the program, effective communication, is critical—it's the only way to ensure that all employees at every location of every Time Warner company will be able to take advantage of the benefits the company offers.[1]

The Work and Family Program at Time Warner is only one component of this organization's very comprehensive employee benefits program. Effective employee benefits programs, like the one at Time Warner, are very important in attracting, motivating, and retaining the appropriate mix of human resources.

HUMAN RESOURCES MANAGEMENT: AN OVERVIEW

The human resource is not only unique and valuable, it is an organization's most important resource. It seems logical that an organization would expend a great deal of effort to acquire and make full use of such a resource, and most organizations do. That effort is now known as *human resources management,* or *HRM.* It has also been called *staffing* and *personnel management.*

Human resources management consists of all the activities involved in acquiring, maintaining, and developing an organization's human resources. As the definition implies, HRM begins with acquisition—getting people to work for the organization. Next, steps must be taken to keep these valuable resources. (This is important; after all, they are the only business resources that can leave the organization at will.) Finally, the human resources should be developed to their full capacity to contribute to the firm.

human resources management all the activities involved in acquiring, maintaining, and developing an organization's human resources

HRM Activities

Each of the three phases of HRM—acquiring, maintaining, and developing human resources—consists of a number of related activities. Acquisition, for example, includes planning, as well as the various activities that lead to hiring new personnel. Altogether, this phase of HRM includes five separate activities:

- *Human resources planning:* determining the firm's future human resources needs
- *Job analysis:* determining the exact nature of the positions to be filled

261

- *Recruiting:* attracting people to apply for positions in the firm
- *Selection:* choosing and hiring the most qualified applicants
- *Orientation:* acquainting new employees with the firm

Maintaining human resources consists primarily of motivating employees to remain with the firm and to work effectively. Motivation was discussed at length in Chapter 8; here we concentrate on some additional aspects of maintaining human resources:

- *Compensation:* rewarding employee effort through monetary payments
- *Benefits:* providing rewards to ensure employee well-being

The development phase of HRM is concerned with improving employees' skills and expanding their capabilities. There are two important activities within this phase:

- *Training and development:* teaching employees new skills, new jobs, and more effective ways of doing their present jobs
- *Performance appraisal:* assessing employees' current and potential performance levels

These activities are discussed in more detail shortly, when we have completed this overview of human resources management.

Responsibility for HRM

In general, human resources management is a shared responsibility of line managers and staff HRM specialists.

In very small organizations, the owner is usually both a line manager and the staff HRM specialist. He or she handles all or most HRM activities. As the firm grows in size, a human resources manager is generally hired to take over most of the staff responsibilities. As growth continues, additional staff positions are added as needed. In firms as large as, say, Bristol-Myers Squibb Co., HRM activities tend to be very highly specialized. There may be separate groups to deal with compensation, training and development programs, and the other staff activities.

Specific HRM activities are assigned to those who are in the best position to perform them. Human resources planning and job analysis are usually done by staff specialists, with input from line managers. Similarly, recruiting and selection are generally handled by staff experts, although line managers are involved in the actual hiring decisions. Orientation programs are usually devised by staff specialists, and the orientation itself is carried out by both staff specialists and line managers. Compensation systems (including benefits) are most often developed and administered by the HRM staff. However, line managers recommend pay increases and promotions. Training and development activities are usually the joint responsibility of staff and line managers. Performance appraisal is the job of the

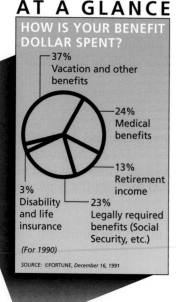

AT A GLANCE

HOW IS YOUR BENEFIT DOLLAR SPENT?

- 37% Vacation and other benefits
- 24% Medical benefits
- 13% Retirement income
- 23% Legally required benefits (Social Security, etc.)
- 3% Disability and life insurance

(For 1990)

SOURCE: ©FORTUNE, December 16, 1991

line manager, although HRM staff personnel design the firm's appraisal system in most organizations.

HUMAN RESOURCES PLANNING

LEARNING OBJECTIVE 2
Identify the steps in human resources planning.

human resources planning
the development of strategies to meet a firm's future human resources needs

Human resources planning is the development of strategies to meet the firm's future human resources needs. The starting point for this planning is the organization's overall strategic plan. From this, human resources planners can forecast the firm's future demand for human resources. Next, the planners must determine whether the needed human resources will be available; that is, they must forecast the supply of human resources within the firm. Finally, they have to take steps to match supply with demand.

Forecasting Human Resources Demand

Forecasts of the demand for human resources in an organization should be based on as much relevant information as planners can gather. The firm's overall strategic plan will provide information about future business ventures, new products, and projected expansions or contractions of particular product lines. Information on past staffing levels, evolving technologies, industry staffing practices, and projected economic trends can also be very helpful.

All this information should be used to determine both the number of employees who will be required and their qualifications—including skills,

T.J. Maxx's homegrown buyers. Off-price chain T.J. Maxx counts on its buyers to purchase goods "opportunistically," whenever and wherever they find a good bargain. It strongly believes that its success depends on its practice of developing its buyers from within the company, giving them a structured in-house training program, and retaining them with good pay, benefits, and a high quality of work life.

experience, and knowledge. Planners use a wide range of methods to forecast specific personnel needs. With one simple method, personnel requirements are projected to increase or decrease in the same proportion as sales revenue. Thus, if a 30 percent increase in sales volume is projected over the next two years, a 30 percent increase in personnel requirements would be forecast for the same period. (This method can be applied to specific positions as well as to the work force in general. It is not, however, a very precise forecasting method.) At the other extreme are elaborate, computer-based personnel planning models used by some larger firms such as Exxon Corporation.

Forecasting Human Resources Supply

The human resources supply forecast must take into account both the present work force and any changes or movements that may occur within it. For example, suppose planners project that, in five years, a firm that currently employs 100 engineers will need to employ a total of 200 engineers. Planners cannot simply assume that they will have to hire 100 engineers over the next five years. During that period, some of the firm's present engineers are likely to be promoted, leave the firm, or move to other jobs within the firm. Thus planners might project the supply of engineers in five years at 87, which means that the firm will have to hire a total of 113 (or more) new engineers.

Two useful techniques for forecasting human resources supply are the replacement chart and the skills inventory. A **replacement chart** is a list of key personnel, along with possible replacements within the firm. The chart is maintained to ensure that top management positions can be filled fairly quickly in the event of an unexpected death, resignation, or retirement. Some firms also provide additional training for employees who might eventually replace top managers.

A **skills inventory** is a computerized data bank containing information on the skills and experience of all present employees. It is used to search for candidates to fill new or newly available positions. For a special project, a manager might be seeking a current employee with an engineering degree, at least six years of experience, and fluency in French. The skills inventory can quickly identify employees who possess such qualifications.

replacement chart a list of key personnel and their possible replacements within the firm

skills inventory a computerized data bank containing information on the skills and experience of all present employees

Matching Supply with Demand

Once they have forecasts of both the demand for personnel and the firm's supply of personnel, planners can devise a course of action for matching the two. When demand is forecast to be greater than supply, plans must be made to recruit and select new employees. The timing of these actions depends on the types of positions to be filled. Suppose we expect to open a new plant in five years. Along with other employees, a plant manager and twenty-five maintenance workers will be needed. We can probably wait quite a while before we begin to recruit maintenance personnel. However, because the job of plant manager is so critical, we may start searching for the right person for that position immediately.

When supply is forecast to be greater than demand, the firm must take steps to reduce the size of its work force. Several methods are available, although none of them is especially pleasant for managers or discharged employees. When the oversupply is expected to be temporary, some employees may be *laid off*—dismissed from the work force until they are needed again.

Perhaps the most humane method for making personnel cutbacks is through attrition. *Attrition* is the normal reduction in the work force that occurs when employees leave the firm. If these employees are not replaced, the work force eventually shrinks to the point where supply matches demand. Of course, attrition may be a very slow process—too slow to really help the firm.

Early retirement is another option that can sometimes be used. Under early retirement, people who are within a few years of retirement are permitted to retire early with full benefits. Depending on the age makeup of the work force, this may or may not reduce the staff enough. As a last resort, unneeded employees are sometimes simply *fired*. Because of its negative impact, this method is generally used only when absolutely necessary.

CULTURAL DIVERSITY IN HUMAN RESOURCES

LEARNING OBJECTIVE 3
Describe cultural diversity and understand some of the challenges and opportunities associated with it.

As a larger number of women, minorities, and immigrants enter the U.S. work force, the workplace is growing more diverse. Based on the *Work Force 2000 Study* conducted by the Hudson Institute, fewer than one-fifth

A company school of the 1990s. Global companies face the challenge of bringing together workers from around the world and keeping them happy in a foreign environment. When Texas Instruments built a semiconductor manufacturing plant in Italy with workers from the United States and Japan, it set up a school for employees' children who here share a common classroom after separate instruction in English and Japanese.

of all persons entering the work force by the year 2000 will be native-born white males. Women will represent approximately 62 percent of all persons entering the work force by the year 2000. Approximately 53 percent will be minorities. Hispanics continue to be the fastest growing population in the United States, and it is estimated that they will represent 27 percent of the net growth of the work force through the year 2000.

Cultural or **workplace diversity** refers to the differences among people in a work force due to race, ethnicity, and gender. This diversity is forcing managers to learn to supervise and motivate people with a broader range of value systems. The increased number of women in the work force, combined with a new emphasis on participative parenting by men, has brought many family-related issues into the workplace. Today's more educated employees also want greater independence and flexibility. In return for their efforts, they want both compensation and a better quality of life.

Although cultural diversity presents a challenge, managers should view it as an opportunity rather than a limitation. When properly managed, cultural diversity can provide competitive advantages for an organization. Table 9.1 shows several competitive advantages that creative management of cultural diversity can offer. A firm that manages diversity properly can develop cost advantages over firms that do not manage diversity well. Moreover, organizations that manage diversity creatively are in a much better position to attract the best personnel. A culturally diverse organization may gain a marketing edge *because* it understands different cultural

cultural (workplace) diversity differences among people in a work force due to race, ethnicity, and gender.

TABLE 9.1   Possible Competitive Advantages of Cultural Diversity

Cost	As organizations become more diverse, the cost of a poor job in integrating workers will increase. Companies that handle this well can thus create cost advantages over those that do a poor job.
Resource acquisition	Companies develop reputations on favorability as prospective employers for women and ethnic minorities. Those with the best reputations for managing diversity will win the competition for the best personnel.
Marketing edge	For multinational organizations, the insight and cultural sensitivity that members with roots in other countries bring to the marketing effort should improve these efforts in important ways. The same rationale applies to marketing to subpopulations domestically.
Creativity	Diversity of perspectives and less emphasis on conformity to norms of the past (which characterize the modern approach to management of diversity) should improve the level of creativity.
Problem solving	Differences within decision and problem-solving groups potentially produce better decisions through a wider range of perspectives and more thorough critical analysis of issues.

Source: Adapted from Taylor H. Cox and Stacy Blake, "Managing Cultural Diversity: Implications for Organizational Competitiveness," *Academy of Management Executive*, Vol. 5, No. 3, (1991), p. 46. Used by permission.

BUSINESS JOURNAL
Managing Cultural Diversity in the Workplace

Gone are the days of the "organization man," the prototype American worker trying his best to look, think, and act the same as every other American worker. Today's work force is made up of many different types of people. Firms can no longer safely assume that every employee walking in the door has similar beliefs or expectations. Whereas North American white males may believe in challenging authority, Asians tend to respect and defer to it. In Hispanic cultures, people often bring music, food, and family to work, a custom North American businesses rarely allow. A job applicant who won't make eye contact during an interview may be rejected for being unapproachable, when according to her culture, she was just being polite.

How can American businesses eliminate the misunderstanding and discrimination that prevent culturally diverse employees from succeeding and still allow those employees to maintain their individuality? In a variety of ways, from formal policies at the executive level to informal celebrations of cultural differences, U.S. firms are tackling the problem. At Monsanto Company, a "Value Diversity" task force raises awareness through sensitivity training, discussions at staff meetings, publications that highlight task force activities, and films. Apple Computer, Inc.'s manager of Multicultural Programs schedules regular workshops to explore what it is like to be a minority in a majority society, and at Xerox Corp., managers are held accountable for the number of minorities employed at every level in every division. Some organizations try to smooth the entry process for new minority employees. To provide them with the skills and experience they need for future advancement, Corning Incorporated rotates new minorities through different jobs for their first five years with the firm. Before being assigned a permanent position at Digital Equipment Corp. (DEC), minorities work at one of two multicultural plants that provide a comfortable learning environment. DEC also honors Black History Week, Hispanic Heritage Week, and other cultural events with special celebrations. The Procter & Gamble Co. uses mentors in its "On-Boarding" program to help minorities adjust more easily to the corporate environment.

In a recent poll of 645 national companies, three-fourths expressed concern for the problems connected with an increasingly diverse work force, but only 29 percent had implemented diversity management programs. When the American Society for Training and Development surveyed 121 human resource development executives at *Fortune 500* companies, 73 percent predicted growing employee diversity within the next few years, but only 15 percent had established formal written policies. Although cultural diversity is a fashionable idea in corporate America today, the number of firms translating thoughts into actions is still rather limited.

groups. Proper guidance and management of diversity in an organization can also improve the level of productive creativity. Workers who bring many different viewpoints to problem solving and decision making may enliven these processes substantially.[2]

Because cultural diversity produces both challenges and advantages, it is important for an organization's employees to know how to cope with it. To accomplish that goal, about 30 percent of U.S. firms are taking action to train their managers to respect and manage diversity, according to one recent study.[3] Diversity training programs may include recruiting minorities, training minorities to be managers, training managers to view diversity positively, teaching English as a second language, providing mentoring programs, and facilitating support groups for immigrants.

As is the case with many organizational goals, a diversity program will be successful only if it is systematic and ongoing and has a strong, sustained commitment from top leadership. Cultural diversity is here to stay. Its impact in organizations is widespread and will continue to grow. Management must learn to meet the challenges and capitalize on the advantages associated with the varying viewpoints and backgrounds of culturally diverse human resources.

JOB ANALYSIS

LEARNING OBJECTIVE 4
Explain the objectives and uses of job analysis.

job analysis   a systematic procedure for studying jobs to determine their various elements and requirements

There is no sense in trying to hire people unless we know what we are hiring them for. In other words, we need to know the exact nature of a job before we can find the right person to do it.

Job analysis is a systematic procedure for studying jobs to determine their various elements and requirements. Consider the position of clerk, for example. In a large corporation, there may be fifty different kinds of clerks' positions. They all may be called "clerks," but each may be different from the others in the activities to be performed, the level of proficiency required for each activity, and the particular set of qualifications that the position demands. These are the things that job analysis focuses on.

You have to know the language. Imagine the job analysis of the scientists at the R. W. Johnson Pharmaceutical Research Institute. Seen here with computer-generated molecular structures, they must understand human physiology as well as complex chemical phenomena.

FIGURE 9.1
Job Description
A job description is a list of the elements that make up a particular position and the tasks that the employee is required to perform.

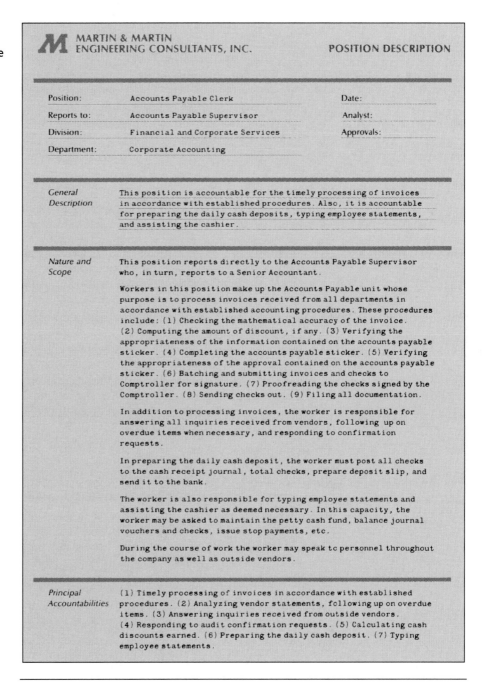

MARTIN & MARTIN
ENGINEERING CONSULTANTS, INC.   POSITION DESCRIPTION

Position:	Accounts Payable Clerk	Date:
Reports to:	Accounts Payable Supervisor	Analyst:
Division:	Financial and Corporate Services	Approvals:
Department:	Corporate Accounting	

General Description

This position is accountable for the timely processing of invoices in accordance with established procedures. Also, it is accountable for preparing the daily cash deposits, typing employee statements, and assisting the cashier.

Nature and Scope

This position reports directly to the Accounts Payable Supervisor who, in turn, reports to a Senior Accountant.

Workers in this position make up the Accounts Payable unit whose purpose is to process invoices received from all departments in accordance with established accounting procedures. These procedures include: (1) Checking the mathematical accuracy of the invoice. (2) Computing the amount of discount, if any. (3) Verifying the appropriateness of the information contained on the accounts payable sticker. (4) Completing the accounts payable sticker. (5) Verifying the appropriateness of the approval contained on the accounts payable sticker. (6) Batching and submitting invoices and checks to Comptroller for signature. (7) Proofreading the checks signed by the Comptroller. (8) Sending checks out. (9) Filing all documentation.

In addition to processing invoices, the worker is responsible for answering all inquiries received from vendors, following up on overdue items when necessary, and responding to confirmation requests.

In preparing the daily cash deposit, the worker must post all checks to the cash receipt journal, total checks, prepare deposit slip, and send it to the bank.

The worker is also responsible for typing employee statements and assisting the cashier as deemed necessary. In this capacity, the worker may be asked to maintain the petty cash fund, balance journal vouchers and checks, issue stop payments, etc.

During the course of work the worker may speak to personnel throughout the company as well as outside vendors.

Principal Accountabilities

(1) Timely processing of invoices in accordance with established procedures. (2) Analyzing vendor statements, following up on overdue items. (3) Answering inquiries received from outside vendors. (4) Responding to audit confirmation requests. (5) Calculating cash discounts earned. (6) Preparing the daily cash deposit. (7) Typing employee statements.

job description a list of the elements that make up a particular job

The job analysis for a particular position typically consists of two parts—a job description and a job specification. A **job description** is a list of the elements that make up a particular job. It includes the duties the jobholder must perform, the working conditions under which the job must be performed, the jobholder's responsibilities (including number and types of subordinates, if any), and the tools and equipment that must be used on the job (see Figure 9.1).

job specification   a list of the qualifications required to perform a particular job

A **job specification** is a list of the qualifications required to perform a particular job. Included are the skills, abilities, education, and experience that the jobholder must have.

The job analysis is the basis for recruiting and selecting new employees—for either existing positions or new ones. It is also used in other areas of human resources management, including evaluation and the determination of equitable compensation levels.

RECRUITING, SELECTION, AND ORIENTATION

LEARNING OBJECTIVE 5
Describe the processes of recruiting, employee selection, and orientation.

In an organization with jobs waiting to be filled, HRM personnel need to (1) find candidates for those jobs and (2) match the right candidate with each job. Three activities are involved: recruiting, selection, and (for new employees) orientation.

Recruiting

recruiting   the process of attracting qualified job applicants

Recruiting is the process of attracting qualified job applicants. Because it is a vital link in a costly process (for example, fees plus expenses paid to private employment agencies can total more than $30,000 for executive positions)[4] recruiting needs to be a systematic rather than haphazard process. One goal of recruiters is to attract the "right" number of applicants. The right number is enough to allow a good match between applicants and open positions, but not so many that matching them requires too much time and effort. For example, if there are five open positions and five applicants, the firm essentially has no choice. It must hire those five applicants (qualified or not) or the positions will remain open. At the other extreme, if several hundred people apply for the five positions, HRM personnel will have to spend weeks processing their applications.

Recruiters may seek applicants outside the firm, within the firm, or both. The source used generally depends on the nature of the position, the situation within the firm, and (sometimes) the firm's established or traditional recruitment policies.

external recruiting   the attempt to attract job applicants from outside the organization

External Recruiting   **External recruiting** is the attempt to attract job applicants from outside the organization. Among the means available for external recruiting are newspaper advertising, recruiting on college campuses and in union hiring halls, using employment agencies, and soliciting the recommendations of present employees. In addition, many people who are looking for work simply apply at the firm's employment office.

Clearly, it is best to match the recruiting means with the kind of applicant being sought. For example, private employment agencies most often handle professional people, whereas public employment agencies (operated by state or local governments) are usually more concerned with operations personnel. Hence we might approach a private agency if we were looking

Come work with some real characters!

Sitting pretty with Hallmark. Recruiting the right people for available positions requires creativity. No one benefits when qualified people apply for jobs in which they just will not fit. With an ad like this, Hallmark is clearly trying to attract certain kinds of job applicants—people who do not take themselves too seriously and would feel comfortable in a world of fantasy.

internal recruiting considering present employees as applicants for available positions

selection the process of gathering information about applicants for a position and then using that information to choose the most appropriate applicant

for a vice president, but we would be more inclined to contact a public agency if we wanted to hire a machinist.

The primary advantage of external recruiting is that it enables the firm to bring in people with new perspectives and varied business backgrounds. It may also be the only way to attract applicants with the required skills and knowledge. A disadvantage of external recruiting is that it is often expensive, especially if private employment agencies must be used. External recruiting may also provoke resentment among present employees.

Internal Recruiting Internal recruiting means considering present employees as applicants for available positions. Generally, current employees are considered for *promotion* to higher-level positions. However, employees may also be considered for *transfer* from one position to another at the same level.

Promoting from within provides strong motivation for current employees and helps the firm to retain quality personnel. General Electric Corporation, Exxon, Bell Telephone Laboratories, and Eastman Kodak Company are companies dedicated to promoting from within. (In cases where there is a strong union, the practice of *job posting,* or informing current employees of upcoming new openings, may be required by the union contract.) The primary disadvantage of internal recruiting is that promoting a current employee leaves another position to be filled. Not only does the firm still incur recruiting and selection costs, but it must also train two employees instead of one.

In many situations, it may be impossible to recruit internally. For example, a new position may be such that no current employee is qualified to fill it. Or the firm may be growing so rapidly that there is no time to go through the reassigning of positions that promotion or transfer require.

Selection

Selection is the process of gathering information about applicants for a position and then using that information to choose the most appropriate applicant. Note the use of the word *appropriate.* In selection, the idea is not to hire the person with the "most" qualifications but rather to choose the applicant with the qualifications that are most appropriate for the job. The actual selection of an applicant often is made by one or more line managers who have responsibility for the position being filled. However, HRM personnel usually help the selection process by developing a pool of applicants and expediting the assessment of these applicants. Common means of obtaining information about applicants' qualifications are employment applications, tests, interviews, references, and assessment centers.

Employment Applications Just about everyone who applies for anything must submit an application. You probably filled one out to apply to your school. An employment application is useful in collecting factual information on a candidate's education, work experience, and personal history (see Figure 9.2). The data obtained from applications are usually used for two purposes: to identify candidates who are worthy of further scrutiny and to familiarize interviewers with applicants' backgrounds.

commission   a payment that is some percentage of sales revenue

Commissions   A **commission** is a payment that is some percentage of sales revenue. Sales representatives and sales managers are often paid entirely through commissions or through a combination of commissions and salary.

bonus   a payment in addition to wages, salary, or commissions, usually an extra reward for outstanding job performance

Bonuses   A **bonus** is a payment in addition to wages, salary, or commissions. Bonuses are really extra rewards for outstanding job performance. They may be distributed to all employees or only to certain employees within the organization. Some firms distribute bonuses to all employees every Christmas. The size of the bonus depends on the firm's earnings and the particular employee's length of service with the firm. Other firms offer bonuses to employees who exceed specific sales or production goals.

To avoid yearly across-the-board salary increases, some organizations individually reward outstanding workers through bonuses. A pay-for-performance approach allows management to control labor costs while encouraging employees to work harder. For example, General Motors Corp. recently overhauled its employee compensation system. GM stopped annual cost-of-living increases for salaried employees and now ranks its employees against each other. An employee's merit pay under the system depends on his or her individual accomplishment relative to that of others.

Traditionally, a good worker was rewarded with a higher base salary. This salary increase was distributed during the year until the next increase. This can be costly to a company—because benefits and pensions are often tied to salaries, labor costs rise exponentially. The current business trend is toward merit payments. A worker gets a bonus, but his or her base salary remains the same. This policy is good for the company because employers can control costs and compensate a worker based on performance. Also, benefit costs can be contained because a lump sum is not added to the salary. Furthermore, employees may perceive lump-sum performance bonuses as more meaningful.

profit sharing   the distribution of a percentage of the firm's profit among its employees

Profit Sharing   **Profit sharing** is the distribution of a percentage of the firm's profit among its employees. The idea is to motivate employees to work effectively by giving them a stake in the company's financial success. Some firms—including Sears, Roebuck and Co.—have linked their profit-sharing plans to employee retirement programs; that is, employees receive their profit-sharing distributions, with interest, when they retire. Olga Company, a maker of lingerie and underwear, places 20 to 25 percent of its annual pretax earnings in a profit-sharing plan for its employees.

Employee Benefits

employee benefit   a reward that is provided indirectly to employees—mainly a service (such as insurance) paid for by the employer or an employee expense (such as college tuition) reimbursed by the employer

An **employee benefit** is a reward that is provided indirectly to employees. Employee benefits consist mainly of services (such as insurance) that are paid for by employers and employee expenses (such as college tuition) that are reimbursed by employers. Nowadays, the average cost of these benefits is more than one-third of the total cost of wages and salaries. Thus a person who earns $15,000 a year is likely to receive, in addition, over $5,000 worth of employee benefits.

Employee benefits take a variety of forms. *Pay for time not worked* covers such things as vacation time, holidays, and sick leave. *Insurance packages* may include health, life, and dental insurance for employees and their families. Some firms pay the entire cost of the insurance package and others share the cost with the employee. The costs of *pension and retirement programs* may also be borne entirely by the firm or shared with the employee.

Some benefits are required by law. For example, employers must maintain *workers' compensation insurance.* This insurance pays medical bills for injuries that occur on the job, and it provides income for employees who are disabled by job-related injuries. Employers must also pay for *unemployment insurance* and must contribute to each employee's federal *Social Security* account.

Other benefits provided by employers include *tuition-reimbursement plans, credit unions, child care,* company *cafeterias* selling reduced-price meals, various *recreational facilities,* and broad *stock option plans* that are available to all employees, not just to top management.[5]

Employees generally want to improve their performance and their compensation as well. It is certainly in the firm's interest to provide opportunities for them to do so. Training and development, then, are important aspects of human resources management.

TRAINING AND DEVELOPMENT

LEARNING OBJECTIVE 7
Explain the purposes and techniques of employee training, development, and performance appraisal.

employee training the process of teaching operations and technical employees how to do their present jobs more effectively and efficiently

management development the process of preparing managers and other professionals to assume increased responsibility in both present and future positions

Training and development are both aimed at improving employees' skills and abilities. However, the two are usually differentiated as follows: **Employee training** is the process of teaching operations and technical employees how to do their present jobs more effectively and efficiently. **Management development** is the process of preparing managers and other professionals to assume increased responsibility in both present and future positions. Thus training and development differ in who is being taught and in the purpose of the teaching. Both are necessary for personal and organizational growth. Companies that hope to stay competitive typically make huge commitments to employee training and development. For example, Motorola, Inc. spends $120 million annually, up from $7 million ten years ago, for employee education and training. Motorola's educational efforts are companywide and range from the basic three R's to technical training, to problem solving, and even interpersonal skills.[6]

Training and Development Methods

A variety of methods are available for employee training and management development. Some of these methods may be more suitable for one or the other, but most can be applied to both. These methods are as follows:

- *On-the-job methods,* in which the trainee learns by doing the work under the supervision of an experienced employee

ETHICAL CHALLENGES
Sexual Harassment on the Job

From the construction site to the secretarial pool, from medical schools to the U.S. Supreme Court, sexual harassment is a fact of life in the American workplace. Anyone—male or female, high- or low-status—can be targeted. In blue-collar jobs, the most common targets are women who are now breaking into fields once controlled by men. In white-collar jobs, employees with lower-status duties are more likely to be targeted—the paralegal rather than the lawyer, the nurse rather than the doctor. Between 1986 and 1990, the number of sexual harassment complaints registered with the Equal Employment Opportunities Commission (EEOC) rose 256 percent. In a recent *Newsweek* poll, 21 percent of women who responded said they had been sexually harassed at work. A 1990 study by the U.S. Department of Defense revealed that 64 percent of the women in the military claim to have been harassed. When the Association of American Colleges took a poll at Harvard University, 32 percent of tenured faculty women and 49 percent of untenured faculty women reported experiencing some form of sexual harassment.

To deal effectively with sexual harassment, managers must have some working definitions of the term. Is it harassment if a supervisor demands that his secretary sleep with him to keep her job? Yes. Is it harassment if he flirts with her, or tells an off-color joke? Maybe. If he tells her she looks nice, is that harassment? Probably not, but not everyone agrees. Although most workers recognize that "unwelcome" is the key word, men and women often find different behaviors unwelcome. Some believe that for a female worker to be harassed, a man must be in a position of greater power and be able to threaten her employment. Others insist that an action must be repeated to be offensive. One

Seattle-based consulting firm recommends that workers ask themselves, "Would you want your mother, sister, or daughter exposed to that?"

In 1986, the U.S. Supreme Court upheld an EEOC ruling that stated that requiring sexual activity as a condition of employment or promotion violates the Civil Rights Act of 1964. Included in the court's definition are two forms of sexual harassment. The first is requiring an employee to trade sex for professional survival, and the second is creating a hostile working environment through unwelcome sexual advances, coercion, favoritism, physical contact, or visual harassment, such as graffiti or pornographic pictures.

Because formal legal procedures are lengthy and expensive, experts agree that the responsibility for addressing the issue rests with employers. A *Working Woman* survey found that 75 percent of *Fortune 500* companies—firms like General Mills, Inc., American Telephone & Telegraph Co., and Dow Chemical—have instituted anti-harassment policies. Corporate policies, however, are only as effective as the supervisors who enforce them, and one-third of those who are harassed are victims of their supervisors. To make sure that workers have somewhere to turn when their supervisors are involved, consulting firms suggest setting up independent committees to investigate harassment. They advise appointing some well-respected person as "harassment officer" and giving that person the power to issue in-house restraining orders forbidding contact between the involved parties during an investigation. If the officer determines that a complaint is valid, disciplinary action can range from required counseling to transfer to termination. Most important, say the consultants, the punishment should fit the crime.

Occupational Safety and Health Act

Passed in 1970, this act is concerned mainly with issues of employee health and safety. For example, the act regulates the degree to which employees can be exposed to hazardous substances. It also specifies the safety equipment that must be provided.

The Occupational Safety and Health Administration (OSHA) was created to enforce this act. Inspectors from OSHA investigate employee complaints regarding unsafe working conditions. They also make spot checks on companies operating in particularly hazardous industries, such as chemicals and mining, to ensure compliance with the law. A firm that is found to be in violation of federal standards can be heavily fined or shut down.

Employee Retirement Income Security Act

This act was passed in 1974 to protect the retirement benefits of employees. It does not require that firms provide a retirement plan. However, it does specify that *if* a retirement plan is provided, it must be managed in such a way that the interests of employees are protected. It also provides federal insurance for retirement plans that go bankrupt.

Affirmative Action

Affirmative action is not one act but is a series of executive orders, issued by the president of the United States. These orders established the requirement for affirmative action in personnel practices. This requirement applies to all employers holding contracts with the federal government. It prescribes that such employers (1) actively encourage job applications from members of minority groups and (2) hire qualified employees from minority groups that are not fully represented in their organizations. Many firms that do not hold government contracts voluntarily take part in this affirmative-action program.

In this chapter we note that although relations between firms and labor unions are an extremely important part of human resources management, they are usually treated separately from HRM. In the next chapter, we discuss this topic in detail.

CHAPTER REVIEW

Summary

Human resources management (HRM) is the set of activities involved in acquiring, maintaining, and developing an organization's human resources. Responsibility for HRM is shared by line and staff managers.

Human resources planning consists of forecasting the human resources that the firm will need and those that it will have available and then planning a course of action to match supply with demand. Attrition, layoffs, early retirement, and (as a last resort) firing can be used to reduce the size of the work force. Supply is increased through hiring.

Cultural or workplace diversity refers to the differences among people in a work force due to race, ethnicity, and gender. With the increase of women, minorities, and immigrants entering the U.S. work force, management is posed with both challenges and competitive advantages. Some organizations are implementing diversity-training programs and working to keep cultural diversity alive. With the proper guidance and management, a culturally diverse organization can prove to be beneficial to all involved.

Job analysis provides a job description and a job specification for each position within the firm. These serve as the basis for recruiting and selecting new employees. Candidates for open positions may be recruited from within or outside the firm. In the selection process, applications, résumés, tests, interviews, references, and assessment centers may be used to obtain information about candidates. This information is then used to select the most appropriate candidate for the job. Newly hired employees should go through a formal or informal orientation program to acquaint them with the firm.

In developing a system for compensating, or paying, employees, management must decide on the firm's general wage level (relative to other firms), the wage structure within the firm, and individual wages. Wage surveys and job analyses are useful in making these decisions. Employees may be paid hourly wages, salaries, or commissions. They may also receive bonuses and profit-sharing payments. Employee benefits, which are nonmonetary rewards to employees, add about one-third to the cost of compensation.

Employee training and management development programs enhance the ability of employees to contribute to the firm. Several training techniques are available. Because training is expensive, its effectiveness should be evaluated periodically.

Performance appraisal, or evaluation, is used to provide employees with performance feedback, to serve as a basis for distributing rewards, and to monitor selection and training activities. Both objective and judgmental appraisal techniques are used. Their results must be communicated to employees if they are to help eliminate job-related weaknesses. A number of laws that affect HRM practices were passed to protect the rights and safety of employees.

Key Terms

You should now be able to define and give an example relevant to each of the following terms:

human resources management	job specification
human resources planning	recruiting
replacement chart	external recruiting
skills inventory	internal recruiting
cultural (workplace) diversity	selection
job analysis	orientation
job description	compensation
	compensation system
	wage survey
	job evaluation

comparable worth	profit sharing
hourly wage	employee benefit
salary	employee training
commission	management development
bonus	performance appraisal

Questions and Exercises

Review Questions

1. List the three main HRM activities and their objectives.
2. In general, on what basis is responsibility for HRM divided between line and staff managers?
3. How is a human resources' demand forecast related to the firm's organizational planning?
4. How do human resources managers go about matching the firm's supply of workers with its demand for workers?
5. What are the major challenges and benefits associated with a culturally diverse work force?
6. How are a job analysis, job description, and job specification related?
7. What are the advantages and disadvantages of external recruiting? of internal recruiting?
8. In your opinion, what are the two best techniques for gathering information about job candidates?
9. Why is orientation an important HRM activity?
10. Explain how the three wage-related decisions result in a compensation system.
11. How is a job analysis used in the process of job evaluation?
12. Suppose you have just opened a new Ford Motor Co. automobile sales showroom and repair shop. Which of your employees would be paid wages, which would receive salaries, and which would receive commissions?
13. What is the difference between the objective of employee training and the objective of management development?
14. Why is it so important to provide feedback after a performance appraisal?

Discussion Questions

1. Why did Time Warner create the Work and Family Program?
2. How does Time Warner benefit from having a highly comprehensive employee benefits program?
3. How accurately can managers plan for future human resources needs?

4. How might an organization's recruiting and selection practices be affected by the general level of employment?

5. Are employee benefits really necessary? Why?

6. What actions would you take, as a manager, if an operations employee with six years of experience on the job refused ongoing training and ignored performance feedback?

7. Why are there so many laws relating to HRM practices? Which are the most important laws, in your opinion?

Exercises

1. Construct a job analysis for the position of "entering first-year student" at your school.

2. Write a newspaper ad to attract applicants for the position of retail salesperson in your small business.

3. Describe the orientation procedure used by a firm that you have worked for or by your school. Then devise an *improved* orientation procedure for that organization.

CASE 9.1

Digital Equipment Corp.'s AIDS Program

Every 54 seconds, someone in the United States contracts the AIDS-causing HIV virus, and 3,000 cases are reported every month. Experts predict these figures will triple in the next few years. Because most of those contracting the virus are of working age—22 to 45 years old—managing AIDS in the workplace is becoming an increasingly critical issue for businesses. Then why do only about 20 percent of large corporations have written AIDS policies? Businesses commonly support programs dealing with socially acceptable chronic illnesses like cancer, but AIDS carries a stigma and attracts few advocates. Pacific Bell and Wells Fargo & Co. defied public opinion years ago by initiating AIDS training programs. Since then, only a handful of major corporations, including Levi Strauss, Bank of America, IBM, and Digital Equipment Corp. (DEC) have dared to join them.

Instituting a written AIDS program is good for workers, but it also makes good business sense. Two years after the U.S. Congress passed the "Americans with Disabilities Act," making it illegal for employers to discriminate against qualified but disabled workers, the number of AIDS discrimination cases skyrocketed from fewer than 400 to more than 95,000. By implementing a written, documented AIDS program, companies become less vulnerable to discrimination lawsuits. And, by reducing fear and prejudice, they keep workers productive. A good policy should tell managers how to act fairly and tell employees what to expect. It should also train managers to implement policy and should educate employees so that they can reduce the spread of the disease and improve relations with infected coworkers.

For years, DEC executives considered implementing some kind of AIDS program, but until an employee came to them and said, "I have AIDS," they did nothing more than talk. At that time, some DEC workers were even afraid to install computer systems in hospitals caring for AIDS patients, believing they could catch it by breathing the air or touching something in the room. From a company with no AIDS policy and no support system, DEC has gone on to become the only major firm in the United States with a corporate department working full-time on the problems of AIDS in the workplace.

DEC's AIDS policy guidelines are simple: Employees with serious illnesses have the right to continue working as long as they can perform their jobs, and medical records are confidential. However, DEC's AIDS Programs office manager is proud of the education program built on this base. The program not only teaches managers to respond skillfully within company guidelines, it also creates a sympathetic environment where workers feel free to tell supervisors about their illnesses. Managers attend mandatory four-hour training sessions that include medical explanations, discussions about employee-relation issues, and videos by medical personnel. Workers learn how the disease is spread and what the law says regarding employee rights. They also learn to deal with psychological problems, such as fear or panic, which can deeply affect personal and professional lives. DEC writes and distributes a pamphlet containing medical facts, company guidelines and benefits, and a list of places to go for help, both inside DEC and in the larger community. To bring the reality of the disease home to its employees, DEC invites people infected with HIV to speak at training sessions. One thirty-five-year-old man relates that when he first came to DEC to talk about his illness, he was one of a panel of three speakers. Of those, he is the only one still alive.

To date, DEC has trained more than half of its 123,000 personnel, both managers and nonmanagers. However, the organization's efforts to halt the spread of AIDS, or at least to alleviate some suffering, don't stop at its own doors. The company sponsors fund-raising events and grants money for AIDS research.

Despite DEC's accomplishments, and those of other firms, AIDS discrimination is still active in the workplace. When a sports superstar shocks the public by revealing that he has the HIV virus, his teammates and coaches stand behind him. When an average worker comes forward, he or she might be told, "leave by the end of the day and don't touch anything on your way out."*

Questions

1. Do most business organizations need an AIDS policy? Why or why not?
2. DEC's AIDS policy guidelines are rather simple and straightforward. Would a different type of organization (hospital, tire manufacturer, grocery store) need a different kind of AIDS policy? Explain.
3. Should an organization's policies and guidelines for AIDS be different from those regarding other types of medical problems? Discuss.

*Based on information from Julia Lawlor, "Working with AIDS," *USA Today*, December 11, 1991, pp. 1B–2B; Art Durity, "The AIDS Epidemic," *Personnel*, April 1991, p. 1; Rhonda West and Art Durity, "Does My Company Need to Worry About AIDS?" *Personnel*, April 1991, p. 5; Stuart Feldman, "When It Comes to AIDS, It's Survival of the Smartest," *Personnel*, April 1991, p. 6; Eleanor Smith, "Train Supervisors to Be AIDS Savvy," *Personnel*, April 1991, p. 7; Stuart Feldman, "A Job for Champions," *Personnel*, April 5, 1991, p. 8; Charles Nau, "ADA Forces Employers to Respond," *Personnel*, April 5, 1991, pp. 9–10; Stuart Feldman, "Three Successful Programs," *Personnel*, April 5, 1991, p. 11; Julia Lawlor, "HIV-Infected Workers Get Little Support," *USA Today*, November 11, 1991, p. B1.

CASE 9.2

HRM: Top Priority at Herman Miller, Inc.

Max DePree, chairman of the $800-million office-furniture manufacturing firm Herman Miller, is optimistic about his company's future. He is confident that Herman Miller can handle the aggression of expanding foreign furniture makers and eventually displace Steelcase Inc., the number-one office-furniture producer in the United States.

Back in 1923, long before employee profit sharing, incentive programs, and human resources management were popular, Max's father and company founder, D. J. DePree, strongly believed in a company ethic that stressed employee involvement and employer compassion. In the ensuing years, employer-employee relationships have been so good at Herman Miller that there has never been a serious attempt to unionize the company. DePree is proud of the trust that exists between management and workers, convinced that caring and sharing are more important than the quest for more and more money. Herman Miller (D. J. DePree named the company after his father-in-law, who gave him the start-up money) may be the only company in the United States with a vice president for people, who supervises human resources and employee relations.

When hiring new employees, Herman Miller managers focus more on a person's character and interpersonal skills than on a résumé. Managers organize employees into work teams with team leaders. Every six months, the leaders evaluate the workers—and the workers evaluate the leaders. To resolve any grievances, company meetings bring together line supervisors and elected team representatives. Workers also have the option of meeting directly with executives. Each employee is involved with cost cutting and product improvement, receiving bonuses that reward individual or group suggestions. In one year alone, worker suggestions saved the company more than $12 million.

Keeping workers satisfied is paramount at Herman Miller, and the company takes measures to make sure that they are. The managerial promotion plan is ethically sound. In the event of a hostile takeover, workers as well as executives will receive "silver parachutes" (large checks) if they lose their jobs. Evidence of the belief that lower executive salaries means higher employee morale can be seen in the CEO's salary, which is limited to twenty times that of the average line worker. Max DePree, who recently stepped down as CEO (he retained his title as chairman), will be the last DePree to head the company. To guard against nepotism, the next generation of DePrees is not allowed to work for the company.

Cost cutting and layoffs—which have led to hard feelings at many large U.S. companies—have actually strengthened the management-worker relationships at Herman Miller as workers and executives work together to achieve company objectives. In the face of the current recession, office furniture orders are down, forcing manufacturers, including Herman Miller, to trim budgets. Rather than laying off staff indiscriminately, Herman Miller implemented a voluntary layoff program. Two hundred workers volunteered to take several weeks' leave without pay.

Max DePree once stated, "Capitalism can only reach its potential when it capitalizes on all workers' gifts and lets them share in the results." The management of his company seems to be deeply dedicated to this idea. Herman Miller's unique management practices and incentive programs have resulted in one of the fastest growth rates of any business in the office furniture industry. Warmth and respect are incorporated into Herman Miller's policies, because the firm believes that in the office furniture business, nice guys certainly don't have to finish last. The executives and workers at Herman Miller have their goals set much higher than that.**

Questions

1. In what ways does a company like Herman Miller benefit from highly favorable employer-employee relationships created by effective HRM activities and programs?

2. Herman Miller appears to provide more employee benefits than do many other companies. What are the advantages and disadvantages of these management practices to the company?

**Based on information from Kenneth Labich, "Hot Company, Warm Culture," *Fortune*, February 27, 1898, pp. 74–76, 78; "Making Open Offices a Little Less Open," *Wall Street Journal*, November 8, 1988, p. B1; Dana Wechsler, "A Comeback in Cubicles," *Forbes*, March 21, 1988, pp. 54, 56; Bob Daily, "Multiple Pay, Multiple Problems," *Business Month*, June 1990, pp. 76–77; and David O. Heenan, "The Right Way to Downsize," *The Journal of Business Strategy*, September-October 1991, pp. 44–47.

Union-Management Relations

LEARNING OBJECTIVES

After studying this chapter you should be able to:

1 Explain how and why labor unions came into being.

2 Discuss the sources of unions' negotiating power and trends in union membership.

3 Identify the main focus of several major pieces of labor-management legislation.

4 Enumerate the steps involved in forming a union, and show how the National Labor Relations Board is involved in the process.

5 Describe the basic elements in the collective bargaining process.

6 Identify the major issues covered in a union-management contract.

7 Explain the primary bargaining tools available to unions and management.

CHAPTER PREVIEW

We open this chapter by reviewing the history of labor unions in this country. Then we turn our attention to organized labor today, noting current membership trends and summarizing important labor-relations laws. We discuss the unionization process—why employees join unions, how a union is formed, and what the National Labor Relations Board does. Collective bargaining procedures are then explained. Next, we consider such issues as employee pay, working hours, security, management rights, and grievance procedures, all of which are issues included in a union-management contract. We close with a discussion of various labor and management negotiating techniques, including strikes, lockouts, mediation, and arbitration.

Union and Management Cooperate at Xerox

Xerox Corp.'s motto, "Team Xerox," isn't just advertising hype. According to the company's manager of public relations, his company has an inseparable partnership with its union, the Amalgamated Clothing and Textile Workers (ACTWU). More than three thousand Xerox manufacturing employees belong to the ACTWU, which cooperates with management to cut costs, increase revenues, improve quality, respond to workers' needs, and keep Xerox competitive. The partnership is working out well for both sides. Xerox and the ACTWU recently signed a three-year contract that guarantees cost-of-living adjustments, increases profit sharing from 6.5 percent to 10 percent, and promises not to lay off workers. In turn, management gets increased employee satisfaction and a commitment to quality that helped to earn Xerox a Malcolm Baldrige Quality Award.

At one time, Xerox reigned supreme in the plain copier market. When you needed something duplicated, you didn't make a copy. You made a Xerox copy. During the late 1970s, however, Japanese competitors such as Sharp and Canon, and U.S. manufacturer International Business Machines Corp. grabbed a substantial chunk of Xerox's market share, reducing it from 90 percent to 43 percent. Japanese companies were selling many copiers for what it cost Xerox to make them, and rework, scrap, excessive inspections, and lost business were costing the company about $2 billion a year.

Instead of saving money by closing plants, subcontracting component parts, and laying off workers, Xerox joined forces with the ACTWU to solve its problems and keep its employees. Xerox's contract with the union states that if management concludes that the company is not manufacturing a product cost-effectively, it will work with the union to establish a study action team composed of union officers, hourly workers, and management personnel. The team attempts to restructure the depart-

ment and cut costs, but if they can't find a way to make a competitive, high-quality product, Xerox is free to subcontract. A job security clause ensures that Xerox will not lay off employees as a result of changes.

Xerox had a chance to put the scheme to a dramatic test. To save about $3 million, the company considered subcontracting its wire harness manufacturing operations, a plan that would eliminate 180 jobs. As mandated in its labor agreement, a study action team proposed alternatives. When implemented, the alternatives not only reduced costs and saved jobs but improved the quality of the wire harnesses, raised worker morale, and intensified worker commitment to Xerox.

At Xerox, whenever a manufacturing glitch or a faulty part threatens product quality, workers are authorized to stop the assembly line until they solve the problem. Management is committed to the concept that its employees are human beings who have more to offer than repetitive, circumscribed, unthinking performance; the ACTWU is committed to working jointly with the company to improve quality. Together, they are revitalizing Xerox and renewing its world-class status.[1]

The cooperation between the ACTWU and Xerox provides greater job satisfaction to the workers, makes the organization more productive, allows Xerox to be more competitive, and thus improves workers' job benefits and security. Not all companies and unions get along as well as the ACTWU and Xerox, however.

labor union an organization of workers acting together to negotiate their wages and working conditions with employers

A **labor union** is an organization of workers acting together to negotiate their wages and working conditions with employers. In the United States, nonmanagement employees have the legal right to form unions and to bargain, as a group, with management. The result of the bargaining process is a *labor contract*, a written agreement that is in force for a set period of time (usually one to three years). The dealings between labor unions and business management, both in the bargaining process and beyond it, are called **union-management relations** or, more simply, **labor relations.**

union-management (or labor) relations the dealings between labor unions and business management, both in the bargaining process and beyond it

There is a dual relationship between labor and management. The two groups have different goals, which tend to place them at odds with each other. But these goals must be attained by the same means—through the production of goods and services. At contract bargaining sessions, the two groups must work together to attain their goals. Perhaps mainly for this reason, antagonism now seems to be giving way to cooperation in union-management relations.

Before we examine how organized labor operates today, we should take a look at its roots in the history of the labor movement.

THE HISTORICAL DEVELOPMENT OF UNIONS

LEARNING OBJECTIVE 1
Explain how and why labor unions came into being.

craft union an organization of skilled workers in a single craft or trade

Until the middle of the nineteenth century, there was very little organization of labor in this country. Groups of workers did occasionally form a **craft union,** which is an organization of skilled workers in a single craft or trade. These unions were usually limited to a single city, and they often lasted only a short time. The first known strike in the United States involved a group of Philadelphia printers who stopped working over demands for higher wages. When the employers granted the printers a pay increase, the group disbanded.

Early History

In the mid-1800s, improved transportation opened new markets for manufactured goods. New manufacturing methods made it possible to supply those markets, and American industry began to grow. The Civil War and the continued growth of the railroads after the war led to further industrial expansion.

Large-scale production required more and more skilled industrial workers. As the skilled labor force grew, craft unions emerged in the more industrialized areas. From these craft unions, three significant labor organizations evolved. See Figure 10.1 for a historical overview of unions and their patterns of membership.

FIGURE 10.1
Historical Overview of Unions
The total number of members for all unions has risen dramatically since 1869, when the first truly national union was organized. The dates of major events in the history of labor unions are singled out along the line of membership change. *(Sources: U.S. Bureau of Labor Statistics and Dictionary of U.S. Labor Organizations, 1986–1987; U.S. Bureau of Labor Statistics,* Current Population Survey of Households, *1991.)*

Knights of Labor   The first significant labor organization to emerge was the Knights of Labor. The *Knights of Labor* was formed as a secret society in 1869 by Uriah Stephens. One major goal of the Knights was to eliminate the depersonalization of the worker that resulted from mass-production technology. Another was to improve the moral standards of both employees and society. The Knights of Labor was the first truly national labor union. Membership increased steadily, and by 1886 the Knights had approximately 700,000 members.

The moralistic goals of the Knights ultimately contributed to its downfall. The group's leaders concentrated so hard on social and economic change that they did not recognize the effects of technological change.

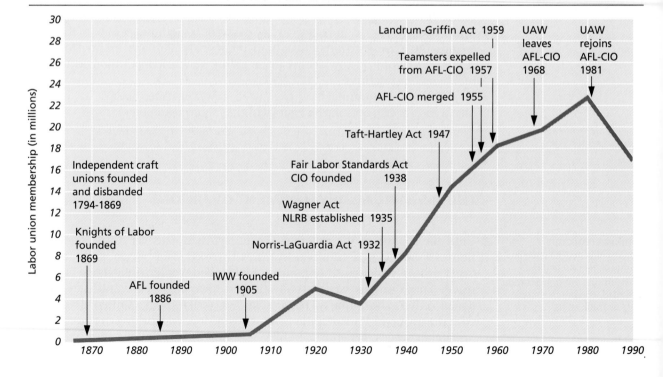

The figure in the salary column approximates the expected annual income after two or three years of service.
1 = $12,000–$15,000; 2 = $16,000–$20,000; 3 = $21,000–$27,000; 4 = $28,000–$35,000; 5 = $36,000 and up.

Educational Requirements	Skills Required	Prospects for Growth
Degree in business or human resources management	Decision making; analytical; communication; interpersonal	Average
Degree in medically related field	Communication; detail; basic office	Average
Bachelor's degree in business or management; on-the-job experience	Communication; problem solving; analytical	Above average
Bachelor's degree; on-the-job experience	Interpersonal; communication; problem solving; analytical	Above average
Bachelor's degree; on-the-job experience	Interpersonal; problem solving	Above average
Some college; degree helpful	Communication; office; interpersonal	Above average
Bachelor's degree in human resources management; master's degree helpful	Communication; decision making; interpersonal	Above average
High school diploma; some college preferred	Communication; detail; basic office skills	Average
High school diploma; some college preferred	Analytical; communication; interpersonal	Average

PART

4

Marketing

The business activities that make up a firm's marketing efforts are those most directly concerned with satisfying customers' needs. In this part, we discuss these activities in some detail. We begin with a general discussion of marketing and the market for consumer goods. Then, in turn, we discuss the four elements that are combined into a marketing mix: product, price, distribution, and promotion. Included in this part are:

An Overview of Marketing

LEARNING OBJECTIVES

After studying this chapter, you should be able to:

1 Know the meaning of *marketing* and explain how it creates utility for purchasers of products.

2 Trace the development of the marketing concept and understand how it is implemented.

3 Understand what markets are and how they are classified.

4 Identify the four elements of the marketing mix and be aware of their importance in developing a marketing strategy.

5 Explain how the marketing environment affects strategic market planning.

6 Describe how market measurement and sales forecasting are used.

7 Distinguish between a marketing information system and marketing research.

8 Identify several factors that may influence buying behavior.

9 Describe three ways of measuring consumer income.

10 Understand the marketing implications of several socioeconomic changes occurring in the United States.

11 Recognize the relative costs and benefits of marketing.

CHAPTER PREVIEW

In this chapter we examine marketing activities that add value to products. We trace the evolution of the marketing concept and describe how organizations practice it. Next, our focus shifts to market classifications and marketing strategy. We analyze the four elements of a marketing mix and also discuss uncontrollable factors in the marketing environment. We consider tools for strategic market planning, including market measurement, sales forecasts, marketing information systems, and marketing research. Then we look at the forces that influence consumer and organizational buying behavior, and the marketing implications of socioeconomic changes. We close with an evaluation of marketing's costs and benefits.

Aiming Gatorade at Children

After a hard workout, exhausted and depleted athletes who want to gulp down an isotonic drink choose Gatorade about 90 percent of the time. Developed in 1965, "America's sports drink" has grown sensationally over the last decade. Recently, however, competitors have become eager to grab some of the $475 million market. PepsiCo, Inc. is test-marketing All Sport, Coke sells four flavors of PowerAde at convenience-store fountains, and Dr Pepper just came out with Nautilus, a low-calorie sports drink made with NutraSweet. Rising to the challenge, Gatorade is targeting untapped markets by increasing its appeal to women, teens, and children.

To attract more diet-conscious women, Gatorade developed Gatorade Light. Teens will be tempted with the brand's newest flavor, Tropical Punch. By sponsoring high-school sporting events on cable TV, Quaker Oats, owner of Gatorade, hopes to reach a large teen-aged audience. It is toward the lunch box set, however, that Gatorade is directing the healthiest portion of its $30-million-a-year ad budget. "My mom knows all about Gatorade," say the new TV commercials. The spots attempt to lure parents, who really bankroll the children's market, by emphasizing that Gatorade quenches a child's thirst with no caffeine and only half the sugar of regular fruit drinks. In commercials featuring basketball legend Michael Jordan playing ball with groups of children, kids are urged to "Be Like Mike—Drink Gatorade." Print ads appearing in national magazines like *Family Circle* and *Woman's Day* promote Gatorade as "a healthy alternative for thirsty kids."

Gatorade's new child-directed advertising comes at a touchy time for children's marketing. The U.S. Food and Drug Administration (FDA), as well as various child-advocacy groups, are demanding that stricter rules govern nutritional claims made on all labels, including those on juice-drink

packages. Critics want the FDA to ban Gatorade ads aimed at children. They assert that there is no evidence the drink is any healthier than water, and parents who buy Gatorade will be wasting money on an unnecessary product. Although Gatorade is the number two seller in the juice-drink category, the Florida Department of Citrus recently revealed that Gatorade contains no vitamin C, and one-tenth the potassium and 36 times the sodium of grapefruit juice. Gatorade may be "what your body needs," say skeptics, but is it what your baby needs?

Analysts predict that in the next few years, sales of sports drinks will reach $12 billion. Children are expected to influence buying decisions associated with about $130 billion in total purchases. Quaker Oats is hoping that by getting millions of children to demand millions of gallons of Gatorade, the company can offset declines it is experiencing in some of its other product categories.[1]

As more competitors enter the sports-drink market, Gatorade is focusing on untapped groups of customers rather than battling major soft-drink companies in head-to-head competition. Marketing encompasses a diverse set of decisions and activities performed by individuals and by both business and nonbusiness organizations. Marketing begins and ends with the customer. The American Marketing Association defines **marketing** as "the process of planning and executing the conception, pricing, promotion, and distribution of ideas, goods, and services to create exchanges that satisfy individual and organizational objectives." The marketing process involves eight major functions and numerous related activities (see Table 11.1). All of these functions are essential if the marketing process is to be effective.

marketing the process of planning and executing the conception, pricing, promotion, and distribution of ideas, goods, and services to create exchanges that satisfy individual and organizational objectives

UTILITY: THE VALUE ADDED BY MARKETING

LEARNING OBJECTIVE 1
Know the meaning of *marketing* and explain how it creates utility for purchasers of products.

utility the ability of a good or service to satisfy a human need

form utility utility created by converting production inputs into finished products

place utility utility created by making a product available at a location where customers wish to purchase it

time utility utility created by making a product available when customers wish to purchase it

possession utility utility created by transferring title (or ownership) of a product to the buyer

As defined in Chapter 7, **utility** is the ability of a good or service to satisfy a human need. A lunch at a Pizza Hut, an overnight stay at a Holiday Inn, and a Mercedes 420 SEL all satisfy human needs. Thus, each possesses utility. There are four kinds of utility.

Form utility is created by converting production inputs into finished products. Marketing efforts may indirectly influence form utility because the data gathered as part of marketing research are frequently used to determine the size, shape, and features of a product.

The three kinds of utility that are directly created by marketing are place, time, and possession utility. **Place utility** is created by making a product available at a location where customers wish to purchase it. A pair of shoes is given place utility when it is shipped from a factory to a department store.

Time utility is created by making a product available when customers wish to purchase it. For example, Halloween costumes might be manufactured in April but not displayed until late September, when consumers start buying them. By storing the costumes until they are wanted, the manufacturer or retailer provides time utility.

Possession utility is created by transferring title (or ownership) of a product to the buyer. For a product as simple as a pair of shoes, ownership

329

TABLE 11.1   Major Marketing Functions

Exchange Functions: All companies such as manufacturers, wholesalers, and retailers buy and sell to market their merchandise.

1. **Buying** includes such functions as obtaining raw materials to make products, knowing how much merchandise to keep on hand, and selecting suppliers.
2. **Selling** creates possession utility by transferring the title of a product from seller to customer.

Physical Distribution Functions: These functions involve the flow of goods from producers to customers. Transportation and storage provide time utility and place utility, and require careful management of inventory.

3. **Transporting** involves selecting a mode of transport that provides an acceptable delivery schedule at an acceptable price.
4. **Storing** goods is often necessary to sell them at the best selling time.

Facilitating Functions: These functions help the other functions take place.

5. **Financing** helps at all stages of marketing. To buy raw materials, manufacturers often borrow from banks or receive credit from suppliers. Wholesalers may be financed by manufacturers, and retailers may receive financing from the wholesaler or manufacturer. Finally, retailers often provide financing to customers.
6. **Standardizing** sets uniform specifications for products or services. **Grading** classifies products by size and quality, usually through a sorting process. Together, standardization and grading facilitate production, transportation, storage, and selling.
7. **Risk taking**—even though competent management and insurance can minimize risks—is a constant reality of marketing because of such losses as bad debt expense, obsolescence of products, theft by employees, and product-liability lawsuits.
8. **Gathering market information** is necessary for making all marketing decisions.

AT A GLANCE

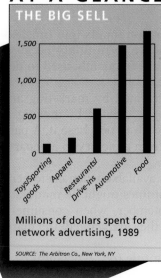

THE BIG SELL

Millions of dollars spent for network advertising, 1989

SOURCE: The Arbitron Co., New York, NY

is usually transferred by means of a sales slip or receipt. For such products as automobiles and homes, the transfer of title is a more complex process. Along with the title to its product, the seller transfers the right to use that product to satisfy a need (see Figure 11.1).

Place, time, and possession utility have real value in terms of both money and convenience. This value is created and added to goods and services through a wide variety of marketing activities—from research indicating what customers want, to product warranties ensuring that customers get what they pay for. Overall, these marketing activities account for about half of every dollar spent by consumers. When they are part of an integrated marketing program that delivers maximum utility to the customer, most of us would agree that they are worth the cost.

Place, time, and possession utility are only the most fundamental applications of marketing activities. In recent years, marketing activities have been influenced by a broad business philosophy known as *the marketing concept.*

THE MARKETING CONCEPT

LEARNING OBJECTIVE 2
Trace the development of the marketing concept and understand how it is implemented.

The process that leads any business to success seems simple. First, the firm must talk to its potential customers to assess their needs for its goods or services. Then the firm must develop a good or service to satisfy those needs. Finally, the firm must continue to seek ways to provide customer satisfaction. This process is an application of the marketing concept, or marketing orientation. As simple as it seems, American business has been slow to accept it.

Evolution of the Marketing Concept

From the start of the Industrial Revolution until the early twentieth century, business effort was directed mainly toward the production of goods. Consumer demand for manufactured products was so great that manufacturers could almost bank on selling everything they produced. Business had a strong *production orientation*, in which emphasis was placed on increased output and production efficiency. Marketing was limited to taking orders and distributing finished goods.

In the 1920s, production began to catch up with demand. Now producers had to direct their efforts toward selling goods to consumers whose basic wants were already satisfied. This new *sales orientation* was characterized by increased advertising, enlarged sales forces, and, occasionally, high-pressure selling techniques. Manufacturers produced the goods they expected consumers to want, and marketing consisted primarily of taking orders and delivering goods, along with personal selling and advertising.

During the 1950s, however, business people started to realize that even enormous advertising expenditures and the most thoroughly proven sales techniques were not enough. Something else was needed if products were

FIGURE 11.1
Types of Utility
Form utility is created by the production process, but marketing creates place, time, and possession utility.

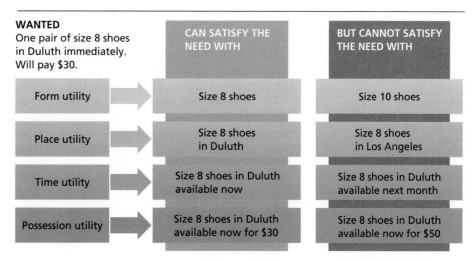

Packaged for playing. If you're headed for a long cruise and you want to listen to your favorite selections from the Beatles or Beethoven, Reader's Digest hopes you will find its musical packages perfectly suit your needs. The company gauges its readers' musical tastes and tries to create packages that will appeal to them, creating not new recordings but new collections.

to sell as well as expected. It was then that business managers recognized that they were not primarily producers or sellers but rather were in the business of satisfying customers' wants. As Phillip E. Benton, Jr., president of Ford Motor Co.'s Automotive Group, states, "What our customers define as quality is what we must deliver. We have re-learned in recent years that the successful automakers consistently provide customers with what they need and want, at a price they feel offers good value, in a product that meets their expectations of safety and quality. Our challenge is to go beyond that—to exceed customer expectations and, indeed, to generate customer enthusiasm."[2] Marketers realized that the best approach was to adopt a customer orientation—in other words, the organization had to first determine what customers need and then develop goods and services to fill those particular needs (see Table 11.2).

marketing concept a business philosophy that involves the entire organization in the process of satisfying customers' needs while achieving the organization's goals

This **marketing concept** is a business philosophy that involves the entire organization in the process of satisfying customers' needs while achieving the organization's goals. All functional areas—research and development, production, finance, human resources, and, of course, marketing—are viewed as playing a role in providing customer satisfaction.

Implementing the Marketing Concept

The marketing concept has been adopted by many of the most successful business firms. Some firms, such as Ford and Apple Computer, have gone through minor or major reorganizations in the process. Because the

TABLE 11.2 Evolution of Customer Orientation
Business managers recognized that they were not primarily producers or sellers but rather were in the business of satisfying customers' wants.

Production Orientation	Sales Orientation	Customer Orientation
Take orders Distribute goods	Increase advertising Enlarge sales force Intensify sales techniques	Determine customer needs Develop goods and services to fill these needs Achieve the organization's goals

marketing concept is essentially a business philosophy, anyone can say, "I believe in it." But to make it work, management must fully adopt and then implement it.

To implement the marketing concept, a firm must first obtain information about its present and potential customers. The firm must determine not only what customers' needs are but also how well those needs are being satisfied by products currently on the market—both its own products and those of competitors. It must ascertain how its products might be improved and what opinions customers have of the firm and its marketing efforts.

The firm must then use this information to pinpoint the specific needs and potential customers toward which it will direct its marketing activities and resources. (Obviously, no firm can expect to satisfy all needs. And not every individual or firm can be considered a potential customer for every product manufactured or sold by a firm.) Next, the firm must mobilize its marketing resources to (1) provide a product that will satisfy its customers; (2) price the product at a level that is acceptable to buyers and that will yield a profit; (3) promote the product so that potential customers will be aware of its existence and its ability to satisfy their needs; and (4) ensure that the product is distributed so that it is available to customers where and when needed.

Finally, the firm must again obtain marketing information—this time regarding the effectiveness of its efforts. Can the product be improved? Is it being promoted properly? Is it being distributed efficiently? Is the price too high? The firm must be ready to modify any or all of its marketing activities on the basis of this feedback.

LEARNING OBJECTIVE 3
Understand what markets are and how they are classified.

market a group of individuals, organizations, or both who have needs for products in a given category and who have the ability, willingness, and authority to purchase such products

MARKETS AND THEIR CLASSIFICATION

A **market** is a group of individuals, organizations, or both that have needs for products in a given category and that have the ability, willingness, and authority to purchase such products. The people or organizations must require the product. They must be able to purchase the product with money,

FOCUS ON SMALL BUSINESS
Fireworks by Grucci: "Bombs Bursting in Air" and a Whole Lot More

Accompanied by the sounds of Jerry Lee Lewis's "Great Balls of Fire," showers of white, red, blue, and green fill the night sky. Golden comets crisscross the dark to Bruce Springsteen's popular "Born in the USA." For about 150 years, the Grucci family has been in the business of entertaining audiences with their fireworks displays. At the Olympics, two U.S. presidential inaugurations, the centennial celebrations of the Brooklyn Bridge and the Statue of Liberty, even at a meeting of the United Arab Emirates in Abu Dhabi, Fireworks by Grucci was there.

The family-owned, family-run firm moved to New York from Begun, Italy, where Angelo Lanzetta had established it in 1850. In the 1970s, two events transformed Fireworks by Grucci from a moderately successful "mom and pop" operation into a world-class, world-renowned firm. In 1976, thousands of cities booked Grucci for U.S. Bicentennial celebrations, and in 1979, the company won the Monte Carlo World Championship of Pyrotechnics. After an explosion killed two family members and destroyed their factory, the Gruccis started purchasing most of their explosive shells from outside suppliers and concentrating their efforts on designing and planning unique shows. Today, Fireworks by Grucci employs thirty-five full-time workers and puts on about two hundred displays every year.

To market their product, the Gruccis rely on word of mouth and brand awareness established by media coverage of their large events. They do not advertise. When the vice president for marketing (a family member, of course) meets with potential clients, whether communities or businesses, he lets a videotape of previous displays do the selling for him. Using this low-key approach has persuaded customers like Lever Bros. Co., PepsiCo, Inc., and Maxwell House Coffee to pay $20,000 to $50,000 for shows at sales meetings and other corporate events. To stage national events, like the Statue of Liberty Centennial Celebration, the Grucci meter ticks away at $2,000 per minute.

Fireworks remain mostly family-run enterprises because they are too small to attract large corporations; learning the business also requires an apprenticeship rather than formal schooling. In the $75 million-a-year market, the Gruccis compete with the Souza family's "Pyro-Spectaculars," and the Zambelli's "Internationale Fireworks." When economic conditions worsen, the competition stiffens. Many communities can no longer afford to pay for the kind of extravaganzas these companies produce. Nevertheless, Grucci's vice president declares that his family are entertainers whose shows will go on in rain, snow, sleet, wind, and cold—everything except fog.

goods, or services that can be exchanged for the product. They must be willing to use their buying power. Finally, they must be socially and legally authorized to purchase the product.

Markets are broadly classified as consumer or industrial markets. These classifications are based on the characteristics of the individuals and organizations within each market. Because marketing efforts vary depending on the intended market, marketers should understand the general characteristics of these two groups.

Consumer markets consist of purchasers and/or individual household members who intend to consume or benefit from the purchased products and who do not buy products to make a profit.

  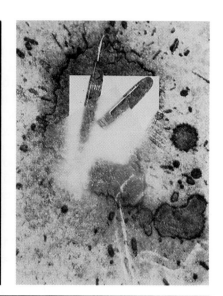

The fountain pen reborn.
Fountain pens virtually disappeared when ballpoints were introduced, but now, with new marketing strategies, they're coming to life again. No one *needs* a fountain pen, but pen makers are convincing consumers that the pens can be "power batons," reflecting their owners' status, class, or sense of style. Buyers are paying up to $345 to give their signatures extra flair.

Industrial markets are grouped broadly into producer, reseller, governmental, and institutional categories. These markets purchase specific kinds of products for use in making other products, for resale, or for day-to-day operations. *Producer markets* consist of individuals and business organizations that buy certain products to use in the manufacture of other products. *Reseller markets* consist of intermediaries such as wholesalers and retailers that buy finished products and sell them for a profit. *Governmental markets* consist of federal, state, county, and local governments. They buy goods and services to maintain internal operations and to provide citizens with such products as highways, education, water, energy, and national defense. Their purchases total billions of dollars each year. *Institutional markets* include churches, not-for-profit private schools and hospitals, civic clubs, fraternities and sororities, charitable organizations, and foundations. Their goals are different from such typical business goals as profit, market share, or return on investment.

DEVELOPING MARKETING STRATEGIES

marketing strategy   a plan that will enable an organization to make the best use of its resources and advantages to meet its objectives

marketing mix   a combination of product, price, distribution, and promotion developed to satisfy a particular target market

A **marketing strategy** is a plan that will enable an organization to make the best use of its resources and advantages to meet its objectives. A marketing strategy consists of (1) the selection and analysis of a target market and (2) the creation and maintenance of an appropriate **marketing mix,** a combination of product, price, distribution, and promotion developed to satisfy a particular target market.

Target Market Selection and Evaluation

target market   a group of persons for whom a firm develops and maintains a marketing mix suitable for the specific needs and preferences of that group

A **target market** is a group of persons for whom a firm develops and maintains a marketing mix suitable for the specific needs and preferences of that group. In selecting a target market, marketing managers examine potential markets for their possible effects on the firm's sales, costs, and profits. The managers attempt to determine whether the organization has the resources to produce a marketing mix that meets the needs of a particular target market and whether satisfying those needs is consistent with the firm's overall objectives. They also analyze the strengths and numbers of competitors already marketing to people in this target market. When selecting a target market, marketing managers generally take either the total market approach or the market segmentation approach.

total market approach   a single marketing mix directed at the entire market for a particular product

Total Market Approach   A company that designs a single marketing mix and directs it at the entire market for a particular product is using a **total market approach** (see Figure 11.2). This approach, also known as an *undifferentiated approach*, assumes that individual customers in the target market for a specific kind of product have similar needs and, therefore, that the organization can satisfy most customers with a single marketing mix. This single marketing mix consists of one type of product with little or no variation, one price, one promotional program aimed at everyone, and one distribution system to reach all customers in the total market. Products that can be marketed successfully with the total market approach include staple food items, such as sugar and salt, and certain kinds of farm produce. A total market approach is useful only in a limited number of situations because for most product categories, buyers have different needs. When customers' needs vary, the market segmentation approach should be used.

FIGURE 11.2 General Approaches for Selecting Target Markets
The total market approach (left) assumes that individual customers have similar needs and that most customers can be satisfied with a single marketing mix. When customers' needs vary, the market segmentation (right) approach should be used.   *(Source: William M. Pride and O. C. Ferrell,* Marketing: Concepts and Strategies, *7/e. Copyright © 1991 by Houghton Mifflin Company. Used by permission.)*

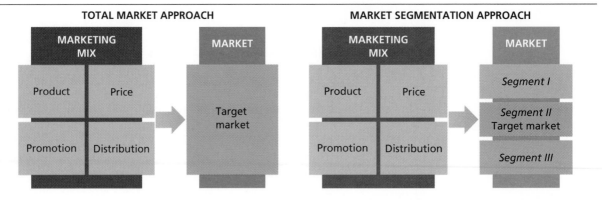

Different types of American families. When *Family Circle* began publication, everyone knew what a "family" was: mother, father, and kids. But now companies realize that they must appeal to the country's many different kinds of families. This ad implies that *Family Circle* came to this realization long ago.

We **always** knew families were

important. But we never dreamed they'd become hip.

FamilyCircle

Market Segmentation Approach   A firm that is marketing 40-foot yachts would not direct its marketing effort toward every person in the total boat market. Some might want a kayak or a canoe. Others might want a speedboat or an outboard-powered fishing boat. Still others might be looking for something resembling a small ocean liner. Marketing efforts directed toward these boat buyers would be wasted.

Instead, the firm would direct its attention toward a particular portion, or *segment*, of the total market for boats. A **market segment** is a group of individuals or organizations, within a market, that share one or more common characteristics. The process of dividing a market into segments is called **market segmentation.** As Figure 11.2 shows, a firm using this approach directs a marketing mix at a segment rather than at the total market. In our example, one common characteristic, or *basis*, for segmentation might be "end use of a boat." The firm would be interested primarily in that market segment whose uses for a boat could lead to the purchase of a 40-foot yacht. Another basis for segmentation might be income; still another might be geographic location. Each of these variables can affect the type of boat an individual might purchase. When choosing a basis for segmentation, it is important to select a characteristic that relates to differences in people's needs for a product. The yacht producer, for example, would not use religion to segment the boat market because people's needs for boats do not vary based on religion, but might use income instead.

Marketers use a wide variety of segmentation bases. Those bases most commonly applied to consumer markets are shown in Table 11.3. Each may be used as a single basis for market segmentation or in combination with other bases.

market segment   a group of individuals or organizations, within a market, that share one or more common characteristics

market segmentation   the process of dividing a market into segments and directing a marketing mix at a particular segment or segments rather than at the total market

TABLE 11.3   Common Bases of Market Segmentation

Product-Related	Demographic	Psychographic	Geographic
Volume usage	Age	Personality	Region
End use	Sex	attributes	Urban, suburban,
Benefit	Race	Motives	rural
expectations	Nationality	Lifestyles	Market density
Brand loyalty	Income		Climate
Price sensitivity	Educational level		Terrain
	Occupation		
	Family size		
	Religion		
	Home ownership		
	Social class		

Source: Adapted from William M. Pride and O. C. Ferrell, *Marketing: Concepts and Strategies,* 7/e. Copyright © 1991 by Houghton Mifflin Company. Used by permission.

Creating a Marketing Mix

LEARNING OBJECTIVE 4
Identify the four elements of the marketing mix and be aware of their importance in developing a marketing strategy.

A business firm controls four important elements of marketing—elements it must combine in such a way as to reach its target market. These are the *product* itself, the *price* of the product, the means chosen for its *distribution,* and the *promotion* of the product. When combined, these four elements form a marketing mix (see the circular area in Figure 11.3).

A firm can vary its marketing mix by changing any one or more of these ingredients. Thus a firm may use one marketing mix to reach one target market and a second, somewhat different marketing mix, to reach another target market. For example, most automakers produce several different types of vehicles and aim them at different market segments based on age and income.

The *product* ingredient of the marketing mix includes decisions about the product's design, brand name, packaging, warranties, and the like. Thus, when McDonald's Corp. decides on brand names, package designs, sizes of orders, flavors of sauces, and recipes, these are all part of the product ingredient.

The *pricing* ingredient is concerned with both base prices and discounts of various kinds. Pricing decisions are intended to achieve particular goals, such as to maximize profit or even to make room for new models. The rebates offered by automobile manufacturers are a pricing strategy developed to boost low auto sales. Product and pricing are discussed in detail in Chapter 12.

The *distribution* ingredient involves not only transportation and storage but also the selection of intermediaries. How many levels of intermediaries should be used in the distribution of a particular product? Should the product be distributed as widely as possible? Or should distribution be restricted to a few specialized outlets in each area? These and other questions related to distribution are considered in Chapter 13.

The *promotion* ingredient focuses on providing information to target markets. The major forms of promotion include advertising, personal selling, sales promotion, and publicity. These four forms are discussed in Chapter 14.

The "ingredients" of the marketing mix are controllable elements. A firm can vary each of them to suit its organizational goals, marketing goals, and target markets. As we extend our discussion of marketing strategy, we will see that the marketing environment includes a number of *uncontrollable* elements.

Marketing Strategy and the Marketing Environment

LEARNING OBJECTIVE 5
Explain how the marketing environment affects strategic market planning.

The marketing mix consists of elements that a firm controls and uses to reach its target market. In addition, the firm has control over such organizational resources as finances and information. These resources, too, may be used to accomplish marketing goals. However, the firm's marketing activities are also affected by a number of external—and generally uncontrollable—forces. As Figure 11.3 illustrates, the forces that make up the external *marketing environment* are:

- *Economic forces*—the effects of economic conditions on customers' ability and willingness to buy
- *Legal forces*—the laws enacted either to protect consumers or to preserve a competitive atmosphere in the marketplace
- *Societal forces*—consumers' social and cultural values, the consumer movement, and environmental concerns

FIGURE 11.3
The Marketing Mix and the Marketing Environment
The marketing mix consists of elements that the firm controls—product, price, physical distribution, and promotion. The firm generally has no control over the external marketing environment. *(Source: Adapted from William M. Pride and O. C. Ferrell,* Marketing: Concepts and Strategies, *7/e. Copyright © 1991 by Houghton Mifflin Company. Used by permission.)*

GLOBAL PERSPECTIVES
MTV Rocks Around the World

By the mid-1980s, cable television was as comfortable in American living rooms as the couch, and MTV was one of its most successful channels. In 53 million U.S. homes, pop music fans—mostly 16 to 34 years old—were tuning in to see and hear superstars like Madonna, Michael Jackson, and Bruce Springsteen. Viacom International Inc., owner of MTV, was thanking the music video channel for about 20 percent of its $1.4 billion in revenue. In the last few years, however, the number of American MTV viewers has not grown at the breakneck speed of the early days. Hoping to attract new audiences while holding on to its loyal market, MTV is concentrating on global expansion. MTV's goal, says the network's CEO, is to be in every home in the world.

MTV's first experiment with foreign licensing was in Japan. At that time, company executives weren't tuned in to overseas expansion and weren't paying much attention to what their Japanese affiliate was doing. However, when one MTV executive saw some Japanese tapes, she decided that they didn't look trendy and sophisticated enough for the MTV image. She negotiated a new deal giving the network tighter quality control and then went on to license MTV in Europe, South America, and Australia. Today, about 200 million fans in about thirty-eight countries enjoy the latest pop videos from around the world.

Like executives at MTV, cable mogul Ted Turner broadcasts his Cable News Network (CNN) all over the world. Unlike MTV, CNN's telecasts are all in English, directed mainly at American travelers, from Toronto to Tokyo. MTV's approach to globalization is more in line with the views of its vice president for new business development. She believes that if MTV is to be successful in business outside of the United States, it needs to be sensitive to other countries' cultures, responding to their musical styles and tastes. Although every broadcast must look like the American MTV, foreign networks employ native video jockeys who highlight locally popular stars. Japanese MTV focused on Japanese and international artists, and the commentary was almost totally in Japanese. On MTV Europe, English is the language of choice, but many of the videos are of European and other international musicians. In Europe, MTV believes it can link its twenty-five-country market with music instead of language.

Recognized as the leading expert on pop music in the United States, MTV wants to become the authority on youth culture all over the world. In this way, insist network executives, MTV will convince record companies that it can launch artists on a worldwide scale, add to its list of international advertisers, like Nike, Levi Strauss, and Fruit of the Loom, and keep hungry competitors like The Jukebox Network at bay.

You can grab it, but you can't shake it.

- *Competitive forces*—the actions of competitors, which are in the process of implementing their own marketing plans
- *Political forces*—government regulations and policies that affect marketing, whether they are directed specifically at marketing or not
- *Technological forces*—in particular, technological changes that can cause a product (or an industry) to become obsolete almost overnight

These forces influence decisions about marketing-mix ingredients. Changes in the environment can have a major impact on existing marketing strategies. In addition, changes in environmental forces may lead to abrupt shifts in the needs of people in the target market.

Strategic Market Planning

The development of a marketing strategy begins with an assessment of the marketing environment. Marketers should gather and analyze all available information concerning the marketing environment, the effectiveness of previous marketing programs or strategies, the firm's present and potential markets and their needs, and the availability of resources. Obviously, marketing research and the firm's system for managing its marketing information play an important role in this first stage of the planning process.

Next, the organization should formulate particular and detailed marketing objectives. These objectives should be consistent with organizational goals. They must also be measurable and realistic—in line with both the marketing situation and available resources.

Then a target market must be selected, and a marketing mix must be designed to reach that market. Here, product, pricing, distribution, and promotional decisions need to be coordinated to produce a unified mix. As we have noted, the marketing strategy must be designed to operate effectively in the dynamic marketing environment.

Finally, the organization must evaluate the performance of its marketing strategy. Both marketing research and the marketing information system come into play as monitoring tools. The information that is obtained should be used to evaluate the strategy and modify it as necessary. This information should also be used to begin the next round of market planning.

MARKET MEASUREMENT AND SALES FORECASTING

LEARNING OBJECTIVE 6
Describe how market measurement and sales forecasting are used.

Measuring the sales potential for specific types of market segments helps an organization make some important decisions. It can evaluate the feasibility of entering new segments. The organization can also decide how best to allocate its marketing resources and activities among market segments in which it is already active. All such estimates should identify the relevant time frame. Short-range estimates cover periods of less than one year; medium-range estimates, one to five years; and long-range estimates, more than five years. The estimates should also define the geographic boundaries of the forecast. For example, sales potential can be estimated for a city, county, state, or group of nations. Finally, analysts should indicate whether their estimates are for a specific product item, a product line, or an entire product category.

sales forecast   an estimate of the amount of a product that an organization expects to sell during a certain period of time, based on a specified level of marketing effort

A company **sales forecast** is an estimate of the amount of a product that an organization expects to sell during a certain period of time, based on a specified level of marketing effort. Managers in different divisions of the organization rely on sales forecasts when they purchase raw materials, schedule production, secure financial resources, consider plant or equipment purchases, hire personnel, and plan inventory levels. Since the accuracy of a sales forecast is so important, organizations often use several forecasting methods, including executive judgments, surveys of buyers or sales personnel, time series analyses, correlation analyses, and market tests. The specific methods used depend on the cost involved, type of product, characteristics of the market, time span of the forecast, purposes for which the forecast is used, stability of historical sales data, availability of the required information, and expertise and experience of forecasters.

MARKETING INFORMATION

LEARNING OBJECTIVE 7
Distinguish between a marketing information system and marketing research.

Accurate and timely information is the foundation of effective marketing—and, in particular, of the marketing concept. A wealth of marketing information is available, both within the firm and from outside sources, but this information must be gathered, analyzed, and put to use by marketing personnel.

There are two general approaches to collecting marketing information. A marketing information system provides information on a continuing basis, whereas marketing research offers information for specific marketing projects.

Marketing Information Systems

marketing information system   a system for managing marketing information that is gathered continually from internal and external sources

A **marketing information system** is a system for managing marketing information that is gathered continually from internal and external sources. Most systems are computer-based because of the amount of data that the system must accept, store, sort, and retrieve. *Continual* collection of data is essential if the system is to incorporate the most up-to-date information.

In concept, the operation of a marketing information system is not complex. Data from a variety of sources are fed into the system. Data from *internal* sources include sales figures, product and marketing costs, inventory levels, and activities of the sales force. Data from *external* sources relate to the firm's suppliers, intermediaries, and customers; competitors' marketing activities; and economic conditions. All these data are stored and processed within the marketing information system. Its output is a flow of information in the form that is most useful for marketing decision making. This information might include daily sales reports by territory and product, forecasts of sales or buying trends, and reports on changes in market share for the major brands in a specific industry. Both the information outputs and their form depend on the requirements of the personnel in the organization.

Marketing Research

marketing research   the process of systematically gathering, recording, and analyzing data concerning a particular marketing problem

Marketing research is the process of systematically gathering, recording, and analyzing data concerning a particular marketing problem. Thus marketing research is used in specific situations to obtain information that is not otherwise available to decision makers. It is an intermittent, rather than a continual, source of marketing information.

A six-step procedure for conducting marketing research is given in Table 11.4. This procedure is particularly well suited to testing new products, determining various characteristics of consumer markets, and

TABLE 11.4   The Six Steps of Marketing Research

1. Define the problem	In this step, the problem is clearly and accurately stated to determine what issues are involved in the research, what questions to ask, and what types of solutions are needed. This is a crucial step that should not be rushed.
2. Make a preliminary investigation	The objective of preliminary investigation is to develop both a sharper definition of the problem and a set of tentative answers. The tentative answers are developed by examining internal information and published data, and by talking with persons who have some experience with the problem. These answers will be tested by further research.
3. Plan the research	At this stage researchers know what facts are needed to resolve the identified problem and what facts are available. They make plans on how to gather needed but missing data.
4. Gather factual information	Once the basic research plan has been completed, the needed information can be collected by mail, telephone, or personal interviews; by observation; or from commercial or government data sources. The choice depends on the plan and the available sources of information.
5. Interpret the information	Facts by themselves do not always provide a sound solution to a marketing problem. They must be interpreted and analyzed to determine the choices that are available to management.
6. Reach a conclusion	Sometimes the conclusion or recommendation becomes obvious when the facts are interpreted. However, in other cases, reaching a conclusion may not be so easy because of gaps in the information or intangible factors that are difficult to evaluate. If and when the evidence is less than complete, it is important to say so.

Source: Adapted from Small Business Administration (Washington, D.C.), *Small Business Bibliography No. 9.*

Nick knows kids. That's the message that Nickelodeon sells to advertisers, and the numbers back the claim. The cable TV network knows what it wants to provide—shows that can let kids be kids, escaping adult worries. To help it create the right programs, it calls on its experts—focus groups of kids who brainstorm ideas and sometimes critique shows all during their development.

evaluating promotional activities. General Foods Corporation makes extensive use of marketing research—in the form of taste tests—to determine whether proposed new products will appeal to consumers.

TYPES OF BUYING BEHAVIOR

buying behavior   the decisions and actions of people involved in buying and using products

consumer buying behavior the purchasing of products for personal or household use, not for business purposes

organizational buying behavior   the purchasing of products by producers, resellers, governmental units, and institutions

Buying behavior may be defined as the decisions and actions of people involved in buying and using products.[3] **Consumer buying behavior** refers to the purchasing of products for personal or household use, not for business purposes. **Organizational buying behavior** is the purchasing of products by producers, resellers, governmental units, and institutions. Since a firm's success depends greatly on buyers' reactions to a particular marketing strategy, it is important to understand buying behavior. Marketing managers are better able to predict consumer responses to marketing strategies and to develop a satisfying marketing mix if they are aware of the factors that affect buying behavior.

Consumer Buying Behavior

LEARNING OBJECTIVE 8
Identify several factors that may influence buying behavior.

Consumers' buying behaviors differ when they buy different types of products. For frequently purchased, low-cost items, a consumer employs routine response behavior, involving very little search or decision-making effort. The buyer uses limited decision making for purchases made occasionally or when more information is needed about an unknown product in a well-known product category. When buying an unfamiliar, expensive item or one that is seldom purchased, the consumer engages in extensive decision making.

A person deciding on a purchase goes through some or all of the steps shown in Figure 11.4. First, the consumer acknowledges that a problem exists. Then the buyer looks for information, which may include brand names, product characteristics, warranties, and other features. Next, the buyer weighs the various alternatives he or she has discovered and then finally makes a choice and acquires the item. In the after-purchase stage, the consumer evaluates the suitability of the product. This judgment will affect future purchases. As Figure 11.4 shows, the buying process is influenced by person-specific factors (demographic, situational), psychological factors (perception, motives, learning, attitudes, personality), and social factors (family, roles, peer groups, social class, culture and subculture).

Organizational-Buying Behavior

Organizational buyers consider a product's quality, its price, and the service provided by suppliers. Organizational buyers are usually better informed than consumers about the products they buy and generally buy in larger quantities. In an organization, a committee or group of people,

FIGURE 11.4 Consumer Buying Decision Process and Possible Influences on the Process
A buyer goes through some or all of these steps when making a purchase.   *(Source: Adapted from William M. Pride and O. C. Ferrell,* Marketing: Concepts and Strategies, 7/e. *Copyright © 1991 by Houghton Mifflin Company. Used by permission.)*

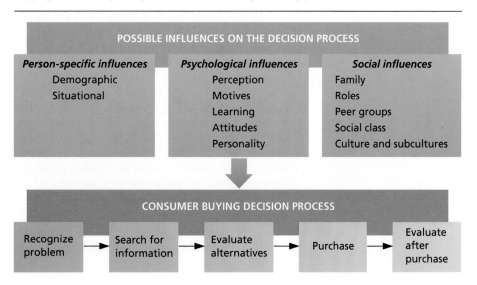

rather than single individuals, often decide on purchases. Committee members must consider the organization's objectives, purchasing policies, resources, and personnel. Organizational buying occurs through description, inspection, sampling, or negotiation.

THE AMERICAN CONSUMER

In this section we examine several measures of consumer income, a major source of buying power. By looking at why, what, where, and when consumers buy, we explain how this income is spent. Our focus then shifts to socioeconomic trends that influence consumption patterns and marketing activities.

Consumer Income

personal income   the income an individual receives from all sources *less* the Social Security taxes the individual must pay

disposable income   personal income *less* all additional personal taxes

discretionary income   disposable income *less* savings and expenditures on food, clothing, and housing

Purchasing power is created by income. However, as every taxpayer knows, not all income is available for spending. For this reason, marketers consider income in three different ways: **Personal income** is the income an individual receives from all sources *less* the Social Security taxes the individual must pay. **Disposable income** is personal income *less* all additional personal taxes. These taxes include income, estate, gift, and property taxes levied by local, state, and federal governments. About 5 percent of all disposable income is saved. **Discretionary income** is disposable income *less* savings and expenditures on food, clothing, and housing. Discretionary income is of particular interest to marketers because consumers have the most choice in spending it. Consumers use their discretionary income to purchase items ranging from automobiles and vacations to movies and pet food.

Of the households headed by a person with five or more years of college education, the average discretionary income is $18,250 per year. Among married couples with both spouses working, the discretionary income averages $13,300 per household.[4]

Why Do Consumers Buy?

Consumers buy with the hope of getting a large amount of current and future satisfaction relative to their buying power. Consumers buy because they would rather have a particular good or service than the money they have to spend to buy it! Several major reasons that consumers may choose to buy a given product are:

1. *They have a use for the product.* Many items fill an immediate "use" need. A kitchen needs pots and pans; a student needs books.

2. *They like the convenience a product offers.* Such items as electric can openers and ice crushers are not essential, but they offer convenience and thus satisfaction.

3. *They believe the purchase will enhance their wealth.* People collect antiques or gold coins as investments as well as for enjoyment. Home owners buy aluminum siding, awnings, and fences to add to the value of their property.

4. *They take pride in ownership.* Many consumers purchase items such as a compact disc player or a gold Rolex watch because such products provide status and pride of ownership as well as utility.

5. *They buy for safety.* Consumers buy health, life, and fire insurance to protect themselves and their families. Smoke detectors, automatic appliance timers, traveler's checks, and similar products also provide safety and protection.

What Do Consumers Buy?

Figure 11.5 shows how consumer spending is divided among various categories of products and services. The average American household spent $27,370 in 1990, according to the latest available data from the Bureau of Labor Statistics. As we have noted, the greatest proportion of disposable income is spent on food, clothing, and shelter. The largest share—$8,521—

FIGURE 11.5
Consumer Spending
What percentage of disposable income is spent on various categories of products and services? *(Source: U.S. Department of Labor, Bureau of Statistics,* Consumer Expenditure Survey, *Third Quarter, 1990; Reprinted by permission of* Wall Street Journal, *©1989, Dow Jones & Company, Inc. All Rights Reserved Worldwide.)*

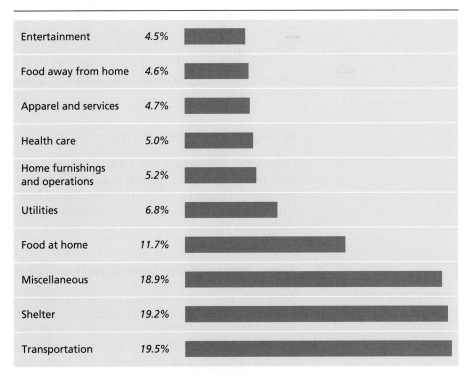

Entertainment	4.5%
Food away from home	4.6%
Apparel and services	4.7%
Health care	5.0%
Home furnishings and operations	5.2%
Utilities	6.8%
Food at home	11.7%
Miscellaneous	18.9%
Shelter	19.2%
Transportation	19.5%

went toward housing and related expenses, such as taxes and furnishings. The second-largest expense was transportation, with families spending an average of $5,337 on cars and other vehicles, insurance, repairs, and public transportation. The average household spent $4,453 on food, including $3,202 to eat at home. Clothing and related services, such as dry cleaning, used up $1,274. Another $1,242 went toward entertainment, and slightly more than $1,358 was spent on health care.[5] (A mere 1 percent of total disposable income amounts to around $30 billion. Thus none of the categories in Figure 11.5 is really small in terms of total dollars spent.)

Where Do Consumers Buy?

Probably the most important factor that influences a consumer's decision about where to buy a particular product is his or her perception of the store. Consumers' general impressions of an establishment's products, prices, and sales personnel can mean the difference between repeat sales and lost business. Consumers distinguish among various types of retail outlets (such as specialty shops, department stores, and discount outlets), and they choose particular types of stores for specific purchases.

Many retail outlets go to a great deal of trouble to build and maintain a particular "image." Products that do not fit the image are not carried. For example, at today's Tiffany & Co. image is everything. When Avon Products, Inc. owned Tiffany from 1979 to 1984, customers were shocked to see cheap glassware and crystal on display. Avon's mismarketing destroyed the once-renowned Tiffany's image and resulted in a $5 million loss in 1984. Today, with new ownership, Tiffany is again selling necklaces worth $7 million, and the Tiffany magic has been recaptured. For fiscal 1991, Tiffany's earnings had climbed to over $36 million.

Consumers also select the businesses they patronize on the basis of location, product assortment, and such services as credit terms, return privileges, and free delivery.

When Do Consumers Buy?

In general, consumers buy when buying is most convenient. Certain business hours have long been standard for establishments that sell consumer products. However, many of these establishments have stretched their hours to include evenings and Sundays. Ultimately, within each area, the consumers themselves control when they do their buying.

Some Noteworthy Demographic Trends

LEARNING OBJECTIVE 10
Understand the marketing implications of several socio-economic changes occurring in the United States.

American consumers are an especially dynamic group. They change their jobs and places of residence, their attitudes, and their lifestyles at a rate that would be alarming in most other countries. Marketers, of course, must keep up with these changes. A shift in population from the cold North to the warm South and Southwest, for example, affects both the marketing

Product and Price

CHAPTER PREVIEW

We look first in this chapter at products. We examine product classifications and describe the four stages, or life cycle, through which every product moves. Next, we illustrate how firms manage products effectively by modifying or deleting existing products and by developing new products. Branding, packaging, and labeling of products are also discussed. Then our focus shifts to pricing. We explain competitive factors that influence sellers' pricing decisions and also explore buyers' perceptions of prices. After considering organizational objectives that can be accomplished through pricing, we outline several methods for setting prices. Finally, we describe pricing strategies by which sellers can reach target markets successfully.

Healthy Choice Snatches a Healthy Market Share

After Mike Harper, CEO of ConAgra, had a heart attack in 1985, his doctors put him on a strict diet. When he complained that all of the healthier prepared foods tasted terrible, his wife whipped him up a bowl of spicy, low-fat, low-salt turkey chili. Some ConAgra managers came to the Harper's for dinner, tried it, and insisted there was a market for flavorful healthy food like that. In 1989, after several years of research and kitchen testing, ConAgra launched Healthy Choice, a line of healthy frozen dinners. Before its sleepy rivals at Kraft General Foods, Inc., Campbell Soup Company, or Stouffer Foods could wake up, Healthy Choice had grabbed 18 percent of the $2.5 billion premium-frozen-dinner market and walked off with an American Marketing Association Edison award for one of the year's best new products.

While Healthy Choice rose to the top, sales of Weight Watcher's frozen dinners slid 30 percent, and Le Menu Healthy sank almost out of sight. How has this product done so well in a slow-growth industry whose shoppers are less brand loyal and more price conscious? In the beginning, ConAgra paid retailers slotting fees to carry its new brand; it continues to trade significant discounts for shelf space. With a $25.7 million ad budget, Healthy Choice dwarfs its competitors' spending. By capitalizing on its premium image with trendy green-and-black packaging and haute cuisine offerings like Dijon chicken and apples in spiced raisin sauce, Healthy Choice attracts upscale customers willing to pay premium prices. Most important for the product's success was ConAgra executives' timely recognition that Americans are becoming more concerned with eating healthy than with losing pounds. By identifying changing consumer concerns before its competitors, Healthy Choice got a jump start in a race it is still winning.

Like the hare in the famous fable, though, Healthy Choice cannot afford to nap while its competitors keep running. Campbell Soup Company recently changed the name of its Le Menu Light Side line to "Le Menu Healthy," increased brand spending by $5 million, and offered a money-back taste test guarantee on one of its entrees. H. J. Heinz's Weight Watchers is launching new frozen items like frosted brownies and bagel breakfast sandwiches, promoting "everyday low prices" on some of its supermarket offerings, and experimenting with selling entrees and breakfast items at some Miami Burger King franchises. Number-one food marketer Kraft General Foods is testing a line of healthier frozen meals, soups, and dairy products called Kraft Alternatives, complete with suspiciously familiar green packaging.

To help make sure that industry analysts are correct in their predictions that sales of Healthy Choice will reach $1 billion in a few years, ConAgra plans to introduce hundreds of new products. Shoppers will soon see Healthy Choice 96 percent lean hamburger, Healthy Choice French bread frozen pizza, and lower-priced Banquet Healthy Balance, featuring down-to-earth items like Salisbury steak and mashed potatoes.[1]

product everything that one receives in an exchange, including all tangible and intangible attributes and expected benefits; it may be a good, service, or idea

A **product** is everything that one receives in an exchange, including all tangible and intangible attributes and expected benefits. A Healthy Choice meal, for example, includes not only a tasty meal, but also a plate and a box with nutritional information and cooking instructions. A car includes a warranty, owner's manual, and perhaps free emergency road service for a year. Some of the intangibles that may go with an automobile include the status associated with ownership and the memories generated from past rides. Developing and managing products effectively is crucial to an organization's ability to maintain successful marketing mixes.

As we noted in Chapter 1, a product may be a good, service, or idea. A *good* is a real, physical thing that we can touch, such as a Healthy Choice meal. A *service* is the result of applying human or mechanical effort to a person or thing. Basically, a service is a change we pay others to make for us. A real estate agent's services result in a change in the ownership of real property. A barber's services result in a change in one's appearance. An idea may take the form of philosophies, lessons, concepts, or advice. Often, ideas are included with a good or service. Thus we might buy a book (a good) that provides ideas on how to lose weight. Or we might join Weight Watchers, for both ideas on how to lose weight and help (services) in doing so.

Our definition of the term *product* is based on the concept of an exchange. In a purchase, the thing that is exchanged for the product is money—an amount of money equal to the *price* of the product. When the product is a good, the price may include such services as delivery, installation, warranties, and training. A good *with* such services is not the same product as the good *without* such services. In other words, sellers set a price for a particular "package" of goods, services, and ideas. When the makeup of that package changes, the price should change as well.

CLASSIFICATION OF PRODUCTS

LEARNING OBJECTIVE 1
Explain what a product is and how products are classified.

Different classes of products are directed at particular target markets. A product's classification largely determines what kinds of distribution, promotion, and pricing are appropriate in marketing the product.

Products can be grouped into two general categories—consumer and industrial. A product purchased to satisfy personal and family needs is a **consumer product.** A product bought for use in a firm's operations or to make other products is an **industrial product.** The buyer's intent—or the ultimate use of the product—determines the classification of an item. Note that a single item can be both a consumer and an industrial product. A broom is a consumer product if you use it in your home. However, the same broom is an industrial product if you use it in the maintenance of your business. After a product is classified as a consumer or industrial product, it can be further categorized as a particular type of consumer or industrial product.

consumer product   a product purchased to satisfy personal and family needs

industrial product   a product bought for use in a firm's operations or to make other products

Consumer Product Classifications

The traditional and most widely accepted system of classifying consumer products consists of three categories: convenience, shopping, and specialty products. These groupings are based primarily on characteristics of buyers' purchasing behavior.

A **convenience product** is a relatively inexpensive, frequently purchased item for which buyers want to exert only minimal effort. Examples include bread, gasoline, newspapers, soft drinks, and chewing gum. The buyer spends little time in planning the purchase of a convenience item or in comparing available brands or sellers.

convenience product   a relatively inexpensive, frequently purchased item for which buyers want to exert only minimal effort

A **shopping product** is an item for which buyers are willing to expend considerable effort on planning and making the purchase. Buyers allocate ample time for comparing stores and brands with respect to prices, product features, qualities, services, and perhaps warranties. Appliances, upholstered furniture, men's suits, bicycles, and stereos are examples of shopping products. These products are expected to last for a fairly long time and thus are purchased less frequently than convenience items.

shopping product   an item for which buyers are willing to expend considerable effort on planning and making the purchase

A **specialty product** possesses one or more unique characteristics for which a significant group of buyers is willing to expend considerable purchasing effort. Buyers actually plan the purchase of a specialty product; they know exactly what they want and will not accept a substitute. In searching for specialty products, purchasers do not compare alternatives. Examples include unique sports cars, a specific type of antique dining table, a rare imported beer, or perhaps special handcrafted stereo speakers.

specialty product   an item that possesses one or more unique characteristics for which a significant group of buyers is willing to expend considerable purchasing effort

One problem with this approach to classification is that buyers may behave differently when purchasing a specific type of product. Thus, a single product can fit into more than one category. To minimize this problem, marketers think in terms of how buyers are most likely to behave when purchasing a specific item.

Industrial Product Classifications

Based on their characteristics and intended uses, industrial products can be classified into the following categories: raw materials, major equipment, accessory equipment, component parts, process materials, supplies, and services.

A slow start. Getting a new product onto the market and earning a profit is more difficult than it might appear. Joseph Wentzell invented a new product to fill a huge need. It's an environmentally safe paint that prevents barnacles and mussels from growing on things in the water. But it has taken Wentzell and his partner years to get EPA approval and financial backing for a product that could make millions.

---

raw material   a basic material that actually becomes part of a physical product; usually comes from mines, forests, oceans, or recycled solid wastes

major equipment   large tools and machines used for production purposes

accessory equipment   standardized equipment used in a variety of ways in a firm's production or office activities

component part   an item that becomes part of a physical product and is either a finished item ready for assembly or a product that needs little processing before assembly

process material   a material that is used directly in the production of another product and is not readily identifiable in the finished product

supply   an item that facilitates production and operations but does not become part of the finished product

A **raw material** is a basic material that actually becomes part of a physical product. It usually comes from mines, forests, oceans, or recycled solid wastes. Raw materials are usually bought and sold according to grades and specifications.

Major equipment includes large tools and machines used for production purposes. Examples of major equipment are lathes, cranes, and stamping machines. Some major equipment is custom-made for a particular organization, but other items are standardized products that perform one or several tasks for many types of organizations.

Accessory equipment is standardized equipment that generally can be used in several ways within a firm's production or office activities. Examples include hand tools, typewriters, fractional-horsepower motors, and calculators. Compared with major equipment, accessory items are usually much less expensive and are purchased routinely with less negotiation.

A **component part** becomes part of a physical product and is either a finished item ready for assembly or a product that needs little processing before assembly. Although it becomes part of a larger product, a component part can often be identified easily. Clocks, tires, and switches are examples of component parts.

A **process material** is used directly in the production of another product; unlike a component part, however, a process material is not readily identifiable. Like component parts, process materials are purchased according to industry standards or to the specifications of the individual purchaser. Examples include industrial glue and food preservatives.

A **supply** facilitates production and operations, but it does not become part of the finished product. Paper, pencils, oils, and cleaning agents are examples.

industrial service   an intangible product that an organization uses in its operations

An **industrial service** is an intangible product that an organization uses in its operations. Examples include financial, legal, marketing research, and janitorial services. Purchasers must decide whether to provide their own services internally or to hire them from outside the organization.

THE PRODUCT LIFE CYCLE

LEARNING OBJECTIVE 2
Discuss the product life cycle and how it leads to new-product development.

product life cycle   a series of stages in which a product's sales revenue and profit increase, reach a peak, and then decline

In a way, products are like people. They are born, they live, and they die. Every product progresses through a **product life cycle,** which is a series of stages in which its sales revenue and profit increase, reach a peak, and then decline. A firm must be able to launch, modify, and delete products from its offering of products in response to changes in product life cycles. Otherwise, the firm's profit will disappear and the firm will fail. Depending on the product, life cycle stages will vary in length. In this section, we discuss the stages of the life cycle and how marketers can use this information.

Stages of the Product Life Cycle

Generally the product life cycle is assumed to be composed of four stages—introduction, growth, maturity, and decline—as shown in Figure 12.1. Some products plunge through these stages rapidly, in a few weeks or months. Others may take years to go through each stage. The Rubicks Cube had a relatively short life cycle. Parker Brothers' *Monopoly* game, which was introduced over fifty years ago, is still going strong.

FIGURE 12.1
Product Life Cycle
The graph shows sales volume and profits during the life cycle of a product. *(Source: Adapted from William M. Pride and O. C. Ferrell,* Marketing: Concepts and Strategies, *7/e. Copyright © 1991 by Houghton Mifflin Company. Used by permission.)*

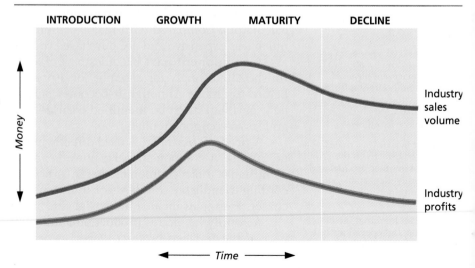

Introduction   In the *introduction stage*, customer awareness and acceptance of the product are low. Sales rise gradually as a result of promotion and distribution activities, but initially high development and marketing costs result in low profit, or even in a loss. There are relatively few competitors. The price is sometimes high, and purchasers are primarily people who want to be "the first on their block" to own the new product. The marketing challenge at this stage is to make potential customers aware of the product's existence and its features, benefits, and uses.

A new product is seldom an immediate success. Marketers must watch early buying patterns carefully and be prepared to modify the new product promptly if necessary. The product should be priced to attract the particular market segment that has the greatest desire and ability to buy the product. Plans for distribution and promotion should suit the targeted market segment. As with the product itself, the initial price, distribution channels, and promotional efforts may need to be adjusted quickly to maintain sales growth during the introduction stage.

Growth   In the *growth stage*, sales increase rapidly as the product becomes well known. Other firms have probably begun to market competing products. The competition and lower unit costs (due to mass production) result in a lower price, which reduces the profit per unit. Note that industry profits reach a peak and begin to decline during this stage. To meet the needs of the growing market, the originating firm offers modified versions of its product and expands its distribution. The 3M Company, the maker of Post-it Notes, has developed a variety of sizes, colors, and designs.

Management's goal in the growth stage is to stabilize and strengthen the product's position by encouraging brand loyalty. To beat the competition, the company may further improve the product or expand the product line to appeal to specialized market segments. Management may also compete by lowering prices if increased production efficiency has resulted in savings for the company. As the product becomes more widely accepted, marketers may be able to broaden the network of distributors. Marketers can also emphasize customer service and prompt credit for defective products. During this period promotional efforts attempt to build brand loyalty among customers.

Maturity   Sales are still increasing at the beginning of the *maturity stage*, but the rate of increase has slowed. Later in this stage the sales curve peaks and begins to decline. Industry profits decline throughout this stage. Dealers' product lines are simplified, markets are segmented more carefully, and price competition increases. The increased competition forces weaker competitors to leave the industry. Refinements and extensions of the original product appear on the market.

During a product's maturity stage, its market share may be strengthened by redesigned packaging or style changes. Also, consumers may be encouraged to use the product more often or in new ways. Pricing strategies are flexible during this stage. Markdowns and price incentives are not uncommon, although price increases to offset production and distribution costs may be used as well. Marketers may offer incentives and assistance of various kinds to dealers to encourage them to support mature products, especially in the face of competition from private-label brands. New promotional efforts and aggressive personal selling may be necessary during this period of intense competition.

Decline   During the *decline stage,* sales volume decreases sharply. Profits continue to fall. The number of competing firms declines, and the only survivors in the marketplace are those firms that specialize in marketing the product. Production and marketing costs become the most important determinant of profit.

When a product adds to the success of the overall product line, the company may retain it; otherwise, management must determine when to eliminate the product. A product usually declines because of technological advances or environmental factors, or because consumers have switched to competing brands. Therefore, few changes are made in the product itself during this stage. Instead, management may raise the price to cover costs, re-price to maintain market share, or lower the price to reduce inventory. Similarly, management will narrow distribution of the declining product to the most profitable existing markets. During this period the company will not give the product a lot of promotion, although the firm may use advertising and sales incentives to slow the product's decline. The company may choose to eliminate less profitable versions of the product from the product line and, eventually, may decide to drop the product entirely.

Using the Product Life Cycle

Marketers should be aware of the life-cycle stage of each product they are responsible for. And they should try to estimate how long the product is expected to remain in that stage. Both must be taken into account in making decisions about the marketing strategy for a product. If a product is expected to remain in the maturity stage for a long time, a replacement product might be introduced later in the maturity stage. If the maturity stage is expected to be short, however, a new product should be introduced much earlier. In some cases, a firm may be willing to take the chance of speeding up the decline of existing products. In other situations, a company will attempt to extend a product's life cycle. For example, General Mills Inc. has extended the life of Bisquick baking mix (launched in the mid-1930s) by significantly improving the product's formulation.

PRODUCT LINE AND PRODUCT MIX

LEARNING OBJECTIVE 3
Define *product line* and *product mix* and be able to distinguish between the two.

product line   a group of similar products that differ only in relatively minor characteristics

In Chapter 7, a **product line** was defined as a group of similar products that differ only in relatively minor characteristics. Generally, the products within a product line are related to each other in the way they are produced, marketed, or used. Parker Brothers, for example, manufactures and sells board games such as *Monopoly* and *Risk*, children's games such as *Winnie the Pooh*, electronic toys for children, and strategy games for adults.

Many organizations tend to introduce new products within existing product lines. This permits them to apply the experience and knowledge that they have acquired to the production and marketing of new products. However, some firms develop entirely new product lines.

product mix   all the products that a firm offers for sale

A firm's **product mix** consists of all the products that the firm offers for sale. Two "dimensions" are often applied to a firm's product mix. The *width* of the mix is a measure of the number of product lines it contains. The *depth* of the mix is a measure of the average number of individual products within each line. These are somewhat vague measures; we speak of a *broad* or a *narrow* mix, rather than a mix of exactly three or five product lines.

Many firms seek new products that will broaden their product mix, just as Mazda Motor Corporation has done with the Miata. By developing new product lines, firms gain additional experience and expertise. Moreover, firms achieve stability by operating within several different markets. Problems in one particular market do not affect a multiline firm nearly as much as they would affect a firm that depended entirely on a single product line.

MANAGING THE PRODUCT MIX

LEARNING OBJECTIVE 4
Identify the methods available for changing a product mix.

To provide products that both satisfy people in a firm's target market or markets and achieve the organization's objectives, a marketer must develop, adjust, and maintain an effective product mix. Seldom can the same product mix be effective for long. Because customers' product preferences and attitudes change, their desire for a product may dwindle or grow. In some cases, a firm needs to alter its product mix to adapt to competition. A marketer may have to eliminate a product from the mix because one or more competitors dominate that product's specific market segment. Similarly, an organization may have to introduce a new product or modify an existing one to compete more effectively. A marketer may expand the firm's product mix to take advantage of excess marketing and production capacity. For whatever reason a product mix is altered, the product mix must be managed to bring about improvements in the mix. There are three major ways to improve a product mix: change an existing product, delete a product, or develop a new product.

Changing Existing Products

product modification   the process of changing one or more of a product's characteristics

Product modification refers to changing one or more of a product's characteristics. For this approach to be effective, several conditions must be met. First, the product must be modifiable. Second, existing customers must be able to perceive that a modification has been made, assuming that

And then the fish said to himself, "Boy, I wish I had arms."

A monitor. One professional diver swims downwards to 200 meters. And features functional diver's fence and authentic there, moreover. So if you're ready to take the plunge, fasten 200-well almost all scuba of your own. Available in new black, aquamarine, red, blue, white and scuba blue. **There's a time and a Swatch for everything.**

A Swatch for all reasons. Once upon a time, a watch was a watch. You wore it everywhere but took it off when you went swimming. Now watchmakers, like Swatch, want their product mix to include a watch for every conceivable buyer and purpose—even for those rare SCUBA divers who go 200 meters deep.

product deletion   the elimination of one or more products from a product line

the modified item is still directed at them. Third, the modification should make the product more consistent with customers' desires so that it provides greater satisfaction.

Existing products can be altered in three primary ways: in quality, function, and aesthetics. *Quality modifications* are changes that relate to a product's dependability and durability and usually are achieved by alterations in the materials or production process. *Functional modifications* affect a product's versatility, effectiveness, convenience, or safety; they usually require redesign of the product. Typical product categories that have undergone extensive functional modifications include home appliances, office and farm equipment, and consumer electronics. *Aesthetic modifications* are directed at changing the sensory appeal of a product by altering its taste, texture, sound, smell, or visual characteristics. Since a buyer's purchasing decision is affected by how a product looks, smells, tastes, feels, or sounds, an aesthetic modification may have a definite impact on purchases. Through aesthetic modifications, a firm can differentiate its product from competing brands and perhaps gain a sizable market share if customers find the modified product more appealing.

Deleting Products

To maintain an effective product mix, an organization often has to eliminate some products. This is called **product deletion.** A weak product costs a firm too much time, money, and resources that could be available for modifying other products or developing new ones. Also, when a weak product generates an unfavorable image among customers, the negative ideas may rub off on other products sold by the firm.

Most organizations find it difficult to delete a product. Some firms drop weak products only after they have become severe financial burdens. A better approach is some form of systematic review of the product's impact on the overall effectiveness of a firm's product mix. Such a review should analyze a product's contribution to a company's sales for a given period. It should include estimates of future sales, costs, and profits associated with the product and a consideration of whether changes in the marketing strategy could improve the product's performance.

A product deletion program can definitely improve a firm's performance. For example, Del Monte once claimed that it had the largest assortment of canned fruits and vegetables nationally. The company recently deleted a number of items that were not achieving adequate sales and profits.

Developing New Products

Developing and introducing new products is frequently time-consuming, expensive, and risky. Thousands of new products are introduced annually. Depending on how one defines it, the failure rate for new products ranges between 60 and 75 percent. Although developing new products is risky, failing to introduce new products can also present hazards. New products are generally grouped into three categories on the basis of their degree of similarity to existing products. *Imitations* are products that are designed to

GLOBAL PERSPECTIVES
Nestlé and Coca-Cola Brew Up a Joint Venture

Recent statistics show that competitors are creeping up on number-one food company, Nestlé. Number-two Unilever and number-three Philip Morris Incorporated are growing faster than the Swiss-based firm. To hold its position, the company is teaming up with American firms to develop and market new product lines. Recently, Nestlé joined forces with Coca-Cola to sell hot and cold canned coffee in Korea. Nestlé is providing coffee-making expertise and globally famous brand names, and Coca-Cola is providing its awesome number-one worldwide distribution system. Hoping to persuade Koreans that coffee is a tasty alternative to soft drinks, these two corporate giants each contributed $100 million to form the Coca-Cola Nestlé Refreshments Company.

In Korea, the canned coffee market is still small, representing only 3 percent of soft drinks sold. Dongsuh Foods Corporation, a joint venture between a Korean food company and Kraft General Foods, Inc. introduced canned coffee in Korea in 1985, and Korea's largest soft-drink company recently came out with canned coffee under the brand Let's Be. Coca-Cola Nestlé Refreshments is not afraid to take on these competitors, confident that being innovative will help them grab market share. Almost 3,000 vending machines all over Seoul will make hot and cold Nescafé easy to find.

The company is dispensing "warming boxes" to all stores carrying the product so that customers can go up to the counter and heat up a can if they want hot coffee instead of cold. Executives believe that offering a choice between hot and cold coffee at the same location, a service rivals don't provide, gives their product the edge.

When the coffee cans appear on Korean grocery shelves, they will have Nestlé's name on them, but not Coca-Cola's. Shoppers can get either regular or rich—which contains more milk—at less than half the price they would pay for a cup of coffee at a restaurant. Differing from other American products advertised on Korean television, Nescafé's ads incorporate traditional Korean music.

If Coca-Cola Nestlé Refreshments is successful in Korea, coffee drinkers will be likely to see canned Nescafé in the United States, Europe, and other parts of Asia, but not in Japan. In that country, where canned coffee is a $5.6 billion business, the two companies are going it alone. Since 1975, Coca-Cola has marketed "Georgia" ready-to-drink coffee in cans in Japan. Nestlé distributes ready-to-drink Nescafé, the number-two seller in Japan, in conjunction with a Japanese partner. In a market where the average Japanese citizen drinks about eight hundred cups of coffee each year, there is probably room for everyone.

be similar to—and to compete with—existing products of other firms. Examples are the various brands of fluoride toothpaste that were developed to compete with Crest. *Adaptations* are variations of existing products that are intended for an established market. Caffeine-free, diet soft drinks are product adaptations. The product refinements and extensions discussed in Chapter 7 are most often considered adaptations, although imitative products may also include some refinement and extension. *Innovations* are entirely new products. They may give rise to a new industry (such as xerography or television) or revolutionize an existing one. The introduction of sound tracks, for example, permanently changed the motion picture industry. Similarly, compact discs have brought major changes to the recording industry. Innovative products take considerable time, effort, and money to develop. They are therefore less common than adaptations and imitations.

quality for a lower price. However, generic products are not necessarily lower in quality. Even though generic brands may have accounted for as much as 10 percent of all grocery sales several years ago, they currently represent less than 1 percent.

Choosing and Protecting a Brand

A number of issues should be considered when selecting a brand name. The name should be easy for customers to say, spell, and recall. Short, one-syllable names such as *Tide* often satisfy this requirement. The brand name should suggest, in a positive way, the product's uses, special characteristics and major benefits and should be distinctive enough to set it apart from competing brands. Choosing the right brand name has become a challenge because many obvious product names have already been used. In 1990, the U.S. Patent and Trademark office registered 56,515 new trademarks, three-and-one-half-times the number registered in 1980.

It is important to select a brand that can be protected through registration, reserving it for exclusive use by a specific firm. Some brands, because of their designs, are more easily infringed on than others. Although registration protects trademarks domestically for ten years and can be renewed indefinitely, a firm should develop a system for ensuring that its trademarks will be renewed as needed. To protect its exclusive right to the brand, the company must ensure that the selected brand will not be considered an infringement on any existing brand already registered with the U.S. Patent and Trademark Office. This task may be complicated by the fact that infringement is determined by the courts, which base their decisions on whether a brand causes consumers to be confused, mistaken, or deceived about the source of the product.

A firm must guard against a brand name becoming a generic term that refers to a general category. Generic terms cannot be protected as exclusive brand names. For example, names such as *yo-yo, aspirin, escalator,* and *thermos*—all brand names at one time—were eventually declared generic terms that refer to product classes. As such, they could no longer be protected. To ensure that a brand name does not become a generic term, the firm should spell the name with a capital letter and use it as an adjective to modify the name of the general product class, as in Jell-o Brand Gelatin. An organization can deal directly with this problem by advertising that its brand is a trademark and should not be used generically. Firms can also use the registered trademark symbol ® to indicate that the brand is trademarked.

Branding Strategies

The basic branding decision for any firm—producer or seller—is whether to brand its products. A producer may market its products under its own brands, private brands, or both. A seller (store) may carry only producer brands, its own brands, or both. Once either type of firm decides to brand, it chooses one of two branding strategies: individual branding or family branding.

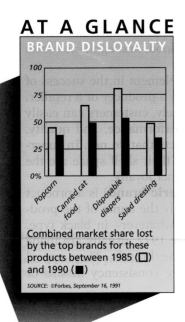

AT A GLANCE
BRAND DISLOYALTY

100
75
50
25
0%

Popcorn
Canned cat food
Disposable diapers
Salad dressing

Combined market share lost by the top brands for these products between 1985 (☐) and 1990 (■)

SOURCE: ©Forbes, September 16, 1991

individual branding   the strategy in which a firm uses a different brand for each of its products

Individual branding is the strategy in which a firm uses a different brand for each of its products. For example, Procter & Gamble uses individual branding for its line of bar soaps, which includes Ivory, Camay, Lava, Zest, Safeguard, and Coast. Individual branding offers two major advantages. A problem with one product will not affect the good name of the firm's other products. And the different brands can be directed toward different segments of the market. For example, Holiday Inns' Hampton Inns are directed toward budget-minded travelers, Residence Inns toward apartment dwellers, and Crown Plazas toward upscale customers.

family branding   the strategy in which a firm uses the same brand for all or most of its products

Family branding is the strategy in which a firm uses the same brand for all or most of its products. Sunbeam, General Electric, IBM, and Xerox use family branding for their entire product mix. A major advantage of family branding is that the promotion of any one item that carries the family brand tends to help all other products with the same brand name. In addition, new products have a head start when their brand name is already known and accepted by customers.

Packaging

packaging   all those activities involved in developing and providing a container for a product

Packaging consists of all those activities involved in developing and providing a container for a product. The package is a vital part of the product. It can make the product more versatile, safer, or easier to use. Through its shape and what is printed on it, a package can influence purchasing decisions.

Packaging Functions   Effective packaging means more than simply putting products in containers and covering them with wrappers. The basic function of packaging materials is to protect the product and maintain its functional form. Fluids such as milk, orange juice, and hair spray need packages that preserve and protect them; the packaging should prevent damage that could affect the product's usefulness and increase costs. Since product tampering has become a problem for marketers of many types of goods, several packaging techniques have been developed to counter this danger. Some packages are also designed to foil shoplifting.

Another function of packaging is to offer consumer convenience. For example, small aseptic packages—individual-size boxes or plastic bags that contain liquids and do not require refrigeration—appeal strongly to children and to young adults with active lifestyles. The size or shape of a package may relate to the product's storage, convenience of use, or replacement rate. Small, single-serving cans of vegetables, for instance, may prevent waste and make storage easier. A third function of packaging is to promote a product by communicating its features, uses, benefits, and image. Sometimes, a reusable package is developed to make the product more desirable. For example, the Cool Whip package doubles as a food-storage container.

Package Design Considerations   Many factors must be weighed when developing packages. Obviously, one major consideration is cost. Although a variety of packaging materials, processes, and designs are available, some are rather expensive. In recent years, buyers have shown a willingness to pay more for improved packaging, but there are limits.

BUSINESS JOURNAL
L'eggs Packaging: Goodbye to the Plastic Egg

Over twenty years ago, L'eggs Products, Inc. became pioneers in marketing women's hosiery. Packaging pantyhose in colorful, eye-catching, egg-shaped containers, the company displayed them all over the country in carousels and on racks in novel places like drugstores, supermarkets, and convenience stores. Widespread availability coupled with the egg's popularity catapulted L'eggs to the top. In a $2.2 billion market, L'eggs controls 55 percent. Only number-two No Nonsense seriously competes nationally for market share. Every year, people buy about 264 million pairs of L'eggs pantyhose in the popular plastic egg-shaped containers.

Although the egg package provides instant brand recognition, consumers will soon witness the end of one of the best-known packages in history. Multipacks of L'eggs pantyhose have been sold in ordinary cardboard packages for some time. Two years of market research, in addition to environmental and financial considerations, have now persuaded the company to abandon the plastic egg

altogether. Rather than wait for criticism from environmental groups, company executives took the initiative. They recognized that the process for recycling the polystyrene egg is not widely available, and the amount of packaging is excessive. Made from recycled cardboard, the new package requires 38 percent less packaging material. The standard-shape package will also save the company money. Because the eggs cannot be neatly stacked together, they create dead space, both in transportation and on retail shelves. After the change, shipping will be easier and less expensive, and 900 L'eggs packages will fit on the same shelf space that previously accommodated 650 eggs.

Citing its easy-to-read labeling, attractiveness, and environmental friendliness, consumers surveyed prefer the new package two-to-one over the old one. Ninety percent recognized the environmental benefits of the new package without any prompting, and response from several grassroots environmental groups has been positive.

Company executives hope to keep their trademark alive by designing the square box with an egg-shaped top and by using the advertising slogan, "A good egg just got better." L'eggs will spend millions of dollars to convert packaging, merchandising, and distribution and to run spot TV ads and special promotions announcing the new design. Apparently, the cost will not be translated to the customer; suggested retail prices will remain the same.

Industry analysts warn that L'eggs risks losing customers by abandoning the egg package. The unique and clever shape has been its most striking feature. Even if Americans do flock to buy L'eggs pantyhose in the new package, they will probably miss having the egg for a container, a toy, or a holiday ornament.

Marketers must also decide whether to package the product in single or multiple units. Multiple-unit packaging can increase demand by increasing the amount of the product available at the point of consumption (in the home, for example). However, multiple-unit packaging does not work for infrequently used products because buyers do not like to tie up their dollars in an excess supply or to store these products for a long time. Multiple-unit packaging can, however, make storage and handling easier (as in the case of six-packs used for soft drinks); it can also facilitate special price offers, such as two-for-one sales. In addition, multiple-unit packaging may increase consumer acceptance of a product by encouraging the buyer to try it several times. On the other hand, customers may hesitate to try the product at all if they are forced to buy several units at one time.

Marketers should consider how much consistency is desirable among an organization's package designs. To promote an overall company image, a firm may decide that all packages must be similar or include one major element of the design. This approach, called *family packaging,* is sometimes used only for lines of products, as with Campbell soups, Weight Watchers' foods, and Planters' nuts. The best policy is sometimes no consistency, especially if a firm's products are unrelated or aimed at vastly different markets.

Packages also play an important promotional role. Through verbal and nonverbal symbols, the package can inform potential buyers about the product's content, uses, features, advantages, and hazards. Firms can create desirable images and associations by choosing particular colors, designs, shapes, and textures. Many cosmetics manufacturers, for example, design their packages to create impressions of richness, luxury, and exclusiveness. The package performs another promotional function when it is designed to be safer or more convenient to use, if such features help stimulate demand.

Packaging must also meet the needs of intermediaries. Wholesalers and retailers consider whether a package facilitates transportation, handling, and storage. Resellers may refuse to carry certain products if their packages are cumbersome.

Finally, firms must consider the issue of environmental responsibility when developing packages. Companies must balance consumers' desires for convenience against desires to preserve the environment. Nearly 50 percent of all garbage consists of discarded plastic packaging, such as Styrofoam containers, plastic soft-drink bottles, carryout bags, and other packaging. Plastic packaging material is not biodegradable, and paper necessitates destruction of valuable forest lands. Consequently, many companies are exploring packaging alternatives and recycling more materials.

Labeling

labeling   the presentation of information on a product or its package

Labeling is the presentation of information on a product or its package. The *label* is the part that contains the information. This information may include the brand name and mark, the registered-trademark symbol ®, the package size and contents, product claims, directions for use and safety precautions, a list of ingredients, the name and address of the manufacturer, and the Universal Product Code symbol, which is used for automated check-out and inventory control.

A number of federal regulations specify information that *must* be included in the labeling for certain products:

- Garments must be labeled with the name of the manufacturer, country of manufacture, fabric content, and cleaning instructions.

- Any food product for which a nutritional claim is made must have nutrition labeling that follows a standard format.
- The ingredients of food products must be listed in order, beginning with the ingredient that constitutes the largest percentage of the product.
- Nonedible items such as shampoos and detergents must carry safety precautions as well as instructions for their use.

Such regulations are aimed at protecting the consumer from both misleading product claims and the improper (and thus unsafe) use of products.

Labels may also carry the details of written or express warranties. An **express warranty** is a written explanation of the responsibilities of the producer in the event that the product is found to be defective or otherwise unsatisfactory. Recently, as a result of consumer discontent (along with some federal legislation), firms have begun to simplify the wording of warranties and to extend their duration. Chrysler Corp.'s 70,000-mile/7-year warranty is featured heavily in that firm's advertising.

Many of the decisions and activities associated with a product have a definite impact on its price. The rest of this chapter is devoted to considerations affecting pricing goals, methods, and strategies.

express warranty   a written explanation of the responsibilities of the producer in the event that the product is found to be defective or otherwise unsatisfactory

THE PRODUCT AND ITS PRICE

LEARNING OBJECTIVE 6
Describe the economic basis of pricing and the means by which sellers can control prices and buyers' perceptions of prices.

You should now realize that a product is more than a thing that we can touch or a change that we can see. Rather, it is a set of attributes and benefits that has been carefully designed to satisfy its market while earning a profit for the seller. But no matter how well a product is designed, it cannot perform its function if it is priced incorrectly. Few people will purchase a product with too high a price, and a product with too low a price will earn little or no profit. Somewhere between too high and too low there is a "proper," effective price for each product. Let's take a closer look at how businesses go about determining what the right price is.

The Meaning and Use of Price

price   the amount of money that a seller is willing to accept in exchange for a product, at a given time and under given circumstances

The **price** of a product is the amount of money that a seller is willing to accept in exchange for a product, at a given time and under given circumstances. At times, the price results from negotiations between buyer and seller. But in many business situations, the price is fixed by the seller. Suppose a seller sets a price of $10 for a particular product. In essence, the seller is saying "Anyone who wants this product can have it here and now, in exchange for $10."

Each interested buyer then makes a personal judgment regarding the utility of the product, often in terms of some dollar value. A particular person who feels that he or she will get at least $10 worth of want satisfaction

No more hard sell. You won't leave this Pontiac dealership worrying that a better negotiator would have gotten a lower price. The dealer gave up his commissioned sales force, dropped his prices, and announced that there would be no negotiation. Sales immediately tripled, although the dealer cut spending on advertising by 85 percent. Buyers evidently like this new type of "good deal."

(or value) from the product is likely to buy it. But if that person can get more want satisfaction by spending $10 in some other way, he or she will not buy it.

Price thus serves the function of *allocator*. First, it allocates goods and services among those who are willing and able to buy them. (As we noted in Chapter 1, the answer to the economic question "For whom to produce?" depends primarily on prices.) Second, price allocates financial resources (sales revenue) among producers according to how well they satisfy customers' needs. And third, price helps customers to allocate their own financial resources among various want-satisfying products.

Can Firms Control Their Prices?

To focus on the issue of the extent to which firms can control their prices, we will take another look at the forces of supply and demand and the actions of firms in a real economy.

supply   the quantity of a product that producers are willing to sell at each of various prices

Supply and Demand—Once Again   In Chapter 1, we defined the **supply** of a product as the quantity of the product that producers are willing to sell at each of various prices. We can draw a graph of the supply relationship for a particular product, say, jeans (see the left graph of Figure 12.3). Note that the quantity supplied by producers *increases* as the price increases along this *supply curve*.

demand   the quantity of a product that buyers are willing to purchase at each of various prices

As defined in Chapter 1, the **demand** for a product is the quantity that buyers are willing to purchase at each of various prices. We can also draw a graph of the demand relationship (see the middle graph of Figure 12.3). Note that the quantity demanded by purchasers *increases* as the price decreases along the *demand curve*.

As noted in Chapter 1, the sellers and buyers of a product interact in the marketplace. We can show this interaction by superimposing the supply curve on the demand curve for our product, as shown in the right graph of Figure 12.3.

FIGURE 12.3
Supply and Demand Curves
Supply curve *(left):* The upward slope means that producers will supply more jeans at higher prices. **Demand curve** *(middle):* The downward slope (to the right) means that buyers will purchase fewer jeans at higher prices. **Supply and demand curves together** *(right):* Point *E* indicates equilibrium in quantity and price for both sellers and buyers.

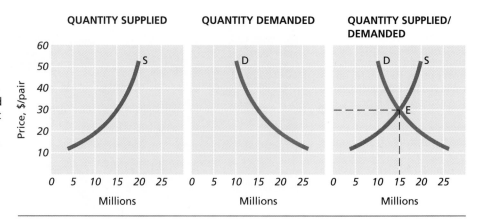

The two curves intersect at point *E,* which represents a quantity of 15 million pairs of jeans and a price of $30 per pair. Point *E* is on the supply curve; thus producers are willing to supply 15 million pairs at $30 each. Point *E* is also on the demand curve; thus buyers are willing to purchase 15 million pairs at $30 each. Point *E* represents *equilibrium.* If 15 million pairs are produced and priced at $30, they will all be sold. And everyone who is willing to pay $30 will be able to buy a pair of jeans.

Prices in the Real Economy   In a (largely theoretical) system of pure competition, no producer has control over the price of its product: All producers must accept the equilibrium price. If they charge a higher price, they will not sell their products. If they charge a lower price, they will lose sales revenue and profits. In addition, the products of the various producers are indistinguishable from each other when a system of pure competition exists. Every bushel of wheat, for example, is exactly like every other bushel of wheat.

In the real economy, producers try to gain some control over price by differentiating their products from similar products. **Product differentiation** is the process of developing and promoting differences between one's product and all similar products. The idea behind product differentiation is to create a specific demand for the firm's product—to take the product out of competition with all similar products. Then, in its own little "submarket," the firm can control price to some degree. Jeans with various designer labels are a result of product differentiation.

Firms also attempt to gain some control over price through advertising. If the advertising is effective, it will increase the quantity demanded. This may permit a firm to increase the price at which it sells its particular output.

In a real market, firms may reduce prices to obtain a competitive edge. A firm may hope to sell more units at a lower price, thereby increasing its total sales revenue. Although each unit earns less profit, total profit may rise.

Finally, the few large sellers in an oligopoly (an industry in which there are few sellers), have considerable control over price, mainly because each

product differentiation   the process of developing and promoting differences between one's product and all similar products

controls a large proportion of the total supply of its product. However, as we pointed out in Chapter 1, this control of price is diluted by each firm's wariness of its competitors.

Overall, then, firms in the real economy do exert some control over prices. How they use this control depends on their pricing goals and their production and marketing costs, as well as on the workings of supply and demand in competitive markets.

Price and Nonprice Competition

Before the price of a product can be set, an organization must decide on what basis it will compete—on the basis of price or some other combination of factors. The choice influences pricing decisions as well as other marketing-mix variables.

price competition an emphasis on setting a price equal to or lower than competitors' to gain sales or market share

Price competition occurs when a seller emphasizes the low price of a product and sets a price that equals or beats competitors' prices. To use this approach most effectively, a seller must have the flexibility to change prices often and must do so rapidly and aggressively whenever competitors change their prices. Price competition allows a marketer to set prices based on demand for the product or in response to changes in the firm's finances. Competitors can do likewise, however, which is a major drawback of price competition. They, too, can quickly match or outdo an organization's price cuts. In addition, if circumstances force a seller to raise prices, competing firms may be able to maintain their lower prices.

nonprice competition competition based on factors other than price

Nonprice competition is based on factors other than price. It is used most effectively when a seller can make its product stand out from the competition by distinctive product quality, customer service, promotion, packaging, or other features. Buyers must be able to perceive these distinguishing characteristics and consider them desirable. Once customers have chosen a brand for nonprice reasons, they may not be as easily attracted to competing firms and brands. In this way a seller can build customers' loyalty to its brand. Price is still an important part of a marketing mix in nonprice competition, but it is possible for a firm to increase a brand's unit sales without lowering its price.

Buyers' Perceptions of Price

In setting prices, managers should consider the price sensitivity of people in the target market. How important is price to them? Is it always "very important"? Members of one market segment may be more influenced by price than members of another. For a particular product, the price may be a bigger factor to some buyers than to others. For example, buyers may be more sensitive to price when purchasing gasoline than when purchasing jeans.

Buyers will accept different ranges of prices for different products; that is, they will tolerate a narrow range for certain items and a wider range for others. Management should be aware of these limits of acceptability and the products to which they apply. The firm should also take

13

Wholesaling, Retailing, and Physical Distribution

After studying this chapter you should be able to:

1 Identify the various channels of distribution that are used for consumer and industrial products.

2 Explain the concept of market coverage.

3 Describe what a vertical marketing system is and identify the types of vertical marketing systems.

4 Discuss the need for wholesalers.

5 Identify the major types of wholesalers and describe the services they perform for retailers and manufacturers.

6 Distinguish among the major types of retail outlets.

7 Explain the wheel of retailing hypothesis.

8 Identify the categories of shopping centers and the factors that determine how shopping centers are classified.

9 Explain the five most important physical distribution activities.

CHAPTER PREVIEW

First in this chapter we examine various channels of distribution—the company-to-company paths that products follow as they move from producer to ultimate user. Then we discuss wholesalers and retailers, two important groups of intermediaries operating within these channels. Next, we examine the types of shopping centers. Finally, we explore the physical distribution function and the major modes of transportation that are used to move goods.

J. C. Penney Pursues Its True Identity

For a long time, J. C. Penney, Inc., America's sixth largest retailer, has struggled with its identity. Rejecting its longtime position as a drab mass merchant, the company moved upscale, transforming itself into a flashier department store chain.

To remake itself, Penney's discarded some departments, expanded its lines of brand-name fashions and cosmetics, and redecorated the stores. During the 1980s, customers bought more than $1.5 billion worth of Penney's sporting goods and appliances, but management decided to drop these departments anyway. That 20 million square feet of store space became departments full of men's, women's, and children's fashions with brand names like Levi's, Oshkosh B'Gosh, Bugle Boy, Haggar, and Van Heusen. At a cost of about $200 million, marble floors, fancy woodwork, and visually appealing displays replaced dreary surroundings. Even Penney's catalog got a face lift and, although you wouldn't mistake it for *Vogue,* it is noticeably more stylish. At first, customers seemed to like the changes; from 1983 to 1989, earnings almost doubled.

Recently, however, business has taken a turn for the worse. In one quarter, profits slid 63 percent and sales went down 3.5 percent. Recession is hurting retailers, but J. C. Penney seems to be suffering more than most chains. The firm can't convince elite suppliers like Liz Claiborne, Inc. and Estée Lauder, Inc. that it has fashion credibility. Although the company has partially succeeded in improving its image, many people still come into Penney's outlets thinking of towels and sheets, not trendy fashion. At the same time that the firm is failing to thrill upscale customers, it is losing its core of loyal price-conscious customers who can no longer afford its prices.

The company is now trying a "middle-of-the-road" strategy, returning to more moderate prices while continuing to add name brands. You can still shop at J. C. Penney for a pair of Levis, but while

you're there, you can also pick up bargains on the company's marked-down, private-label clothing. The retailer's new ad agency created a series of television spots that emphasize value over fashion by showing ordinary people shopping at Penney's stores. Company executives believe that somewhere between the fashion department store it tried to become and the mass merchandiser it once was, is a retailing niche just right for the value-conscious consumers of the 1990s.[1]

More than two million firms in the United States help move products from producers to consumers. Of all marketers, retail firms that sell directly to consumers are the most visible. Store chains like J. C. Penney, Sears, Roebuck and Co., and Wal-Mart Stores, Inc. operate retail outlets where consumers make purchases. Other retailers, like Avon Products and Electrolux, send their salespeople to the homes of customers. Still others, like Lands' End, Inc. and L. L. Bean, Inc. sell through catalogs or through both catalogs and stores.

In addition, there are more than half a million wholesalers that sell merchandise to other firms. Most consumers know little about these firms that work "behind the scenes" and rarely sell directly to consumers.

These and other intermediaries are concerned with the transfer of both products and ownership. They thus help create the time, place, and possession utilities that are so important in marketing. As we will see, they also perform a number of services for their suppliers and their customers.

Before we look closely at some of these important intermediaries, we should get an idea of the various channels—some simple, some complex—through which products are distributed to customers.

CHANNELS OF DISTRIBUTION

channel of distribution (or **marketing channel**) a sequence of marketing organizations that directs a product from the producer to the ultimate user

A **channel of distribution,** or **marketing channel,** is a sequence of marketing organizations that directs a product from the producer to the ultimate user. Every marketing channel begins with the producer and ends with either the consumer or the industrial user.

middleman (or **marketing intermediary**) a marketing organization that links a producer and user within a marketing channel

A marketing organization that links a producer and user within a marketing channel is called a **middleman,** or **marketing intermediary.** For the most part, middlemen are concerned with the transfer of *ownership* of products. A **merchant middleman** (or, more simply, a *merchant*) is a middleman that actually takes title to products by buying them. A **functional middleman,** on the other hand, helps in the transfer of ownership of products but does not take title to the products.

merchant middleman a middleman that actually takes title to products by buying them

functional middleman a middleman that helps in the transfer of ownership of products but does not take title to the products

Different channels of distribution are generally used to move consumer and industrial products. The six most commonly used channels are illustrated in Figure 13.1.

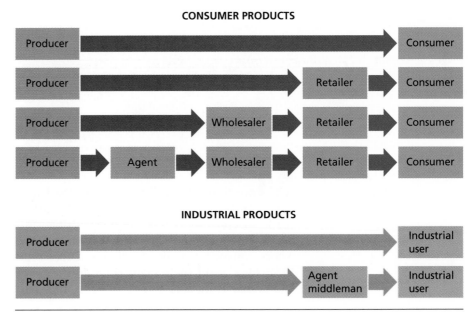

Channels for Consumer Products

Producer to Consumer   This channel, which is often called the *direct channel*, includes no marketing intermediaries. Practically all services, but very few consumer goods, are distributed through the direct channel. However, the sellers of some consumer goods, such as Avon Products, Mary Kay Cosmetics, and Fuller Brush, prefer to sell directly to consumers.

Producers sell directly to consumers for several reasons. They can better control the quality and price of their products. They don't have to pay (through discounts) for the services of intermediaries. And they can maintain closer ties with consumers.

retailer   a middleman that
buys from producers or other
middlemen and sells to
consumers

Producer to Retailer to Consumer   A **retailer** is a middleman that buys from producers or other middlemen and sells to consumers. Producers sell directly to retailers when retailers can buy in large quantities. This channel is most often used for products that are bulky, such as furniture and automobiles, for which additional handling would increase selling costs. It is also the usual channel for perishable products, such as fruits and vegetables, and for high-fashion products that must reach the consumer in the shortest possible time.

wholesaler   a middleman that
sells products to other firms

Producer to Wholesaler to Retailer to Consumer   This channel is known as the *traditional channel*, because most consumer goods (especially convenience goods) pass through wholesalers to retailers. A **wholesaler** is a middleman that sells products to other firms. These firms may be retailers, industrial users, or other wholesalers. A producer uses wholesalers when its products are carried by so many retailers that the producer cannot deal with all of them.

FOCUS ON SMALL BUSINESS
Performance Bicycle's Road to Success

When the United States Cycling Team competed in Barcelona, Spain, at the 1992 Olympics, members raced on bikes made by their official sponsor, Performance Bicycles. Starting as a mail-order business offering bicycle parts and accessories out of a basement, Performance mushroomed into a $50-million-a-year enterprise. The largest single retailer of cycling gear in the United States, the North Carolina-based firm employs more than five hundred people who mail about ten million catalogs and sell ten to fifteen thousand bicycles a year. Fourteen Performance retail outlets from California to North Carolina each gross over $1 million a year. Forty-five-year-old owner, Gary Snook, insists his company's rise is not an overnight success story. He attributes Performance's achievements to a step-by-step strategy and lots of plain hard work.

While studying for his doctorate in finance at the University of North Carolina, Snook wanted to start a business as a sideline. Doing his research, Snook determined that, although cycling was on the rise, avid cyclists were not satisfied with average bike shops. After borrowing a book called *How to Start a Mail-Order Business* from the public library and studying successes like L. L. Bean, Inc. and Land's End, Inc., Snook, together with his wife and brother, launched Performance Bicycles. In its second year of business, sales at Performance reached $3.2 million, but for Snook, that was just the beginning. Only a few years after he expanded the catalog to include cycling clothes, over 44 percent of those responding to a *Bicycling Magazine* survey said they owned Performance apparel. Retail stores came next, with Snook opening 6,000-square-foot stores where shoppers enjoy hands-on examination of clothes, helmets, handlebars, wheels, toe clips,

pedals, pumps, seats, and more. Snook never finished his Ph.D., but he has gone on to run his company with awe-inspiring results.

Gary Snook's general strategy is to go slowly: Examine the risks at every stage, decide if the potential rewards are great enough to take the risk, test the market, and if tests are successful, only then proceed. Snook was able to identify a niche and excel at filling it. When he began, his research told him that no mail-order cycling firm focused on affordable quality and customer service, so Performance offers fair prices, a twenty-four-hour, toll-free number, and a 100 percent money-back guarantee. To keep prices affordable, Snook produces his own apparel instead of ordering it from outside manufacturers. A pair of cycling shorts, for example, that would sell for $24.95 can be reduced to $19.95. Some cycling socks come with an 18,000-mile guarantee. Performance prides itself on quick, reliable service to mail-order customers. The managing editor of *Bicycle*, who often orders from Performance, recently remarked that the company has never bungled an order.

Asked about the secret of his success, Snook answers that he is just a good businessman who saw an opening in a market and worked day and night to fill it. Work is an understatement. For the first six months of operation, Gary and his wife, Sharon, never left the house at the same time; someone had to be home to answer the phone. They stayed up late filling orders and were back at it by 7 a.m. every day of the week, every week of the year. Now that the company has so many employees and is so successful, does Snook relax by riding his bicycle? No. He says he doesn't have time to ride because he is working all the time.

Producer to Agent to Wholesaler to Retailer to Consumer Producers may use agents to reach wholesalers. Agents are functional middlemen that do not take title to products and that are compensated by commissions paid by producers. This channel is used for products that are sold through thousands of outlets to millions of consumers. Often, these products are inexpensive, frequently purchased items. For example, millions of consumers buy candy bars, which are sold through numerous outlets. Some candy

Working with multiple channels. Liz Claiborne is the largest women's apparel manufacturer in the world, and it uses many different channels to get its products to customers. Buyers can find Claiborne clothes in department stores and in the company's own boutiques and factory outlet stores. Ads, products, and the stores themselves are differentiated by price and by target audience.

bars are sold through agents to wholesalers who, in turn, supply them to retail stores and vending machines. This channel is also used for highly seasonal products (such as Christmas tree decorations) and by producers that do not have their own sales forces.

Multiple Channels for Consumer Goods   Often a manufacturer uses different distribution channels to reach different market segments. A manufacturer uses multiple channels, for example, when the same product is sold to consumers and industrial users. Multiple channels are also used to increase sales or to capture a larger share of the market. With the goal of selling as much merchandise as possible, both Firestone Tire & Rubber Co. and The Goodyear Tire & Rubber Company market their tires through their own retail outlets as well as through independent service stations and department stores.

Channels for Industrial Products

Producers of industrial products generally tend to use short channels. We will outline the two that are most commonly used.

Producer to Industrial User   In this direct channel, the manufacturer's own sales force sells directly to industrial users. Heavy machinery, large computers, and major equipment are usually distributed in this way. The very short channel allows the producer to provide customers with expert and timely services, such as delivery, machinery installation, and repairs.

Manufacturer to Agent Middleman to Industrial User   This channel is employed by manufacturers to distribute such items as operating supplies, accessory equipment, small tools, and standardized parts. The agent is an independent intermediary between the producer and the user. Generally, agents represent sellers.

Market Coverage

LEARNING OBJECTIVE 2
Explain the concept of market coverage.

How does a producer decide which distribution channels (and which particular intermediaries) to use? Like every other marketing decision, this one should be based on all relevant factors. These include the firm's production capability and marketing resources, the target market and buying patterns of potential customers, and the product itself. After evaluating these factors, the producer can choose a particular *intensity of market coverage*. Then the producer selects channels and intermediaries to implement that coverage (see Figure 13.2).

intensive distribution   the use of all available outlets for a product

Intensive distribution is the use of all available outlets for a product. The producer that wants to give its product the widest possible exposure in the marketplace chooses intensive distribution. The manufacturer saturates the market by selling to any intermediary of good financial standing that is willing to stock and sell the product. For the consumer, intensive distribution means being able to shop at a nearby store and spending minimum time to find the product in the store. Many convenience goods, including candy, gum, and cigarettes, are distributed intensively.

FIGURE 13.2
Market Coverage
The number of outlets a producer chooses for a product depends on the type of product. Batteries, for example, are distributed intensively.

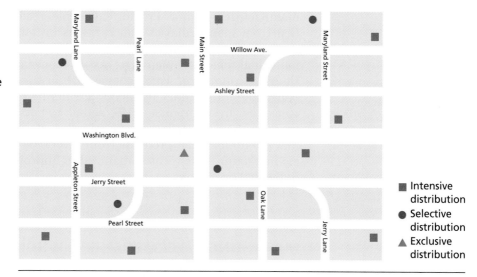

■ Intensive distribution
● Selective distribution
▲ Exclusive distribution

---

selective distribution the use of only a portion or percentage of the available outlets for a product in each geographic area

Selective distribution is the use of only a portion or percentage of the available outlets for a product in each geographic area. Manufacturers of goods such as furniture, major home appliances, and clothing typically prefer selective distribution. Franchisers also use selective distribution in granting franchises for the sale of their goods and services in a specific geographic area.

exclusive distribution the use of only a single retail outlet for a product in a large geographic area

Exclusive distribution is the use of only a single retail outlet for a product in a large geographic area. Exclusive distribution is usually limited to very prestigious products. It is appropriate, for instance, for specialty goods such as expensive pianos, fine china, and automobiles. The producer usually places many requirements (inventory levels, sales training, service quality, warranty procedures) on exclusive dealers.

Vertical Marketing Systems

LEARNING OBJECTIVE 3
Describe what a vertical marketing system is and identify the types of vertical marketing systems.

vertical channel integration the combining of two or more stages of a distribution channel under a single firm's management

vertical marketing system (VMS) a centrally managed distribution channel resulting from vertical channel integration

Vertical channel integration occurs when two or more stages of a distribution channel are combined and managed by one firm. A **vertical marketing system (VMS)** is a centrally managed distribution channel resulting from vertical channel integration. This merging eliminates the need for certain intermediaries. One member of a marketing channel may assume the responsibilities of another member, or it may actually purchase the operations of that member. For example, a large-volume discount retailer that ships and warehouses its own stock directly from manufacturers does not need a wholesaler. Total vertical integration occurs when a single management controls all operations from production to final sale. Oil companies that own wells, transportation facilities, refineries, terminals, and service stations exemplify total vertical integration.

There are three types of VMSs: administered, contractual, and corporate. In an *administered VMS*, one of the channel members dominates the other members, perhaps because of its large size. Under its influence, the channel members collaborate on production and distribution. A powerful manufacturer, such as Procter & Gamble, receives a great deal of cooperation from intermediaries that carry its brands. Although the goals of the entire system are considered when decisions are made, control rests with individual channel members, as in conventional marketing channels. Under a *contractual VMS*, cooperative arrangements and the rights and obligations of channel members are defined by contracts or other legal measures. In a *corporate VMS*, actual ownership is the vehicle by which production and distribution are joined. A grocery-store chain, for example, may obtain its bread products from several of its own bakeries. Most vertical marketing systems are organized to improve distribution by combining individual operations.

MARKETING INTERMEDIARIES: WHOLESALERS

LEARNING OBJECTIVE 4
Discuss the need for wholesalers.

Wholesalers may be the most misunderstood of marketing intermediaries. Producers sometimes try to eliminate them from distribution channels by dealing directly with retailers or consumers. Yet wholesalers provide a variety of essential marketing services. It may be true that wholesalers themselves can be eliminated, but their functions cannot. These functions *must* be performed by some organization within the distribution channel or by the consumer or ultimate user.

Justifications for Marketing Intermediaries

The press, consumers, public officials, and other marketers often charge wholesalers, at least in principle, with inefficiency and parasitism. Consumers in particular feel strongly that the distribution channel should be made as short as possible. They assume that the fewer the intermediaries in a distribution channel, the lower the price.

Those who believe that the elimination of wholesalers would bring about lower prices, however, do not recognize that the services wholesalers perform would still be needed. Those services would simply be provided by other means, and consumers would still bear the costs. Moreover, all manufacturers would have to keep extensive records and employ enough personnel to deal with a multitude of retailers individually. Even with direct distribution, products might be considerably more expensive because prices would reflect the costs of producers' inefficiency. Figure 13.3 shows that sixteen contacts could result from the efforts of four buyers purchasing the products of four producers. With the assistance of an intermediary, only eight contacts would be necessary.

To illustrate further the useful role of wholesalers in the marketing system, assume that all wholesalers in the candy industry were abolished. With more than 1.3 million retail businesses to contact, candy manufacturers could be making as many as a million sales calls or more just to maintain the present level of product visibility. Hershey Foods Corp., for example, would have to set up warehouses all over the country, organize a

FIGURE 13.3
Efficiency Provided by an Intermediary
The services of an intermediary reduce the number of contacts, or exchanges, between producers and buyers, thereby increasing efficiency. *(Source: Adapted from William M. Pride and O. C. Ferrell,* Marketing: Concepts and Strategies, *7/e. Copyright © 1991 by Houghton Mifflin Company. Used by permission.)*

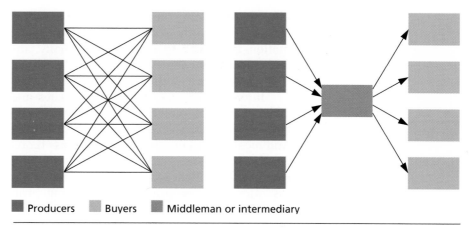

■ Producers   ■ Buyers   ■ Middleman or intermediary

fleet of trucks, purchase and maintain thousands of vending machines, and deliver all of its own candy. Sales and distribution costs for candy would soar. Candy producers would be contacting and shipping products to thousands of small businesses, instead of to a few food brokers, large retailers, and merchant wholesalers. The high costs of this inefficiency would be passed on to consumers. Candy bars would be more expensive and perhaps in short supply.

Wholesalers are more efficient and economical not only for manufacturers but also for consumers. Because their elimination is proposed from both ends of the marketing channel, however, wholesalers should perform only those functions that are genuinely in demand. To stay in business, wholesalers should also take care to be efficient and productive and to provide high-quality services to other channel members.

Wholesalers' Services to Retailers

Wholesalers help retailers by buying in large quantities and then selling to retailers in smaller quantities and by delivering goods to retailers. They also stock—in one place—the variety of goods that retailers would otherwise have to buy from many producers. And wholesalers provide assistance in three other vital areas: promotion, market information, and financial help.

Promotion   Most wholesalers help promote the products they sell to retailers. These services are usually either free or performed at cost. Some wholesalers are major sources of display materials designed to stimulate "impulse buying." They may also help retailers build effective window, counter, and bin displays; they may even donate their own employees to work on the retail sales floor during special promotions.

Market Information   Wholesalers are a constant source of market information. Wholesalers have numerous contacts with local businesses and distant suppliers. In the course of these dealings, they accumulate information about consumer demand, prices, supply conditions, new developments within the trade, and even industry personnel. Most of this information is relayed to retailers informally, through the wholesaler's sales force. However, some wholesalers distribute bulletins or newsletters to their customers as well.

Information regarding industry sales and competitive prices is especially important to all firms. Dealing with a number of suppliers and many retailers, a wholesaler is a natural "clearinghouse" for such information. And most wholesalers are willing to pass it on to their customers.

Financial Aid   Most wholesalers provide a type of financial aid that retailers often take for granted. By making prompt and frequent deliveries, wholesalers enable retailers to keep their own inventory investments small in relation to sales. Such indirect financial aid reduces the amount of operating capital retailers need.

In some trades, wholesalers extend direct financial assistance through long-term loans. Most wholesalers also provide help through delayed billing, giving customers thirty to sixty days *after delivery* to pay for merchandise. Wholesalers of seasonal merchandise may offer even longer payment periods. For example, a wholesaler of lawn and garden supplies may deliver seed to retailers in January but not bill them for it until May.

Wholesalers' Services to Manufacturers

Some of the services that wholesalers perform for producers are similar to those provided to retailers. Others are quite different.

Providing an Instant Sales Force   A wholesaler provides its producers with an instant sales force so that producers' sales representatives need not call on retailers. This can result in large savings for producers. For example, Procter & Gamble and General Foods Corp. would have to spend millions of dollars each year to field a sales force that could call on all the retailers that sell their numerous products. Instead, these producers rely on wholesalers to sell and distribute their products to retailers.

Reducing Inventory Costs   Wholesalers purchase goods in sizable quantities from manufacturers and store these goods for resale. By doing so, they reduce the amount of finished goods inventory that producers must hold and, thereby, the cost of carrying inventories.

Assuming Credit Risks   When producers sell through wholesalers, it is the wholesalers who extend credit to retailers, make collections from retailers, and assume the risks of nonpayment. These services reduce the producers' cost of extending credit to customers and the resulting bad debt expense.

Furnishing Market Information   Just as they do for retailers, wholesalers supply market information to the producers they serve. Valuable information accumulated by wholesalers may concern consumer demand, the producers' competition, and buying trends.

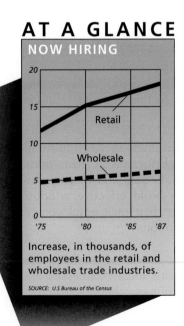

AT A GLANCE

NOW HIRING

Increase, in thousands, of employees in the retail and wholesale trade industries.

SOURCE: U.S Bureau of the Census

Types of Wholesalers

LEARNING OBJECTIVE 5
Identify the major types of wholesalers and describe the services they perform for retailers and manufacturers.

Wholesalers generally fall into three categories: merchant wholesalers; commission merchants, agents, and brokers; and manufacturers, sales branches, and offices. Of these, merchant wholesalers constitute the largest portion. They account for about 58 percent of wholesale sales, four-fifths of all wholesale employees, and four out of every five establishments.[2]

merchant wholesaler a middleman that purchases goods in large quantities and then sells them to other wholesalers or retailers and to institutional, farm, government, professional, or industrial users

Merchant Wholesalers A **merchant wholesaler** is a middleman that purchases goods in large quantities and then sells them to other wholesalers or retailers and to institutional, farm, government, professional, or industrial users. Merchant wholesalers usually operate one or more warehouses where they receive, take title to, and store goods. These wholesalers are sometimes called *distributors* or *jobbers.*

Most merchant wholesalers are businesses composed of salespeople, order takers, receiving and shipping clerks, inventory managers, and office personnel. The successful merchant wholesaler must analyze available products and market needs. It must be able to adapt the type, variety, and quality of the products it stocks to changing market conditions.

full-service wholesaler a middleman that performs the entire range of wholesaler functions

Merchant wholesalers may be classified as full-service or limited-service wholesalers, depending on the number of services they provide. A **full-service wholesaler** performs the entire range of wholesaler functions described earlier in this section. These functions include delivering goods, supplying warehousing, arranging for credit, supporting promotional activities, and providing general customer assistance.

general merchandise wholesaler a middleman that deals in a wide variety of products

limited-line wholesaler a middleman that stocks only a few product lines

specialty-line wholesaler a middleman that carries a select group of products within a single line

limited-service wholesaler a middleman that assumes responsibility for a few wholesale services only

Under this broad heading are the general merchandise wholesaler, limited-line wholesaler, and specialty-line wholesaler. A **general merchandise wholesaler** deals in a wide variety of products, such as drugs, hardware, nonperishable foods, cosmetics, detergents, and tobacco. A **limited-line wholesaler** stocks only a few product lines, in groceries, lighting fixtures, or drilling equipment, for example. A **specialty-line wholesaler** carries a select group of products within a single line. Food delicacies such as shellfish represent the kind of product handled by this wholesaler.

In contrast to a full-service wholesaler, a **limited-service wholesaler** assumes responsibility for a few wholesale services only. Other marketing tasks are left to other channel members or consumers. This category includes cash-and-carry wholesalers, truck wholesalers, rack jobbers, drop shippers, and mail-order wholesalers.

commission merchant a middleman that carries merchandise and negotiates sales for manufacturers

agent a middleman that expedites exchanges, represents a buyer or a seller, and often is hired permanently on a commission basis

Commission Merchants, Agents, and Brokers Commission merchants, agents, and brokers are functional middlemen. Functional middlemen do not take title to products. They perform a small number of marketing activities and are paid a commission that is a percentage of the sales price.

A **commission merchant** usually carries merchandise and negotiates sales for manufacturers. In most cases, commission merchants have the power to set the prices and terms of sales. After a sale is made, they either arrange for delivery or provide transportation services.

An **agent** is a middleman that expedites exchanges, represents a buyer or a seller, and often is hired permanently on a commission basis. When agents represent producers, they are known as *sales agents* or *manufacturer's agents*. As long as the products represented do not compete, a sales agent may represent one or several manufacturers on a commission basis. The agent solicits orders for the manufacturers within a specific territory. As a rule, the manufacturers ship the merchandise and bill the customers directly. The manufacturers also set the prices and other conditions of the sales. What do the manufacturers gain by using a sales agent? The sales agent provides immediate entry into a territory, regular calls on customers, selling experience, and a known, predetermined selling expense (a commission that is a percentage of sales revenue).

broker a middleman that specializes in a particular commodity, represents either a buyer or a seller, and is likely to be hired on a temporary basis

A **broker** is a middleman that specializes in a particular commodity, represents either a buyer *or* a seller, and is likely to be hired on a temporary basis. However, food brokers, which sell grocery products to resellers, generally have long-term relationships with their clients. Brokers may perform only the selling function or both buying and selling, using established contacts or special knowledge of their fields.

manufacturer's sales branch essentially a merchant wholesaler that is owned by a manufacturer

Manufacturers' Sales Branches and Offices A **manufacturer's sales branch** is, in essence, a merchant wholesaler that is owned by a manufacturer. Sales branches carry stock, extend credit, deliver goods, and offer help in promoting products. Their customers are retailers, other wholesalers, and industrial purchasers.

Because sales branches are owned by producers, they stock primarily the goods manufactured by their own firms. Selling policies and terms are usually established centrally and then transmitted to branch managers for implementation.

manufacturer's sales office essentially a sales agent owned by a manufacturer

A **manufacturer's sales office** is essentially a sales agent owned by a manufacturer. Sales offices may sell goods manufactured by their own firms and also certain products of other manufacturers that complement their own product lines. For example, Hiram Walker & Sons imports wine from Spain to increase the number of products its sales offices can offer to wholesalers.

MARKETING INTERMEDIARIES: RETAILERS

LEARNING OBJECTIVE 6
Distinguish among the major types of retail outlets.

Retailers are the final link between producers and consumers. Retailers may buy from either wholesalers or producers. They sell not only goods but also such services as repairs, haircuts, and tailoring. Some retailers sell both. Sears, Roebuck sells consumer goods, financial services, and repair services for home appliances bought at Sears.

Of the more than 1.3 million retail firms in the United States, about 90 percent have annual sales of less than $1 million.[3] On the other hand, there are giants that realize well over $1 million per day in sales revenue. Table 13.1 lists the twenty largest retail firms, the cities where their headquarters are located, and their approximate sales revenues and yearly profits. Figure 13.4 shows retail sales categorized by major merchandise type and the percentage of total sales for each type.

TABLE 13.1 The Twenty Largest Retail Firms in the United States

Rank	Company	Sales	Profits
		($ millions)	($ millions)
1	Wal-Mart (Bentonville, Ark.)	$32,601.6	$1,291.0
2	K mart (Troy, Mich.)	32,070.0	756.0
3	Sears, Roebuck (Chicago)	31,986.0	257.4
4	American Stores (Salt Lake City)	22,155.0	182.4
5	Kroger Co. (Cincinnati)	20,261.0	82.4
6	J. C. Penney (Dallas)	16,365.0	557.0
7	Safeway Stores (Oakland, Calif.)	14,873.0	87.1
8	Dayton Hudson (Minneapolis)	14,739.0	412.0
9	A&P (Montvale, N.J.)	11,391.0	151.0
10	May (St. Louis)	10,035.0	500.0
11	Woolworth (New York)	9,789.0	317.0
12	Winn-Dixie Stores (Jacksonville, Fla.)	9,744.5	152.6
13	Melville (Rye, N.Y.)	8,686.8	664.2
14	Southland Corporation (Dallas)	8,347.7	276.6
15	Albertsons (Boise, Idaho)	8,218.6	233.8
16	R. H. Macy (New York)	7,266.8	215.2
17	Campeau (Toronto, Canada)	7,137.4	271.4
18	Supermarkets General Holdings (Carteret, N.J.)	6,126.0	41.5
19	Walgreen Co. (Deerfield, Ill.)	6,048.0	174.6
20	Publix Super Markets (Lakeland, Fla.)	5,800.0	172.6

Source: "State of the Industry," *Chain Store Age Executive,* August 1991, p. 5A. Reprinted by permission from *Chain Store Age Executive,* (August 1991). Copyright Lebhar-Friedman, Inc., Park Avenue, New York, NY 10022.

Classes of In-Store Retailers

independent retailer　a firm that operates only one retail outlet

One way to classify retailers is by ownership—in particular, by the number of stores owned and operated by the firm. An **independent retailer** is a firm that operates only one retail outlet. Approximately 79 percent of retailers are independent, and they account for about 48 percent of all retail sales.[4] One-store operators, like all small businesses, generally provide personal service and convenient locations.

chain retailer　a company that operates more than one retail outlet

A **chain retailer** is a company that operates more than one retail outlet. By adding outlets, chain retailers attempt to reach new geographic markets. As sales increase, chains may buy in larger quantities and thus take advantage of quantity discounts. They also wield more power in their dealings with suppliers. About 21 percent of retailers operate chains, and they account for about 52 percent of all retail sales revenue.[5]

A better way to classify in-store retailers is by type of store. Each of the following types of stores may be owned independently or by a chain.

department store　a retail store that (1) employs twenty-five or more persons and (2) sells at least home furnishings, appliances, family apparel, and household linens and dry goods, each in a different part of the store

Department Stores　These are large retail establishments consisting of several parts, or departments, that sell a wide assortment of products. According to the U.S. Bureau of the Census, a **department store** is a retail store that (1) employs twenty-five or more persons and (2) sells at least home

FIGURE 13.4
Retail Sales Categorized by Merchandise Type
The numbers in this graph represent the percentage of total sales for each merchandise type.   *(Source:* Monthly Retail Trade: Sales and Inventories, *December 1990, U.S. Bureau of the Census, p. 10.)*

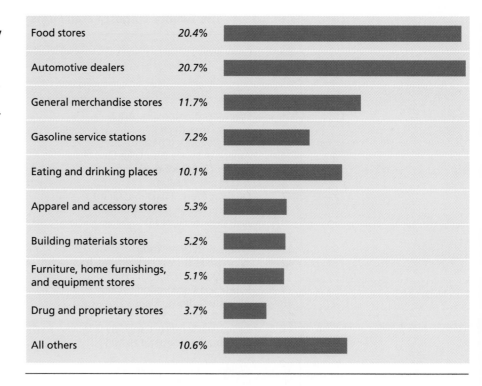

Food stores	20.4%
Automotive dealers	20.7%
General merchandise stores	11.7%
Gasoline service stations	7.2%
Eating and drinking places	10.1%
Apparel and accessory stores	5.3%
Building materials stores	5.2%
Furniture, home furnishings, and equipment stores	5.1%
Drug and proprietary stores	3.7%
All others	10.6%

furnishings, appliances, family apparel, and household linens and dry goods, each in a different part of the store. Marshall Fields in Chicago (and several other cities), Harrods in London, and Au Printemps in Paris are examples of large department stores. Sears, Roebuck and J. C. Penney are also department stores.

Department stores are distinctly service-oriented. Along with the goods they sell, they provide credit, delivery, personal assistance, liberal return policies, and a pleasant atmosphere. They are, for the most part, shopping stores. That is, consumers compare merchandise, price, quality, and service in competing department stores before they buy.

discount store   a self-service, general-merchandise outlet that sells goods at lower-than-usual prices

Discount Stores   A **discount store** is a self-service, general-merchandise outlet that sells goods at lower-than-usual prices. These stores can offer lower prices by operating on lower markups; locating their retail showrooms in large, low-rent areas; and offering minimal customer services. To keep prices low, discount stores operate on the basic principle of high turnover of such items as appliances, toys, clothing, automotive products, and sports equipment. To attract customers, many discount stores also offer some food items at low prices. Popular discount stores include K mart, Wal-Mart, Dollar General, and Target.

As competition among discount stores has increased, some discounters have improved their services, store environments, and locations. As a consequence, many of the better-known discount stores have assumed the characteristics of department stores. This has boosted their prices and blurred the distinction between some discount stores and department stores.[6]

catalog discount showroom
a retail outlet that displays well-known brands and sells them at discount prices through catalog sales within the store

Catalog Discount Showrooms   A **catalog discount showroom** is a retail outlet that displays well-known brands and sells them at discount prices through catalog sales within the store. Colorful catalogs are available in the showroom (and sometimes by mail). The customer selects the merchandise, either from the catalog or from the showroom display. Then the customer fills out an order form provided by the store and hands the form to a clerk. The clerk retrieves the merchandise from a room that is located away from the selling area and that serves as a warehouse. Well-known national and regional catalog showrooms include Service Merchandise, Consumers Distributing, W. Bell, and Best Products.

specialty store   a retail outlet that sells a single category of merchandise

Specialty Stores   A **specialty store** is a retail outlet that sells a single category of merchandise. Specialty stores may sell shoes, men's or women's clothing, baked goods, children's wear, photo equipment, flowers, or books. Most specialty stores cater to local markets, remain small, and are individually owned. However, there are a few large specialty chains, such as Radio Shack, Toys "Я" Us, and Hickory Farms of Ohio. Regardless of their size, all specialty stores offer specialized knowledge and service to their customers.

supermarket   a large self-service store that sells primarily food and household products

Supermarkets   A **supermarket** is a large self-service store that sells primarily food and household products. It stocks canned, fresh, frozen, and

Filling the gap. Why is The Gap "the nation's hottest retailer"? Head to your local mall and see if you can figure it out. Evidently the chain's owners saw a "gap" between expensive retailers of traditional dress clothes and bargain basement purveyors of denim jeans. So they filled that gap with stores that let you dress up casually.

processed foods, paper products, and cleaning products. Supermarkets may also sell such items as housewares, toiletries, toys and games, drugs, stationery, books and magazines, plants and flowers, and small items of clothing.

Supermarkets are large-scale operations that emphasize low prices and one-stop shopping for household needs. The first self-service food market opened fifty years ago. It grossed only $5,000 per week, with an average sale of just $1.31.[7] Today, a supermarket has minimum annual sales of at least $2 million. Current top-ranking supermarkets include Safeway Stores, Inc., Kroger, Winn-Dixie, Jewel, Lucky, and A&P.

superstore   a large retail store that carries not only food and nonfood products ordinarily found in supermarkets but also additional product lines

Superstores   A **superstore** is a large retail store that carries not only food and nonfood products ordinarily found in supermarkets but also additional product lines that include housewares, hardware, small appliances, clothing, personal-care products, garden products, and automotive merchandise. Superstores also provide a number of services to entice customers. Typical services include automotive repair, snack bars/restaurants, film developing, and limited banking. Although the superstore concept originated in Europe, it is relatively new to the United States. Sam Walton established Dallas-based Hypermart USA to focus on high volume, low prices, and one-stop shopping for most consumer merchandise.

convenience store   a small food store that sells a limited variety of products but remains open well beyond the normal business hours

Convenience Stores   A **convenience store** is a small food store that sells a limited variety of products but remains open well beyond the normal business hours. Almost 70 percent of the people who use convenience stores live within a mile of the store. Convenience stores are popular and are growing in number. White Hen Pantry, 7-Eleven, Circle K, and Open Pantry stores, for example, are found in most areas, as are independent convenience stores. The limited stock that these stores offer and the high prices they must charge to stay open for long hours, seven days a week, keep them from becoming a threat to supermarkets.

warehouse store   a minimal-service retail food outlet

Warehouse Stores   A **warehouse store** is a minimal-service retail food outlet. These stores appeared in the early 1970s to test discount pricing as a marketing strategy in food retailing. Escalating grocery prices in the 1970s and early 1980s made these low-price outlets extremely appealing. Many were successful.

In warehouse stores, such as Mrs. Clark's Foods and Pick 'N Save, the merchandise is left in packing cases on pallets on the floor. Prices are displayed on the cases but are not individually marked on the items. Customers may be expected to provide the paper bags or cartons in which to take their purchases home. The stores themselves are located in low-rent buildings and have large inventories on the premises.

Warehouse Clubs   The warehouse club is a large-scale, members-only, selling operation that combines cash-and-carry wholesaling features with discount retailing. Small-business owners account for about 60 percent of a typical warehouse club's sales. For a nominal annual fee (usually about

BUSINESS JOURNAL

Warehouse Club Customers Get Low-Price Thrills Instead of Frills

The Jones family piles into the car for a 50-mile trip to the store. They plan to stock up on basics, like a 50-pound bucket of detergent, a 20-pack of toilet paper, and a 40-pound sack of dog food. They'll probably pick up food items, too—perhaps several gigantic boxes of cereal and a 5-pound block of cheese. While there, they'll check out the price of a new refrigerator and tires for the car, and maybe splurge on some houseplants. The Joneses can shop for all of these items—plus office and automotive supplies, clothing, electronic equipment, even champagne or a baby grand piano—under one roof because they are members of a warehouse club. More than four hundred warehouse club outlets attract price-conscious shoppers all over the United States. The combined sales of the nine major chains reached over $22 billion in one year, making it the fastest growing retail segment in the country.

These huge warehouses have grown to challenge department stores, grocery stores, and regular discount chains. Almost everything they sell—and they sell almost everything—comes in industrial-size packages and quantities. Shoppers find limited selections of high-quality, nationally recognized brands like General Foods, Sony, and Procter & Gamble at about half the price they would pay at regular discount stores. What they won't find is decor, sales assistance, deliveries, or help getting their purchases to the car. They might have to dodge a forklift while craning their necks to spot something at the top of a towering stack, and they won't be able to pay with a credit card.

Warehouse club customers come in two varieties—business members and individual members. Average business customers spend about $1,000 each visit, and individuals about $75. Business members, whose purchases account for more than 60 percent of sales, are usually companies too small to buy directly from manufacturers. Most outlets designate exclusive business-member shopping hours. Individuals who want access to great bargains pay yearly dues (about $25) to get cards that let them in the door. The requirement of a card reduces the number of potential customers, but the warehouse club benefits through fewer bad checks and built-in customer commitment to come back.

Some of the major warehouse clubs include Costco Wholesale Club, Price Company, PACE Membership Warehouse, Inc. (owned by K mart Corp.), and Sam's Club, started by the late retailing genius, Sam Walton. Although all chains are basically the same, offering 3,000–4,000 deeply discounted items in bare-bones surroundings, each one strives to stand out from the crowd. Some Costco outlets sell cars at fixed prices prearranged with local car dealers. Price is exploring the possibility of selling pizza and yogurt. Sam's, the current market leader, is experimenting with a full line of fresh produce and meat. Although customers believe that warehouse clubs offer value, it is uncertain whether or not they are loyal to one chain over another. In Texas and the Northeast, where all the major clubs will soon be opening outlets, this question will soon be put to the test.

$25), small retailers may purchase products at wholesale prices for business use or for resale. Warehouse clubs also sell to ultimate consumers who are affiliated with government agencies, credit unions, schools, hospitals, and banks. Instead of paying a membership fee, individual consumers pay about 5 percent more on each item than do small-business owners.

Warehouse clubs offer the same types of products offered by discount stores, but in a limited range of sizes and styles. Since their product lines are shallow and sales volumes high, warehouse clubs can offer a broad range of merchandise, including nonperishable foods, beverages, books, appliances, housewares, automotive parts, hardware, furniture, and sundries. The sales volume of most warehouse clubs is four to five times that of a typical department store. With stock turning over at an average rate of eighteen times each year, warehouse clubs sell their goods before manufacturers' payment periods are up, thus reducing their need for capital.

To keep their prices 20 to 40 percent lower than those of supermarkets and discount stores, warehouse clubs provide few services. They generally advertise only through direct mail. Their facilities often have concrete floors and aisles wide enough for using forklifts. Merchandise is stacked on pallets or displayed on pipe racks. All payments must be in cash, and customers must transport purchases themselves. Examples of warehouse club chains are Costco Warehouse Clubs, Price Company, PACE Membership Warehouses, Sam's Club (owned by Wal-Mart Stores), and BJ's Warehouse Club (owned by Ames Corporation).

Kinds of Nonstore Retailers

Nonstore retailers are retailers that do not sell in conventional store facilities. Instead they sell door to door, through the mail, or through vending machines.

door-to-door retailer   a retailer that sells directly to consumers in their homes

Door-to-Door Retailers   A **door-to-door retailer** is one that sells directly to consumers in their homes. The seller's representative calls on the potential customer at home and demonstrates the product. If a sale is made, she or he writes up the order and often delivers the product to the purchaser. Encyclopedias (Encyclopaedia Britannica, Encyclopedia Americana); cosmetics and toiletries (Avon, Mary Kay); kitchenware (Tupperware); and vacuum cleaners (Electrolux) have been successfully sold door to door.

Avon Products, Inc. is the world's largest direct-selling retailer. Avon representatives sell cosmetics, fragrances and toiletries, jewelry, and accessories in consumers' homes. Avon doesn't tamper with its winning combination: The selling method it uses today was first developed when the firm was founded in 1886.

mail-order retailer   a retailer that solicits orders by mailing catalogs to potential customers

Mail-Order Retailers   A **mail-order retailer** is one that solicits orders by mailing catalogs to potential customers. To make a purchase, the customer fills out an enclosed order form and mails it to the firm. Lately, more and more mail-order firms are taking orders via toll-free telephone calls and charging the orders to customers' credit cards.

As a selling technique, catalogs work. According to the Direct Marketing Association, an industry trade group, Americans buy approximately $40 billion worth of merchandise through the mail per year. And most of this merchandise is selected from catalogs. In the last five years, mail-order sales have been increasing by about 10 percent a year; in the last ten years, sales have increased by approximately $25 billion. The annual increase in traditional retail sales is only 5 percent. The Sharper Image Corp., Land's End, Inc., L. L. Bean, Inc., and Spiegel are all mail-order retailers that compete with traditional retailers for customers.

Vending Machines Vending machines dispense convenience goods automatically when customers deposit the appropriate amount of money. Vending machines do not require sales personnel, and they permit twenty-four-hour service. They can be placed in convenient locations in office buildings, educational institutions, motels and hotels, shopping malls, and service stations.

The machines make available a wide assortment of goods. They can supply candy, cigarettes, soups, sandwiches, fresh fruits, yogurt, chewing gum, postage stamps, hot and cold beverages, perfume and cosmetics, and golf balls. They are even used to sell travel insurance at airports and around-the-clock banking services at convenient urban and suburban locations.

What drawbacks plague the vending-machine business? For one thing, malfunctioning is a costly and frustrating problem, as is vandalism. The machines must also be serviced frequently to operate properly. Together, repairs and servicing result in a very high cost for vending-machine selling—often more than one-third of sales revenue.

The Wheel of Retailing

LEARNING OBJECTIVE 7
Explain the wheel of retailing hypothesis.

wheel of retailing a hypothesis that suggests that new retail operations usually begin at the bottom—in price, profits, and prestige—and gradually move up the cost/price scale, competing with newer businesses that are evolving in the same way

Newly developing retail businesses strive for a secure position in the ever-changing retailing environment. One theory attempts to explain how types of retail stores originate and develop. The **wheel of retailing** hypothesis suggests that new retail operations usually begin at the bottom—in price, profits, and prestige. In time, their facilities become more elaborate, their investments increase, and their operating costs go up. Finally, the retailers emerge at the top of the cost/price scale, competing with newer businesses that are evolving in the same way.[8]

In Figure 13.5, the wheel of retailing describes the development of department and discount stores. Department stores such as Sears were originally high-volume, low-cost retailers competing with general stores and other small businesses. As the costs of services rose in department stores, discount stores began to fill the low-price retailing niche. Now many discount stores, in turn, are following the pattern by expanding services, improving locations, upgrading inventories, and raising prices.

Like most hypotheses, the wheel of retailing may not be universally applicable. The theory cannot predict what new retailing developments will occur, or when, for example. In industrialized, expanding economies, however, the hypothesis does help explain retailing patterns.

opening day drew 26,000 customers who backed up traffic on the New Jersey Turnpike for nine miles and bought $1 million worth of merchandise. Although IKEA's customers are attracted by the clean lines and bright colors of its sophisticated Scandinavian furniture, the primary reason for its success is its low prices—prices 25 to 50 percent below those of competitors. Customers can pick up a dining table for $59 or a sofa bed for $169.

IKEA, the brain child of Swedish entrepreneur Ingvar Kamprad, relies on a simple but highly successful formula: Sell quality, unassembled furniture at low prices to as many people as possible. To do this, IKEA farms out its product designs to the most efficient suppliers it can find. Almost 90 percent of IKEA's inventory is exclusive, conceived in Sweden by twenty in-house designers and produced in almost fifty countries by suppliers that work closely with IKEA designers to meet strict specifications. Items must be machine-made, attractive, economical, and, of course, packable. They must also withstand the company's rigid durability tests. IKEA currently carries about twelve thousand items that are produced by 1,800 suppliers; it is seeking out still more suppliers in the United States.

Kamprad also originated IKEA's knockdown packaging in the early 1950s, after observing the cumbersome distribution system of the Swedish furniture industry. Today's flat-pack technology has reduced IKEA's handling and warehousing costs by more than 50 percent. IKEA's giant central warehouse in Almhult, Sweden, is staffed with three people, thirteen robots, and a line of computerized forklifts. A keyboard operator electronically directs the forklifts and robots to load movable pallets with the appropriate merchandise and to transport them to the trucking area.

Skillful site selection is another factor in the company's worldwide success. IKEA looks just outside big cities for inexpensive land near major highways. This tactic allows the company to target customers who live within ninety minutes of a store. Because IKEA customers often spend half a day at the stores anyway, they don't seem to mind the driving distance.

An IKEA store is something like a grocery warehouse, complete with special shopping carts. Aisles are wide and easy to navigate. The U.S. stores display furniture and large items upstairs in individual room settings. Downstairs are a Swedish restaurant, a children's playroom, baby-changing facilities providing free diapers, and the IKEA Marketplace—a showroom of lamps, fabrics, housewares, and accessories. Each of the twelve thousand store items bears a tag listing its price, materials, and assembly. In the self-service area, a customer locates the appropriate flat boxes in warehouse stacks, carts purchases to the check-out counter, and then loads them in the car. Every article of furniture comes with a free Allen wrench, the only tool required for assembly. Shipping, arranged with outside contractors, is available for a fee.

IKEA acknowledges that customers are often inconvenienced by out-of-stock items. That annoyance doesn't seem to threaten the company's success. There are currently ninety IKEA stores operating in twenty-two countries, including recent additions in Hungary and Poland. In the next few years, at least eight outlets will open on both coasts in the United States. Every year, IKEA mails more than 60 million catalogs worldwide, in twelve languages. In the last four years, sales have added up to $3.2 billion, rising 35 percent in one year alone. *Money* magazine named IKEA the 1990 Store of the Year, and *Advertising Age* presented the company with the magazine's first ever Retail Marketing Campaign of the Year award. IKEA is proving itself the right store for the value-conscious 1990s.*

Questions

1. Although the median, after-tax profit for the U.S. retailing industry is 2.7 percent, IKEA's after-tax profit is 7 percent. How can IKEA price its merchandise as much as 50 percent lower than that of its competitors and still earn more money than they do?

2. What are the major advantages and disadvantages of using flat-pack technology—for IKEA and for its customers?

*Based on information from Peter Fuhrman, "The Workers' Friend," *Forbes*, March 21, 1988, pp. 124+; Kimberley Carpenter, "Help Yourself," *Working Woman*, August 1986, p. 56; Lindsay Gruson, "IKEA Venture in USA a Hit," *New York Times*, March 22, 1986, Sec. L37; Mary Krienke, "IKEA = Simple Good Taste," *Stores*, April 1986, pp. 56–59; Jennifer Lin, "IKEA's U.S. Translation," *Stores*, April 1986, pp. 60+; Kevin Maney, "Customers Flood USA IKEA Outlets," *USA Today*, November 4, 1986, p. B1; Eleanor Johnson Tracy, "Shopping Swedish-Style Comes to the U.S.," *Fortune*, January 20, 1986, p. 63; Alison Fahey, "IKEA Building a Loyal Following with Style, Price," *Advertising Age*, January 28, 1991, p. 23; Diane Harris, "Money's Store of the Year," *Money*, December 1990, pp. 144–146, 148–150; William E. Sheeline, "IKEA's Got 'Em Lining Up," *Fortune*, March 11, 1991, p. 72; Phil Patton, "The World 'Я ' Us," *Esquire*, October 1990, p. 47.

CASE 13.2

Mrs. Fields: The Cookies Aren't Crumbling

For Debbie Fields—founder of Mrs. Fields Cookies— the first day of business was terrible. By noon, when she had not sold a single cookie, she decided it was time to do something. So she loaded a tray with freshly baked cookies, walked up and down the street outside her Palo Alto, California, store and gave her cookies away to potential customers. Her strategy worked. At the end of her first day she had made $75. Today, Mrs. Fields Inc. is the world's best-known maker of cookies, operating in thirty-six states and six countries, including Japan and Australia; employing about five thousand workers; and generating almost $90 million in annual sales revenue. Unlike many cookie retailers, the company has not franchised any of its stores. Instead, all stores are company-owned, a policy enabling management to ensure that Mrs. Fields' famous standards of quality are maintained in all retail outlets. To facilitate consistent management, the firm developed "Retail Operations Intelligence" (ROI), computer software that allows managers worldwide to have daily contact with company headquarters.

After about a decade of success, lower cookie sales due to increasing competition and too many new stores paying soaring rents led to operating losses of more than $15 million. According to financial analysts, Mrs. Fields illustrates problems that can develop when a single-product company experiences rapid expansion.

Debbie Fields and her husband and company CEO, Randy Fields, took action to reverse the downward trend. First they delegated the running of the business to professional managers, like head-of-operations Paul Baird, a former top executive with Godfather's Pizza. Then the company began evolving into a specialty foods retailer that sells more than just cookies. After acquiring La Petite Boulangerie, a chain of bakeries, from PepsiCo, Mrs. Fields opened more than thirty new combination stores that offer not only cookies but also such items as muffins, bagels, soups, and sandwiches. A recent licensing agreement with a division of Marriott Corporation paves the way for about sixty new Mrs. Fields shops that will operate in highway plazas and airports. Ambrosia Chocolates agreed to make and market semisweet chocolate baking chips under the Mrs. Fields name. To pave the way for increased global expansion, the firm has recently entered into a joint-venture agreement with Paris-based Midial S.A. to market products with the Mrs. Fields

and La Petite Boulangerie names in the new twelve-nation European Community. In return for the European marketing rights, Mrs. Fields received $10 million. Under negotiation is a deal with supermarket chains to create in-store bakeries that will make and sell Mrs. Fields products.

The new strategy is a risky one, say financial analysts, because Mrs. Fields is getting away from the company's "core" business—selling gourmet cookies. For example, because the new combination stores are three times as large as the old cookie shops, they cost more to operate. In addition, the company has had to absorb the costs of opening new combination stores and retraining employees.

Randy Fields believes growth and change will make Mrs. Fields more profitable than ever. The company closed ninety-five, or about 16 percent, of the cookie stores that were either operating at a loss or overlapping the customer base of the new combination stores. Profits from the remaining cookie outlets have risen about 17 percent, and in one year, the first combination stores generated about $6 million in sales.**

Questions

1. Most companies like Mrs. Fields would have expanded by franchising their retail outlets. What are the advantages of company-owned stores? What are the disadvantages?

2. Originally, Mrs. Fields Cookies was a single-product company. What are the potential risks and benefits associated with expansion into combination stores?

3. Why would Mrs. Fields enter a joint venture with Paris-based Midial S.A. to market the Mrs. Fields and La Petite Boulangerie names in Europe?

**Based on information from "Tough Cookies?" *Fortune,* February 13, 1989, p. 112; Tom Richman, "Their System . . . ," *Inc.,* April 1989, p. 100; Buck Brown, "How the Cookie Crumbled at Mrs. Fields," *Wall Street Journal,* January 26, 1989, p. B1; "Mrs. Fields Automates the Way the Cookie Sells," *Chain Store Executive,* April 1988, pp. 73–74+; Mark Lewyn, "Executive Tales, Told by the Book," *USA Today,* October 12, 1987, p. 1; Nancy Rivera Brooks, "To Entrepreneur, Success Tastes Sweet," *Los Angeles Times,* September 4, 1986, Section IV, p. 1; Diane Filipowski, "1991 Optima Awards," *Personnel Journal,* January 1991, p. 49; Paul Quinn, "Innovation," *Personnel Journal,* January 1991, p. 56; Katherine Weisman, "Succeeding by Failing," *Forbes,* June 25, 1990, p. 160.

Promotion

CHAPTER PREVIEW

In this chapter we introduce four promotion methods and describe how they are used in an organization's marketing plans. First, we examine the role of advertising in the promotion mix. We discuss different types of advertising, the process of developing an advertising campaign, and social and legal concerns in advertising. Next, we consider several categories of personal selling, noting the importance of effective sales management. We also look at sales promotion—why firms use it and which sales promotion techniques are most effective. Then, we explain how both publicity and public relations can be used to build sales. Finally, we illustrate how these four promotion methods are combined in an effective promotion mix.

Taster's Choice Instant Coffee: Stay Tuned for the Next Episode

A beautiful, sophisticated woman with a British accent runs out of coffee for a dinner party she is giving. Hoping to borrow some, she knocks on a neighbor's door. When the door opens, she comes face to face with a handsome man who lends her his Taster's Choice Instant Coffee. Although instant coffee is the subject of this television commercial, what is really brewing is romantic tension and sexual innuendo.

In what television viewers have come to label the "Taster's Choice Soap Opera," the two characters, Tony and Sharon, meet in a second spot when she returns the instant coffee, and in a third one when he shows up late to a dinner party, is seated next to her, and invites her to dinner at his place. Will she go? Like any respectable soap opera, viewers have to tune in next time to find out—and more "next times" are in the works. Even viewers who aren't particular about their brand of coffee like the commercials and are eager to know what will happen next. *USA Today* and the *New York Times* have allotted space to that question, but Taster's Choice is guarding the story line so closely that even the stars don't know.

In England, where Nestlé markets Gold Blend, the British edition of Taster's Choice, television viewers have been watching the romance grow for the last four years. In episode seven the couple shared a kiss, and the whole country is waiting to see if episode eight will be a wedding. Tony and Sharon's coffee-based relationship made headlines in London tabloids, and eighteen months after the ads debuted, sales of Gold Blend had risen by 20 percent.

Nestlé is counting on its ads to do the same for sagging sales in the $1.1 billion instant coffee category in the United States. With growing concern over the effects of caffeine and increasing popularity of gourmet beans, sales of supermarket brands are down about 9.4 percent. Strategists at Taster's Choice believe that the witty and clever dialogue and ongoing sexual possibilities in their commercials will get coffee drinkers so emotionally involved with the product that they will become loyal Taster's Choice customers. In another instant coffee commercial, a husband and wife are both drinking coffee in the morning, and the husband asks, "Why is your coffee darker than mine?" Consumers answered, "Who cares?" Do they care about Tony and Sharon and Taster's Choice? Stay tuned.[1]

The makers of Taster's Choice instant coffee are using interesting television commercials as well as other advertising efforts to gain market share in an industry in which demand is gradually declining. Advertising is one ingredient a firm can use in its promotion programs.

promotion communication intended to inform, persuade, or remind an organization's target markets of the organization or its products

Promotion is communication intended to inform, persuade, or remind an organization's target markets of the organization or its products. The promotion with which we are most familiar—advertising—is intended to inform, persuade, or remind us to buy particular products. But there is more to promotion than advertising, and it is used for other purposes as well. Charities use promotion to inform us of their need for donations, to persuade us to give, and to remind us to do so in case we have forgotten. Even the Internal Revenue Service uses promotion (in the form of publicity) to remind us of its April 15 deadline for filing tax returns.

promotion mix the particular combination of promotion methods a firm uses in its promotional campaign to reach a target market

A **promotion mix** is the particular combination of promotion methods a firm uses in its promotional campaign to reach a target market. The makeup of a mix depends on many factors, including the characteristics of the target market. We shall discuss these factors toward the end of this chapter, after we have examined the promotion methods of advertising, personal selling, sales promotion, and publicity (which is closely related to public relations).

THE ROLE OF PROMOTION

LEARNING OBJECTIVE 1
Understand the role of promotion.

Promotion is commonly the object of two misconceptions. On the one hand, people take note of highly visible promotional activities, such as advertising and personal selling, and conclude that these make up the entire field of marketing. On the other hand, people sometimes consider promotional activities to be unnecessary, expensive, and the cause of higher prices. Neither view is accurate.

The role of promotion is to facilitate exchanges directly or indirectly by informing individuals, groups, or organizations and influencing them to accept a firm's products. To expedite exchanges directly, marketers convey information about a firm's goods, services, and ideas to particular market segments. To bring about exchanges indirectly, marketers address interest groups (such as environmental and consumer groups), regulatory agencies,

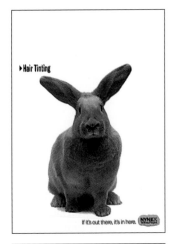

> Hair Tinting

If it's out there, it's in here. **NYNEX**

Promotion isn't always what you think. Watching a NYNEX ad is a little like watching a detective show or listening to a good joke—you try to figure it out before the end. NYNEX isn't selling rabbits or dyes with its painful puns. It's promoting the whole concept of Yellow Pages, convincing potential advertisers and customers that, yes, you can find *everything* in the Yellow Pages.

advertising   a paid, nonpersonal message communicated to a select audience through a mass medium

investors, and the general public concerning a company and its products. The broader role of promotion, therefore, is to maintain positive relationships between a company and various groups in the marketing environment.

Marketers frequently design promotional communications, such as advertisements, for specific groups, although some may be directed at wider audiences. Several different messages may be communicated simultaneously to different market segments. For example, Exxon Corporation may address customers about a new motor oil, inform investors about the firm's financial performance, and update the general public on the firm's environmental efforts to clean up the Alaskan shoreline.

Marketers must carefully plan, implement, and coordinate promotional communications to make the best use of them. The effectiveness of promotional activities depends greatly on the quality and quantity of information available to marketers about the organization's marketing environment (see Figure 14.1). If marketers want to influence customers to buy a certain product, for example, they must know who these customers are likely to be and how they make purchase decisions for that type of product. Marketers must gather and use information about particular audiences to communicate successfully with them.

THE PROMOTION MIX: AN OVERVIEW

Marketers can use several promotional methods to communicate with individuals, groups, and organizations. The methods that are combined to promote a particular product make up the promotion mix for that item.

Advertising, personal selling, sales promotion, and publicity are the four major elements in an organization's promotion mix (see Figure 14.2). Two, three, or four of these ingredients are used in a promotion mix, depending on the type of product and target market involved.

Advertising is a paid, nonpersonal message communicated to a select audience through a mass medium. The key words in the definition are *nonpersonal*, which excludes personal selling by a sales force, and *paid*, which excludes publicity. Advertising is so flexible that it can reach a very large

FIGURE 14.1
Information Flows Into and Out of an Organization
A promotional activity's effectiveness depends on the information available to marketers. *(Source: Adapted from William M. Pride and O. C. Ferrell,* Marketing: Concepts and Strategies, *8/e. Copyright © 1993 by Houghton Mifflin Company. Used by permission.)*

FIGURE 14.2
Possible Ingredients for an Organization's Promotion Mix
Depending on the type of product and target market involved, two or more of these ingredients are used in a promotion mix. *(Source: Adapted from William M. Pride and O. C. Ferrell,* Marketing: Concepts and Strategies, *8/e. Copyright © 1993 by Houghton Mifflin Company. Used by permission.)*

personal selling   personal communication aimed at informing customers and persuading them to buy a firm's products

sales promotion   the use of activities or materials as direct inducements to customers or salespersons

publicity   a nonpersonal message delivered in news-story form through a mass medium, at no charge

target group or a small, carefully chosen target audience. **Personal selling** is personal communication aimed at informing customers and persuading them to buy a firm's products. It is more expensive to reach one person through personal selling than through advertising, but this method provides immediate feedback and is often more persuasive than advertising. **Sales promotion** is the use of activities or materials as direct inducements to customers or salespersons. It adds extra value to the product or increases the customer's incentive to buy the product. **Publicity** is a nonpersonal message delivered in news-story form through a mass medium, at no charge. Magazine, newspaper, radio, and television stories about a company's new stores, products, or personnel changes are examples of publicity. Although marketers do not pay outright for such media coverage, there are nonetheless definite costs associated with the preparation and distribution of news releases.

ADVERTISING

In 1990 organizations spent $128 billion on advertising in the United States.[2] Figure 14.3 shows how advertising expenditures and employment in advertising have increased since 1972. In recent years, the growth of advertising has subsided to some extent.

Types of Advertising by Purpose

LEARNING OBJECTIVE 2
Explain the purposes of the three types of advertising.

Depending on its purpose and message, advertising may be classified into three groups. Selective advertising promotes specific brands of products

FIGURE 14.3
Growth of Advertising Expenditures and of Employment in Advertising
Total advertising expenditures and employment in advertising have been steadily increasing since 1972. Both are expected to continue to rise in the 1990s. *(Source: Reprinted with permission of* Advertising Age, *May 6, 1991, Copyright Crain Communications, Inc. All rights reserved.)*

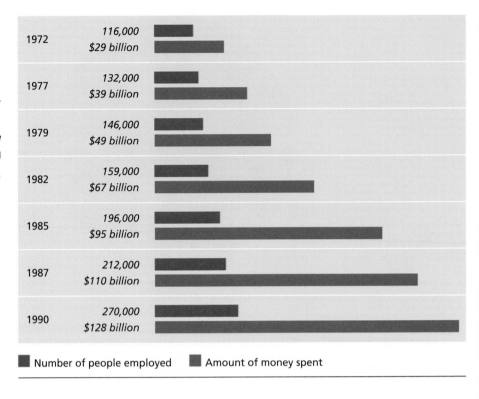

and services. Institutional advertising is image-building advertising for a firm. And primary-demand advertising is industry (rather than brand) advertising.

Selective Advertising **Selective** (or **brand**) **advertising** is advertising that is used to sell a particular brand of product. It is by far the most common type of advertising, and it accounts for the lion's share of advertising expenditures. Producers use brand-oriented advertising to convince us to buy their products, from Bubble Yum to Buicks.

> **selective (or brand) advertising** advertising that is used to sell a particular brand of product

Selective advertising that aims at persuading consumers to make purchases within a short time is called *immediate-response advertising*. Most local advertising is of this type. It generally promotes products with immediate appeal, such as fans or air conditioners during an unusually hot summer. Selective advertising aimed at keeping a firm's name or product before the public is called *reminder advertising*.

Comparative advertising, which has become more popular over the last decade, compares specific characteristics of two or more identified brands. Of course, the comparison always shows the advertiser's brand to be best. Comparative advertising is now fairly common among manufacturers of deodorants, toothpaste, butter, tires, and automobiles. Comparisons are often based on the outcome of surveys or research studies. Though competing firms act as effective watchdogs against each other's advertising claims, and regulations on comparative advertising are stringent, a certain sophistication on the consumer's part concerning claims based on "scientific studies" and various statistical manipulations is worth cultivating. Comparative advertising is illegal or at least unacceptable in a number of countries.

institutional advertising advertising designed to enhance a firm's image or reputation

Institutional Advertising Institutional advertising is advertising designed to enhance a firm's image or reputation. Many public utilities and larger firms, such as AT&T and the major oil companies, use part of their advertising dollars to build goodwill rather than to stimulate sales directly. A positive public image helps an organization to attract not only customers but also employees and investors.

primary-demand advertising advertising whose purpose is to increase the demand for *all* brands of a good or service

Primary-Demand Advertising Primary-demand advertising is advertising whose purpose is to increase the demand for *all* brands of a good or service. Trade and industry associations, such as the American Dairy Association ("Milk: It Does a Body Good.") and the Association of American Railroads ("Who Needs America's Railroads? We All Do."), are the major users of primary-demand advertising. Their advertisements promote broad product categories, such as beef, milk, pork, potatoes, and prunes, without mentioning specific brands.

Advertising Media

LEARNING OBJECTIVE 3
Describe the advantages and disadvantages of the major advertising media.

advertising media the various forms of communication through which advertising reaches its audience

The **advertising media** are the various forms of communication through which advertising reaches its audience. They include newspapers, magazines, television, radio, direct mail, and outdoor displays. Figure 14.4 shows how organizations allocate their advertising expenditures among the various media. Note that *electronic media*—television and radio—account for less than 30 percent of all media expenditures.

FIGURE 14.4
Comparison of Advertising Media in Terms of Advertising Expenditures
About 47 cents of every dollar spent on advertising are consumed in newspaper and television advertising. *(Source: Reprinted with permission from* Advertising Age, *May 6, 1991. Copyright Crain Communications, Inc. All rights reserved; U.S. Industrial Outlook 1991—Professional Services, p. 52–53.)*

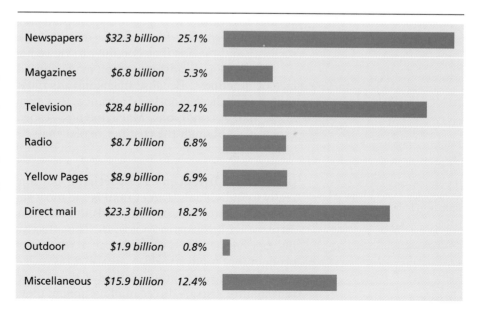

Newspapers	$32.3 billion	25.1%
Magazines	$6.8 billion	5.3%
Television	$28.4 billion	22.1%
Radio	$8.7 billion	6.8%
Yellow Pages	$8.9 billion	6.9%
Direct mail	$23.3 billion	18.2%
Outdoor	$1.9 billion	0.8%
Miscellaneous	$15.9 billion	12.4%

Newspapers Newspaper advertising accounts for about 25 percent of all advertising expenditures. More than half is purchased by local retailers. Newspaper advertising is used so extensively by retailers because it is reasonable in cost. Furthermore, because it provides only local coverage, advertising dollars are not wasted in reaching people who are outside the store's market area. It is also timely. Ads can usually be placed the day before they are to appear.

There are some drawbacks, however, to newspaper advertising. It has a short life span; newspapers are generally read through once and then discarded. Color reproduction in newspapers is usually poor; thus most ads must be run in black and white. Finally, marketers cannot target specific demographic markets through newspaper ads because the newspaper is read by such a broad spectrum of people.

Newspapers carry more cooperative advertising than other print media. **Cooperative advertising** is advertising in which the cost is shared by a producer and one or more local retailers. The costs are shared because the advertising benefits both the producer, whose products are promoted, and the retailer, which reaches its customers through the advertising.

cooperative advertising advertising in which the cost is shared by a producer and one or more local retailers

Magazines The advertising revenues of magazines have been climbing dramatically since 1976. In 1990 they reached $6.8 billion, or about 5.3 percent of all advertising expenditures.

Advertisers can reach very specific market segments through ads in special-interest magazines. A boat manufacturer has a ready-made consumer audience in subscribers to *Yachting* or *Sail*. Producers of cameras and photographic equipment advertise primarily in *Travel & Leisure* or *Popular Photography*. A number of more general magazines like *Time* and *Cosmopolitan* publish regional editions, which provide advertisers with geographic flexibility as well.

Magazine advertising is more prestigious than newspaper advertising, and it provides high-quality color reproduction. In addition, magazine advertisements have a longer life span than those in other media. Issues of *National Geographic*, for example, may be kept for months or years by subscribers, and the ads they contain are viewed over and over again.

The major disadvantages of magazine advertising are high cost and lack of timeliness. Because magazine ads must normally be prepared more than two to three months in advance, they cannot be adjusted to reflect the latest market conditions. Magazine ads—especially full-color ads—are also expensive, although the cost per reader may compare favorably with that of other media.

direct-mail advertising promotional material mailed directly to individuals

Direct Mail **Direct-mail advertising** is promotional material mailed directly to individuals. Direct mail is the most selective medium: Mailing lists are available (or can be compiled) to reach almost any target market, from airplane enthusiasts to zoologists. The effectiveness of direct-mail advertising can be measured easily because recipients either buy or don't buy the product that is advertised.

The success of direct-mail advertising depends on appropriate and current mailing lists. A direct-mail campaign may fail if the mailing list is outdated and the mailing does not reach the right people. In addition, this

Trying to borrow an image.
Baseball used to have such a solid, All-American image that baseball players were almost sure bets in ads. But with many baseball players making headlines that cause their coaches to cringe, baseball is trying to rebuild its own image. This Minnesota Twins ad uses the popularity of the Young Guns movies to promote its new, young, likable stars.

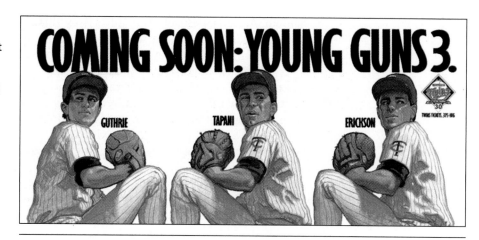

medium is relatively costly. Nevertheless, direct-mail advertising expenditures in 1990 amounted to more than $23 billion, or about 18 percent of the total.

Outdoor Advertising **Outdoor advertising** consists of short promotional messages on billboards, posters, and signs. In 1990 outdoor advertisers spent $1.9 billion, or slightly less than 1 percent of total advertising expenditures, on outdoor advertising.

Sign and billboard advertising allows the marketer to focus on a particular geographic area; it is fairly inexpensive. However, because most of it is directed toward a mobile audience, the message must be limited to a few words. The medium is especially suitable for products that lend themselves to pictorial display.

outdoor advertising short promotional messages on billboards, posters, and signs, and in skywriting

Television Television is the newest advertising medium, and it ranks second only to newspapers in total revenue. In 1990, 22.1 percent of advertising expenditures, or $28 billion, went to television. Approximately 98 percent of American homes have at least one color television set, which is used an average of seven hours each day.[3] The average U.S. household can receive nearly twenty-eight TV channels, including cable and pay stations, according to Nielson Media Research. Fifty-four percent of households receive twenty or more channels, and 39 percent can get between seven and nineteen channels.[4] Television obviously provides a massive market for advertisers.

Television advertising is the primary medium for larger firms whose objective is to reach national or regional markets. A national advertiser may buy *network time*, which guarantees that its message will be broadcast by hundreds of local stations affiliated with the network. And both national and local firms may buy *local time* on a single station that covers a particular geographic area.

Advertisers may *sponsor* an entire show, alone or with other sponsors. Or they may buy *spot time* for a single 10- , 20- , 30- , or 60-second commercial during or between programs. To an extent, they may select their audience by choosing the day of the week and the time of day their ads will be

shown. Anheuser-Busch, Inc. advertises Budweiser Beer and Noxell Corporation advertises Noxema shaving cream during the TV football season because the majority of viewers are men, who are likely to use these products.

Television advertising rates are based on the number of people expected to be watching when the commercial is aired. In 1989, a thirty-
second network commercial aired during the National Basketball Association Championships cost over $150,000, and a commercial of the same
length ran $850,000 for Superbowl XXVI.

Unlike magazine advertising, and perhaps like newspaper ads, television advertising has a short life. If a viewer misses a commercial, it is
missed forever. Viewers may also become indifferent to commercial messages. Or they may use the commercial time as a break from viewing, thus
missing the message altogether. Remote-control devices make it especially
easy to avoid television commercials.

Radio Advertisers spent about $8.7 billion, or 6.8 percent of total expendi-
tures, on radio advertising in 1990. Like magazine advertising, radio advertising offers selectivity. Radio stations develop programming for—and are
tuned in by—specific groups of listeners. There are almost half a billion radios in the United States (about six per household), which makes radio the
most accessible medium.

Radio can be less expensive than other media. Actual rates depend on
geographic coverage, the number of commercials contracted for, the time
period specified, and whether the station broadcasts on AM, FM, or both.
Even small retailers are able to afford radio advertising.

LEARNING OBJECTIVE 4
Identify the major steps in
developing an advertising
campaign.

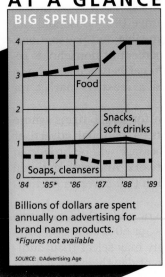

AT A GLANCE
BIG SPENDERS

Billions of dollars are spent
annually on advertising for
brand name products.
*Figures not available

SOURCE: ©Advertising Age

Major Steps in Developing an Advertising Campaign

An advertising campaign is developed in several stages. These stages may
vary in number and the order in which they are implemented, depending
on the company's resources, product, and audiences. A campaign in any organization, however, will include the following steps in some form.

1. Identify and Analyze the Advertising Target The advertising target is
the group of people toward which advertisements are directed. To pinpoint
the advertising target and develop an effective campaign, marketers must
analyze such information as the geographic distribution of consumers;
their age, sex, race, income, and education; and their attitudes toward both
the advertiser's product and competing products. How marketers use this
information will be influenced by the features of the product to be advertised and the nature of the competition. Precise identification of the advertising target is crucial to the proper development of subsequent stages and,
ultimately, to the success of the campaign itself.

2. Define the Advertising Objectives The goals of an advertising campaign should be stated precisely and in measurable terms. The objectives
should include the current position of the firm, indicate how far and in
what direction from that original reference point the company wishes to
move, and specify a definite period of time for the achievement of the

ETHICAL CHALLENGES

Sex in Advertising—Has It Gone Too Far?

For years, advertising flirted with sexual innuendoes but avoided being sexually explicit. Then, in a Calvin Klein jeans ad, actress Brooke Shields asked the question, "Want to know what comes between me and my Calvins?" The answer, "Nothing," raised eyebrows, sold jeans, and paved the way for a new generation of sexually provocative advertising.

Ever since a beautiful woman first posed on the hood of a new model automobile, or a handsome man first rode his horse over a mountain and lit up a cigarette, advertisers have been satisfied that sex sells products. From coffee to clothing, advertising contains sexual innuendo. A series of Bugle Boy ads currently running on MTV shows more women dressed in bikinis and tight skirts than men wearing Bugle Boy jeans. In Maidenform underwear ads, women squirm and stuff their way into constricting underwear fashions from the past. Beer marketers are notorious for relying on sexy men and women to sell their product. When the "Swedish Bikini Team," a group of shapely blonds in skimpy bathing suits, joins a group of men drinking Old Milwaukee Beer, the implication is clear—drinking this brand of beer attracts beautiful women. Although these ads range from humorous and inoffensive to obviously sexist, others cross the line into what many call crass, soft-core pornography. The epitome of advertising that provokes an uproar was Calvin Klein's explicit ad insert in *Vanity Fair* magazine. On 116 textless—and many

say tasteless—pages of advertising that would make anyone's grandmother blush, readers saw naked bodies, tattoos, and motorcycles, but not many jeans.

For Calvin Klein's marketers, shocking and outraging some people is permissible if it means selling more jeans. Other advertising executives, however, ask themselves if it is ethical to offend for the sake of profit. To get expert advice and increase awareness, agencies are hiring consultants and holding seminars on sex in advertising. As a result, many sexist, exploitative, or degrading ads are disappearing. There are those, however, who argue that if the public really objected to this type of ad, the products they promote wouldn't sell. In addition, they insist, it's the role of advertisers to market products, not to serve as America's social conscience.

Issues to Consider

1. Is it ethical to use sex in advertising to attract attention when sex is not related to the product, such as in an advertisement for industrial equipment or life insurance? Explain. What about for products related to sex, such as perfume or jeans?

2. From an ethical standpoint, what factors influence how sexually explicit an advertisement should be?

goals. Advertising objectives that focus on sales will stress increasing sales by a certain percentage or dollar amount, or expanding the firm's market share. Communication objectives will emphasize increasing product or brand awareness, improving consumer attitudes, or conveying product information.

3. Create the Advertising Platform An advertising platform includes the important selling points or features that an advertiser wishes to incorporate into the advertising campaign. These features should be those that are important to consumers in their selection and use of a product and, if possible, those features that competing products lack. Although research into consumer opinions is expensive, it is the most productive way to determine the issues of an advertising platform.

4. Determine the Advertising Appropriation The advertising appropriation is the total amount of money designated for advertising in a given period. This stage is critical to the success of the campaign because advertising efforts based on an inadequate budget will understimulate customer demand, and a budget too large will waste a company's resources. Advertising appropriations may be based on last year's sales or forecasted plan, on what competitors spend on advertising, or on executive judgment.

5. Develop the Media Plan A media plan specifies exactly which media will be used in the campaign and when advertisements will appear. The primary concern of the media planner is to reach the largest possible number of persons in the advertising target for each dollar spent, though cost effectiveness is not easy to measure. In addition to cost, media planners must consider the location and demographics of people in the advertising target, the content of the message, and the characteristics of the audiences reached by various media. The media planner begins with general media decisions, selects subclasses within each medium, and finally chooses particular media vehicles for the campaign.

6. Create the Advertising Message The content and form of a message are influenced by the product's features, the characteristics of people in the advertising target, the objectives of the campaign, and the choice of media. An advertiser must consider these factors to choose words and illustrations that will be meaningful and appealing to persons in the advertising target. The copy, or words, of an advertisement will vary depending on the media choice but should attempt to move the audience through attention, interest, desire, and action. Artwork and visuals should complement copy by attracting the audience's attention and communicating an idea quickly.

7. Evaluate Advertising Effectiveness A campaign's success should be measured, in terms of its original objectives, before, during, and/or after the campaign ends. An advertiser should at least be able to estimate whether sales or market share went up because of the campaign or whether any change occurred in customer attitudes or brand awareness. Data from past and current sales, responses to coupon offers, and customer surveys administered by research organizations are some of the ways in which advertising effectiveness can be evaluated.

Advertising Agencies

advertising agency   an independent firm that plans, produces, and places advertising for its clients

Advertisers can plan and produce their own advertising with help from media personnel, or they can hire advertising agencies. An **advertising agency** is an independent firm that plans, produces, and places advertising for its clients. Many larger ad agencies offer help with sales promotion and publicity as well. The media usually pay a commission of 15 percent to advertising agencies. Thus the cost to the agency's client can be quite moderate. The client may be asked to pay for selected services the agency performs. Other methods for compensating agencies are also used.

Firms that do a lot of advertising may use both an in-house advertising department and an independent agency. This approach gives the firm the advantage of being able to call on the agency's expertise in particular areas of advertising. The agency also brings a fresh viewpoint to the firm's products and advertising plans.

Table 14.1 lists the nation's twenty leading advertisers, in all media. In 1990 the number-one honor went to Procter & Gamble.

Social and Legal Considerations in Advertising

Critics of U.S. advertising have two main arguments—that it is wasteful and that it can be deceptive. Although advertising (like any other activity) can be performed inefficiently, it is far from wasteful. Let's look at the evidence:

- Advertising is the most effective and the least expensive means of communicating product information to millions of individuals and firms.

- Advertising encourages competition and is, in fact, a means of competition. It thus leads to the development of new and improved products, wider product choices, and lower prices.

TABLE 14.1 Advertising Expenditures and Sales Volume for the Top 20 National Advertisers (in millions of dollars)

Rank	Company	Advertising Expenditures	Sales (millions)	Advertising Expenditures as Percentage of Sales
1	Procter & Gamble Co.	$2,284.5	$15,276	15.0
2	Philip Morris Cos.	2,210.2	36,014	6.1
3	Sears, Roebuck & Co.	1,507.1	55,972	2.7
4	General Motors Corp.	1,502.8	86,967	1.7
5	Grand Metropolitan PLC	882.6	8,025	11.0
6	PepsiCo Inc.	849.1	14,047	6.0
7	AT&T Co.	796.5	37,285	2.1
8	McDonald's Corp.	764.1	3,871	19.7
9	K mart Corp.	693.2	32,070	2.2
10	Time Warner	676.9	8,550	7.9
11	Eastman Kodak Co.	664.8	20,229	3.3
12	Johnson & Johnson	653.7	5,427	12.0
13	RJR Nabisco	636.1	12,125	5.2
14	Nestlé SA	635.9	36,511	1.7
15	Warner-Lambert Co.	630.8	2,445	25.8
16	Ford Motor Co.	616.0	56,902	1.1
17	Toyota Motor Corp.	580.7	71,400	0.8
18	Kellogg Co.	577.7	3,044	19.0
19	Unilever NV	568.9	8,680	6.6
20	General Mills	539.0	6,377	8.5

Source: Reprinted with permission from *Advertising Age*, September 25, 1991. Copyright Crain Communications, Inc. All rights reserved.

- Advertising revenues support our mass communications media—newspapers, magazines, radio, and television. This means that advertising pays for much of our news coverage and entertainment programming.
- Advertising provides job opportunities in fields ranging from sales to film production. Total employment within the advertising industry stood at 236,000 in 1989.[5]

Along with pure fact, advertising tends to include some exaggeration, stretching of the truth, and occasional deception. Consumers usually spot such distortion in short order. Also, various government and private agencies scrutinize advertising for false or deceptive claims or offers. At the national level, the Federal Trade Commission, the Food and Drug Administration, and the Federal Communications Commission oversee advertising practices. Advertising may also be monitored by state and local agencies, Better Business Bureaus, and industry associations. These organizations have varying degrees of control over advertising, but their overall effect has been a positive one.

PERSONAL SELLING

Personal selling is the most adaptable of all promotion methods because the person who is presenting the message can modify it to suit the individual buyer. However, personal selling is also the most expensive promotion method.

Most successful salespeople are able to communicate with people on a one-to-one basis and are strongly motivated. They strive to have a thorough knowledge of the products they offer for sale. And they are willing and able to deal with the details involved in handling and processing orders. Sales managers tend to emphasize these qualities in recruiting and hiring, as well as in the other human resources management activities discussed in Chapter 9.

Many selling situations demand the personal contact and adaptability of personal selling. This is especially true of industrial sales, where single purchases may amount to millions of dollars. Obviously, sales of that size must be based on carefully planned sales presentations, personal contact between buyers and sellers, and thorough negotiations.

Kinds of Salespersons

LEARNING OBJECTIVE 5
Recognize the various kinds of salespersons, the steps in the personal-selling process, and the major sales management tasks.

Because most businesses employ different salespersons to perform different functions, marketing managers must select the kinds of sales personnel that will be most effective in selling the firm's products. Salespersons may be identified as order getters, order takers, and support personnel. A single individual can, and often does, perform all three functions.

GETTING AHEAD IN BUSINESS
Making Effective Sales Calls

A recent survey by Communispond Incorporated, a New York-based management consulting firm, asked 255 salespeople to identify the most difficult and unpleasant aspects of their jobs. Forty-nine percent of the respondents put "making a sales call" at the top of the "hate list." Forty-one percent revealed that these calls usually resulted in failure to make a sale. Yet as time becomes more constrained for clients and salespeople as well and travel costs soar, the ability to make a successful sale with one, perhaps brief, call carries increasing weight. Planning your sales call in detail tremendously increases your chances of success. Here are some essential things to do to make your sales call effective.

DO YOUR HOMEWORK

- Assess your prospective customer's beliefs, desires, and needs to the extent possible.
- Know exactly how your service or product meets your customer's needs.
- Focus your presentation on conveying that information.

The more you know, the more confidence you express, and confidence goes a long way toward winning a client.

PLAN YOUR PRESENTATION

- Make an outline to help organize your thoughts.
- Be clear and to the point.
- Discard nonessentials—anything extra takes up too much of your client's time.
- Be sure to include three things your client needs to know:
  (1) What your product or service is.
  (2) What your product or service will do for your client.
  (3) What your product or service will cost.

Try to imagine all possible objections that your client might have and any problems that might come up during the presentation, and plan your solutions.

MAKE YOUR PRESENTATION

- Listen first to what your client has to say and then do your own talking—something the customer says might change what you want to say.
- Start with the most important issues.
- Briefly explain your strategies for meeting your client's needs.
- Use concrete examples—they paint the best picture.
- Let your client talk as much as he or she wants.
- Keep track of the time you spend talking—finishing quickly is best.
- Never lecture your client—this is boring and insulting.
- Never patronize your client—this is demeaning.

Carefully choose the way you express questions and ideas. For example, asking, "How much do you plan to invest?" is much less threatening than asking, "How much can you afford?"

CLOSE YOUR PRESENTATION

- You can be prepared with a preplanned phrase that wraps things up—"Why don't we check our calendars and set a time for delivery?"
- You can initiate an action that says, without words, that the sale is closed—start filling out the necessary forms.
- You can ask for the order and write it up—it's a simple and direct way to close.

Long or short, well-executed or not, the time comes in every sales call to close. Even for seasoned salespeople, this can be a difficult and awkward moment.

A well-researched and well-planned sales call may still lack essential ingredients for success. First, remember that no amount of preparation can take the place of a display of enthusiasm for the product or service and a sincere expression of commitment to the client. Second, keep in mind that the sales call doesn't really end when you walk out the door. A follow-up call indicates true interest and fosters a long-term business relationship.

Selling in a "man's world." Saleswomen have long been accepted in such areas as retailing and real estate, but a woman who puts on a hard hat and tries to sell to industry faces a new set of challenges. The problem, of course, is stereotypes, not what's under the hard hat, and women use their individual strengths and strategies to destroy the stereotypes and win acceptance.

During a demonstration, the salesperson may suggest that the prospect try out the product personally. The demonstration and product trial should underscore specific points made during the presentation.

Answering Objections The prospect is likely to raise objections or ask questions at any time. This gives the salesperson a chance to eliminate objections that might prevent a sale, to point out additional features, or to mention special services the company offers.

Closing the Sale To close the sale, the salesperson asks the prospect to buy the product. This is considered the critical point in the selling process. Many experienced salespeople make use of a *trial closing*, in which they ask questions that are based on the assumption that the customer is going to buy the product. The questions, "When would you want delivery?" and "Do you want the standard or the deluxe model?," are typical of trial closings. They allow the reluctant prospect to make a purchase without having to say, "I'll take it."

Following Up The salesperson must follow up after the sale to ensure that the product is delivered on time, in the right quantity, in good condition, and in proper operating condition. During follow-up, the salesperson also makes it clear that he or she is available in case problems develop. Follow-up leaves a good impression and eases the way toward future sales. Hence it is essential to the selling process. The salesperson's job does not end with a sale. It continues as long as the seller and the customer maintain a working relationship.

Managing Personal Selling

A firm's success often hinges on the competent management of its sales force. Without a strong sales force—and the sales revenue it brings in—a business will soon fail.

Sales managers have responsibilities in a number of areas. They must set sales objectives in concrete, quantifiable terms, specifying a certain period of time and a certain geographic area. They must adjust the size of the sales force in accord with changes in the firm's marketing plan and changes in the marketing environment. Sales managers must attract and hire effective salespersons. They must develop a training program and decide where, when, how, and for whom the training will be conducted. They must formulate a fair and adequate compensation plan to keep qualified employees. They must motivate salespersons to boost their productivity. They must define sales territories and determine scheduling and routing of the sales force. Finally, sales managers must evaluate the operation as a whole through sales reports, communications with customers, and invoices.

SALES PROMOTION

LEARNING OBJECTIVE 6
Describe sales promotion objectives and methods.

Sales promotion consists of activities or materials that are direct inducements to customers or salespersons. Sales promotion techniques are used primarily to enhance and supplement other promotion methods. In this role they can have a significant impact on sales of consumer products. The dramatic increase in recent spending for sales promotion shows that marketers have recognized the potential of this promotion method. Many firms now include year-round sales promotions as part of their overall promotion mix.

Sales Promotion Objectives

Sales promotion activities may be used singly or in combination, both offensively and defensively, to achieve one goal or a set of goals. Marketers use sales promotion activities and materials for a number of purposes:

1. To draw new customers
2. To encourage trial purchases of a new product
3. To invigorate the sales of a mature brand
4. To boost sales to current customers
5. To reinforce advertising

6. To increase traffic in retail stores

7. To steady irregular sales patterns

8. To build up reseller inventories

9. To neutralize competitive promotional efforts

10. To improve shelf space and displays[6]

Some of these objectives focus on reseller demand; some, on consumer demand; and some, on both resellers and consumers. Any sales promotion objective should be in keeping with the organization's general goals and with its marketing and promotion objectives.

Sales Promotion Methods

consumer sales promotion method a sales promotion method designed to attract consumers to particular retail stores and to motivate them to purchase certain new or established products

trade sales promotion method a sales promotion method designed to encourage wholesalers and retailers to stock and actively promote a manufacturer's product

Most sales promotion methods can be classified as promotion techniques either for consumer sales or for trade sales. A **consumer sales promotion method** attracts consumers to particular retail stores and motivates them to purchase certain new or established products. A **trade sales promotion method** encourages wholesalers and retailers to stock and actively promote a manufacturer's products. Incentives such as money, merchandise, marketing assistance, or gifts are commonly awarded to resellers who buy products or respond positively in other ways.

A number of factors enter into marketing decisions about which, and how many, sales promotion methods to use. Of greatest importance are the objectives of the promotional effort. Product characteristics—size, weight, cost, durability, uses, features, and hazards—and target-market profiles—age, gender, income, location, density, usage rate, and buying patterns—must likewise be considered. Distribution channels and availability of appropriate resellers also influence the choice of sales promotion methods, as do the competitive and regulatory environments. Let's now discuss a few important sales promotion methods.

refund a return of part of the purchase price of a product

Refunding A **refund** is a return of part of the purchase price of a product. Usually the refund is offered by the producer to those consumers who send in a coupon along with a specific proof of purchase. (A refund is sometimes called a *manufacturer's rebate*.) Refunding is a relatively low-cost promotion method. It was formerly used mainly for new product items, but is now applied to a wide variety of products.

cents-off coupon a coupon that reduces the retail price of a particular item by a stated amount at the time of purchase

Couponing A **cents-off coupon** is a coupon that reduces the retail price of a particular item by a stated amount at the time of purchase. These coupons may be worth anywhere from a few cents to more than $1. They are reproduced in newspapers and magazines and/or sent to consumers by direct mail. More and more firms now use coupons. About 280 billion coupons were distributed in 1990. Of these, fewer than 3 percent were redeemed by consumers.[7] The average value of a coupon increased from 29 cents in 1987 to 49 cents in 1990.[8] Coupons seem to work best for new or improved product items. The largest single category of coupons is health and beauty aids, followed by prepared foods, frozen and refrigerated foods, cereals, and household products. Stores in some areas even deduct double or triple the value of manufacturers' coupons from the purchase price, as a sales promotion technique of their own. Coupons may also offer free merchandise, either with or without an additional purchase of the product.

sample   a free package or container of a product

Sampling   A **sample** is a free package or container of a product. Samples may be offered through coupons, by direct mailing, or at *in-store demonstrations*. Although sampling ensures that consumers will try the product, it is the most expensive sales promotion technique. It gives best results when used with new products.

premium   a gift that a producer offers the customer in return for using its product

Premiums   A **premium** is a gift that a producer offers the customer in return for using its product. A producer of packaged foods may, for instance, offer consumers a cookbook as a premium. Most airlines offer free travel to business customers after a certain number of paid trips or air miles.

point-of-purchase display promotional material placed within a retail store

Point-of-Purchase Displays   A **point-of-purchase display** is promotional material placed within a retail store. The display is usually located near the product being promoted. It may actually hold merchandise (as do L'eggs' hosiery displays) or inform customers about what the product offers and encourage them to buy it. Most point-of-purchase displays are prepared and set up by manufacturers and wholesalers.

trade show   an industrywide exhibit at which many sellers display their products

Trade Shows   A **trade show** is an industrywide exhibit at which many sellers display their products. Some trade shows are organized exclusively for dealers—to permit manufacturers and wholesalers to show their latest lines to retailers. Others are consumer promotions designed to stimulate buying interest in the general public. Among the latter are boat shows, home shows, and flower shows put on each year in large cities.

PUBLICITY AND PUBLIC RELATIONS

LEARNING OBJECTIVE 7
Discuss the types and uses of publicity and the requirements for effective use of publicity.

Publicity, as mentioned earlier, is a nonpersonal message in news story form delivered through a mass medium, free of charge. Publicity differs from advertising in two ways: It is free (the media do not get paid for it), and its content and timing are not controlled by the firm. When it enhances the image of the firm or its products, publicity can be an effective form of promotion.

public relations   all activities whose objective is to create and maintain a favorable public image

Public relations consists of all activities whose objective is to create and maintain a favorable public image. In one sense, publicity is a part of public relations—the "information" part. Actually, good public relations generally results in good publicity and thus a favorable image.

Public-relations activities are many and varied, including the sponsorship of programs on public television and radio, and the sponsorship of events (including the Olympics). Although approximately two-thirds of the

Eat and ogle. Hollywood restaurants have long attracted patrons more interested in seeing the stars than in eating the food. Now Planet Hollywood, a restaurant and movie museum in New York City, is trying to cash in on meal-time star-gazing. Backers Arnold Schwarzenegger, Sylvester Stallone, and Bruce Willis promised to be seen often at the restaurant, making it the place to be seen.

funds spent for event-sponsorship support sports events, companies also sponsor festivals, popular music, plays, and social causes.[9] These and other public-relations efforts tend to build sales indirectly by showing that the sponsor is a "good citizen."

Types of Publicity

news release a typed page of generally fewer than 300 words provided by an organization to the media as a form of publicity

feature article a piece (of up to 3,000 words) prepared by an organization for inclusion in a particular publication

captioned photograph a picture accompanied by a brief explanation

press conference a meeting at which invited media personnel hear important news announcements and receive supplementary textual materials and photographs

Several approaches to publicity are available to marketers. The **news release,** one of the most widely used types of publicity, is generally one typed page of about three hundred words provided by an organization to the media. The release includes the firm's name, address, phone number, and contact person. The **feature article,** which may run as long as three thousand words, is usually written for inclusion in a particular publication. The **captioned photograph,** a picture accompanied by a brief explanation, is an effective way to illustrate a new or improved product. The **press conference** allows invited media personnel to hear important news announcements and to receive supplementary textual materials and photographs. Finally, letters to the editor, special newspaper or magazine editorials, films, and tapes may be prepared and distributed to appropriate media for possible use.

At times, a single type of publicity will be adequate for a promotion mix. At other times, publicity will predominate in a mix, and the marketer will capitalize on several avenues of publicity. The specific kinds of publicity chosen depend on the composition of the target audience, the response of media personnel, the significance of the news item, and the nature and quantity of information to be communicated.

The Uses of Publicity

Businesses may use publicity for only one purpose or for several purposes. Publicity can raise public awareness of a company's products or activities. It can maintain a desired level of visibility for an organization. It can show a forward-looking company to its best advantage and help to downplay a negative image as well. Table 14.2 lists some of the issues that can be addressed by publicity releases.

Using Publicity Effectively

A company's publicity efforts should be thorough, well-organized, and regular. The program should be led by a designated individual or department within the business or by a public relations firm.

Because publicity functions often require personal communications with editors, reporters, and other media personnel, good professional relationships with these individuals are essential. Their advice can help ensure that a business's publicity program meshes well with the workings of the media.

A firm striving for effective publicity should review its news items carefully to avoid releasing those that are insignificant or poorly written. News items that do not meet media standards are usually rejected by media personnel.

TABLE 14.2 Possible Issues for Publicity Releases

Changes in marketing personnel	Packaging changes
Support of a social cause	New products
Improved warranties	Creation of a new slogan
Reports on industry conditions	Research developments
New uses for established products	Company's history and development
Product endorsements	Employment, production, and sales records
Winning of quality awards	
Company name changes	Award of contracts
Interviews with company officials	Opening of new markets
Improved distribution policies	Improvements in financial position
International business efforts	Opening of an exhibit
Athletic event sponsorship	History of a brand
Visits by celebrities	Winners of company contests
Reports on new discoveries	Logo changes
Innovative marketing activities	Speeches of top management
Economic forecasts	Merit awards to the organization
	Anniversary of inventions

GLOBAL PERSPECTIVES
Promoting Coke Around the World

When Coca-Cola aired a television commercial featuring children from around the world holding hands and singing together, the theme was global harmony, not global marketing. However, in the decades since that ad encouraged the world to sing and drink Coke, selling products worldwide has become essential in many industries. To advertise around the world, U.S. companies usually adopt one of two general strategies. They either generate campaigns in native languages to appeal to individual cultures, or they take a universal approach, using similar themes and ads everywhere from Europe to Asia to South America. Coca-Cola uses the second tactic because its marketers believe they can count on Coke's powerful brand name to make it recognizable without words in just about any country on the globe.

According to the company's president, the United States is Coke's test market for the rest of the world. Exporting its successful theme, "Can't beat the real thing; can't beat the feeling," Coke recently produced nine TV spots for international release. These ads don't say much, but in thirty or sixty seconds they show lots of people pouring and drinking lots of Coke. What's inside the bottle, say Coke's advertising executives, needs no translation. In French ads, young French people drink Coke at the beach, while dancing, and during exercise, but all the dialogue is in English. On familiar red-and-white signs at restaurants and on street vendors' carts throughout Germany, "You can't beat the real thing" stands out clearly in English. In Taiwan, where Coke controls 69 percent of the soft-drink market, and Brazil, where that figure is 60 percent, Coke's commercials and signs are all in English. Although some Europeans criticize Coca-Cola's international advertising for being too "American," the firm believes that successes abroad prove that its strategy is working.

Experts agree that the international soft-drink market is wide open. Consider, for example, that American soft-drink lovers already consume an average of three and a half cans of Coke products every week, but the French drink only about half a can in that amount of time. By intensifying its global advertising efforts, Coke hopes that the whole world soon will be drinking Coke, making a wish from the old song come true.

includes some advertising, some sales promotion to attract consumers to stores, and much personal selling.

The size, geographic distribution, and socioeconomic characteristics of the target market play a part in the composition of a product's promotion mix. If the market is small, personal selling will probably be the most important element in the promotion mix. This is true of organizations that sell to small industrial markets and businesses that use only a few wholesalers to market their products. Companies that need to contact millions of potential customers, however, will emphasize sales promotion and advertising because these methods are relatively inexpensive. The age, income, and education of the target market will also influence the choice of promotion techniques. For example, with less educated consumers, personal selling may be more effective than ads in newspapers or magazines.

In general, industrial products require personal selling, whereas consumer goods depend on advertising. This is not true in every case, however. The price of the product also influences the composition of the promotion mix. Since consumers often want the advice of a salesperson on an expensive product, high-priced consumer goods may call for more personal selling. Similarly, advertising and sales promotion may be more crucial to marketers of seasonal items because having a year-round sales force is not always appropriate.

The cost and availability of promotion methods are important factors in the development of a promotion mix. Although national advertising and sales promotion activities are expensive, the cost per customer may be quite small if the campaign succeeds in reaching large numbers of people. In addition, local advertising outlets—newspapers, magazines, radio and television stations, and outdoor displays—may not be that costly for a small, local business. In some situations, a firm may find that no available advertising medium reaches the target market effectively.

This chapter concludes our discussion of marketing. In the next chapter we begin our examination of information for business by discussing management information and computers.

CHAPTER REVIEW

Summary

Promotion is communication that is intended to inform, persuade, or remind an organization's target markets of the organization or its products. The major promotion-mix ingredients are advertising, personal selling, sales promotion, and publicity. The role of promotion is to facilitate exchanges directly or indirectly and to help an organization maintain favorable relationships between itself and groups in the marketing environment.

Advertising is a paid, nonpersonal message communicated to a select audience through a mass medium. Selective advertising promotes a particular brand of product. Institutional advertising is image-building advertising for a firm. Primary-demand advertising promotes the products of an entire industry rather than a single brand.

The major advertising media are newspapers, magazines, direct mail, outdoor advertising, television, and radio. Newspapers account for the greatest part of advertising expenditures, with television running a

fairly close second. Magazine advertising is perhaps the most prestigious, and direct mail is certainly the most selective medium. Radio and magazine advertising can also be quite selective, and radio is relatively inexpensive.

An advertising campaign is developed in several stages. A firm's first task is to identify and analyze its advertising target. The goals of the campaign must also be clearly defined. Then the firm must develop the advertising platform, or statement of important selling points, and determine the size of the advertising budget. The next steps are to develop a media plan and create the advertising message itself. Finally, the effectiveness of the advertising campaign should be evaluated before, during, and/or after the campaign ends.

A firm may develop its own advertising, hire an advertising agency to plan and produce its ads, or both. Advertising is monitored by federal, state, and local agencies and industry organizations.

Personal selling is a personal communications process aimed at informing customers and persuading them to buy a firm's products. It is the most adaptable promotion method: The message can be modified by the salesperson to fit each buyer. Three major kinds of salespersons are order getters, order takers, and support personnel. The six steps in the personal-selling process are prospecting, approaching the prospect, making the presentation, answering objections, closing the sale, and following up. Sales managers get directly involved in setting sales force objectives; recruiting, selecting, and training salespersons; compensating and motivating sales personnel; creating sales territories; and evaluating sales performance.

Sales promotion is the use of activities and materials as direct inducements to customers and salespersons. Examples include refunding, couponing, sampling, offering premiums, setting up point-of-purchase displays, and taking part in trade shows.

Public-relations, or image-building, activities include the sponsorship of programs and events that are of interest to the general public. Publicity is a nonpersonal message in news story form delivered through a mass medium at no charge. It is transmitted to the media via news releases, feature articles, captioned photographs, and press conferences.

A promotional campaign is a plan for combining and using advertising, personal selling, sales promotion, and publicity to achieve one or more marketing goals. Campaign objectives are developed from marketing objectives. Then the promotion mix is developed on the basis of the organization and its marketing objectives, the nature of the target market, the product characteristics, and the feasibility of various promotional methods.

Key Terms

You should now be able to define and give an example relevant to each of the following terms:

promotion
promotion mix
advertising
personal selling
sales promotion
publicity
selective (or brand)
  advertising
institutional advertising
primary-demand
  advertising
advertising media
cooperative advertising
direct-mail advertising

outdoor advertising
advertising agency
order getter
creative selling
order taker
sales support personnel
missionary salesperson
trade salesperson
technical salesperson
consumer sales
  promotion method
trade sales promotion
  method
refund

cents-off coupon
sample
premium
point-of-purchase display
trade show
public relations

news release
feature article
captioned photograph
press conference
promotional campaign
positioning

Questions and Exercises

Review Questions

1. What is the difference between a marketing mix and a promotion mix? How are they related?
2. What is the major role of promotion?
3. How are selective, institutional, and primary-demand advertising different from each other? Give an example of each.
4. What is cooperative advertising? What sorts of firms use it?
5. List the four major print media, and give an advantage and a disadvantage of each.
6. What types of firms use each of the two electronic media?
7. Outline the main steps required to develop an advertising campaign.
8. Why would a firm use an ad agency if it had its own advertising department?
9. Identify and give examples of the three major types of salespersons.
10. Explain how each step in the personal-selling process leads to the next step.
11. What are the major tasks involved in managing a sales force?
12. In your opinion, what are the three most effective techniques for sales promotion? How does each of these techniques supplement advertising?
13. What is the difference between publicity and public relations? What is the purpose of each?
14. Why is promotion particularly effective in positioning a product? in stabilizing or increasing sales?
15. What factors determine the specific promotion mix that should be used?

Discussion Questions

1. Why is the maker of Taster's Choice instant coffee using romantic-type advertisements?
2. What other forms of promotion (besides advertising) are used by coffee marketers?
3. Discuss the pros and cons of comparative advertising from the viewpoint of (a) the advertiser, (b)

the advertiser's competitors, and (c) the target market.

4. Which kinds of advertising—in which media—influence you most? Why?

5. Which kinds of retail outlets or products require mainly order taking by salespeople?

6. Why would a producer offer refunds or cents-off coupons rather than simply lowering the price of its products?

7. During the 1980s, customers were very receptive to certain types of sales promotion methods. Why?

8. How does the publicity that business firms seek help the general public?

9. What steps should a company take to avoid negative publicity?

10. What kind of promotion mix might be used to extend the life of a product that has entered the declining stage of its product life cycle?

Exercises

1. Describe, sketch, or photocopy one example of each of the following types of advertisements. Explain briefly what makes it an example of its particular type.
   a. Immediate-response (selective)
   b. Reminder (selective)
   c. Institutional
   d. Primary-demand
   e. Local
   f. Cooperative

2. Briefly describe four different point-of-purchase displays you have seen. For each, give the type of display, the product and brand displayed or promoted, and your evaluation of the effectiveness of the display.

3. Choose a particular product that was not discussed in the chapter. From your overall knowledge of the product, outline a promotion mix for it. That is, determine what percentage of your total promotion budget you would allocate to each promotion method, at whom the promotion would be directed, and the media you would use. Give your reason for each decision.

CASE 14.1

Nabisco's Winning Sales Force

In almost any grocery store in the United States, you will find shelves full of Nabisco's Oreos, Teddy Grahams, Chips Ahoy!, Ritz Crackers, and Wheat Thins.

Challengers come and go, but these favorites never get lost in the shuffle. The ninety-five-year-old Nabisco Biscuit Company, a subsidiary of RJR Nabisco, Inc., has a knack for coming up with popular products. Eight of the top ten selling brands in the cookie/cracker category are Nabisco offerings, adding up to one billion pounds sold every year. Does this achievement prove that a really good product "sells itself"? Nabisco's four-thousand-person sales force says no. They believe their extraordinary success is the result of extensive training, dedicated customer service, and personal commitment to the product and the company—not just a reputation for selling delicious cookies. Recently winning *Sales and Marketing Management's* "Best Sales Force Survey" award affirms Nabisco's belief in and reliance on its salespeople.

Good training gives Nabisco's people an edge when they go into the field. The company spends about $1 million a year to hold thirteen strategy meetings for sales personnel. At these sessions, salespeople learn current sales figures and set new goals together; plan sales and marketing strategies; find out about new products, upcoming promotions, and advertising campaigns; and work together to improve their selling skills. To make these meetings as effective and interesting as possible, Nabisco consulted with a firm specializing in sales force development and surveyed one hundred sales managers to determine the factors that contribute to a good sales meeting. The company's response to the information it received includes better manager preparation, more guest speakers, more and higher-quality visual aids, and most important, more sales representative participation. Nabisco works hard to ensure that its salespeople leave with knowledge they can put to use.

Equipped with exceptional training, sales personnel go out and provide their customers with exceptional service. Using available data from their laptop computers, salespeople often share with outlet managers information to help boost sales, such as who their customers are, what the average purchases are, and how to create the most effective product mix. Eliminating the inconvenience of requiring trips to a central warehouse, Nabisco delivers products directly to its customers, a service that most of its competitors do not provide. Salespeople will sometimes set up the cookie/cracker department themselves, picking the best location and putting the boxes on the shelves.

Nabisco's salespeople are highly committed to their company, in part because their personal input and involvement are highly valued. Communication is good between the decision makers in the marketing department and the sales reps. By talking to one another, marketers get frequent feedback, and sales reps get the satisfaction of knowing that their ideas and suggestions carry weight. To facilitate individual involvement, Nabisco decentralizes its national sales meetings. Holding them in different geographic locations every year means more people can attend. By breaking meetings down into smaller, less intimidating, groups, more people are willing to talk.

Another way Nabisco keeps involvement high and generates enthusiasm is by rewarding people for a good sales record. Breaking from the tradition of giving a gift—an all-expense-paid vacation, for example— to a single person who sells the most, the company instead ties salaries and bonuses to individualized sales goals. The more that salespeople meet or exceed these goals (and 75 percent of them do), the more money they make. The motivation to keep selling is self-directed and long term, and every Nabisco salesperson can be a winner.

Nabisco sales personnel are proud of their jobs, their products, and their company. In addition to winning the "Best Sales Force" award, they won high marks for retaining existing accounts and bringing in new ones. The Nabisco sales organization recently posted record sales of $2.5 billion, boosting the company's earnings 19 percent and giving it a 44 percent share of the market.*

Questions

1. What factors contribute to having a successful sales meeting?
2. How does Nabisco motivate its sales force?
3. Why is an effective sales force so important to a company like Nabisco?

*Based on information from "When the Chips Were Down, Nabisco Didn't Crumble," *Sales and Marketing Management*, June 1990, pp. 64–76; Robert H. Klein, "Nabisco Packages a Meeting for Field Managers," *Sales and Marketing Management*, November 11, 1985, pp. 88–90; Judann Dagnoli and Judith Graham, "Aggressive Marketer to Head RJR," *Advertising Age*, March 20, 1989, p. 4; "Inside Nabisco's Cookie Machine," *Adweek's Marketing Week*, March 18, 1991, pp. 22–23.

CASE 14.2

Icon Acoustics Markets High-quality Products Using Low-cost Promotion

When Dave Fokos, the thirty-year-old owner of Icon Acoustics, graduated from Cornell University with a degree in electrical engineering, he went to work designing loudspeakers for Conrad-Johnson. During his tenure there, he was the principal designer for thirteen different speaker models. Although successful at what he was doing, Fokos envisioned a different kind of loudspeaker company of his own, a company that would build high-quality speakers and sell them at fair prices. He would use Teflon-insulated wire and gold-plated input jacks. He would get his tweeters from Norway and his woofers from Germany. In 1989, Fokos rented 3,500 square feet of space in the Massachusetts countryside and founded Icon Acoustics.

Fokos loved listening to music played on a high-quality sound system, but, like others with the same appetite, he couldn't afford the kind of speakers that would give him what he wanted to hear. He also recognized that, even in large cities, customers didn't have much choice of brands. If only seventy brands were available in New York City, how many could there be in Bismarck, North Dakota? Finally, Fokos believed that, because manufacturers focused their attention on retailers instead of on individual customers, stereo buyers weren't receiving the quality of service they deserved. Knowing that Icon Acoustics should provide quality, affordability, widespread availability, and customer service was the easy part. What would prove more difficult was figuring out a way to do it.

Fokos is able to keep his own expenses down and his prices in the reasonable realm by spending as little as possible on promotion. Rather than selling to retailers, which means 100-percent dealer markups and higher prices, Fokos sells direct from his factory. By calling a toll-free phone number, customers get a postage-paid, thirty-day, no-obligation home trial— what the company calls "the 43,200-minute, no pressure audition." The appeal of a free home trial promotes Icon's speakers without requiring lots of advertising dollars to convince customers. Speakers are available from Seattle to Miami, and, because they talk directly to the manufacturer, customers get better service.

Saving money by relying on word of mouth to get its message across, Icon's promotion is based almost entirely on reviews and feature articles in stereo consumer magazines and attendance at trade shows where stereo lovers gather. Fokos occasionally places inexpensive bare-bones ads in trade magazines, and he once invested a more substantial sum in a four-color display ad in *Stereo Review's Buyers Guide*, a publication boasting a circulation of 506,000. When it came to company stationery, business cards, and brochures, however, Fokos spent almost $40,000. He wanted to make sure that those distinctive cards and brochures convey the same distinctive image his speakers convey.

By employing its strategy of relying on low-cost promotion, can Icon effectively reach potential customers? With more than 325 specialty stereo makers fighting over a limited market, can Fokos sell enough Lumens at $795 a pair and Parsecs at $1,795 a pair to stay in business? The jury is still out. Although 1991 revenues totaled $303,000, the company also had a $50,000 bank loan payment due. Fokos admits wondering sometimes if the stress is worth it. Then he looks at the back of one his speakers and reads the hand-lettered label saying, "This speaker was hand-crafted by Dave Fokos," and decides that the answer is yes.**

Questions

1. What are the major ingredients in Icon's promotion mix?
2. Evaluate Fokos's decision to minimize the use of advertising in Icon's promotion mix.

**Based on information from Julian Hirsch, "Icon Parsec Speaker System," *Stereo Review*, April 1991; Michael O'Connell, "Icon Making Some Noise Out of Billerica," *Lowell (Mass.) Sun*, August 19, 1990, pp. 33–34; Edward O. Welles, "Sound Strategy," *Inc.*, May 1991, pp. 46–48, 50, 55; Press release from High-End Hi-Fi Show, 1990.

Career Profile

Job Title	Job Description	Salary Range
Advertising account executive	Responsible for managing the development and implementation of the client's advertising campaign; must know client's product and marketing plans and agency's resources for carrying out plans; plans the advertising campaign and creates its components; has the job of selling the client on the planned advertising campaign; goes to location to oversee the production of commercials; must ensure that artists, copywriters, and production people meet the schedule	4
Advertising manager	Develops advertising to reach organizations' customers; one-person staff in some companies; responsible for the administration of a large budget; coordinates the activities of the department to meet deadlines and schedules; places the company's advertising in the appropriate media; handles day-to-day administration of the department; represents the company in its dealings with an agency	5
Manufacturer's salesperson	Interests wholesale and retail buyers and purchasing agents in products; spends much time traveling; keeps prospective buyers up-to-date with sales promotions and prices; helps buyers with technical problems; works with engineers adapting products to customers' needs	4
Marketing researcher	Plans and designs research projects; conducts interviews and fact-gathering operations; tabulates and analyzes findings	4
Media buyer	Must be well informed about costs and audiences of various media; works with account executives to decide how to reach the target audience for the client's product; buys media time and space	2
Public relations specialist	Helps business, governments, universities, hospitals, schools, and other organizations build positive relationships with their various publics; handles the press, political campaigns, and employee relations; understands the attitudes and concerns of customers, employees, and various publics and communicates this to management; contacts media that might print or air materials; develops information packets	3
Store manager	Manages a multitude of store operations including personnel, ordering, displays, selling, accounting, and advertising	4
Wholesale or retail buyers	Purchases merchandise for resale; usually specializes in acquiring one or two lines of merchandise; needs to be knowledgeable about the products and what will appeal to consumers; keeps up with inventories; checks on competitive sales activities; helps to determine customer trends and interests; helps in planning sales promotions	3

The figure in the salary column approximates the expected annual income after two or three years of service.
1 = $12,000–$15,000; 2 = $16,000–$20,000; 3 = $21,000–$27,000; 4 = $28,000–$35,000; 5 = $36,000 and up.

Educational Requirements	Skills Required	Prospects for Growth
Bachelor's degree in business or liberal arts	Communication; problem solving; interpersonal	Average
Bachelor's degree in business or liberal arts	Communication; decision making; interpersonal; marketing skills	Average
Some college; degree preferred; on-the-job experience	Communication; marketing skills; interpersonal; time management	Above average
College degree; on-the-job experience	Analytical; communication	Average
Some college; on-the-job experience	Communication; decision making; interpersonal	Limited
College degree; on-the-job experience	Writing; public speaking; interpersonal; communication; time management; problem solving	Average
College degree; on-the-job experience	Office; decision making	Average
Varies; college preferred; on-the-job experience	Communication; interpersonal; decision making; marketing skills	Below average

PART
5

Information for Business

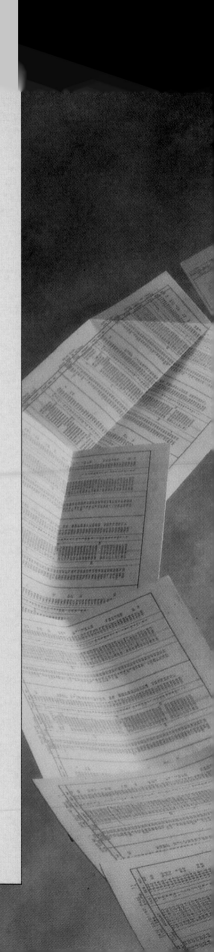

The subject of this part is information, the fourth of our business resources. First we discuss computers and the different kinds of information that are necessary for effective decision making. Then we examine the role of accounting and how financial information is collected, processed, and presented. Included in this part are:

CHAPTER 15 Management Information and Computers

CHAPTER 16 Accounting

Management Information and Computers

LEARNING OBJECTIVES

After studying this chapter you should be able to:

1 Describe what information is and how it differs from data.

2 Summarize the development of the computer.

3 Explain the difference between computer hardware and computer software.

4 Describe the impact that computers have had on business.

5 Discuss management's information requirements.

6 State the four functions of a management information system.

7 Specify the various sources of business data.

8 Explain how a management information system uses statistics to turn data into information.

CHAPTER PREVIEW

In this chapter, we take a closer look at management information and computers. First, we look at the difference between data and information. Then we see how computers help managers transform data into information. We also consider the present and future impact of computers on business. Next, we analyze what types of information managers need. Finally, we examine the components of a management information system (MIS) and show how the system can be used to aid managers in the decision-making process.

The Chips Are Down, and Intel's a Good Bet

Since the introduction of personal computers, small microprocessor chips—the brains inside computers—have dramatically transformed banking, transportation, communications, and just about every other industry almost overnight. And although people recognize popular computer names like International Business Machines Corp., Compaq Computer, and Zenith, they don't recognize Intel Corp.—the company that manufactures more than 75 percent of the chips used in personal computers.

California-based Intel Corp. was founded in 1968 by three engineers: Robert Noyce, the co-inventor of the integrated circuit; Gordon Moore; and Andrew Grove, Intel's current chief executive officer. During the 1970s, the small company began to grow, and it used initial profits to fund an aggressive research and development program. In 1981, the firm's research efforts paid off when IBM chose the Intel 8088 chip for its first Personal Computer. During the first part of the 1980s, IBM's PCs became the standard for the computer industry. As a result, the demand for Intel's chips soared, and so did Intel's sales and profits. Once again Intel invested in research, and in 1985 it introduced the 80386 chip—commonly known as the 386. Between 1985 and the end of 1991, Intel sold an estimated fourteen million 386 chips. During the same period, Intel earned over $2 billion in profits from its 386 chips.

To date, the 386 is the most profitable chip in the history of the computer industry—and all the profits belonged to Intel until 1990. That's when a federal court decision opened the door for such competitors as Advanced Micro Devices, NexGen Microsystems, Chips & Technologies, and Cyrix to begin manufacturing their own 386 chips, which are often referred to as clones. To compete with its new competitors, Intel began to lower prices. In late 1991, Intel's 386 chip sold for $200, about 25 per-

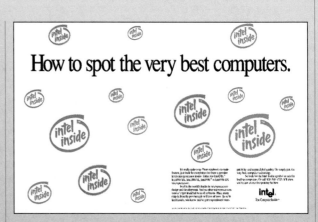

cent less than in mid-1990. As a result of lower prices, the firm's profits began to decline.

Not one to throw in the towel, Intel began fighting back with an aggressive marketing campaign built around the "Intel Inside" slogan. This campaign was designed not only to build name recognition with computer buyers but also to get consumer buyers to request genuine Intel parts. There already is some evidence that consumers prefer computers with Intel chips. According to retailers, if two computers are side by side and one has an Intel 386 chip and the other a 386 clone, customers will choose Intel every time.

Intel is also relying on its R&D program to provide the technological edge needed to beat its new competitors. About the time competitors introduced their 386 clones, Intel began selling its new, improved 486 chip. Although sales for the 486 were slow in the first part of the 1990s, orders have picked up as more computer manufacturers are beginning to use the new chip. And Intel is already planning to develop a superfast 586 chip. According to industry experts, it will take years and multimillion dollar investments for competitors to develop microprocessors that will compete with Intel's new products.[1]

Intel's current problems are common among firms that operate in the highly competitive computer-information industry. Over the past twenty years, this industry has undergone dramatic changes. And yet, Andrew Grove, Intel's current CEO, is optimistic that Intel's research and development efforts will enable the firm to become even more competitive in an ever-changing industry. In fact, Intel's engineers are already working on new microprocessor chips and other component parts that will enable computer manufacturers to build the next generation of computers. Once developed, these new computers will provide even more information than today's best computer systems.

As we noted in Chapter 1, information is the basic material from which plans are developed and decisions are made. To help their managers obtain and use information, most firms establish management information systems. The recent "computer revolution" has expanded the capabilities and capacities of such systems and, therefore, their usefulness.

THE NEED FOR MANAGEMENT INFORMATION

LEARNING OBJECTIVE 1
Describe what information is and how it differs from data.

data numerical or verbal descriptions that usually result from measurements of some sort

information data presented in a form that is useful for a specific purpose

In many contexts the terms *data* and *information* are used interchangeably, but they differ in important ways. **Data** are numerical or verbal descriptions that usually result from measurements of some sort. (The word *data* is plural; the singular form is *datum*.) An individual's current wage level, a firm's net after-tax profit last year, and the retail prices for automobiles currently produced in the United States are all data. Most people think of data as being numerical only, but they can be nonnumerical as well. A description of an individual as a "tall, athletic woman with short, dark hair" would certainly qualify as data.

Information is data presented in a form that is useful for a specific purpose. Suppose a human resources manager wants to compare the wages paid to male and female employees by the firm over a period of seven years. The manager might begin with a stack of computer printouts listing every person employed by the firm, along with each employee's current and past wages. The manager would be hard-pressed to make any sense of the mass of names and numbers. Such printouts consist of data rather than information.

Now suppose the manager causes the computer to compute and graph the average wage paid to men and that paid to women in each of the seven years. The resulting graph (see Figure 15.1) is information because the manager can use it for the purpose at hand—to compare wages paid to men with those paid to women over the seven-year period.

The wage data from the printouts became information when they were summarized in the chart. Large sets of data often must be summarized if they are to be at all useful, but this is not always the case. If the manager in our example had wanted to know only the wage history of a specific employee, that information would be contained in the original computer

FIGURE 15.1
Data versus Information
Data are numerical or verbal descriptions that usually result from measurements; information is data presented in a form useful for a specific purpose.

	Jan	Feb	March	April	May	June	July	Aug	Sept	Oct	Nov	Dec	Totals
Female Employees													
Employee 1	1,150	1,150	1,150	1,150	1,150	1,150	1,200	1,200	1,200	1,200	1,200	1,300	$14,200
Employee 2	1,400	1,400	1,400	1,400	1,400	1,400	1,400	1,400	1,400	1,400	1,400	1,400	$16,800
Employee 3	1,600	1,600	1,600	1,600	1,800	1,800	1,800	1,800	1,800	1,900	1,900	1,900	$21,100
Employee 4	1,200	1,200	1,200	1,200	1,200	1,200	1,250	1,250	1,250	1,250	1,250	1,250	$14,700
Male Employees													
Employee 5	1,800	1,800	1,800	1,800	1,800	1,800	1,800	1,800	1,800	1,800	1,800	1,800	$21,600
Employee 6	2,000	2,000	2,000	2,000	2,000	2,000	2,100	2,100	2,100	2,100	2,100	2,100	$24,600
Employee 7	1,900	1,900	1,900	1,900	1,900	1,900	1,950	1,950	1,950	1,950	2,000	2,000	$23,200
Employee 8	2,400	2,400	2,400	2,400	2,400	2,400	2,500	2,500	2,500	2,500	2,500	2,500	$29,400

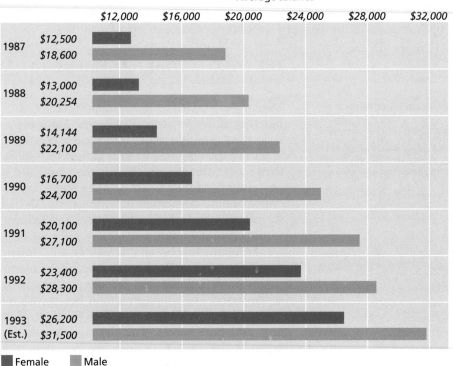

Average salaries

Year	Female	Male
1987	$12,500	$18,600
1988	$13,000	$20,254
1989	$14,144	$22,100
1990	$16,700	$24,700
1991	$20,100	$27,100
1992	$23,400	$28,300
1993 (Est.)	$26,200	$31,500

■ Female   ■ Male

printout. That is, the data (the employee's name in the listing) would already be in the most useful form for the manager's purpose; they would need no further processing.

The average company maintains a great deal of data—personnel, inventory, sales, accounting, and other types—that can be transformed into information. Often, each type of data is stored in individual departments within the organization. In a large organization, each type of data is more effectively used when it is organized into a database. A **database** is a single collection of data that is stored in one place and can be used by people throughout the organization to make decisions. In addition to just storing data in one place, the organization must establish procedures for gathering, updating, and processing facts in the database. Computers can help ensure that the facts in a database are up to date and available when employees and managers need them.

database a single collection of data that is stored in one place and can be used by people throughout the organization to make decisions

HISTORICAL DEVELOPMENT OF THE COMPUTER

LEARNING OBJECTIVE 2
Summarize the development of the computer.

Until perhaps twenty-five years ago, most data and information were stored using manual systems. Records were kept in written form, and clerical personnel were responsible for collecting, filing, retrieving, and processing the data required by managers. Today, most clerical tasks are completed with the aid of a computer.

A **computer** is an electronic machine that can accept, store, manipulate, and transmit data in accordance with a set of specific instructions. Moreover, it can store large amounts of data, process them very rapidly with perfect accuracy, and transmit (or present) results in a variety of ways. For example, Carter Hawley Hale Stores Inc. is a large corporation

computer an electronic machine that can accept, store, manipulate, and transmit data in accordance with a set of specific instructions

Putting the horse to work. Anxious to keep up with the latest technology, many businesses purchase new computers but wind up feeling as though they've bought a Trojan horse, something that looked good but leads to disaster. The software company that created this ad offers to solve such problems by "retraining" computers to do the work companies want them to do.

that owns several retail companies, including The Broadway, Emporium, and Weinstock's on the West Coast. Altogether, Carter's management must keep track of approximately one hundred stores and more than eight million items of merchandise. To deal with this, Carter's management invested $75 million in a computer center near Los Angeles to keep track of all the buying, pricing, and inventory-control data and to provide management with the information it needs to run the retail network.

The Evolution of Computers

Today, large firms such as Carter Hawley Hale use computers on a daily basis, and even some small businesses rely on the daily use of computers. This was not always the case, however. Even after computers were developed and mass-produced, most were too large and too expensive for most businesses. Although the computer is a relatively recent invention, its development rests on centuries of research (see Figure 15.2).

Early Technological Developments   Since the beginning of recorded history, people have had difficulty calculating answers to mathematical problems. One early mechanical calculating device, the abacus, was developed by Chinese merchants before the birth of Christ. Composed of several wires, each strung with ten beads, the abacus enabled merchants to calculate solutions to mathematical problems and store the results.

In the seventeenth century, the slide rule was developed through the work of John Napier and William Oughtred. And the first real mechanical "calculator" was developed in 1642 by the Frenchman Blaise Pascal. Later in the same century, the German Gottfried von Liebniz developed a mechanical device that would not only add and subtract but also multiply, divide, and calculate square roots.

In the early 1800s, Charles Babbage, a British mathematician, designed a machine that could perform mathematical calculations and store the intermediate results in a memory unit—the forerunner of today's computer. Babbage called his device the *difference engine*. Later, Babbage designed a similar machine called the *analytical engine* that could perform addition, subtraction, multiplication, or division based on instructions coded on cards. Both the difference and analytical engines contained many features similar to those found in today's modern computers. As a result, Babbage is often called the father of modern computer technology.

In the late 1880s, the U.S. government commissioned Herman Hollerith to develop a system that could process the 1890 census data. His punch card system (based on Babbage's original concept) reduced the time required to process the 1890 census data to two and a half years. (It had taken seven and a half years to process the 1880 census data manually.) Later, Hollerith founded the Tabulating Machine Company to manufacture and sell punch card equipment to businesses. The Tabulating Machine Company eventually changed its name and today is known as International Business Machines (IBM).

In 1944 Howard Aiken of Harvard University, in collaboration with IBM and the U.S. War Department, embarked on a joint project to manufacture the Mark I computer. It was not a true electronic computer because

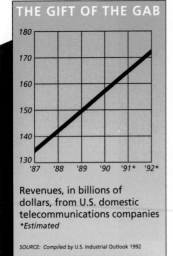

AT A GLANCE

THE GIFT OF THE GAB

180
170
160
150
140
130

'87   '88   '89   '90   '91*   '92*

Revenues, in billions of dollars, from U.S. domestic telecommunications companies
*Estimated

SOURCE: Compiled by U.S. Industrial Outlook 1992

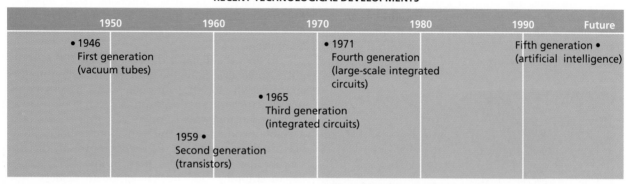

EARLY TECHNOLOGICAL DEVELOPMENTS

Before Christ	1600		1700	1800	1900
Babylonian Empire: Abacus		• 1673 Improved calculator: Liebniz • 1642 Calculator: Pascal • 1633 Slide rule: Oughtred • 1617 Predesssor to slide rule: Napier		1890 • Census punchcards: Hollerith • 1820's–1830's Difference engine and analytic engine: Babbage	• 1944 Mark 1 computer: Aiken

RECENT TECHNOLOGICAL DEVELOPMENTS

1950	1960	1970	1980	1990	Future
• 1946 First generation (vacuum tubes)	1959 • Second generation (transistors)	• 1971 Fourth generation (large-scale integrated circuits) • 1965 Third generation (integrated circuits)		Fifth generation • (artificial intelligence)	

FIGURE 15.2
A Chronology of Technological Developments
Many significant developments led up to the invention of the electronic computers widely used today.

it relied on electromagnetic relays and mechanical counters to perform mathematical calculations. Nevertheless, this device did open the door for the development of the electronic computer.

Recent Technological Developments Today's electronic computers are the result of five stages (sometimes called generations) of research and development. The first generation of computers (1946 to 1958) relied on glass vacuum tubes to control the internal operations of the computer. The vacuum tubes, which were quite large, generated a great deal of heat. As a result, the overall computer was huge and required special air conditioning to compensate for the excessive heat buildup.

The second generation (1959 to 1964) began when tiny, electronic transistors replaced vacuum tubes. Transistors greatly reduced the size of the computer and also helped solve the heat problem that plagued first-generation computers. In addition, transistors were more reliable, required less maintenance, and processed data much faster than had the vacuum tubes. High-speed printers and card readers were introduced during the second generation. Finally, second-generation computers were programmed with high-level languages such as FORTRAN (*FOR*mula *TRAN*slation) and COBOL (*CO*mmon *B*usiness *O*riented *L*anguage).

The third generation (1965 to 1971) began when computer manufacturers started using integrated circuits (ICs), small silicon chips containing

GLOBAL PERSPECTIVES
Apple and Sony's Strategic Alliance

Consumers looking at the PowerBook 100 laptop computer immediately recognize the Apple Computer, Inc. logo. What most consumers don't realize is that the 5.1-pound, notebook-sized portable computer was manufactured by Japan's Sony Corp. Apple—the company famous for going it alone in the computer industry—asked Sony to manufacture its new laptop computer for a reason. According to Apple officials, the company did not have enough product engineers to develop and manufacture *all* the new products the company had planned to introduce in 1991 and 1992. And faced with the possibility that competitors could beat Apple to the marketplace if they didn't move quickly, the Apple/Sony alliance made sense.

Apple chose Sony because Sony already manufactures many of the components (disk drives, monitors, and power supplies) that Apple uses to manufacture its Macintosh computers. And according to Apple officials, Sony's experience in manufacturing small electronic products could pay off in manufacturing the new notebook-sized laptops. Sony, on the other hand, wanted to learn more about manufacturing and marketing personal computers.

To turn the idea for the PowerBook 100 into reality, Apple gave Sony the basic plans, including the specifications for the computer chips necessary to manufacture the small computer. Sony took it from there and transformed Apple's research efforts into a viable product. Just thirteen months later, Sony was manufacturing the PowerBook 100 on the assembly line. Shortly after that, in late 1991, Apple began shipping "its" new machine to dealers. According to most dealers, Apple's new PowerBook 100 is expected to be a big hit with Macintosh users who have been waiting as long as two years for a small laptop computer that would be compatible with other computers in Apple's product line.

Based on the success of the first Apple/Sony alliance, the two companies are exploring other projects that blend Apple's computer expertise with Sony's experience in electronic consumer products. By cooperating with Sony, Apple can reduce the amount of time required to produce and market new products. And according to Apple CEO John Sculley, to be successful in today's ever-changing computer industry, you must be able to introduce and market new products quickly.

a network of transistors. Integrated circuits were quite a bit faster and more reliable than the single transistors used in the second generation. And yet, because of improved technology, they were also less expensive than second-generation transistors. Third-generation computers had more storage capacity and greater compatibility of computer components. The concept of remote terminals that communicate with a central computer became a reality at this time.

The fourth generation (1971 to the present) began when computer manufacturers began using large-scale, integrated (LSI) circuits. LSI circuits are silicon superchips that contain thousands of small transistors. As a result of LSI circuits, fourth-generation computers are smaller than those manufactured during the third generation. Both the Apple and the IBM personal computers were developed during the fourth generation. Also, increased storage and even greater compatibility were characteristics of computers manufactured during this period.

To date, we have experienced four generations of computer development. Now, many experts believe we are entering the *fifth generation*—computers that can simulate human decision making. All through this chapter, we stress that computers must be programmed or given step-by-step instructions to complete a specific task because a computer doesn't have common sense or the ability to think on its own. This may change in the near future. Today, researchers are studying the human brain in an attempt to learn how people reason and think. For years, scientists have known that the human brain is more efficient than any computer in terms of storage capacity, data retrieval, and information processing. The researchers' goal is to duplicate the same processes with a computer and thus create a form of artificial intelligence.

artificial intelligence   a combination of computer hardware and software that exhibits the same type of intelligence as human beings

Artificial intelligence is a combination of computer hardware and software that exhibits the same type of intelligence as human beings. According to John Sculley, Apple's chairman, "the really interesting stuff begins in the 1990s."[2] Tomorrow's computer technology will be everywhere because personal computers will be as popular as phones—especially in all sorts of consumer and health products. The practical applications for artificial intelligence generated by a computer are unlimited. For example, a computer may be able to examine cells from the human body and determine which genetic factors cause cancer and other dreaded diseases.

Today, artificial intelligence is one of the fastest-growing, high-tech fields. Many companies in the computer field are investing large amounts of money to either develop artificial-intelligence systems or purchase existing systems developed by other companies. Later in this chapter, we examine additional technological developments and how they will affect society.

COMPUTER HARDWARE AND SOFTWARE

LEARNING OBJECTIVE 3
Explain the difference between computer hardware and computer software.

The computers used in business today are generally categorized according to size: mainframes, minicomputers, and microcomputers. In the next section, we examine each type. Then we discuss the difference between computer hardware and computer software—the two components that are required for a computer to process data into information.

Types of Computers

The *mainframe computer* is the large, powerful, and expensive (usually costing more than $1 million) computer traditionally identified with the largest businesses. IBM established its reputation by manufacturing mainframe computers. Mainframes, which may be as big as a good-sized room, can handle huge quantities of data, perform a variety of operations on these data in fractions of a second, and provide output information in several different forms. Huge organizations, like Exxon Corporation, Ford Motor Co., or the U.S. government, have the most need for mainframe computers. The largest and most powerful mainframe computers are sometimes referred to as *supercomputers*. These very large computers are used almost exclusively by universities and government agencies that are heavily involved in research activities that require large memories and high-speed processing. Today, IBM is the largest producer of mainframe computers.

Minicomputers are smaller (more or less desk-sized) computers that revolutionized the industry and made computers available to most firms. These self-contained systems can be purchased for less than $10,000, and prices continue to drop steadily. With a minicomputer, most businesses can now maintain very sophisticated information systems that were previously beyond their reach. Currently, IBM and Digital Equipment Corporation account for almost half of all minicomputer sales.

The *microcomputer*, sometimes referred to as a personal computer, is a desktop-sized computer. It was made possible by the development of *microprocessor chips*, a fraction of an inch in size, that contain all the electronic circuitry required to perform large-scale data processing. Microcomputers sell for as little as several hundred dollars or as much as a few thousand dollars and are available in portable, laptop, and hand-held models. Although microcomputers are often purchased for use in the home, many smaller firms find them completely satisfactory for their limited needs. Companies like IBM, Compaq Computer Corporation, and Apple Computer, Inc. make microcomputers for the small-business market.

Computer Hardware

Most computers and computer systems consist of five basic components (see Figure 15.3). The **input unit** is the device used to enter data into a computer. In the past, data were fed to computers on punched cards, which were "read" by the input unit. Few modern systems use this method. Instead, data are entered manually via a keyboard (much like a typewriter keyboard) or electronically through the use of a mouse, light pen, touch pad, or optical scanners. Currently, voice recognition as an input device is being developed by a number of manufacturers. When fully developed, voice recognition will make use of a computer easier for almost anyone.

input unit   the device used to enter data into a computer

The **memory** (or **storage unit**) is the part of a computer that stores all data entered into the computer and processed by it. One measure of a computer's power is the amount of data that can be stored within it at one time. This memory capacity is given in bytes: One byte is the capacity to store one character. One kilobyte (1 Kbyte) is the capacity to store 1,024 characters, and one megabyte (1 Mb) is the capacity to store 1,024,000 characters. A personal computer with two megabytes of main memory is thus capable of storing over 450 pages of this book.

memory (or storage unit) the part of a computer that stores all data entered into the computer and processed by it

The **control unit** is the part of a computer that guides the entire operation of the computer. It transfers data and sends processing directions to

control unit   the part of a computer that guides the entire operation of the computer

FIGURE 15.3
How a Computer Works
A computer is a machine that accepts, stores, manipulates, and transmits data in accordance with a set of specific instructions. Most computers consist of five basic components.

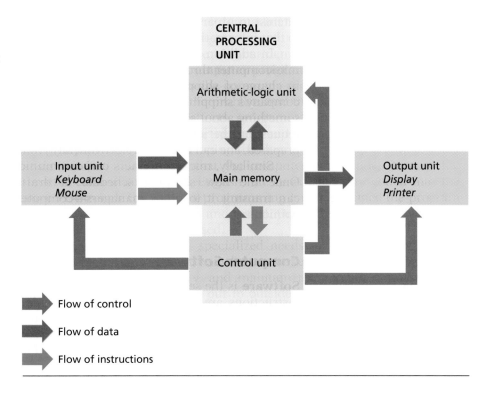

the various other units, in the proper sequence to carry out the instructions of the user.

The **arithmetic-logic unit** is the part of a computer that performs mathematical operations, comparisons of data, and other types of data transformations.

The **output unit** is the mechanism by which a computer transmits processed data to the user. Most commonly, computer output is printed on paper or displayed on a monitor, a televisionlike screen.

All these components make up the computer's **hardware,** the electronic equipment or machinery used in a computer system. Hence, the keyboard used to enter data; the arithmetic-logic, control, and storage units; and the monitor are all hardware.

Computer Networks

The concept of networking is perhaps the greatest boon to management decision making since the low-cost computer. A **computer network** is a system in which several computers can either function individually or communicate with each other. A typical business network revolves around a mainframe or minicomputer, which serves as the basic computer system for all areas and levels of the firm. In addition, each key manager has her or his own microcomputer. These smaller computers have sufficient capacity to store up-to-date information that the managers require on a regular basis. That is, each microcomputer maintains records that are of primary

arithmetic-logic unit the part of a computer that performs mathematical operations, comparisons of data, and other types of data transformations

output unit the mechanism by which a computer transmits processed data to the user

hardware the electronic equipment or machinery used in a computer system

computer network a system in which several computers can either function individually or communicate with each other

THE IMPACT OF COMPUTERS ON BUSINESS

As the cost of computer memory (or storage) drops and the availability of
sophisticated software packages grows, more and more businesses are becoming computer literate. The kinds of analyses, research, and recordkeeping that were once available only to the very largest organizations—if they
were available at all—are now within reach of all but the smallest and least
sophisticated businesses.

Current Business Applications

Today, software has been developed to satisfy almost every business need.
The most common types of software for business applications include
packages in the following areas:

- Database management
- Graphics
- Spreadsheets
- Word processing
- Accounting and bookkeeping
- Computer-aided design (CAD)
- Computer-aided engineering (CAE)
- Computer-aided manufacturing (CAM)
- Computer-aided instruction (CAI)
- Desktop publishing

Four of the most popular packages (database management, graphics,
spreadsheets, and word processing) are described in the following sections.

Database Management Programs   Earlier in this chapter, we defined a
database as a single collection of data that are stored in one place and can
be used by people throughout the organization to make decisions. Forty
years ago, a company like Eastman Kodak Company stored its data in file
cabinets and then retrieved data when needed. Any manipulation to transform the data contained in each file folder into useful information would
be completed manually—usually by the manager who needed the information in the first place.

Today, database management software allows users to electronically
store and transform data into information. Data can be sorted by different
criteria; for example, typical data for a firm's personnel department might
include criteria such as each worker's age, gender, salary, and years of
service. If management needs to know the names of workers who have at
least fifteen years of experience and are at least fifty years old, an employee using database management software can print a list of such employees in a matter of minutes. Although this example involves data
required for personnel decisions, the same type of manipulation of data for

other departments within a business is possible with database management software. In addition to building its own database, a company can also subscribe to on-line computer services that enable users to access large external databases.

Graphics Programs   Whether you play a video game or watch a computerized scoreboard at a football stadium, you are viewing computer-generated graphics. A **graphics program** enables users to display and print data and conclusions in graphic form. From a business standpoint, graphics can be used for oral or written presentations of financial analyses, budgets, sales projections, and the like.

graphics program   a software package that enables the user to display (and often print) data and conclusions in graphic form

Typically, graphics software allows the user to select a type of visual aid from a menu of available graphic options. The user enters the numerical data, such as sales figures, to be illustrated. The computer program then converts the data into a graph, bar chart, or pie chart. (Graphs, bar charts, and pie charts are discussed later in this chapter.)

Although visual aids have always been available, their use was restricted because someone had to take the time to draw them. With the aid of a graphics program, the computer can generate drawings in seconds.

Spreadsheet Programs   In the late 1970s, Daniel Bricklin and Robert Frankston, two business students, developed VisiCalc—a software package that enabled computer users to generate electronic spreadsheets. A **spreadsheet program** is a software package that allows the user to organize numerical data into a grid of rows and columns. Typically, spreadsheet software such as VisiCalc and Lotus 1-2-3 allows users to build a spreadsheet by using commands such as *create, format, enter, move, insert, compute, save, delete,* and *print*.

spreadsheet program   a software package that allows the user to organize numerical data into a grid of rows and columns

A billion-dollar smile. With a net worth exceeding $6 billion, Bill Gates may be the richest man in America. His company, Microsoft Corp., dominates the market for personal computer operating systems. Its latest big hit, Windows, gives IBM-style PCs the graphics look of Apple's Macintosh. It sold 9 million copies in the first 20 months, becoming a billion-dollar business itself.

Formulas entered into the spreadsheet allow the computer to perform mathematical calculations automatically. For example, a manager may want to project sales and expenses for the next accounting period. Numerical data for both sales and expenses are entered into the computer, and the spreadsheet software calculates the dollar amount of profit or loss based on the assumptions that the manager entered into the computer. Spreadsheet software can also be used to answer "what if" questions. By changing data to match new assumptions, the manager can see how the change will affect other data contained in the spreadsheet. This same manager might want to calculate the firm's profits based on projections that sales will increase 5, 10, and 15 percent. In this case, three additional spreadsheets could be prepared, based on each set of assumptions. In fact, any variable contained in the spreadsheet could be changed and, within seconds, new information could be generated to aid the manager in the decision-making process.

word processing program   a software package that allows the user to store written documents (letters, memos, reports) in the computer memory or on a disk

Word Processing Programs   A **word processing program** allows the user to store written documents (letters, memos, reports) in the computer memory or on a disk. Once entered, the material can be revised, edited, deleted, or printed. No longer is it necessary to spend long hours retyping entire documents. Only the changed portions need to be entered into the computer before the document is reprinted. In addition, materials that have been stored on a disk can be used at a later date. For example, most firms use a collection letter to urge prompt payment of past-due amounts. A word processing program can be used to send a personalized copy of the letter to all overdue accounts through the use of sort and merge features. Mail-order firms and direct-mail marketing firms make extensive use of these features to appeal to customers. Tens, hundreds, or thousands of letters—each sent to a selected individual—can be prepared from one master document.

Future Business Applications

In Chapter 1, information was described as the resource that tells the managers of the business how effectively the material, human, and financial resources are being utilized. The need for information will continue to increase in the future. Computers have already transformed us into an information society. An information society exists when large groups of employees generate or depend on information to perform their jobs.

Most offices are already equipped with word processing equipment. Today, messages and correspondence can be prepared on a word processor and then sent electronically to their destinations. This type of communication, sometimes called *electronic mail*, will increase in the future. The use of computer terminals for graphics, recordkeeping, data entry, and other office functions will also increase.

The ability to access information will enable more people to work at home with a personal computer linked to the mainframe or minicomputer at the office. Working at home will provide a type of flexibility that is needed in special situations. For example, the ability to work at home enables working parents to raise families without sacrificing their careers.

BUSINESS JOURNAL
Computers: The Next Generation

Automobiles, jet engines, and color televisions changed the world when they became available. Now, it's time to add the personal computer to the list. Since the personal computer was introduced almost fifteen years ago, typewriters have become almost obsolete, secretaries have become word processors, and small-business owners have gained access to information that was once available only to large corporations. Young, upstart firms like Apple Computer, Inc., NeXT, Inc., and Microsoft Corp. have matured and now compete on an equal basis with established, old-line firms like International Business Machines Corp., Digital Equipment Corp., and Hewlett-Packard Co. During this same period, overall industry sales have increased to over $100 billion a year, and experts predict that the demand for computers and software will continue to increase for at least the next decade. Although there is a lot of disagreement on specific changes that will take place within the computer industry, most experts do agree that the computer will become even more important both at the office and at home thanks to several changes.

TECHNOLOGICAL CHANGES

During the next ten years, computer-chip makers will continue to increase the amount of memory that can be stored on a computer chip. As a result, one superchip of the future will be able to store as many facts as the most advanced personal computers available today. This development will enable manufacturers to produce even smaller computers. Both laptops and notebooks—small, battery-powered, portable computers that can process information much as today's personal computers

do—will become more available because of lower prices. Pentops—notebook-sized computers that can read handwriting—will also be available at affordable prices. By the mid-1990s, small computers will be upgraded to understand spoken commands.

IMPROVED SOFTWARE

There is already a big push by major computer companies to develop a new operating system to replace *MS-DOS*—the operating system used with most IBM and IBM-compatible computers. The new operating systems will enable computers to understand handwriting and spoken commands. This new operating system will also improve the computer's graphics capabilities and ability to reproduce the human voice and stereo sounds. To date, Microsoft and a joint venture between Apple Computer and IBM show the greatest potential for turning initial research into a viable operating system.

INCREASED CONSUMER APPLICATIONS

All kinds of household products will use emerging computer technologies. For starters, experts already predict that toasters, televisions, video recorders, microwave ovens, and many other appliances will be able to respond to spoken commands by the year 2000. Interactive computers will open up a whole new world of information and entertainment, for both children and adults. And the next generation of computers will replace not only traditional telephones but also cellular telephones and fax machines. In fact, according to computer experts, the list of consumer products that will be affected by improved computer technology is endless.

Working at home may also offer an attractive alternative for people with some types of physical handicaps or other special needs.

Although we have emphasized information in this section, production of manufactured goods is still necessary for our survival. Computer-aided design and computer-aided manufacturing programs will continue to automate the way that manufactured goods are produced. Computers are already being used to control automated equipment. In fact, some computers control entire assembly lines. Robots and robotlike equipment are common in the automobile, steel, and other manufacturing industries. For example, General Motors Corp., Ford Motor Company, and Chrysler Corp. use robots to paint automobiles, weld automobile bodies, and perform other jobs on assembly lines. And, robots are often used when the work is dangerous.

The factory of the future will make increased use of automation and robotics. Thus it will have fewer employees, and all employees will be required to work with computers. As a result, a certain amount of job displacement and unemployment will result from the increased use of computers. In many cases, the computer will simply take over the routine jobs. Although experts predict a significant number of new jobs in the computer industry and related fields, employees who don't know how to use a computer, or those who refuse to learn, will be at a definite disadvantage.

Most experts predict that in the future computers will affect every aspect of human life. They will be as common as the toaster, the television, and the automobile. We have tried to describe the most obvious technological trends and how computers affect business, but the advances in medicine, transportation, conservation of natural resources, and all other areas of human life as we know it today are just as spectacular. It is safe to say that every aspect of your life will be affected by the changes that will take place in the development of computer technology in your lifetime.

Now that we understand how computers transform data into information, it is time to examine a management information system (MIS).

THE MANAGEMENT INFORMATION SYSTEM

management information system (MIS)   a system that provides managers with the information they need to perform management functions as effectively as possible

Where do managers get the information they need? In many organizations, the answer lies in a **management information system (MIS),** which is a means of providing managers with the information they need to perform management functions as effectively as possible (see Figure 15.4).

If this sounds like the marketing information system discussed in Chapter 11, the similarity is intended. In many firms, the MIS is combined with a marketing information system so that it can provide information based on a wide variety of data. In fact, it makes little sense to have separate information systems for the various management areas. After all, the goal is to provide needed information to all managers.

Managers' Information Requirements

LEARNING OBJECTIVE 5
Discuss management's information requirements.

Managers have to plan for the future, implement their plans in the present, and evaluate the results against what has been accomplished in the past. Thus they need access to information that summarizes future possibilities, the present situation, and past performance. Of course, the specific types of information they need depend on their area of management and on their level within the firm.

FIGURE 15.4
Management Information System (MIS)
After an MIS is installed, a user can get information directly from the MIS without having to go through other people in the organization. (*Source: Ricky W. Griffin,* Management, *3rd ed. Copyright © 1990 by Houghton Mifflin Company, p. 673. Used by permission.*)

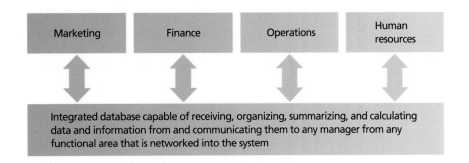

In Chapter 5 we identified five areas of management: finance, operations, marketing, human resources, and administration. Financial managers are obviously most concerned with their firms' finances. They study its debts and receivables, cash flow, future capitalization needs, financial ratios, and other accounting information. Of equal importance to financial managers is information about the present state of the economy and predictions of business conditions for the near future.

Operations managers are concerned with present and future sales levels and with the availability of the resources required to meet sales forecasts. They need to know the cost of producing their firms' goods and services, including inventory costs. And they are involved with new-product planning. They must also keep abreast of any new production technology that might be useful to their firm.

Marketing managers need to have detailed information about their firms' product mix and the products offered by competitors. Such information includes prices and pricing strategies, new and projected promotional campaigns, and new products that competitors are test-marketing. Information concerning target markets, current and projected market share, new and pending product legislation, and developments within channels of distribution is also important to marketing managers.

Human resources managers must be aware of anything that pertains to their firms' employees and employment in general—from plant safety to the unemployment rate. Key examples include current wage levels and benefits packages both within their firms' and in firms that compete for valuable employees; current legislation and court decisions that affect employment practices; union activities; and their firms' plans for growth, expansion, or mergers.

Administrative managers are responsible for the overall management of their organizations. Thus they are concerned with the coordination of information—just as they are concerned with the coordination of material, human, and financial resources. First, administrators must ensure that subordinates have access to the information they need to do their jobs. And second, they must ensure that the information is used in a consistent manner. Suppose, for example, that the operations group for General Electric Co. is designing a new plant to manufacture consumer electronic products to be opened in five years. GE's management will want answers to many questions: Is the capacity of the plant consistent with marketing plans based on economic projections? Will human resources managers be able to staff the plant on the basis of their employment forecasts? And will projected sales generate enough income to cover the expected cost of financing?

Size and Complexity of the System

A management information system (MIS) must be tailored to the needs of the organization it serves. In some firms there may be a tendency to save on initial costs by developing a system that is too small or simple. Such a system generally ends up serving only one or two management levels or a single department—the one that gets its data into the system first. Managers in other departments "give up" on the system as soon as they find that it cannot accept or process their data. They either look elsewhere for information or do without.

Almost as bad is an MIS that is too large or too complex for the organization. Unused capacity and complexity do nothing but increase the cost of owning and operating the system. In addition, a system that is difficult to use may not be used at all. Managers may find that it is easier to maintain their own records. Or, again, they may try to operate without information that could be helpful in their decision making.

Obviously, much is expected of an effective MIS. Let's examine the four functions that an MIS must perform to provide the information that managers need.

FUNCTIONS OF THE MANAGEMENT INFORMATION SYSTEM

LEARNING OBJECTIVE 6
State the four functions of a management information system.

To provide information, a management information system must perform four specific functions. It must collect data; store and then update the data; process the stored data into information; and present information to users of the system (see Figure 15.5).

Obviously, data must be collected if they are to be available for storing, processing, and presentation. The data entered into the system must be *relevant* to the needs of the firm's managers. And, perhaps most important, these data must be *accurate*. Irrelevant data are simply useless; inaccurate data can be disastrous.

The system must be capable of storing data until they are needed. And it must be able to update stored data to ensure that the information presented to managers is *timely*. An operations manager for Goodyear Tire & Rubber Company, for instance, cannot produce finished goods with last week's work-in-process inventory. She or he needs to know what is available today.

Much of the power of a management information system stems from its ability to transform data into useful information. The system must be

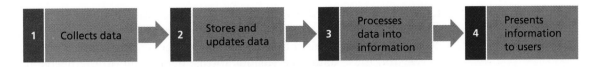

FIGURE 15.5   Four MIS Functions
Every MIS must be tailored to the organization it serves and must perform four functions.

capable of processing data in different ways to meet the particular needs of different managers.

Finally, the system must be capable of presenting the information in a *usable form*. That is, the method of presentation—tables, graphs, or charts, for example—must be appropriate for the information itself and the uses to which it will be put.

Collecting Data

LEARNING OBJECTIVE 7
Specify the various sources of business data.

The first step in using an MIS is to gather the data needed to establish the firm's *data bank*. This data bank should include all past and current data that may be useful in managing the firm. The data themselves can be obtained from within the firm and from outside sources.

Internal Sources of Data   Typically, the majority of the data gathered for an MIS come from internal sources. The most common internal sources of information include company records, reports, managers, and conferences and meetings.

Past and present accounting data can provide information about the firm's customers, creditors, and suppliers. Similarly, sales reports are a source of data on sales and sales patterns, pricing strategies, and the level and effectiveness of promotional campaigns during past years. Various management and financial reports and the minutes of committee meetings can also yield valuable information for an MIS.

Personnel records are useful as a source of data on wage and benefits levels, hiring patterns, employee turnover, and other human resources variables. Production and inventory records can be used to reconstruct patterns of production, inventory movement, costs, and the like.

Present and past forecasts should also be included in the MIS, with data indicating how well these forecasts predicted actual events. Similarly, specific plans and management decisions—regarding capital expansion and new-product development, for example—should be made a part of the system.

The firm's managers can supply additional data about its economic and legal situations. For instance, financial managers can provide information about the firm's credit rating. Legal personnel can add data regarding lawsuits and the firm's compliance with government regulations.

External Sources of Data   External sources of management data include customers, suppliers, bankers, trade and financial publications, industry conferences, and firms that specialize in gathering data for organizations.

Again, these data take various forms, depending on the needs and requirements of the firm and its managers. A marketing research company may be used to acquire forecasts pertaining to product demand, consumer tastes, and other marketing variables. Suppliers are an excellent source of information about the future availability and costs of raw materials and parts used by the firm.

Bankers can often provide valuable economic insights and projections. The information furnished by trade publications and industry conferences is usually concerned as much with the future as with the present. Both are valuable sources of data on competitors and production technology.

Legal issues and court decisions that may affect the firm are occasionally discussed in local newspapers and, more often, in specialized publications such as the *Wall Street Journal, Fortune,* and *Business Week.* Government publications like the *Monthly Labor Review* and the *Federal Reserve Bulletin* are also quite useful as sources of external data.

Cautions in Collecting Data   Three cautions should be observed in collecting data for an MIS. First, the cost of obtaining data from such external sources as marketing research firms can be quite high. In all cases—whether the data come from internal or external sources—the cost of obtaining data should be weighed against the potential benefits that having the data will confer on the firm.

Second, although computers do not make mistakes, the people who use them can make or cause errors. By simply pushing the wrong key on a computer keyboard, a technician can change an entire set of data, along with the information it contains. Data—from whatever source—should always be viewed in light of the manager's judgment. When data (or information) and judgment disagree, the data should be checked.

Third, outdated or incomplete data usually yield inaccurate information. Data collection is an ongoing process. New data must be added to the data bank, either as they are obtained or in regularly scheduled updates.

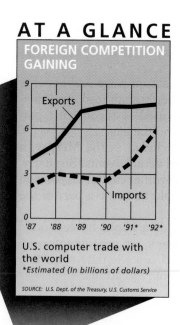

AT A GLANCE

FOREIGN COMPETITION GAINING

U.S. computer trade with the world
Estimated (In billions of dollars)

SOURCE: U.S. Dept. of the Treasury, U.S. Customs Service

Storing and Updating Data

Computers are especially well suited for both storing and rapidly updating MIS data. Large mainframes, minicomputers, and even microcomputers can store a great deal of data. However, that storage capacity is generally used for the particular data that are being processed at any given time (and for the processing instructions). When data are stored for an MIS, the computer is used only to transfer the data to magnetic tapes, hard disks, or floppy disks. Usually, the programmer enters the data into the computer, which transfers it to a tape or disk. When the tape or disk is full, the programmer removes it from the machine, makes a note about which data it contains, stores the tape or disk on a shelf, and (if necessary) continues with another tape or disk. When the data stored on a particular disk are

ETHICAL CHALLENGES

Problems at TRW Credit Bureaus

Inaccurate credit reports can keep consumers from obtaining a home mortgage, an automobile loan, or even a job. And as more and more retailers, banks, and employers rely on credit bureaus to screen either potential credit customers or future employees, the number of complaints has risen dramatically. In fact, inaccurate credit reports are now the number-one consumer complaint, according to the Federal Trade Commission.

One of the three largest credit bureaus in the United States—Cleveland-based TRW Inc.—has been particularly hard hit with consumer lawsuits in fourteen different states. Most lawsuits are the result of TRW's failure to correct inaccurate or incomplete information quickly enough. According to officials at TRW, the company does everything it can to ensure the accuracy of its credit reports. But with files on 170 million Americans, the firm admits that some mistakes are inevitable. In response to the rising number of complaints, TRW has revamped its Consumer-assistance Department and now provides a free annual credit report to consumers who ask for one. Under the current Fair Credit Reporting Act, only consumers who have been denied credit because of information contained in a credit report are entitled to a free report. All other consumers have had to pay a $5 to $15 fee for a report. According to company officials, giving away credit reports is the easiest way for TRW to demonstrate that the information contained in its files is accurate.

Consumer groups admit that TRW's response to the complaints is a good beginning but say it's only the first step. They believe that an industry with more than $1 billion in annual sales revenue should be more responsive to consumers. Specifically, consumer advocates argue that credit bureaus should ensure that consumers get quick service when correcting inaccurate information in their credit files. (Consumers who currently complain to the Federal Trade Commission have already contacted a credit bureau an average of five times without resolving the issue.) Also, consumer advocates want to strengthen the existing Fair Credit Reporting Act and give more power to the Federal Trade Commission—the agency responsible for enforcing current legislation. Finally, they argue, it should be easier for consumers to sue credit bureaus that provide lenders, bankers, and prospective employers with inaccurate credit information.

Issues to Consider

1. With files on 170 million Americans, TRW admits that some mistakes are inevitable. From an ethical standpoint, what should management do to eliminate or reduce the incorrect information contained in the firm's credit reports?

2. Both the U.S. Senate and the House of Representatives are considering additional federal legislation to police the consumer credit industry. Could increased government legislation lead to more ethical decisions by managers in a firm like TRW Inc.?

needed, the disk is reinserted into the computer. At this point, the data are ready to be processed by the computer.

Manual Updating To update stored data manually, a programmer inserts the proper tape or disk into the computer, locates the data that are to be changed, and provides the new data. The computer automatically replaces the older data with the new.

The frequency with which data are updated depends on how fast they change and how often they are used. When it is vital to have current data, updating may occur daily. Otherwise, new data may be collected and held for updating at a certain time each week or, perhaps, each month.

Automatic Updating   In automatic updating, the system itself updates the existing data bank as new information becomes available. The data bank, usually in the form of hard disks, is permanently connected to the MIS. The computer automatically finds the proper disk and replaces the existing data with the new data.

For example, Giant Food, a Washington, D.C.-based grocery store chain, has installed cash registers that automatically transmit, to a central computer, information regarding each item sold. The computer adjusts the store's inventory records accordingly. At any time of the day, the manager can get precise, up-to-the-minute information on the inventory of every item sold by the store. In some systems, the computer may even be programmed to reorder items whose inventories fall below some specified level.

Forms of Updating   We have been discussing the type of updating in which new data are *substituted for* old data. Although this is an efficient type of updating in terms of the use of storage space, it does result in the loss of the old data. In a second form of updating, new data are *added to* the old data—much as a new file folder is placed between two folders that are already in a drawer. (In fact, on a magnetic tape or disk, existing data are actually spread apart by the computer to accommodate the new data.) The form of updating a firm uses will depend entirely on whether the existing data will be needed in the future.

Processing Data

data processing   the transformation of data into a form that is useful for a specific purpose

Data are collected, stored in an MIS, and updated under the assumption that they will be of use to managers. Some data are used in the form in which they are stored. This is especially true of verbal data—a legal opinion, for example. Other data require processing to extract, highlight, or summarize the information they contain. **Data processing** is the transformation of data into a form that is useful for a specific purpose. For verbal data, this processing consists mainly of extracting the pertinent material from storage and combining it into a report.

Most business data, however, are in the form of numbers—large groups of numbers, such as daily sales volumes or annual earnings of workers in a particular city. Such groups of numbers are difficult to handle and to comprehend, but their contents can be summarized through the use of statistics.

statistic   a measure that summarizes a particular characteristic for an entire group of numbers

Statistics as Summaries   A **statistic** is a measure that summarizes a particular characteristic for an entire group of numbers. In this section we discuss the most commonly used statistics (or statistical measures), using the data given in Figure 15.6. This figure contains only eleven items of data, which simplifies our discussion. Most business situations would deal with

```
Rondex Corporation
Employee salaries for
the month of April 199x

Employee              Monthly salary
=============================================

Thomas P. Ouimet       $ 3,500
Marina Ruiz              3,500
Ronald F. Washington     3,000
Sarah H. Abrams          3,000
Kathleen L. Norton       3,000
Martin C. Hess           2,800
Jane Chang               2,500
Margaret S. Fernandez    2,400
John F. O'Malley         2,000
Robert Miller            2,000
William G. Dorfmann      1,800
Total                  $29,500
```

FIGURE 15.6
Statistics
A statistic is a measure that summarizes a particular characteristic for an entire group of numbers.

tens or hundreds of items. Fortunately, computers can be programmed to process such large groups of numbers quickly. Managers are free to concern themselves mainly with the information that results.

The number of items in a set of data can be reduced by developing a frequency distribution. A **frequency distribution** is a listing of the number of times each value appears in the set of data. For the data in Figure 15.6, the frequency distribution is as follows:

frequency distribution   a listing of the number of times each value appears in a set of data

Monthly salary	Frequency
$3,500	2
3,000	3
2,800	1
2,500	1
2,400	1
2,000	2
1,800	1

It is also possible to obtain a grouped frequency distribution:

Salary range	No. of employees
$3,000–$3,500	5
2,500– 2,999	2
2,000– 2,499	3
1,500– 1,999	1

Note that summarizing the data into a grouped frequency distribution has reduced the number of data items by approximately 60 percent.

Measures of Size and Dispersion   The arithmetic mean, median, and mode are measures of the size (or magnitude) of values in a set of data. Perhaps the most familiar statistic is the arithmetic mean, which is commonly called the *average*.

arithmetic mean   the sum of all the values of a set of data, divided by the number of items in the set

The **arithmetic mean** of a set of data is the sum of all the data values, divided by the number of items in the set. The sum of employee salaries given in Figure 15.6 is $29,500. The average (arithmetic mean) of employee salaries is $2,681.82 ($29,500 ÷ 11 = $2,681.82).

median   the value that appears at the exact middle of a set of data when the data are arranged in order

The **median** of a set of data is the value that appears at the exact middle of the data when they are arranged in order. The data in Figure 15.6 are already arranged from the highest value to the lowest value. Their median is thus $2,800, which is exactly halfway between the top and bottom values.

mode   the value that appears most frequently in a set of data

The **mode** of a set of data is the value that appears most frequently in the set. In Figure 15.6, the $3,000 monthly salary appears three times, which is more times than any other salary amount appears. Thus, $3,000 is the mode for this set of data.

Although the mean, or arithmetic average, is the most commonly used statistical measure of size, it may be distorted by a few extremely small or large values in the set of data. In this case, a manager may want to rely on the median, mode, or both to describe the values in a set of data. Managers often use the median to describe dollar values or income levels when the

Worth a thousand numbers. Geographic information systems represent a relatively new way in which computers can make information more useful. The systems combine maps with other information, like population data, to enable users to figure out the best newspaper delivery routes, accurate homeowners' insurance rates, or, in this case, what effect a new competitor will have on a store's patronage.

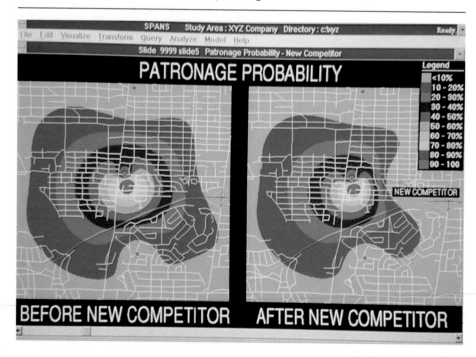

arithmetic average for the same numbers is distorted. In a similar fashion, marketers often use the mode to describe a firm's most successful or popular product when average sales amounts for a group of products would be inaccurate or misleading.

Although size (or magnitude) is an important characteristic of the items in a set of data, size alone does not describe the set. Another characteristic that is often summarized is the dispersion, or spread, of the items within the set. The simplest measure of dispersion is the **range,** which is the difference between the highest value and the lowest value in a set of data. The range of the data in Figure 15.6 is $3,500 –$1,800 = $1,700.

range   the difference between the highest value and the lowest value in a set of data

The smaller the range of the numbers in a set of data, the closer the values are to the mean—and, thus, the more effective the mean is as a measure of those values. Other measures of dispersion that are used to describe business data are the *variance* and the *standard deviation*. These are somewhat more complicated than the range, and we shall not define or calculate them here. However, you should remember that larger values of both the variance and the standard deviation indicate a greater spread among the values of the data.

With the proper software, a computer can provide these and other statistical measures almost as fast as a user can ask for them. How they are used is then up to the manager. Although statistics provide information in a much more manageable form than raw data, they can be interpreted incorrectly. Note, for example, that the average of the employee salaries given in Figure 15.6 is $2,681.82, yet not one of the employee salaries is exactly equal to that amount. This distinction between actual data and the statistics that describe them is an important one that should never be disregarded.

Presenting Information

Processed data should be presented in the form in which they have the most informational value. Verbal information may be presented in list or paragraph form. Employees are often asked to prepare formal business reports. A typical business report includes (1) an introduction, (2) the body of the report, (3) the conclusions, and (4) the recommendations.

The *introduction* section, which sets the stage for the remainder of the report, describes the problem to be studied in the report, identifies the research techniques that were used, and previews the material that will be presented in the report. The *body of the report* should objectively describe the facts that were discovered in the process of completing the report. The body should also provide a foundation for the conclusions and the recommendations. The *conclusions* should contain statements of fact that describe the findings contained in the report. They should be specific, practical, and based on the evidence contained in the report. The *recommendations* section presents suggestions on how the problem might be solved. Like the conclusions, recommendations should be specific, practical, and based on the evidence.

Visual and tabular displays may be necessary in a formal business report. For example, numerical information and combinations of numerical

FIGURE 15.7
Typical Visual Displays Used in Business Presentations
Visual displays help business people to present information in a form that can be easily understood.

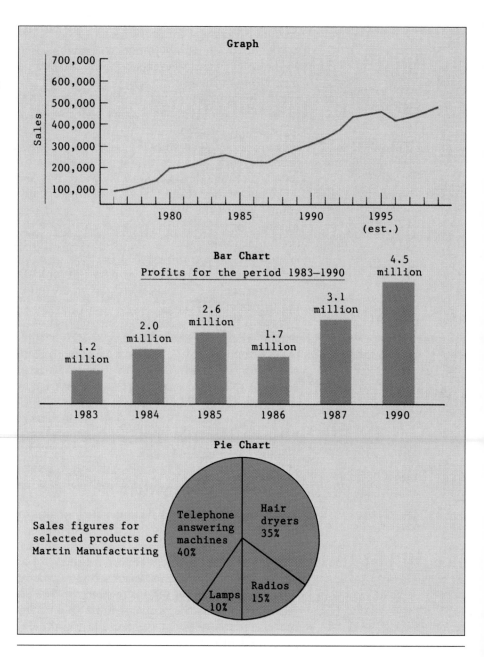

and verbal information are most easily and effectively presented in diagrams and tables.

Visual Displays A **visual display** is a diagram that represents several items of information in a manner that makes comparison easier or reflects trends among the items. The most accurate visual display is a *graph,* in which values are plotted to scale on a set of axes. Graphs are most effective for presenting information about a single variable that changes with time (such as variations in the gross national product over the last forty years). Graphs tend to emphasize trends as well as peaks and low points in the value of the variable. Figure 15.7 illustrates examples of visual displays generated by a computer.

In a *bar chart,* each value is represented as a vertical or horizontal bar. The longer a bar, the greater the value. This type of display is useful for presenting values that are to be compared. The eye can quickly pick out the longest or shortest bar, or even those that seem to be of average size.

A *pie chart* is a circle ("pie") that is divided into "slices," each of which represents a different item. The circle represents the whole—for example, total sales. The size of each slice shows the contribution of that item to the whole. The larger the slice, the larger the contribution. By their nature, pie charts are most effective in displaying the relative size or importance of various items of information.

tabular display a display used to present verbal or numerical information in columns and rows

Tabular Displays A **tabular display** is used to present verbal or numerical information in columns and rows. It is most useful in presenting information about two or more related variables (for example, variations in both sales volume and size of sales force by territory).

Tabular displays generally have less impact than visual displays. Moreover, the data contained in most two-column tables (like Figure 15.6) can be displayed visually. However, displaying the information that could be contained in a three-column table would require several bar or pie charts. In such cases, the items of information are easier to compare when they are presented in a table. Information that is to be manipulated—for example, to calculate loan payments—is also usually displayed in tabular form.

In this chapter, we have explored the role of the computer in business and have outlined some functions and requirements of an MIS. In Chapter 16, we examine the accounting process, which is a major source of information for business.

CHAPTER REVIEW

Summary

Data are numerical or verbal descriptions, whereas information is data presented in a form that is useful for a specific purpose. Generally, information is more effectively used when it is organized into a database. A database is a single collection of data that are stored in one place and can be used by people throughout the organization to make decisions.

Today, business, government, and other organizations depend on computers to process data and to make information available for decision making. A computer is an electronic machine that can accept, store, manipulate, and transmit data in accordance with a set of specific instructions. Although computers are a relatively recent invention, we have already seen five generations of computers. Currently, firms can choose mainframe computers, minicomputers, or microcomputers to match their information needs. Each of these machines consists of at least one input unit, a memory, a control unit, an arithmetic-logic unit, and an output unit. Today, the largest mainframe computers are called supercomputers, whereas the smallest microcomputers are referred to as laptops or notebooks. Firms can also establish a computer network—a system in which several computers can either function individually or communicate with each other.

Computers require software, or programs, which are operating instructions. Software may be either custom- or ready-made. Today, software has been developed to satisfy almost every business need. Database management programs can store and transform data into information. Data contained in a database program can also be sorted by selected criteria. Graphics programs make it possible to display in graph form data and conclusions. Spreadsheets are software packages that allow users to organize data into a grid of rows and columns. Spreadsheets allow managers to answer "what if" questions by changing data to match new assumptions. Word processing programs allow users to store documents in the computer's memory or on a disk. Once entered, the material can be revised, edited, deleted, printed, or simply used at a later date. Most experts predict that in the future computers will affect every aspect of human life. Specific trends that will affect business include the increase in available information, the use of automation, and the need for employees that know how to use a computer.

A management information system (MIS) is a means of providing managers with the information they need to perform management functions as effectively as possible. The data that are entered into the system must be relevant, accurate, and timely. The information provided by the system must be all of these—and it must be in usable form as well. Managers in different areas of a business generally require information pertaining to their own areas. The management information system itself should match the firm it serves in capacity and complexity.

The four functions performed by an MIS are collecting data, storing and updating data, processing data, and presenting information. Data may be collected from such internal sources as accounting documents and other financial records, conferences and meetings, and sales and production records. External sources include customers, suppliers, bankers, publications, and information-gathering organizations.

With a computer, data can be stored on magnetic tapes and disks and used whenever they are needed. Data should be updated regularly to maintain their timeliness and accuracy. Updating can be accomplished manually or via computer.

Data processing is the MIS function that transforms stored data into a form that is useful for a specific purpose. Large groups of numerical data are usually processed into summary numbers called statistics. The arithmetic mean, median, and mode are measures of the sizes of values in a set of data. The range is a measure of the dispersion, or spread, of the data values. Although statistics can provide information in a manageable form, the user is responsible for correctly interpreting statistics.

Finally, the processed data (which can now be called information) must be presented for use. Verbal information is generally presented in list or paragraph form. Typically, the components of a business report are the introduction, the body of the report, the conclusions, and the recommendations. Numerical information is most often displayed in graphs and charts or tables.

Key Terms

You should now be able to define and give an example relevant to each of the following terms:

data	flow chart
information	graphics program
database	spreadsheet program
computer	word processing program
artificial intelligence	management information system (MIS)
input unit	
memory (or storage) unit	data processing
control unit	statistic
arithmetic-logic unit	frequency distribution
output unit	arithmetic mean
hardware	median
computer network	mode
software	range
computer programmer	visual display
	tabular display

Questions and Exercises

Review Questions

1. What is the difference between data and information? Give one example of accounting data and one example of accounting information.
2. In basic terms, what is a database? How is it used in a business?
3. Briefly describe the history of computers.
4. List the five primary components of a computer, and briefly state the function of each.
5. What is meant by the term *computer network*?

6. What are the advantages of ready-made software? What are the disadvantages?

7. How do businesses use database management programs, graphics programs, spreadsheet programs, and word processing programs?

8. In your own words, define a management information system (MIS).

9. How do the information requirements of managers differ by management area?

10. Why must a management information system (MIS) be tailored to the needs of the organization it serves?

11. List the four functions of a MIS.

12. List several internal and several external sources of data.

13. What kinds of data might be updated by substituting new data for old data? by adding new data to old data?

14. What are the differences among the mean, median, and mode of a set of data? How can a few extremely small or large numbers affect the mean?

15. Data set A has a mean of 20 and a range of 10; data set B has the same mean and a range of 4. In which data set are the values closer to each other in size? How do you know?

16. What are the components of a typical business report?

Discussion Questions

1. Intel Corp. invests between 10 and 15 percent of annual sales on research and development. How has the company's R&D effort enabled Intel to compete in the computer-information industry?

2. Based on a federal court decision in 1990, competitors like Advanced Micro Devices began selling 386 chips. In your opinion, is competition between Intel and other computer parts manufacturers good for the industry? Why?

3. How can confidential data (such as the wages of individual employees) be kept confidential but be made available to managers who need them?

4. Why are computers so well suited to management information systems? What are some things that computers *cannot* do in dealing with data and information?

5. Do managers really need all the kinds of information discussed in this chapter? If not, which kinds can they do without?

6. How do you think computer technology will change in the next ten years?

Exercises

1. Leaf through a few magazines to find advertisements for three different brands of computers. For each brand, list the product attributes stressed in the ads. Then state whether each attribute would be important in an MIS, and why.

2. Choose a bar chart, a pie chart, or a graph, and display the data given in Figure 15.6. Why did you choose this method of presentation?

CASE 15.1

A Compaq Guide for Recovery

Less than four years after it was founded in 1982, Compaq Computer Corporation made the *Fortune* 500 list of America's top industrial companies. Compaq's rise to this prestigious list—the fastest in the list's thirty-two-year history—provides a perfect example of how the free-market system should function. The firm's founders—Bill Murto, Jim Harris, and Rod Canion—identified a need and then produced a product to meet that need.

The young company took its first crucial step in product development by choosing to follow the lead of International Business Machines Corp. (IBM), whose PCs set the standard for personal computers. Until Compaq was founded, smaller companies that survived the intense competition with IBM had done so by stressing price over quality as a way to differentiate their products from IBM's. But Compaq took another crucial step by deciding to differentiate itself from the clones by matching IBM's quality instead of undercutting their prices.

Compaq spent three years in the position of apprentice—learning from the master, IBM. Then in 1985 Compaq prepared to strike out on its own. It worked hard to produce the first personal computer based on the Intel Corp. 80386 computer chip. Compaq read the market well for its first big, independent step. It realized that IBM would be reluctant to bring out a machine based on the new chip because this new generation of computers would steal business from IBM's existing product line. And Compaq's early success proved that customers would respond to its approach—building quality computers compatible with machines already in use.

During the 1980s, sales and profits almost doubled each year. Then in 1991, Compaq—the company known for setting growth records—stopped growing. Annual sales dropped almost 15 percent, and the company announced plans for its first-ever employee lay-offs. Finally, on October 23, the company announced that it would post a $70 million loss for the third quarter of 1991. Although many factors contributed to Compaq's slowdown, the major reasons cited for the firm's reduced sales revenues were reduced corporate sales because of the sluggish economies in both the United States and Europe, coupled with stiff price cutting by competitors.

To solve Compaq's problems, its board of directors decided to replace Rod Canion—one of the original founders and the firm's current chief executive officer. The board chose Eckhard Pfeiffer, the executive who built the company's European division into a $2 billion-a-year operation. The board also approved plans to reorganize the company into two units. One unit would produce and market "plain vanilla PCs" that would compete head on with computer discounters. The other unit would concentrate on the research and development necessary to produce and market more sophisticated state-of-the-art computer systems.

According to industry experts, Compaq is still a strong company with a better new-product record than any other firm in the computer industry. While competitors spend 3 to 4 percent of sales on R&D, Compaq still invests more than 7 percent. Compaq's management team is counting on this technological edge to help the firm introduce new products with technical superiority and at the same time improve the firm's bottom-line profit amount.*

Questions

1. Many computer companies have tried to compete with IBM by offering clones at low prices. In contrast, Compaq chose to compete by matching IBM's quality. What are the disadvantages and advantages of Compaq's decision?

2. To solve the firm's problems, the board of directors approved plans to divide Compaq into separate units. One unit would produce and market plain vanilla PCs. The other unit would produce and market more sophisticated computer systems. Is this a good strategy for a firm that is known for its quality image? Why?

*Based on information from Mark Ivey, "Compaq's New Boss Doesn't Even Have Time to Wince," *Business Week*, November 11, 1991, p. 41; Mark Ivey, "Can Rod Canion Stop Compaq's Erosion?" *Business Week*, November 4, 1991, p. 134+; Richard A. Shaffer, "How Compaq Can Recover," *Forbes*, August 5, 1991, p. 98; Patrick Honan and Russ Lockwood, "Big Manufacturers Thinking Small," *Personal Computing*, November 1988, pp. 112–113; and Joel Kotkin, "The 'Small Team' at Compaq Computer," *Inc.*, February 1986, p. 48.

CASE 15.2

The Good and Bad News at Microsoft Corporation

First the good news: Microsoft Corp., led by thirty-six-year-old William Gates, is the most successful software firm in the world. Founded in 1975, when Gates was just nineteen, the firm now has annual sales revenues in excess of $1.5 billion. And with a 24 percent after-tax profit margin, the firm is debt free and has accumulated over $500 million in cash.

The firm's early success was tied to a partnership with International Business Machines Corp. (IBM) that began in the early 1980s. When IBM introduced its first Personal Computer, Microsoft supplied the operating system—*MS-DOS*—that guides the inner workings of the personal computer. Before long, all IBM's competitors with the exception of Apple Computer, Inc. followed suit, and *MS-DOS* became the standard operating system for the industry.

Microsoft's initial success with operating systems enabled the firm to branch out into application software. Today, the firm introduces either a new software program or an upgraded/improved software program on the average of once a month. And with the introduction of *Windows*—an all-in-one software program that enables users to integrate electronic mail, graphics, word processing, and other application programs—Microsoft's sales will increase for at least the next two to three years.

Now the bad news: The successful partnership between IBM and Microsoft is on the rocks. Problems between the two firms are numerous, but the straw that broke the camel's back came in early 1991 when Microsoft abandoned a new operating system called *OS/2*. *OS/2* had been a joint research project for both IBM and Microsoft. IBM needed the new operating system to power its most advanced personal computers. But after three years of disappointing sales, Microsoft began to market its *Windows* software package to compete with the *OS/2* operating system. Sales for the *Window*'s software were phenomenal—over 4 million copies the first year. During the same period, fewer than 600,000 copies of *OS/2* were sold.

Because Microsoft's management chose to market *Windows*, IBM's management felt betrayed. Instead of working with Microsoft on new software research projects, IBM struck deals with Apple, Lotus Development Corp., and other software firms. Not expecting a reconciliation with IBM anytime soon, Microsoft struck its own deal with Digital Equipment Corp. to develop new software application programs to accompany

Windows. In addition, Microsoft is also forging ahead with a major research project to develop a new operating system called *New Technology* (NT) to replace *MS-DOS.* Even with its break from IBM, Microsoft seems destined to keep its number-one spot in the software industry for years to come if the software firm's new application programs and *New Technology* operating system are half as successful as *MS-DOS* has been.**

Questions

1. Founded just over fifteen years ago, Microsoft's annual sales revenues are now in excess of $1.5 billion. What factors led to Microsoft's phenomenal success?
2. Based on the information presented in this case, how has the break between IBM and Microsoft affected new product development at each company?
3. One of Microsoft's major research projects is the development of a new operating system called *New Technology.* How can the *New Technology* operating system help Microsoft retain its number-one position in the software industry?

**Based on information from Kathy Rebello, "Microsoft," *Business Week*, February 24, 1992, pp. 60–64; "DEC and Microsoft Do Windows," *Business Week*, November 18, 1991, p. 52; Julie Pitta, "What's Good for IBM," *Forbes*, August 5, 1991, pp. 90–91; Brenda Dalglish, "A High-Tech Alliance," *Maclean's*, July 15, 1991, pp. 26–27; Richard Landry, "Microsoft's Choice," *PC World*, June 1991, pp. 21–22; Deidre A. Depke and Evan I. Schwartz, "Big Blue Makes a Big Commitment," *Business Week*, April 22, 1991, p. 33; and Kathleen K. Wiegner and Julie Pitta, "Can Anyone Stop Bill Gates?" *Forbes*, April 1, 1991, p. 108.

Accounting

LEARNING OBJECTIVES

After studying this chapter you should be able to:

1 Explain what accounting is and what accountants do.

2 Discuss the accounting equation and the concept of double-entry book-keeping.

3 List the steps of the accounting cycle.

4 Read and interpret a balance sheet.

5 Read and interpret an income statement.

6 Summarize why managers, lenders, and investors compare present financial statements with those prepared for past accounting periods.

7 Use financial ratios to reveal how a business is doing.

CHAPTER PREVIEW

We begin this chapter with an overview of the accounting process. We identify different classifications of accountants and see how their work is important both to a firm's managers and to individuals and groups outside a firm. Then we focus on the basics of an accounting system—the accounting equation, double-entry bookkeeping, and the process by which raw data are organized into financial statements. Next, we examine the three most important financial statements: the balance sheet, the income statement, and the statement of cash flows. Finally, we show how accounting information can be expressed numerically—as financial ratios—and what these ratios say about a firm's operations.

Defensive Accounting at the Big Six

For most investors, creditors, government officials, and corporate executives, an unqualified audit by an accounting firm means that everything is *OK* and the accountants have found nothing wrong. That's what Lincoln Savings got—an unqualified audit—from its accounting firm. A year later, Lincoln collapsed. And according to one source, the only thing unqualified about Lincoln was the extent of the damage.[1] Thousands of investors who—at least partly on the strength of the firm's financial audit—had invested in uninsured junk bonds issued by Lincoln lost millions. To make matters worse, Lincoln's collapse could cost taxpayers $2.5 billion.

What went wrong? Why didn't the accountants spot the financial irregularities that led to Lincoln's collapse? According to officials at Ernst & Young, the accounting firm that audited Lincoln's books, nothing went wrong from an auditing standpoint. The accountants argue that the purpose of an audit is not to determine the safety and financial stability of the firm being audited, but only to see if it complied with generally accepted accounting principles. But Federal Deposit Insurance Corporation (FDIC) officials disagree. The FDIC contends that the accountants should have found financial irregularities. They believe that Lincoln was on the edge of bankruptcy when accountants allowed the thrift to show profits that in reality just were not there. And based on this theory, the FDIC filed a multimillion-dollar lawsuit against Lincoln's auditors.

While maintaining its innocence, Ernst & Young agreed to pay the government over $40 million to settle this case in 1991. According to William Gladstone, the co-chief executive officer for Ernst & Young, "The S&L problems were not caused by the auditors, but rather resulted from economic downturns, extremely weak government accounting rules, and fraud that was hidden from the accountants."[2]

Ernst & Young is not the only accounting firm to face lawsuits and large damage awards resulting from audits that were performed for businesses that later failed. Coopers & Lybrand was hit with a $200 million punitive damage award for a faulty audit of now-bankrupt MiniScribe Corporation. Although this case was eventually settled out of court for an undisclosed amount, Coopers & Lybrand spent millions to settle the case. And KPMG Peat Marwick paid over $65 million for an allegedly faulty audit of an English firm. In fact, five of the six largest accounting firms in the United States have encountered similar legal problems.

Now, faced with the possibility of future lawsuits, the "Big Six" accounting firms (Arthur Andersen, Ernst & Young, Deloitte & Touche, KPMG Peat Marwick, Coopers & Lybrand, and Price Waterhouse) are more careful about the audit services they perform for their clients. In some cases, these firms will reject an account if they suspect that there may be problems. They have also taken steps to increase their own professional, internal review of the audit before it is released to the client, investors, or government regulators. Finally, they have taken steps to ensure that both clients and potential users understand just what an audit does do and what it does not do. According to a number of industry sources, most accountants realize they are now under the gun to tighten audit procedures and eliminate many of the problems that have led to lawsuits and large court settlements. And accountants are quick to point out that these same activities will enhance a profession that is built on trust.[3]

Just the thought that either management or a firm's accountants have *cooked the books* sends chills through investors, creditors, and government officials. As a result, large accounting firms like Ernst & Young have taken steps to ensure that the information they provide not only to corporate executives, but also to investors, creditors, and government officials, is accurate. After all, the basic product that an accounting firm sells is information—information that must meet clients' needs.

Today, it is impossible to manage a business operation without accurate and timely accounting information. Managers and employees, lenders, suppliers, stockholders, and government agencies all rely on the information contained in two financial statements, each no more than one page in length. These two reports—the balance sheet and the income statement—are concise summaries of a firm's activities during a specific time period. Together, they represent the results of perhaps tens of thousands of transactions that have occurred during the accounting period.

Standard accounting methods (described later in this chapter) have been developed for summarizing and presenting data in financial reports. This is to ensure that each item in each report means the same thing to everyone who reads it. Moreover, the form of the financial statements is pretty much the same for all businesses, from a neighborhood video arcade to giant conglomerates like General Motors Corp. and Coca-Cola. This information has a variety of uses, both within the firm and outside it. However, first and foremost, accounting information is management information. As such, it is of most use to those responsible for managing the operation of the firm.

ACCOUNTING AND ACCOUNTANTS

Accounting is the process of systematically collecting, analyzing, and reporting financial information. Because of its great value, business owners have been concerned with financial information for hundreds of years: The first book of accounting principles was written in 1494, by an Italian monk named Paciolo.

Modern accounting in the United States can be traced back to the establishment of the American Institute of Certified Public Accountants

- *Lenders* require at least the information contained in the firm's financial statements before they will commit themselves to either short- or long-term loans. *Suppliers* generally ask for such information before they will extend trade credit to a firm.
- *Stockholders* must, by law, be provided with a summary of the firm's financial position in each annual report. In addition, *potential investors* must be provided with financial statements in the prospectus for each securities' issue.
- *Government agencies* require a variety of information pertaining to the firm's tax liabilities, payroll deductions for employees, and new issues of stocks and bonds.

The firm's accounting system must be able to provide all this information, in the required form. An important function of accountants is to ensure that such information is accurate and thorough enough to satisfy these outside groups.

THE ACCOUNTING PROCESS

LEARNING OBJECTIVE 2
Discuss the accounting equation and the concept of double-entry bookkeeping.

Accounting can be viewed as a system for transforming raw financial *data* into useful financial *information*. In this section, we see how such a system operates. Then, in the next three sections, we describe the three most important financial statements provided by the accounting process.

The Accounting Equation

The accounting equation is a simple statement that forms the basis for the accounting process. It shows the relationship among the firm's assets, liabilities, and owners' equity.

assets   the items of value that a firm owns

liabilities   a firm's debts and obligations—what it owes to others

owners' equity   the difference between a firm's assets and its liabilities—what would be left over for the firm's owners if its assets were used to pay off its liabilities

- **Assets** are the items of value that a firm owns—cash, inventories, land, equipment, buildings, patents, and the like.
- **Liabilities** are the firm's debts and obligations—what it owes to others.
- **Owners' equity** is the difference between a firm's assets and its liabilities—what would be left over for the firm's owners if its assets were used to pay off its liabilities.

accounting equation   the basis for the accounting process: Assets = liabilities + owners' equity

The relationship among these three terms is almost self-evident: Owners' equity = assets – liabilities. By moving terms algebraically, we obtain the standard form of the **accounting equation:**

$$\text{Assets = liabilities + owners' equity}$$

Implementation of this equation begins with the recording of raw data—that is, the firm's day-to-day financial transactions. It is accomplished through the double-entry system of bookkeeping.

Fear of accounting. Many people who are not accounting experts become terrified when it's time to do taxes or "the books." Makers of an accounting software package used this picture to sell their product to "any client who doesn't understand double-entry." Such packages have not put CPAs out of business, but they have reduced this particular fear of numbers.

Quicken. The ideal software for any client who doesn't understand double-entry.

The Double-Entry Bookkeeping System

double-entry bookkeeping a system in which each financial transaction is recorded as two separate accounting entries to maintain the balance shown in the accounting equation

Double-entry bookkeeping is a system in which each financial transaction is recorded as two separate accounting entries to maintain the balance shown in the accounting equation. Most often, one entry changes the left (assets) side of the equation, and the other entry changes the right (liabilities + owners' equity) side. However, for a few types of transactions, the two entries change only one side of the equation. This occurs, for example, when cash (an asset) is used to purchase equipment (another asset).

Suppose John Thompson and Maria Martin each invest $25,000 in cash to start a new business. Before they make these investments, both sides of the accounting equation are equal to zero. The firm has no assets, no liabilities, and no owners' equity. The results of their investments are shown as transaction *A* in Figure 16.1. Cash (an asset) is increased by $50,000; owners' equity is also increased by a total of $50,000 to balance the increase in assets.

Note that the entries for this transaction are not lumped together as one asset increase and one owners' equity increase. Instead, the entries are placed in separate *accounts*, which show exactly what is being increased. Here the investments are cash, so the *Cash* account is increased. Similarly, under owners' equity, there is one account for Thompson and one for Martin.

Three additional transactions are shown in Figure 16.1:

- In transaction *B*, a bank loan of $10,000 was used to purchase equipment. The loan is a liability, and the equipment is an asset.

- In transaction *C*, inventory worth $5,000 was purchased on credit. The inventory is an asset, and the amount owed is a liability.

	ASSETS			=	LIABILITIES		+	OWNERS' EQUITY	
	Cash	Equipment	Inventory	=	Bank Loans	Suppliers	+	Thompson	Martin
Transaction A *(cash investment)*	+$50,000	–0–	–0–	=	–0–	–0–	+	+$25,000	+$25,000
	$50,000 +	–0– +	–0–	=	–0– +	–0–	+	$25,000 +	$25,000
Transaction B *(equipment purchase via bank loan)*	–0–	+$10,000	–0–	=	+$10,000	–0–		–0–	–0–
	$50,000 +	$10,000 +	–0–	=	$10,000 +	–0–	+	$25,000 +	$25,000
Transaction C *(credit purchase of inventory)*	–0–	–0–	+$5,000	=	–0–	+$5,000		–0–	–0–
	$50,000 +	$10,000 +	$5,000	=	$10,000 +	$5,000	+	$25,000 +	$25,000
Transaction D *(partial payoff of loan)*	–$ 5,000	–0–	–0–	=	–$ 5,000	–0–		–0–	–0–
	$45,000 +	$10,000 +	$5,000	=	$ 5,000 +	$5,000	+	$25,000 +	$25,000

FIGURE 16.1
Four Business Transactions Recorded Using the Double-Entry System
Double-entry bookkeeping is used to balance the accounting equation (assets = liabilities + owners' equity).

- In transaction *D*, $5,000 in cash was used to pay off part of the bank loan. The payoff decreases cash, an asset; the reduction of the loan amount decreases a liability.

Follow through each of these transactions in Figure 16.1 to make sure you understand why each entry is recorded as shown. Also note that, after all four transactions, assets total $60,000, and liabilities and owners' equity total $60,000. Thus the books are still balanced. That is, assets are indeed equal to liabilities plus owners' equity.

The Accounting Cycle

LEARNING OBJECTIVE 3
List the steps of the accounting cycle.

In the typical accounting system, raw data are transformed into financial statements in five steps. The first three—analysis, journalizing, and posting—are performed on a continual basis throughout the accounting period. The last two—preparation of the trial balance and of the financial statements—are performed at the end of the accounting period.

Analyzing Source Documents   The basic accounting data are contained in *source documents,* which are the receipts, invoices, sales slips, and other documents that show the dollar values of day-to-day business transactions. The accounting cycle begins with the analysis of each of these documents. The purpose of the analysis is to determine which accounts are affected by the documents and how they are affected.

Journalizing the Transactions   Every financial transaction is next recorded in a journal—a process that is called *journalizing.* Transactions must be recorded in the firm's general journal or in specialized journals. The **general journal** is a book of original entry in which typical transactions are

general journal   a book of original entry in which typical transactions are recorded in order of their occurrence

recorded in order of their occurrence. An accounting system may also include *specialized journals* for specific types of transactions that occur frequently. Thus a retail store might have cash receipts, cash disbursements, purchases, and sales journals in addition to its general journal. Today, large, medium-sized, and even small businesses use a computer when journalizing accounting entries.

Posting Transactions   Next the information recorded in the general journal or specialized journals is transferred to the general ledger. The **general ledger** is a book of accounts containing a separate sheet or section for each account. The process of transferring journal entries to the general ledger is called **posting.**

general ledger a book of accounts containing a separate sheet or section for each account

posting the process of transferring journal entries to the general ledger

trial balance a summary of the balances of all general ledger accounts at the end of the accounting period

Preparing the Trial Balance   A **trial balance** is a summary of the balances of all general ledger accounts at the end of the accounting period. To prepare a trial balance, the accountant determines and lists the balances for all ledger accounts. If the trial balance totals are correct, the accountant can proceed to the financial statements. If not, there is a mistake somewhere, which the accountant must find and correct before proceeding.

Preparing Financial Statements and Closing the Books   The firm's financial statements are prepared from the information contained in the trial balance. This information is presented in a standardized format to make the statements as generally accessible as possible to the various parties who may be interested in the firm's financial affairs.

Once these statements have been prepared and checked, the firm's books are "closed" for the accounting period. A new accounting cycle is then begun for the next period.

Now let us consider the two most important financial statements generated by the accounting process, the balance sheet and the income statement.

THE BALANCE SHEET

LEARNING OBJECTIVE 4
Read and interpret a balance sheet.

balance sheet (or statement of financial position) a summary of a firm's assets, liabilities, and owners' equity accounts at a particular time, showing the various dollar amounts that enter into the accounting equation

A **balance sheet** (or **statement of financial position**), is a summary of a firm's assets, liabilities, and owners' equity accounts at a particular time, showing the various dollar amounts that enter into the accounting equation. The balance sheet must demonstrate that the accounting equation does indeed balance. That is, it must show that the firm's assets are equal to its liabilities plus its owners' equity. As previously noted, the balance sheet is prepared at least once a year. Most firms also have balance sheets prepared semiannually, quarterly, or monthly.

Figure 16.2 shows the balance sheet for Northeast Art Supply, a small corporation that sells picture frames, paints, canvases, and other artists' supplies to retailers in New England. Note that assets are reported at the top of the statement, followed by liabilities and owners' equity. Let us work through the accounts in Figure 16.2, from top to bottom.

FIGURE 16.2
Balance Sheet
A balance sheet summarizes a firm's accounts at a particular time, showing the various dollar amounts that enter into the accounting equation and showing that the equation balances. Note that assets ($340,000) equal liabilities plus owners' equity ($340,000).

NORTHEAST ART SUPPLY, INC.

Balance Sheet
December 31, 199x

ASSETS

Current assets			
Cash		$ 59,000	
Marketable securities		10,000	
Accounts receivable	$ 40,000		
Less allowance for doubtful accounts	2,000	38,000	
Notes receivable		32,000	
Merchandise inventory		41,000	
Prepaid expenses		2,000	
Total current assets			$182,000
Fixed assets			
Delivery equipment	$110,000		
Less accumulated depreciation	20,000	$ 90,000	
Furniture and store equipment	62,000		
Less accumulated depreciation	15,000	47,000	
Total fixed assets			137,000
Intangible assets			
Patents		$ 6,000	
Goodwill		15,000	
Total intangible assets			21,000
Total assets			$340,000

LIABILITIES AND STOCKHOLDERS' EQUITY

Current liabilities			
Accounts payable	$ 35,000		
Notes payable	25,000		
Salaries payable	4,000		
Taxes payable	6,000		
Total current liabilities		$ 70,000	
Long-term liabilities			
Mortgage payable on store equipment	$ 40,000		
Total long-term liabilities		40,000	
Total liabilities			$110,000
Stockholders' equity			
Common stock, 10,000 shares at $15 Par value		$150,000	
Retained earnings		80,000	
Total owners' equity			230,000
Total liabilities and owners' equity			$340,000

Assets

On a balance sheet, assets are listed in order, from the *most liquid* to the *least liquid*. The **liquidity** of an asset is the ease with which it can be converted into cash.

liquidity   the ease with which an asset can be converted into cash

Current Assets   **Current assets** are cash and other assets that can be quickly converted into cash or that will be used in one year or less. Because cash is the most liquid asset, it is listed first. Following that are *marketable*

current assets   cash and other assets that can be quickly converted into cash or that will be used in one year or less *securities*—stocks, bonds, and so on—that can be converted into cash in a matter of days. These are temporary investments of excess cash that Northeast Art Supply doesn't immediately need.

Next are the firm's receivables. Its *accounts receivables,* which result from the issuance of trade credit to customers, are generally due within sixty days. However, the firm expects that some of these debts will not be collected. Thus it has reduced its accounts receivables by a 5 percent *allowance for doubtful accounts.* The firm's *notes receivables* are receivables for which customers have signed promissory notes. They are generally repaid over a longer period of time when compared with the firm's accounts receivables.

Northeast's *merchandise inventory* represents the value of goods that are on hand for sale to customers. These goods are listed as current assets because they will be sold in one year or less. Since Northeast Art Supply is a wholesale operation, the inventory listed in Figure 16.2 represents finished goods ready for sale to retailers. For a manufacturing firm, merchandise inventory can also represent raw materials that will become part of a finished product, or work in process that has been partially completed but requires further processing.

prepaid expenses assets that have been paid for in advance but have not yet been used

Northeast's last current asset is **prepaid expenses,** which are assets that have been paid for in advance but have not yet been used. An example is insurance premiums. They are usually paid at the beginning of the policy year for the whole year. The unused portion (say, for the last four months of the policy year) is a prepaid expense—a current asset. For Northeast Art, all current assets total $182,000.

Keeping track. These rolls of Weyerhauser newsprint are bound across the Pacific, part of over $1 billion in pulp and paper products that the company exports from North America each year. A forest products company like Weyerhauser faces some tricky accounting to keep track of its trees, which may not be converted into a marketable product for decades.

well, if they existed. As illustrated in Figure 16.2, current and long-term liabilities total $110,000.

Owners' Equity   For a sole proprietorship or partnership, the owners' equity is shown as the difference between assets and liabilities. In a partnership, each partner's share of the ownership is reported separately by each owner's name. For a corporation, the owners' equity is usually referred to as *stockholders' equity* or *shareholders' equity*. It is shown as the total value of its stock, plus retained earnings that have accumulated to date.

Northeast Art Supply has issued only common stock. Its value is shown as its par value ($15) times the number of shares outstanding (10,000). In addition, $80,000 of Northeast's earnings have been reinvested in the business since it was founded. Thus, owners' equity totals $230,000.

As the two grand totals show, Northeast's assets and the sum of its liabilities and owners' equity are equal—at $340,000.

THE INCOME STATEMENT

LEARNING OBJECTIVE 5
Read and interpret an income statement.

income statement   a summary of a firm's revenues and expenses during a specified accounting period

An **income statement** is a summary of a firm's revenues and expenses during a specified accounting period. The income statement is sometimes called the *earnings statement* or the *statement of income and expenses*. It may be prepared monthly, quarterly, semiannually, or annually. An income statement covering the previous year must be included in a corporation's annual report to its stockholders.

Figure 16.3 shows the income statement for Northeast Art Supply. Note that it consists of four sections. Generally, revenues *less* cost of goods sold *less* operating expenses *equals* net income from operations.

Revenues

revenues   dollar amounts received by a firm

gross sales   the total dollar amount of all goods and services sold during the accounting period

Revenues are dollar amounts received by a firm. Northeast obtains its revenues solely from the sale of its products. The revenues section of its income statement begins with gross sales. **Gross sales** are the total dollar amount of all goods and services sold during the accounting period. From this amount are deducted the dollar amounts of

- *Sales returns,* or merchandise returned to the firm by its customers
- *Sales allowances,* or price reductions offered to customers who accept slightly damaged or soiled merchandise
- *Sales discounts,* or price reductions offered by manufacturers and suppliers to customers who pay their bills promptly

net sales   the actual dollar amount received by a firm for the goods and services it has sold, after adjustment for returns, allowances, and discounts

The remainder is the firm's net sales. **Net sales** are the actual dollar amounts received by the firm for the goods and services it has sold, after adjustment for returns, allowances, and discounts. For Northeast Art, net sales are $451,000.

FIGURE 16.3
Income Statement
An income statement summarizes the firm's revenues and expenses during a specified accounting period—one month, three months, six months, or a year.

NORTHEAST ART SUPPLY, INC.

Income Statement
For the Year Ended
December 31, 199x

Revenues			
Gross sales		$465,000	
Less sales returns and allowances	$ 9,500		
Less sales discounts	4,500	14,000	
Net sales			$451,000
Cost of goods sold			
Beginning inventory, January 1, 199x		$ 40,000	
Purchases	$346,000		
Less purchase discounts	11,000		
Net purchases		335,000	
Cost of goods available for sale		$375,000	
Less ending inventory December 31, 199x		41,000	
Cost of goods sold			334,000
Gross profit on sales			117,000
Operating expenses			
Selling expenses			
Sales salaries	$ 20,000		
Advertising	6,000		
Sales promotion	2,500		
Depreciation—store equipment	3,000		
Miscellaneous selling expenses	1,500		
Total selling expenses		$ 33,000	
General expenses			
Office salaries	$ 28,500		
Rent	8,500		
Depreciation—delivery equipment	4,000		
Depreciation—office furniture	1,500		
Utilities expense	2,500		
Insurance expense	1,000		
Miscellaneous expense	500		
Total general expenses		46,500	
Total operating expenses			79,500
Net income from operations			$ 37,500
Less interest expense			2,000
Net income before taxes			$ 35,500
Less federal income taxes			5,325
Net income after taxes			$ 30,175

Cost of Goods Sold

According to Figure 16.3, Northeast began its accounting period with a merchandise inventory that cost $40,000 (see *beginning inventory* under *cost of goods sold*). During the period, the firm purchased, for resale, merchandise worth $346,000. But, after taking advantage of *purchase discounts*, it paid only $335,000 for this merchandise. Thus, during the year, Northeast had *goods available for sale* valued at $40,000 + $335,000 = $375,000.

At the end of the accounting period, Northeast had an *ending inventory* of $41,000. Thus it had sold all but $41,000 worth of the available goods.

The *cost of goods sold* by Northeast was therefore $375,000 *less* $41,000, or $334,000.

This is the standard method of determining the cost of the goods sold by a retailing or wholesaling firm during an accounting period. It may be summarized as follows:

cost of goods sold   the cost of the goods a firm has sold during an accounting period; equal to beginning inventory *plus* net purchases *less* ending inventory

gross profit on sales   a firm's net sales *less* the cost of goods sold

$$\text{Cost of goods sold} = \frac{\text{beginning}}{\text{inventory}} + \frac{\text{net}}{\text{purchases}} - \frac{\text{ending}}{\text{inventory}}$$

A manufacturer must include its raw-materials inventories, work-in-process inventories, and direct manufacturing costs in this computation.

A firm's **gross profit on sales** is its net sales *less* the cost of goods sold. For Northeast, gross profit on sales was $117,000.

Operating Expenses

operating expenses   those costs that do not result directly from the purchase or manufacture of the products a firm sells

selling expenses   costs related to the firm's marketing activities

A firm's **operating expenses** are those costs that do not result directly from the purchase or manufacture of the products it sells. They are generally classed as either selling expenses or general expenses.

Selling expenses are costs related to the firm's marketing activities. They include salaries for members of the sales force, advertising and other promotional expenses, and the costs involved in operating stores. For Northeast Art, selling expenses total $33,000.

general expenses   costs that are incurred in managing a business

General expenses are costs incurred in managing a business. They are sometimes called *administrative expenses*. Typical general expenses are the salaries of office workers and the costs of maintaining offices. A catchall account called *miscellaneous expense* is usually included in the *general expenses* section of the income statement. For Northeast Art, general expenses total $46,500. Now it is possible to total both selling and general expenses for Northeast Art. As illustrated in Figure 16.3, total operating expenses are $79,500.

The easy part of the job. To executives in the petroleum industry, finding, tapping, and delivering their product must sometimes seem like the easy part when compared to handling the financial aspects of the business. The industry is affected by unique tax provisions, and the value of its assets—and how much it's allowed to charge for them—can fluctuate overnight.

Net Income

net income   the profit earned (or the loss suffered) by a firm during an accounting period, after all expenses have been deducted from revenues

Net income is the profit earned (or the loss suffered) by a firm during an accounting period, after all expenses have been deducted from revenues. In Figure 16.3, Northeast's *net income from operations* is computed as gross profit on sales ($117,000) *less* total operating expenses ($79,500). For Northeast Art, net income from operations totals $37,500. From this, an *interest expense* of $2,000 is deducted to give a *net income before taxes* of $35,500. The interest expense is deducted in this section of the income statement because it is not an operating expense. Rather, it is an expense that results from financing the business.

Northeast's *federal income taxes,* based on its pretax income, are $5,325. Although these taxes may or may not be payable immediately, they are definitely an expense that must be deducted from income. This leaves Northeast with a *net income after taxes* of $30,175. This amount may be used to pay a dividend to stockholders, retained or reinvested in the firm, used to reduce the firm's debts, or all three.

THE STATEMENT OF CASH FLOWS

statement of cash flows illustrates the effect on cash of the operating, investing, and financing activities of a company for an accounting period

Cash generation is the life blood of business. In 1987 the Securities and Exchange Commission (SEC) and the Financial Accounting Standards Board (FASB) required all publicly traded companies to include a **Statement of Cash Flows** with their annual reporting requirements. The statement of cash flows illustrates the effect on cash of the operating, investing, and financing activities of a company for an accounting period. It provides information concerning a company's cash receipts and cash payments during the accounting period and is organized into three activities: operations, investing, and financing.

Cash Flows from Operating Activities. This first section of the statement addresses the firm's primary revenue generating activities—providing goods and services. The Net Income (from the Income Statement) is adjusted by adding back any non-cash expenses (such as Depreciation Expense). Additional adjustments are made based on changes in the working capital accounts (current assets and current liabilities). The end result gives the true cash flows from operating activities.

Cash Flows from Investing Activities. The second section is concerned with the net cash flow from acquiring and disposing of non-current assets. This includes the purchase and sale of property, plant, equipment, long-term investments, and intangible assets.

Cash Flows from Financing Activities. The third and final section deals with the cash flow from all financing activities. It reports changes in long-term liability and Owner's Equity accounts. This includes long-term borrowing and repayments, the sale and repurchase of the company's own stock and cash dividends.

The totals of all three activities are added to the beginning cash balance to equal the ending cash balance. The cash flow statement, along with the balance sheet and income statement, illustrate such things as the results of past decisions, the business' ability to pay debts and dividends, and finance growth internally.

ANALYZING FINANCIAL STATEMENTS

LEARNING OBJECTIVE 6
Summarize why managers, lenders, and investors compare present financial statements with those prepared for past accounting periods.

As we have seen, a firm's balance sheet provides a "financial picture" of the firm at a particular time. Its income statement summarizes its operations during one accounting period. Both can provide answers to a variety of questions about the firm's ability to do business and stay in business, its profitability, its value as an investment, and its ability to repay its debts.

Even more information can be obtained by comparing present financial statements with those prepared for past accounting periods. Such comparisons permit managers (and other interested people) to (1) pick out trends in growth, borrowing, income, and other business variables and (2) determine whether the firm is on the way to accomplishing its long-term goals. Most corporations include, in their annual reports, comparisons of the important elements of their financial statements for recent years. One such comparison is shown in Figure 16.4.

FIGURE 16.4
Comparisons of Present and Past Financial Statements
Most corporations include in their annual reports comparisons of the important elements of their financial statements for recent years. *(Source: Allied-Signal, 1991 Annual Report, pp. 20–25. Used by permission.)*

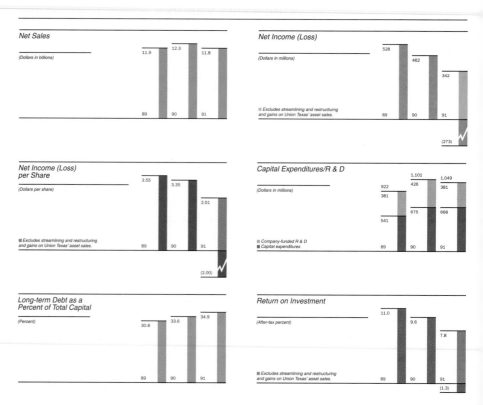

Many firms also compare their financial results with those of competing firms and with industry averages. Comparisons are possible as long as accountants follow the basic rules of accounting, often referred to as *generally accepted accounting principles (GAAP)*. Except for minor differences in the format and terms used in each financial statement, the balance sheet and income statement for The Procter & Gamble Co. (Case 16.2) are similar to the balance sheet and income statement for similar large corporations in the industry. Comparisons give managers a general idea of a firm's relative effectiveness and its standing within the industry. For example, a manager at IBM would read the financial reports for Digital Equipment Corp., Hewlett-Packard Co., and Compaq Computer to get a good idea of IBM's position within the office automation/computer fields. Competitors' financial statements can be obtained from their annual reports—if they are public corporations. Industry averages are published by reporting services such as The Dun & Bradstreet Corp. and Standard & Poor's, as well as by some industry trade associations.

Still another type of analysis involves computation of the financial ratios discussed in the next section.

FINANCIAL RATIOS

LEARNING OBJECTIVE 7
Use financial ratios to reveal how a business is doing.

financial ratio a number that shows the relationship between two elements of a firm's financial statements

A **financial ratio** is a number that shows the relationship between two elements of a firm's financial statements. Many of these ratios can be formed, but only about a dozen or so have real meaning. Those that we discuss are generally grouped as profitability ratios, short-term financial ratios, activity ratios, and long-term debt ratios. The information required to form these ratios is found in the balance sheet and the income statement (or, in our examples, in Figures 16.2 and 16.3). Like the individual elements in the financial statements, these ratios can be compared with the firm's past ratios, with those of competitors, and with industry averages.

Profitability Ratios

A firm's net income after taxes indicates whether the firm is profitable. It does not, however, indicate how effectively the firm's resources are being used. For this latter purpose, three ratios can be computed.

net profit margin a financial ratio that is calculated by dividing net income after taxes by net sales

Net Profit Margin   **Net profit margin** is a financial ratio that is calculated by dividing net income after taxes by net sales. For Northeast Art Supply,

$$\text{Net profit margin} = \frac{\text{net income after taxes}}{\text{net sales}} = \frac{\$30,175}{\$451,000}$$

$$= 0.067, \text{ or } 6.7\%$$

The net profit margin indicates how effectively the firm is transforming sales into profits. Today, the average net profit margin for all business firms is between 4 and 5 percent. With a net profit margin of 6.7 percent,

of the firm's inventories do not enter into the calculation. Inventories are "removed" from current assets because they are not converted into cash as easily as other current assets. For Northeast Art Supply,

$$\text{Acid-test ratio} = \frac{\text{current assets} - \text{inventory}}{\text{current liabilities}}$$

$$= \frac{\$182,000 - \$41,000}{\$70,000} = \frac{\$141,000}{\$70,000} = 2.01$$

For all businesses, the desired acid-test ratio is 1.0. Northeast Art Supply is above average with a ratio of 2.01, and the firm should be well able to pay its current liabilities. To increase a low ratio, a firm would have to repay current liabilities, obtain additional cash from investors, or convert current liabilities to long-term debt.

Activity Ratios

Two activity ratios permit managers to measure how many times per year a company collects its accounts receivable or sells its inventory. Both the accounts receivable turnover ratio and the inventory turnover ratio are described below.

accounts receivable turnover a financial ratio that is calculated by dividing net sales by accounts receivable; measures the number of times a firm collects its accounts receivable in one year

Accounts Receivable Turnover   A firm's **accounts receivable turnover** is the number of times the firm collects its accounts receivable in one year. If the data are available, this ratio should be calculated using a firm's net credit sales. Since data for Northeast Art Supply's credit sales are unavailable, this ratio can be calculated by dividing net sales by accounts receivable. Then,

$$\text{Accounts receivable turnover} = \frac{\text{net sales}}{\text{accounts receivable}} = \frac{\$451,000}{\$38,000}$$

$$= 11.9 \text{ times each year}$$

Northeast Art Supply collects its accounts receivable 11.9 times each year, or about every 30 days. If a firm's credit terms call for credit customers to pay up in 25 days, a collection period of 30 days is considered acceptable. There is no meaningful average for this measure, mainly because credit terms differ among companies. As a general rule, however, a low accounts receivable turnover ratio can be improved by pressing for payment of past-due accounts and by tightening requirements for prospective credit customers.

inventory turnover a financial ratio that is calculated by dividing the cost of goods sold in one year by the average value of the inventory; measures the number of times the firm sells and replaces its merchandise inventory in one year

Inventory Turnover   A firm's **inventory turnover** is the number of times the firm sells and replaces its merchandise inventory in one year. It is approximated by dividing the cost of goods sold in one year by the average value of the inventory.

The average value of the inventory can be found by adding the beginning and ending inventory values (as given on the income statement) and

GETTING AHEAD IN BUSINESS
Can a Firm's Annual Report Help You Invest?

Most annual reports are notorious for playing up the positive and soft-pedaling the negative. In reality, the true story behind the information contained in an annual report is not in the upbeat letter from the chairman of the board or in the glossy pictures—it's in the financial statements and footnotes contained in the back of the annual report.

START WITH THE FINANCIAL STATEMENTS

The key to sound investing is doing your homework. Too many investors simply take the advice of stock brokers or investment counselors and don't bother to check out a hot tip before spending their money. Here are some things you can watch for when you evaluate a potential investment.

Determine Whether the Firm Is Profitable

According to the experts, you should look at the firm's income statement and determine if the company is earning a profit or not.

Look for Significant Trends

Specific items on a firm's financial statements can be compared with the same items for previous accounting periods. On the statement of financial position, look at trends for current assets, current liabilities, inventories, total liabilities, and owners' equity. On the income statement, look at trends for sales, expenses, and profits or losses.

Calculate Financial Ratios

The following ratios can provide insight into the financial health of a company:*

- *Current ratio*   Measures a firm's ability to pay its current liabilities

- *Debt-to-assets ratio*   Measures whether a company has too much debt

- *Inventory turnover*   Measures how many times each year a firm sells its merchandise inventory

- *Net profit margin*   Measures how effectively the firm is transforming sales into profits

- *Earnings per share*   Measures the amount the firm earned for each share of stock owned by investors

Examine the Footnotes

The footnotes may be the most important part of the annual report. According to author and money manager Kenneth L. Fisher, that's where companies bury the bodies and where the fewest folks find them—in the fine print.**

WATCH FOR RED FLAGS

Learn to spot "red flags" that warn you that the firm's future may not be too rosy. Such flags may be the words they choose to report information. The word *challenges* is more acceptable than the word *problems* to describe troubles that are foreseen in the company's future. The word *contingencies* is often used in annual reports as a fancy term for problems such as lawsuits. Above all, watch for the phrases *except for . . .* and *despite the . . .* Finally, beware of unrealistic, overly enthusiastic boasts and projections. If the present is bleak, it's usually easy to predict that the future will be better.

*Specific instructions on how to calculate each of these ratios are included at the end of this chapter.

**Kenneth L. Fisher, "Thanks Dad," *Forbes*, August 8, 1988, p. 122.

dividing the sum by 2. For Northeast Art Supply, this comes out to $40,500. Then,

$$\text{Inventory turnover} = \frac{\text{cost of goods sold}}{\text{average inventory}} = \frac{\$334,000}{\$40,500}$$

$$= 8.2 \text{ times each year}$$

Northeast Art Supply sells and replaces its merchandise inventory 8.2 times each year, or about once every month and a half.

The higher a firm's inventory turnover, the more effectively it is using the money invested in inventory. The average inventory turnover for all firms is about 9 times per year, but turnover rates vary widely from industry to industry. For example, supermarkets may have turnover rates of 20 or higher, whereas turnover rates for furniture stores are generally well below the national average. The quickest way to improve inventory turnover is to order merchandise in smaller quantities at more frequent intervals.

Long-Term Debt Ratios

Two financial ratios are of particular interest to lenders of long-term funds. They indicate the degree to which a firm's operations are financed through borrowing.

debt-to-assets ratio   a financial ratio that is calculated by dividing total liabilities by total assets; indicates the extent to which the firm's borrowing is backed by its assets

Debt-to-Assets Ratio   The **debt-to-assets ratio** is calculated by dividing total liabilities by total assets. It indicates the extent to which the firm's borrowing is backed by its assets. For Northeast Art Supply,

$$\text{Debt-to-assets ratio} = \frac{\text{total liabilities}}{\text{total assets}} = \frac{\$110,000}{\$340,000} = 0.32, \text{ or } 32\%$$

Northeast's debt-to-assets ratio of 32 percent means that slightly less than one-third of its assets are financed by creditors. For all businesses, the average debt-to-assets ratio is 33 percent.

The lower this ratio is, the more assets the firm has to back up its borrowing. Northeast has $3 in assets with which to repay each $1 of borrowing. A high debt-to-assets ratio can be reduced by restricting both short-term and long-term borrowing, by securing additional financing from stockholders, or by reducing dividend payments to stockholders.

debt-to-equity ratio   a financial ratio calculated by dividing total liabilities by owners' equity; compares the amount of financing provided by creditors with the amount provided by owners

Debt-to-Equity Ratio   The **debt-to-equity ratio** is calculated by dividing total liabilities by owners' equity. It compares the amount of financing provided by creditors with the amount provided by owners. For Northeast Art Supply,

$$\text{Debt-to-equity ratio} = \frac{\text{total liabilities}}{\text{owners' equity}} = \frac{\$110,000}{\$230,000} = 0.48, \text{ or } 48\%$$

A debt-to-equity ratio of 48 percent means that creditors have provided about 48 cents of financing for every dollar provided by owners.

The debt-to-equity ratio for business in general ranges between 33 and 50 percent. The larger this ratio, the riskier the situation is for lenders. A high debt-to-equity ratio can be reduced by paying off debts or by increasing the owners' investment in the firm.

Northeast's Financial Ratios: A Summary

The formulas we used to analyze Northeast Art Supply's financial statements are listed in Table 16.3, along with the ratios we calculated. Northeast seems to be in good financial shape. Its net profit margin, current ratio, and acid-test ratio are all above average. Its other ratios are about average, although its inventory turnover could be improved. To do so, Northeast might consider ordering smaller quantities of merchandise at shorter intervals. Of course, the resulting decrease in inventory holding costs would have to be balanced against increased ordering costs and the possible cost of stock-outs.

This chapter ends our discussion of accounting information. In Chapter 17, we begin our examination of business finances by discussing money, banking, and credit.

TABLE 16.3   Summary of Financial Ratios for Northeast Art Supply

Ratio	Formula	Northeast Art Supply	Overall Business Average
Profitability Ratios			
Net profit margin	$\dfrac{\text{net income after taxes}}{\text{net sales}}$	6.7%	4%–5%
Return on equity	$\dfrac{\text{net income after taxes}}{\text{owners' equity}}$	13%	12%–15%
Earnings per share	$\dfrac{\text{net income after taxes}}{\text{common stock shares outstanding}}$	$3.02 per share	—
Short-Term Financial Ratios			
Working capital	current assets less current liabilities	$112,000	—
Current ratio	$\dfrac{\text{current assets}}{\text{current liabilities}}$	2.6	2.0
Acid-test ratio	$\dfrac{\text{current assets} - \text{inventory}}{\text{current liabilities}}$	2.01	1.0
Activity Ratios			
Accounts receivable turnover	$\dfrac{\text{net sales}}{\text{accounts receivable}}$	11.9	—
Inventory turnover	$\dfrac{\text{cost of goods sold}}{\text{average inventory}}$	8.2	9
Long-Term Debt Ratios			
Debt-to-assets ratio	$\dfrac{\text{total liabilities}}{\text{total assets}}$	32%	33%
Debt-to-equity ratio	$\dfrac{\text{total liabilities}}{\text{owners' equity}}$	48%	33%–50%

CHAPTER REVIEW

Summary

Accounting is the process of systematically collecting, analyzing, and reporting financial information. Bookkeeping is essentially recordkeeping that is a part of the overall accounting process. A private accountant is employed by a specific organization to operate its accounting system and to interpret accounting information. A public accountant performs these functions for various individuals or firms, on a professional-fee basis. Accounting information is used primarily by management, but it is also demanded by creditors, suppliers, stockholders, and government agencies.

The accounting process is based on the accounting equation: Assets = liabilities + owners' equity. Double-entry bookkeeping ensures that the balance shown by the equation is maintained.

There are five steps in the accounting process: (1) Source documents are analyzed to determine which accounts they affect. (2) Each transaction is recorded in a journal. (3) Each journal entry is posted in the appropriate general ledger accounts. (4) At the end of each accounting period, a trial balance is prepared to make sure that the accounting equation is in balance at the end of the period. (5) Financial statements are prepared from the trial balance. Once statements are prepared, the books are closed. A new accounting cycle is then begun for the next accounting period.

The balance sheet, or statement of financial position, is a summary of a firm's assets, liabilities, and owners' equity accounts at a particular time. This statement must demonstrate that the equation is in balance. On the balance sheet, assets are categorized as current (convertible to cash in a year or less), fixed (to be used or held for more than one year), or intangible (valuable solely because of the rights or advantages they confer). Similarly, current liabilities are those that are to be repaid in one year or less, and long-term liabilities are debts that will not be repaid for at least one year. For a sole proprietorship or partnership, owners' equity is reported by the owner's name in the last section of the balance sheet. For a corporation, the value of common stock, preferred stock, and retained earnings is reported in the owners' equity section.

An income statement is a summary of a firm's financial operations during a specified accounting period. On the income statement, the company's gross profit on sales is computed by subtracting the cost of goods sold from net sales. Operating expenses are then

deducted to compute net income from operations. Finally, nonoperating expenses and income taxes are deducted to obtain the firm's net income after taxes.

The information contained in these two financial statements becomes more meaningful when it is compared with corresponding information for previous years, for competitors, and for the industry in which the firm operates. A number of financial ratios can also be computed from this information. These ratios provide a picture of the firm's profitability, its short-term financial position, its activity in the area of accounts receivables and inventory, and its long-term debt financing. Like the information on the firm's financial statements, the ratios can and should be compared with those of past accounting periods, those of competitors, and those representing the average of the industry as a whole.

Key Terms

You should now be able to define and give an example relevant to each of the following terms:

accounting	depreciation
bookkeeping	intangible assets
private (or nonpublic) accountant	goodwill
	current liabilities
public accountant	accounts payable
certified public accountant (CPA)	notes payable
assets	long-term liabilities
liabilities	income statement
owners' equity	revenues
accounting equation	gross sales
double-entry bookkeeping	net sales
general journal	cost of goods sold
general ledger	gross profit on sales
posting	operating expenses
trial balance	selling expenses
balance sheet (or statement of financial position)	general expenses
	net income
liquidity	financial ratio
current assets	net profit margin
prepaid expenses	return on equity
fixed assets	earnings per share
	working capital
	current ratio

acid-test ratio
accounts receivable
 turnover

inventory turnover
debt-to-assets ratio
debt-to-equity ratio

Questions and Exercises

Review Questions

1. What is the difference between accounting and bookkeeping? How are they related?
2. What are certified public accountants? What functions do they perform?
3. List four groups that use accounting information and briefly explain why each has an interest in this information.
4. State the accounting equation and list two specific examples of each term in the equation.
5. How is double-entry bookkeeping related to the accounting equation? Briefly, how does it work?
6. Briefly describe the five steps of the accounting cycle, in order.
7. What is the principal difference between a balance sheet and an income statement?
8. How are current assets distinguished from fixed assets? Give two examples of each.
9. Why are fixed assets depreciated on a balance sheet?
10. Can a single debt (for example, a promissory note) be part current liability and part long-term liability? Explain.
11. Explain how a retailing firm would determine the cost of goods sold during an accounting period.
12. How does a firm determine its net income after taxes?
13. Explain the calculation procedure for and the significance of each of the following ratios:
    a. One profitability ratio
    b. One short-term financial ratio
    c. One activity ratio
    d. One long-term debt ratio

Discussion Questions

1. According to Ernst & Young officials, the purpose of an audit is not to determine the safety and financial stability of the firm being audited, but only to see if they've complied with generally accepted accounting principles. Do you agree or disagree with this statement? Why?
2. Five of the six largest accounting firms in the United States have been sued for negligence. As a result, these accounting firms have taken steps to reduce their exposure to potential problems.

Based on the information presented in the opening case, do these steps protect the accounting firms, the users of the accounting information, or both?

3. Bankers usually insist that prospective borrowers submit audited financial statements along with a loan application. Why should financial statements be audited by a CPA?
4. What can be said about a firm whose owners' equity is a negative amount? How could such a situation come about?
5. Do the balance sheet and the income statement contain all the information you might want as a potential lender or stockholder? What other information would you like to have?
6. Which do you think are the two or three most important financial ratios? Why?
7. Why is it so important to compare a firm's financial statements and ratios with those of previous years, those of competitors, and the average of all firms in the industry in which the firm operates?

Exercises

1. Table 16.4 lists the ledger account balances for the Green Thumb Garden Shop, which was started

TABLE 16.4   Account Balances for Green Thumb Garden Shop

Accounts	Amounts
Cash	$ 7,500
Accounts receivables	3,500
Inventory	20,000
Equipment	15,000
Accumulated depreciation	2,000
Accounts payable	11,000
Long-term debt—equipment	10,000
Owners' equity	23,000
Sales	48,000
Cost of goods sold	23,000
Sales salaries expense	8,500
Advertising expense	1,500
Depreciation expense	2,000
Rent expense	6,000
Utilities expense	1,500
Insurance expense	1,000
Miscellaneous expense	500
Income taxes	600

just one year ago. From that information, prepare a balance sheet and an income statement for the business.

2. Using the financial statements you prepared in Exercise 1 and the material on ratio analysis presented in this chapter, evaluate the financial health of the Green Thumb Garden Shop. Explain how the firm's finances could be improved.

CASE 16.1

The Arthur Andersen Worldwide Organization

According to Lawrence A. Weinbach, CEO and managing partner at The Arthur Andersen Worldwide Organization, "It isn't how big you are but how well you serve your clients' needs."* With annual revenues of more than $2.3 billion, this philosophy has enabled his company to become the largest accounting firm in the world. And while this philosophy applies to all businesses, it is especially apt for an accounting firm. The basic product an accounting firm sells is information—information that must meet clients' needs.

Arthur Andersen derives about 60 percent of its revenues from its U.S. operations, but attracting new business in North America has never been more difficult. As a result of a large number of corporate mergers, the number of companies needing auditing has diminished. To keep current U.S. clients or attract new ones, accounting firms have had to cut their fees. In response, Arthur Andersen is focusing on increasing the value of its services to clients and is initiating a wide range of financial consulting services, which are generating revenue growth.

At the same time, Arthur Andersen is continuing to concentrate on restructuring its global operations. First, the firm consolidated its worldwide operations into three geographic areas: Europe, Asia, and the Americas. Then, Arthur Andersen realigned its services along distinct business lines reflecting the diverse client needs in the global marketplace. Two business units were established: Arthur Andersen, which provides audit, tax, and financial consulting services; and Andersen Consulting, which provides information technology and computer consulting services.

Although most people think of accounting when they hear the name *Arthur Andersen*, the firm has been involved in the information and computer consulting field for years. As far back as 1954, it installed the first commercial computer system at the General Electric Co. Today, Andersen Consulting is the most successful consulting unit of its kind, with annual revenues over

$1 billion. And it is easy to see why the firm expanded into information and computer consulting—it's very profitable. Just one major contract—such as improving a product distribution system—may generate more than $20 million in fees. In contrast, an audit contract for a firm of the same size typically yields less than $5 million.**

Questions

1. According to Lawrence Weinbach, CEO for Arthur Andersen, an accounting firm must meet its clients' needs. How can Arthur Andersen or any accounting firm achieve this goal?
2. In your own words, describe what Arthur Andersen is doing to retain its number one ranking among accounting firms.
3. In the past ten years, most of the "big six" accounting firms have tried to diversify their operations. Why do you think Arthur Andersen chose to diversify into the information and computer consulting fields?

*Quoted in Jeffrey M. Laderman, "When One Plus One Equals No. 1," *Business Week*, June 5, 1989, p. 94.

**Based on information from Rahul Jacob, "Can You Trust That Audit?" *Fortune*, November 18, 1991, pp. 191–192+; "Civil War at Arthur Andersen," *The Economist*, August 17, 1991, pp. 66–67; "Price Andersen or Price Waterhouse," *The Economist*, September 30, 1989, p. 84; and Lois Therrien, "How Arthur Andersen Became a High-Tech Hotshot," *Business Week*, April 25, 1988, p. 125; Jeffrey M. Laderman, "When One Plus One Equals No. 1," *Business Week*, June 5, 1989, p. 94; Kathleen A. Behof, "An Identity Crisis at Arthur Andersen," *Business Week*, July 24, 1989, pp. 20–21.

CASE 16.2

Procter & Gamble

The Procter & Gamble Co. is today one of the world's leading producers of packaged consumer goods. The company produces laundry and cleaning products, personal care products, food and beverage products, and pulp and chemicals. International operations represented approximately 46 percent of the company's net sales for the fiscal year ended June 30, 1989. Net sales are more than $27 billion.

The following are Procter & Gamble's consolidated (summarized) statement of earnings and consolidated balance sheet.*

*Procter & Gamble's consolidated statement of earnings and consolidated balance sheet are taken from the 1991 Procter & Gamble Annual Report, pp. 17–18. Used with permission.

Consolidated Statement of Earnings

Year Ended June 30 (millions of dollars except per-share amounts)		1991
Income	Net sales	$27,026
	Interest and other income	380
		$27,406

Costs and Expenses

	Cost of products sold	16,081
	Marketing, administrative, and other expenses	8,243
	Interest expense	395
		24,719
Earnings Before Income Taxes		2,687
Income Taxes		914
Net Earnings		$1,773
Per Common Share		
	Net earnings	$4.92
	Dividends	$1.95

Consolidated Balance Sheet

June 30 (millions of dollars)		1991

Assets
Current Assets

	Cash and cash equivalents	$1,384
	Accounts receivable, less allowance for doubtful accounts of $29 in 1991	3,024
	Inventories	3,190
	Prepaid expenses and other current assets	837
		8,435
Property, Plant, and Equipment		8,273
Goodwill and Other Intangible Assets		2,882
Other Assets		878
Total		$20,468

Liabilities and Shareholders' Equity
Current Liabilities

	Accounts payable—trade	$2,045
	Accounts payable—other	375
	Accrued liabilities	1,807
	Taxes payable	537
	Debt due within one year	1,969
		6,733
Long-Term Debt		4,111
Other Liabilities		578
Deferred Income Taxes		1,310
Shareholders' Equity		
	Convertible Class A preferred stock	1,995
	Common stock—shares outstanding: 1991–338,089,360	338
	Additional paid-in capital	609
	Currency translation adjustments	(56)
	Reserve for employee stock ownership plan debt retirement	(1,925)
	Retained earnings	6,775
		7,736
Total		$20,468

Questions

1. Using the financial information provided in this case, calculate the following ratios for Procter & Gamble.
   a. Current ratio
   b. Acid-test ratio
   c. Net profit margin
   d. Return on equity
2. Based on your analysis of available information, how would you describe Procter & Gamble's current financial condition? What actions, if any, would you consider taking to improve it? Explain your recommendations.

Career Profile

Job Title	Job Description	Salary Range
Accountant—corporate	Analyze source documents and journalize accounting entries for a private business; post journal entries to ledger accounts; prepare a trial balance and financial statements for each accounting period; and close the accounting books at the end of each accounting period	3–4
Accounting—private practice	Provide accounting services to businesses and individuals for a fee; offer bookkeeping, accounting, auditing services, and help with taxes; consult with small business owners and individuals on accounting and financial matters	4–5
Bookkeeper	Work for either a private business or accounting firm; talk with clients; use computerized accounting systems to process daily accounting entries; post journal entries to ledger accounts; prepare a trial balance at the end of the accounting period	1–2
Computer application engineer	Design either hardware or software applications to perform a specific task; test and debug computer applications to ensure that programs or equipment do what they are supposed to do; communicate with other engineers, marketing personnel, and others involved in product development and application	3
Computer operator	Use available software programs to process data into information; prepare reports based on original input data; communicate with managers and other personnel who need processed information	1–2
Computer—repair technician	Provide repair service on either an in-house basis or for customers on a fee basis; analyze and diagnose problems with computer equipment; perform necessary repairs; complete accuracy checks to ensure equipment is correctly repaired	2
Computer—systems analyst	Serve as a communication link between managers and programmers; identify needs that can be served by computers; develop computer applications that help managers achieve goals; determine hardware and software needs	3–4
Financial controller	Establish company-wide financial and administrative goals and objectives; work with the company's stockholders; communicate the company's position on financial matters to all interested parties; approve the firm's annual operating budget; invest the company's excess funds in order to maintain the safety factor while maximizing financial return	4–5
Salesperson—computer software or hardware	Analyze customer needs; make sales presentation to potential buyers; demonstrate hardware, software, or both; answer questions and overcome objections; provide follow-up service after the sale	3–4

The figure in the salary column approximates the expected annual income after two or three years of service. 1 = $12,000–$15,000; 2 = $16,000–$20,000; 3 = $21,000–$27,000; 4 = $28,000–$35,000; 5 = $36,000 and up.

Educational Requirements	Skills Required	Prospects for Growth
Bachelor's degree in accounting; master's degree preferred	Computer; problem solving; quantitative; analytical/diagnostic; conceptual; critical thinking	Greatest
Bachelor's degree; state exam for Certified Public Accountant status; master's degree helpful	Computer; problem solving; quantitative; analytical/diagnostic; conceptual; critical thinking	Average
High-school diploma; some college preferred	Computer; problem solving; quantitative	Limited
Bachelor's degree in business and computer science	Problem solving; analytical/diagnostic; technical; conceptual; critical thinking	Average
Two years of college in data processing; on-the-job experience	Computer; problem solving; quantitative; technical	Greatest
High school diploma; some technical training required; on-the-job experience	Communication; problem solving; technical	Greatest
College degree; master's degree preferred; on-the-job experience	Communication; problem solving; analytical/diagnostic; technical; conceptual; critical thinking	Above Average
College degree in finance or accounting; on-the-job experience	Leadership; decision making; interpersonal; quantitative; analytical/diagnostic; conceptual	Limited
Some college; degree helpful	Communication; computer; analytical/diagnostic; technical; conceptual	Average

PART

6

Finance and Investment

In this part, we are concerned with still another business resource—money. First we discuss the functions and forms of money and the financial institutions that are part of the U.S. monetary system. Then we examine the concept and methods of financial management, for both firms and individuals. Finally, we explore the means by which some types of financial losses can be minimized. Included in this part are:

CHAPTER 17 Money, Banking, and Credit

CHAPTER 18 Financial Management

CHAPTER 19 Securities Markets

CHAPTER 20 Risk Management and Insurance

Money, Banking, and Credit

LEARNING OBJECTIVES

After studying this chapter you should be able to:

1 Identify the functions and important characteristics of money.

2 Describe the differences between commercial banks and other financial institutions in the banking industry.

3 Identify the primary services provided by commercial banks and other financial institutions.

4 Summarize how the Federal Reserve System regulates the money supply.

5 Describe the Fed's role in clearing checks, controlling and inspecting currency, and administering selective credit controls.

6 Explain the function of the Federal Deposit Insurance Corporation (FDIC), Savings Association Insurance Fund (SAIF), and National Credit Union Association (NCUA).

7 Discuss the importance of credit and credit management.

CHAPTER PREVIEW

In this chapter we take a good look at money and the financial institutions that create and handle it. We begin by outlining the purposes of money in a society and the characteristics of money that make it an acceptable means of payment for products, services, and resources. Then we turn our attention to the banking industry—commercial banks, savings and loan associations, credit unions, and other institutions that offer financial services. Next, we consider the role of the Federal Reserve System in maintaining a healthy economy. We also describe the safeguards established by the federal government to protect depositors against recent bank failures. In closing, we examine credit transactions, sources of credit information, and effective collection procedures.

Morgan Guaranty Trust—The Tortoise That Won the Banking Race

In 1861, J. P. Morgan, the New York financier, began J. P. Morgan and Company, Inc. Through the years, the company's principal subsidiary—Morgan Guaranty Trust Company—became a conservative bank known for tradition and teamwork. Today, after 130 years, Morgan Guaranty Trust has more than $100 billion in assets and is the most profitable commercial bank in the United States. In 1991, the bank earned more than $1 billion—up a staggering 36 percent when compared with earnings for 1990. It is also the only major bank to retain its *AAA* rating from credit-rating firms. And, according to *Fortune* magazine, Morgan Guaranty Trust is the most highly respected bank in the commercial banking category.

Although it may be hard to believe, given Morgan Guaranty Trust's currently impressive statistics, the bank's record is not unblemished. Like most commercial banks, Morgan Guaranty Trust lent billions of dollars to third-world nations during the 1970s and 1980s. Later, anticipating repayment problems, the bank set aside huge reserves to cover 65 percent of its loans to third-world nations. As a result, Morgan announced a $1.3 billion loss in 1989.

But Morgan Guaranty Trust executives learned from their mistakes. When a number of large commercial banks rushed to finance questionable loans for real estate and corporate mergers in the last part of the 1980s, Morgan's executives recalled their painful experience with third-world nations. Morgan Guaranty Trust just watched from the sidelines. Both competitors and critics argued that the bank had become too conservative and that executives at Morgan were too set in their ways to compete in the changing banking industry.

Then in 1990, Morgan Guaranty Trust's conservative philosophy began to pay off. While other commercial banks were writing off billions of dollars for nonperforming real estate and merger loans, Morgan Guaranty Trust emerged as one of the safest and most financially secure banks in the United States. The bank used this success to build for the future. According to bank executives, the bank used both its reputation and financial stability to attract the best corporate customers—firms like The Procter & Gamble Co., PepsiCo, Inc., and American Brands. It also began to expand its banking functions in Japan, Germany, France, Kuwait, Saudi Arabia, and other foreign nations.

To further strengthen Morgan Guaranty Trust's role as a "full-service" bank, executives at J. P. Morgan and Company began investment banking activities—selling both debt and stock issues for corporate clients through a subsidiary called J. P. Morgan Securities. The Federal Reserve Board approved Morgan Securities's application for investment banking activities in September 1990. Morgan Guaranty Trust (through Morgan Securities) was then able to compete head to head with European banks that regularly sell new debt and stock issues for clients in addition to its regular commercial banking activities.[1]

With record bank failures, it's nice to see that one bank—Morgan Guaranty Trust—is not only financially sound but also extremely profitable. Morgan Guaranty Trust is now in a position to become a global power in the banking industry, whereas other banks are just struggling to survive. Unfortunately, the statistics on bank failures are real and they have depositors worried.

Just the thought of depositing money in a bank and then losing it because the bank becomes insolvent makes people nervous, but it does illustrate how important banks, savings and loan associations, credit unions, and other financial institutions are today.

Most people regard a bank or similar financial institution as a place to deposit or borrow money. In return for depositing their money, they receive interest. When they borrow money, they must pay interest. Individuals may borrow to buy a home, a car, or some other high-cost item. In this case, the resource that will be transformed into money to repay the loan is the individual's labor.

Businesses also transform resources into money. A business firm (even a new one) may have a valuable asset in the form of a product idea. If the idea is a good one, and the firm (or its founder) has a good reputation, a bank will probably lend it the money to develop, produce, and market the product. The loan—with interest—will be repaid out of future sales revenue. In this way, both the firm and the bank will earn a reasonable profit.

In each of these situations, the borrower needs the money now and has the ability to repay it later. But also, in each situation, the money will be used to *purchase something*, and it will be repaid through the use of *resources*.

WHAT IS MONEY?

barter system   a system of exchange in which goods or services are traded directly for other goods or services

The members of some remote societies exchange goods and services through barter, without using money. A **barter system** is a system of exchange in which goods or services are traded directly for other goods or services. One family may raise vegetables and herbs on a plot of land, and another may weave cloth. To obtain food, the family of weavers trades cloth for vegetables, provided that the farming family is in need of cloth.

535

money   anything used by a society to purchase products, services, or resources

The trouble with the barter system is that the two parties in an ex-change must need each other's products at the same time, and the two products must be roughly equal in value. It may work well when few products, primarily the necessities of life, are available. But even very isolated societies soon develop some sort of money to eliminate the inconvenience of trading by barter.

Money is anything used by a society to purchase products, services, or resources. The members of the society receive money for their products or resources. Then they either hold that money or use it to purchase other products or resources, when and how they see fit. Different groups of people have used all sorts of objects as money—whale's teeth, stones, beads, copper crosses, clam shells, and gold and silver, for example. Today, the most commonly used objects are metal coins and paper bills, which together are called *currency*.

The Functions of Money

LEARNING OBJECTIVE 1
Identify the functions and im-portant characteristics of money.

We have already noted that money aids in the exchange of goods and services for resources. And it does. But that's a rather general (and somewhat theoretical) way of stating money's function. Now, let's look at three *specific* functions of money in any society.

Sheets of yen. These inspectors probably appreciate more than do most people the necessary attributes of currency. The yen in these sheets must be durable, easily portable, and difficult to counterfeit. Government treasurers around the world have evolved a variety of methods of meeting these goals.

medium of exchange anything that is accepted as payment for products, services, and resources

Serves as a Medium of Exchange   A **medium of exchange** is anything that is accepted as payment for products, services, and resources. This definition looks very much like the definition of money. It is meant to, because the primary function of money is to serve as a medium of exchange. The key word here is *accepted*. As long as the owners of products, services, and resources accept money in an exchange, it is performing this function. Of course, these owners accept it because they know it is acceptable to the owners of other products, services, and resources, which *they* may wish to purchase. For example, the family in our earlier example can sell their vegetables and use the money to purchase cloth from the weavers. This eliminates the problems associated with the barter system.

measure of value a single standard or "yardstick" that is used to assign values to, and compare the values of, products, services, and resources

Serves as a Measure of Value   A **measure of value** is a single standard or "yardstick" that is used to assign values to, and compare the values of, products, services, and resources. Money serves as a measure of value because the prices of all products, services, and resources are stated in terms of money. It is thus the "common denominator" we use to compare products and decide which we will buy. Imagine the difficulty you would have in deciding whether you could afford new shoes if they were priced in terms of yards of cloth or pounds of vegetables—especially if your employer happened to pay you in toothbrushes.

Represents a Store of Value   Money received by an individual or firm need not be used immediately. It may be held and spent later. Hence money serves as a **store of value,** or a means for retaining and accumulating wealth. This function of money comes into play whenever we hold on to money—in a pocket, a cookie jar, a savings account, or whatever.

store of value a means for retaining and accumulating wealth

Value that is stored as money is affected by fluctuations in the economy. One of the major problems caused by inflation is a loss of stored value: As prices go up in an inflationary period, money loses value. Suppose you can buy a Sony stereo system for $1,000. Your $1,000 has a value equal to the value of that system. But let us suppose that you wait a while and don't buy the stereo immediately. If the price goes up to $1,100 in the meantime because of inflation, you can no longer buy the stereo with your $1,000. Your money has *lost* value because it is now worth less than the stereo. To determine the effect of inflation on purchasing power, economists often refer to a consumer price index like the one illustrated in Figure 17.1.

Important Characteristics of Money

To be acceptable as a medium of exchange, money must be fairly easy to use, it must be trusted, and it must be capable of performing the three functions we mentioned earlier. Together, these requirements give rise to five essential characteristics.

Divisibility   The standard unit of money must be divisible into smaller units to accommodate small purchases as well as large ones. In the United States, our standard is the dollar, and it is divided into one-hundredths,

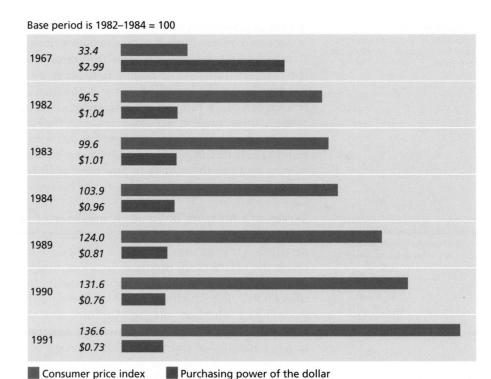

Base period is 1982–1984 = 100

Year	CPI	Purchasing power
1967	*33.4* / *$2.99*	
1982	*96.5* / *$1.04*	
1983	*99.6* / *$1.01*	
1984	*103.9* / *$0.96*	
1989	*124.0* / *$0.81*	
1990	*131.6* / *$0.76*	
1991	*136.6* / *$0.73*	

■ Consumer price index   ■ Purchasing power of the dollar

FIGURE 17.1   The Consumer Price Index and the Purchasing Power of the Consumer Dollar (Base Period: 1982–1984 = 100)
Inflation causes a loss of money's stored value. As the consumer price index goes up, the purchasing power of the consumer's dollar goes down.   *(Source:* Economic Report of the President, *United States Printing Office, Washington, D.C., 1990, p. 359, and* Federal Reserve Bulletin, *November 1991, p. A50.)*

AT A GLANCE

SAVINGS & LOANS IN THE RED

The '80s saw an unprecedented number of banks that were closed or assisted by the federal government due to insolvency.

SOURCE: FDIC

one-twentieths, one-tenths, one-fourths, and one-halves through the issuance of coins (pennies, nickels, dimes, quarters, and half-dollars, respectively). These allow us to make purchases of less than a dollar and of odd amounts greater than a dollar. Other nations have their own currencies: the franc in France, the mark in Germany, and the yen in Japan, to mention a few.

Portability   Money must be small enough and light enough to be carried easily. For this reason, paper currency is issued in larger *denominations*—multiples of the standard dollar unit. Five-, ten-, twenty-, fifty-, and hundred-dollar bills make our money convenient for almost any purchase.

Stability   Money should retain its value over time. When it does not (during periods of high inflation), people tend to lose faith in their money. They may then turn to other means of storing value (such as gold and jewels, works of art, and real estate). In extreme cases, they may use such items as a medium of exchange as well. They may even resort to barter. During the recent upheavals in Russia, farmers have traded farm products for cigarettes because the value of cigarettes is more stable than the Russian economy.

Durability   The objects that serve as money should be strong enough to last through reasonable usage. No one would appreciate (or use) dollar bills that disintegrated as they were handled or coins that melted in the sun. To increase the life expectancy of paper currency, most nations use special paper with a high fiber content.

Difficulty of Counterfeiting   If a nation's currency were easy to counterfeit—that is, to imitate or fake—its citizens would be uneasy about accepting it as payment. Even genuine currency would soon lose its value, because no one would want it. Thus the countries that issue currency do their best to ensure that it is very hard to reproduce. Typically, countries use special paper and watermarks and designs printed on the currency to discourage counterfeiting.

The Supply of Money: M₁, M₂, and M₃

How much money is there in the United States? Before we can answer that question, we need to define a couple of familiar concepts.

demand deposit an amount that is on deposit in a checking account

A **demand deposit** is an amount that is on deposit in a checking account. It is called a *demand* deposit because it can be claimed immediately—on demand—by presenting a properly made-out check, withdrawing cash from an automated teller machine (ATM), or transferring money between accounts.

time deposit an amount that is on deposit in an interest-bearing savings account

A **time deposit** is an amount that is on deposit in an interest-bearing savings account. Financial institutions generally permit immediate withdrawal of money from savings accounts. However, they can require written notice prior to withdrawal. The time between notice and withdrawal is what leads to the name *time* deposits.

Time deposits are not immediately available to their owners, but they can be converted to cash easily. For this reason, they are called *near-monies*. Other near-monies include short-term government securities, government bonds, and the cash surrender values of insurance policies.

Now we can discuss the question of how much money there is in the United States. There are three main measures of the supply of money—M_1, M_2, and M_3.

The M_1 *supply of money* consists only of currency and demand deposits. (It is thus based on a narrow definition of money.) By law, currency must be accepted as payment for products and resources. Checks are accepted as payment because they are convenient, convertible to cash, and generally safe.

The M_2 *supply of money* consists of M_1 (currency and demand deposits) plus certain specific securities and small-denomination time deposits. Another common definition of money—M_3—consists of M_1 and M_2 plus large time deposits of $100,000 or more. The definitions of money that include the M_2 and M_3 supplies are based on the assumption that time deposits are

GETTING AHEAD IN BUSINESS
The Time Value of Money Concept

The old saying goes: "I've been rich and I've been poor, but believe me, rich is better." Being rich doesn't guarantee happiness, but the accumulation of money does provide financial security and is a goal worthy of pursuit. Regardless of how much money you want or what you want to use the money for, the time value of money concept can help you obtain your financial goals.

The time value of money is a concept that recognizes that money can be invested and can earn interest over a period of time. For example, assume you invest $10,000 in a certificate of deposit or other investments like stocks, mutual funds, or bonds that pay 5 percent interest. If you let your interest accumulate, your initial $10,000 investment is worth $10,500 at the end of one year. At the end of five years, your investment is worth $12,762.81. At the end of ten years, your investment has increased to $16,288.94. In this example, you have received $6,288.94 in interest over a ten-year period of time as a result of letting your interest compound and grow. You can use the money you accumulate to achieve any goal you value—college tuition, financing a major purchase like a car or a home, another investment, or retirement income.

THE RULE OF 72

Many people are afraid of mathematical calculations, but the Rule of 72 provides a quick, easy method to estimate how long it takes an investment to double in value. Divide the number 72 by the interest rate for any investment. Thus, an investment that pays 6 percent will double in value in 12 years (72 ÷ 6 = 12 years).

HOW YOU CAN BECOME A MILLIONAIRE

Today, there are more than one million millionaires in the United States, and you too, can become a millionaire. Here's a plan guaranteed to work. Assume you are 25 years old and you invest $4,000 each year for the next forty years in an investment that provides an 8 percent return each year. When you reach 65, your investment will be worth $1,036,240. Over a forty-year period of time, you will have invested a total of $160,000 ($4,000 × 40 = $160,000). The remaining $876,240 is the result of letting your investment accumulate and compound for forty years.

A WORD OF CAUTION

For this plan to work, you must be 25 years old and willing to invest $4,000 a year for forty years. If you skip investments or use the money before you reach 65, or if the interest rate falls below 8 percent, your investment would be worth less than $1 million. This example illustrates the time value of money concept, but it does not tell you what your money will buy when you reach retirement age. Certainly, inflation and increasing prices over the next forty years (both topics discussed in this chapter) should be taken into consideration. Nevertheless, it is important to realize that for as little as $333 a month over a forty-year period, you, too, can become a millionaire.

easily converted to cash for spending. Figure 17.2 shows the elements of the M_1, M_2, and M_3 supplies. About 21 percent is coins, paper currency, and demand deposits; and the remaining 79 percent is time deposits and certain specific securities.

We have, then, at least three measures of the supply of money. (Actually, there are other measures as well, which may be broader or narrower than M_1, M_2, and M_3.) So the answer to our original question is that the amount of money in the United States depends very much on how we

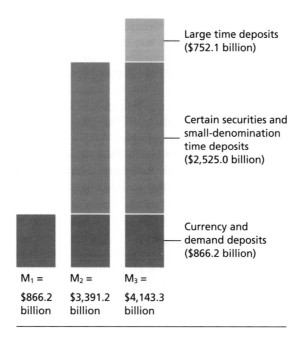

Large time deposits
($752.1 billion)

Certain securities and
small-denomination
time deposits
($2,525.0 billion)

Currency and
demand deposits
($866.2 billion)

$M_1 =$ $M_2 =$ $M_3 =$

$866.2 $3,391.2 $4,143.3
billion   billion   billion

FIGURE 17.2
The Supply of Money
Three measures of the money supply are M_1, which includes currency and demand deposits; M_2, which includes M_1 plus certain specific securities and small-denomination time deposits; and M_3, which includes M_1, M_2, plus time deposits of $100,000 or more. (*Source:* Federal Reserve Bulletin, *November 1991, p. A13.*)

measure it. Generally, economists, politicians, and bankers tend to focus on M_1 or some variation of M_1.

We have seen that a very large part of the money that exists in this country is deposited in banks and other financial institutions. Let us now examine the banking industry.

THE AMERICAN BANKING INDUSTRY

LEARNING OBJECTIVE 2
Describe the differences between commercial banks and other financial institutions in the banking industry.

During the 1980s, a record number of banks, savings and loan associations, and credit unions failed. Unfortunately, this trend is likely to continue for at least the first part of the 1990s. Banks, savings and loan associations, and credit unions fail because a large percentage of their loans go bad and cannot be repaid. Although no individual state is immune, most of the recent failures have occurred in either agricultural or oil-producing states. The New England states have also experienced a large number of failures in the first part of the 1990s. And, in a number of cases, fraud and questionable management practices have played an important role in the current crisis. To help solve the problem, Congress has passed a bailout plan that is the largest federal rescue in history. The total cost for the government's plan is estimated to be $500 billion, or about $3,000 per taxpayer.[2]

NOW account   an interest-bearing checking account; *NOW* stands for Negotiable Order of Withdrawal

which became effective on January 1, 1981, they have been able to offer NOW accounts to attract depositors. A **NOW account** is an interest-bearing checking account. (*NOW* stands for Negotiable Order of Withdrawal.)

During the 1980s, high interest rates, coupled with a reduced demand for homes and an increase in nonperforming loans and foreclosures, led to financial difficulties for many S&Ls. Much of their lending is in the form of low-interest, long-term home-mortgage loans, which were issued to finance the purchase of homes during the 1960s and 1970s. Those older loans generate very little revenue, compared with more recent loans. In addition, because few people were taking out mortgages in the early 1980s, S&Ls were not able to lend money at the higher interest rates of that time period. As a result, S&Ls were squeezed between the higher interest rates they paid to their depositors and the lower interest rates they received from their loans. As we mentioned earlier in this section, a large number of the troubled financial institutions are S&Ls. In fact, the Resolution Trust Corporation—a recently created federal agency—expects to liquidate or sell one thousand weak or insolvent S&Ls by the end of 1992.[4] Though estimates vary, it may take as long as ten years to dispose of some troubled S&Ls.

Today, there are approximately 2,500 savings and loan associations in the United States.[5] Federal associations are chartered under provisions of the Home Owners' Loan Act of 1933 and are supervised by the Office of Thrift Supervision—a branch of the U.S. Treasury. Approximately 40 percent of all S&Ls have federal charters and the remaining 60 percent are chartered and supervised by state authorities.

credit union   a financial institution that accepts deposits from, and lends money to, only those people who are its members

Credit Unions   A **credit union** is a financial institution that accepts deposits from, and lends money to, only those people who are its members. Usually the membership is composed of employees of a particular firm, people in a particular profession, or those who live in a community served by a local credit union. Some credit unions require that members purchase at least one share of ownership, at a cost of about $5 to $10. Credit unions generally pay higher interest on deposits than commercial banks and S&Ls, and they may provide loans at lower cost. Credit unions are regulated by the Federal Credit Union Administration.

mutual savings bank   a bank that is owned by its depositors

Mutual Savings Banks   A **mutual savings bank** is a bank that is owned by its depositors. Located primarily in the Northeast, mutual savings banks accept deposits and lend money for home mortgages. The approximately five hundred mutual savings banks in this country have no stockholders.[6] Their profits are distributed to depositors. They operate much like S&Ls and are controlled by state banking authorities.

Organizations That Perform Banking Functions   There are three other types of financial institutions that are not actually banks but that are nevertheless involved in various banking activities to a limited extent.

- *Insurance companies* provide long-term financing for office buildings, shopping centers, and other commercial real estate projects through-

TABLE 17.2 Methods Used by the Federal Reserve System to Control the Money Supply and the Economy

Method Used	Immediate Result	End Result
Regulating reserve requirement 1. Fed **increases** reserve requirement	Less money for banks to lend to customers—reduction in overall money supply	Economic slowdown
2. Fed **decreases** reserve requirement	More money for banks to lend to customers—increase in overall money supply	Increased economic activity
Regulating the discount rate 1. Fed **increases** the discount rate	Less money for banks to lend to customers—reduction in overall money supply	Economic slowdown
2. Fed **decreases** the discount rate	More money for banks to lend to customers—increase in overall money supply	Increased economic activity
Open-market operations 1. Fed **sells** government securities and bonds	Less money for banks to lend to customers—reduction in overall money supply	Economic slowdown
2. Fed **buys** government securities and bonds	More money for banks to lend to customers—increase in overall money supply	Increased economic activity

the United States are cleared in this way. The remainder are either presented directly to the paying bank or processed through local clearinghouses. Through the use of electronic equipment, most checks can be cleared within two or three days.

Control and Inspection of Currency As paper currency is handled, it becomes worn or dirty. The typical one-dollar bill has a life expectancy of less than one year (larger denominations usually last longer because they are handled less). When member banks deposit their surplus cash in a Federal Reserve Bank, the currency is inspected. Bills that are unfit for further use are separated and destroyed. The destruction process is usually as follows:

- Holes are drilled in each corner of the bills by one group of employees.
- The bills are then cut in half by a second group of employees.
- Each half is pulverized by a third group.
- The end result is barely recognizable as paper. It is recycled and used for such things as wrapping paper and roofing material.

Suppose Ms. Henderson of Albany, NY, buys a painting from an art dealer in Sacramento, CA. She sends her check. . .

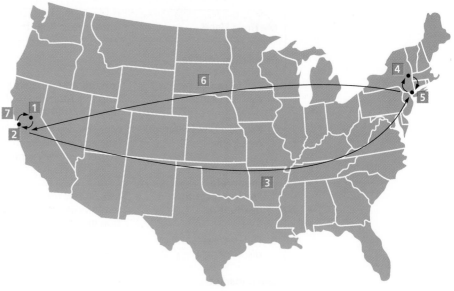

1. The dealer deposits the check in his account at a Sacramento bank.

2. The Sacramento bank deposits the check for credit in its account with the Federal Reserve Bank of San Francisco.

3. The Federal Reserve Bank of San Francisco sends the check to the Federal Reserve Bank of New York for collection.

4. The Federal Reserve Bank of New York forwards the check to the Albany bank, which deducts the amount of the check from Ms. Henderson's account.

5. The Albany bank authorizes the Federal Reserve Bank of New York to deduct the amount of the check from its deposit account with the Federal Reserve Bank.

6. The Federal Reserve Bank of New York pays the Federal Reserve Bank of San Francisco by payment from its share in the interdistrict settlement fund.

7. The Federal Reserve Bank of San Francisco credits the Sacramento bank's deposit account, and the Sacramento bank credits the art dealer's account.

FIGURE 17.4   Clearing a Check Through the Federal Reserve System
Approximately one-half of all U.S. checks are cleared this way, a process that usually takes two to three days.   (*Source: Federal Reserve Bank of New York,* The Story of Checks, *6th ed., 1983, p. 11.*)

Selective Credit Controls   The Federal Reserve System has the responsibility for implementing the Truth-in-Lending Act, which was passed by Congress in 1968. This act requires lenders to clearly state the annual percentage rate and total finance charge for a consumer loan. It also prohibits discrimination in lending based on race, color, sex, marital status, religion, or national origin.

The Federal Reserve System is also responsible for setting the margin requirements for certain stock transactions. The *margin* is the minimum portion of the selling price that must be paid in cash. (The investor may borrow the remainder.) The current margin requirement is $2,000, or 50 percent. Thus if an investor purchases $4,000 worth of stock, he or she must pay at least $2,000 cash. The remaining $2,000 may be borrowed from the brokerage firm or some other financial institution.

THE FDIC, SAIF, AND NCUA

LEARNING OBJECTIVE 6
Explain the function of the Federal Deposit Insurance Corporation (FDIC), Savings Association Insurance Fund (SAIF), and National Credit Union Association (NCUA).

During the Depression, a number of banks failed and their depositors lost all their savings. To make sure that this does not happen again (and to restore public confidence in the banking industry), Congress organized the *Federal Deposit Insurance Corporation (FDIC)* in 1933. The primary purpose of the FDIC is to insure deposits against bank failure. All banks that are members of the Federal Reserve System are required to belong to the FDIC. Nonmember banks are allowed to join if they qualify. Insurance premiums are paid by the banks.

The FDIC insures all accounts in each member bank for up to $100,000 per depositor. An individual depositor may obtain additional coverage by

Rhode Islanders see red. Although all Americans are paying for the savings and loan bailout, no one has suffered more from the banking crisis than citizens of Rhode Island. Governor Bruce Sundlun closed 45 banks and credit unions when the state deposit insurance system collapsed. But what most outraged depositors was that a group of insiders withdrew $5 million just before the governor made the announcement.

opening separate accounts in different banks. Individuals who deposit their money in savings and loan associations or credit unions receive similar protection. The newly created *Savings Association Insurance Fund (SAIF)*—funded by the FDIC—insures deposits in savings and loan associations. Formerly, the now defunct Federal Savings and Loan Insurance Corporation (FSLIC) was charged with this responsibility. The *National Credit Union Association (NCUA)* insures deposits in credit unions.

The FDIC, SAIF, and NCUA have improved banking in the United States. When any one of these organizations insures an institution's deposits, it reserves the right to periodically examine that institution's operations. For example, the FDIC has established regional centers in Tennessee, California, and Texas to monitor the large number of banks that are in trouble in those parts of the country. If a bank, S&L, or credit union is found to be poorly managed, it is reported to the proper banking authority. In extreme cases, the FDIC, SAIF, or NCUA can cancel its insurance coverage. This is a particularly unwelcome action. It causes many depositors to withdraw their money from the bank, S&L, or credit union and discourages most prospective depositors from opening an account.

Lending to individuals and firms is a vital function of banks. And deciding wisely to whom it will extend credit is one of the most important activities of any institution. The material in the next section explains the different factors that are used to evaluate credit applicants.

EFFECTIVE CREDIT MANAGEMENT

credit immediate purchasing power that is exchanged for a promise to repay it, with or without interest, at a later date

Credit is immediate purchasing power that is exchanged for a promise to repay it, with or without interest, at a later date. A credit transaction is a two-sided business activity that involves both a borrower and a lender. The borrower is most often a person or firm that wishes to make a purchase. The lender may be a bank, some other lending institution, or business firm selling merchandise or services on credit.

For example, suppose you obtain a bank loan to buy a $40,000 Porsche automobile. You, as the borrower, obtain immediate purchasing power. In return, you agree to certain terms that are imposed by the bank. As the lender, the bank requires that you make a down payment, make monthly payments, pay interest, and purchase insurance to protect the car until the loan is paid in full. That is, you promise to repay the purchasing power, pay interest for its use, and protect the collateral until the loan is repaid.

Banks lend money because they are in business for that purpose. The interest they charge is what provides their profit. There are at least two reasons why other businesses extend credit to their customers. First, some customers simply cannot afford to pay the entire amount of their purchase immediately, but they *can* repay credit in a number of smaller payments, stretched out over some period of time. Second, some firms are forced to sell goods or services on credit to compete effectively when other firms offer credit to their customers.

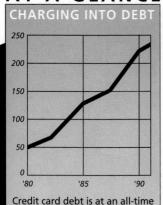

AT A GLANCE

CHARGING INTO DEBT

Credit card debt is at an all-time high — a sign that consumers are living beyond their means.
1991 estimated (In billions of dollars)

SOURCE: ©FORTUNE, January 27, 1992

500,000 Americans file for personal bankruptcy each year. To help such people avoid personal bankruptcy, counselors at more than 550 local CCCS offices help clients assess their current financial situation and create a plan for repaying outstanding debts. Although each case is different, most CCCS counselors begin by establishing a realistic budget of income and expenditures. In addition to establishing a realistic budget, CCCS counselors also provide information on the pitfalls of unwise credit buying and the real cost of credit purchases.

In more extreme cases, the counselor can recommend CCCS's debt-management program. When the debt-management program is used, the CCCS counselor works with the clients' creditors to create a new debt-repayment schedule with lower monthly payments spread out over a longer period of time. The client then makes regular monthly payments to the CCCS, which in turn pays off creditors. In most cases, the debt-management program is designed to pay off the clients' debt within two to three years.**

Questions

1. Consumers often complain that it is *too* easy to get credit cards. Why would this be a problem for some consumers?

2. Americans consistently use credit cards to purchase everyday items. What are the advantages and disadvantages of using credit cards?

3. Because the CCCS is funded by contributions from local businesses, their credit counseling is usually free. Why would local businesses help sponsor a program like the CCCS?

**Based on information from Charles E. Cohen, "The Last Charge," *Ladies' Home Journal*, June 1991, pp. 118+; Jack Kapoor, Les R. Dlabay, and Robert J. Hughes, *Personal Finance* (Homewood, IL: Richard D. Irwin, 1991), pp. 203–205; Guy Murdoch, "Credit Counseling," *Consumers' Research*, March 1991, p. 2; Theodore P. Roth, "Sorry, Your Card Is No Good," *Time*, April 9, 1990, p. 62; and "Your Credit Rating," *Consumer Reports*, October 1990, p. 648.

CHAPTER

18

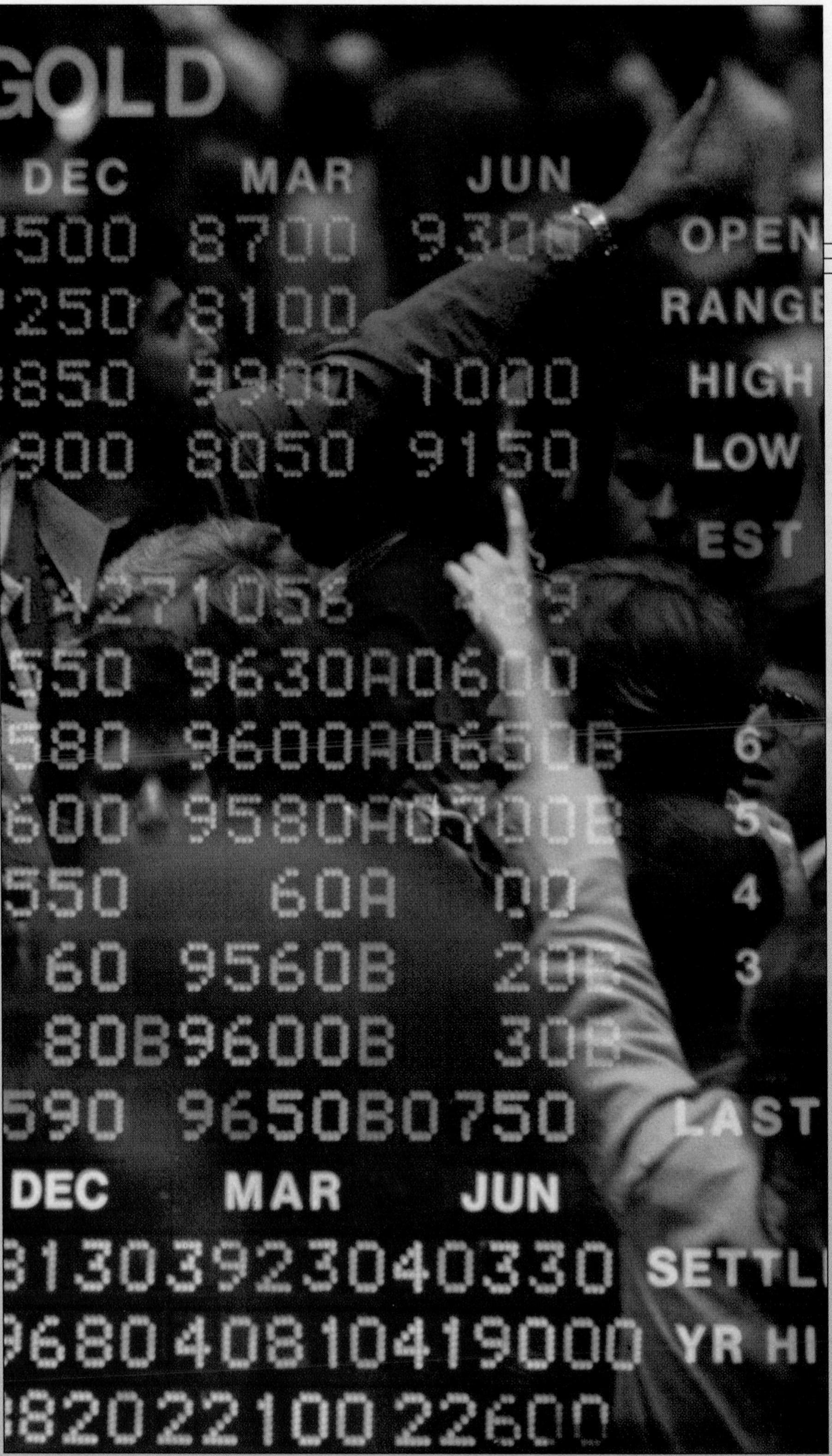

Financial Management

LEARNING OBJECTIVES

After studying this chapter you should be able to:

1 Explain the need for financing and financial management in business.

2 Summarize the process of planning for financial management.

3 Describe the relative advantages and disadvantages of different methods of short-term financing.

4 Evaluate the advantages and disadvantages of equity financing and debt financing from the corporation's standpoint.

5 Discuss the importance of using funds effectively.

CHAPTER PREVIEW

In this chapter we concentrate on the acquisition and efficient use of money. Initially, we focus on two needs of business organizations: the need for money to start a business and keep it going, and the need to manage that money effectively. We also look at how firms develop financial plans and evaluate financial performance. Then, we compare various methods of obtaining short-term financing—money that will be used for one year or less, usually to pay a firm's bills until customers pay theirs, or to cover production costs until the goods are sold. We also examine sources of long-term financing, which a firm may require for expansion, new-product development, or replacement of equipment.

Morgan Stanley

In the past, Morgan Stanley—a Wall Street financial firm that helps large corporations sell new stock and bond issues—has been known as a top-notch securities firm with an ultra-conservative management team. In fact, critics even said that Morgan Stanley was too staid in its "pinstriped" ways to compete with more aggressive firms like Drexel Burnham Lambert, Merrill Lynch, and a host of others involved in the takeovers, mergers, and acquisitions so numerous during the 1980s. Now, in the 1990s, Morgan Stanley's conservative management philosophy has enabled the firm to become one of the most profitable firms on Wall Street, while avoiding many of the problems that other firms more involved in takeover activities have experienced. With assets of over $50 billion and annual sales revenues in excess of $5 billion, Morgan Stanley's return on owners' equity has averaged 30 percent for the past five years.

The Morgan Stanley firm was originally part of the J. P. Morgan banking company. But in 1934, the United States Congress enacted the Glass-Steagall Act requiring commercial banks to separate traditional banking (accepting deposits, processing checks, and making loans) from investment banking (selling new issues of corporate stocks and bonds). In order to comply with the Glass-Steagall Act, Henry Morgan and Harold Stanley resigned from the J. P. Morgan Company and established Morgan Stanley. Today, Morgan Stanley, with 6,700 employees, has offices in the United States, Canada, Japan, Australia, and most European nations.

According to industry analysts there are at least three reasons why Morgan Stanley is so successful. First, the firm chooses its clients with great care. Stanley's list of clients reads like the Who's Who of American business and includes firms like General Motors, U.S. Steel, General Electric, Du Pont, and the Boston Celtics. And Morgan Stanley's clients are devoted; they trust a firm known for its integrity.

ONEX corporation

has sold its interest in

Beatrice

Beatrice Foods Canada

to an affiliate of

Merrill Lynch Capital Partners, Inc.

The undersigned acted as financial advisor to Onex Corporation in this transaction.

MORGAN STANLEY & CO.
Incorporated

November 26, 1991

The second reason why Morgan Stanley is successful is that the firm has expanded its global operations. Rather than just having an office in a foreign country and doing business the "American" way, Morgan Stanley becomes part of the local business community by hiring local employees. For example, over 80 percent of the firm's employees in its Japanese office are from Japan. This international approach to staffing results in improved communications with foreign customers. And this international approach is good for Morgan Stanley; over 40 percent of the firm's annual revenues come from foreign operations.

The third—and maybe most important—reason for Morgan Stanley's success is the firm's ability to attract and keep the best people. In many cases, Morgan Stanley recruits only top graduates with the best grade point averages. In other cases, Morgan Stanley recruits employees from other firms who want to work for one of the best investment bankers on Wall Street.[1]

FIGURE 18.4
Budget Comparison for Newton's Clothing Store
Budget comparisons can point up areas that require additional planning or careful investigation.

NEWTON'S CLOTHING STORE
Sales Budget Update   First Quarter, 199x

Department	First-quarter estimate	Actual sales	Dollar difference
Infants'	$ 50,000	$ 45,600	$-4,400
Children's	45,000	48,200	+3,200
Women's	35,000	36,300	+1,300
Men's	20,000	21,100	+1,100
Totals	$150,000	$151,200	$+1,200

need to take corrective action (such as promoting infants' wear more vigorously).

It is important to realize that the decision to borrow money does not mean that a firm is in financial trouble. On the contrary, astute financial management often means regular, responsible borrowing of many different kinds to meet different needs. In the next two sections we examine the sources of short- and long-term financing available to businesses.

SOURCES OF SHORT-TERM FINANCING

LEARNING OBJECTIVE 3
Describe the relative advantages and disadvantages of different methods of short-term financing.

Short-term financing is usually easier to obtain than long-term financing for three reasons: The shorter repayment period means there is less risk of nonpayment. The dollar amounts of short-term loans are usually smaller than those of long-term loans. And a close working relationship normally exists between the short-term borrower and the lender.

Most lenders do not require collateral for short-term financing. When they do, it is usually because they are concerned about the size of a particular loan, the borrowing firm's poor credit rating, or the general prospects of repayment. It may be the case that a financially weak firm will have difficulty securing short-term financing even when it is willing to pledge collateral to back up a loan.

Sources of Unsecured Short-Term Financing

unsecured financing   financing that is not backed by collateral

Unsecured financing is financing that is not backed by collateral. A company seeking unsecured short-term capital has several options. They include trade credit, promissory notes, bank loans, commercial paper, and commercial drafts.

Trade Credit   In Chapter 13 we noted that wholesalers may provide financial aid to retailers by allowing them thirty to sixty days (or more) in which to pay for merchandise. This delayed payment, which may also be granted by manufacturers, is a form of credit known as *trade credit* or the *open-book account*. More specifically, **trade credit** is a payment delay that a supplier grants to its customers.

trade credit   a payment delay that a supplier grants to its customers

Between 80 and 90 percent of all transactions between businesses involve some trade credit. Typically, the purchased goods are delivered along with a bill (or invoice) that states the credit terms. If the amount is paid on time, no interest is generally charged. In fact, the seller may offer a cash discount to encourage prompt payment. The terms of a cash discount are specified on the invoice. For instance, "2/10, net 30" means that the customer may take a 2 percent discount if the invoice is paid within 10 days of the invoice date; if the bill is paid between 11 and 30 days, the customer must pay the entire (or net) amount.

Promissory Notes Issued to Suppliers   A **promissory note** is a written pledge by a borrower to pay a certain sum of money to a creditor at a specified future date. Suppliers uneasy about extending trade credit may be less reluctant to offer credit to customers that sign promissory notes. Unlike trade credit, however, promissory notes usually require the borrower to pay interest. Although repayment periods may extend to one year, most promissory notes specify 60 to 180 days. A typical promissory note is shown in Figure 18.5. Note that the customer buying on credit (Richland Company) is called the *maker* and is the party that issues the note. The business selling the merchandise on credit (Shelton Company) is called the *payee*.

promissory note   a written pledge by a borrower to pay a certain sum of money to a creditor at a specified future date

A promissory note offers two important advantages to the firm extending the credit. First, a promissory note is a legally binding and enforceable document. Second, most promissory notes are negotiable instruments that can be sold when the money is needed immediately. For example, the note shown in Figure 18.5 will be worth $820 at maturity. If it chose, the Shelton Company could discount, or sell, the note to its own bank. The price would be slightly less than $820, because the bank charges a fee for the service—hence the term *discount*. Shelton would have its money immediately, and the bank would collect the $820 when the note matured.

Unsecured Bank Loans   Commercial banks offer unsecured short-term loans to their customers at interest rates that vary with each borrower's credit rating. The **prime interest rate** (sometimes called the *reference rate*) is the lowest rate charged by a bank for a short-term loan. This lowest rate is generally reserved for large corporations with excellent credit ratings. Organizations with good to high credit ratings may pay the prime rate plus 2 percent. Firms with questionable credit ratings may have to pay the prime rate plus 4 percent. Of course, if the banker feels loan repayment may be a problem, the borrower's loan application may be rejected.

prime interest rate   the lowest rate charged by a bank for a short-term loan

Banks generally offer short-term loans through promissory notes, a line of credit, or a revolving credit agreement. *Promissory notes* that are written to banks are similar to those discussed in the last section.

TABLE 18.2   Comparison of Short-Term Financing Methods

Type of Financing	Cost	Repayment Period	Businesses That May Use It	Comments
Trade credit	Low, if any	30 to 60 days	All businesses	Usually no finance charge.
Promissory note issued to suppliers	Moderate	1 year or less	All businesses	Usually unsecured but requires legal document; issued by borrower.
Unsecured bank loan	Moderate	1 year or less	All businesses	A line of credit or revolving credit agreement may be used.
Commercial paper	Moderate	1 year or less	Large corporations with high credit ratings	Available only to large firms.
Commercial draft	Moderate	1 year or less	Generally used by manufacturers and wholesalers	Issued by seller and accepted by buyer; has value and can be sold.
Secured loan	High	1 year or less	Firms with questionable credit ratings	Inventory or accounts receivable may be used as collateral.
Factoring	High	None	Firms that have large numbers of credit customers	Accounts receivable are sold to a factor.

firm receives instant feedback on whether the factor will purchase the account. Generally, customers whose accounts receivable have been factored are given instructions to make their payments directly to the factor.

Cost Comparisons

Table 18.2 compares the various types of short-term financing. As you can see, trade credit is the least expensive. Generally, the less favorable a firm's credit rating, the more likely that it will have to use a higher-cost means of financing. Factoring of accounts receivable is the highest-cost method shown.

For many purposes, short-term financing suits a firm's needs perfectly. In other cases, however, long-term financing may be more appropriate.

SOURCES OF LONG-TERM FINANCING

LEARNING OBJECTIVE 4
Evaluate the advantages and disadvantages of equity financing and debt financing from the corporation's standpoint.

Sources of long-term financing vary with the size and type of business. If the business is a sole proprietorship or partnership, equity capital is acquired by the business when the owner or owners invest money in the business. For corporations, equity-financing options include the sale of stock and the use of profits not distributed to owners. The available debt-financing options are the sale of corporate bonds and long-term loans.

Equity Financing

Some equity capital is used to start every business—sole proprietorship, partnership, or corporation. In the case of corporations, equity capital is provided by stockholders who buy shares in the company.

There are at least two reasons why equity financing is attractive to large corporations. First, the corporation need not repay money obtained from the sale of stock. Occasionally a corporation buys back its own stock, but only because such an investment is in its own best interest. In 1991, Diasonics—a high-tech manufacturer of x-ray and ultrasound systems— began to purchase shares of its own stock with uninvested profits. According to management, the purchase of 14.5 million shares was the best investment available at that particular time.[5]

A second advantage of equity financing is that a corporation is under no legal obligation to pay dividends to stockholders. As mentioned in Chapter 3, a *dividend* is a distribution of earnings to the stockholders of a corporation. Investors purchase the shares of stock of many corporations primarily for the dividends they pay. However, for any reason (if a company has a bad year, for example), the board of directors can vote to omit dividend payments. Earnings are then retained for use in funding business operations. Thus a corporation need not even pay for the use of equity capital. Of course, the corporate management may hear from unhappy stockholders if expected dividends are omitted too frequently.

There are two types of stock: common and preferred. Each type has advantages and drawbacks as a means of long-term financing.

Timberland goes public—and global. Jeffrey B. Swartz is the grandson of the founder of the Abington Shoe Co. The company changed its name to Timberland in 1978, but an even bigger step was selling shares of stock in 1987. With the long-term financing that move provided, Timberland went global, its sales boomed, and now it cannot keep up with Japanese demand for its boots.

FOCUS ON SMALL BUSINESS
Small Businesses Sell Stock to Raise Equity Capital

To some people who own their own businesses, "going public" may seem like the pot of gold at the end of the rainbow. They sell off millions of tiny pieces of the company they've created, and suddenly that creation makes them very rich. It *can* work that way, but many business people find that turning the dream into gold is more difficult than it appears.

For one thing, it takes an average of three years for a small company to prepare financial statements, get registered with the Securities and Exchange Commission, and select an investment banker willing to market a new stock issue. The investment banker plays a crucial role in taking a company public. As the underwriter, the banker agrees to buy the company's new shares or at least to do its best to find buyers. As adviser, the banker helps the company through the regulatory process and figures out how many shares to offer and at what price. As marketer, the banker spreads the word about the company and rouses investors' interest.

A second factor that must be considered is timing. Typically, companies selling stock for the first time wait for the stock market to take an upturn and for stocks in general to increase in value. If most stocks already on the market are overpriced, investors usually become hungry for new stock issues.

A third factor—the expenses of going public—can keep a company's owners from cashing in on their dreams. A small company going public can expect to pay $200,000 to lawyers, accountants, and printers. Even more important are the fees, ranging from 2 to 12 percent of the money raised, that a company must pay to an investment banker.

To many company executives, the most disturbing part of going public is that they themselves must become public figures. Instead of making decisions on their own and taking responsibility for their own successes and failures, executives of a public company make decisions that are watched by government agencies and that affect thousands of shareholders. Making the company's finances public can be especially traumatic—"like getting undressed in public"—says one newly public figure.

Despite these drawbacks, hundreds of privately owned companies go public every year, raising cash to expand operations and increasing their credibility with other companies and the public at large. It seems the success of some companies keeps the dream alive. For instance, Liz Claiborne, Inc. raised more than $22 million when it sold its first stock issue. And it's not hard to figure out why investors wanted to buy the company's stock. The stock was originally offered at $0.79 a share when adjusted for stock splits. It recently sold for more than $40 a share.

---

common stock   stock whose owners may vote on corporate matters, but whose claims on profits and assets are subordinate to the claims of others

Common Stock   A share of **common stock** represents the most basic form of corporate ownership: Common-stock owners may vote on corporate matters, but their claims on profits and assets are subordinate to those of preferred-stock owners. A common-stock certificate for Houghton Mifflin Company is shown in Figure 18.7. In return for the financing provided by selling common stock, management must make certain concessions to stockholders that may restrict or change corporate policies. By law, every corporation must hold an annual meeting, at which the holders of common stock may vote for the board of directors and approve (or disapprove) major corporate actions. Among such actions are

1.   Amendments to the corporate charter or bylaws.
2.   Sale of certain assets.

FIGURE 18.7   A Common-Stock Certificate
Capital is provided to the company by stockholders when they purchase shares of stock
(equity) in the company.   *(Source: Used with permission of Houghton Mifflin Company.)*

3. Mergers and acquisitions.

4. Issuing of preferred stock or bonds.

5. Changes in the amount of common stock issued.

pre-emptive rights the rights of current stockholders to purchase any new stock that the corporation issues before it is sold to the general public

Many states require that a provision for pre-emptive rights be included in the charter of every corporation. **Pre-emptive rights** are the rights of current stockholders to purchase any new stock that the corporation issues before it is sold to the general public. By exercising their pre-emptive rights, stockholders are able to maintain their current proportion of ownership of the corporation. This may be important when the corporation is small and management control is a matter of concern to stockholders.

Money acquired through the sale of common stock is thus essentially cost-free, but few investors will buy common stock if they cannot foresee some return on their investment. Information on how individuals can make money with stock investments is provided in Chapter 19.

preferred stock stock whose owners usually do not have voting rights, but whose claims on profits and assets have precedence over those of common-stock owners

Preferred Stock   As noted in Chapter 3, the owners of **preferred stock** usually do not have voting rights, but their claims on dividends and assets precede those of common-stock owners. If the board of directors approves dividend payments, holders of preferred stock must receive their dividends before holders of common stock are paid dividends. And when compared with common stockholders, preferred stockholders have first claim (after creditors) on corporate assets if the firm is dissolved or declares bankruptcy. Even so, like common stock, preferred stock does not represent a debt that must be legally repaid.

The dividend to be paid on a share of preferred stock is known before the stock is purchased. It is stated, on the stock certificate, either as a percentage of the par value of the stock or as a dollar amount of money. The **par value** of a stock is an assigned (and often arbitrary) dollar value printed on the stock certificate. For example, Pitney Bowes—a U.S. manufacturer of office and business equipment—issued 4 percent preferred stock with a par value of $50. The annual dividend amount is $2 per share (4 percent × $50 par value = $2 annual dividend).

par value an assigned (and often arbitrary) dollar value printed on the face of a stock certificate

A corporation usually issues one type of common stock, but it may issue many types of preferred stock with varying dividends or dividend rates. For example, Ohio Edison has one common-stock issue but six preferred-stock issues with different dividend amounts for each type of preferred stock.

On occasion, a corporation may decide to call in or buy back an issue of preferred stock when management believes it can issue new preferred stock at a lower dividend rate—or possibly common stock with no specified dividend. When this occurs, management has two options. First, they can buy shares in the market—just like another investor purchases shares of the preferred-stock issue. Second, practically all preferred stock is *callable* at the option of the corporation; that is, the corporation can buy back the stock. When the corporation exercises a call provision, the investor usually receives a call premium. A **call premium** is a dollar amount over par value that the corporation has to pay an investor for redeeming either preferred stock or a corporate bond. (Corporate bonds are discussed later in this chapter.) When considering the two options, management will naturally obtain the preferred stock in the less costly way.

call premium a dollar amount over par value that the corporation has to pay an investor for redeeming either preferred stock or a corporate bond

Added Features for Preferred-Stock Issues To make their preferred stock more attractive to investors, some corporations include cumulative, participating, and convertible features in various issues.

Cumulative preferred stock is preferred stock on which any unpaid dividends accumulate and must be paid before any cash dividend is paid to the holders of common stock. For example, Atlantic Richfield Co. has issued cumulative preferred stock that pays $3 per year. Let's suppose that in 1992 Atlantic Richfield is faced with a substantial loss, and the board of directors votes to omit dividends on both common- and preferred-stock issues. In 1993, however, the board of directors decides that profits are high enough to pay the required preferred dividend, as well as a $2 per-share dividend on its common stock. The holders of the cumulative preferred stock must receive $6 per share ($3 for 1992 and $3 for 1993) before holders of common stock can receive their $2-per-share dividend declared for 1993.

cumulative preferred stock preferred stock on which any unpaid dividends accumulate and must be paid before any cash dividend is paid to the holders of common stock

Participating preferred stock is preferred stock whose owners share in the corporation's earnings, along with the owners of common stock.

participating preferred stock preferred stock whose owners share in the corporation's earnings, along with the owners of common stock

FIGURE 18.8   A Corporate Bond
A corporate bond is a corporation's written pledge that it will repay on the date of
maturity a specified amount of money, with interest.   *(Source: Used with permission of
Baltimore Gas and Electric Company.)*

registered bond   a bond that
is registered in the owner's
name by the issuing company

coupon bond   a bond whose
ownership is not registered by
the issuing company

corporation pays interest to the bond owner—usually every six months—at
the stated rate. The method used to pay bondholders their interest depends
on whether they own registered or coupon bonds. A **registered bond**—like
the Baltimore Gas and Electric bond—is a bond that is registered in the
owner's name by the issuing company. Interest checks for registered bonds
are mailed directly to the bondholder of record. When a registered bond is
sold, it must be endorsed by the seller before ownership can be transferred
on the company books. A **coupon bond,** sometimes called a *bearer bond,* is
a bond whose ownership is not registered by the issuing company. To collect interest on a coupon bond, bondholders must clip a coupon and then
redeem it by following procedures outlined by the issuer. At the maturity
date, the bond owner returns the bond to the corporation and receives cash
equaling its face value. Coupon bonds are less secure than registered
bonds. If coupon bonds are lost or stolen, interest may be collected and the
bonds may be redeemed by anyone who finds them. For this reason, most
corporate bonds are registered.

Repayment Provisions for Corporate Bonds   Maturity dates for bonds generally range from fifteen to forty years after the date of issue. In the event
that the interest is not paid or the firm becomes insolvent, bond owners'

claims on the assets of the corporation take precedence over both common and preferred stockholders. Some bonds are callable before the maturity date. For these bonds, the corporation usually pays the bond owner a call premium. The amount of the premium is specified, along with other provisions, in the bond indenture. The **bond indenture** is a legal document that details all the conditions relating to a bond issue.

bond indenture   a legal document that details all the conditions relating to a bond issue

From the corporation's standpoint, financing through a bond issue differs considerably from equity financing. Interest must be paid periodically—usually every six months. In the eyes of the Internal Revenue Service, interest is a tax-deductible business expense. Furthermore, corporate bonds must be redeemed for their face value at maturity. If the corporation defaults on (does not pay) either of these payments, owners of bonds could force the firm into bankruptcy.

A corporation may use one of three methods to ensure that it has sufficient funds available to redeem a bond issue. First, it can issue the bonds as **serial bonds,** which are bonds of a single issue that mature on different dates. For example, Seaside Productions used a twenty-five-year, $50-million bond issue to finance its expansion. None of the bonds matures during the first fifteen years. Thereafter, 10 percent of the bonds mature each year, until all the bonds are retired at the end of the twenty-fifth year. Second, the corporation can establish a sinking fund. A **sinking fund** is a sum of money to which deposits are made each year for the purpose of redeeming a bond issue. When H. J. Heinz sold a $50-million bond issue, the company agreed to contribute $3 million to a sinking fund each year until the bond's maturity in the year 2007. Third, a corporation can pay off an old bond issue by selling new bonds. Although this may appear to perpetuate the corporation's long-term debt, a number of utility companies and railroads have used this repayment method.

serial bonds   bonds of a single issue that mature on different dates

sinking fund   a sum of money to which deposits are made each year for the purpose of redeeming a bond issue

A corporation that issues bonds must also appoint a **trustee,** which is an independent firm or individual that acts as the bond owners' representative. A trustee's duties are most often handled by a commercial bank or other large financial institution. The corporation must report to the trustee periodically regarding its ability to make interest payments and eventually redeem the bonds. In turn, the trustee transmits this information to the bond owners, along with its own evaluation of the corporation's ability to pay.

trustee   an independent firm or individual that acts as the bond owners' representative

Most corporate bonds are debenture bonds. A **debenture bond** is a bond backed only by the reputation of the issuing corporation. To make its bonds more appealing to investors, however, a corporation may issue mortgage bonds. A **mortgage bond** is a corporate bond secured by various assets of the issuing firm. Or the corporation can issue convertible bonds. A **convertible bond** can be exchanged, at the owner's option, for a specified number of shares of the corporation's common stock. Westinghouse Electric Corp.'s 2007 bond issue is convertible. Each bond can be converted to 64.5 shares of the company's common stock. The corporation can gain in two ways by issuing convertible bonds. They usually carry a lower interest rate than nonconvertible bonds. And once a bond owner converts a bond to common stock, the corporation no longer has to redeem it.

debenture bond   a bond backed only by the reputation of the issuing corporation

mortgage bond   a corporate bond that is secured by various assets of the issuing firm

convertible bond   a bond that can be exchanged, at the owner's option, for a specified number of shares of the corporation's common stock

Long-Term Loans   Many businesses finance their long-range activities with loans from commercial banks, insurance companies, pension funds, and other financial institutions. Manufacturers and suppliers of heavy equipment and machinery may also provide long-term financing by granting extended credit terms to their customers.

When the loan repayment period is longer than one year, the borrower must sign a term-loan agreement. A **term-loan agreement** is a promissory note that requires a borrower to repay a loan in monthly, quarterly, semiannual, or annual installments.

term-loan agreement   a promissory note that requires a borrower to repay a loan in monthly, quarterly, semiannual, or annual installments

Long-term business loans are normally repaid in three to seven years. The interest rate and other specific terms are often based on such factors as the reasons for borrowing, the borrowing firm's credit rating, and the value of collateral. Although long-term loans may occasionally be unsecured, in most cases the lender requires some type of collateral. Acceptable collateral includes real estate, machinery, and equipment. Lenders may also require that borrowers maintain a minimum amount of working capital.

Cost Comparisons

Table 18.3 compares the different types of equity and long-term debt financing. Obviously, the least expensive type of financing is through an issue of common stock. The most expensive is a long-term loan.

TABLE 18.3   Comparison of Long-Term Financing Methods

Type of Financing	Repayment?	Repayment Period	Interest/ Dividends	Businesses That May Use It
Equity				
1. Common stock	No	None	Dividends not required	All corporations that sell stock to investors
2. Preferred stock	No	None	Dividends not required but must be paid before common stockholders receive any dividends	Larger corporations that have an established investor base of common stockholders
Debt				
1. Corporate bond	Yes	Usually 15 to 40 years	Interest rates between 7% and 12%, depending on economic conditions and the financial stability of the company issuing the bonds	Larger corporations that investors trust
2. Long-term loan	Yes	Usually 3 to 7 years (up to 15 years)	Interest rates between 8% and 14%, depending on economic conditions and the financial stability of the company requesting the loan	All firms that can meet the lender's repayment and collateral requirements

1991 FRONTRUNNER–BUSINESS

Helene Hahn
Film Industry Executive

Photography by Joyce Tenneson

SARA LEE CORPORATION

Honored money-raiser.
Helene Hahn joined Walt Disney Studios in 1984, becoming the first woman to run the business and legal divisions of a major film studio. As an executive vice president responsible for over 4000 employees, she has helped raise over $1 billion in motion picture financing. For her pioneering work, Hahn received Sara Lee Corp.'s Frontrunner Award.

A WORD ABOUT THE USES OF FUNDS

LEARNING OBJECTIVE 5
Discuss the importance of using funds effectively.

In this chapter we have mentioned a variety of business uses of funds. They range from the payment of recurring expenses, such as rent, wages, and the cost of raw materials, to the payment of such one-time costs as plant expansions and mergers. In general, a business uses funds to pay for the resources it needs to produce and market its products.

The effective use of finances, as we have noted, is an important function of financial management. To some extent, financial management can be viewed as a two-sided problem. On one side, the uses of funds often dictate the type or types of financing needed by a business. On the other side, the activities that a business can undertake are determined by the types of financing available. Financial managers must ensure that funds are available when needed, that they are obtained at the lowest possible cost, and that they are used as efficiently as possible. And, finally, financial managers must ensure that funds are available for the repayment of debts in accordance with lenders' financing terms. Prompt repayment is essential to protect the firm's credit rating and its ability to obtain financing in the future.

To a great extent, firms are financed through the investments of individuals—money that people have deposited in banks or have used to purchase stocks, mutual funds, and bonds. In Chapter 19, we look at securities markets and how they help people invest their money in business.

CHAPTER REVIEW

Summary

Financial management consists of those activities that are concerned with obtaining money and using it effectively. Short-term financing is money that will be used for one year or less. Although there are many short-term needs, cash flow and inventory are two problems that deserve special attention. Long-term financing is money that will be used for more than one year. Such financing may be required for starting a business, expansion, new-product development, or replacement of production facilities. Proper financial management can ensure that money is available when it is needed and that it is used efficiently, in keeping with organizational goals.

A financial plan begins with the organization's goals and objectives. Next these goals and objectives are "translated" into budgets that detail expected income and expenses. From these budgets, which may be combined into an overall cash budget, the financial manager determines what funding will be needed and where it may be obtained. The four principal sources of financing are sales revenue, equity capital (derived from the sale of common and preferred stock), debt capital, and proceeds from the sale of assets. Once the needed funds have been obtained, the financial manager is responsible for ensuring that they are properly used. This is accomplished through a system of monitoring and evaluating the firm's financial activities.

Most short-term financing is unsecured. That is, no collateral is required. Sources of unsecured short-term financing include trade credit, promissory notes issued to suppliers, unsecured bank loans, commercial paper, and commercial drafts. Sources of secured short-term financing include loans secured by inventory or accounts receivable. It is also possible to sell receivables to factors. Trade credit is the least expensive source of short-term financing; there is no interest charge. The cost of financing through other sources generally depends on the source and on the credit rating of the firm that requires the financing. Factoring is generally the most expensive approach.

Long-term financing may be obtained as equity capital or debt capital. For a corporation, equity capital is obtained by selling either common or preferred stock. Common stock is voting stock; holders of common stock elect the corporation's directors and must approve equity funding plans. Holders of preferred stock usually do not vote on corporate matters, but they must be paid a specified dividend before holders of common stock are paid any dividends. Another source of equity funding is retained earnings, which is the portion of a business's profits that is reinvested in the corporation.

Sources of long-term debt financing are the sale of corporate bonds and long-term loans. Money realized from the sale of bonds must be repaid when the bonds mature. In addition, interest must be paid on that money from the time the bonds are sold until maturity. Maturity dates for bonds generally range from fifteen to forty years, but long-term loans are generally repaid in three to seven years. The rate of interest for long-term loans usually depends on the financial status of the borrower, the reason for borrowing, and the kind of collateral pledged to back up the loan.

Key Terms

You should now be able to define and give an example relevant to each of the following terms:

financial management	par value
short-term financing	call premium
cash flow	cumulative preferred
long-term financing	stock
financial plan	participating preferred
budget	stock
zero-base budgeting	convertible preferred
equity capital	stock
debt capital	retained earnings
unsecured financing	corporate bond
trade credit	maturity date
promissory note	registered bond
prime interest rate	coupon bond
revolving credit agreement	bond indenture
commercial paper	serial bonds
commercial draft	sinking fund
floor planning	trustee
accounts receivable	debenture bond
factor	mortgage bond
common stock	convertible bond
pre-emptive rights	term-loan agreement
preferred stock	

Questions and Exercises

Review Questions

1. How does short-term financing differ from long-term financing? Give two business uses of each of these types of financing.
2. What is the function of budgets in financial planning?
3. What is zero-base budgeting? How does it differ from the traditional concept of budgeting?
4. How does a financial manager monitor and evaluate a firm's financing?
5. What are the four general sources of financing?
6. How is unsecured financing different from secured financing?
7. How important is trade credit as a source of short-term financing? How does trade credit differ from other kinds of short-term financing?
8. What is the difference between a line of credit and a revolving credit agreement?
9. Distinguish between a commercial draft and a promissory note. Why would a supplier require either of these?
10. Explain how factoring works. Of what benefit is factoring to a firm that sells its receivables?
11. What are the advantages of financing through the sale of stock? What are pre-emptive rights?
12. Explain each of the following features of preferred stock:
    a. The cumulative feature
    b. The participating feature
    c. The convertible feature
13. Where do a corporation's retained earnings come from? What are the advantages of this type of financing?
14. Describe the three methods used to ensure that funds are available to redeem corporate bonds at maturity.
15. For the corporation, what are the advantages of corporate bonds when compared with long-term loans?

Discussion Questions

1. During the 1980s, Morgan Stanley was criticized for being too conservative. Now, in the 1990s, the firm is one of the most respected and most profitable on Wall Street. In your own words, describe the events that led to Morgan Stanley's transformation.
2. According to the experts, Morgan Stanley is one of the most successful American financial firms in the global marketplace. What specific actions has management taken to encourage international growth in foreign countries?
3. What does a financial manager do? How can she or he monitor a firm's financial success?
4. If you were the financial manager of Newton's Clothing Store, what would you do with the excess cash that the firm expects to have in the second and fourth quarters? (See Figure 18.3.)
5. Why would a supplier offer both trade credit and cash discounts to its customers?
6. Why would a lender offer unsecured loans when it could demand collateral?
7. In what circumstances might a large corporation sell stock rather than bonds to obtain long-term financing? In what circumstances would it sell bonds rather than stock?

Exercises

1. Suppose you are responsible for setting a bank's interest rates. Your prime rate is 7 percent. Determine the interest rate you would charge a new, medium-sized firm for:
   a. A six-month unsecured loan
   b. Loans on a revolving credit agreement (Also specify the commitment fee.)
   c. A three-month loan secured by the firm's accounts receivable
   d. A five-year loan secured by the firm's land and buildings
   Explain briefly how you arrived at each interest rate.
2. You want to borrow funds to finance next year's college expenses. Set up a budget showing your expected income and expenses, and determine how much money you will need to borrow. Then outline a plan for repaying the borrowed funds. Provide enough detail to convince your financing source to advance you the money.

CASE 18.1

Dun & Bradstreet's Commercial Credit Reports

As the nation's largest commercial credit bureau, The Dun & Bradstreet Corp. (known as D&B in the business community) maintains credit information on 9.5 million U.S. companies. And with more than 90 percent of the market, D&B has a virtual monopoly in the commercial credit-information industry. In fact, D&B

receives over 90,000 requests each day for credit information to help business firms decide whether to extend short-term financing to another company or sell merchandise to another company on credit.

On the basis of the information contained in a D&B credit report, a business can better judge whether a customer will pay promptly. The most easily accessible source of information is the *Dun & Bradstreet Reference Book*. Information is given on a firm's line of business, net worth, and credit rating. The current D&B credit rating system is illustrated in Table 18.4. A firm with a *CC2* rating has estimated financial strength, based on net worth, of $75,000 to $125,000, with an overall composite credit appraisal of "Good." Dun & Bradstreet composite credit appraisals range from "High" to "Limited" and are based on a firm's repayment history, financial strength, and management personnel. Although the prospects of repayment for firms in each category vary, firms rated "High" or "Good" generally repay their credit obligations. Firms rated "Fair" are less likely to repay credit obligations. Most lenders and suppliers are reluctant to extend credit to firms with a limited credit rating.

It is also possible to obtain a more extensive credit report that includes all of the above plus additional information on a firm's sales, assets, debts, bank balances, number of employees, and facts relating to whether the firm is behind on its bills or not. Finally, there is a section on the company's history, with background information on the officers of the company.

Users sometimes complain that the information in D&B reports is inaccurate, outdated, or incomplete. In addition, users complain that much of the information included in D&B's reports is self-reported by the business owners themselves. The company admits that only a portion of its information has been audited or checked for accuracy. And, since a decision to sell merchandise on credit or extend short-term financing may be based entirely on the information contained in a D&B report, inaccuracies can have serious repercussions.

D&B counters that some mistakes are inevitable because it maintains credit information on 9.5 million businesses in the United States. To reduce customer complaints, D&B is developing a new quality-control system to monitor virtually all credit reports. Also, the company has begun conducting research to measure customer satisfaction. Although the company cannot guarantee the accuracy, completeness, or timeliness of credit reports, D&B management insists that its theme is "Quality First."*

TABLE 18.4   Dun & Bradstreet's Credit Rating System

Composite Credit Appraisal			
High	Good	Fair	Limited
1	2	3	4
Estimated Financial Strength			
5A	Over	$50,000,000	
4A	$10,000,000 to	50,000,000	
3A	1,000,000 to	10,000,000	
2A	750,000 to	1,000,000	
1A	500,000 to	750,000	
BA	300,000 to	500,000	
BB	200,000 to	300,000	
CB	125,000 to	200,000	
CC	75,000 to	125,000	
DC	50,000 to	75,000	
DD	35,000 to	50,000	
EE	20,000 to	35,000	
FF	10,000 to	20,000	
GG	5,000 to	10,000	
HH	Up to	5,000	

Source: Key to Dun & Bradstreet ratings used by permission. Copyright Dun & Bradstreet.

Questions

Assume that you are the owner of Mountain-Top Fashions, a small, Denver-based manufacturing company that specializes in women's sportswear. You receive an order for $22,500 worth of merchandise from a retailer in Seattle, Washington. You have never sold to this retailer before, and you have no idea whether the customer will pay for the merchandise.

1. If the Seattle retailer has a FF3 rating in the *Dun & Bradstreet Reference Book,* would you sell your merchandise on a credit basis?
2. What type of information would you expect to find in an extensive D&B credit report on this retailer?
3. In the above situation, what other information would you want before making a decision to sell your merchandise on a credit basis? Where could you find this information?

*Based on information from Anne Murphy, "How to Read a Credit Report," *Inc.,* June 1990, pp. 68–69; Jeffrey Rothfeder, "Damage Control at Dun & Bradstreet," *Business Week,* November 27, 1989, pp. 187–188+; Johnnie L. Roberts, "Dun's

Credit Reports, Vital Tool of Business Can Be Off the Mark," *Wall Street Journal*, October 5, 1989, p. A1+; and *Moody's Handbook of Common Stocks*, Summer 1991.

CASE 18.2

RJR Nabisco's Refinancing Plan

In 1989, Kohlberg Kravis Roberts—the top takeover firm of the 1980s—paid $25 billion for RJR Nabisco, Inc. To obtain the financing needed for the buyout, Kohlberg Kravis Roberts sold high-interest-rate bonds totaling $6 billion. The interest expense alone cost the company $2.5 million a day, or about $100,000 an hour each day. Since the record-breaking buyout, RJR Nabisco's executives have managed the massive debt and the related interest expense by boosting sales revenue and reducing operational expenses, selling assets, issuing stock, and refinancing some of the high-interest-rate bonds.

According to Louis Gerstner, chairman of the board, the company has refused to cut back on marketing and product-development activities. Products like Oreos and Fig Newton cookies, Ritz Crackers, and Camel and Winston cigarettes have continued to generate record sales revenues. In addition, new products like Teddy Grahams Breakfast Bears and Life Savers Holes have boosted the company's sales revenues by approximately $600 million a year. At the same time, RJR Nabisco has slashed expenses by eliminating 2,300 jobs in its factories, reducing the corporate staff, and eliminating six corporate jets.

To further strengthen RJR Nabisco's balance sheet, Gerstner sold International Nabisco Brands, Del Monte Foods, and other unwanted assets for $5.6 billion. Then, in April 1991, the company sold 100 million shares of common stock that brought in an additional $1.1 billion. According to management, selling common stock was an especially attractive option because equity financing does not have to be repaid. Finally, the corporation replaced some of its high-interest bonds with a $750 million, 10.5 percent bond issue. Because of overall low interest rates on comparable investments, investor demand was so strong for RJR Nabisco's new bond issue that the company increased the offering to $1.5 billion.

According to financial analysts, RJR Nabisco's operations have always been profitable, but financial problems have taken their toll. Now the company hopes to save $400 to $500 million a year because of its refinancing plan. According to Chairman Gerstner, one of the major objectives of the refinancing plan was to take the financial pressure off the company so that management can run the company's day-to-day operations and take advantage of new opportunities for expansion.**

Questions

1. RJR management resisted the temptation to reduce marketing and product-development activities during the recent financial crisis. How has this decision affected the company's financial statements?
2. As part of its refinancing plan, RJR Nabisco sold 100 million shares of common stock. For the corporation, what are the advantages of selling stock?
3. Despite the fact that a number of companies have defaulted on bond issues in the first part of the 1990s, RJR Nabisco was able to sell new bonds. As an investor, would you purchase RJR Nabisco's new 10.5 percent bonds? Why?

**Based on information from "Louis Gerstner's Script for a Debt-Defying Drama at RJR," *U.S. News & World Report*, May 20, 1991, p. 61; "The Acquisitor Strikes Again," *Time*, May 6, 1991, p. 48; "RJR Nabisco: Junk Buyers at the Gate," *Newsweek*, April 29, 1991, p. 48; Jeffrey M. Laderman and Laura Zinn, "Investors Can't Get Enough of Those Stocks," *Business Week*, April 29, 1991, p. 74; Judith H. Dobrzynski, "RJR Gives Itself Some Running Room," *Business Week*, July 30, 1990, p. 60; Carolyn Friday, "RJR Tries to Salvage Its Junk," *Newsweek*, July 2, 1990, p. 38; and Judith H. Dobrzynski, "Would $2 Billion Buy Faith in RJR Nabisco?" *Business Week*, April 9, 1990, pp. 70–71.

CHAPTER

19

Securities Markets

CHAPTER PREVIEW

To begin, we examine the process of buying and selling securities, noting the functions of securities exchanges and stock brokerage firms. Then we outline the reasons for developing a personal investment plan and point out several factors that should be considered in any potential investment. Next, we present several types of traditional investments. In addition, we consider high-risk investment techniques—that is, investments that can lead to large gains but are also quite speculative. We also explain how to obtain and interpret financial information from newspapers, brokerage firms, and periodicals. Finally, we discuss the evolution of state and federal laws governing the sale of stocks and bonds.

Charles Schwab and Company

According to some investors, Charles Schwab and Company is the Wal-Mart of Wall Street firms that buy and sell stocks and other investments for their customers. In fact, Schwab is the largest *discount* brokerage firm in the world with more than 1.4 million customers, 3,000 employees in more than 120 U.S. offices, annual revenues of over $600 million, and yearly net income in excess of $17 million. And despite its reputation for lower fees and commissions, the San Francisco firm has earned a reputation for being one of the most customer-oriented firms in the industry.

The Schwab company began discount transactions on May 1, 1975—the same day that the Securities and Exchange Commission (SEC) abolished the fixed commissions charged by all brokerage firms. In *theory*, the fees and commissions that customers paid for buying and selling securities became negotiable after the SEC's action. In *reality*, most brokerage firms negotiated fees with their more active and wealthy customers. Small customers, on the other hand, often paid higher commissions after deregulation. To attract these dissatisfied customers—especially those who knew what they wanted to buy or sell—Schwab offered fees and commissions that were about one-half those offered by competing brokerage firms. Customers began switching to Schwab and the firm became successful almost overnight.

By the early 1980s, Schwab needed capital to expand and to open new branch offices across the United States. To gain the needed capital, Schwab agreed to a friendly takeover by BankAmerica Corporation. But the marriage between the large commercial bank and the discount brokerage firm didn't last. So in 1987, Charles R. Schwab, the firm's current chief executive officer, agreed to repurchase the discount brokerage firm from BankAmerica. Later that year, the Schwab company "went public" and sold eight million shares of

stock to the general public to raise capital. But just when Schwab had the capital it needed to expand and establish branch offices throughout the United States, the stock market took a real dive in the last part of 1987. Individual investors became scared and as a result Schwab's sales revenues and profits both plummeted.

From their 1987 experience, Schwab executives realized that the firm had to offer new services while finding ways to trim operating costs. In the early 1990s, the firm broadened its product mix to include checking accounts, credit cards, certificates of deposit, retirement accounts, cash-management services, and even mutual funds. To lower operating costs, management began to invest in state-of-the-art computer equipment. As a result of this investment in technology, coupled with other cost-cutting measures, Schwab's break-even point is now just 10,000 transactions a day. And with daily transactions of nearly 19,000, the firm is more profitable than ever. Today, most people agree that the Schwab company is more than just a discount brokerage firm. It is now a top-notch financial firm for people who want to take charge of their own finances.[1]

T oday, Charles Schwab and Company has over 120 U.S. offices that help more than 1.4 million customers buy and sell securities. Without the brokerage services offered by Charles Schwab and similar, competing brokerage firms, it would be difficult, if not impossible, for the average person to buy and sell securities.

HOW SECURITIES ARE BOUGHT AND SOLD

LEARNING OBJECTIVE 1
Describe how securities are bought and sold through brokerage firms and securities exchanges.

To purchase a sweater, you simply walk into a store that sells sweaters, choose one, and pay for it. To purchase stocks, bonds, mutual funds, and many other investments, you have to work through a representative—your stockbroker. In turn, your broker must buy or sell for you in either the primary or secondary market.

The Primary Market

primary market a market in which an investor purchases financial securities (via an investment bank or other representative) directly from the issuer of those securities

investment banking firm an organization that assists corporations in raising funds, usually by helping sell new security issues

The **primary market** is a market in which an investor purchases financial securities (via an investment bank or other representative) directly from the issuer of those securities. An **investment banking firm** is an organization that assists corporations in raising funds, usually by helping sell new security issues. An example of a financial security sold through the primary market is the common-stock issue sold by Microsoft Corp. Investors bought this stock through brokerage firms acting as agents for the investment banking firm Goldman Sachs; the money (almost $60 million) they paid for common stock flowed to Microsoft.[2]

For a large corporation, the decision to sell securities is often complicated, time-consuming, and expensive. Such companies usually choose one of two basic methods. The company may choose to have an investment banking firm handle the stock issue, or it may choose to sell directly to current stockholders.

Large firms that need a lot of financing often use an investment banking firm to sell and distribute the new security issue. Analysts for the investment bank examine the corporation's financial condition to determine whether the company is financially sound and how difficult it will be to sell the new stock issue. If the analysts for the investment banking firm are satisfied that the new issue is a good risk, the bank will buy the securities and then resell them to the investment bank's customers—commercial banks, insurance companies, pension funds, mutual funds, and the general public. The investment banking firm generally charges a fee of 2 to 12 percent of the gross proceeds received by the corporation issuing the securities. The size of the commission depends on the financial health of the corporation issuing the new securities and the size of the new security issue. The commission allows the investment bank to make a profit while guaranteeing that the corporation will receive the needed financing.

The second method used by a corporation trying to obtain financing through the primary market is to sell directly to current stockholders. Usually, promotional materials describing the new security issue are mailed to current stockholders. These stockholders may then purchase securities directly from the corporation. Why would a corporation try to sell its own securities? The most obvious reason is to avoid the investment bank's commission. Of course, a corporation's ability to sell a new security issue without the aid of an investment banking firm is tied directly to the public's perception of the corporation's financial health.

The Secondary Market

secondary market   a market for existing financial securities that are currently traded between investors

After securities are originally sold through the primary market, they are traded on a regular basis through the secondary market. The **secondary market** is a market for existing financial securities that are currently traded between investors. Usually, secondary-market transactions are completed through a securities exchange or the over-the-counter market.

securities exchange   a marketplace where member brokers meet to buy and sell securities

Securities Exchanges   A **securities exchange** is a marketplace where member brokers meet to buy and sell securities. The securities sold at a particular exchange must first be *listed,* or accepted for trading, at that exchange. Generally, securities issued by nationwide corporations are traded at either the New York Stock Exchange or the American Stock Exchange. The securities of regional corporations are traded at smaller *regional exchanges,* located in Chicago, San Francisco, Philadelphia, Boston, and several other cities. The securities of very large corporations may be traded at more than one of these exchanges. Securities of firms may also be listed on foreign securities exchanges—in Tokyo, London, or Paris, for example.

The largest and best-known securities exchange in the United States is the New York Stock Exchange (NYSE). It handles about 50 percent of all stock bought and sold in the United States. The NYSE lists approximately 2,250 securities issued by more than 1,500 corporations, with a total market value of $3 trillion.[3] The actual trading floor of the NYSE, where listed securities are bought and sold, is approximately the size of a football field. A glass-enclosed visitors' gallery lets people watch the proceedings below and, on a busy day, the floor of the NYSE can best be described as organized confusion. Yet, the system does work and enables brokers to trade an average of more than 165 million shares per day.

Before a corporation's stock is approved for listing on the New York Stock Exchange, the firm must meet five criteria (see Figure 19.1).

CRITERIA				
Annual earnings before taxes: $2.5 million	Shares of stock held publicly: 1.1 million	Market value of publicly held stock: $18 million	Number of stockholders owning at least 100 shares: 2,000	Value of net tangible assets: $18 million

FIGURE 19.1
Criteria a Firm Must Meet Before Being Listed on the New York Stock Exchange
Approximately 1,500 corporations are currently listed on the New York Stock Exchange. *(Source:* Chase, C. David, Chase Investment Performance Digest (Chase Global Data, 289 Great Road, Acton, Mass. 01720), 1990 edition, p. 70. *Used by permission.)*

over-the-counter (OTC) market   a network of stockbrokers who buy and sell the securities of corporations that are not listed on a securities exchange

The American Stock Exchange handles about 5 percent of U.S. stock transactions. Regional exchanges and the over-the-counter market account for the remainder. The American and regional exchanges and the over-the-counter market have generally less stringent listing requirements than the NYSE.

The Over-the-Counter Market   The **over-the-counter (OTC) market** is a network of stockbrokers who buy and sell the securities of corporations that are not listed on a securities exchange. Each broker usually specializes, or *makes a market,* in the securities of one or more specific firms. These brokers—sometimes referred to as specialists—are generally aware of the prices of securities traded through the over-the-counter market and of investors willing to buy or sell them. Most OTC trading is conducted by telephone. Currently, more than 4,900 stocks are traded over the counter. Since 1971, the brokers and dealers operating in the OTC market have used a computerized quotation system called *NASDAQ*—the National Association of Securities Dealers Automated Quotation system. NASDAQ displays current price quotations on terminals in subscribers' offices.

The Role of the Stockbroker

account executive   an individual—sometimes called a *stockbroker* or *registered representative* —who buys or sells securities for clients

An **account executive**—sometimes called a *stockbroker* or *registered representative*—is an individual who buys or sells securities for clients. (Actually, *account executive* is the more descriptive title because account executives handle all securities—not only stocks. Choosing an account executive can be difficult for at least three reasons. First, you must exercise a shrewd combination of trust and mistrust when you approach an account executive. Remember that you are interested in the broker's recommendations to increase your wealth, but the account executive is interested in your investment trading as a means to swell commissions. Unfortunately, some account executives are guilty of churning—a practice that generates commissions by excessive buying and selling of securities.

Second, you must decide if you need a full-service broker or a discount broker. A full-service broker charges more but gives you personal investment advice. He or she can provide you with research reports from Moody's Investors Service, Standard & Poor's Corporation, and Value Line Inc.—all companies that specialize in providing investment information to investors. A full-service broker should also provide additional reports prepared by the brokerage firm's financial analysts. A discount broker simply executes buy and sell orders, usually over the phone. Most discount brokers offer no investment advice; you must make your own investment decisions.

Learning the capitalists' game. In 1991, the Polish stock market opened in, of all places, the old Communist Party headquarters. The exchange is modeled after France's Bourse and funded by Great Britain. It began by trading shares in five companies, once a week, but expected to handle many of the 3,500 companies that the government owned and plans to privatize.

Finally, you must consider the factor of compatibility. It is always wise to interview several potential account executives. During each interview, ask some questions to determine if you and the account executive understand each other. You must be able to communicate the types of investments that interest you, your expected rate of return, and the amount of risk you are willing to take to achieve your goals. If you become dissatisfied with your investment program, do not hesitate to discuss your dissatisfaction with the account executive. If your dissatisfaction continues, you may even find it necessary to choose another account executive.

Account executives are employed by stock brokerage firms, such as Merrill Lynch & Co., Inc., Dean Witter Reynolds, and Prudential-Bache Securities. To trade at a particular exchange, a brokerage firm must be a member of that exchange. The NYSE has a limited membership of 1,366 members, or "seats," as they are often called. Although seats on the NYSE are rarely sold, in 1989 a seat sold for $675,000.

The Mechanics of a Transaction   Once an investor and his or her account executive have decided on a particular transaction, the investor gives the account executive an order for that transaction. A **market order** is a request that a stock be purchased or sold at the current market price. The broker's representative on the exchange's trading floor will try to get the best possible price, and the trade will be completed as soon as possible.

A **limit order** is a request that a stock be bought or sold at a price equal to or better (lower for buying, higher for selling) than some specified price. Suppose you place a limit order to *sell* Home Depot common stock at $55 per share. Your broker's representative sells the stock only if the price

market order   a request that a stock be purchased or sold at the current market price

limit order   a request that a stock be bought or sold at a price that is equal to or better than some specified price

is $55 per share or *more*. If you place a limit order to *buy* Home Depot at $55, the representative buys it only if the price is $55 per share or *less*. Limit orders may or may not be transacted quickly, depending on how close the limit price is to the current market price. Usually, a limit order is good for one day, one week, one month, or good until canceled (GTC).

Investors can also choose to place a discretionary order. A **discretionary order** is an order to buy or sell a security that lets the broker decide when to execute the transaction and at what price. Financial planners advise against using a discretionary order for two reasons. First, a discretionary order gives the account executive a great deal of authority. If the account executive makes a mistake, it is the investor who suffers the loss. Second, financial planners argue that only investors (with the help of their account executives) should make investment decisions.

A typical stock transaction includes the five steps shown in Figure 19.2. The entire process, from receipt of the selling order to confirmation of the completed transaction, takes about twenty minutes.

Commissions Brokerage firms are free to set their own commission charges. Like other businesses, however, they must be concerned with the fees charged by competing firms. Full-service brokers generally charge higher fees than discount brokers.

On the trading floor, stocks are traded in round lots. A **round lot** is a unit of 100 shares of a particular stock. Table 19.1 shows typical commission charges for some round-lot transactions. An **odd lot** is fewer than 100

discretionary order   an order to buy or sell a security that lets the broker decide when to execute the transaction and at what price

round lot   a unit of 100 shares of a particular stock

odd lot   fewer than 100 shares of a particular stock

FIGURE 19.2   Steps in a Typical Stock Transaction
A typical stock transaction takes about twenty minutes.

1   Account executive receives customer's order to sell stock and relays order to stock-exchange representative.

2   Firm's clerk signals transaction from booth to partner on stock-exchange floor.

3   Floor partner goes to trading post where stock is traded with a stock-exchange member with an order to buy. Generally 10 or 12 issues are traded at each trading post.

4   Floor partner signals transaction back to clerk in booth. Sale is recorded on card inserted into card reader and transmitted to ticker.

5   Sale appears on ticker, and confirmation is phoned to account executive, who notifies customer.

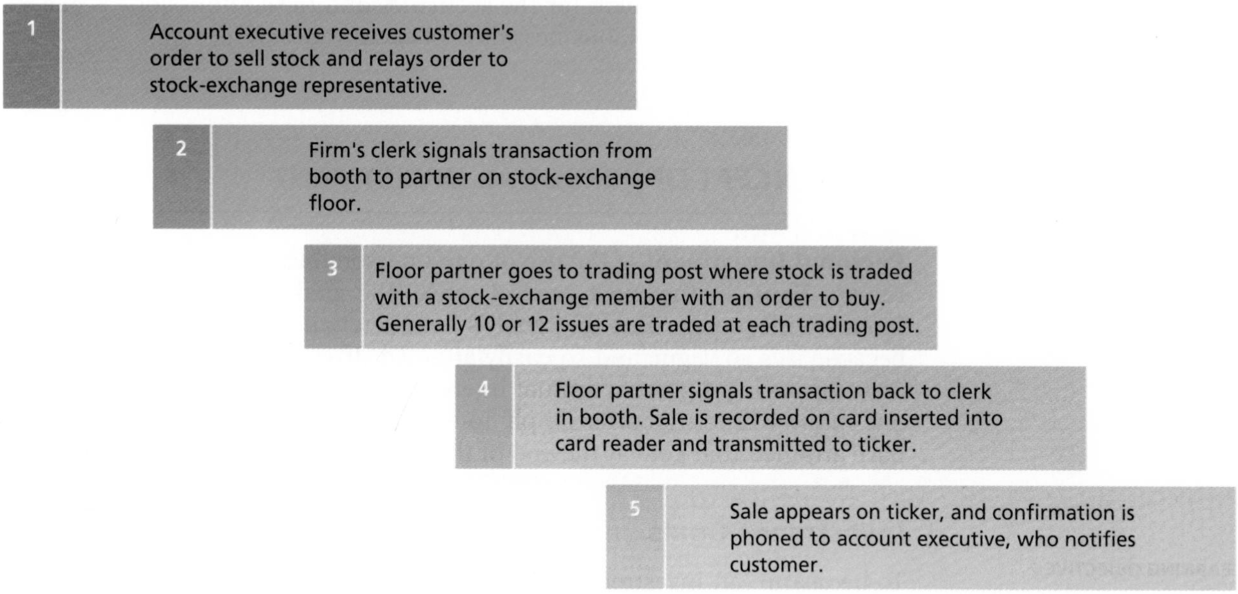

Brokerage Firm	Commissions 100 shares of a $30 stock
Full-Service	
Dean Witter	$84
A.G. Edwards	$83
Edward D. Jones	$87
Merrill Lynch	$86
Paine Webber	$89
Prudential Securities	$90
Shearson Lehman	$83
Smith Barney	$91
Discount	
Charles Schwab	$55
Fidelity	$48
Quick & Reilly	$49

TABLE 19.1
Typical Commissions Charged by Full-Service and Discount Brokers

Source: Joshua Mendes, "Getting the Most from Brokers," *1992 Investor's Guide/Fortune,* © 1991 The Time Inc. Magazine Company. All rights reserved.

shares of a particular stock. Brokerage firms generally charge higher per-share fees for trading in odd lots, primarily because several odd lots must be combined into round lots before they can actually be traded through the exchange.

Commissions for trading bonds, commodities, and options are usually lower than those for trading stocks. The charge for buying or selling a $1,000 corporate bond is typically $10. With the exception of some mutual funds, the investor generally pays a commission when buying *and* when selling securities. Payment for the securities and for commissions is generally required within five business days of each transaction.

THE CONCEPT OF PERSONAL INVESTMENT

personal investment the use of one's personal funds to earn a financial return

Personal investment is the use of one's personal funds to earn a financial return. Thus, in the most general sense, the goal of investing is to earn money with money. But that goal is completely useless for the individual, because it is so vague and so easily attained. If you place $100 in a savings account paying 4 percent annual interest, your money will earn 33 cents in one month. If your goal is simply to earn money with your $100, you will have attained that goal at the end of the month. Then what do you do?

Investment Goals

LEARNING OBJECTIVE 2
Develop a personal investment plan.

To be useful, an investment goal must be specific and measurable. It must be tailored to the individual so that it takes into account his or her particular financial circumstances and needs. It must also be oriented toward the future, because investing is usually a long-term undertaking. Finally, an investment goal must be realistic in terms of the economic conditions that prevail and the investment opportunities that are available.

Some financial planners suggest that investment goals be stated in terms of money: "By January 1, 1999, I will have total assets of $80,000." Others believe that people are more motivated to work toward goals that are stated in terms of the particular things they desire: "By May 1, 1999, I will have accumulated enough money so that I can take a year off from work to travel around the world." Like the goals themselves, the way they are stated depends on the individual.

The following questions can be helpful in establishing valid investment goals.

1. What financial goals do I want to achieve?
2. How much money will I need, and when?
3. Is it reasonable to assume that I can obtain the amount of money I will need to meet my investment goals?
4. Do I expect my personal situation to change in a way that will affect my investment goals?
5. What economic conditions could alter my investment goals?
6. Am I willing to make the necessary sacrifices to ensure that my investment goals are met?
7. What are the consequences if I don't obtain my investment goals?

A Personal Investment Plan

Once you have formulated specific goals, investment planning is similar to planning for a business. If your goals are realistic, investment opportunities will be available to implement them. Investment planning begins with the assessment of these opportunities—including the potential return and risk involved in each. At the very least, this requires some expert advice and careful study. Many investors turn to lawyers, accountants, bankers, or insurance agents. The problem of finding qualified help is compounded by the fact that many people who call themselves "financial planners" are in reality nothing more than salespersons for various financial investments, tax shelters, or insurance plans.

A true financial planner has had at least two years of training in securities, insurance, taxation, real estate, and estate planning and has passed a rigorous examination. As evidence of training and successful completion of the qualifying examination, the Institute of Financial Planners in Denver allows individuals to use the designation Certified Financial Planner (CFP). Similarly, the American College in Bryn Mawr, Pennsylvania, allows individuals who have completed the necessary requirements to use the designation Chartered Financial Consultant (ChFC). Most CFPs and ChFCs don't sell a particular investment product or charge commissions for their investment recommendations. Instead, they charge consulting fees that range from $75 to $125 an hour.

608 Part 6 Finance and Investment

Unattractive numbers. Why was the stock market hitting new highs during the recession of the early 1990s? One reason was that the alternative investments were paying so poorly. Banks lowered long-stable interest rates on their savings accounts, and rates on certificates of deposit and money market funds, popular during more inflationary times, dropped so low that even cautious savers began to put their money elsewhere.

Many financial planners suggest that an investment program should begin with the accumulation of an "emergency fund"—a certain amount of money that can be obtained quickly in case of immediate need. This money should be deposited in a savings account at the highest available interest rate. The amount of money that should be salted away in the emergency fund varies from person to person. However, most financial planners agree that an amount equal to three to six months' living expenses is reasonable.[4]

After the personal emergency account is established, the individual may invest additional funds according to his or her investment plan. Some additional funds may already be available, or money for further investing may be saved out of earnings. In addition to savings, other investment alternatives are chosen by a process of evaluation and elimination and combined into a comprehensive personal investment plan.

Once a plan has been put into operation, the investor must monitor it and, if necessary, modify it. The most successful investors spend hours each week evaluating their own investments and investigating new investment opportunities. An investor's circumstances and economic conditions are both subject to change. Hence all investment programs should be reevaluated regularly.

Four Important Factors in Personal Investment

LEARNING OBJECTIVE 3
Explain how the factors of safety, income, growth, and liquidity affect an individual's investment alternatives.

How can the individual (or a financial planner) tell which investments are "right" for an investment plan and which are not? One way to start is to match potential investments with investment goals in terms of four factors: safety, income, growth, and liquidity.

The Safety Factor Safety in an investment means minimal risk of loss. Investment goals that require a steady increase in value or a fairly certain annual return are those that stress safety. In general, they are implemented with the more conservative investments, such as savings accounts, whose

GETTING AHEAD IN BUSINESS
Measuring Investment Risk

Millions of Americans buy stocks or bonds, purchase mutual funds, or make even more speculative investments. These investments all have one thing in common—investment risk. The following brief quiz, adapted from one prepared by the T. Rowe Price group of mutual funds, can help you as an investor discover how comfortable you are with varying degrees of risk. Other things being equal, your risk tolerance score is a useful guide for decisions about the types of investments you include in a personal financial plan—while also allowing yourself a peaceful night's sleep. A primer on the ABCs of investing is available from T. Rowe Price, 100 East Pratt Street, Baltimore, MD 21202 (800-638-5600).

1. You're the winner on a TV game show. Which prize would you choose?
   - ☐ $2,000 in cash (1 point).
   - ☐ A 50 percent chance to win $4,000 (3 points).
   - ☐ A 20 percent chance to win $10,000 (5 points).
   - ☐ A 2 percent chance to win $100,000 (9 points).
2. You're down $500 in a poker game. How much more would you be willing to put up to win the $500 back?
   - ☐ More than $500 (8 points).
   - ☐ $500 (6 points).
   - ☐ $250 (4 points).
   - ☐ $100 (2 points).
   - ☐ Nothing—you'll cut your losses now (1 point).
3. A month after you invest in a stock, it suddenly goes up 15 percent. With no further information, what would you do?
   - ☐ Hold it, hoping for further gains (3 points).
   - ☐ Sell it and take your gains (1 point).
   - ☐ Buy more—it will probably go higher (4 points).
4. Your investment suddenly goes down 15 percent

one month after you invest. Its fundamentals still look good. What would you do?
   - ☐ Buy more. If it looked good at the original price, it looks even better now (4 points).
   - ☐ Hold on and wait for it to come back (3 points).
   - ☐ Sell it to avoid losing even more (1 point).
5. You're a key employee in a start-up company. You can choose one of two ways to take your year-end bonus. Which would you pick?
   - ☐ $1,500 in cash (1 point).
   - ☐ Company stock options that could bring you $15,000 next year if the company succeeds, but will be worthless if it fails (5 points).

Your total score: _____

Scoring

5–18 points:
More Conservative Investor. You prefer to minimize financial risks. The lower your score, the more cautious you are. When you choose investments, look for high credit ratings, well-established records, and an orientation toward stability. Avoid bonds with the very highest yields; they pay those yields because they involve bigger risks. In stocks and real estate, look for a focus on income.

19–30 points:
Less Conservative Investor. You are willing to take more chances in pursuit of greater rewards. The higher your score, the bolder you are. When you invest, look for high overall returns within the appropriate time category. You may want to consider bonds with the steepest yields and lower credit ratings, the stocks of newer companies, and real estate investments that use mortgage debt.

safety is guaranteed up to $100,000 by the FDIC, SAIF, or NCUA (see Chapter 17).

Other relatively safe investments include highly rated corporate and municipal bonds and the stocks of certain highly regarded corporations—sometimes called "blue-chip stocks." These corporations are generally industry leaders that have provided stable earnings and dividends over a number of years. Examples include Du Pont, Xerox, and General Electric.

To implement goals that stress higher dollar returns on their investments, investors must generally give up some safety. How much risk should they take in exchange for how much return? This question is almost impossible to answer for someone else, because the answer depends so much on the individual and his or her investment goals. However, in general, *the potential return should be directly related to the assumed risk.* That is, the greater the risk assumed by the investor, the greater the potential monetary reward should be.

As we will see shortly, there are a number of risky—and potentially profitable—investments. They include some stocks, commodities, and stock options. The securities issued by new and growing corporations usually fall in this category. When originally sold, the stock of Computer-Tabulating-Recording Company was considered a risky investment. Today the company is known as International Business Machines (IBM), and its stock is part of most conservative investment portfolios.

The Income Factor   Savings accounts, certificates of deposit, corporate and government bonds, and certain stocks pay a predictable amount of interest or dividends each year. Such investments are generally used to implement investment goals that stress periodic income.

Investors in savings accounts, certificates of deposit, and bonds know exactly how much income they will receive each year. The dividends paid to stockholders can and do vary, even for the largest and most stable corporations. However, a number of corporations have built their reputations on a policy of paying dividends every three months. (The firms listed in Table 19.2 have paid dividends to their owners for at least eighty-five years.) The stocks of these corporations are often purchased primarily for income.

TABLE 19.2   Corporations That, Through Mid-1991, Had Made Consecutive Dividend Payments for at Least 85 Years

Corporation	Dividends Since	Type of Business
American Telephone and Telegraph	1881	Telephone utility
Borden, Inc.	1899	Foods
Commonwealth Edison Company	1890	Electric utility
Du Pont (E.I.) de Nemours	1904	Chemicals
Exxon Corporation	1882	Chemical & petroleum products
General Electric Company	1899	Electrical equipment
Norfolk Southern Corp.	1901	Railroad
PPG Industries, Inc.	1899	Glass
Procter & Gamble Company	1891	Soap products

Source: *Standard & Poor's Stock Market Encyclopedia,* August 1991, published by Standard & Poor's Corporation, 25 Broadway, New York, N.Y. 10004. Reprinted with permission.

The Growth Factor To investors, *growth* means that their investments will increase or appreciate in value. For example, a corporation that is in the process of growing usually pays a small cash dividend or no dividend at all. Instead, profits are reinvested in the business (as retained earnings) to finance additional expansion. In this case, the corporation's stockholders receive little or no income from their investments, but the value of their stock increases as the corporation grows.

Investment goals that stress growth, or an increase in the value of the investment, can be implemented by purchasing the stocks of such "growth corporations." During the 1980s, firms in the electronics, energy, and health-care industries showed the greatest growth. They are expected to continue growing in the 1990s. Individual firms within these industries may grow at a slower or faster rate than the industry as a whole—or they may not grow at all.

For investors who carefully choose their investments, both mutual funds and real estate may offer substantial growth possibilities. More speculative investments like strategic metals, gemstones, and collectibles (antiques and paintings) offer less predictable growth possibilities, whereas investments in commodities and stock options usually stress immediate returns as opposed to continued growth. Generally, corporate and government bonds are not purchased for growth.

liquidity the ease with which an asset can be converted into cash

The Liquidity Factor **Liquidity** is the ease with which an asset can be converted into cash. Investments range from cash or cash equivalents (like investments in government securities or money-market accounts) to the other extreme of frozen investments, where it is impossible to get your money. Checking and savings accounts are liquid investments because they can be quickly converted into cash. Another type of bank account—a certificate of deposit—is not as liquid as a checking or savings account. There are penalties for withdrawing money from this type of account before the maturity date.

Although you may be able to sell other investments quickly, you might not regain the amount of money you originally invested because of market conditions, economic conditions, or many other reasons. For example, the owner of real estate may have to lower the asking price to find a buyer for a property. Finding a buyer for investments in certain types of collectibles may also be difficult.

Different kinds of investments offer different combinations of safety, income, growth, and liquidity. Keep the nature of this important "mix" in mind as we consider the following investment alternatives.

TRADITIONAL INVESTMENT ALTERNATIVES

LEARNING OBJECTIVE 4
Identify the advantages and disadvantages of the traditional investment alternatives: savings accounts, bonds, stocks, mutual funds, and real estate.

In this section and the next, we look at some investments that are available to investors. A number of the investments listed in Table 19.3 have already been discussed. Others have only been mentioned and will be examined in more detail. Still others may be completely new to you.

Traditional	High risk
Bank accounts	Buying stock on margin
Corporate and government bonds	Selling short
Common stock	Trading in commodities
Preferred stock	Trading in options
Mutual funds	
Real estate	

TABLE 19.3
Investment Alternatives
Traditional investments involve less risk than high-risk investments.

Bank Accounts

Bank accounts that pay interest—and are therefore investments—include passbook savings accounts, certificates of deposit, and NOW accounts. These were discussed in Chapter 17. They are the most conservative of all investments, and they provide safety and either income or growth. That is, the interest paid on bank accounts can be withdrawn to serve as income, or it can be left on deposit to earn additional interest and increase the size of the bank account.

Figure 19.3 illustrates the concept of compound interest, which is a feature of most savings accounts and certificates of deposit. As illustrated in Figure 19.3, an initial $5,000 deposit invested at 5 percent is worth $8,144 at the end of ten years. The depositor has received $3,144 in interest over a ten-year period of time as a result of letting the interest compound and grow. A word of caution: Both the time the money is on deposit and the interest rate can affect the dollar value the depositor receives at the end of a specified time.

Corporate and Government Bonds

In Chapter 18 we discussed the issuing of bonds by corporations to obtain financing. The U.S. government and state and local governments also issue bonds, for the same reason. In addition, many government and municipal bonds are tax free, which enables owners to earn income that is exempt from federal income taxes. Both corporate and government bonds may be purchased through brokers or, in some cases, directly from the issuer.

Because they are a form of long-term debt financing that must be repaid, bonds are generally considered a more conservative investment than either preferred or common stock. But they are less conservative than bank accounts. They are primarily long-term, income-producing investments. Between the time of purchase and the maturity date, the bondholder will receive interest payments—usually every six months—at the stated interest rate. For example, assume you purchase a $1,000 bond issued by Westinghouse Electric and the interest rate for this bond is 9 percent. In this situation, you receive interest of $90 ($1,000 × .09 = $90) a year from the corporation. The interest is paid every six months in $45 installments.

FIGURE 19.3
Investment in a Bank Account
This chart shows how $5,000 will grow, depending on the duration of the deposit and on the rate of interest (when both the original amount—or principal—and the interest payments remain in the account).

FIXED SAVINGS (STARTING BALANCE = $5,000)

Balance at end of year

Rate (%)	1	5	10
5	$5,250	$6,381	$8,144
6	5,300	6,691	8,954
7	5,350	7,013	9,836
8	5,400	7,347	10,795
9	5,450	7,693	11,839
10	5,500	8,053	12,969

Most beginning investors think that a $1,000 bond is always worth $1,000. In reality, the price of corporate and government bonds may fluctuate until the bond's maturity date. Changes in the overall interest rates in the economy are the primary cause of most bond price fluctuations. For example, when overall interest rates in the economy are rising, the market value of existing bonds typically declines. They may then be purchased for less than their face value. By holding such bonds until maturity, or until interest rates decline (causing the bond's market value to increase), bond owners can realize some profit through the growth of their investments.

Convertible bonds generally carry a lower interest rate than nonconvertible bonds—by about 1 to 2 percent. In return for accepting a lower interest rate, holders of convertible bonds have the opportunity to benefit through investment growth. For example, assume an investor purchases a $1,000 corporate bond that is convertible to 40 shares of the company's common stock. This means the investor could convert the bond to common stock whenever the price of the company's stock is $25 (1,000 ÷ 40 = $25) or higher. In reality, there is no guarantee that bondholders will convert to common stock even if the market value of the common stock does increase to $25 or higher. The reason for not exercising the conversion feature is quite simple. As the market value of the common stock increases, the price of the convertible bond also increases. By not converting to common stock, bondholders enjoy interest income from the bond in addition to increased bond value caused by the price movement of the common stock.

The safety of a particular bond issued by a particular firm or government depends very much on the financial strength of the issuer. For example, in 1983, Washington Public Power Supply was unable to pay off its debt on municipal bonds worth more than $2 billion, and thousands of investors lost money. Several years ago, New York City was on the verge of *defaulting* on (failing to redeem) an issue of bonds that was about to mature. Strong financial measures and new loans saved the city and the bondholders, but the experience affected the market value of all New York City bonds. Recently, financial planners have warned that the number of

to provide the holders of preferred stocks with safety and a predictable income.

In addition, owners of preferred stock may also gain through special features offered with some preferred stock issues. First, owners of *cumulative* preferred stocks are assured that omitted dividends will be paid to them before common stockholders receive any dividends. Second, owners of *participating* preferred stock may earn more than the specified dividend if the firm has a good year. The participating feature enables preferred stockholders to share in surplus profit, along with common stockholders, after the designated amounts have been paid to both classes of stockholders. Finally, owners of *convertible* preferred stock may profit through growth as well as from dividends. Thus, if the value of a firm's common stock increases, the market value of its convertible preferred stock also grows. Convertibility allows the owner of convertible preferred stock to combine the lower risk of preferred stock with the possibility of greater speculative gain through conversion to common stock.

Mutual Funds

mutual fund   a professionally managed investment vehicle that combines and invests the funds of many individual investors

A **mutual fund** combines and invests the funds of many investors, under the guidance of a professional manager. The major advantages of a mutual fund are its professional management and its *diversification*, or investment in a wide variety of securities. Diversification spells safety, because an occasional loss incurred with one security is usually offset by gains from other investments.

Mutual-Fund Shares and Fees   A *closed-end* mutual fund sells shares (in the fund) to investors only when the fund is originally organized. And only a specified number of shares are made available at that time. Once all the shares are sold, an investor can purchase shares only from some other investor who is willing to sell them. The mutual fund itself is under no obligation to buy back shares from investors. Shares of closed-end mutual funds are traded on the floor of stock exchanges.

An *open-end* mutual fund issues and sells new shares to any investor who requests them. It also buys back shares from investors who wish to sell all or part of their holdings. Investors are free to buy and sell shares at the net asset value plus a small commission. The **net asset value (NAV)** per share is equal to the current market value of the mutual fund's portfolio minus the mutual fund's liabilities, divided by the number of outstanding shares. For most mutual funds, NAV is calculated at least once a day and is reported in newspapers and financial publications.

net asset value (NAV)   current market value of the mutual fund's portfolio minus the mutual fund's liabilities, divided by the number of outstanding shares

With regard to costs, there are three types of mutual funds: load, low-load, and no-load funds. An individual who invests in a *load fund* pays a sales charge every time he or she purchases shares. This charge is typically 7 to 8.5 percent of the investment. A low-load fund, as the name implies, charges a lower commission than a load fund. Commissions for low-load funds range between 1 and 3 percent of the investment. The purchaser of shares in a *no-load fund* pays no sales charges at all. No-load funds offer the same type of investment opportunities that load funds and low-load

ETHICAL CHALLENGES
Legal Problems at First Investors Corporation

According to Margaret and Don Blackwell, their mutual fund investment was one of the biggest disappointments in their lives. In May 1989, they invested $84,000—over half of their family's savings—in First Investors Corporation's Fund for Income. Two years later, their investment was worth less than $55,000. What went wrong?

WHY PEOPLE CHOSE FIRST INVESTORS

The Blackwells weren't the only ones who lost money by investing in First Investors' Fund for Income or the firm's High Yield Fund. In fact, First Investors had more than 270,000 clients, who may lose a total of $500 million. According to clients, sales agents for First Investors Corporation made promises that just weren't true. For example, clients were told they couldn't lose, because the investments in the fund were government insured. Still other clients were led to believe that the 12 to 14 percent yields on these two funds were guaranteed.

TWO STATES FILED LAWSUITS AGAINST FIRST INVESTORS

Based on a large number of complaints and preliminary evidence, the states of New York and Massachusetts filed fraud charges against First Investors Corporation and seven of its top executives. The lawsuit claimed that First Investors used misleading sales tactics that targeted inexperienced investors. The suit also claimed that the firm failed to disclose the fact that both funds invested heavily in volatile junk bonds issued by corporations with questionable investment ratings. According to Robert Abrams, the New York attorney general, "These were the junkiest of the junk bonds, yet investors who asked specific questions about them were lied to."*

FIRST INVESTORS' RESPONSE

In a brief statement, First Investors said, "The two states' claims are 'without merit. The company will vigorously defend itself, and is confident that it will prevail.'"** According to company officials, information about the type of investments in each fund was available to clients. They also noted that there are two risks associated with junk bond investments. First, investors must consider the risk of default—junk bonds are less likely to be repaid at maturity. Second, there is an increased risk that interest payments on junk bonds will not be made. If either of these risks becomes a reality, the value of shares in a mutual fund with junk bond investments will decrease. Finally, the company was quick to point out, the reason mutual funds with junk bonds provide high yields is because of the risk involved.

Issues to Consider

1. When selling shares in a mutual fund, to what extent is a firm like First Investors Corporation obligated to tell clients about potential investment risks?

2. If you were a manager at First Investors, what could you do to ensure that the sales agents in your department were acting ethically?

3. Ironically, many financial analysts are beginning to recommend some high-quality, junk-bond mutual funds. Based on what you have learned, would you invest in a junk-bond mutual fund?

*Richard Behar, "At the End of Milken's Junk-food Chain," *Time*, December 3, 1990, p. 84.

**Jonathan Clements, "Two States Sue to Recover Huge Losses on Junk Funds," the *Wall Street Journal*, November 9, 1990, p. C1.

Thus, investors can presently borrow up to half the cost of a stock purchase. But why would they want to do so? Simply because they can buy twice as much stock by buying on margin. Suppose an investor expects the market price of a certain stock to increase in the next month or two. Let's say this investor has enough money to purchase 500 shares of the stock. But if she buys on margin, she can purchase an additional 500 shares. If the price of the stock increases by $5 per share, her profit will be $5 × 500, or $2,500 if she pays cash. But it will be $5 × 1,000, or $5,000 if she buys on margin. That is, by buying her shares on margin, she will earn double the profit (less the interest she pays on the borrowed money and customary commission charges).

leverage   the use of borrowed funds to increase the return on an investment

The use of borrowed funds to increase the return on an investment is called **leverage.** The investor's profit is earned by both the borrowed funds and the investor's own money. The investor retains all the profit and pays interest only for the temporary use of the borrowed funds. Note that the stock purchased on margin serves as collateral for the borrowed funds.

If all goes as expected, investors can increase their profits by using leverage—buying stocks on margin. However, margin investors are subject to two problems. First, if the market price of the purchased stock does not increase as quickly as expected, interest costs mount and eventually drain the investor's profit. Second, if the price of the purchased stock falls, the leverage works against the investor. That is, because the margin investor has purchased twice as much stock, he or she loses twice as much money.

Moreover, any decrease in the value of a stock bought using leverage is considered to come out of the investor's own funds, not out of the borrowed funds. If the stock's market value decreases to approximately half its original price, the investor will receive a *margin call* from the brokerage firm. The investor must then provide additional cash or securities to restore the value of the investor's portion to its original amount. If he or she cannot do so, the stock is sold and the proceeds are used to pay off the loan. Any funds remaining after the loan is paid off are returned to the investor.

Selling Short

buying long   buying stock with the expectation that it will increase in value and can then be sold at a profit

selling short   the process of selling stock that an investor does not actually own but has borrowed from a stockbroker and will repay at a later date

Normally, investors buy stocks expecting that they will increase in value and can then be sold at a profit. This procedure is referred to as **buying long.** However, many securities decrease in value, for various reasons. More risk-oriented investors can use a procedure called *selling short* to make a profit when the price of an individual stock is falling. **Selling short** is the process of selling stock that an investor does not actually own but has borrowed from a stockbroker and will repay at a later date. The idea is to sell at today's higher price and then buy later at a lower price.

To make a profit from a short transaction, the investor must proceed as follows:

1. Arrange to borrow a certain number of shares of a particular stock from a brokerage firm.

2. Sell the borrowed stock immediately, assuming that its price will drop in a reasonably short time.

3. After the price drops, buy the same number of shares that were sold in step 2.

4. Give the newly purchased stock to the brokerage firm in return for the stock borrowed in step 1.

The investor's profit is the difference between the amount received in step 2 and the amount paid in step 3. For example, assume that you think that Sony Corp. stock is overvalued at $40 a share. You also believe the stock will decrease in value over the next three to four months. You call your broker and arrange to borrow 100 shares of Sony stock (step 1). The broker then sells your borrowed Sony stock for you at the current market price of $40 a share (step 2). Also assume that three months later, the Sony stock is selling for $33 a share. You instruct your broker to purchase 100 shares of Sony stock at the lower price (step 3). The newly purchased Sony stock is used to repay the borrowed stock (step 4). In this example, you made $700 by selling short ($4,000 selling price – $3,300 purchase price = $700 profit). Naturally, the $700 profit must be reduced by the commissions you paid to the broker for buying and selling the Sony stock.

People often ask where the broker obtains the stock for a short transaction. The broker probably borrows the stock from other investors who have purchased Sony stock through a margin arrangement or from investors who have left stock certificates on deposit with the brokerage firm. As a result, the person who is selling short must pay any dividends declared on the borrowed stock. The most obvious danger, of course, is that a loss can result if the stock's market value increases instead of decreases. If the market price of the stock increases after the investor has sold it in step 2, he or she loses money.

Trading in Commodities

The ownership of certain commodities (including cattle, hogs, pork bellies, various grains, sugar, coffee, frozen concentrated orange juice, cotton, gold, silver, and copper) is traded on a regular basis through organized exchanges. The world's major commodity exchanges are in New York, London, and Chicago. The buying and selling of commodities for immediate delivery is called **spot trading.** However, most commodities transactions involve a future delivery date. A **futures contract** is an agreement to buy or sell a commodity at a guaranteed price on some specified future date.

spot trading   the buying and selling of commodities for immediate delivery

futures contract   an agreement to buy or sell a commodity at a guaranteed price on some specified future date

Commodity trading is much riskier than trading in securities because prices fluctuate widely. Almost any change in economic conditions, supply and demand, or even the weather affects commodity prices. An unexpected freeze in Florida can cause the price of orange juice futures to soar. An exceptionally good harvest can have the opposite effect on grain and cotton futures. Rumors, natural disasters, and political events can also propel commodity prices upward or downward very quickly. The continual price

Thriving on information. The Chicago Mercantile Exchange, like other investment and exchange markets, depends on reliable, up-to-date information. Computers need to exchange data, customers must be able to talk to brokers, and the Exchange staff must keep in constant touch with colleagues in London and Tokyo. The local telephone company provides a special backup system to make sure all calls go through.

movements and relatively low margin requirements tend to attract numbers of speculators to the commodity markets. These same characteristics make the commodity markets too risky for most investors.

Trading in Options

option   the right to buy or sell a specified amount of stock at a specified price within a certain period of time

An **option** is the right to buy or sell a specified amount of stock at a specified price within a certain period of time. Options are purchased and sold by investors who expect the price of a stock to change.

A *call option* gives the purchaser the right to *buy* 100 shares of a specific stock at a specified price within a specified time. Call options are sold by owners of stock. They are purchased by investors who expect the market price of the stock to increase beyond the amount specified in the call. If this occurs, the call purchaser exercises the call (buys the stock at a specified price) and then sells it on the open market for a profit. If the call purchaser does not exercise the call before it expires, she or he loses the cost of the option.

A *put option* gives the purchaser the right to *sell* 100 shares of a specific stock at a specified price within a specified time. Put options are purchased by investors who expect the market price of the stock to fall below the guaranteed price. If this occurs before the option expires, the put purchaser buys the stock at the lower market price and then sells it at the higher price guaranteed by the put. Again, if the put is not exercised before it expires, the purchaser loses the cost of the option.

Now that we know something about the traditional and high-risk investments that are available, let's take a look at the sources of information that can help you evaluate a potential investment.

SOURCES OF FINANCIAL INFORMATION

LEARNING OBJECTIVE 6
Use the various sources of financial information, especially newspaper stock quotations and stock indexes.

A wealth of information is available to investors. Sources include newspapers, brokerage-firm reports, business periodicals, corporate reports, and investors' services. For example, most local newspapers carry several pages of business news, including reports of securities transactions. The *Wall Street Journal* (published on weekdays) and *Barron's* (published once a week) are devoted almost entirely to financial and economic news. Both include complete coverage of transactions on all major securities exchanges.

Newspaper Coverage of Securities Transactions

Securities transactions are reported as long tables of figures that tend to look somewhat forbidding. However, they are easy to decipher when you know what to look for. Because transactions involving listed stocks, OTC stocks, and bonds are reported differently, we shall examine all three types of reports.

Listed Common and Preferred Stocks   Transactions involving listed common and preferred stocks are reported together in the same table. This table usually looks like the top section of Figure 19.4. Parts of a dollar are traditionally quoted as fractions rather than as cents. Thus ⅛ means $0.125, or 12.5 cents, and ¾ means $0.75, or 75 cents. Stocks are listed alphabetically. Your first task is to move down the table to find the stock you're interested in. Then, to read the transaction report, or *stock quotation*, you read across the table. The last row in the table in Figure 19.4 gives detailed information about General Electric Co. (Each numbered entry in the list above the enlarged stock table refers to a numbered column of the stock table.)

If a corporation has more than one stock issue, the common stock is always listed first. Preferred stock, as indicated by the letters *pf* in the stock column, is listed below the firm's common stock issue.

Over-the-Counter Stocks   Financial information about stocks traded in the over-the-counter stock market is reported in one of two ways. Current financial information may be reported in tables just like the one illustrated in Figure 19.4. A second method is illustrated in Figure 19.5. When this format is used, less information about a particular over-the-counter stock is given, but relevant information about a stock's volume, bid price, asked

FIGURE 19.4
Reading Stock Quotations for Listed Common Stocks
At the top of the figure, a portion of the stock quotations for the New York Stock Exchange as reported by the *Wall Street Journal* is reproduced. The same information is enlarged at the bottom of the figure. The itemized list in the middle is used to explain what the numbers in each column of the figure mean. *(Source: Newspaper at top of figure is the* Wall Street Journal, *February 5, 1992, p. C4. Reprinted by permission of the* Wall Street Journal, © *1992 Dow Jones & Company, Inc. All rights reserved worldwide.)*

52 Weeks Hi	Lo	Stock	Sym	Div	Yld %	PE	Vol 100s	Hi	Lo	Close	Net Chg
↓x 13½	7¼	GenCorp	GY	.60	4.4	14	x2507	13⅞	13	13½	+ ½
36¼	24⅜	Genentech	GNE		...	70	3439	27½	26¾	27⅛	+ ⅝
29⅞	18¾	GenAmInv	GAM	3.16e	11.3	...	446	28	27⅝	28	+ ¼
24¾	16½	GenCinema	GCN	.52	2.7	...	1561	20	19¼	19⅜	− ½
4	2⅛	GenData	GDC		...	67	734	4	3⅞	4	+ ⅛
61½	23⅝	GenDynam	GD	1.00	1.7	7	1049	58¾	58	58⅜	− ⅜
80¾	62	GenElec	GE	2.20	2.9	15	11365	77⅛	75⅝	76⅞	+ ⅞

1. Highest price paid for one share of General Electric during the past 52 weeks: $80¾
2. Lowest price paid for one share of General Electric during the past 52 weeks: $62
3. Abbreviated name of the company: GenElec
4. Ticker symbol or letters that identify a stock for trading: GE
5. Total dividends paid per share during the last 12 months: $2.20
6. Yield percentage, or the percentage of return based on the current dividend and current price of the stock: $2.20 ÷ $76.875 = .029 = 2.9%
7. Price-earnings (PE) ratio—the price of a share of stock divided by the corporation's earnings per share of stock outstanding over the last 12 months: 15 ("..." indicates that the company is operating at a loss and there are no earnings.)
8. Number of shares of General Electric traded during the day, expressed in hundreds of shares: 1,136,500
9. Highest price paid for one share of General Electric during the day: $77⅛, or $77.125
10. Lowest price paid for one share of General Electric during the day: $75⅝, or $75.625
11. Price paid in the last transaction of the day: $76⅞, or $76.875
12. Difference between the price paid for the last share today and the price paid for the last share on the previous day: ⅞, or $0.875 (In Wall Street terms, General Electric "closed up ⅞" on this day.)

1	2	3	4	5	6	7	8	9	10	11	12
52 Weeks Hi	Lo	Stock	Sym	Div	Yld %	PE	Vol 100s	Hi	Lo	Close	Net Chg
13½	7¼	GenCorp	GY	.60	4.4	14	x2507	13⅞	13	13½	+ ½
36¼	24⅜	Genentech	GNE		...	70	3439	27½	26¾	27⅛	+ ⅝
29⅞	18¾	GenAmInv	GAM	3.16e	11.3	...	446	28	27⅝	28	+ ¼
24¾	16½	GenCinema	GCN	.52	2.7	...	1561	20	19¼	19⅜	- ½
4	2⅛	GenData	GDC		...	67	734	4	3⅞	4	+ ⅛
61½	23⅝	GenDynam	GD	1.00	1.7	7	1049	58¾	58	58⅜	- ⅜
80¾	62	GenElec	GE	2.20	2.9	15	11365	77⅛	75⅝	76⅞	+ ⅞

price, and net change is reported. Thus, for American Education common stock, Figure 19.5 shows that 3,100 shares were traded on this day. The first price, or *bid price,* is the price a buyer has offered to pay for one share of a particular stock. The *asked price* is the price at which a seller offered to sell one share of a particular stock. American Education had a bid price of $4 and an asked price of $4¾ or $4.75. In addition to price, the table includes information about current dividends and net change.

Bonds Purchases and sales of bonds are reported in tables like that shown at the top of Figure 19.6. In bond quotations, prices are given as a percentage of the face value, which is usually $1,000. Thus, to find the actual price paid, you must multiply the face value ($1,000) by the quotation listed in

Stock & Div	Sales 100s	Bid	Asked	Net Chg.
AAcft	5663	7/8	31/32	−15/32
AmAset	1	2 3/8	2 7/8	...
AmBio	552	3	3 1/8	...
AmBiogn	704	10 7/8	11 1/8	+ 7/8
ABiog wtB	727	6 1/4	6 1/2	+ 1
AmBiom	50	11 3/8	12	...
AmBio wt	105	3 1/4	3 3/4	...
ABsCpt	268	2 1/8	2 3/8	...
AmDrg	309	3 1/8	3 1/4	− 1/16
AmEduc	31	4	4 3/4	− 1/2

1. Abbreviated name of the company and dividends, if any, paid by the company during the last 12 months
2. Number of shares traded during the day, expressed in hundreds of shares
3. Amount a seller could receive for a share of stock
4. Amount for which a buyer could purchase a share of stock
5. Difference between the bid price today and the bid price on the previous day

1	2	3	4	5
Stock & Div	Vol. 100s	Bid	Asked	Net Chg.
AAcft	5663	7/8	31/32	− 15/32
AmAset	1	2 3/8	2 7/8	...
AmBio	552	3	3 1/8	...
AmBiogn	704	10 7/8	11 1/8	+ 7/8
ABiog wtB	727	6 1/4	6 1/2	+ 1
AmBiom	50	11 3/8	12	...
AmBio wt	105	3 1/4	3 3/4	...
ABsCpt	268	2 1/8	2 3/8	...
AmDrg	309	3 1/8	3 1/4	− 1/16
AmEduc	31	4	4 3/4	− 1/2

FIGURE 19.5 Reading Stock Quotations for Over-the-Counter Stocks
At the top of Figure 19.5, a portion of the stock quotations for over-the-counter stocks as reported by the *Wall Street Journal* is reproduced. The same information is enlarged at the bottom of the figure. The itemized list at the top on the right side is used to explain what the numbers in each column of the figure mean. *(Source: Newspaper at the top of the figure is the* Wall Street Journal, *February 5, 1992, p. C6. Reprinted by permission of the* Wall Street Journal, *© 1992 Dow Jones & Company, Inc. All rights reserved worldwide.)*

the newspaper. For example, a price quoted as 84 translates to a selling price of $840 ($1,000 × 84 percent = $840). The last row of Figure 19.6 gives detailed information (again, by column number) for the Eastman Kodak Corporation bond that pays 8⅝ percent interest and matures in 2016.

Other Sources of Financial Information

In addition to newspaper coverage, other sources offer detailed and varied information about investment alternatives. Typical sources of information include brokerage-firm reports, business periodicals, corporate reports, and investors' services.

Brokerage-Firm Reports Brokerage firms employ financial analysts to prepare detailed reports on individual corporations and their securities. Such reports are based on the corporation's sales, earnings, management, and planning, plus other information on the company, its industry, and

- A *utility average,* computed from the prices of fifteen utility stocks
- A *composite average,* computed from the prices of the sixty-five stocks included in the industrial, transportation, and utility averages

The Standard & Poor's 500 Stock Index and the New York Stock Exchange Index include more stocks than the Dow Jones averages. Thus they tend to reflect the stock market more fully. The *Standard & Poor's 500 Stock Index* is an average of the prices of 400 industrial, sixty transportation and utility, and forty financial stocks. The *New York Stock Exchange Composite Index* is computed from the prices of all stocks listed on the NYSE, weighted to reflect the number and value of outstanding shares.

It should be apparent that vast sums of money are involved in securities trading. In an effort to protect investors from unfair treatment, both federal and state governments have acted to regulate securities trading.

REGULATION OF SECURITIES TRADING

LEARNING OBJECTIVE 7
Explain how federal and state authorities regulate trading in securities.

Government regulation of securities trading began as a response to abusive and fraudulent practices in the sale of stocks and bonds. The states were the first to react, early in this century. Later, federal legislation was passed to regulate the interstate sale of securities.

State Regulation

The first state law regulating the sale of securities was enacted in Kansas in 1911. Within a few years, several other states had passed similar laws. Today, most states require that new issues be registered with a state agency and that brokers and securities dealers operating within the state be licensed. The states also provide for the prosecution of individuals accused of the fraudulent sale of stocks, bonds, and other securities.

blue-sky laws   state laws that regulate securities trading

The state laws that regulate securities trading are often called **blue-sky laws.** They are designed to protect investors from purchasing securities backed up by nothing but the "clear blue sky."

Federal Regulation

The *Securities Act of 1933,* sometimes referred to as the *Truth in Securities Act,* provides for full disclosure of important facts about corporations issuing new securities. Such corporations are required to file a *registration statement* containing specific information about the corporation's earnings, assets, and liabilities; its products or services; and the qualifications of its top management. Publication of the prospectus is also a requirement of this act.

GLOBAL PERSPECTIVES
Should You Invest in Global Securities?

Only a few years ago, putting your money in a foreign investment was like betting on the horses or playing the slot machines in Las Vegas. Today, many financial analysts suggest that there are at least two reasons why you should consider placing 10 to 30 percent of your assets in global investments.

PERFORMANCE AND REDUCED RISK

While the U.S. stock market had a total return of 325 percent during the 1980s, at least eleven foreign stock markets outperformed the U.S. market. In fact, stock markets in both Japan and Sweden had returns in excess of 1,100 percent. Even the stock market in Great Britain had more than a 400 percent increase during this same period.

Second, it may be possible to reduce risks if you choose the right global investments. Simply put, what drives the U.S. economy is often different from what drives the economy in a foreign nation. By diversifying with global investments, you may be able to reduce your losses should the U.S. economy take a nosedive.

GLOBAL INVESTMENT ALTERNATIVES

An investor who wants to go international has a choice between purchasing shares of stock in individual foreign firms or shares in a global mutual fund. Most financial analysts recommend global mutual funds for small investors with less than $200,000 to invest. In the United States there are more than one hundred stock funds and more than fifty bond funds that invest partly or entirely abroad. And there are more than forty funds that invest in stocks of a single nation or geographic region.

A WORD OF CAUTION

Investors who want to go international must evaluate foreign investments just as they would U.S. investments. Evaluating foreign firms may be even more difficult because reliable accounting information on foreign firms is often scarce. Of course, you can get an annual report, but you won't know if the foreign firm uses the same accounting procedures used by U.S. firms.

It is usually easier to obtain reliable information about global mutual funds. Typically, you can obtain a prospectus, an annual report, and other information by calling a toll-free telephone number. *Forbes, Kiplinger's Personal Finance Magazine, Money,* and other financial magazines also provide information about global mutual fund investments. An additional source of information is the list of funds investing in specific foreign countries, published each week in *Barron's,* in the Monday edition of the *Wall Street Journal,* and in the Saturday edition of the *New York Times.*

Securities and Exchange Commission (SEC)   the agency that enforces federal securities regulations

The *Securities Exchange Act of 1934* created the **Securities and Exchange Commission (SEC),** which is the agency that enforces federal securities regulations. The operations of the SEC are directed by five commissioners, who are appointed by the president of the United States. The 1934 act gave the SEC the power to regulate trading on all national securities exchanges. It also requires that corporations' registration statements be brought up to date periodically. Finally, this act requires brokers and securities dealers to register with the SEC.

Eight other federal acts have been passed primarily to protect investors:

National Association of Securities Dealers (NASD)   the organization responsible for the self-regulation of the over-the-counter securities market

- The *Maloney Act of 1938* made it possible to establish the **National Association of Securities Dealers (NASD)** to oversee the self-regulation of the over-the-counter securities market.
- The *Investment Company Act of 1940* placed investment companies that sell mutual funds under the jurisdiction of the SEC.
- The *Investment Advisers Act of 1940* required financial advisors with more than fifteen clients to register with the SEC.
- The *Federal Securities Act of 1964* extended the SEC's jurisdiction to include companies whose stock is sold over the counter, if they have total assets of at least $1 million or have more than 500 stockholders of any one class of stock.
- The *Securities Investor Protection Act of 1970* created the *Securities Investor Protection Corporation (SIPC).* The SIPC provides insurance of up to $500,000 for securities and up to $100,000 for cash left on deposit with a brokerage firm that later fails. The SIPC is, in essence, the securities-market equivalent of the FDIC and the SAIF (discussed in Chapter 17).
- The *Securities Amendments Act of 1975* empowered the SEC to supervise the development of a national securities market system. In addition, the law prohibited fixed commissions.
- The *Insider Trading Sanctions Act of 1984* strengthened the penalty provisions of the Securities Exchange Act of 1934. Under the 1984 act, people are guilty of insider trading if they use information that is available only to account executives or other brokerage-firm employees. This act also expanded the SEC's authority by empowering it to investigate such illegal acts.
- The *Insider Trading and Securities Fraud Enforcement Act of 1988* made the top management of brokerage firms responsible for reporting to the SEC any transaction that was based on inside information. In addition, this act empowered the SEC to levy fines of up to $1 million for failure to report such trading violations.

In Chapter 20, we discuss the protection of finances and other assets from the hazards involved in simply existing. As you will see, these hazards include fire, theft, accident, and the legal liability for injury to others. The potential effect of hazards on firms and individuals can be minimized through effective risk management.

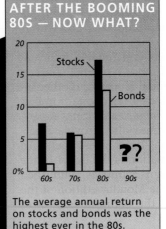

AT A GLANCE

AFTER THE BOOMING 80S — NOW WHAT?

The average annual return on stocks and bonds was the highest ever in the 80s.

SOURCE: *Ibbotson Associates*

CHAPTER REVIEW

Summary

Stocks may be purchased in either the primary or the secondary market. The primary market is a market in which an investor purchases financial securities (via an investment bank or other representative) directly from the issuer of those securities. Usually, an investment banking firm—an organization that assists corporations in raising funds—is involved in the marketing and distribution process. A corporation can also obtain equity financing by selling securities directly to current stockholders.

The secondary market involves transactions for existing securities that are currently traded between investors and are usually bought and sold through a securities exchange or the over-the-counter market. Securities exchanges are marketplaces where members buy and sell securities for their clients. The New York Stock Exchange is the largest in the United States; it accounts for about 50 percent of stock bought and sold in the United States. Other securities exchanges include the American Stock Exchange and several regional exchanges. The over-the-counter market is a network of account executives (stockbrokers) who buy and sell the securities that are not traded in exchanges. If you invest in securities, chances are that you will use the services of an account executive who works for a brokerage firm. Most full-service account executives not only process your orders to buy and sell securities but also provide valuable information and advice. For these services, they are paid a commission based on the size and value of the transaction. An investor should choose an account executive who is ethical, compatible, and able to provide the level of service required by the investor.

Personal-investment planning begins with formulating measurable and realistic investment goals. A personal investment plan is then designed to implement those goals. Many financial planners suggest, as a first step, that the investor establish an emergency fund equivalent to three to six months' living expenses. Then additional funds may be invested according to the investment plan. Finally, all investments should be carefully monitored and, if necessary, the investment plan should be modified.

Depending on their particular investment goals, investors seek varying degrees of safety, income, growth, and liquidity from their investments. Safety is, in essence, freedom from the risk of loss. Generally, the greater the risk, the greater should be the potential return on an investment. Income is the periodic return from an investment. Growth is an increase in the value of the investment. Liquidity is defined as the ease with which an asset can be converted into cash.

Among the traditional investment alternatives are bank accounts, corporate bonds, government bonds, common stock, preferred stock, mutual funds, and real estate. High-risk investment techniques can provide greater returns, but they entail greater risk of loss. They include buying stock on margin, selling short, and trading in commodities and options.

Information on securities and the firms that issue them can be obtained from newspapers, brokerage-firm reports, business periodicals, corporate reports, and investors' services. Most local newspapers report daily securities transactions and stock indexes, or averages. The averages indicate price trends but reveal nothing about the performance of individual stocks.

State and federal regulations protect investors from unscrupulous securities trading practices. Federal laws, which are enforced by the Securities and Exchange Commission, require the registration of new securities, the publication and distribution of prospectuses, and the registration of brokers and securities dealers. These laws apply to securities listed on the national security exchanges, to mutual funds, and to some OTC stocks.

Key Terms

You should now be able to define and give an example relevant to each of the following terms:

primary market	stock dividend
investment banking firm	market value
secondary market	bull market
securities exchange	bear market
over-the-counter (OTC) market	stock split
	mutual fund
account executive (or stockbroker)	net asset value (NAV)
	high-risk investment
market order	margin requirement
limit order	leverage
discretionary order	buying long
round lot	selling short
odd lot	spot trading
personal investment	futures contract
liquidity	

option
prospectus
stock average (or stock index)
blue-sky laws

Securities and Exchange Commission (SEC)
National Association of Securities Dealers (NASD)

Questions and Exercises

Review Questions

1. What is the difference between the primary market and the secondary market?
2. When a corporation decides to sell stock, what is the role of an investment banking firm?
3. What is the difference between a securities exchange and the over-the-counter market?
4. What steps are involved in purchasing a stock listed on the NYSE?
5. What steps are involved in developing a personal investment plan?
6. What is an investment "emergency fund," and why is it recommended?
7. What is meant by the safety of an investment? What is the tradeoff between safety and return on the investment?
8. In general, what kinds of investments provide income? What kinds provide growth?
9. How can the interest on savings accounts be used either as income or for growth?
10. Characterize the purchase of corporate bonds as an investment, in terms of safety, income, growth, and liquidity.
11. How does a stock dividend differ from a stock split from an investor's point of view?
12. An individual may invest in stocks either directly or through a mutual fund. How are the two investment methods different?
13. What are the risks and rewards of purchasing stocks on margin?
14. When would a speculator sell short? buy a call option? buy a put option?
15. In what ways are newspaper stock quotations useful to investors? In what ways are stock averages useful?
16. What is the Securities and Exchange Commission? What are its principal functions?

Discussion Questions

1. In less than twenty years, Charles Schwab and Company has become the largest discount brokerage firm in the world. What factors have made this firm successful in such a short time?

2. Assume that you want to invest $7,500 in Disney common stock. Would you prefer a discount brokerage firm like Charles Schwab or a full-service brokerage firm. Why?
3. What personal circumstances might lead some investors to emphasize income rather than growth in their investment planning? What might lead them to emphasize growth rather than income?
4. Suppose you have just inherited 500 shares of IBM common stock. What would you do with or about it, if anything?
5. For what reasons might a corporation's executives be *unwilling* to have their firm's securities listed on an exchange?
6. What kinds of information would you like to have before you invest in a particular common or preferred stock? From what sources can you get that information?
7. Federal laws prohibit corporate managers from making investments that are based on "inside information"—that is, special knowledge about their firms that is not available to the general public. Why are such laws needed?

Exercises

1. Using recent newspaper stock quotations, fill in the following table for common stocks only.

Newspaper: _____

Date: _____

	Dividend	P-E Ratio	Closing Price	Net Change
American Express (AmExpress)	_____	_____	_____	_____
General Dynamics (GenDynam)	_____	_____	_____	_____
General Motors (GenMotors)	_____	_____	_____	_____

a. Which of the three stocks would be the best investment for someone whose investment plan stresses income? Why?
b. Which stock would seem to be best for an investment plan that stresses growth? (If you need more information to answer this, explain what information you need.)
c. Can you tell from this information which stock offers the most safety? Explain.

2. Municipal bonds (those issued by cities) generally pay a lower rate of interest than corporate bonds. Through library research, determine why this is so—and why municipal bonds are still attractive to investors.

CASE 19.1

Bond Choices: Chiquita or Amoco?

Are bonds safer than common or preferred stock? The answer to that question depends on such factors as who issued the bond, the likelihood the bond will be repaid at maturity, the conditions contained in the bond agreement, and the future outlook for the firm or government agency that issued the bond. Most investors rely on two financial services, Standard & Poor's Corporation and Moody's Investors Service, to provide ratings for corporate bonds. Standard & Poor's bond ratings range from *AAA* (the highest) to *D* (the lowest). Moody's bond ratings range from *Aaa* (the highest) to *C* (the lowest). For most investors, a bond rated *A* or better is probably as safe as a blue-chip stock, whereas a bond rated *B* or lower could be as risky as the most speculative stock. Bonds that receive the *C* and *D* rating are bonds of poor standing. Such issues may be in default and may include issues where the company is behind on either interest, principal repayment, or both.

A large number of corporations have sold bonds to provide debt financing for expansion, research and development, debt retirement, or many other reasons. From the investor's standpoint, these bond issues range from ultraconservative to extremely speculative investments. Financial information about two such bond issues is provided below.

Chiquita Brands International
Face value—$1,000
Maturity date—2003
Interest rate—11.875%
Current market price— $1,050
Current yield—11.2%

Amoco Corporation
Face value—$1,000
Maturity date—2005
Interest rate—8.38%
Current market price— $1,008
Current yield—8.3%

Chiquita Brands International is a leading marketer, producer, and processor of fresh fruits and vegetables. The company has demonstrated its ability to earn profit over the last ten years. In fact, the company earned record profits of $93 million in 1990. Earnings per share were $2.23, and during this particular year the company paid $0.35 per share in dividends to shareholders. The Moody's rating for the Chiquita

Brands bond is *Ba*, which means that it is a speculative bond when compared with more conservative bond issues, and the Standard and Poor's rating for this bond is *BB*, which stands for speculative bond issues.

The Amoco Corporation is a leading petroleum and chemical company with worldwide operations in more than forty different countries. This company also has a history of profits over the last ten years. In 1990 (the last year for which complete financial information is available), Amoco earned $1.9 billion on sales revenues of $31.6 billion. Earnings per share were $3.77, and during this particular year the company paid $2.04 per share in dividends to shareholders. According to Moody's, the Amoco bond is rated *Aaa*, which means this bond is judged to be of the highest quality. The Standard and Poor's rating for this bond is *AAA*—the highest rating assigned for any corporation issuing bonds.*

Questions

1. How important are the bond ratings issued by Moody's and Standard & Poor's?
2. The 11.2 percent current yield for the Chiquita Brands bond is almost 3 percent higher than the current yield for the Amoco bond. Is the additional 3 percent worth the added risks involved in purchasing the lower-rated Chiquita Brands bond?
3. The Chiquita Brands bond matures in 2003; the Amoco bond matures in 2005. As the maturity dates approach, what should happen to the market price of each bond? Why?
4. What other information would you need to evaluate these two bonds? Where would you get this information?

*Based on information from *Standard and Poor's Bond Guide*, December 1991, Standard & Poor's Corporation, Publishers, 25 Broadway, New York, NY 10004; *Barron's*, October 28, 1991, pp. 109, 111; *Moody's Handbook of Common Stock*, Fall 1991, Moody's Investors Service, 99 Church Street, New York, NY 10007; *Moody's Bond Record*, September 1991, Moody's Investors Service, 99 Church Street, New York, NY 10007; Geoffrey A. Hirt and Stanley B. Block, *Fundamentals of Investment Management* (Homewood, Ill.: Richard D. Irwin, 1990), p. 310; and John Paul Newport, Jr., "Junk Bonds Face the Big Unknown," *Fortune*, May 22, 1989, pp. 129–130.

CASE 19.2

General Motors Corporation

In this chapter, we have stressed the importance of evaluating potential investments. Now, it's your turn to

FIGURE 19.7
Research Report on General Motors Corporation
Detailed financial information about most major corporations is available from companies like Moody's Investors Service. *(Source:* Moody's Handbook of Common Stocks, *Summer, 1991 ed., Moody's Investors Service, 99 Church Street, New York, NY 10007. Tel (212) 553-0300. Used by permission.)*

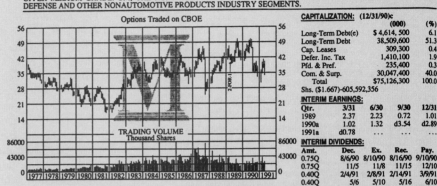

GENERAL MOTORS CORPORATION

LISTED	SYM.	LTPS♦	STPS♦	IND. DIV.	REC. PRICE	RANGE (52-WKS.)	YLD.
NYSE	GM	81.9	86.5	$1.60*	36	51 - 30	4.4%

UPPER MEDIUM GRADE. GM, THE NO. 1 AUTO MAKER, ALSO PRODUCES PRODUCTS AND SERVICES IN THE DEFENSE AND OTHER NONAUTOMOTIVE PRODUCTS INDUSTRY SEGMENTS.

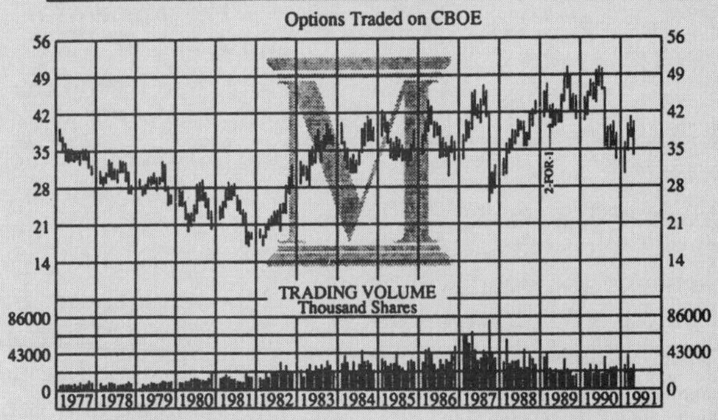

CAPITALIZATION: (12/31/90)c

	(000)	(%)
Long-Term Debt(e)	$ 4,614, 500	6.1
Long-Term Debt	38,509,600	51.3
Cap. Leases	309,300	0.4
Defer. Inc. Tax	1,410,100	1.9
Pfd. & Pref.	235,400	0.3
Com. & Surp.	30,047,400	40.0
Total	$75,126,300	100.0

Shs. ($1.667)-605,592,356

INTERIM EARNINGS:

Qtr.	3/31	6/30	9/30	12/31
1989	2.37	2.23	0.72	1.01
1990a	1.02	1.32	d3.54	d2.89
1991a	d0.78	...	...	...

INTERIM DIVIDENDS:

Amt.	Dec.	Ex.	Rec.	Pay.
0.75Q	8/6/90	8/10/90	8/16/90	9/10/90
0.75Q	11/5	11/8	11/15	12/10
0.40Q	2/4/91	2/8/91	2/14/91	3/9/91
0.40Q	5/6	5/10	5/16	6/10

BACKGROUND:

General Motors Corporation is the world's largest auto maker operating through its Chevrolet, Pontiac, Cadillac, Buick, Oldsmobile, GMC Truck and internationally via Holden, OPEL and Vauxhall. GMAC operates the financial and insurance segment of the Company. The other product segments consist of military vehicles, radar and weapons, guided missiles systems, satellites; the design installation and operation of business information and telecommunications systems as well as the design, manufacturer of locomotives engines for drilling, marine applications.

RECENT DEVELOPMENTS:

For the quarter ended 3/31/91, net loss totaled $376.5 million compared with net income of $710 million last year. Revenues decreased 3% to $29.19 billion. Results for 1991 included a gain of $403 million from the sale of a New York building and a gain of $303 million from the change of accounting for inventories. The poor performance reflects depressed sales in the domestic automotive operation, the shift in product mix towards lower-priced models and costly sales incentives. Expansion into new markets and growth in existing areas of business boosted profits in Electronic Data Systems. Operating profits in GMAC and GM Hughes Electronics fell 9% and 38%, respectively.

PROSPECTS:

Despite the drop in interest rates, sales of domestically built vehicles remain depressed. Furthermore, competitive pricing pressures combined with a declining European automotive market cloud the near-term outlook. Compliance with stringent environmental standards which include longer warranties on pollution equipment, higher fuel economy per vehicle and lower emission of hydrocarbons will boost operating costs. Meanwhile, further workforce reductions, temporary plant shutdowns and consolidation of manufacturing units continue. Strong results from Electronic Data System and GMAC will help the Company endure the downturn.

STATISTICS:

YEAR	GROSS REVS. ($mill.)	OPER. PROFIT MARGIN %	RET. ON EQUITY %	NET INCOME ($mill.)	WORK CAP. ($mill.)	SENIOR CAPITAL ($mill.)	SHARES (000)	EARN. PER SH.$	DIV. PER SH.$	DIV. PAY. %	PRICE RANGE	P/E RATIO	AVG. YIELD %
81	62,791	0.6	1.9	333.4	1,161	4,377.5	594,400	0.54	1.20	N.M.	29 - 16⅞	42.5	5.2
82	60,026	1.6	5.3	962.7	1,658	5,028.7	624,720	1.55	1.20	77	32⅛ - 17	15.9	4.9
83	74,582	7.4	18.0	3,730.0	5,891	3,805.4	631,422	5.92	1.40	24	40 - 28	5.7	4.1
84	83,890	5.6	18.9	4,517.0	6,276	3,028.5	635,008	7.11	2.38	33	41⅜ - 30½	5.1	6.6
85	96,372	4.4	13.4	3,999.0	1,958	4,829.0	637,706	6.14	2.50	41	42½ - 32⅛	6.1	6.7
86	102,814	1.4	9.6	b2,945.0	3,920	4,325.3	638,768	b4.11	2.50	61	44¼ - 29⅞	9.0	6.7
87	101,782	2.5	10.7	b3,550.9	14,243	4,549.8	625,308	b5.03	2.50	50	47 - 25	7.2	6.9
c88	123,642	5.4	16.4	4,856.3	31,582	36,388.2	612,913	7.17	2.50	35	44 - 30	5.2	6.8
89	126,932	5.0	12.0	4,224.3	17,230	36,944.1	604,300	6.33	2.50	39	50½ - 39⅛	7.1	5.6
90	**124,705**	**d**	**d**	**ad1,985.7**	**10,815**	**39,054.3**	**605,592**	**ad4.09**	**3.00**	**—**	**50½ - 33⅛**	**—**	**7.2**

♦Long-Term Price Score —Term Price Score; see page 4a. STATISTICS ARE AS ORIGINALLY REPORTED. Adjusted for 2-for-1 stock split 3/89. a-Incl. net charge of $2.10 billion related to restructuring, 1990; and a net gian of $403 mill. from asset sales and a gain of $306.5 mill. from an acct'g. change, 1991. b-Includes net charges of $1.29 billion ($1.10 per sh.) from closing and restructuring of certain operations in 1986 and $292 million in 1987. c-Includes subsidiaries and GMAC. e-GM only.

INCORPORATED:
October 13, 1916 — Delaware

PRINCIPAL OFFICE:
3044 W. Grand Blvd.
Detroit, MI 48202
Tel.: (313) 556-5000

ANNUAL MEETING:
Fourth Friday in May

NUMBER OF STOCKHOLDERS:
Com. & Pfd. 924,000
Class E 427,000
Class H 497,000

TRANSFER AGENT(S):
First Chicago Trust Co. of NY
National Trust Co. Ltd., Toronto, Ont.
National Trust Co. Ltd., Montreal Quebec.

REGISTRAR(S):

INSTITUTIONAL HOLDINGS:
No. of Institutions: 868
Shares Held: 237,310,737

OFFICERS:
Chairman & C.E.O.
R. C. Stempel
Vice Chairmen
J. F. Smith, Jr.
R. J. Schultz
President
L. E. Reuss
E.V.P.-Fin. & C.F.O.
R. T. O'Connell
Secretary & Gen. Coun.
P. H. Zalecki

try your skill at evaluating an investment in General Motors Corp. Assume that on Thursday, October 17, 1991, you prepared a personal investment plan and established an emergency fund equal to three months' living expenses. Also assume that you had saved $5,000, to be used to purchase General Motors' common stock. To help evaluate your investment in General Motors, carefully examine the research report (Figure 19.7) taken from the Summer 1991 issue of *Moody's Handbook of Common Stocks*.

Questions

1. Based on the Moody's research report, would you buy General Motors' common stock? Justify your answer.

2. What other investment information would you need to evaluate General Motors Corporation? Where would you obtain this information?

3. On Thursday, October 17, 1991, the common stock for General Motors Corporation was selling for $37.50 a share.* Using a recent newspaper, determine the current price for a share of General Motors' common stock. Based on this information, would your General Motors' investment have been profitable if you had purchased the common stock for $37.50 a share? Why?

*Price information for a share of General Motors' common stock was taken from *The Wall Street Journal* on October 18, 1991, p. C4.

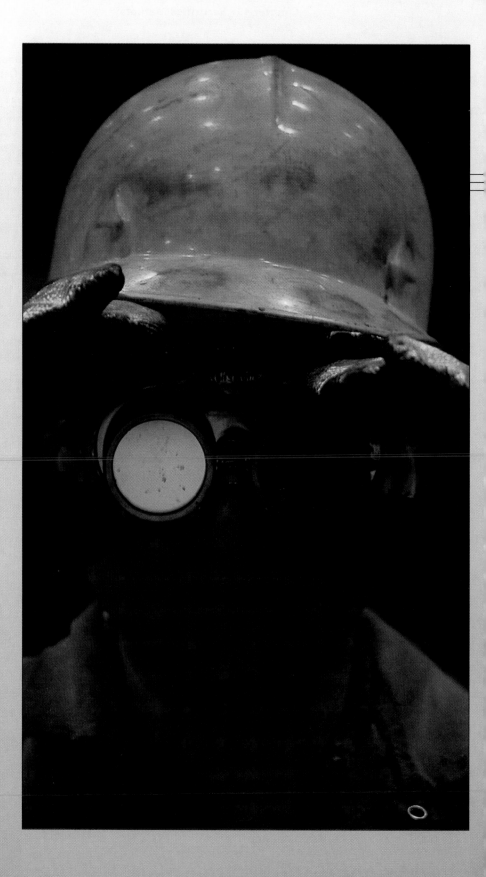

Risk Management and Insurance

LEARNING OBJECTIVES

After studying this chapter you should be able to:

1 Explain what risk is, and understand the difference between a pure and a speculative risk.

2 Appraise the four general techniques of risk management: avoidance, reduction, assumption, and the shifting of risk to an insurer.

3 Discuss the principles underlying insurance and the insurability of risks.

4 Distinguish the types of insurance that can be used to protect businesses and individuals against property and casualty losses.

5 Describe the types of insurance available to individuals.

6 Analyze the advantages and disadvantages of term, whole, endowment, and universal life insurance.

CHAPTER PREVIEW

We open this chapter by defining two broad categories of risk: pure risks and speculative risks. Then we examine several methods of risk management available to individuals and businesses and consider situations for which each method is appropriate. Next, we turn our attention to insurance companies—organizations that agree to assume responsibility for certain kinds of risks in exchange for payment of a fee. We see how insurance companies determine which risks they will cover and what prices they will charge for coverage. Then we list the major types of insurance against loss of property and losses owing to accidents. We close the chapter with a comparison of several kinds of life insurance.

Career Profile

PART 6   Career Opportunities in Finance, Investment, and Insurance

Job Title	Job Description	Salary Range
Actuary	Determine probability of loss in specific situations; calculate premium amounts that provide enough revenue to cover losses and operating expenses, and provide reasonable profits for the company; communicate with managers, agents, and the firm's accounting staff	3–4
Bank officer and manager	Ensure that banking activities are carried out efficiently and without error; supervise employees; communicate with bank customers; approve both loans and expenditures; maintain financial records to ensure that the bank is in compliance with government regulations	3–4
Claims adjuster	Adjust claims when customers incur losses; maintain accurate insurance records; oversee disbursement of payments to customers; communicate with upper level managers and other insurance firm employees	2
Credit manager	Oversee activities of credit department employees; maintain control of credit records; communicate with credit applicants, other employees, and firms requesting credit information about credit applicants; ensure that the firm complies with government regulations	2–3
Financial analyst	Evaluate financial performance of corporations; write research reports that are distributed to brokerage firm customers; make predictions on which securities will increase or decrease in value; communicate with managers, stockbrokers, and other brokerage firm employees	4–5
Insurance agent	Communicate with customers; evaluate potential risks for customers; determine appropriate coverage to reduce or transfer customer risk to insurance company; follow up activities with both customers and insurance companies; maintain accurate records for each customer	3–4
Investment banker	Help corporations obtain both equity and debt financing; evaluate the financial health of corporations; ensure that a new security issue meets all government regulations; choose appropriate methods to advertise and distribute new security issues; maintain relations with prior customers that may desire additional financing in the future	5
Stockbroker (account executive)	Provide investment advice and recommendations to individual customers; evaluate the financial performance of stocks, bonds, mutual funds, and other investment alternatives; maintain accurate and complete financial records for individual customers; provide follow-up services for all customers; adhere to all government regulations that affect securities transactions	4–5

The figure in the salary column approximates the expected annual income after two or three years of service.
1 = $12,000–$15,000; 2 = $16,000–$20,000; 3 = $21,000–$27,000; 4 = $28,000–$35,000; 5 = $36,000 and up.

Educational Requirements	Skills Required	Prospects for Growth
Bachelor's or master's degree in math, business, or statistics	Computer; decision making; quantitative; conceptual; critical thinking	Average
College degree; master's degree preferred; on-the-job experience	Communication; leadership; decision making; interpersonal; quantitative; conceptual; critical thinking	Below average
Some college preferred; on-the-job training	Communication; computer; problem solving; technical; conceptual	Average
College degree; on-the-job experience	Communication; leadership; decision making; interpersonal; conceptual; critical thinking	Below average
College degree; on-the-job experience; master's degree helpful	Computer; problem solving; interpersonal; quantitative; analytical; critical thinking	Below average
Bachelor's degree preferred	Communication; computer; interpersonal; critical thinking	Below average
College degree; master's degree helpful; on-the-job experience	Computer; problem solving; interpersonal; quantitative; analytical; conceptual; critical thinking	Below average
Bachelor's degree; on-the-job experience	Communication; computer; quantitative; analytical; conceptual; critical thinking	Average

PART

7

The Business Environment and International Issues

This final part of *Business* covers two topics that affect the operations of every firm: the legal aspects of business and the relationship between business and government in the United States. It also treats a topic that is steadily increasing in importance: the benefits, problems, and methods of international trade. Finally, the last chapter of the text provides information useful for planning your career, including career preparation, résumé writing, and interviewing. Included in this part are:

Business Law

LEARNING OBJECTIVES

After studying this chapter you should be able to:

1 Explain how law comes into being and how it is administered by the courts.

2 Summarize what constitutes a valid and enforceable contract and the principal remedies for breach of contract.

3 Discuss the major provisions of property law, especially those regarding the transfer of title to property.

4 State what a negotiable instrument is and how it is endorsed for transfer.

5 Explain the agent-principal relationship.

6 Know how bankruptcy is initiated and resolved.

CHAPTER PREVIEW

Our initial task in this chapter is to examine the judicial, legislative, and administrative sources of law. We also describe the functions of the federal and state court systems in administering the law. Then we discuss the major categories of law that apply to business activities. These categories include (1) contract law, governing agreements between individuals or businesses; (2) property law, relating to rights of ownership; (3) laws that regulate the use of such negotiable instruments as checks, promissory notes, and commercial paper; (4) agency laws, under which agents may agree to work on behalf of individuals or organizations in a business relationship; and (5) bankruptcy laws, designed to protect both debtors and creditors.

News Flash: Kermit the Frog Sues Mickey Mouse

How could lovable, animated characters like Kermit the Frog and Mickey Mouse end up in a lawsuit? That's a question that executives at Walt Disney were asking themselves on April 17, 1991, when Henson Associates filed a multimillion-dollar lawsuit against the Disney Corporation. Henson Associates accused Disney of copyright and trademark infringement. According to officials at Henson, Disney was never given legal permission to use Kermit the Frog, Miss Piggy, and the other animated characters most often referred to as the Muppets, on Disney merchandise, brochures, books, and in theme parks. Disney officials denied the charges and claimed that Henson's claims were a distortion of the facts.

Legal problems for Henson Associates and Disney actually began back in 1989 when Disney offered to purchase Henson Associates from Jim Henson—the creator of Kermit, Miss Piggy, and the other Muppet characters. According to Disney chief executive officer, Michael Eisner, the merger was "a business association made in family entertainment heaven." Disney viewed the Muppet characters as a valuable asset that could be used again and again to entertain future generations of children. For Jim Henson, the $150 million deal was a way to ensure that his beloved characters would have a happy home with Disney—a company that has built a $6 billion empire based on animated characters and the entertainment industry. Although initial negotiations moved slowly, Henson Associates began working on several projects for Disney including Muppet attractions at Disney World and a special effects, 3-D movie about Kermit, Miss Piggy, and the other Muppets.

Then on May 16, 1990, Jim Henson (age 53) died unexpectedly. After Henson's untimely death, both negotiations and work on special projects for Disney continued. But seven months later, in December 1990, negotiations between the two firms collapsed when Disney reduced the purchase price by about $25 million. Henson Associates made a counteroffer; Disney officials refused. And the entertainment deal of the decade was off.

After the negotiations broke off, Henson Associates asked Disney to limit the use of the Muppet characters at Disney World. Disney argued that an implied contract existed between the two firms because Jim Henson had signed a letter of intent and because Disney's use of the characters began before Henson's death. According to Disney, this implied agreement gave them the right to continue using the Muppet characters. That's when Henson Associates sued.

Less than a month later, the lawsuit was dropped when officials for Henson and Disney worked out details for a new contractual agreement. According to industry sources, Henson Associates agreed to let Disney show the new 3-D movie and use a stage show starring Kermit the Frog and Miss Piggy for an eighteen-month period. In return, Disney agreed to pay Henson Associates approximately $10 million.[1]

According to legal experts, there is no sharp distinction between business law and other kinds of law. The term *business law* simply applies to those laws that primarily affect business activities and practices. Such laws set standards of behavior for both businesses and individuals. They set forth the rights of the parties in exchanges and various types of agreements. And they provide remedies in the event that one business (or individual) believes it has been injured by another.

For example, Henson Associates believed that it was monetarily injured when the Walt Disney Company used Kermit the Frog, Miss Piggy, and the other Muppet characters on Disney merchandise, brochures, books, and in theme parks without legal permission. As a result, Henson Associates sued Disney for copyright and trademark infringement. A month later, Henson Associates and the Disney Corporation resolved their differences, dropped the lawsuit, and entered into a new contractual agreement.

Four ideas are critical here. First, Henson Associates' case against Disney was based on existing laws. Second, Henson Associates sought a remedy to its complaint within the court system, the purpose of which is to hear and decide such cases. Third, both parties agreed to settle the case before it was tried in a court of law. Fourth, the parties entered a new contractual arrangement that was beneficial for both firms. We will discuss all four ideas in this chapter.

LAWS AND THE COURTS

LEARNING OBJECTIVE 1
Explain how law comes into being and how it is administered by the courts.

law   a rule developed by a society to govern the conduct of, and relationships among, its members

A **law** is a rule developed by a society to govern the conduct of, and relationships among, its members. In the United States, the supreme law of the land is the U.S. Constitution. No federal, state, or local law is valid if it violates the U.S. Constitution. In addition to the U.S. Constitution, laws are developed and administered at all three levels of government (federal, state, and local). The entire group of laws dealing with a particular subject, or arising from a particular source, is often called a *body of law*. Some examples are business law, contract law, and common law.

Sources of Laws

Each level of government derives its laws from two major sources: (1) judges' decisions, which make up common law, and (2) legislative bodies, which enact statutory laws.

common law   the body of law created by the court decisions rendered by judges; also known as *case law* or *judicial law*

Common Law   **Common law,** also known as *case law* or *judicial law,* is the body of law created by the court decisions rendered by judges. Common law began as custom and tradition in England, and it was enlarged by centuries of English court decisions. It was transported to America during the colonial period and, since then, has been further enlarged by the decisions of American judges.

This growth of common law is founded on the doctrine of *stare decisis,* a Latin term that is translated as "to stand by a previous decision." The doctrine of *stare decisis* is a practical source of law for two reasons. First, this doctrine allows the courts to be more efficient. A judge's decision in a case may be used by other judges as the basis for later decisions. The earlier decision thus has the strength of law and is, in effect, a source of law. Second, the doctrine of *stare decisis* makes law more stable and predictable. If someone brings a case to court *and* the facts are the same as those in a case that has already been decided, the court will make a decision based on the previous legal decision. The court may depart from the doctrine of *stare decisis* if the facts in the current case differ from those in an earlier case or if business practices, technology, or the attitudes of society have changed.

statute   a law passed by the U.S. Congress, a state legislature, or a local government

statutory law   all the laws that have been enacted by legislative bodies

Statutory Law   A **statute** is a law passed by the U.S. Congress, a state legislature, or a local government. **Statutory law,** then, consists of all the laws that have been enacted by legislative bodies. Many aspects of common law have been incorporated into statutory law and, in the process, made more precise.

Uniform Commercial Code (UCC)   a set of laws designed to eliminate differences among state regulations affecting business and to simplify interstate commerce

For businesses, one very important part of statutory law is the Uniform Commercial Code. The **Uniform Commercial Code (UCC)** is a set of laws designed to eliminate differences among state regulations affecting business and to simplify interstate commerce. The UCC consists of ten articles, or chapters, that cover sales, commercial paper, bank deposits and collections, letters of credit, transfers of title, securities, and transactions that involve collateral. It has been adopted with variations in all fifty states. The state statutes that were replaced by the UCC generally varied from state to state and caused problems for firms that did business in more than one state.

administrative law   the regulations created by government agencies established by legislative bodies

Today, most legal experts have expanded the concept of statutory law to include administrative law. **Administrative law** consists entirely of the regulations created by government agencies established by legislative bodies. The Nuclear Regulatory Commission, for example, has the power to set specific requirements for nuclear power plants. It can even halt the construction or operation of plants that do not meet such requirements. These requirements thus have the force and effect of law. Some well-known federal agencies are the Federal Communications Commission, Federal Aviation Administration, Equal Employment Opportunity Commission, and

Nothing but the truth.
Health and Human Services Secretary Louis Sullivan joins Food and Drug Administration Commissioner David Kessler to announce new regulations intended to topple what Sullivan calls the "tower of Babel" created by food-industry-packaging claims. Regulations to define the meanings of words like *fresh* and *light* are expected to save consumers billions in food and health care costs.

Environmental Protection Agency. State and local agencies also enact laws that both businesses and individuals must obey. For example, each state has a Bureau of Motor Vehicles that develops specific rules for the operation of motor vehicles within that state.

Most regulatory agencies hold hearings that are similar to court trials. Evidence is introduced, and the parties involved are represented by legal counsel. Moreover, the decisions of these agencies may be appealed in state or federal courts.

Public Law and Private Law: Crimes and Torts

public law the body of law that deals with the relationships between individuals or businesses and society

crime a violation of a public law

Public law is the body of law that deals with the relationships between individuals or businesses and society. A violation of a public law is called a **crime.** Among the crimes that can affect a business are the following:

- Burglary, robbery, and theft (discussed in Chapter 20)
- Embezzlement, or the unauthorized taking of money or property by an employee, agent, or trustee
- Forgery, or the false signing or changing of a legal document with the intent to alter the liability of another person
- The use of inaccurate weights, measures, or labels
- The use of the mails to defraud, or cheat, an individual or business
- The receipt of property that has been stolen
- The filing of a false and fraudulent income tax return

GLOBAL PERSPECTIVES
Legal Aspects of the Foreign Corrupt Practices Act

Suppose you are sales manager for the international department of a U.S. manufacturing firm involved in foreign trade, and you receive the following letter:

> Dear _____:
>
> We wish to inform you of a business opportunity in _____. We work in the Foreign Trade Ministry which has an urgent need for the supply of _____. We want to advise you on obtaining this contract in return for getting our own commission for this transaction. . . .
>
> The Ministry wants a company that is capable of handling the order and also capable of cooperating with officials in the Ministry who will receive a percentage of 20 percent of the total amount of the contract. . . .
>
> When typing your quotation, remember to add the 20 percent of the cost to your price which is to be shared by appropriate officials of the Ministry. Please rest assured that we are in charge of the awarding of the contract. . . .

Would you recognize the request for a bribe? Most sales managers—and for that matter—most business executives would immediately realize that the above letter is asking for a bribe. And if they were to agree to the terms of the letter, they would be violating the U.S. Foreign Corrupt Practices Act.

Basically, the Foreign Corrupt Practices Act (FCPA) makes it unlawful for a firm (and those acting on behalf of the firm) to offer or pay anything of value to any foreign official (and certain other foreigners) for the purpose of obtaining or retaining business. The FCPA contains the following basic provisions:

- *Who is covered?*   The provisions of the FCPA apply to any individual who is a citizen or resident of the United States or any entity that has its principal place of business in the United States.
- *Payments*   The FCPA prohibits paying, offering, or promising to pay money or anything of value.
- *Corrupt intent*   An illegal payment must be intended to persuade the recipient to *misuse* his or her official position to wrongfully direct business to the person or firm making the payment.
- *Recipient*   This act extends only to corrupt payments made to a foreign official, a foreign political party or party official, or any candidate for foreign political office.
- *Third-party payments*   The FCPA prohibits corrupt payments through intermediaries if the person or business making the payment knows that all or a portion of the payment will go directly or indirectly to a foreign official.
- *Sanctions against bribery*   Criminal penalties for violations of this act include imprisonment and fines and may be imposed on business firms, employees of the firms, or the firms' agents.

Although this act is somewhat vague, the consequences of violation can be very serious. It is imperative that U.S. firms devise a specific procedure for compliance with the Foreign Corrupt Practices Act.

Those accused of crimes are prosecuted by a federal, state, or local government.

private law   the body of law that governs the relationships between two or more individuals or businesses

tort   a violation of a private law

Private law is the body of law that governs the relationships between two or more individuals or businesses. A violation of a private law (which is, in essence, a violation of another's rights) is called a **tort.** For example, the courts have ruled that Eastman Kodak Company was guilty of infringing on the patent rights owned by Polaroid Corp. Thus, Eastman Kodak committed a tort, or a violation of private law. In some cases, a single illegal act—such as shoplifting—can be both a crime and a tort.

The purpose of private law is to provide a remedy for the party that is injured by a tort. In most cases, the remedy is monetary damages to compensate the injured party and punish the person committing the tort.

Torts may result either from intentional acts or from negligence. Such acts as shoplifting and embezzlement are intentional torts. **Negligence** is a failure to exercise reasonable care, resulting in injury to another. Suppose the driver of a delivery truck loses control of the truck, and it damages a building. A tort has been committed, and the owner of the building may sue both the driver and the driver's employer to recover the cost of the necessary repairs.

negligence   a failure to exercise reasonable care, resulting in injury to another

An important area of tort law deals with *product liability*—manufacturers' responsibility for negligence in designing, manufacturing, or providing operating instructions for their products. Toyota Motor Sales USA Inc. was slapped with a $43 million judgment in a case involving a rear-end collision of a Toyota station wagon that resulted in the deaths of three people. After a lengthy court trial, the jury decided the car was improperly designed when originally built. Toyota Motor Sales USA has indicated it will seek a new trial or appeal the decision.[2] In some cases, product liability has been extended to mean strict product liability. **Strict product liability** is a legal concept that holds a manufacturer responsible for injuries caused by its products even if the manufacturer was not negligent. An injured party need only prove that the product was defective, that the defect existed at the time it left the seller's hands, and that an injury occurred because of the defect.

strict product liability   the legal concept that holds that a manufacturer is responsible for injuries caused by its products even if it was not negligent

The Court System

The United States has two separate and distinct court systems. The federal court system consists of the Supreme Court of the United States, which was established by the Constitution, and other federal courts that were created by Congress. In addition, each of the fifty states has established its own court system. Figure 21.1 shows the makeup of both the federal court system and a typical state court system.

The Federal Court System   Federal courts generally hear cases that involve

- Questions of constitutional law.
- Federal crimes or violations of federal statutes.
- Property valued at $50,000 or more between citizens of different states, or between an American citizen and a foreign nation.
- Bankruptcy; the Internal Revenue Service; the postal laws; or copyright, patent, and trademark laws.
- Admiralty and maritime cases.

The United States is divided into federal judicial districts. Each state includes at least one district court, and more populous states have two or more. A district court is a **court of original jurisdiction,** which is the first

court of original jurisdiction   the first court to recognize and hear testimony in a legal action

contract   a legally enforceable agreement between two or more competent parties who promise to do, or not to do, a particular thing

should understand what a valid contract is and how a contract is fulfilled or violated.

A **contract** is a legally enforceable agreement between two or more competent parties who promise to do, or not to do, a particular thing. The parties to a contract may be individuals or businesses. An *implied contract* is an agreement that results from the actions of the parties rather than from specific promises. For example, a person who orders dinner at a local restaurant assumes that the food will be served within a reasonable time and will be fit to eat. The restaurant owner, for his or her part, assumes that the customer will pay for the meal.

Most contracts are more explicit and formal than that between a restaurant and its customers: An *express contract* is one in which the parties involved have made oral or written promises about the terms of their agreement.

Requirements for a Valid Contract

To be valid and legally enforceable, a contract must meet five specific requirements, as follows: (1) voluntary agreement, (2) consideration, (3) legal competence of all parties, (4) lawful subject matter, and (5) proper form.

voluntary agreement   a contract requirement consisting of an *offer* by one party to enter into a contract with a second party and *acceptance* by the second party of all the terms and conditions of the offer

Voluntary Agreement   **Voluntary agreement** consists of both an *offer* by one party to enter into a contract with a second party and *acceptance* by the second party of all the terms and conditions of the offer. Both the offer and the acceptance should be given in specific terms that would enable a reasonable person to understand the contract agreement. If any part of the offer is not accepted, there is no contract. And, if it can be proved that coercion, undue pressure, or fraud was used to obtain a contract, it may be voided by the injured party.

Unless the method of acceptance is specified in the offer, a contract can be accepted orally or in writing. Generally, acceptance must occur

Simulating space. This simulation laboratory owned by a division of Rockwell International is testing Space Station Freedom's power system design, a step toward the goal of having a permanently manned space station in orbit by 1996. To reach that goal, a government agency, the National Aeronautics & Space Administration, contracts with thousands of private companies like Rockwell.

within a reasonable time. If the offer calls for acceptance by a specific date, acceptance after that date does *not* result in a binding contract.

Consideration   A contract is a binding agreement only when each party provides something of value to the other party. The value or benefit that one party furnishes to the other party is called **consideration.** This consideration may be money, property, a service, or the promise not to exercise a legal right. However, the consideration given by one party need not be equal in dollar value to the consideration given by the other party. As a general rule, the courts will not void a contract just because one party got a bargain.

consideration   the value or benefit that one party to a contract furnishes to the other party

Legal Competence   All parties to a contract must be legally competent to manage their own affairs *and* must have the authority to enter into binding agreements. The courts generally will not require minors, persons of unsound mind, or those who entered into contracts while they were intoxicated to comply with the terms of their contracts. The intent of the legal competence requirement is to protect individuals who may not have been able to protect themselves. In particular, minors can void (or nullify) contracts to which they are parties (except contracts for such necessities of life as food and shelter) at any time before they reach the age of majority. In some states, minors can void a contract even after reaching the age of majority. The business person is nevertheless bound by the terms and conditions of the contract.

Lawful Subject Matter   A contract is not legally enforceable if it involves an unlawful act. Certainly, a person who contracts with an arsonist to burn down a building cannot go to court to obtain enforcement of the contract. Equally unenforceable is a contract that involves **usury,** which is the practice of charging interest in excess of the maximum legal rate. In many states, a lender who practices usury is denied the right to recover any interest at all. In a few states, such a lender may recover the maximum legal interest. And in still other states, the person borrowing the money may recover damages equal to double or triple the excessive interest amount. Other contracts that may be unlawful include promissory notes resulting from illegal gambling activities, contracts to bribe public officials, agreements to perform services without required licenses, and contracts that restrain trade or eliminate competition.

usury   the practice of charging interest in excess of the maximum legal rate

Proper Form of Contract   Although contracts may be oral, it is safer to commit them to writing. A written contract is visible evidence of its terms, whereas an oral contract is subject to the memories and interpretations of the parties involved. Businesses generally draw up all contractual agreements in writing so that differences can be resolved readily if a dispute develops. Figure 21.2 shows that a contract need not be complicated to be legally enforceable.

A written contract must contain the names of the parties involved, their signatures, the purpose of the contract, and all terms and conditions to which the parties have agreed. Changes to a written contract should be

FIGURE 21.2
Contract Between a Business and a Customer
Notice that the requirements for a valid contract are satisfied and that the contract takes the proper form by containing the names of the parties involved, their signatures, the purpose of the contract, and all terms and conditions.

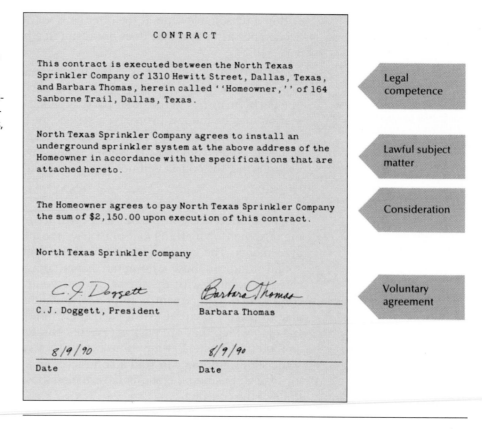

made in writing and should be initialed by all parties. They should be written directly on the original contract or attached to it.

The *Statute of Frauds,* which has been passed in some form by all states, requires that certain types of contracts be in writing to be enforceable. These include contracts dealing with

- The exchange of land or real estate.
- The sale of goods, merchandise, or personal property valued at $500 or more.
- The sale of securities, regardless of the dollar amount.
- Acts that will not be completed within one year after the agreement is made.
- A promise to assume someone else's financial obligation.
- A promise made in contemplation of marriage.

Performance and Nonperformance

performance   the fulfillment of all obligations by all parties to the contract

Ordinarily, a contract is terminated by **performance,** which is the fulfillment of all obligations by all parties to the contract. Occasionally, however, performance may become impossible. Death, disability, or bankruptcy, for

GETTING AHEAD IN BUSINESS
Home Improvements: The Need for a Contract

The success of any remodeling project depends on two factors: the choice of the right contractor, and the existence of a detailed written contract that describes what the contractor is going to do. If either factor is ignored, disaster can strike, as Sandra and Mike Jackson discovered.

After the arrival of their second child, the Jacksons needed more space in their two-bedroom home. They looked in the home section of the *Houston Chronicle* and found the name of a contractor. The contractor came to their home and gave them an estimate. Because the contractor was eager to start work immediately, the Jacksons did not insist on a written contract—that's when their problems started. According to the Jacksons, the contractor wouldn't listen to their ideas and refused to make the changes that would turn the space into their ideal bedroom. Finally, after thirteen months, he did finish the job. But six months later, the glass door he had installed began to leak both air and water, and the Jacksons called him to come repair the leak. To their surprise, they found he had declared bankruptcy and had left the home-remodeling business.

According to consumer advocates, the Jacksons made two mistakes. First, they should have been more careful when they chose their contractor. Most experts suggest that before you talk to any contractor, you should crystallize your dreams into concrete plans that a contractor can understand. Then, with specific plans in hand, talk with more than one contractor and get bids from each of them. Ask each contractor for a list of customers you can call to see if they were satisfied with the contractor's work. Also, walk through at least one remodeling project the contractor has completed. If possible, choose a contractor who belongs to either the National Association of Home Builders or the National Association of the Remodeling Industry. Above all, don't let a contractor pressure you to sign a contract prematurely.

The Jacksons's second mistake was to fail to insist on a written contract. For $5.95, the American Homeowners Foundation (1724 S. Quincy St., Arlington, VA 22204) will provide an eight-page model contract that you can use when negotiating your contract. Any remodeling contract should describe exactly what the contractor is going to do, all the materials that will be used, the complete financial terms of the agreement and the payment schedule, the starting and completing dates, and any other conditions that are relevant to the remodeling project. All special requests, oral promises, or conditions should be included in the written contract. Although most experts recommend including an arbitration clause in the contract to resolve any disputes, the best way to avoid problems is to get answers to your questions before you sign anything.

example, may legally excuse one party from a contractual obligation. But what happens when one party simply does not perform according to a legal contract?

breach of contract   the failure of one party to fulfill the terms of a contract when there is no legal reason for that failure

A **breach of contract** is the failure of one party to fulfill the terms of a contract when there is no legal reason for that failure. In such a case, it may be necessary for the other parties to the contract to bring legal action to discharge the contract, obtain monetary damages, or require specific performance.

discharge by mutual assent   when all parties agree to void a contract

Discharge by mutual assent is the termination of a contract when all parties agree to void a contract. Any consideration received by the parties must be returned when a contract is discharged by mutual assent.

damages   a monetary settlement awarded to a party injured through a breach of contract

Damages are a monetary settlement awarded to a party injured through a breach of contract. When damages are awarded, an attempt is made to place the injured party in the position it would be in if the contract had been performed. Suppose A contracts to paint B's house for $1,500. Then A breaches the contract, and B must hire C to paint the house for $2,000. B can sue A for $500, the additional cost he or she had to pay to achieve what was expected as a result of the original contract—a newly painted house.

specific performance   the legal requirement that the parties to a contract fulfill their obligations according to the contract (as opposed to settlement via payment of damages)

Specific performance is the legal requirement that the parties to a contract fulfill their obligations according to the contract (as opposed to settlement via payment of damages). Generally, the courts require specific performance if a contract calls for a unique service or product that cannot be obtained from another source. For example, only one artist may be capable of designing and creating a specific piece of art. In this case, the court may order the artist to create the artwork at the price agreed on in the original contract.

Most individuals and firms enter into a contract because they expect to live up to its terms. Very few end up in court. When they do, it is usually because one or more of the parties did not understand all the conditions of the agreement. Thus it is imperative to know what you are signing before you sign it. If there is any doubt, get legal help! A signed contract is very difficult—and often very costly—to void.

Sales Agreements

sales agreement   a type of contract by which ownership is transferred from a seller to a buyer

A **sales agreement** is a special (but very common) type of contract by which ownership is transferred from a seller to a buyer. Article 2 of the UCC (entitled "Sales") provides much of our sales law, which is derived from both common and statutory law. It covers the sale of goods only. It does not cover the sale of stocks and bonds, personal services, or real estate. Among the topics included in Article 2 are rights of the buyer and seller, acceptance and rejection of an offer, inspection of goods, delivery, transfer of ownership, and warranties.

Article 2 provides that a sales agreement may be binding even when one or more of the general contract requirements is omitted. For example, a sales agreement is legally binding when the selling price is left out of the agreement. Article 2 requires that the buyer pay the reasonable value of the goods at the time of delivery. Key considerations in resolving such issues are the actions and business history of the parties and any customary sales procedures within the particular industry.

express warranty   a written explanation of the responsibilities of the producer (or seller) in the event that a product is found to be defective or otherwise unsatisfactory

Article 2 also deals with warranties—both express and implied. As we saw in Chapter 12, an **express warranty** is a written explanation of the responsibilities of the producer (or seller) in the event that a product is found to be defective or otherwise unsatisfactory. An express warranty may also include the seller's representations concerning such product characteristics as age, durability, and quality. A *full warranty* exists when the producer or seller guarantees to fix or replace a defective product within a reasonable time without cost to the customer. A *limited warranty* exists when the producer or seller does not offer the complete protection of a full warranty. A product's limited warranty must be disclosed to the customer.

implied warranty   a guarantee that is imposed or required by law

An **implied warranty** is a guarantee that is imposed or required by law. In general, the buyer is entitled to assume that

1. The merchandise offered for sale has a clear title and is not stolen.
2. The merchandise is as advertised.
3. The merchandise will serve the purpose for which it was manufactured and sold.

Any limitation to an express or implied warranty must be clearly stated so the buyer can understand any exceptions or disclaimers.

PROPERTY LAW

property   anything that can be owned

Property is anything that can be owned. The concept of private ownership of property is fundamental to the free-enterprise system. Our Constitution guarantees to individuals and businesses the right to own property and to use it in their own best interest.

Kinds of Property

real property   land and anything permanently attached to it

Property is legally classified as either real property or personal property. **Real property** is land and anything permanently attached to it. The term also applies to water on the ground and minerals and natural resources beneath the surface. Thus, a house, a factory, a garage, and a well are all considered real property.

The degree to which a business is concerned with real-property law depends on its size and type of business. The owner of a small jewelry store needs only a limited knowledge of real-property law. But a national jewelry-store chain might employ several real estate experts with extensive knowledge of real-property law, property values, and real estate zoning ordinances throughout the country.

personal property   all property other than real property

Personal property is all property other than real property. Personal property—such as inventories, equipment, store fixtures, an automobile, or a book—has physical or material value. It is referred to as *tangible personal property*. Thus, tangible personal property is movable and can be felt, tasted, or seen. Property that derives its value from a legal right or claim is called *intangible personal property*. Examples include stocks and bonds, receivables, trademarks, patents, and copyrights.

As we noted in Chapter 12, a trademark is a brand that is registered with the U.S. Patent and Trademark Office. Registration guarantees the owner the exclusive use of the trademark for ten years. At the end of that time, the registration can be renewed for additional ten-year periods. If necessary, the owner must defend the trademark from unauthorized use—usually through legal action. McDonald's was recently forced to do exactly that, when the trademark "Big Mac" was used by another fast-food outlet in a foreign country.

patent   the exclusive right to make, use, or sell a newly invented product or process

A **patent** is the exclusive right to make, use, or sell, or to license others to make and sell, a newly invented product or process. Patents are granted by the U.S. Patent and Trademark Office for a period of seventeen years.

A major league agent. Dennis Gilbert never made it out of the minor leagues as a center-fielder, but as an agent for others his batting average is impressive. In the winter of 1991–1992, Gilbert earned $3 million by negotiating two expensive contracts—a $29 million agreement between Bobby Bonilla and the New York Mets and a $25.5 million deal between Danny Tartabull and the New York Yankees.

act. For this reason, a written contract describing the conditions and limits of the agency relationship is extremely important to both parties.

A **power of attorney** is a legal document that serves as evidence that an agent has been appointed to act on behalf of a principal. In the majority of states in the United States, a power of attorney is required in agency relationships involving the transfer of real estate, as well as in other specific situations.

An agent is responsible for carrying out the principal's instructions in a professional manner, for acting reasonably and with good judgment, and for keeping the principal informed of progress according to their agreement. The agent must also be careful to avoid a conflict involving the interests of two or more principals. The agency relationship is terminated when its objective is accomplished, at the end of a specified time period, or in some cases, when either party renounces the agency relationship. The agent's actual authority ends when the principal tells the agent that his or her authority has been revoked. The principal must also notify third parties, those with whom the agent has dealt on a regular basis, of the agent's termination.

power of attorney   a legal document that serves as evidence that an agent has been appointed to act on behalf of a principal

BANKRUPTCY LAW

LEARNING OBJECTIVE 6
Know how bankruptcy is initiated and resolved.

bankruptcy   a legal procedure designed both to protect an individual or business that cannot meet its financial obligations and to protect the creditors involved

Bankruptcy is a legal procedure designed both to protect an individual or business that cannot meet its financial obligations and to protect the creditors involved. The Bankruptcy Reform Act was enacted in 1978 and was subsequently amended in July 1984. This act is divided into nine parts, called chapters, which explain the procedures for resolving a bankruptcy

(Boston: PWS-Kent Publishing Company, 1990), p. 366; and Robert N. Corley and William J. Robert, *Principles of Business Law*, 10th. ed. (Englewood Cliffs, NJ: Prentice-Hall, 1975), p. 343.

CASE 21.2

The "New" Federated Department Store Chain

Financial problems for the Allied and Federated department stores began in 1986 when Robert Campeau—the successful Canadian real estate developer and chairman of the board of the Campeau Corporation—acquired Allied Stores Corporation for $3.7 billion. The Allied stores included the Bon Marche (39 stores), Jordan Marsh (26 stores), Maas Brothers (38 stores), and Stern's (24 stores).

Two years later, Robert Campeau acting on behalf of the Campeau Corporation became involved in a bidding war with the R. H. Macy & Co., Inc. department-store chain in an attempt to purchase the Federated chain. Federated Department Stores, Inc. included Abraham & Straus (15 stores), Bloomingdale's (17 stores), Burdines (39 stores), Lazarus (46 stores), Rich's/Goldsmith (24 stores), and other stores. Although Campeau was able to purchase the Federated chain for $6.6 billion, this transaction was the beginning of the end. Faced with long-term debts that some experts estimated to be in excess of $12 billion, the Campeau Corporation immediately had financial problems. The stores could not generate enough cash to pay even the interest on the massive long-term debts.

As a result, Campeau spokeswoman Carol Sanger announced that Campeau's Allied and Federated Department Stores were filing for protection under Chapter 11 of the U.S. Bankruptcy Reform Act on January 15, 1990. The bankruptcy—the largest in the history of retailing—affected 100,000 employees in 261 stores and more than 50,000 lenders, bondholders, and merchandise suppliers who were owed money. The bankruptcy petition allowed Federated and Allied to suspend interest payments on bonds and other long-term debts. The stores could then use the cash to pay suppliers—a move that ensured continued shipments of merchandise needed by individual stores to attract customers during the firm's reorganization.

In May 1991—almost sixteen months after the bankruptcy filing—the management for Allied and Federated stores proposed a reorganization plan that would eventually pare outstanding debt to between $1.5 billion and $2 billion. Under the plan, creditors would receive approximately 60 cents on the dollar, with the remainder paid in stock in a *new* Cincinnati-based holding company known as Federated Department Stores, Inc.

The new Federated chain will operate 243 stores with approximately 88,000 employees. Although the Allied and Federated chains' financial problems are still huge, the firm's management team is optimistic. And according to most financial analysts, the firm's financial problems were not the result of poor management, poor merchandising practices, or operating losses. Instead, they were caused by the debt financing needed to purchase both chains. Simply put, Robert Campeau paid too much for the Federated and Allied stores.**

Questions

1. In 1986 Robert Campeau purchased the Allied Stores Corporation. In 1988 he purchased the Federated Department Store chain. Then, in 1990, the Campeau stores were forced to file for protection under Chapter 11 of the U.S. Bankruptcy Reform Act. Given the information presented in this case, briefly describe the problems that Campeau encountered since acquiring Allied Stores Corp. in 1986.

2. Most financial analysts are quick to point out that Campeau's financial problems are not the result of poor management, poor merchandising practices, or operating losses, but resulted from too much debt financing. In what ways could Campeau's financial problems affect management decisions?

**Based on information from Laura Zinn, "Minding the Stores," *Business Week*, May 6, 1991, p. 36; John Daly, "A Fallen Tycoon," *Maclean's*, May 13, 1991, p. 38; John Greenwald, "How Do You Spell Relief?" *Time*, January 22, 1990, pp. 48–49; Todd Mason, "It'll Be a Hard Sell," *Business Week*, January 29, 1990, pp. 30–31; and "Bankruptcy Petition Brings Fresh Risks for Allied, Federated," the *Wall Street Journal*, January 16, 1990, p. A1.

Government Assistance, Regulation, and Taxation

CHAPTER PREVIEW

We begin this chapter by describing how government supports business activities—through its information services, its funded research efforts, and its enormous purchasing power. We also examine several important laws that support business by prohibiting monopolies and restraints on competition. Next, we review the definition of natural monopoly introduced in Chapter 1. We explain how the government permits the existence of certain natural monopolies but carefully regulates their activities. Then we consider the deregulation movement, noting some of the arguments for and against deregulation. We conclude the chapter with a discussion of federal, state, and local taxes—the primary means by which governments at all levels finance their activities.

The President's Council on Competitiveness

The President's Council on Competitiveness was created to ensure that American business firms remain competitive in the global marketplace. Since its inception in 1989, the Council has examined at least fifty major federal regulations that directly impact American business firms. In many cases, the Council has either blocked or substantially changed regulations that created unfair burdens on American firms.

According to political observers, the Council uses a cost/benefit test to determine if a regulation is needed or not. Simply put, if the cost of implementation exceeds the benefits derived from a regulation, the Council will ask that the federal agency sponsoring the regulation change the regulation to make it more cost effective. The Council also has the power to order that the agency drop the regulation. For example, the Council recently ordered the Environmental Protection Agency (EPA) to drop its proposed ban on the incineration of lead batteries because the regulation did not pass the cost/benefit test. The Council also asked the EPA to make more than 100 changes in the 1990 Clean Air Act. According to Council members, the EPA's Clean Air Act would cost American manufacturers millions of dollars at a time when profits for many firms are already depressed. And, in an effort to encourage scientific and technological progress, the Council has proposed new guidelines that would speed the approval of new prescription drugs.

Currently, the Council is chaired by the Vice President of the United States. Additional members of the Council include the Secretary of the Treasury, the Secretary of the Department of Commerce, the Attorney General, the Director for the Office of Management and Budget, the Chief of Staff, and the Chairperson of the Council of Economic Advisors. So far, Council members have adopted a philosophy that there are too many regulations and that eliminating at least some of the regulations

will make American firms more competitive. And of course, fewer regulations is good news for business owners—especially when the news comes from the Vice President and members of a committee with as much political clout as this committee has.

Opponents disagree and accuse the Council of being soft on industry. A growing number of agency officials and politicians argue that all the Council on Competitiveness has done is weaken existing laws against pollution and eliminate many of the rules that would help guarantee new drugs to be safe and effective. According to opponents, the Council and its staff are not experts and are not qualified to evaluate—let alone revise—federal regulations. These same people believe that further action by the Council on Competitiveness could lead to serious environmental and consumer problems in the years ahead.

Members of the Council counter by stressing that the goal of the agency is to improve the nation's competitiveness, and not to shelter industry from regulation. Members are also quick to point out that the cost of regulation is usually passed on to consumers in the form of higher prices. And according to Allan B. Hubbard, the executive director of the Council, "our whole effort is to protect the consumer and the American worker."[1]

Today, the government's relationship with business is twofold. First, government at the federal, state, and local levels support and encourage business activities. Second, government is charged with the responsibility to oversee or regulate business activities. Sometimes, there is conflict. The President's Council on Competitiveness, for example, was created to ensure that American firms remain competitive in the global marketplace by either changing or eliminating some government regulations. And while the Council's original purpose seems worthwhile, opponents argue that the Council has overstepped its bounds and is soft on industry. These same opponents argue that more regulations are needed in order to protect not only the environment, but also the American consumer. In this chapter we examine this twofold relationship between government and business. We begin by looking at ways that government is supportive of business. Then, we describe the methods used to regulate business.

GOVERNMENT SUPPORT OF BUSINESS

LEARNING OBJECTIVE 1
Discuss the ways in which government can assist business firms.

Government regulations and actions that restrict certain business activities may, at the same time, support other activities. The breakup of American Telephone & Telegraph Co. (AT&T) was calculated to restrict the operations of that firm but it also opened up new markets to the firms that are now producing telephone equipment in competition with Western Electric Company, Incorporated. And the "equal access" portion of the consent decree directly benefited such firms as GTE, U.S. Sprint Communications, and MCI Communications Corp. These firms are now able to compete with AT&T on a more or less equal footing.

Not all government regulations are of this nature. Many of them (and some critics say *too many* of them) are intended primarily to restrict business activities, for various reasons. We discuss government regulation and deregulation in some detail later in the chapter. Here, our main point is simply that at least some government regulations do function in support of business activities.

In addition, government supports business by providing information and assistance, funding research, and acting as the largest customer of American business firms.

Making its pitch to the police. The government's importance as a major purchaser results in ads like this one from Bell Helicopter Textron. Arms of the government, especially law enforcement agencies, are major purchasers of helicopters, so Bell made sure that this ad, run in *Governing* magazine, featured a helicopter already being used by a police department.

Providing Information and Assistance to Business

The U.S. government may be the world's largest collector and user of information. Much of this information is of value to businesses and is available at minimal cost.

The U.S. Census Bureau, for example, collects and can provide a wealth of marketing data:

- Demographic data showing the population distribution by age, sex, race, geographic area, educational level attained, occupation, and income
- Housing data by type and year of construction, size, building materials, and the like

The Census Bureau also provides information on manufacturing and agricultural activity, government spending, and the availability of natural resources. To inform businesses about the types of data and reports that are available, the bureau publishes an annual *Catalog of U.S. Census Publications*.

Other U.S. government publications that can be valuable sources of business information include the *Survey of Current Business* and *Business America* from the Department of Commerce, the *Monthly Labor Review* from the Department of Labor, and the *Federal Reserve Bulletin*.

The Internal Revenue Service and the Small Business Administration provide not only information but also direct assistance. (As we saw in Chapter 4, the SBA provides management assistance and financial help to qualifying businesses.) Finally, state and local governments provide information and aid (including tax reductions and help with low-cost financing) to firms that are, or expect to be, located within their borders.

Funding Research

Every year the federal government and private business each spend over $70 billion on research. Some government-funded research is done at federal institutions such as the Centers for Disease Control in Atlanta. However, the greater portion of government-funded research is performed independently at colleges and universities under government grants.

For example, the federal government is (and has been, for some time) funding research into the causes of and potential cures for cancer. This research, which is taking place at a number of universities and medical schools around the country, is simply too expensive to be funded by individual firms. Because the research is being financed with public funds, the results it yields become part of the *public domain*. That is, they become the property of all citizens—and in particular, of those who can use the results to produce cancer-fighting drugs and apparatus.

Government funding is not limited to research into diseases. In the 1940s, for example, the federal government began to finance basic research into a phenomenon called semiconduction. This research eventually led to the development of the transistor, which you may recall from Chapter 15 is

FOCUS ON SMALL BUSINESS
Small Businesses Can Sell to Uncle Sam

Each year, Uncle Sam contracts for more than $165 billion in goods and services needed to operate the federal government. Approximately $30 billion, or 20 percent of the total, is reserved for small businesses. Although these dollar amounts are impressive, many small-business owners that have dealt with the U.S. government warn that getting a government contract with Uncle Sam is not easy. In fact, many small-business owners admit that, compared with getting the contract, doing the work is a piece of cake.

RESOURCES THAT CAN HELP YOU GET GOVERNMENT BUSINESS

According to the experts, most small-business owners who have been awarded government contracts started at district Small Business Administration (SBA) offices located throughout the United States. SBA staff members can explain the government's complex procurement process. Also, both the SBA and the U.S. Department of Defense (DOD) sponsor procurement conferences designed to help small-business owners understand the government's bidding process. A telephone call to either government agency can put your company's name on the government's mailing list for notice of such meetings.

In addition to the SBA and the DOD, the following publications can also provide information about the government procurement process.

1. *The U.S. Government Purchasing and Sales Directory* can help you determine whether the government needs your product or service. This publication is available from the Superintendent of Documents, U.S. Government Printing Office, Washington, DC 20402-9371.

2. *The Federal Acquisitions Regulation* states all the rules for bidding on government contracts. This publication is also available from the Superintendent of Documents, U.S. Government Printing Office, Washington, DC 20402-9371.

3. *The Commerce Business Daily* is the publication in which the federal government advertises for bids on goods and services that exceed $25,000. This publication, available at most libraries, also lists contract awards. This information is especially useful if you're interested in subcontracting for a government contractor.

A WORD OF CAUTION

Before making your bid for a government contract, examine the government's specifications. The federal government requires strict compliance to contract specifications. Also keep in mind that government contractors are required to comply with equal-opportunity laws, environmental laws, and a host of other regulations and laws. A small business that fails to comply with such requirements can lose its contract.

Even if turned down, try to learn from the experience. Contact the agency that turned you down and ask why you were rejected. Finally, remember to keep trying if you don't get a government contract the first time. Perseverance pays off.

---

the basis of the modern electronics industry. Present government-funded research may lead to entirely new industries and jobs in the decades to come.

Buying the Products of Business

The U.S. government is the largest single purchaser of goods and services in the world. Table 22.1 shows projected federal spending for 1992 and 1993 by department. A single purchase may range in size from a few hundred dollars for office supplies or furniture to more than a billion dollars

TABLE 22.1   Budget of the United States by Department (in billions of dollars)

Department or Other Unit	1992 Estimate	1993 Estimate
Legislative branch	3.0	3.0
Judiciary	2.1	2.7
Executive Office of the President	0.2	0.3
Funds appropriated to the president	25.4	13.9
Agriculture	62.1	60.1
Commerce	2.6	2.6
Defense—military	278.3	277.9
Defense—civilian	40.5	42.3
Education	29.6	28.6
Energy	16.1	17.0
Health and Human Services	588.1	638.8
Housing and Urban Development	25.6	24.3
Interior	6.5	6.4
Justice	10.2	10.4
Labor	33.2	34.6
State	5.7	5.2
Transportation	33.5	34.1
Treasury	300.0	316.2
Environmental Protection Agency	6.0	5.2
General Services Administration	0.3	0.2
National Aeronautics and Space Administration	15.7	17.2
Office of Personnel Management	61.2	65.2
Veterans Administration	33.2	33.9
Other agencies	116.3	23.5
Allowances	0.1	0.1
Undistributed offsetting receipts	−118.0	−134.8
Total Outlays	1,577.5	1,528.9

Source: Executive Office of the President and Office of Management and Budget, *Budget of the United States Government: FY 1992,* Part 7, p. 63.

for new aircraft. The federal government is the largest customer of many firms, and it is the only customer of some.

In addition, there are fifty state governments, 3,042 county governments, 19,200 cities, 16,691 townships, 14,721 school districts, and 29,532 special districts in this country.[2] Together, their total expenditures *exceed* the federal budget. Their needs run from paper clips to highways, from janitorial services to the construction of high-rise office buildings. And they purchase what they need from private businesses. Besides buying both products and services from private businesses, the federal, state, and local governments help businesses by ensuring that they can operate in a competitive environment. In the next section, we examine the specific regulations that help ensure competition among business firms.

FEDERAL REGULATIONS TO ENCOURAGE COMPETITION

LEARNING OBJECTIVE 2
State the reasons for—and content of—the major federal antitrust laws.

Most states have laws to encourage competition, but for the most part, these laws duplicate federal laws. Therefore we discuss only federal legislation designed to encourage competition. A substantial body of federal law has been developed to guard against monopolies, price fixing, and similar restraints on competition. These laws protect consumers by ensuring that they have a choice in the marketplace. The same laws protect businesses by ensuring that they are free to compete.

The need for such laws became apparent in the late 1800s, when monopolies or trusts developed in the sugar, whiskey, tobacco, shoe, and oil industries, among others. A **trust** is a business combination that is created when one firm obtains control of competing firms by purchasing their stock or their assets. Eventually, the trust gains control of the entire industry and can set prices and manipulate trade to suit its own interests. As a result, there is a need for antitrust laws.

trust a business combination that is created when one firm obtains control of competing firms by purchasing their stock or their assets

One of the most successful trusts was the Standard Oil Trust, created by John D. Rockefeller in 1882. Until 1911, the Standard Oil Trust controlled between 80 and 90 percent of the petroleum industry. The firm earned extremely high profits primarily because it had obtained secret price concessions from the railroads that shipped its products. Very low shipping costs, in turn, enabled the firm to systematically eliminate most of its competition by deliberately holding prices down. Once this was accomplished, Standard Oil quickly raised its prices.

In response to public outcry against such practices—and prices— Congress passed the Sherman Antitrust Act in 1890. Since then, Congress has enacted a number of other laws designed to protect American businesses and consumers from monopolies.

The Sherman Antitrust Act (1890)

The objectives of the *Sherman Antitrust Act* are to encourage competition and to prevent monopolies. The act specifically prohibits any contract or agreement entered into for the purpose of restraining trade. Its two most important provisions are

- *Section 1:* Every contract combination, in the form of trust or otherwise, or conspiracy, in restraint of trade or commerce among the several states, or with foreign nations, is hereby declared to be illegal.

- *Section 2:* Every person who shall monopolize or attempt to monopolize, or combine or conspire with any other person or persons to monopolize any part of the trade or commerce . . . shall be deemed guilty of a misdemeanor.[3]

Specific business practices prohibited by the Sherman Antitrust Act include price fixing, allocation of markets among competitors, and boycotts in restraint of trade. **Price fixing** is an agreement between two businesses as to the prices to be charged for goods. A **market allocation** is an agreement to divide a market among potential competitors. A **boycott in restraint of trade** is an agreement between businesses not to sell to, or buy from, a particular entity.

Power to enforce the Sherman Antitrust Act was given to the Department of Justice, which may bring legal action against businesses suspected of violating its provisions. In 1911, the Standard Oil Trust was broken up into thirty-nine independent companies to restore an acceptable level of competition within the oil industry. The Sherman Antitrust Act was also used to break up the Northern Securities Company in 1904 and the American Tobacco Company in 1911. It was, in fact, part of the basis for the Justice Department's 1949 and 1974 suits against AT&T. Today, the Sherman Act is still the cornerstone, or foundation, used to encourage competition and to break up large businesses that monopolize trade.

An amendment to the Sherman Antitrust Act, the *Antitrust Procedures and Penalties Act of 1974,* made violation of the Sherman Act a felony rather than a misdemeanor. It provides for fines of up to $100,000 and prison terms of up to three years for individuals convicted of antitrust violations. The act also provides that a guilty corporation may be fined up to $1 million and may be sued by competitors or customers for treble monetary damages plus attorneys' fees.

The Clayton Act (1914)

Because the wording of the Sherman Antitrust Act is somewhat vague, it could not be used to halt specific monopolistic tactics. Congress therefore enacted the *Clayton Act* in 1914. This legislation identifies and prohibits five distinct practices that had been used to weaken trade competition:

- **Price discrimination,** the practice in which producers and wholesalers charge larger firms a lower price for goods than they charge smaller firms. The price differential had been used by large firms to gain a competitive edge and, in many cases, to force small firms out of business. (The Clayton Act does, however, allow quantity discounts.)
- The **tying agreement,** which is a contract that forces an intermediary to purchase unwanted products along with the products it actually wants to buy. This practice was used to "move" a producer's slow-selling merchandise along with its more desirable merchandise. Twentieth Century-Fox Film Corp., for example, was fined under the Clayton Act for forcing theater chains to rent a less popular motion picture along with one that promised to be highly successful.[4]

price fixing   an agreement between two businesses as to the prices to be charged for goods

market allocation   an agreement to divide a market among potential competitors

boycott in restraint of trade an agreement between businesses not to sell to or buy from a particular entity

price discrimination   the practice in which producers and wholesalers charge larger firms a lower price for goods than they charge smaller firms

tying agreement   a contract that forces an intermediary to purchase unwanted products along with the products it actually wants to buy

- The **binding contract,** an agreement that requires an intermediary to purchase products from a particular supplier, not from the supplier's competitors. In return for signing a binding contract, the intermediary was generally given a price discount.

- The **interlocking directorate,** an arrangement in which members of the board of directors of one firm are also directors of a competing firm. This arrangement is prohibited if either firm has total capital in excess of $1 million. Thus, for example, a person may not be a director of American Airlines Inc. and Delta Air Lines Inc. at the same time. The threat to competition created by such a situation is obvious.

- The **community of interests,** the situation in which one firm buys the stock of a competing firm to reduce competition between the two. This tactic was used to create the giant trusts of the late 1800s. Acquisition of stock may result in either a horizontal or vertical merger. If it *may* substantially lessen competition or tend to create a monopoly, it is unlawful. (Remember, a horizontal merger is a merger between firms that make and sell similar products in similar markets. A vertical merger is a merger between firms that operate at different but related levels in the production and marketing of a single product.)

The Federal Trade Commission Act (1914)

In 1914 Congress also passed the *Federal Trade Commission Act,* which states that "Unfair methods of competition in commerce are hereby declared unlawful." This act also created the **Federal Trade Commission (FTC),** a five-member committee charged with the responsibility of investigating illegal trade practices and enforcing antitrust laws.

At first, the FTC was limited to enforcement of the Sherman Antitrust, Clayton, and FTC Acts. However, in 1938, in the *Wheeler-Lea Amendment* to the FTC Act, Congress gave the FTC the power to eliminate deceptive business practices—including those aimed at consumers rather than competitors. This early "consumer legislation" empowered the FTC to deal with a variety of unfair business tactics without having to prove that they endangered competition.

The FTC may act on its own or on complaints lodged by businesses or individuals. The first step is to investigate the accused firm and its business practices. After its investigation, the commission can issue a **cease and desist order,** which is an order to refrain from an illegal practice. If the business does not refrain, it can be fined $5,000 a day. If the practice is still continued, the FTC may, with the aid of the Justice Department, bring suit against the violating firm.

The Robinson-Patman Act (1936)

Although the Clayton Act prohibits price discrimination, it does permit quantity discounts. This provision turned out to be a major loophole in the law: It was used by large chain retailers to obtain sizable price concessions that gave them a strong competitive edge over independent stores. To correct this imbalance, the *Robinson-Patman Act* was passed by Congress in 1936. This law specifically prohibits

- Price differentials that "substantially" weaken competition, unless they can be justified by the actual lower selling costs associated with larger orders
- Advertising and promotional allowances (a form of discount), unless they are offered to small retailers as well as large retailers

The Robinson-Patman Act is more controversial than most antitrust legislation. Many economists believe the act tends to discourage price competition rather than to eliminate monopolies. In any case, there have been relatively few convictions under the act because the burden of proof is on the injured party—and that is most often small business owners, who often lack the time and financial resources necessary to take legal action.

The Celler-Kefauver Act (1950)

The Clayton Act prohibited building a trust by purchasing the stock of competing firms. To get around that prohibition, however, a firm could still purchase the *assets* of its competitors. The result was the same: the elimination of competition.

This gigantic loophole was closed by the *Celler-Kefauver Act,* which prohibits mergers through the purchase of assets if these mergers will tend to reduce competition. The act also requires all proposed mergers to be approved by both the FTC and the Justice Department.

The Antitrust Improvements Act (1976)

The laws we have discussed were enacted "after the fact"—to correct abuses. In 1976 Congress passed the *Antitrust Improvements Act* to strengthen previous legislation. This law provided additional time for the FTC and the Justice Department to evaluate proposed mergers, and it expanded the investigative powers of the Justice Department. It also authorized the attorneys general of individual states to prosecute firms accused of price fixing and to recover monetary damages for *consumers.* The major antitrust legislation is summarized in Table 22.2.

The Present Antitrust Environment

The problem with antitrust legislation and its enforcement is that it is hard to define exactly what an appropriate level of competition is. For example, a particular merger may be in the public interest because it increases the efficiency of an industry. But it may be harmful at the same time because it reduces competition. There is really no rule of law (or of economics) that can be used to determine which of these two considerations is more important in a given case.

Three factors tend to influence the enforcement and effectiveness of antitrust legislation at the present time. The first is the growing presence of

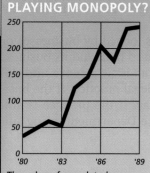

AT A GLANCE

PLAYING MONOPOLY?

The value of completed mergers and acquisitions rose 734% from 1980 to 1989, but the number of mergers rose only 231%. In 1989, 3,602 businesses were sold.
(In billions of dollars)

SOURCE: *MLR Publishing Co., Philadelphia, PA*

TABLE 22.2   Summary of Antitrust Legislation

Government Legislation	Major Provisions	Purpose
Sherman Antitrust Act of 1890	Outlaws business monopolies	To prevent a corporation from systematically eliminating competition by forcing competing firms out of the industry
Clayton Act of 1914	Prohibits five common business practices used to reduce competition	To outlaw (1) price discrimination, (2) tying agreements, (3) binding contracts, (4) interlocking directorates, and (5) community of interests
Federal Trade Commission Act of 1914	Empowers a five-member commission to investigate illegal trade practices (strengthened by the Wheeler-Lea Amendment)	To outlaw unfair trade practices and deceptive advertising
Robinson-Patman Act of 1936	Provides for improved competition between small and large retailers	To prohibit unfair pricing and to make sure promotional assistance and advertising are available to both small and large customers
Celler-Kefauver Act of 1950	Prevents one company from buying the assets of competing companies	To prevent mergers that would weaken competition; enforced by both the Federal Trade Commission and the Justice Department
Antitrust Improvements Act of 1976	Strengthens previous antitrust legislation	To provide additional time for the FTC and the Justice Department to evaluate proposed mergers

foreign firms in American markets. Foreign firms have increased competition in America and thus have made it more difficult for any firm to monopolize an industry. Second, most antitrust legislation must be interpreted by the courts because it is often vague and open-ended. Thus the attitude of the courts has a lot to do with the effectiveness of these laws. And third, political considerations often determine how actively the FTC and the Justice Department pursue antitrust cases. For example, a number of large corporate mergers were allowed during the 1980s when Ronald Reagan was president. The political factor may very well be the primary determinant of the antitrust environment at any given time.

But what about those monopolies that our government *does* allow to exist and flourish? In the next section, we see what makes them different and how they are regulated.

FEDERAL REGULATION OF NATURAL MONOPOLIES

LEARNING OBJECTIVE 3
Describe how the federal government regulates natural monopolies.

natural monopoly   an industry requiring huge investments in capital and for which duplication of facilities would be wasteful and, thus, not in the public interest

In Chapter 1, a **natural monopoly** is defined as an industry requiring huge investments in capital and for which duplication of facilities would be wasteful and, thus, not in the public interest. In such industries, the government may permit one or very few firms to operate. Then it carefully regulates their activities, prices, and profits. Such regulation is aimed at ensuring that natural monopolies earn reasonable profits but do not take advantage of their unique positions. The three major regulated monopolies are the public utilities, communications, and transportation industries.

Public Utilities

Provision of electricity to homes and businesses within an area requires the installation of expensive generating equipment, transmission lines, transformers, and protective equipment. Constant maintenance of these installations is also necessary. Moreover, electricity is most efficiently generated in large quantities. Duplication of equipment for generating and distributing electricity within a geographic area would be wasteful. Prices would be higher than they are at present, but profits would be lower. The quality of service would eventually deteriorate.

For these reasons, a single supplier of electricity is licensed to operate in each geographic area. Its operations are generally controlled by a city or state utilities commission that must, for example, approve any proposed rate increases. The **Federal Energy Regulatory Commission** oversees the *interstate* operations of firms that sell electricity or natural gas, or operate gas pipelines. The nuclear power plants operated by public utilities are licensed and regulated by the Nuclear Regulatory Commission.

Federal Energy Regulatory Commission   the federal agency that oversees the *interstate* operations of firms that sell electricity or natural gas, or operate gas pipelines

Communications

Radio and television stations are monopolies in the sense that each has the exclusive right to broadcast on a particular frequency within a specified area. Telephone and telegraph companies also fall within our definition of a regulated monopoly. All are regulated by either state or federal agencies.

The **Federal Communications Commission (FCC)** is the federal agency responsible for the interstate regulation of communications. It was created by Congress in 1934, primarily to license radio stations and set rates for interstate telephone and telegraph services. At present, the FCC is also responsible for the licensing and regulation of television stations, cable television networks, and ham and CB radio operators.

Federal Communications Commission (FCC)   the federal agency responsible for the interstate regulation of communications, including television, radio, telephone, and telegraph

Transportation

Various abuses in the late nineteenth century—primarily by the railroads—led to the passage of the Interstate Commerce Act in 1887. This act was really the first major piece of federal regulatory legislation. It created the **Interstate Commerce Commission (ICC),** which is responsible for licensing carriers to operate in specific geographic areas, for establishing safety stan-

Interstate Commerce Commission (ICC)   the federal agency responsible for the licensing and regulation of carriers

dards for interstate carriers, and for approving mergers of transportation firms. Originally, its main function was to police the railroads. Since then its scope has been expanded to include trucks, buslines, and all other interstate carriers.

Until 1984, the Civil Aeronautics Board (CAB) set and approved airfares, licensed airlines to serve particular airports, and established standards of service for air carriers. As part of the deregulation movement (which we discuss later), the CAB was phased out of existence on December 31, 1984. Today, regulation of the airline industry is the responsibility of the Transportation Department and the Federal Aviation Administration (FAA).

Critics have argued that regulation of the transportation industry tends to benefit the carriers rather than their customers. In fact, the ICC, Transportation Department, and FAA have been criticized for not paying enough attention to the needs of consumers. As a result, each group is coming under sharp attack for ignoring pressing problems in the transportation industry.

OTHER AREAS OF REGULATION

It is impossible to manage even a small business without being affected by local, state, and federal regulations. And it is just as impossible to describe all the government regulations that affect business. In addition to the two broad areas discussed here, we have examined a variety of regulations in other chapters (and there are more in the next chapter). Chapter 2 discussed laws and regulations dealing with the physical environment and consumerism; Chapter 3, organization of business entities; Chapter 9, personnel and employee relations; Chapter 10, union-management relations;

Forever clean? Getting all branches of a single government to agree on a regulation is often difficult, so forging an agreement among many governments may seem impossible. Yet there is now hope that the governments of the world will agree to keep Antarctica the world's least polluted continent by signing an accord to ban mining there for at least thirty years.

Chapter 19, securities; Chapter 21, trademarks, patents, and copyrights; and Chapter 23, international trade.

By now, you may think that there must be a government regulation to govern any possible situation. Actually, government regulations increased from the 1930s through the 1970s. The country then entered a deregulation period that lasted over twenty years. In the next section, we examine the effects of deregulation and the current status of the deregulation movement.

THE DEREGULATION MOVEMENT

deregulation   the process of removing existing regulations, forgoing proposed regulations, or reducing the rate at which new regulations are enacted

Deregulation is the process of removing existing regulations, forgoing proposed regulations, or reducing the rate at which new regulations are enacted. A movement to deregulate business began in the 1970s and continued into the 1990s.

The primary aim of the movement is to minimize the complexity of regulations that affect business and the cost of compliance. Today, many Americans believe the federal government is now out of control and out of touch with the needs of average citizens. These same people often complain that the federal government has too many employees and spends too much money. At the time of publication, the U.S. government

- Employed approximately 3.1 million civilian workers (in addition to 2.1 million military personnel).
- Spent more than $1.5 trillion a year, which is approximately $6,000 for every person in the United States.

Critics also complain that too many government agencies regulate business activities. In the 1970s alone, twenty new federal agencies were formed. (The average for the previous sixty years was about six new agencies per decade.) More than one hundred federal agencies are currently responsible for enforcing a staggering array of regulations. And at least fifteen federal agencies now have a direct impact on business firms. These agencies are listed in Table 22.3, with the activities they regulate.

The Cost of Regulation

Advocates of deregulation argue that there would be more protest if consumers really knew how much government regulations cost. It has been estimated that federal spending for enforcing regulations costs the taxpayers $12 billion a year, whereas compliance with all of these regulations costs businesses $100 billion each year.[5] One recent study found that government regulations cost the average American $725 each year.[6] And for some Americans who make large purchases, the total cost for government regulations is even higher. According to economist Robert Crandall, approxi-

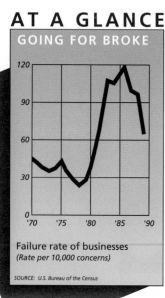

AT A GLANCE

GOING FOR BROKE

Failure rate of businesses
(Rate per 10,000 concerns)

SOURCE: U.S. Bureau of the Census

May 18, 1991, pp. 312–314; Otis Port, "Sematech May Give America's Middleweights a Fighting Chance," *Business Week,* December 10, 1990, p. 186; Lee Smith, "Can Consortiums Defeat Japan?" *Fortune,* June 5, 1989, pp. 245–246+; and John Walsh, "Texas Wins R&D Center," *Science,* January 15, 1988, p. 248.

CASE 22.2

A Tax Cut for Capital Gains?

Under the Tax Reform Act of 1986—the last major revision of the Internal Revenue Code—capital gains resulting from the sale of real estate, small businesses, financial securities, and most other long-term assets are taxed as ordinary income. With one exception, these long-term gains are treated just like wages, interest, or any other income that a taxpayer might receive in a one-year period. The exception is that the maximum tax rate for capital gains is capped at 28 percent under current law.

During his presidential campaign, George Bush promised that he would push for a substantial reduction in the amount of taxes Americans paid on capital gains. The overall goal of his proposal was to encourage Americans to make long-term investments because of preferential tax treatment. When elected, he proposed a maximum tax rate of 19.6 percent on capital gains resulting from the sale of long-term assets held for more than three years.

President Bush's proposal has received mixed reactions from both Republicans and Democrats. Advocates of the proposal argue that a reduction in the taxes paid on capital gains is good for the economy because it will lead to increased savings and investments. They believe most profits derived from the sale of long-term assets would be reinvested. Thus, the economy would quickly expand because of the additional investment capital. Advocates also point out that a capital-gains tax cut would encourage investors to take their money out of tax loopholes, tax shelters, and tax-exempt bonds and put it into new taxable investments. Finally, advocates argue, almost anyone who must report capital gains on a long-term investment would benefit from this tax reduction. According to the U.S. Treasury Department, 50 percent of all taxpayers will report capital gains during their lifetime.*

On the other side of the debate are the opponents of President Bush's plan, who argue that it is just another political giveaway program for the rich. More than 50 percent of all the benefits that result from the reduced tax on capital gains goes to people who make more than $200,000 a year, opponents argue. They also maintain that the majority of Americans oppose a change in the way capital gains are taxed. A 1991 *Business Week*/Harris Poll indicates that 54 percent of those surveyed are against a big cut in capital-gains taxes.** Finally, opponents say, it doesn't make much sense to cut *any* taxes as long as the federal deficit is nearly $300 billion a year.

In 1989, Congress struck down a capital-gains tax proposal. Then, in 1991, the issue was revived when President Bush created a new bipartisan fact-finding commission to study the taxation of capital gains. At the time of publication, this major tax issue was still under consideration.***

Questions

1. Advocates of President Bush's plan argue that a reduction in taxes on long-term capital gains is good for the economy. Do you agree? Why?
2. At the time of publication, President Bush and congressional leaders were still debating the capital gains taxation issue. Using information obtained in the library, determine how capital gains are taxed under current tax laws. Then, in your own words, describe your findings.

*Peter L. Spencer, "The Capital Gains Tax Cut," *Consumers' Research,* November 1989, p. 30.
**"Prescriptions for a Sick Economy," *Business Week,* December 2, 1991, p. 32.
***Based on information from Jack Kemp, "Cutting Capital Gains Taxes," *USA Today,* May 1991, pp. 38–39; "Nothing," the *New Republic,* February 5, 1991, pp. 7–8; "Strait of the Union," *National Review,* February 25, 1991, p. 16; Robert J. Samuelson, "Bush's Capital Gains Obsession," *Newsweek,* October 1, 1990, p. 32; Larry Martz, "A Tax-Cut Stampede," *Newsweek,* February 5, 1990, pp. 18–20.

International Business

LEARNING OBJECTIVES

After studying this chapter you should be able to:

1 Explain the economic basis for international business.

2 Discuss the restrictions that nations place on international trade, the objectives of these restrictions, and their results.

3 Outline the extent of international trade and the organizations that are working to foster it.

4 Define the methods by which a firm can organize for, and enter, international markets.

5 Analyze the main considerations in international marketing.

6 Identify the institutions that help firms and nations to finance international business.

CHAPTER PREVIEW

We describe international trade in this chapter in terms of specialization, whereby each country trades the surplus goods and services it produces most efficiently for products in short supply. We also outline the restrictions that nations place on products from other countries and present some of the advantages and disadvantages of such restrictions. In addition, we discuss the social, cultural, legal, and economic factors that must be considered by firms intending to market products in other countries. Finally, we list some of the institutions that provide the complex financing necessary for modern international trade.

Exporting Pays Off

The Intermark Group of Rolling Hills, California, does not export—it shows other firms how to do it. James C. McKay developed the concept of a business services company that would help its clients maximize their sales effectiveness both in the United States and in international markets. He established Intermark five years ago and is its chairman. About half of Intermark's clients are U.S. firms hoping to expand their exports. Intermark has fifty employees and maintains offices in several countries.

McKay explains, "A client comes to us and says, 'Hey, what countries should we go out and sell to?' We do market research and help identify the best overseas markets. We deal with every type of product, service, and technology."

One of Intermark's clients is Ramtron International Corporation of Colorado Springs, Colorado, a newcomer to exporting. Ramtron retained Intermark to assist with the marketing of its memory chip technology and to establish manufacturing partners here and abroad. Intermark helped set up a multimillion-dollar codevelopment and licensing agreement between Ramtron and ITT Semiconductors in Germany. The agreement led to similar agreements with Seico Epson and NMB Semiconductors Ltd. of Japan.

Kauai Kookie Kompany owners, Norman and Mabel Hashisaka of Eleele, Kauai, Hawaii, have also profited by exporting. They were successful proprietors of the Kakui Nut Tree Inn Restaurant, where they featured a special macadamia nut cookie for dessert. Japanese tourists were draining their cookie supply by taking home boxes of cookies, and the Hashisakas knew further demand existed in Japan. They ignored popular views about the difficulty of doing business in Japan and set about a step-by-step export plan, including taking samples of their products to trade fairs in Tokyo and Osaka. Now, just over three years later, the Kompany has expanded its product line to salad dressings, and it ships not only to Hawaii, California, and Washington but also to Japan, Guam, and Saipan.

The Hashisakas' business operates one facility with twenty-two employees, where up to 50,000 cookies are baked daily on a continuous twenty-four-hour schedule. The good news is that Kauai Kookie is another American company doing a very successful business abroad. The bad news is it can't keep up with the demand—perhaps the best bad news a business can get.

American oral care giant, Colgate-Palmolive Co., is a $5.7 billion, global, consumer products company that markets its Colgate toothpaste in more than 160 countries. In the last decade, the company has increased its share of the world market to more than 40 percent.

In many growth markets around the world, Colgate is building new facilities to manufacture and market its products. The company recently built a toothpaste plant in Turkey, a bleach plant in the Dominican Republic, a fully automated warehouse in Germany, a major new soap facility in India, a new detergent complex in Australia, and a new toothpaste plant in Eastern Europe.[1]

Careers in Business

LEARNING OBJECTIVES

After studying this chapter you should be able to:

1   Describe the factors that influence an individual's career choice.

2   Identify trends in employment in today's changing job market.

3   Summarize occupational search strategies used to find job opportunities.

4   Prepare a cover letter and résumé.

5   Describe the interview process.

6   Summarize the factors that lead to career growth and advancement.

CHAPTER PREVIEW

In this chapter, we examine the factors that influence an individual's career choices. We also look at trends in employment and at some methods that a job applicant can use to find job opportunities. Next, we focus on the tools a job applicant uses to get a job: application letters, résumés, and job interviews. Finally, we look at what it takes to be successful in today's changing job market.

Job Search Techniques That Work

Jobs, jobs, jobs. They're out there, but sometimes the search for the *perfect* position can seem endless. Take the case of thirty-year-old Mike Logan. After graduating from a community college, Mike went to work in the purchasing department for a General Motors assembly plant in Michigan. Within three years, he received two promotions and became a supervisor with responsibility for seventeen employees. He liked the work and the pay was good. But then in 1990, Mike was laid off. After four months it became obvious that he would not be called back. After another eight months, he finally obtained a job as a sales representative for a firm that supplies parts to General Motors, Ford, and Chrysler. According to Mike, searching for a job was one of the most difficult things he had done in his whole life.

Unfortunately, Mike Logan's experience is not that uncommon. But there are a number of actions you can take to make obtaining your next career position a little easier.

First, *before starting your job search, take time to analyze your strengths and weaknesses*. The people who get the best jobs are the ones who have the most to offer an employer. Take a good look at what you have to offer a prospective employer. Specific factors to evaluate include your health and appearance, employment experience, attitude, skills, willingness to adapt, and of course, your job-seeking abilities. Then, talk to former coworkers, friends, even relatives, and ask for their honest appraisals of your strengths and weaknesses. If this analysis reveals problem areas, take the time to polish the areas of concern. For Sandra Martin, an unemployed, mid-level executive, it was necessary to go back to college and learn the basic computer skills that would make her more employable.

Second, *build a network of people who can help you*. According to career counselors, most jobs—some estimates run as high as 90 percent—are filled through word of mouth.[1] Establish a referral database of everyone you know who could either hire you or provide information that may lead to a new job. Debbie Barcelona found that she received the most help when she made specific requests for names, addresses, phone numbers, and introductions to prospective employers.

Third, *make sure your letter of application and résumé are up-to-date and accurate*. Once you discover a job opening, it's time for action. Usually the first step is to mail a letter of application and a résumé. Take the time to customize both the letter of application and the résumé to meet the needs of the prospective employer. After looking for a job for five months, James Fostor revised his résumé and got a job within two weeks. His new résumé sounded exciting and stressed the special skills that his new employer—Texas Instruments—needed.

Fourth, *fine tune your interview skills*. If, after reading your letter of application and résumé, the prospective employer is interested, you will probably be called in for an interview. For Martha Evans, a mock interview helped her fine tune her communication skills and build self-confidence. More important, she got an entry-level position in a large bank within ten days of her mock-interview practice session.[2]

Words like *excited, challenged, scared,* and *frustrated* have been used to describe a job search. But the fact is that everyone who is employed must have looked for a job at one time or another. In fact, according to the Bureau of Labor Statistics, today's job applicants will change jobs over ten times during their career. And by the year 2000, graduates will experience at least four complete career changes. Therefore, the job search techniques presented in the opening case and the employment information that follows will be of lasting value. Let's begin our discussion with a look at the factors affecting an individual's career choices.

THE IMPORTANCE OF CAREER CHOICES

LEARNING OBJECTIVE 1
Describe the factors that influence an individual's career choice.

It's likely that you will spend more time at work than at any other single place during your lifetime. It therefore makes sense to spend those hours doing something you enjoy. Unfortunately, some people just work at a *job* because they need money to survive. Other people choose a *career* because there is a commitment not only to a profession but also to their own interests and talents. Whether you are looking for a job or a career, you will need to do some careful planning. During that planning, you should examine your own values and other personal factors that may affect your career choice.

Personal Factors Influencing Career Choices

Before you choose your career or job, you need to have a pretty good idea of who you are, what motivates you, and what skills you can offer an employer. The following four questions may help you decide what you consider to be important in your life.

1. *What types of activities do you enjoy?* This question could be asked another way: What excites you? Although most people know what they enjoy in a general way, a number of interest inventories exist, which can help you determine specific interests and activities that can help

you land a job leading to a satisfying career. In some cases, it may help just to list the interests or activities you enjoy, along with those you dislike. Watch for patterns that may influence your career choices.

2. *What do you do best?*   All jobs in all careers require employees to be able to "do something." It is extremely important to assess what you do best. Be honest with yourself about your ability to succeed in a specific job. It may help to make a list of your strongest job-related skills. Also try looking at your skills from an employer's perspective. What can you do that an employer would be willing to pay for?

3. *What kind of education will you need?*   The amount of education you need is determined by the type of career you choose. In some careers, it is impossible to get an entry-level position without at least a college degree. In other careers, technical or hands-on skills are more important than formal education. Generally, more education increases your potential earning power, as illustrated in Figure 24.1.

4. *Where do you want to live?*   When you enter the job market, you may want to move to a different part of the country. According to the *Occupational Outlook Handbook,* the western and southern sections of the United States will experience the greatest population increase between now and the year 2000. The population in the midwestern section of the country will stay about the same, whereas the northeastern section will decrease slightly in population. These population changes will affect job prospects in each of those areas.

Before entering the job market, most people think they are free to move any place they want. In reality, job applicants may be forced to move to the town, city, or metropolitan area that has available jobs. Each of the ten cities listed in Table 24.1 received high scores not only on the economy factor but also on other factors that can improve the overall quality of life for those who do obtain jobs there.

FIGURE 24.1   Education and Income
For most Americans, the average income they earn is tied to the number of years of education they have obtained.   *(Source:* The Statistical Abstract of the United States, *1991, p. 459.)*

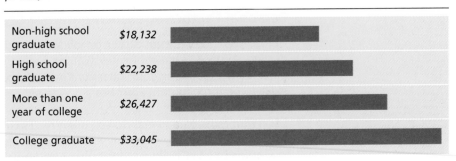

Non-high school graduate	$18,132
High school graduate	$22,238
More than one year of college	$26,427
College graduate	$33,045

first-year salary. It is quite common today for employers to pay the fee. When the employee must pay the fee, it is usually paid in installments over a twelve-month period. Obviously, most employees would prefer that the employer pay the fee.*

Questions

1. What types of questions could a job applicant like Bart Blackburn use to evaluate an employment agency?
2. Although employment agencies can help you get your foot in the door, you are the one who must go through the interview process. How can you convince prospective employers that you are the best applicant for the job?
3. Why would an organization use an employment agency instead of recruiting and hiring its own employees?

*Based on information from "Don't Be Fooled by Job Scams," *Glamour*, May 1991, p. 92; Sheila S. Harrison, "Star Search," *Black Enterprise*, April 1990, p. 74+; Lisa J. Moore, "Putting an Agency on the Job," *U.S. News & World Report*, May 29, 1989, p. 73; and Larry Reibstein, "Employment-Agency Scams," *Newsweek*, February 20, 1989, p. 40.

CASE 24.2

Moving Up Through the Glass Ceiling

Women executives and women who want to be executives face many difficulties. One particular difficulty is moving up through the "glass ceiling." The term *glass ceiling* refers to an imaginary barrier that separates women from top-management positions. According to an eighteen-month U.S. Labor Department study, the height of the glass ceiling varies from one company to the next, but it is often not much higher than entry-level for women employees.

According to the results of the Labor Department study, women were passed over for promotions to higher-level managerial positions for the following specific reasons:

1. Lack of early managerial training for prospective female managers
2. Corporate recruiting practices that rely on word-of-mouth referrals from male managers who recommend other males
3. The use of executive search firms, sometimes referred to as *headhunters*, who fail to pursue qualified female managerial candidates

4. The fact that female managers have often been passed over or have not volunteered for high-visibility projects that provide both exposure and the broad range of experience needed by the organization

Some women do break through the "glass ceiling," however, and become important assets to their companies. Women are especially successful in high-tech, high-growth industries, where they seem to be promoted more quickly than in other fields. The publishing industry also has a history of being receptive to women executives. Health services, social services, the retail-clothing business, and education have large numbers of women in executive positions. Other industries—such as steel, railroads, and mining—have a disproportionately low number of women in top management.

Despite the fact that a few women executives have managed to break through the glass ceiling, a significant amount of research indicates that problems still exist. For example, at the time of this writing, women hold 38 percent of all managerial positions in the United States. Yet these overall statistics are misleading because only three of every one hundred top-level executives are women. There is also still a large gap between the salaries women managers earn and the salaries earned by men in the same positions. According to the most recent wage surveys, women earn approximately 70 cents for every $1 that male managers earn.**

Questions

1. From the material presented in this case, it is obvious that employment discrimination still exists. Assume that you are a job applicant in a discriminatory environment. What can you do to market yourself?
2. Assume that you are a female employee in a lower-level managerial position. What can you do to keep your career on track and to get promotions that will lead to senior management positions?

**Based on information from Paul R. Krugman, "The Painful Cost of Workplace Discrimination," *U.S. News & World Report*, November 4, 1991, p. 63; Susan B. Garland, "How to Keep Women Managers on the Corporate Ladder," *Business Week*, September 2, 1991, p. 64; Susan B. Garland, "Throwing Stones at the 'Glass Ceiling,'" *Business Week*, August 19, 1991, p. 29; Dawn M. Baskerville, "Breaking Through the Glass Ceiling," *Black Enterprise*, August 1991, p. 37; and Amy Saltzman, "Trouble at the Top," *U.S. News & World Report*, June 17, 1991, pp. 40–42+.

Career Profile

Job Title	Job Description	Salary Range
City manager	Coordinate the day-to-day operation of local governments; provide leadership for employees; appoint department heads and supervisors; prepare annual budgets and other financial reports	5
Economic analyst	Track economic data; assist senior analysts in the preparation of reports on the impact of economic changes in a given community, state, or the nation; communicate information to politicians, business managers, and other interested parties	2–3
Economist	Analyze the costs of producing and marketing goods and services; use mathematical models to develop economic theories; prepare reports for profit and non-profit organizations; assess economic conditions in the United States and abroad	3–4
Export manager	Direct foreign sales; negotiate sales with foreign countries; arrange payments; handle transportation of goods; prepare foreign correspondence	3–4
Government chief executive	Appoint people to head departments, such as finance, highways, health, police, recreation; oversee the work of civil servants; prepare budgets; ensure that resources are used properly to encourage economic growth	4–5
Import/export agent	Manage import-export activities for clients; coordinate payments between foreign and domestic buyers and sellers; supervise workers in the shipping and receiving departments; oversee the assessment of import and export duties; determine documents required in foreign trade	3
Paralegal or legal assistant	Perform all the functions of a lawyer other than accepting clients, setting legal fees, giving legal advice or presenting a case in court; investigate the facts of the case; prepare draft documents such as contracts, mortgages, separation agreements, and trust instruments	2–3
Tax attorney	Counsel clients as to their legal rights and obligations; suggest particular courses of action related to tax matters; represent clients in criminal and civil trials; interpret the law and its application; use computers to make tax computations and explore alternative tax strategies for clients	4–5
Urban and regional planner	Develop programs to provide for growth and revitalization of urban, suburban and rural communities; help local officials make decisions on social, economic, and environmental problems; formulate capital improvement plans to construct new school buildings, housing, and other public projects	3–4

The figure in the salary column approximates the expected annual income after two or three years of service. 1 = $12,000–$15,000; 2 = $16,000–$20,000; 3 = $21,000–$27,000; 4 = $28,000–$35,000; 5 = $36,000 and up.

Educational Requirements	Skills Required	Prospects for Growth
Bachelor's or master's degree	Interpersonal; analytical; decision-making	Below average
Bachelor's degree in economics	Computer; communication; problem solving; quantitative; critical thinking	Average
Bachelor's degree in economics	Communication; computer; quantitative; interpersonal; analytical; critical thinking	Above average
Bachelor's degree; on-the-job experience	Communication; interpersonal; decision making; conceptual; critical thinking	Above average
Bachelor's degree in public administration; financial management; master's degree preferred	Communication; problem solving; leadership; decision-making; analytical; conceptual; critical thinking	Average
Bachelor's degree; on-the-job experience	Interpersonal; communication; problem solving; analytical; technical; conceptual	Above average
Associate's or bachelor's degree; on-the-job experience	Communication; computer; problem solving; technical; conceptual	Above average
Bachelor's degree plus at least three years of law school; on-the-job experience	Communication; computer; problem solving; quantitative; analytical; conceptual	Above average
Master's degree in urban or regional planning, on-the-job experience	Communication; computer; decision making; problem solving; analytical; conceptual	Average

NOTES

CHAPTER 1

[1]Based on information from *Moody's Handbook of Common Stocks*, 1991–1992 Winter Edition, Moody's Investors Service, 99 Church Street, New York, N.Y. 10007; "Some New Blocks for Blockbuster," *Business Week*, December 2, 1991, p. 44; Alan Deutschman, "America's Fastest Risers," *Fortune*, October 7, 1991, pp. 46–48; Gail DeGeorge, "Blockbuster's Grainy Picture," *Business Week*, May 20, 1991, pp. 40–41; "A Video Titan Gets Bigger," *U.S. News and World Report*, December 3, 1990, p. 15; and Erik Calonius, "Meet the King of Video," *Fortune*, June 4, 1990, p. 208. [2]Adapted from "The Origins of Enterprise in America," *Exxon U.S.A.*, third quarter, 1976, pp. 8–11.

CHAPTER 2

[1]Based on information from Borden, Inc., Annual Report, pp. 16–19. [2]Rick Wartzman, "Northrop Agrees to Pay About $9 Million to Settle Suit by Two Whistle-Blowers," *Wall Street Journal*, June 24, 1991, p. A3. [3]O.C. Ferrell and Larry G. Gresham, "A Contingency Framework for Understanding Ethical Decision Making in Marketing," *Journal of Marketing*, Summer 1985, pp. 87–96. [4]"Engineers' Duty to Speak Out," *The Nation*, June 28, 1986, p. 880. [5]John J. Fialka, "Employee Charges United Technologies Bribed Two Saudi Princes in Helicopter Sale," *Wall Street Journal*, October 7, 1991, p. A16. [6]Ellen Joan Pollock, "Jury Orders Merrell-Dow to Pay $33.8 Million in Suit Over Nausea Drug," *Wall Street Journal*, October 7, 1991, p. B7. [7]Bridget O'Brian, "Jury Sets Damages at $15 Million in Texaco Case," *Wall Street Journal*, October 4, 1991, p. B12. [8]"Air Pollution: New Approach Needed to Resolve Safety Issues for Vapor Recovery Systems," U.S. General Accounting Office, Report 91–171, (Washington D.C., June 28, 1991), p. 10. [9]"Superfund: More Settlement Authority and EPA Controls Could Increase Cost Recovery," *Reports and Testimony*, August 1991, p. 10. [10]"Fascinating Facts," *Wellness Letter*, University of California at Berkeley, 7:10, July 1991, p. 1. [11]"Water Pollution: Stronger Efforts Needed by EPA to Control Toxic Water Pollution," U.S. Congress. House. Committee on Government Operations, *Report to the Chairman, Environment, Energy, and Natural Resources Subcommittee*, General Accounting Office, (Washington D.C., July 1991), p. 8. [12]*Ibid.* [13]"Acid Rain Affects Coastal Waters Too," *Environment*, June 1988, p. 22. [14]Merrill McLoughlin, "Our Dirty Air," *U.S. News & World Report*, June 12, 1989, p. 54. [15]"A Biodegradable Recyclable Future," *The Economist*, January 7, 1989, pp. 61–62. [16]Faye Rice, "Where Will We Put All That Garbage?" *Fortune*, April 11, 1988, pp. 96–100. [17]"A Biodegradable Recyclable Future," pp. 61–62. [18]*Ibid.* [19]David Landis, "Tighter Rules Put Squeeze on Firms," *USA Today*, May 26, 1989, pp. B-1–B-2.

CHAPTER 3

[1]Based on information from William J. Cook, "Rebuilding Big Blue," *U.S. News & World Report*, December 23, 1991, pp. 48–50; "Starched Collars, Pink People," *U.S. News & World Report*, December 23, 1991, p. 50; "It's Official: IBM and Apple Tie the Knot," *Business Week*, October 14, 1991, p. 54; Deidre A. Depke, "IBM-Apple Could Be Fearsome," *Business Week*, October 7, 1991, pp. 28–30; Deidre A. Depke, "IBM and Apple: Can Two Loners Learn to Say "Teamwork'?," *Business Week*, July 22, 1991, p. 25; Bill Powell, "'The Deal of the Decade'," *Newsweek*, July 15, 1991, p. 40; and Brenda Dalglish, "A High-Tech Alliance," *Maclean's*, July 15, 1991, p. 27. [2]"M&M Products Purchased by Boston Minority Firm," *Jet*, July 17, 1989, pp. 16–17. [3]Cindy Skrzycki, "Why Nonprofit Businesses Are Booming," *U.S. News & World Report*, January 16, 1984, p. 65. [4]Judith H. Dobrzynski, "You Just Can't Mail Out 132 Prospectuses Anymore," *Business Week*, January 28, 1991, pp. 62–64. [5]Jaclyn Fierman, "Deals of the Year," *Fortune*, January 28, 1991, pp. 90–92+.

CHAPTER 4

[1]Based on information from Meg Cox, "Little Rap-Music Magazine Has Big Aims," *Wall Street Journal*, September 25, 1991, p. B1; Anthony Tommasini, "Yo! Harvard Hip-Hop," *Boston Globe*, January 28, 1990, pp. B35–36; and Elizabeth Mehren, "Head of the Class in College of Letters, Arts and Rap," *Los Angeles Times*, April 16, 1990, p. F1. [2]*The State of Small Business: A Report of the President*, 1990, pp. 9–11. [3]Ibid., p. xii. [4]Ibid., pp. 15–19. [5]Small Business Administration, *Annual Report*, 1990, p. 16. [6]Ibid., p. 38. [7]"Here's Help for Women," *USA Today*, May 11, 1989, p. 4B. [8]Mark Robichaux, "Teens in Business Discover Credibility Is Hard to Earn," *Wall Street Journal*, June 9, 1989, pp. B1–B2. [9]Small Business Administration, *Annual Report*, 1990, p. 46. [10]*Report of the Committee on Small Business*, House of Representatives, Ninety-Ninth Congress, January 2, 1987, p. 22. [11]Small Business Administration, *Annual Report*, 1990, p. 20. [12]John R. Emshwiller, "Enterprise," *Wall Street Journal*, December 26, 1990, p. B1. [13]Paul D. Lovett, "Meetings That Work: Plans Bosses Can Approve," *Harvard Business Review*, November-December 1988, pp. 38–41, 44. [14]Marc Leepsonn, "Building a Business: A Matter of Course," *Nation's Business*, April 1988, pp. 42–43. [15]Small Business Administration, *Annual Report*, 1990, p. 50. [16]*Small Business: Development Centers Meet Needs of Most Clients*, U.S. General Accounting Office, U.S. Senate, Committee on Small Business, Brief Report to the Chairman, Washington, D.C., November 1989, p. 15. [17]*The Small Business Advocate*, Small Business Administration, Office of Advocacy, September 1991, p. 10. [18]*The Universal Almanac*, 1991, p. 231. [19]Al Urbanski, "The Franchise Option," *Sales and Marketing Management*, February 1988, pp. 28–33. [20]Jeanne Saddler, "Franchise Pacts Can End in Suits Over Contracts," *Wall Street Journal*, January 15, 1991, p. B1. [21]Ibid.

CHAPTER 5

[1]Based on information from Martha M. Hamilton, "Short-Haul Airline Is Sitting Tall," *Washington Post*, August 8, 1991,

pp. B10, B13; Peter T. Elsworth, "Southwest Air's New Push West," *New York Times*, June 16, 1991; Jim Castelli, "Finding the Right Fit," *HR Magazine*, September 1990, pp. 38–41; Michael Hiestand, "Flying the Wacky Skies With Southwest's CEO," *Adweek's Marketing Week*, July 10, 1989, p. 31; Subrata N. Chakravarty, "Hit 'Em Hardest With the Mostest," *Forbes*, September 16, 1991, pp. 48–50. [2]Henry Mintzberg, "The Manager's Job: Folklore and Fact," *Harvard Business Review*, July-August 1975, pp. 49–61. [3]Michael Cieply, "Meanwhile, Back in Marysville," *Forbes*, March 12, 1984, p. 127. [4]Terrence Deal and Allan Kennedy, *Corporate Culture* (Reading, Mass.: Addison-Wesley, 1982). [5]Ricky W. Griffin, *Management*, 3d ed. (Boston: Houghton Mifflin Company, 1990), pp. 475–476. [6]Robert Kreitner, *Management*, 5th edition (Boston: Houghton Mifflin Company, 1992) p. 462. [7]Griffin, *Management*, p. 125. [8]Kreitner, *Management*, pp. 226–230. [9]John A. Byrne, "Business Is Bountiful for Elite Headhunters," *Business Week*, April 18, 1988, p. 28. [10]Fred Steingraber, "Total Quality Management: A New Look at a Basic Issue," *Vital Speeches of the Day*, May 1990, pp. 415–416.

CHAPTER 6

[1]Based on information from "Bruegger's Bagel Bakery, Burlington, Vt.," *Modern Baking*, July 1990, pp. 4, 61–62; Julie Ritzer Ross, "How Bruegger's Turns Managers into Partners," *Modern Baking*, September 1990, pp. 102–107; Bruce G. Posner, "Raising the Stakes," *Inc.*, March 1990, pp. 100–102. [2]Robert Kreitner, *Management* 5th ed. (Boston: Houghton Mifflin Company, 1992) p. 96. [3]"Lessons from a Successful Intrapreneur," *Journal of Business Strategy*, March-April 1988, pp. 20–24.

CHAPTER 7

[1]Based on information from Maria Shao, Robert Neff, and Jeffrey Ryser, "For Levi's, a Flattering Fit Overseas," *Business Week*, November 5, 1990, pp. 76–77; Margaret Price, "Pitfalls Are Plentiful in Hungarian Market," *Pensions and Investments*, March 4, 1991, p. 1, 31; Natalia Wolniansky and Leon P. Garry, "A New Hungarian Spring?" *Management Review*, July 1991, pp. 37–40; Steven Greenhouse, " In a Failed Hungarian Factory, Jeans succeed," *New York Times*, November 10, 1990; Charles T. Powers, "Levi Strauss Sews Up Enthusiastic Support for Factory in Polish City," *Los Angeles Times*, July 9, 1991; and "A Levi Strauss Plant in Poland", *USA Today*, November 15, 1991. [2]Tim Studt, "$158 Billion and Holding for U.S. R&D in 1991," *R&D Magazine*, January 1991, pp. 38–44. [3]Robert Kreitner, *Management*, 5th ed. (Boston: Houghton Mifflin Company, 1992), p. 598. [4]The least-cost order quantity is found by applying the equation $EOQ = \sqrt{2RC/S}$, where R is the total yearly demand in units, C is the cost of processing an order, and S is the annual storage cost per unit. [5]Kreitner, *Management*, p. 160. [6]Ibid., p. 97. [7]U.S. Department of Labor, *Monthly Labor Review*, July 1991, p. 92.

CHAPTER 8

[1]Based on information from Orel Hershiser, *Out of the Blue*, (Brentwood, TN: Wolgemuth & Hyatt, Inc., 1989), pp. 7–13; Brian Dumaine, "Business Secrets of Tommy LaSorda," *Fortune*, July 3, 1989, pp. 130–132, 135; Tim Kurkjian, "Tommy's Team," *Sports Illustrated*, March 4, 1991, pp. 18–23. [2]Douglas McGregor, *The Human Side of Enterprise* (New York: McGraw-Hill, 1960). [3]William Ouchi, *Theory Z*

(Reading, MA: Addison Wesley, 1981). [4]Ricky W. Griffin, *Management*, 3rd ed. (Boston: Houghton Mifflin Company, 1990), pp. 245–246.

CHAPTER 9

[1]Based on information from "Work and Family," *Bureau of National Affairs, Inc.*, Washington D.C., 1991; Stephanie Lawrence, "What Is Benefits Communication?" *Personnel Journal*, February 1990, pp. 65–67; Time Warner, "Work and Family Program," 1991. [2]Taylor H. Cox and Stacy Blake, "Managing Cultural Diversity: Implications for Organizational Competitiveness," *Academy of Management Executive* 5, no. 3 (1991) pp. 45–56. [3]"A Sampling of Diversity Programs," *Training and Development Journal*, March 1991, p. 43. [4]Jeffrey J. Hallet, "Why Does Recruitment Cost So Much?" *Personnel Administrator*, December 1986, pp. 22–26. [5]David Craig, "Stock Plans Gain Favor as New Benefit," *USA Today*, Sept. 24, 1991, p. B1. [6]William Wiggenhorn, "Motorola U: When Training Becomes an Education," *Harvard Business Review*, July-August 1990, pp. 71–83. [7]Robert Kreitner, *Management*, 5th ed. (Boston: Houghton Mifflin Company, 1992), pp. 327–328.

CHAPTER 10

[1]Based on information from Peter Lazes et al., "Xerox and the ACTWU: Using Labor-Management Teams to Remain Competitive," *National Productivity Review*, Summer 1991, pp. 339–349; Norman E. Rickard, Jr., "The Quest for Quality: A Race Without a Finish Line," *Industrial Engineering*, January 1991, pp. 25–27; Anne Ritter, "Are Unions Worth the Bargain?" *Personnel*, February 1990, pp. 12–14; Dan Cordtz, "Listening to Labor," *Financial World*, September 2, 1991, pp. 44–47.

CHAPTER 11

[1]Based on information from Laura Bird, "Gatorade for Kids," *Adweek's Marketing Week*, July 15, 1991, pp. 4–5; Michael Lev, "Gatorade Sponsoring High School Games," *New York Times*, October 9, 1990; Kevin Goldman, "Gator Raiding's on the Mind of Coke, Pepsi," *Wall Street Journal*, August 2, 1990; Julie Liesse, "Quaker Stays Course Amid Woes," *Advertising Age*, August 6, 1990, pp. 3, 36; Stuart Elliot, "It's Official: Michael Jordan Is Now Promoting Gatorade," *New York Times*, August 9, 1991; Barbara Holsomback, "Dr Pepper Pumping Up Nautilus," *Adweek*, September 9, 1991, pp. 1, 4. [2]Ford Motor Company, *Annual Report, 1988*, p. 6. [3]James F. Engel, Roger D. Blackwell, and Paul W. Miniard, *Consumer Behavior* (Hinsdale, Ill.: Dryden Press, 1990), p. 3. [4]Statistical Abstract of the United States, 1991, p. 453. [5]*Wall Street Journal*, August 21, 1989, p. B1. [6]Jon Berry, "Forever Single," *Adweek's Marketing Week*, October 15, 1990, pp. 20–24. [7]Laura Zinn, "Home Alone—with $660 Billion," *Business Week*, July 29, 1991, pp. 75–77. [8]Bickley Townsend, "Beyond the Boom," *American Demographics*, June 1989, p. 40. [9]*American Demographics*, March 1989, p. 15. [10]Ibid. [11]Allen M. Clark, "Trends That Will Impact New Products," *Journal of Consumer Marketing*, Winter 1991, pp. 35–40.

CHAPTER 12

[1]Based on information from Fara Warner, "The Forgotten Majority," *Adweek's Marketing Week*, September 23, 1991, pp.

16–17; Fara Warner, "The Diet-Food Frenzy," *Adweek's Marketing Week*, August 19, 1991, pp. 4–5; Julie Liesse and Jundann Dagnoli, "Kraft, Campbell on Health Kick," *Advertising Age*, February 11, 1991, pp. 1, 44; Judann Dagnoli and Julie Liesse, "'Healthy' Frozen Foods Launch Offensive," *Advertising Age*, September 2, 1991, pp. 1, 45; Richard Gibson, "ConAgra Plans Several New Lines of 'Healthy' Food," *Wall Street Journal*, September 19, 1991, p. B4; Lois Therrien, "ConAgra Turns Up the Heat in the Kitchen," *Business Week*, September 2, 1991, pp. 58–60; Howard Schlossberg, "Pepperidge Farms Wins Grand Edison," *Marketing News*, May 4, 1990, p. 12. [2]Peter D. Bennett, ed. *Dictionary of Marketing Terms* (Chicago: American Marketing Foundation, 1988), p. 18. [3]Neal Templin and Joseph B. White, "Ford Motor Ventures into Value Pricing," *Wall Street Journal*, September 18, 1991, p. B1.

CHAPTER 13

[1]Based on information from Cyndee Miller, "Sears, Penney Revamp Catalogues to Compete with Specialty Books," *Marketing News*, April 1, 1991, pp. 1, 6; Allan J. Magrath, "Born-Again Marketing," *Across The Board*, June 1991, pp. 33–36; Christy Fisher and Jon Lafayette, "Why Penney's Moved to Bozell," *Advertising Age*, June 17, 1991, pp. 3, 48; Christy Fisher, "Penney's Pinching," *Advertising Age*, September 2, 1991, p. 42; Stephanie Anderson, "Trapped Between the Up and Down Escalators," *Business Week*, August 26, 1991, pp. 49–50. [2]*U.S. Statistical Abstract*, 1991, p. 779. [3]*Ibid.* p. 767. [4]Barry Berman and Joel R. Evans, *Retail Management: A Strategic Approach*, 4th ed. (New York: Macmillan, 1989), pp. 68–69. [5]*Ibid.* [6]William M. Pride and O. C. Ferrell, *Marketing: Basic Concepts and Decisions*, 7th ed. (Boston: Houghton Mifflin Company, 1991), p. 368. [7]*Chain Store Age/Supermarkets*, July 1983, p. 11. [8]Stanley C. Hollander, "The Wheel of Retailing," *Journal of Marketing*, July 1960, p. 37. [9]Adapted from John F. Magee, *Physical Distribution Systems* (New York: McGraw-Hill, 1967), p. 73.

CHAPTER 14

[1]Based on information from Bernice Kanner, "The Secret Life of the Female Consumer," *Working Woman*, December 1990, pp. 69–72; Judann Dagnoli and Elena Bowes, "A Brewing Romance," *Advertising Age*, April 8, 1991, p. 22; Barbara Lippert, "A Coffee Break from Taster's Choice," *Adweek's Marketing Week*, May 6, 1991, p. 29; Tim Allis, Laura Sanderson Healy, and Lorenzo Benet, "Sex by the Cupful," *People*, May 20, 1991, pp. 94–95. [2]*Advertising Age*, May 6, 1991, p. 16. [3]Newton W. Minow, "Television: How Far Has It Come?" *Vital Speeches of the Day*, July 1, 1991, pp. 552–556. [4]*Wall Street Journal*, June 7, 1989, p. B1. [5]*U.S. Statistical Abstract*, 1991, p. 410. [6]Terence A. Shimp, *Promotion Management and Marketing Communications* (Hinsdale, Ill.: The Dryden Press, 1990), pp. 524–525. [7]Scott Hume and Patricia Strand, "FSI Coupon Redemption Hits Wall," *Advertising Age*, March 18, 1991, p. 41. [8]Laurie Petersen, "Clutter Anyone?" *Adweek's Marketing Week*, April 8, 1991, pp. 22, 24. [9]Scott Hume and Marcy Magiera, "Patrons of the Arts," *Advertising Age*, June 3, 1991, p. 36.

CHAPTER 15

[1]Gary Hoover, Alta Campbell, and Patrick J. Spain, eds., *Hoover's Handbook of American Business 1992* (Emeryville,

CA: Publishers Group West, 1991), p. 315; Julie Pitta, "Live by the Clone, Die by the Clone," *Forbes*, October 28, 1991, pp. 109–110; Russell Mitchell, "Intel Isn't Taking This Lying Down," *Business Week*, September 30, 1991, pp. 32–33; Robert Buderi, ed., "U.S. Chipmakers Grab a Bigger Piece of the Pie," *Business Week*, June 24, 1991, p. 113; Richard A. Shaffer, "Intel Lives," *Forbes*, September 30, 1991, p. 164; and Warren Cohen, "Spending on Tomorrow Today," *U.S. News & World Report*, July 22, 1991, pp. 45–46. [2]Deidre A. Depke, "PCs: What the Future Holds," *Business Week*, August 12, 1991, pp. 58–64.

CHAPTER 16

[1]Scott Shuger and Ned Martel, "The High Cost of Unaccountable Accounting," *The Washington Monthly*, January, 1990, p. 26. [2]Steven Waldman, "The Other S&L Culprits," *Newsweek*, October 29, 1990, p. 54. [3]Based on information from Lee Berton, "Legal-Liability Awards Are Frightening Smaller CPA Firms Away From Audits," *Wall Street Journal*, March 3, 1992, p. B1+; Gary Hoover, Alta Campbell, and Patrick J. Spain, eds., *Hoover's Handbook of American Business 1992*, (Emeryville, CA.: The Reference Press, Inc., 1991), p. 244; "Audit at Your Peril," *Time*, February 18, 1991, p. 57; "A Failure of Principles?," *Time*, December 17, 1990, p. 71; Steven Waldman, "The Other S & L Culprits," *Newsweek*, pp. 54–55; Scott Shuger and Ned Martel, "The High Cost of Unaccountable Accounting," *The Washington Monthly*, January, 1990, pp. 26–27.

CHAPTER 17

[1]Kate Ballen, "America's Most Admired Corporations," *Fortune*, February 10, 1992, p. 64; John Meehan, "Mighty Morgan," *Business Week*, December 23, 1991, pp. 64–69; "New Morgan, Old Verities," *Business Week*, December 23, 1991, p. 104; Laura Jereski, "Good News at Last," *Forbes*, October 28, 1991, p. 44; "Winners and Losers," *The Economist*, March 2, 1991, pp. 76–77; Penelope Wang, "Six Gems Amid the Rubble," *Money*, January, 1991, pp. 56–57; and Jack Egan, "Betting on Bulletproof Banks," *U.S. News & World Report*, January 21, 1991, p. 83. [2]Frank McCoy, "The World's Biggest Fire Sale," *Black Enterprise*, June 1991, p. 267. [3]Mark S. Hoffman, ed., *The World Almanac and Book of Facts 1991* (New York: Pharos Books, 1990), p. 127. [4]Terence P. Pare, "How to Hold Down S&L Losses," *Fortune*, February 11, 1991, p. 100. [5]*Statistical Abstract of the United States 1990*, U.S. Department of the United States, Bureau of Census, 1990, p. 500. [6]John W. Wright, ed., *The Universal Almanac 1991* (New York: Andrews and McMeel, 1990), p. 219. [7]*Ibid.*, p. 217.

CHAPTER 18

[1]Geoffrey Smith, "$183 Million for the Celts? Now That's a Stretch," *Business Week*, February 24, 1992, pp. 86–87; Gary Hoover, Alta Campbell, and Patrick J. Spain, eds., *Hoover's Handbook of American Business 1992*, (Emeryville, CA: Publishers Group West, 1991), p. 390; "Morgan Stanley Group Inc.," *Moody's Handbook of Common Stocks*, Winter 1991–92, Moody's Investors Service, 99 Church Street, New York N.Y. 10007; Matthew Schifrin, "Bull in Morgan's China Shop," *Forbes*, February 19, 1990, pp. 94–98; Frederick Ungeheuer, "We Don't Have to Have All of Our Cake Today," *Time*, February 26, 1990, p. 52. [2]Jordan E. Goodman, "Come Soar with Companies That Are Dumping Their Debt," *Money*, July,

1991, p. 60. ³Judith H. Dobrzynski, "Would $2 Billion Buy Faith in RJR Nabisco?," *Business Week*, April 9, 1990, p. 70. ⁴David Zigas, "Junk Is Ripping Into Commercial Paper," *Business Week*, March 26, 1990, p. 84+. ⁵"Why the Buybacks at Diasonics?," *Business Week*, February 4, 1991, p. 80. ⁶Wilbur W. Widicus and Thomas E. Stitzel, *Personal Investing*, 5th. ed. (Homewood, IL.: Irwin, 1989), p. 162. ⁷*General Motors Annual Report*, 1990, p. 27. ⁸*Exxon Annual Report*, 1990, p. 39.

CHAPTER 19

¹Thomas Jaffe, ed., "Tough Act to Follow," *Forbes*, January 6, 1992, p. 292; *Moody's Handbook of Common Stocks*, Winter 1991-1992, Moody's Investors Service, 99 Church Street, New York, N.Y. 10007; Gary Hoover, Alta Campbell, and Patrick J. Spain, *Hoover's Handbook of American Business 1992*, (Emeryville, CA: Publishers Group West, 1991), p. 172; Gene Marcial, "This Discount Broker Looks Like a Bargain," *Business Week*, June 17, 1991, p. 92; Dan Moreau, "Change Agents," *Changing Times*, October, 1990, p. 112; and Maria Shao, "Suddenly, the Envy of the Street Is . . . Schwab?," *Business Week*, March 19, 1990, p. 102. ²Mark Hulbert, "Getting Taken," *Forbes*, June 24, 1991, p. 218. ³Chase, C. David. *Chase Global Investment Almanac* (Homewood, IL.: Chase Global Data and Research, Inc. and Dow Jones-Irwin, 1989), p. 94. ⁴Beth Kobliner, "Tight Times for 20-Somethings," *Money*, August 1991, p. 56.

CHAPTER 20

¹Based on information from Sears, Roebuck and Co., *Annual Report*, 1990, pp. 6–7; Sears, Roebuck and Co., *Sears Today*, n.d., n.p.; *News from Sears, Roebuck and Co.*, October 23, 1991, n.p.; Alfred G. Haggerty, "Allstate Invests in Collision Avoidance System," *National Underwriter Property & Casualty*, August 5, 1991, p. C12; Kenneth Reich, "Allstate Wants to Trim Number of New Car Policies," *Los Angeles Times*, June 8, 1991, p. D1. ²*U.S. Industrial Outlook 1991*, U.S. Department of Commerce, pp. 50–51. ³"Proper Precautions Trim Product Liability Risks," *Inc.*, May 1980, p. 131. ⁴*Source Book of Health Insurance Data: 1991–1992* (Health Insurance Association of America). ⁵Jack R. Kapoor, Les R. Dlabay, and Robert J. Hughes, *Personal Finance*, 2nd ed. (Homewood, Ill.: Richard D. Irwin, 1991), p. 375. ⁶*U.S. Industrial Outlook 1991*, U.S. Department of Commerce, pp. 50–51.

CHAPTER 21

¹Based on information from Gary Hoover, Alta Campbell, and Patrick J. Spain, eds., *Hoover's Handbook of American Business 1992*, (Emeryville, CA., The Reference Press, Inc., 1991), p. 559; Harris Collingwood, ed., "No Hard Feelings, Miss Piggy," *Business Week*, May 13, 1991, p. 52; "Kermit the Frog and Mickey Mouse," *U.S. News & World Report*, May 13, 1991, p. 21; Larry Reibstein, "Kermit vs. Mickey Mouse," *Newsweek*, April 29, 1991, pp. 42–43; Lisa Gubernick, "Did Mickey Shaft Kermit?," *Forbes*, April 29, 1991, p. 44; Harris Collingwood, "Gosh, the Muppets vs. Mickey!" *Business Week*, April 29, 1991, p. 40; "K. Frog v M. Mouse," *The Economist*, April 20, 1991, p. 75; and "Even Kermit Has His Price," *Time*, September 11, 1989, p. 59. ²"Black Woman Wins $43 Million in Accident Suit," *Jet*, January 8, 1990, pp. 10–11. ³Summarized from 11 USC 507 (1–6).

CHAPTER 22

¹Michael Duffy, "Need Friends in High Places?," *Time*, November 4, 1991, p. 25. Based on information from Steven Waldman and Mary Hager, "A Quayle Hunts the Watchdogs," *Newsweek*, January 6, 1992, p. 34; Tim Smart, "Quayle's Pet Project Is Looking More Like a Liability," *Business Week*, December 23, 1991, p. 39; Douglas Harbrecht, "Dan Quayle, Regulation Terminator," *Business Week*, November 4, 1991, p. 31; Paul Rauber, *Sierra*, September/October 1991, pp. 42–43+; and Jim Sibbison, "Dan Quayle, Business's Backdoor Boy," *The Nation*, July 29, 1991, p. 1+. ²*Statistical Abstract of the United States 1991*, 111th ed.," U.S. Department of Commerce, p. 278. ³See Sherman Act 15 U.S.C.A., Sec. 1–7. ⁴Keith Davis, William C. Frederick, and Robert L. Blomstrom, *Business and Society*, 4th ed. (New York: McGraw-Hill, 1980), pp. 263–264. ⁵*Economic Report of the President* (Washington, D.C.: U.S. Government Printing Office, 1989), pp. 188–195. ⁶John W. Merline, "Regulatory Rebound," *Consumers' Research*, January 1991, p. 38. ⁷*Ibid.* ⁸"Deregulation: A Fast Start for the Reagan Strategy," *Business Week*, March 9, 1981, p. 63. ⁹*Economic Report of the President* (Washington, D.C.: U.S. Government Printing Office, 1989), pp. 188–189. ¹⁰Albert R. Karr and Muriel McQueen, "Adjusting Course," *Wall Street Journal*, November 27, 1989, p. 1+. ¹¹Merline, *op.cit.* ¹²Murray Weidenbaum, "The Consumer's Stake in Deregulation," *Vital Speeches of the Day*, January 1, 1991, p. 188. ¹³Based on information from the Internal Revenue Service and the Alcohol, Tobacco, and Firearms Department of the U.S. Treasury on December 27, 1991.

CHAPTER 23

¹Based on information from Colgate-Palmolive Company, *Annual Report, 1990*, pp. 1–16; "Exporting Pays Off," *Business America*, June 17, 1991, p. 24; "Exporting Pays Off," *Business America*, November 4, 1991, p. 21; "Exporting Pays Off," *Business America*, May 6, 1991, p. 22. ²"U.S. Customs Blocks Suspected Chinese Prison Labor Goods," *Wall Street Journal*, October 7, 1991, p. B7D. ³*Business America*, April 22, 1991, p. 5. ⁴Joseph B. White and Bob Davis, "U.S. Says Japan is 'Dumping' In Minivan War," *Wall Street Journal*, December 23, 1991, pp. B1+. ⁵Ibid. ⁶Nayan Chanda, "Pressure Mounts for U.S. to Lift Embargo on Vietnam, But Obstacles Still Loom," *Wall Street Journal*, December 20, 1991, p. 3B. ⁷James Bovard, "Torpedo Shipping Protection," *Wall Street Journal*, November 26, 1991, p. A14. ⁸"American Free Trade Policy: Rhetoric or Reality?" *Imprimis*, August 1989, p. 2. ⁹Joseph B. White and Bob Davis, "U.S. Says Japan is "Dumping' in Minivan War," *Wall Street Journal*, December 23, 1991, p. B6. ¹⁰The *Economic Report of the President*, February 1991, pp. 240–241. ¹¹Linda C. Hunter, "U.S. Trade Protection: Effects on the Industrial and Regional Composition of Employment," *Economic Review*, Federal Reserve Bank of Dallas, January 1990, pp. 1–11. ¹²"U.S. Trade Facts," *Business America*, May 6, 1991, p. 10. ¹³John E. Jelacic, "The International Economic Outlook in 1992," *U.S. Industrial Outlook 1991*, U.S. Department of Commerce/International Trade Administration, p. 7. ¹⁴Robin Knight and David Lawday, "Boarding the European Bandwagon," *U.S. News & World Report*, December 9, 1991, pp. 42–43. ¹⁵Lawrie Hays, "Russia Removes Price Controls on Most Goods," *Wall Street Journal*, January 2, 1992, p. 3. ¹⁶Ameritech, *Annual Report, 1990*, p. 8. ¹⁷Peter F. Drucker, "Secrets of the U.S. Export Boom," *Wall Street Journal*, Au-

gust 1, 1991, p. A12. [18]Louis J. Murphy, "Negotiations Are at Work in Geneva to Conclude the Uruguay Round," *Business America*, September 23, 1991, p. 12. [19]Mark M. Nelson and Martin DuBois, "Pact Expands Europe's Common Market," *Wall Street Journal*, October 23, 1991, and "European Trade Blocs OK Merger," *Chicago Tribune*, November 23, 1991, Section 3, p. 1. [20]Roger W. Wallace, "North American Free Trade Agreement: Generating Jobs for Americans," *Business America*, April 8, 1991, p. 3. [21]General Mills, Inc., *Annual Report, 1991*, pp. 2, 12–13. [22]Caleb Solomon, "Pennzoil Enters Joint Venture in Russia to Produce, Export Oil as Early as '92," *Wall Street Journal*, December 24, 1991, p. A2. [23]Colgate-Palmolive Company, *Third Quarter Report, 1991*, pp. 3–4. [24]Peter G. Peterson, "Japan's 'Invasion': A Matter of 'Fairness'," *Wall Street Journal*, November 3, 1989, p. A12. [25]Carl A. Gerstacker, *A Look at Business in 1990* (Washington, D.C.: U.S. Government Printing Office, November 1990), pp. 274–275. [26]Adapted from *Business Week*, December 6, 1976, pp. 91–92.

CHAPTER 24

[1]Kathryn Stechert, "The High-Level Job Search," *Working Woman*, October, 1986, p. 120. [2]Based on information from Betty Winston Baye, *Essence*, October 1991, p. 69+; Laurel Allison Touby, "Reality Check," *Seventeen*, August, 1991, pp. 112–115; "Getting Back to Work if Your Job Quits You," *Occupational Outlook Quarterly*, Summer 1991, p. 33; Max Carey, "How to Assess a Job Offer," *Occupational Outlook Quarterly*, Winter 1990/1991, pp. 19–23; Madeline and Robert Swain, "How Long a Job Search Takes," *Working Woman*, August 1988, pp. 76–77+; and Kathryn Stechert, "The High-Level Job Search," *Working Woman*, October 1986, pp. 120–122+.

CREDITS

Box Credits

CHAPTER 1 (continued from p. iv)

"So You Wanna Be a Mail-Order Star," *Business Week*, July 1, 1991, pp. 66–67; Julie Pitts, "Computer Crow," *Forbes*, June 10, 1991, p. 10; and Banning Kent Lary, "An 'Instinct' for Computer Success," *Nation's Business*, April 1991, pp. 46–47. **26** Based on information from George M. Taber, "Rx for Russia: Shock Therapy," *Time*, January 27, 1992, p. 37; Malcolm Gray, "'How Will I Survive?'" *Maclean's*, January 20, 1992, pp. 24–26; Rae Corelli, "New Year's Shock," *Maclean's*, January 13, 1992, pp. 18–19; Malcolm Gray, "Red Star Falling," *Maclean's*, December 30, 1991, pp. 12–14; and Boris Yeltsin, "Russia Will Revive," *Vital Speeches of the Day*, September 1, 1991, pp. 677–678. **31** Based on information from "Con Games That Target the Elderly," *Consumer's Research*, September 1991, pp. 30–32; Dallas Galvin, "Mail Fraud and Telescams," *New Choices*, September 1991, pp. 34–35; "Buyer Beware," *Kiplinger's Personal Finance Magazine*, July 1991, p. 28; Richard L. Stern and Reed Abelson, "The Second-Oldest Industry," *Forbes*, June 24, 1991, p. 236; and "Scams Target Believers," *Christianity Today*, May 27, 1991, p. 57.

CHAPTER 2

44 Based on information from O. C. Ferrell and John Fraedrich, *Business Ethics: Ethical Decision Making and Cases* (Boston: Houghton Mifflin, 1991), pp. 154–160; Colgate-Palmolive Company, *1990 Annual Report*, p. 40; and John J. Fialka, "Employee Charges United Technologies Bribed Two Saudi Princes in Helicopter Sale," *Wall Street Journal*, October 7, 1991, p. A16. **47** Adapted from Robert Hughes and Jack Kapoor, *Business*, (Chicago: Rand McNally, 1980), p. 540. **63** Based on information from Melanie Griffin and Thomas H. Hanna, "Resolved: Consumers Benefit from Stronger Fuel Efficiency Legislation," *At Home with Consumers*, The Direct Selling Education Foundation, (Washington D.C., September 1991), pp. 1–6.

CHAPTER 3

75 Based on information from Bruce W. Nelan, "Desperate Moves," *Time*, September 2, 1991, pp. 25–26+; Suddeutsche Zeitung, "Crime and Violence Already on the Rise," *World Press Review*, February 1991, pp. 16–17; Richard I. Kirkland, Jr., "Can Capitalism Save Perestroika?" *Fortune*, July 30, 1990, p. 137; Lee Smith, "Can You Make Any Money in Russia?" *Fortune*, January 1, 1990, pp. 103–104+; and Alan S. Blinder, "Let's Help the East Bloc by Exporting Entrepreneurs," *Business Week*, January 29, 1990, p. 20. **82** Based on information from Lloyd Gite, "Living and Working Together," *Glamour*, April 1991, p. 128; Ronaleen R. Roha, "Enterprising Couples," *Changing Times*, December 1990, pp. 73–76; Dalton Narine, "Wives and Husbands Who Work Together," *Ebony*, March 1990, pp. 35–36+; Kevin D. Thompson, "Married . . . with Business," *Black Enterprise*, April 1990, p. 47+; and Linda Lee Small and Susan McHenry, "For Love and Money," *New Choices*, January 1990, pp. 45–48. **97** Based on information from Judith H. Dobrzynski, "Takeovers Used to Be Too Easy. Now They're Too Hard," *Business Week*, April 22, 1991, p. 29; "Balance Sheet Surgeons," *World Press Review*, April 1991, p. 40; Judith H. Dobrzynski, "'You Just Can't Mail Out 132 Prospectuses Anymore'," *Business Week*, January 28, 1991, pp. 62–64; Larry Light, "For Buyers with Cash, It's a Shopper's Delight," *Business Week*, January 28, 1991, p. 63; and Jaclyn Fierman, "Deals of the Year," *Fortune*, January 28, 1991, pp. 90–92.

CHAPTER 4

111 Source: Your Personal Assessment, *Small Business Management Training Instructor's Handout* (Washington, D.C.: The U.S. Small Business Administration, Office of Business Development) n.p., n.d. **116** Based on information from Lena H. Sun, "China's Premier Urges Tight Controls, Slow Reform," *Washington Post*, March 25, 1991, p. 12; Allison E. W. Conner, "Private Sector Shrinking under Intense Criticism and Increasing Controls," *East Asian Executive Reports: China*, December 15, 1989, p. 10; Adi Ignatius, "A Tiny Chinese Venture into Capitalism Feels Icy Chills in Wake of Crackdowns," *Wall Street Journal*, March 8, 1990, p. B2; and Sheila Melvin, "China's Entrepreneurs: Keeping the Faith after Tiananmen," *Freeman*, October 1991, pp. 380–386. **124** Source: U.S. Department of Commerce, *Franchise Opportunities Handbook* (Washington, D.C.: U.S. Government Printing Office, June 1991), pp. 11–12.

CHAPTER 5

151 Based on information from Nancy K. Austin, "Race Against Time—and Win," *Working Woman*, November 1990, pp. 48, 50, 52, 54; Spencer Hud, "Making Meetings More Meaningful," *Washington Post*, July 1, 1990, p. H3; Peter Passell, "Time Is Money and Other Things," *New York Times*, December 19, 1990, p. D2; Jane Applegate, "An Organized Effort to Cut through the Clutter," *Washington Post*, February 4, 1991. **154** Based on information from Dana Milbank, "Alcoa's President, Fetterolf, Leaves Firm over Differences with Chairman O'Neill," *Wall Street Journal*, July 31, 1991; Laura Sessions Stepp, "New Test of Values at Alcoa," *Washington Post*, August 4, 1991; Laura Sessions Stepp, "In Search of Ethics," *Washington Post*, March 31, 1991. **161** Based on information from Brad Stratton, "A Different Look at the Baldrige Award," *Quality Progress*, February 1991, pp. 17–20; J. M. Juran, "Strategies for World-Class Quality," *Quality*

Progress, March 1991, pp. 81–85; Ron Zemke, "Bashing the Baldrige," *Training*, February 1991, pp. 29–34, 36, 38–39; Micheline Maynard, "No Price Tag on Being Best, Winners Show," *USA Today*, October 10, 1991, pp. 1B–2B; Micheline Maynard, "Glory and Pain of Taking the Prize," *USA Today*, October 10, 1991, p. 2B; Philip B. Crosby and Curt Reimann, "Criticism and Support for the Baldrige Award," *Quality Progress*, May 1991, pp. 41–44; Mark Ivey and John Carey, "The Ecstasy and the Agony," *Business Week*, October 21, 1991, p. 40.

CHAPTER 6

172 Based on information from "The World's Biggest Industrial Corporations: How They Performed in 1990," *Fortune*, July 29, 1991, pp. 237–286; Jane Sasseen, "GM Moves up a Gear," *International Management*, February 1991, pp. 46–47, 49; "America's New King of Europe's Roads," *Economist*, March 9, 1991, pp. 63–64, 70; Paul A. Eisenstein, "In Ex-Communist Bloc, World's Big Automakers See New Plants, Markets," *Christian Science Monitor*, November 29, 1990, p. 7; James Risen, "General Motors Turns to Europe for Its Future," *Los Angeles Times*, August 2, 1990; Alex Taylor, III, "Can GM Remodel Itself," *Fortune*, January 13, 1992, pp. 26–29; 32–34. **176** Based on information from "Business Ethics Get Renewed Push," *Wall Street Journal*, February 6, 1990; Erika Penzer, "Doing the Right Thing," *Incentive*, April 1991, pp. 60–62; Keith Bradsher, "Nynex to Establish Office to Address Ethical Issues," *New York Times*, August 3, 1990; John D. Bishop, "The Moral Responsibility of Corporate Executives for Disasters," *Journal of Business Ethics* 10 (1991), pp. 377–383; Betsy Weisendanger, "Doing the Right Thing," *Sales & Marketing Management*, March 1991, pp. 82–83; Andrew S. Grove, "What's the Right Thing? Everyday Ethical Dilemmas," *Working Woman*, June 1990, pp. 16, 18, 20; Ronni Sandroff, "How Ethical Is American Business?" *Working Woman*, September 1990, pp. 113–114, 116, 129; David R. Francis, "Prevent Trouble by Improving Ethics," *Christian Science Monitor*, June 14, 1991. **186** Based on information from Roger Fritz, "Career Key: How to Influence Your Boss," *Supervisory Management*, August 1990, pp. 10–11; Suzanne B. Laporte, "Surviving the Big Bad Boss," *Working Woman*, March 1991, pp. 38, 40; Hendrie Weisinger, "How Should You Criticize Your Boss? Carefully." *Working Woman*, February 2, 1990, pp. 90–91, 122–123; Judith Waldrop, "Meet the New Boss," *American Demographics*, June 1991, pp. 26–27, 29, 32–33; Adele Scheele, "The Bad Boss: Can You Make Him Better?" *Working Woman*, June 1991, pp. 26, 28; Marc B. Rubner, "More Workers Prefer a Man in Charge," *American Demographics*, June 1991, p. 11.

CHAPTER 7

200 Based on information from Michael Dobbs, "In Moscow, Running out of Socks," *Washington Post*, June 22, 1991; Klas Bergman, "A Factory Impatient for Reforms," *CSM*, April 12, 1990; Esther B. Fein, "Reactors to Cartons: Soviets Make a Factory Less Military," *New York Times*, July 27, 1991; Justin Burke, "Marxist Cloud May Linger behind the Party," *Christian Science Monitor*, August 29, 1991. **207** Based on information from Nelson Antosh, "Aluminum Adds Strength to Quanex Mix," *Houston Chronicle*, September 30, 1991, p. 4B; Peter Nulty, "The Less-Is-More Strategy," *Fortune*, December 2, 1991, pp. 102, 106; Frank Bocchino, "Nichols-Homeshield Builds Outside the Building Market," *Metal Center News*,

November 1991; Quanex Corporation, *Annual Report*, 1990; *Fourth Quarter Report*, 1991. **214** Based on information from Robert Ronstadt, "Just-in-Time and Small Business Evolution," *Entrepreneurship Theory and Practice*, Summer 1990, pp. 51–65; Charles R. O'Neal and Kate Bertrand, "Developing a Winning JIT Marketing Strategy," *Small Business Reports*, October 1991, pp. 68–71; R. Anthony Inman and Satishi Mehra, "The Transferability of Just-in-Time Concepts to American Small Business," *Interfaces*, March–April 1990, pp. 30–37; Damodar Y. Golhar, Carol L. Stamm, and Wayland P. Smith, "JIT Implementation in Small Manufacturing Firms," *Production and Inventory Management Journal*, Second Quarter, 1990, pp. 44–48.

CHAPTER 8

234 Based on information from Charles A. Jaffe, "Management by Fun," *Nation's Business*, January 1990, pp. 58–60; Marjorie S. Allison, "Funny Business," *Incentive*, March 1991, pp. 41–43; Julia Lawlor, "Employee Encouraged to Lighten Up," *USA Today*, September 23, 1991, pp. B1–2; Anne M. Russell and Lorraine Calvacca, "Should You Be Funny at Work?" *Working Woman*, pp. 74–75, 126, 128. **244** Based on information from Martha E. Mangelsdorf, "Managing the New York Force," *Inc.*, January 1990, pp. 79–81, 83; Nina Simonds, "An Easter Surprise from Harbor Sweets," *Boston Globe*, March 30, 1988; Ruth Mehrtens Galvin, "Sybaritic to Some, Sinful to Others, But How Sweet It Is!" *Smithsonian*, February, 1986. **253** Based on information from Gary N. Powell and Lisa A. Mainiero, "What Managers Need to Know about Office Romances," *Leadership and Organization Development Journal 11*, no. 1 (1990), i–iii; Lee Colby, "Regulating Love," *Personnel*, June 1991, p. 23; Andrew S. Grove, "Office Romance: How to Handle the Heat," *Working Woman*, December 1990, pp. 24, 26–27; Ellen Rapp, "Dangerous Liaisons," *Working Woman*, February 1991, pp. 56–61.

CHAPTER 9

267 Based on information from "A Sampling of Diversity Programs," *Training & Development Journal*, March 1991, pp. 40–44; Abby Livingston, "12 Companies That Do the Right Thing," *Working Woman*, January 1991, pp. 57, 59–60; Shari Caudron, "Monsanto Responds to Diversity," *Personnel Journal*, November 1990, pp. 72–80; Constance Gemson, "How to Cultivate Today's Multi-Cultural Work Force," *Employment Relations Today*, Summer 1991, pp. 157–160. **275** Based on information from Adele Scheele, "How to Get the Raise You Want," *Working Woman*, January 1991, p. 71; Marilyn Moats Kennedy, "Can You Ask for a Raise Right Now?" *Glamour*, February 2, 1990, p. 85; "Getting Your Point Across to Each Group," *Working Woman*, July 1991, p. 47; Anita Gates, "How to Be the One They Promote," *Working Woman*, October 1990, pp. 100, 102–105. **286** Based on information from Stephen J. Adler, "Suits over Sexual Harassment Prove Difficult Due to Issue of Definition," *Wall Street Journal*, October 9, 1991, pp. B1, B4; Tamar Lewin, "Ruling on Pinups as Sexual Harassment: What Does It Mean?" *New York Times*, February 8, 1991; Julia Lawlor and Kevin Maney, "Harassment Not Sole Root of Tension," *USA Today*, October 11, 1991; Barbara Kantrowitz et al., "Striking a Nerve," *Newsweek*, October 21, 1991, pp. 34–38, 40; Joann S. Lublin, "Companies Try a Variety of Approaches to Halt Sexual Harassment on the Job," *Wall Street Journal*, October 11, 1991, pp. B1, B3; Nancy Gibbs, "Office Crimes," *Time*, October 21, 1991, pp. 52–54,

63–64; "Harassment: Views in the Workplace," *Wall Street Journal*, October 10, 1991.

CHAPTER 10

207 Based on information from Paul Jarley and Jack Fiorito, "Unionism and Changing Employee Views toward Work," *Journal of Labor Research*, Summer 1991, pp. 223–229; John S. Heywood, "Who Queues for a Union Job?" *Industrial Relations*, Winter 1990, pp. 119–134; Anne Ritter, "Are Unions Worth the Bargain?" *Personnel*, February 1990, pp. 12–14; "America's Trade Unions Return from the Dead," *The Economist*, February 10, 1990, pp. 66–67; Victor Kamber, Keith Geiger, Albert Shanker, et al., "Are Unions Dead?" *Business and Society Review*, Summer 1990, pp. 4–10; Bureau of Labor Statistics, "Union Members in 1990," *United States Department of Labor News*, February 6, 1991. **309** Based on information from Rhonda Rhodes, "The NLBR Bargaining Rules: Why Employees Turn to Unions," *Trustee*, July 1990, pp. 20–21; Jonathan Tasini, "Local Heroes," *Village Voice*, February 6, 1990, p. 59; "ANA Wins Battle for VA Nurses' Right to Bargain," *American Journal of Nursing*, July 1991, p. 72; "Splinter, Divide, and Organize," *Industry Week*, June 4, 1990, p. 14; "Supreme Court Upholds Health Care Bargaining Unit Rule," *Personnel Journal*, July 1991, pp. 22–23. **316** Based on information from "Manning the Mines with Foreign Workers," *Business Korea*, April 1991, p. 15; "All Losers, No Winners," *Business Korea*, February 1991, p. 26; "In Need of a Fair Referee," *Business Korea*, March 1991, pp. 34–35; "In Search of Common Goals," *Business Korea*, April 1991, pp. 16, 18.

CHAPTER 11

334 Based on information from "Philip Butler: Grucci's Rocket Scientist," *Sales & Marketing Management*, July 1991, pp. 22–23; Alex Kozlov, "First Family of Fireworks," *Discover*, July 1990, pp. 40–45; "Fireworks Fizzle," *Wall Street Journal*, June 28, 1990; Andrew H. Malcolm, "Our Towns," *New York Times*, July 2, 1991; John R. Enswiler, "For Fireworks Families, Passing the Torch Is Tradition," *Wall Street Journal*, September 5, 1990; Press Release Packet, Fireworks by Grucci, 1991. **340** Based on information from Sara Nelson, "What's the Big Idea," *Working Woman*, July 1990, pp. 96, 98, 108; Andy Fry, "The Year of European Media Revolutions," *Marketing*, March 28, 1991, pp. 25–26; Peter Newcomb, "Music Video Wars," *Forbes*, March 4, 1991, pp. 68, 70. **349** Based on information from Joann A. Lublin, "WPP's Scali Gives up the Volvo Account," *Wall Street Journal*, November 14, 1990, p. B6; Krystal Miller, "Such an Ad Was Almost Certain to Make Somebody Hit the Roof," *Wall Street Journal*, November 8, 1990, p. B1; "Volvo Settles with Texas," *Wall Street Journal*, November 6, 1990, p. B10; "Taking 'EM for a Ride," *Time*, November 19, 1990, p. 85; David Kiley, "Candid Camera: Volvo and the Art of Deception," *Adweek's Marketing Week*, November 12, 1990, pp. 4–5; Raymond Serafin and Gary Levin, "Ad Industry Suffers Crushing Blow," *Advertising Age*, November 12, 1990, pp. 1, 76–77; Stuart Elliot, "Ad Agency Quits Over Volvo Ad," *USA Today*, November 14, 1990, p. 1; Raymond Serafin and Jennifer Lawrence, "Four More Volvo Ads Scrutinized," *Advertising Age*, November 26, 1990, p. 3; and "As Volvo Sales Slide, Do Ads Share Blame?" *Wall Street Journal*, December 3, 1990, p. B1; David Kiley, "The FTC Sends a Post-Volvo Message to Marketers," *Adweek's Marketing Week*, February 18, 1991, p. 10; Raymond Serafin, "No More 'Monsters'," *Advertising Age*, September 23, 1991, pp. 1, 42.

CHAPTER 12

369 Based on information from Laurel Wentz, "Nestlé Sweet on Int'l Partnerships," *Advertising Age*, December 12, 1990, p. 31; Damon Darlin, "Coke, Nestlé Launch First Coffee Drink," *Wall Street Journal*, October 1, 1991, pp. B1, B6; Martha Groves, "Nestlé, Coke, Plan Joint Venture for Ready-Made Coffee and Teas," *Los Angeles Times*, November 30, 1990. **376** Based on information from Laurie Petersen, "Shed the Egg, Spare the Image," *Adweek's Marketing Week*, July 15, 1991, p. 9; "A Good Egg Gets Better," *Time Magazine*, July 22, 1991, p. 51; Anthony Ramirez, "L'eggs Makes Big Switch: From Plastic to Cardboard," *New York Times*, July 10, 1991, pp. D1, D7; Pat Sloan, "L'eggs Egg Cracks," *Advertising Age*, July 15, 1991, p. 16; "L'eggs to Scrap Plastic Egg Package," *Marketing News*, August 19, 1991, p. 20; "L'eggs to Eliminate Egg Containers," *Los Angeles Times*, July 10, 1991, p. D2. **382** Based on information from Cara Appelbaum, "The Man in the Grayish Rayon Suit," *Adweek's Marketing Week*, September 30, 1991, p. 20; Julia Lawlor, "Survey: Office Attire Lightens Up," *USA Today*, September 17, 1991; Troy Segal, "Executive Fall Fashion," *Business Week*, September 24, 1990; Paula S. Gray, "Working on Motherhood," *Black Enterprise*, July 1990, pp. 70–73.

CHAPTER 13

399 Based on information from Edward O. Welles, "A Quantified Success," *Inc.*, August 1991, pp. 54–56, 58–60; Marla Cohen, "Bike Shop Rolls Out a Champ," *Chapel Hill (NC) News and Observer*, May 16, 1991; Wendy Bounds, "Business Grew from Home," *Chapel Hill (NC) Herald*, May 9, 1991; Neil Koomen, "He's Helping the Olympic Biking Team," *Hendersonville Times-News*, May 20, 1991; Selected company information provided by Performance Bicycles, Inc. **411** Based on information from Dori Jones Yang, "Bargains by the Forklift," *Business Week*, July 15, 1991, p. 152; Dori Jones Yang, "Corn Flakes, Aisle 1. Cadillacs, Aisle 12," *Business Week*, April 29, 1991, pp. 68–70; Debra Chanil, "Wholesale Club Update," *DM*, November 1990, pp. 58–62; Steve Weinstein, "The Power of the Club," *Progressive Grocer*, February 1991, pp. 26–28, 30, 32; Howard C. Gelbtuch, "The Warehouse Club Industry," *Appraisal Journal*, pp. 153–159; Richard S. Bragaw, "Pioneering the Wholesale Club Concept," *DM*, November 1990, pp. 42, 44, 48; Karen Blumenthal, "Shopping Clubs Ready for Battle in Texas Market," *Wall Street Journal*, October 24, 1991. **419** Based on information from Karen Levine, "Making Money from Home," *Parents*, November 1991, pp. 89–92; Thomas V. Bonoma, "This Snake Rises in Bad Times," *Marketing News*, February 18, 1991, p. 16; Eric Schine, "100,000 FundAmerica Customers Couldn't Be Wrong, Could They?" *Business Week*, September 3, 1990, pp. 40, 42; Paul Klebnikov, "The Power of Positive Inspiration," *Forbes*, December 9, 1991, pp. 244–249; Richard L. Stern and Mary Beth Grover, "Pyramid Power?" *Forbes*, November 11, 1991, pp. 139, 142, 147–148.

CHAPTER 14

437 Based on information from Joanne Lipman, "Sexy or Sexist? Recent Ads Spark Debate," *Wall Street Journal*, September 30, 1991, pp. B1, B3; Tim Allis, Laura Sanderson Healy, and Lorenzo Benet, "Sex by the Cupful," *People*, May 20, 1990, pp. 94–95; Alex Prud'homme, "What's It All about, Calvin?" *Time*, September 23, 1991, p. 44; Barbara Lippert, "Calvin Klein, Masturbation and Jeans," *Adweek*, September 16, 1991, pp. 39–40; Bob Garfield, "It's Hot! It's Sexy! It's

Drop-Dead Calvin Klein!" *Advertising Age*, September 23, 1991, p. 46; Joe Mandese, "Olympic Test for CBS," *Advertising Age*, November 25, 1991, p. 2. **441** Based on information from James E. Lukazsweski and Paul Ridgeway, "To Put Your Best Foot Forward, Start by Taking These 21 Steps," *Sales and Marketing Management*, June 1990, pp. 84–86; Wendy Cole, "Taking the Chill Out of Calling Cold," *Working Woman*, October 1989, pp. 32–33; Winston Marsh, "Selling Strategies," *Australian Accountant*, December 1989, pp. 16–19. **452** Based on information from Alison Fahey and Gary Levin, "Coke Plans 'Real Thing' Global Attack," *Advertising Age*, August 5, 1991, pp. 1, 36; John Marcom, Jr., "Cola Attack," *Forbes*, November 26, 1990, pp. 48–49; Walecia Konrad, "The Real Thing Is Getting Real Aggressive," *Business Week*, November 26, 1990, pp. 94, 96, 100, 104; Bruce Crumley, "French Cola Wars," *Advertising Age*, December 12, 1990, p. 22; Ferdinand Protzman, "Coke's Splash in Eastern Germany," *New York Times*, May 3, 1991, pp. D1, D6.

CHAPTER 15

470 Based on information from Brenton Schlender, "Apple's Japanese Ally," *Fortune*, November 4, 1991, p. 151+; Kathy Rebello, "Apple Gets a Little More Help from Its Friends," *Business Week*, October 28, 1991, p. 132; Tom Koppel, "Reading Books Byte by Byte," *Scientific American*, June 1991, pp. 116–117; and "Sony Apple Negotiating Laptop Deal," *New York Times*, October 1, 1990, p. D1. **479** Based on information from Brenton R. Schlender, "The Future of the PC," *Fortune*, August 26, 1991, pp. 40–44+; John W. Verity, "Multimedia Computing: PCs That Do Everything but Walk the Dog," *Business Week*, August 12, 1991, p. 62; and Deidre A. Depke, "PCs: What the Future Holds," *Business Week*, August 12, 1991, pp. 58–64. **489** Based on information from "States Sue TRW over Credit-Reporting Practices," *Consumer Reports*, November, 1991, p. 710; "Credit Check," *Black Enterprise*, November 1991, p. 34; "Free Credit Reports for All," *U.S. News & World Report*, October 28, 1991, p. 90; "TRW Will Give Consumers Free Peeks," *Business Week*, October 28, 1991, p. 45; John Schwartz, "Consumer Enemy No. 1," *Newsweek*, October 28, 1991, p. 42; and Evan I. Schwartz, "Credit Bureaus: Consumers Are Stewing—and Suing," *Business Week*, July 29, 1991, pp. 69–70.

CHAPTER 16

501 Based on information from Bradford McKee, "Finding the System That Fits Your Firm," *Nation's Business*, May 1991, p. 9; Richard Morochove, "Budget-Wise Accounting," *PC World*, November 1990, pp. 187–189+; Ripley Hotch, "The Most Desired, Troubling Category of Programs," *Nation's Business*, September 1990, p. 50+; and Ralph Soucie and William Flora, "Hot Picks in Small Business Accounting," *PC World*, March 1989, pp. 108–113. **511** Based on information from Harris Collingwood, ed., "Why K mart's Good News Isn't," *Business Week*, March 18, 1991, p. 40; Kathleen Kerwin, "L.A. Gear Is Tripping over Its Shoelaces," *Business Week*, August 20, 1990, p. 30; Philip E. Fess and Carl S. Warren, *Accounting Principles*, 16th ed. (Cincinnati: South-Western, 1990), pp. 354–361; Belverd E. Needles, Henry R. Anderson, and James C. Caldwell, *Principles of Accounting*, 4th ed. (Boston: Houghton Mifflin Company, 1990) pp. 431–436; Gary Hector, "Cute Tricks on the Bottom Line," *Fortune*, April 24, 1989, p. 194. **521** Based on information from Rahul Jacob, "Can You Trust That Audit?" *Fortune*, November 18, 1991, pp. 191–192; Wiley Wodard, "How to Read Finan-

cial Reports," *Black Enterprise*, May 1989, pp. 90–92+; Gary Hector, "Cute Tricks on the Bottom Line," *Fortune*, April 24, 1989, p. 193+; and Robin Micheli, "A Few Key Items in an Annual Report Can Tell You a Lot," *Money*, March 1988, p. 181; Kenneth L. Fisher, "Thanks Dad," *Forbes*, August 8, 1988, p. 122.

CHAPTER 17

540 Based on information from Jack Egan, "Savings," *U.S. News & World Report*, July 15, 1991, p. 60; Kevin McCormally, "The Saying That a Bird in Hand Is Worth Two in the Bush Applies to Money, Too," *Changing Times*, August 1989, p. 16; Clint Willis, "Mastering the Math behind Your Money," *Money*, May 1989, pp. 129–130+; and John Steele Gordon, "The Problem of Money and Time," *American Heritage*, May–June, 1989, pp. 57–58+. **545** Based on information from Margaret Carlson, "Then There Was One," *Time*, March 11, 1991, p. 69; Paula Dwyer, "The Worst Is Probably Over for the Keating Five," *Business Week*, February 4, 1991, p. 63; Carol J. Loomis, "Pornography in Finance," *Fortune*, January 1, 1990, pp. 67–68; Howard Rudnitsky, "Good Timing, Charlie," *Forbes*, November 27, 1989, pp. 140–142+; Rich Thomas and Eleonor Clift, "Asleep at the S&L Switch," *Newsweek*, December 11, 1989, p. 71; Tom Morganthau, "The S&L Scandal's Biggest Blowout," *Newsweek*, November 6, 1989, pp. 35–36; and Margaret Carlson, "Keating Takes the Fifth," *Time*, December 4, 1989, p. 46. **558** Based on information from David Hage and Jack Egan, "Was the Fed Asleep on BCCI?" *U.S. News & World Report*, August 19, 1991, pp. 56–58; Jack Egan, "How BCCI Banked on Global Secrecy," *U.S. News & World Report*, August 19, 1991, pp. 58–59; Susan Detzer, "How to Avoid Another BCCI," *U.S. News & World Report*, August 12, 1991, p. 33; Marci McDonald, "A Bank of Scandal," *Maclean's*, August 5, 1991, pp. 24–25+; Robert Kuttner, "Controlling the Climate That Let BCCI Bloom," *Business Week*, July 2, 1991, p. 16; and Mark Maremont, "The Long and Winding Road to BCCI's Dead End," *Business Week*, July 22, 1991, pp. 54–55.

CHAPTER 18

572 Based on information from Ronald Grover, "Lights, Camera, Auction," *Business Week*, December 10, 1990, pp. 27–28; Janice Castro, "Let Us Entertain You," *Time*, December 10, 1990, pp. 68–70; Patricia Chisholm, "It Came from Japan II," *Maclean's*, December 10, 1990, p. 48; Ronald Grover, "Even for Michael Ovitz, $8 Billion Is a Big Deal," *Business Week*, October 15, 1990, p. 114. **585** Based on information from Philip W. Taggart and Roy Alexander, "Deciding Whether to Go Public," *Nation's Business*, May 1991, pp. 51–52; Jeffrey M. Laderman and Laura Zinn, "Investors Can't Get Enough of Those Stocks," *Business Week*, April 29, 1991, pp. 74+; Mark Hulbert, "Getting Taken," *Forbes*, June 24, 1991, pp. 216+; Leslie Helm, "A Wake-Up Call for Initial Public Offerings," *Business Week*, May 8, 1989, pp. 40–41; Charles M. Bartlett, Jr., "Survival of the Few," *Forbes*, June 26, 1989, pp. 266–267; and Jeffrey M. Laderman, "Timing Is Everything When You Go Public," *Business Week*, November 3, 1986, p. 120. **588** Based on information from Gane G. Martial, "Not for the Weak of Knee," *Business Week*, June 24, 1991, p. 80; Claire Poole, "There's an IPO Buyer Every Minute," *Forbes*, June 24, 1991, p. 222+; Mark Hulbert, "Getting Taken," *Forbes*, June 24, 1991, p. 216+; Jeffrey Laderman, "Think You've Found the Next Microsoft?" *Business Week*, May 13, 1991, pp. 114–115; and Jeffrey M. Laderman and

Laura Zinn, "Investors Can't Get Enough of Those Stocks," *Business Week,* April 29, 1991, pp. 74–75.

CHAPTER 19

609 Source: "Asset-Mix Worksheet," T. Rowe Price, Mutual Funds, 100 Pratt Street, Baltimore, MD 21201. **617** Based on information from Prashanta Misra, "It's Alive! The Junk Monster Rises from Dead Again," *Money,* May 1991, p. 49+; Michael Fritz, "An Unhappy Tale," *Forbes,* March 19, 1990, p. 196; and Arthur S. Hayes and Ellen Joan Pollock, "Law Section," *Wall Street Journal,* November 15, 1990, p. B6. **629** Based on information from David Carey, "Why Investors Should Go Global," *Fortune/1991 Investor's Guide,* Fall 1991, p. 97+; David Dreman, "How to Diversify Abroad," *Forbes,* July 22, 1991, p. 324; "How to Make World Your Oyster," *Fortune,* July 15, 1991, p. 33; Mark Hulbert, "Innocents Abroad," *Forbes,* April 15, 1991, p. 143; Manuel Schiffres, "Great Ways To Go Global," *Changing Times,* February 1991, pp. 37–40; John P. Dessauer, "How to Succeed in Global Investing," *World Monitor,* January 1991, pp. 30–34.

CHAPTER 20

647 Based on information from *The Actuarial Profession: Picture Yourself Making a Terrific Choice* (Schaumburg, IL.: Society of Actuaries and the Casualty Actuarial Society 1991), pp. 5–11; Jack R. Kapoor, Les R. Dlabay, and Robert J. Hughes, *Personal Finance,* 2nd ed. (Homewood, IL.: Richard D. Irwin, 1991), p. 318; Personal interview, Rebecca Chase-Warren, library technical assistant, Society of Actuaries, October 28, 1991. **656** Based on information from Janet L. Shikles, "Long-Term Care Insurance: Risks to Consumers Should Be Reduced," *Statement Before the Subcommittee on Health Committee on Ways and Means,* April 11, pp. 1–23; Kevin Anderson, Democratic Leaders Urge Small Steps to Insurance Reform," *USA Today,* October 25, 1991, p. 8B; "Choosing Long-Term Health Care," *Wheaton Journal,* October 9, 1991, p. 12; "U.S. Health Care Spending Increased 10.5% in 1990," *Wall Street Journal,* October 3, 1991, p. B4; Kevin Anderson, "Middle Class: Health Care Ails," *USA Today,* October 14, 1991, p. B2; and "Long-Term Care Insurance: Avoiding the Pitfalls," *Research Reports,* American Institute for Economic Research, October 7, 1991, pp. 111–112. **659** Based on information from Chales A. Bowsher, "U.S. Health Care Spending: Trends, Contributing Factors, and Proposals for Reform," *Statement before the Committee on Ways and Means,* April 17, 1991, pp. 1–23; Ron Winslow, "Health Costs," *Wall Street Journal,* March 27, 1991, p. B1; "Trends in Health Expenditures by Medicare and the Nation." *Congressional Budget Office,* January 1991, n.p.; Jack Hadley, "Comparison of Uninsured and Privately Insured Hospital Patients," *Journal of the American Medical Association,* January 16, 1991, p. 374; and "Health and Medical Service," *U.S. Industrial Outlook,* 1991, pp. 44–51.

CHAPTER 21

676 Based on information from Arthur Aronoff, "Complying with the Corrupt Practices Act," *Business America,* February 11, 1991, pp. 10–11. **683** Based on information from Sherry Harowitz, "Remodeling without the Aspirin," *Kiplinger's Personal Finance Magazine,* July 1991, pp. 36–39; "Ten Tips That Can Save You Money," *Money,* May 1991, pp. 96–97; Sherry Horowitz, "Your Home," *Changing Times,* April 1991, p. 24+;

"Home Remodeling: Getting It Done Right," *Consumer's Research,* September 1989, pp. 34–36; "Hiring a Contractor," *Better Homes and Gardens,* June 1989, p. 85. **693** Based on information from "Uncommon Law," *National Review,* September 9, 1991, p. 14+; Michael Kinsley, "Quayle's Case," *New Republic,* September 9, 1991, p. 4; David Gergen and Ted Gest "Ruling on Quayle v. Lawyers," *U.S. News and World Report,* August 26, September 2, 1991, p. 44; and Bob Cohn, "The Lawsuit Cha-Cha," *Newsweek,* August 26, 1991, pp. 58–59.

CHAPTER 22

703 Based on information from Mary Beth Marklein, "Selling to Uncle Sam," *Nation's Business,* March 1991, pp. 29–30; "Winning Your Share of Federal Business," *Nation's Business,* March 1991, p. 30; Brian W. O'Connor, "More Woes for Black Business," *Black Enterprise,* January 1991, p. 23; June Easter Bahls, "A Demanding Customer," *Nation's Business,* March 1990, pp. 29–30. **715** Based on information from Michael Waldman, "Bad Cops," *New Republic,* September 9, 1991, p. 11; Gloria Borger, "An Easy Way to Fix the Ethics Mess," *U.S. News & World Report,* September 2, 1991, p. 42; Scott Shuger, "Stopping the Next Sununu," *Newsweek,* July 8, 1991, p. 9; and Francis Wilkinson, "Rules of the Game: The Senate's Money Politics," *Rolling Stone,* August 8, 1991, pp. 31–34+. **720** Based on information from Albert Ellentuck, "Preserving the Evidence," *Nation's Business,* May 1991, p. 66; Laura Saunders, "Why Apr. 15 Is Getting Worse and Worse," *Forbes,* March 18, 1991, pp. 84–87; "Three Financial Records You Must Keep Long-Term," *Nation's Business,* January 1991, p. 66; Nancy Henderson, "Weeding out Your Home Files," *Changing Times,* January 1991, pp. 41–43.

CHAPTER 23

731 Based on information from "Exporting Pays off," *Business America,* September 23, 1991, p. 22. **742** Based on information from "EC–U.S. Trade Relations," *A Guide to the European Community,* EC Delegation to the United States, 1991, pp. 24–25; Janice L. Boucher, "Europe 1991: A Closer Look," *Economic Review,* Federal Reserve Bank of Atlanta, July–August 1991, pp. 23–38; George O. Orban, "Europe's Protectionist Industrial Policy," *Wall Street Journal,* July 15, 1991, p. A10; Janice L. Boucher, "Europe 1992: An American Perspective," *Economic Review,* Federal Reserve Bank of Atlanta, November–December 1991, pp. 26–30; Kymberly K. Hockman, "The Last Barrier to the European Market," *Wall Street Journal,* October 7, 1991, p. A14; and Don R. Wright, "The EC Single Market in 1991—Status Report," *Business America,* February 25, 1991, pp. 12–13. **750** Based on information from Cheryl Horst, "Watch Those Hands," *Daily Herald* (Carol Stream, IL), November 14, 1991, Sec. 8, pp. 1–2; "Blunders Abroad," *Nation's Business,* March 1989, pp. 54–55; "The Old Sexism in the New China," *U.S. News & World Report,* April 24, 1989, pp. 36–38; and "Understand and Heed Cultural Differences," *Business America,* Vol. 112, No. 2, Special Edition, 1991, pp. 26–27.

CHAPTER 24

765 Based on information from Betsy Streisand, "A Baptism by Fire," *U.S. News & World Report,* November 11, 1991, pp. 84–87; Katherine Burton, "Getting a Global MBA," *U.S. News & World Report,* November 11, 1991, p. 87; "Who Studies Where," *The World Monitor,* September 1991, p. 10; and

John Brademas, "A Moment to Seize," *Vital Speeches of the Day*, May 1, 1991, pp. 432–435. **771** Based on information from Kenneth Labich, "Take Control of Your Career," *Fortune*, November 18, 1991, pp. 87–88; Amy Saltzman, "Smart Moves," *U.S. News & World Report*, November 11, 1991, pp. 62–64; Bruce Nussbaum, "A Career Survival Kit," *Business Week*, October 7, 1991, p. 98+; and Bruce Nussbaum, "I'm Worried about My Job!" *Business Week*, October 7, 1991, pp. 94–97.

PHOTO CREDITS

continued from p. iv.

buying long buying stock with the expectation that it will increase in value and can then be sold at a profit (19)

call premium the dollar amount over par value that the corporation has to pay an investor for redeeming either preferred stock or a corporate bond (18)

capacity the amount of input a facility can process or output it can produce in a given time (7)

capital all the financial resources, buildings, machinery, tools, and equipment that are used in an organization's operations (1)

capital-intensive technology one in which machines and equipment do most of the work (7)

capitalism an economic system in which individuals own and operate the majority of businesses that provide goods and services (1)

captioned photograph a picture accompanied by a brief explanation (14)

carrier a firm that offers transportation services (13)

cash flow the movement of money into and out of an organization (18)

cash surrender value an amount that is payable to the holder of a whole life insurance policy if the policy is canceled (20)

catalog discount showroom a retail outlet that displays well-known brands and sells them at discount prices through catalog sales within the store (13)

caveat emptor a Latin phrase meaning "let the buyer beware" (2)

cease and desist order an order to refrain from an illegal practice (22)

centralized organization an organization that systematically works to concentrate authority at the upper levels of the organization (6)

cents-off coupon a coupon that reduces the retail price of a particular item by a stated amount at the time of purchase (14)

certificate of deposit a document stating that the bank will pay the depositor a guaranteed interest rate for money left on deposit for a specified period of time (17)

certified public accountant (CPA) an individual who has met state requirements for accounting education and experience and has passed a rigorous three-day accounting examination (16)

chain of command the line of authority that extends from the highest to the lowest levels of an organization (6)

chain retailer a firm that operates more than one retail outlet (13)

channel of distribution (or marketing channel) a sequence of marketing organizations that directs a product from the producer to the ultimate user (13)

check a written order for a bank or other financial institution to pay a stated dollar amount to the business or person indicated on the face of the check (17)

close corporation a corporation whose stock is owned by relatively few people and is not traded in stock markets (3)

closed shop a workplace in which workers must join the union before they are hired, outlawed by the Taft-Hartley Act (10)

coinsurance clause a part of a fire insurance policy that requires the policyholder to purchase coverage at least equal to a specified percentage of the replacement cost of the property to obtain full reimbursement for losses (20)

collateral real or personal property that a firm or individual owns and that is pledged as security for a loan (17)

collective bargaining the process of negotiating a labor contract with management (10)

commercial bank a profit-making organization that accepts deposits, makes loans, and provides related services to its customers (17)

commercial draft a written order requiring a customer (the *drawee*) to pay a specified sum of money to a supplier (the *drawer*) for goods or services (18)

commercial paper short-term promissory notes issued by large corporations (18)

commission a payment that is some percentage of sales revenue (9)

commission merchant a middleman that carries merchandise and negotiates sales for manufacturers but does not take title to the goods it sells (13)

common law also known as case law or judicial law is the body of law created by the court decisions rendered by judges (21)

common stock stock owned by individuals or firms who may vote on corporate matters, but whose claims on profit and assets are subordinate to the claims of others (3, 18)

community of interests the situation in which one firm buys the stock of a competing firm to reduce competition between the two (22)

community shopping center a planned shopping center that includes one or two department stores and some specialty stores, along with convenience stores (13)

comparable worth a concept that seeks equal compensation for jobs requiring about the same level of education, training, and skills (9)

comparative advantage the ability to produce a specific product more efficiently than any other products (23)

compensation the payment that employees receive in return for their labor (9)

compensation system the policies and strategies that determine employee compensation (9)

competition a rivalry among businesses for sales to potential customers (1)

component part an item that becomes part of a physical product and is either a finished item ready for assembly or a product that needs little processing before assembly (12)

compressed workweek an arrangement whereby an employee works a full forty hours per week, but in less than the standard five days (6)

computer an electronic machine that can accept, store, manipulate, and transmit data in accordance with a set of specific instructions (15)

computer network a system in which several computers can either function individually or communicate with each other (15)

computer programmer a person who develops the step-by-step instructions that are contained in a computer program (15)

conceptual skill the ability to conceptualize and think in abstract terms (5)

consideration the value or benefit that one party to a contract furnishes to the other party (21)

consumer buying behavior the purchasing of products for personal or household use, not for business purposes (11)

consumer goods products purchased by individuals for personal consumption (1)

consumer product a product purchased to satisfy personal and family needs (12)

consumer sales promotion method a sales promotion method designed to attract consumers to particular retail stores and motivate them to purchase certain new or established products (14)

consumerism all those activities intended to protect the rights of consumers in their dealings with business (2)

consumers individuals who purchase goods or services for their own personal use rather than to resell them (1)

contract a legally enforceable agreement between two or more competent parties who promise to do, or not to do, a particular thing (21)

control unit the part of a computer that guides the entire operation of the computer (15)

controlling the process of evaluating and regulating ongoing activities to ensure that goals are achieved (5)

convenience product a relatively inexpensive, frequently purchased item for which buyers want to exert only minimal effort (12)

convenience store a small food store that sells a limited variety of products but remains open well beyond the normal business hours (13)

convertible bond a bond that can be exchanged, at the owner's option, for a specified number of shares of the corporation's common stock (18)

convertible preferred stock preferred stock that may be exchanged *at the stockholder's option* for a specified number of shares of common stock (18)

cooperative an association of individuals or firms whose purpose it is to perform some business function for all its members (3)

cooperative advertising advertising whose cost is shared by a producer and one or more local retailers (14)

copyright the exclusive right to publish, perform, copy, or sell an original work (21)

corporate bond a corporation's written pledge that it will repay a specified amount of money, with interest (18)

corporate charter a contract between the corporation and the state, in which the state recognizes the formation of the artificial person that is the corporation (3)

corporate code of ethics a guide to acceptable and ethical behavior as defined by an organization (2)

corporate culture the inner rites, rituals, heroes, and values of a firm (5)

corporate officer the chairman of the board, president, executive vice president, corporate secretary and treasurer, or any other top executive appointed by the board of directors (3)

corporation an artificial person created by law, with most of the legal rights of a real person, including the right to start and operate a business, to own or dispose of property, to borrow money, to sue or be sued, and to enter into binding contracts (3)

cost of goods sold the cost of the goods a firm has sold during an accounting period; equal to beginning inventory *plus* net purchases *less* ending inventory (16)

coupon bond a bond whose ownership is not registered by the issuing company (18)

court of limited jurisdiction a court that hears only specific types of cases (21)

court of original jurisdiction the first court to recognize and hear testimony in a legal action (21)

craft union an organization of skilled workers in a single craft or trade (10)

creative selling selling products to new customers and increasing sales to present customers (14)

credit immediate purchasing power that is exchanged for a promise to repay it, with or without interest, at a later date (17)

credit union a financial institution that accepts deposits from, and lends money to, only those people who are its members (17)

crime a violation of a public law (21)

cultural diversity the differences among people in a work force due to race, ethnicity, and gender

cumulative preferred stock preferred stock on which any unpaid dividends accumulate and must be paid before any cash dividend is paid to the holders of common stock (18)

currency devaluation the reduction of the value of a nation's currency relative to the currencies of other countries (23)

current assets cash and other assets that can be quickly converted into cash or that will be used in one year or less (16)

current liabilities debts that will be repaid in one year or less (16)

current ratio a financial ratio that is computed by dividing current assets by current liabilities (16)

customs (or import) duty a tax on a particular foreign product entering a country (22)

damages a monetary settlement awarded to a party that is injured through a breach of contract (21)

data numerical or verbal descriptions that usually result from measurements of some sort (15)

data processing the transformation of data into a form that is useful for a specific purpose (15)

database a single collection of data that are stored in one place and can be used by people throughout the organization to make decisions (15)

debenture bond a bond backed only by the reputation of the issuing corporation (18)

debt capital money obtained through loans (18)

debt-to-assets ratio a financial ratio that is calculated by dividing total liabilities by total as-

sets; indicates the extent to which the firm's borrowing is backed by its assets (16)

debt-to-equity ratio a financial ratio that is calculated by dividing total liabilities by owners' equity; compares the amount of financing provided by creditors with the amount provided by owners (16)

decentralized organization an organization in which management consciously attempts to spread authority widely in the lower levels of the organization (6)

decision making the process of developing a set of possible alternative solutions and choosing one alternative from among that set (5)

decisional role a role that involves various aspects of management decision making (5)

deed a written document by which the ownership of real property is transferred from one person or organization to another (21)

delegation the assigning of part of a manager's work and power to a subordinate (6)

demand the quantity of a product that buyers are willing to purchase at each of various prices (1, 12)

demand deposit an amount that is on deposit in a checking account (17)

democratic leader one who holds final responsibility but also delegates authority to others, who help determine work assignments; communication is active upward and downward (5)

department store a retail store that (1) employs twenty-five or more persons and (2) sells at least home furnishings, appliances, family apparel, and household linens and dry goods, each in a different part of the store (13)

departmentalization the process of grouping jobs into manageable units according to some reasonable scheme (6)

departmentalization basis the scheme or criterion by which jobs are grouped into units (6)

departmentalization by customer the grouping together of all activities according to the needs of the various customer groups (6)

departmentalization by function the grouping together of all jobs that relate to the same organizational activity (6)

departmentalization by location the grouping together of all activities according to the geographic area in which they are performed (6)

departmentalization by product the grouping together of all activities related to a particular product or product group (6)

depreciation the process of apportioning the cost

of a fixed asset over the period during which it will be used (16)

deregulation the process of removing existing regulations, foregoing proposed regulations, or reducing the rate at which new regulations are enacted (22)

design planning the development of a plan for converting a product idea into an actual commodity ready for marketing (7)

diagnostic skill the ability to assess a particular situation and identify its causes (5)

direct-mail advertising promotional material that is mailed directly to individuals (14)

directing the combined processes of leading and motivating (5)

discharge by mutual assent when all parties agree to void a contract (21)

discount a deduction from the price of an item (12)

discount rate the interest rate that the Federal Reserve System charges for loans to member banks (17)

discount store a self-service general-merchandise outlet that sells goods at lower than usual prices (13)

discretionary income disposable income less savings and expenditures on food, clothing, and housing (11)

discretionary order an order to buy or sell a security that lets the broker decide when to execute the transaction and at what price (19)

disposable income personal income less all additional personal taxes (11)

dividend a distribution of earnings to the stockholders of a corporation (3)

domestic corporation a corporation in the state in which it is incorporated (3)

domestic system a method of manufacturing in which an entrepreneur distributed raw materials to various homes, where families would process them into finished goods to be offered for sale by the merchant entrepreneur (1)

door-to-door retailer a retailer that sells directly to consumers in their homes (13)

double-entry bookkeeping a system in which each financial transaction is recorded as two separate accounting entries to maintain the balance shown in the accounting equation (16)

dumping exportation of large quantities of a product at a price lower than that of the same product in the home market (23)

earnings per share a financial ratio that is calculated by dividing net income after taxes by the number of shares of common stock outstanding (16)

economic community an organization of nations formed to promote the free movement of resources and products among its members and to create common economic policies (23)

economic model of social responsibility the view that society will benefit most when business is left alone to produce and market profitable products that are needed by society (2)

economics the study of how wealth is created and distributed (1)

economy the system through which a society answers the two economic questions—how wealth is created and distributed (1)

electronic funds transfer (EFT) system a means for performing financial transactions through a computer terminal or telephone hookup (17)

embargo a complete halt to trading with a particular nation or in a particular product (23)

employee benefit a reward that is provided indirectly to employees—mainly a service (such as insurance) paid for by the employer or an employee expense (such as college tuition) reimbursed by the employer (9)

employee training the process of teaching operations and technical employees how to do their present jobs more effectively and efficiently (9)

endorsement the payee's signature on the back of a negotiable instrument (21)

endowment life insurance life insurance that provides protection and guarantees the payment of a stated amount to the policyholder after a specified number of years (20)

entrepreneur a person who risks time, effort, and money to start and operate a business (1)

Environmental Protection Agency (EPA) the federal agency charged with enforcing laws designed to protect the environment (2)

Equal Employment Opportunity Commission (EEOC) a government agency with the power to investigate complaints of employment discrimination and the power to sue firms that practice it (2)

equity capital money received from the sale of shares of ownership in the business (18)

equity theory a theory of motivation based on the premise that people are motivated first to achieve and then to maintain a sense of equity (8)

esteem needs the human requirements for respect, recognition, and a sense of one's own accomplishment and worth (8)

ethics the study of right and wrong and of the morality of choices made by individuals (2)

excise tax a tax on the manufacture or sale of a particular domestic product (22)

exclusive distribution the use of only a single retail outlet for a product in each geographic area (13)

expectancy theory a model of motivation based on the assumption that motivation depends on how much we want something and on how likely we think we are to get it (8)

Export-Import Bank of the United States an independent agency of the U.S. government whose function is to assist in financing the exports of American firms (23)

exporting selling and shipping raw materials or products to other nations (23)

express warranty a written explanation of the responsibilities of the producer (or seller) in the event that a product is found to be defective or otherwise unsatisfactory (12, 21)

extended coverage insurance protection against damage caused by wind, hail, explosion, vandalism, riots or civil commotion, falling aircraft, and smoke (20)

external recruiting the attempt to attract job applicants from outside the organization (9)

factor a firm that specializes in buying other firms' accounts receivable (18)

factors of production three categories of resources: land, labor, capital (1)

factory system a system of manufacturing in which all of the materials, machinery, and workers required to manufacture a product are assembled in one place (1)

family branding the strategy in which a firm uses the same brand for all or most of its products (12)

feature article a piece (of up to 3,000 words) prepared by an organization for inclusion in a particular publication (14)

Federal Communications Commission (FCC) the federal agency responsible for the interstate regulation of communications, including radio, television, telephone, and telegraph (22)

Federal Energy Regulatory Commission the federal agency that oversees the interstate operations of firms that sell electricity or natural gas, or operate gas pipelines (22)

Federal Reserve System the government agency responsible for regulating the United States banking industry (17)

Federal Trade Commission (FTC) a five-member committee charged with the responsibility of investigating illegal trade practices and enforcing antitrust laws (22)

fidelity bond an insurance policy that protects a business from theft, forgery, or embezzlement by its employees (20)

financial management all those activities that are concerned with obtaining money and using it effectively (18)

financial manager a manager who is primarily responsible for the organization's financial resources (5)

financial plan a plan for obtaining and using the money that is needed to implement an organization's goals (18)

financial ratio a number that shows the relationship between two elements of a firm's financial statements (16)

fire insurance insurance that covers losses due to fire (20)

fixed assets assets that will be held or used for a period longer than one year (16)

fixed cost a cost that is incurred no matter how many units of a product are produced or sold (12)

flexible manufacturing system (FMS) a recent development in automation that combines robotics and computer-aided manufacturing in a single system (7)

flexible workweek an arrangement in which each employee chooses the hours during which he or she will work, subject to certain limitations (6)

floor planning a method of financing where the title to merchandise is given to lenders in return for short-term financing (18)

flow chart a graphic description of the types and sequences of operations in a computer program (15)

foreign corporation a corporation in any state in which it does business except the one in which it is incorporated (3)

foreign-exchange control a restriction on the amount of a particular foreign currency that can be purchased or sold (23)

form utility utility that is created by converting production inputs into finished products (7, 11)

franchise a license to operate an individually owned business as though it were part of a chain of outlets or stores (4)

franchisee a person or organization purchasing a franchise (4)

franchising the actual granting of a franchise (4)

franchisor   an individual or organization granting a franchise (4)

free enterprise   the system of business in which individuals are free to decide what to produce, how to produce it, and at what price to sell it (1)

free-market economy   an economic system in which individuals and firms are free to enter and leave markets at will (1)

frequency distribution   a listing of the number of times each value appears in a set of data (15)

full-service wholesaler   a middleman that performs the entire range of wholesaler functions (13)

functional middleman   a middleman that helps in the transfer of ownership of products but does not take title to the products (13)

futures contract   an agreement to buy or sell a commodity at a guaranteed price on some specified future date (19)

Gantt chart   a graphic scheduling device that displays the tasks to be performed on the vertical axis and the time required for each task on the horizontal axis (7)

General Agreement on Tariffs and Trade (GATT)   an international organization whose goal is to reduce or eliminate tariffs and other barriers to world trade (23)

general expenses   costs that are incurred in managing a business (16)

general journal   a book of original entry in which typical transactions are recorded in order of their occurrence (16)

general ledger   a book of accounts that contains a separate sheet or section for each account (16)

general merchandise wholesaler   a middleman that deals in a wide variety of products (13)

general partner   a person who assumes full or shared responsibility for operating a business (3)

generic product (or brand)   a product with no brand at all (12)

goal   an end state that the organization is expected to achieve (5)

goal setting   the process of developing and committing an organization to a set of goals (5)

goodwill   the value of a firm's reputation, location, earning capacity, and other intangibles that make the business a profitable concern (16)

government-owned corporation   a corporation owned and operated by a local, state, or federal government (3)

grapevine   the informal communications network within an organization (6)

graphics program   a software package that enables the user to display and print data and conclusions in graphic form (15)

grievance procedure   a formally established course of action for resolving employee complaints against management (10)

gross domestic product (GDP)   the total dollar value of all goods and services produced by citizens physically located within a country (1)

gross national product (GNP)   the total dollar value of all goods and services produced by all citizens of a country for a given time period (1)

gross profit on sales   a firm's net sales *less* the cost of goods sold (16)

gross sales   the total dollar amount of all goods and services sold during the accounting period (16)

hard-core unemployed   workers with little education or vocational training and a long history of unemployment (2)

hardware   the electronic equipment or machinery used in a computer system (15)

health maintenance organization (HMO)   an insurance plan that directly employs or contracts with selected physicians and hospitals to provide health-care services in exchange for a fixed, prepaid monthly premium (20)

health-care insurance   insurance that covers the cost of medical attention, including hospital care, physicians' and surgeons' fees, prescription medicines, and related services (20)

hierarchy of needs   Maslow's sequence of human needs in the order of their importance (8)

high-risk investment   an investment that is made in the hope of earning a relatively large profit in a short time (19)

hourly wage   a specific amount of money paid for each hour of work (9)

human resources management   all the activities involved in acquiring, maintaining, and developing an organization's human resources (9)

human resources manager   a person charged with managing the organization's formal human resources programs (5)

human resources planning   the development of strategies to meet a firm's human resources needs (9)

hygiene factors   job factors that reduce dissatisfaction when present to an acceptable degree, but do not necessarily result in high levels of motivation, according to the motivation-hygiene theory (8)

implied warranty a guarantee that is imposed or required by law (21)

import duty (or tariff) a tax that is levied on a particular foreign product entering a country (23)

import quota a limit on the amount of a particular good that may be imported into a country during a given period of time (23)

importing purchasing raw materials or products in other nations and bringing them into one's own country (23)

income statement a summary of a firm's revenues and expenses during a specified accounting period (16)

incorporation the process of forming a corporation (3)

independent retailer a firm that operates only one retail outlet (13)

individual branding the strategy in which a firm uses a different brand for each of its products (12)

industrial product a product bought for use in a firm's operations or to make other products (12)

industrial service an intangible product that an organization uses in its operations (12)

industrial union an organization of both skilled and unskilled workers in a single industry (10)

inflation a general rise in the level of prices (1)

informal group a group created by the members themselves to accomplish goals that may or may not be relevant to the organization (6)

informal organization the pattern of behavior and interaction that stems from personal rather than official relationships (6)

information data that are presented in a form that is useful for a specific purpose

informational role a role in which the manager either gathers or provides information (5)

injunction a court order requiring a person or group either to perform some act or to refrain from performing some act (10)

inland marine insurance insurance that protects against loss or damage to goods shipped by rail, truck, airplane, or inland barge (20)

input unit the device used to enter data into a computer (15)

inspection the examination of output to control quality (7)

institutional advertising advertising designed to enhance a firm's image or reputation (14)

insurable risk a risk that insurance companies will assume (20)

insurance the protection against loss that is afforded by the purchase of an insurance policy (20)

insurance policy the contract between an insurer and the person or firm whose risk is assumed (20)

insurer (or insurance company) a firm that agrees, for a fee, to assume financial responsibility for losses that may result from a specific risk (20)

intangible assets assets that do not exist physically but that have a value based on legal rights or advantages that they confer on a firm (16)

intensive distribution the use of all available outlets for a product (13)

interlocking directorate an arrangement in which members of the board of directors of one firm are also directors of a competing firm (22)

internal recruiting considering present employees as applicants for available positions (9)

international business all business activities that involve exchanges across national boundaries (23)

International Monetary Fund (IMF) an international bank that makes short-term loans to countries experiencing balance-of-payment deficits (23)

interpersonal role a role in which the manager deals with people (5)

interpersonal skill the ability to deal effectively with other people (5)

Interstate Commerce Commission (ICC) the federal agency responsible for the licensing and regulation of carriers (22)

intrapreneur an entrepreneur working in an organizational environment who develops an idea into a product and manages the product within the firm (6)

inventory stocks of goods and materials (7)

inventory control the process of managing inventories in such a way as to minimize inventory costs, including both holding costs and potential stockout costs (7, 13)

inventory turnover a financial ratio that is calculated by dividing the cost of goods sold in one year by the average value of the inventory; measures the number of times the firm sells and replaces its merchandise inventory in one year (16)

investment banking firm an organization that assists corporations in raising funds, usually by helping sell new security issues (19)

involuntary bankruptcy a bankruptcy procedure initiated by creditors (21)

job analysis a systematic procedure for studying jobs to determine their various elements and requirements (9)

job description a list of the elements that make up a particular job (9)

job enlargement giving a worker more things to do within the same job (6)

job enrichment providing workers with both more tasks to do and more control over how they do their work (6)

job evaluation the process of determining the relative worth of the various jobs within a firm (9)

job rotation the systematic shifting of employees from one job to another (6)

job security protection against the loss of employment (10)

job sharing an arrangement whereby two people share one full-time position (6)

job specialization the separation of all organizational activities into distinct tasks and the assignment of different tasks to different people (6)

job specification a list of the qualifications required to perform a particular job (9)

joint venture a partnership that is formed to achieve a specific goal or to operate for a specific period of time (3)

jurisdiction the right of a particular union to organize particular workers (10)

just-in-time inventory system a system designed to ensure that materials or supplies arrive at a facility just when they are needed (7)

labeling the presentation of information on a product or its package (12)

labor union an organization or workers acting together to negotiate their wages and working conditions with employers (10)

labor-intensive technology one in which people must do most of the work (7)

laissez-faire capitalism an economic system characterized by private ownership of property, free entry into markets, and the absence of government intervention (1)

laissez-faire leader one who waives responsibility and allows subordinates to work as they choose with a minimum of interference; communication flows horizontally among group members (5)

law a rule developed by a society to govern the conduct of, and relationship among, its members (21)

leadership the ability to influence others (5)

leading the process of influencing people to work toward a common goal (5)

lease an agreement by which the right to use real property is temporarily transferred from its owner, the landlord, to a tenant (21)

leverage the use of borrowed funds to increase the return on an investment (19)

liabilities a firm's debts and obligations—what it owes to others (16)

licensing a contractual agreement in which one firm permits another to produce and market its product and use its brand name in return for a royalty or other compensation (23)

life insurance insurance that pays a stated amount of money on the death of the insured individual (20)

limit order a request that a stock be bought or sold at a price that is equal to or better than some specified price (19)

limited liability a feature of corporate ownership that limits each owner's financial liability to the amount of money he or she has paid for the corporation's stock (3)

limited partner a person who contributes capital to a business but is not active in managing it; this partner's liability is limited to the amount that he or she has invested (3)

limited-line wholesaler a middleman that stocks only a few product lines (13)

limited-service wholesaler a middleman that assumes responsibility for a few wholesale services only (13)

line management position a position that is part of the chain of command and that includes direct responsibility for achieving the goals of the organization (6)

line of credit a loan that is approved before the money is actually needed (17)

liquidity the ease with which an asset can be converted into cash (16, 19)

lockout a firm's refusal to allow employees to enter the workplace (10)

long-term financing money that will be used for longer than one year (18)

long-term liabilities debts that need not be repaid for at least one year (16)

lower-level manager a manager who coordinates and supervises the activities of operating employees (5)

mail-order retailer a retailer that solicits orders by mailing catalogs to potential customers (13)

maintenance shop a workplace in which an employee who joins the union must remain a union member as long as he or she is employed by the firm (10)

major equipment large tools and machines used for production purposes (12)

management the process of coordinating the resources of an organization to achieve the primary goals of the organization (5)

management by objectives (MBO) a motivation technique in which a manager and his or her subordinates collaborate in setting goals (8)

management development the process of preparing managers and other professionals to assume increased responsibility in both present and future positions (9)

management excellence an approach to management that promotes feelings of excellence in employees (5)

management information system (MIS) a system that provides managers with the information they need to perform management functions as effectively as possible (15)

managerial hierarchy the arrangement that provides increasing authority at higher levels of management (6)

manufacturer (or producer) brand a brand that is owned by a manufacturer (12)

manufacturer's sales branch essentially a merchant wholesaler that is owned by a manufacturer (13)

manufacturer's sales office essentially a sales agent that is owned by a manufacturer (13)

margin requirement the proportion of the price of a stock that cannot be borrowed (19)

market a group of individuals, organizations, or both who have needs for products in a given category and who have the ability, willingness, and authority to purchase such products (11)

market allocation an agreement to divide a market among potential competitors (22)

market order a request that a stock be purchased or sold at the current market price (19)

market price in pure competition, the price at which the quantity demanded is exactly equal to the quantity supplied (1)

market segment a group of individuals or organizations, within a market, that share one or more common characteristics (11)

market segmentation the process of dividing a market into segments and directing a marketing mix at a particular segment or segments rather than at the total market (11)

market value the price of one share of a stock at a particular time (19)

marketing the process of planning and executing the conception, pricing, promotion, and distribution of ideas, goods, and services to create exchanges that satisfy individual and organizational objectives (11)

marketing concept the business philosophy that involves the entire organization in the process of satisfying customers' needs while achieving the organization's goals (11)

marketing information system a system for managing marketing information that is gathered continually from internal and external sources (11)

marketing manager a manager who is responsible for facilitating the exchange of products between the organization and its customers or clients (5)

marketing mix a combination of product, price, distribution, and promotion developed to satisfy a particular target market (11)

marketing research the process of systematically gathering, recording, and analyzing data concerning a particular marketing problem (11)

marketing strategy a plan that will enable an organization to make the best use of its resources and advantages to meet its objectives (11)

markup the amount that a seller adds to the cost of a product to determine its basic price (12)

materials handling the actual physical handling of goods, in warehousing as well as during transportation (13)

matrix structure an organizational structure that combines vertical and horizontal lines of authority by superimposing product departmentalization on a functionally departmentalized organization (6)

maturity date the date on which the corporation is to repay the borrowed money (18)

measure of value a single standard or "yardstick" that is used to assign values to, and compare the values of, products, services, and resources (17)

median the value that appears at the exact middle of a set of data when the data are arranged in order (15)

mediation the use of a neutral third party to assist management and the union during their negotiations (10)

medium of exchange anything that is accepted as payment for products, services, and resources (17)

memory (or storage unit) that part of a computer that stores all data entered into the computer and processed by it (15)

merchant middleman a middleman that actually takes title to products by buying them (13)

merchant wholesaler a middleman that purchases goods in large quantities and then sells them to other wholesalers or retailers and to institutional, farm, government, professional, or industrial users (13)

merger the purchase of one corporation by another (3)

middle manager a manager who implements the strategy and major policies developed by top management (5)

middleman (or marketing intermediary) a marketing organization that links a producer and user within a marketing channel (13)

minority a racial, religious, political, national, or other group regarded as different from the larger group of which it is a part, often singled out for unfavorable treatment (2)

mission the means by which an organization is to fulfill its purpose (5)

missionary salesperson a salesperson—generally employed by a manufacturer—who visits retailers to persuade them to buy the manufacturer's products (14)

mixed economy an economy that exhibits elements of both capitalism and socialism (1)

mode the value that appears most frequently in a set of data (15)

money anything used by a society to purchase products, services, or resources (17)

monopolistic competition a market situation in which there are many buyers along with relatively many sellers who differentiate their products from the products of competitors (1)

monopoly a market (or industry) with only one seller (1)

morale a person's attitude toward his or her job, superiors, and the firm itself (8)

mortgage bond a corporate bond that is secured by various assets of the issuing firm (18)

motivating the process of providing reasons for people to work in the best interests of the organization (5)

motivation the individual, internal process that energizes, directs, and sustains behavior; the personal "force" that causes one to behave in a particular way (8)

motivation factors job factors that increase motivation, but whose absence does not necessarily result in dissatisfaction according to the motivation-hygiene theory (8)

motivation-hygiene theory the idea that satisfaction and dissatisfaction are distinct and separate dimensions (8)

multilateral development bank (MDB) an internationally supported bank that provides loans to developing countries to help them grow (23)

multinational enterprise a firm that operates on a worldwide scale, without ties to any specific nation or region (23)

multiple-unit pricing the strategy of setting a single price for two or more units (12)

mutual fund a professionally managed investment vehicle that combines and invests the funds of many individual investors (19)

mutual insurance company an insurance company that is collectively owned by its policyholders and is thus a cooperative (20)

mutual savings bank a bank that is owned by its depositors (17)

National Alliance of Business (NAB) a joint business-government program to train the hardcore unemployed (2)

National Association of Securities Dealers (NASD) the organization responsible for the self-regulation of the over-the-counter securities market (19)

national bank a commercial bank that is chartered by the U.S. Comptroller of the Currency (17)

National Labor Relations Board (NLRB) the federal agency that enforces the provisions of the Wagner Act (10)

natural monopoly an industry requiring huge investments in capital and within which duplication of facilities would be wasteful and, thus, not in the public interest (1, 22)

need a personal requirement (8)

negligence a failure to exercise reasonable care, resulting in injury to another (21)

negotiable instrument a written document that (1) is a promise to pay a stated sum of money and (2) can be transferred from one person or firm to another (21)

neighborhood shopping center a planned shopping center consisting of several small convenience and specialty stores (13)

net asset value current market value of a mutual fund's portfolio minus the mutual fund's liabilities divided by the number of shares outstanding (19)

net income the profit earned (or the loss suffered) by a firm during an accounting period, after all expenses have been deducted from revenues (16)

net profit margin a financial ratio that is calculated by dividing net income after taxes by net sales (16)

net sales the actual dollar amount received by a firm for the goods and services it has sold, after adjustment for returns, allowances, and discounts (16)

news release a typed page of generally fewer than 300 words provided by an organization to the media as a form of publicity (14)

no-fault auto insurance a method of paying for losses suffered in an automobile accident; enacted by state law, requires that those suffering injury or loss be reimbursed by their own insurance companies, without regard to who was at fault in the accident (20)

nonprice competition competition that is based on factors other than price (12)

nontariff barrier a nontax measure imposed by a government to favor domestic over foreign suppliers (23)

not-for-profit corporation a corporation that is organized to provide a social, educational, religious, or other service rather than to earn a profit (3)

notes payable obligations that have been secured with promissory notes (16)

NOW account an interest-bearing checking account; NOW stands for Negotiable Order of Withdrawal (17)

objective a specific statement detailing what an organization intends to accomplish as it goes about its mission (5)

ocean marine insurance insurance that protects the policyholder against loss or damage to a ship or its cargo on the high seas (20)

odd lot fewer than 100 shares of a particular stock (19)

odd pricing the strategy of setting prices at odd amounts that are slightly below an even or whole number of dollars (12)

oligopoly a market situation (or industry) in which there are few sellers (1)

open corporation a corporation whose stock is traded openly in stock markets and can be purchased by any individual (3)

open-market operations the buying and selling of U.S. government securities by the Federal Reserve System for the purpose of controlling the supply of money (17)

operating expenses those costs that do not result directly from the purchase or manufacture of the products a firm sells (16)

operational planning the development of plans for utilizing production facilities and resources (7)

operations management all the activities that managers engage in for the purpose of producing goods and services (7)

operations manager manager who creates and manages the systems that convert resources into goods and services (5)

option the right to buy or sell a specified amount of stock at a specified price within a certain period of time (19)

order getter a salesperson who is responsible for selling the firm's products to new customers and increasing sales to present customers (14)

order processing those activities that are involved in receiving and filling customers' purchase orders (13)

order taker a salesperson who handles repeat sales in ways that maintain positive relationships with customers (14)

organic structure a management system founded on cooperation and knowledge-based authority (6)

organization a group of two or more people working together in a predetermined fashion to achieve a common set of goals (6)

organization chart a diagram that represents the positions and relationships within an organization (6)

organizational buying behavior the purchasing of products by producers, governmental units, institutions, and resellers (11)

organizational height the number of layers, or levels, of management in a firm (6)

organizational structure a fixed pattern of (1) positions within an organization and (2) relationships among those positions (6)

organizing the grouping of resources and activities to accomplish some end result in an efficient and effective manner (5)

orientation the process of acquainting new employees with an organization (9)

outdoor advertising short promotional messages on billboards, posters, and signs, and in skywriting (14)

output unit the mechanism by which a computer transmits processed data to the user (15)

over-the-counter (OTC) market a network of stockbrokers who buy and sell the securities of corporations that are not listed on securities exchange (19)

overtime time worked in excess of forty hours in one week; under some union contracts, it can be time worked in excess of eight hours in a single day (10)

owners' equity the difference between a firm's assets and its liabilities—what would be left over for the firm's owners if its assets were used to pay off its liabilities (16)

packaging all those activities involved in developing and providing a container for a product (12)

par value an assigned (and often arbitrary) dollar value printed on the face of a stock certificate (18)

participating preferred stock preferred stock whose owners share in the corporation's earnings, along with the owners of common stock (18)

partnership an association of two or more persons to act as co-owners of a business for profit (3)

patent the exclusive right to make, use, sell, or license others to make or sell a newly invented product or process (21)

penetration pricing the strategy of setting a low price for a new product (12)

performance the fulfillment of all obligations by all parties to the contract (21)

performance appraisal the evaluation of employees' current and potential levels of performance to allow superiors to make objective human resource decisions (9)

personal income the income an individual receives from all sources less the Social Security taxes that the individual must pay (11)

personal investment the use of one's personal funds to earn a financial return (19)

personal property all property other than real property (21)

personal selling personal communication aimed at informing customers and persuading them to buy a firm's products (14)

PERT (Program Evaluation and Review Technique) a technique for scheduling a process or project and maintaining control of the schedule (7)

physical distribution all those activities concerned with the efficient movement of products from the producer to the ultimate user (13)

physiological needs the things human beings require for survival (8)

picketing marching back and forth in front of one's place of employment with signs informing the public that a strike is in progress (10)

piece-rate system a compensation system under which employees are paid a certain amount for each unit of output they produce (8)

place utility utility that is created by making a product available at a location where customers wish to purchase it (11)

plan an outline of the actions by which an organization intends to accomplish its goals (5)

planned economy an economy in which the answers to the three basic economic questions (what, how, and for whom) are determined, to some degree, through centralized government planning (1)

planning the processes involved in developing plans (5)

planning horizon the period during which a plan will be in effect (7)

plant layout the arrangement of machinery, equipment, and personnel within a facility (7)

point-of-purchase display promotional material that is placed within a retail store (14)

policy a general guide for action in a situation that occurs repeatedly (5)

pollution the contamination of water, air, or land through the actions of people in an industrialized society (2)

positioning the development of a product image in buyers' minds relative to the images they have of competing products (14)

possession utility utility that is created by transferring title (or ownership) of a product to the buyer (11)

posting the process of transferring journal entries to the general ledger (16)

power of attorney a legal document that serves as evidence that an agent has been appointed to act on behalf of a principal (21)

pre-emptive rights the rights of current stockholders to purchase any new stock that the corporation issues before it is sold to the general public (18)

preferred provider organizations (PPOs) offer the services of doctors and hospitals at discount rates or give breaks in copayments and deductibles (20)

preferred stock stock whose owners usually do not have voting rights, but whose claims on dividends and assets precede those of common-stock owners (3, 18)

premium a gift that a producer offers the customer in return for using its product (14)

premium the fee charged by an insurance company (20)

prepaid expenses assets that have been paid for in advance but not yet used (16)

press conference a meeting at which invited media personnel hear important news announcements and receive supplementary textual materials and photographs (14)

prestige pricing the strategy of setting a high price to project an aura of quality and status (12)

price the amount of money that a seller is willing to accept in exchange for a product, at a given time and under given circumstances (12)

price competition an emphasis on setting a price equal to or lower than competitors' to gain sales or market share (12)

price discrimination the practice in which producers and wholesalers charge larger firms a lower price for goods than they charge smaller firms (22)

price fixing an agreement between two businesses as to the prices to be charged for goods (22)

price lining the strategy of selling goods only at certain predetermined prices that reflect definite price breaks (12)

price skimming the strategy of charging the highest-possible price for a product during the introduction stage of its life cycle (12)

primary market a market in which an investor purchases financial securities (via an investment bank or other representative) from the issuer of those securities (19)

primary-demand advertising advertising whose purpose is to increase the demand for all brands of a good or service (14)

prime interest rate the lowest rate charged by a bank for a short-term loan (18)

principle of indemnity In the event of a loss, an insured firm or individual cannot collect, from the insurer, an amount greater than the actual dollar amount of the loss. (20)

private accountant an accountant who is employed by a specific organization (16)

private law the body of law that governs the relationships between two or more individuals or businesses (21)

process material a material that is used directly in the production of another product and is not readily identifiable in the finished product (12)

product everything that one receives in an exchange, including all tangible and intangible attributes and expected benefits; it may be a good, service, or idea (12)

product deletion the elimination of one or more products from a product line (12)

product design the process of creating a set of specifications from which a product can be produced (7)

product differentiation the process of developing and promoting differences between one's product and all similar products (12)

product liability insurance insurance that protects the policyholder from financial losses due to injuries suffered by others as a result of using the policyholder's products (20)

product life cycle a series of stages in which a product's sales revenue and profit increase, reach a peak, and then decline (12)

product line a group of similar products that differ only in relatively minor characteristics (7)

product line a group of similar products that differ only in relatively minor characteristics (12)

product mix all the products that a firm offers for sale (12)

product modification the process of changing one or more of a product's characteristics (12)

production the process of converting resources into goods, services, or ideas (7)

productivity the average level of output per unit of time per worker (1, 7)

productivity the average output per hour for all workers in the private business sector (5)

profit what remains after all business expenses have been deducted from sales revenue (1)

profit sharing the distribution of a percentage of the firm's profit among its employees (9)

progressive tax a tax that requires the payment of an increasing proportion of income as the individual's income increases (22)

promissory note a written pledge by a borrower to pay a certain sum of money to a creditor at a specified future date (18)

promotion communication that is intended to inform, persuade, or remind an organization's target markets of the organization or its products (14)

promotion mix the particular combination of promotion methods that a firm uses in its promotional campaign to reach a target market (14)

promotional campaign a plan for combining and using the four promotion methods— advertising, personal selling, sales promotion,

owned and operated for profit and is not dominant in its field (4)

Small Business Administration (SBA) a governmental agency that assists, counsels, and protects the interests of small businesses in the United States (4)

Small Business Development Center (SBDC) a university-based group that provides individual counseling and practical training to owners of small businesses (4)

Small Business Institute (SBI) a group of senior and graduate students in business administration who provide management counseling to small businesses (4)

Small Business Investment Company (SBIC) a privately owned firm that provides venture capital to small enterprises that meet its investment standards (4)

social audit a comprehensive report of what an organization has done, and is doing, with regard to social issues that affect it (2)

social needs the human requirements for love and affection and a sense of belonging (8)

social responsibility the recognition that business activities have an impact on society, and the consideration of that impact in business decision making (2)

socioeconomic model of social responsibility the concept that business should emphasize not only profits, but the impact of its decisions on society (2)

software the set of instructions that tells a computer what to do (15)

sole proprietorship a business that is owned (and usually operated) by one person (3)

span of management (or span of control) the number of subordinates who report directly to one manager (6)

specialization the separation of a manufacturing process into distinct tasks and the assignment of different tasks to different individuals (1)

specialty product an item that possesses one or more unique characteristics for which a significant group of buyers is willing to expend considerable purchasing effort (12)

specialty store a retail outlet that sells a single category of merchandise (13)

specialty-line wholesaler a middleman that carries a select group of products within a single line (13)

specific performance the legal requirement that the parties to a contract fulfill their obligations according to the contract (as opposed to settlement via payment of damages) (21)

speculative investment an investment that is made in the hope of earning a relatively large profit in a short time (19)

speculative risk a risk that accompanies the possibility of earning a profit (20)

spot trading the buying and selling of commodities for immediate delivery (19)

spreadsheet program a software package that allows the user to organize numerical data into a grid of rows and columns (15)

staff management position a position created to provide support, advice, and expertise within an organization (6)

standard of living a loose, subjective measure of how well off an individual or a society is, mainly in terms of want satisfaction through goods and services (1)

standard operating procedure (SOP) a plan that outlines the steps to be taken in a situation that arises again and again (5)

standing committee a relatively permanent committee charged with performing some recurring task (6)

state bank a commercial bank that is chartered by the banking authorities in the state in which it operates (17)

statistic a measure that summarizes a particular characteristic for an entire group of numbers (15)

statute a law that is passed by the U.S. Congress, a state legislature, or a local government (21)

statutory law all the laws that have been enacted by legislative bodies (21)

stock the shares of ownership of a corporation (3)

stock average (or stock index) an average of the current market prices of selected stocks (19)

stock dividend a dividend in the form of additional stock (19)

stock insurance company an insurance company that is owned by stockholders and is operated to earn a profit (20)

stock split the division of each outstanding share of a corporation's stock into a greater number of shares (19)

stockholder a person who owns a corporation's stock (3)

store (or private) brand a brand that is owned by an individual wholesaler or retailer (12)

store of value a means for retaining and accumulating wealth (17)

strategy an organization's broadest set of plans,

developed as a guide for major policy setting and decision making; it defines what business the company is in or wants to be in and the kind of company it is or wants to be (5)

strict product liability the legal concept that holds that a manufacturer is responsible for injuries caused by its products even if it was not negligent (21)

strike a temporary work stoppage by employees, calculated to add force to their demands (10)

strikebreaker a nonunion employee who performs the job of a striking union member (10)

supermarket a large self-service store that sells primarily food and household products (13)

superstore a large retail store that carries not only food and nonfood products ordinarily found in supermarkets but also additional product lines (13)

supply an item that facilitates production and operations but does not become part of the finished product (12)

supply the quantity of a product that producers are willing to sell at each of various prices (1, 12)

syndicate a temporary association of individuals or firms, organized to perform a specific task that requires a large amount of capital (3)

tabular display a display used to present verbal or numerical information in columns and rows (15)

tactical plan a small-scale, short-range plan developed to implement a strategy (5)

target market a group of persons for whom a firm develops and maintains a marketing mix suitable for the specific needs and preferences of that group (11)

task force a committee established to investigate a major problem or pending decision (6)

technical salesperson a salesperson who assists the company's current customers in technical matters (14)

technical skill a specific skill needed to accomplish a specialized activity (5)

technology the knowledge and process required to transform input resources into outputs such as specific products (7)

term life insurance life insurance that provides protection to beneficiaries for a stated period of time (20)

term-loan agreement a promissory note that requires a borrower to repay a loan in monthly, quarterly, semiannual, or annual installments (18)

Theory X a concept of employee motivation generally consistent with Taylor's scientific management; assumes that employees dislike work and will function only in a highly controlled work environment (8)

Theory Y a concept of employee motivation generally consistent with the ideas of the human relations movement; assumes that employees accept responsibility and work toward organizational goals if by so doing they also achieve personal rewards (8)

Theory Z the belief that some middle ground between Ouchi's Type A and Type J practices is best for American business (8)

time deposit an amount that is on deposit in an interest-bearing savings account (17)

time utility utility that is created by making a product available when customers wish to purchase it (11)

top manager an upper-level executive who guides and controls the overall fortunes of the organization (5)

tort a violation of a private law (21)

total cost the sum of the fixed costs and the variable costs attributed to a product (12)

total market approach a single marketing mix directed at the entire market for a particular product (11)

total quality management the coordination of efforts directed at improving customer satisfaction, increasing employee participation and empowerment, forming and strengthening supplier partnerships, and facilitating an organization atmosphere of continuous quality improvement. (5)

total revenue the total amount received from sales of a product (12)

trade credit a payment delay that a supplier grants to its customers (18)

trade deficit an unfavorable balance of trade (23)

trade name the complete and legal name of an organization (12)

trade sales promotion method a sales promotion method designed to encourage wholesalers and retailers to stock and actively promote a manufacturer's product (14)

trade salesperson a salesperson—generally employed by a food producer or processor—who assists customers in promoting products, especially in retail stores (14)

trade show an industrywide exhibit at which many sellers display their products (14)

trademark a brand that is registered with the

U.S. Patent and Trademark Office and is thus legally protected from use by anyone except its owner (12, 21)

transportation the shipment of products to customers (13)

trial balance a summary of the balances of all general ledger accounts at the end of the accounting period (16)

trust a business combination that is created when one firm obtains control of competing firms by purchasing their stock or their assets (22)

trustee an independent firm or individual that acts as the bond owners' representative (18)

tying agreement a contract that forces an intermediary to purchase unwanted products along with the products it actually wants to buy (22)

Uniform Commercial Code (UCC) a set of laws designed to eliminate differences among state regulations affecting business and to simplify interstate commerce (21)

uninsurable risk a risk that insurance firms will not assume (20)

union security protection of the union's position as the employees' bargaining agent (10)

union shop a workplace in which new employees must join the union after a specified probationary period (10)

union-management (or labor) relations the dealings between labor unions and business management, both in the bargaining process and beyond it (10)

universal life insurance life insurance that combines insurance protection with an investment plan that offers a potentially greater return than that guaranteed by a whole life insurance policy (20)

unlimited liability a legal concept that holds a sole proprietor personally responsible for all the debts of his or her business (3)

unsecured financing financing that is not backed by collateral (18)

usury the practice of charging interest in excess of the maximum legal rate (21)

utility the ability of a good or service to satisfy a human need (7, 11)

variable cost a cost that depends on the number of units produced (12)

venture capital money that is invested in small (and sometimes struggling) firms that have the potential to become very successful (4)

vertical channel integration the combining of two or more stages of a distribution channel under a single firm's management (13)

vertical marketing system (VMS) a centrally managed distribution channel resulting from vertical channel integration (13)

visual display a diagram that represents several items of information in a manner that makes comparison easier or reflects trends among the items (15)

voluntary agreement a contract requirement consisting of an offer by one party to enter into a contract with a second party and acceptance by the second party of all the terms and conditions of the offer (21)

voluntary bankruptcy a bankruptcy procedure initiated by an individual or business that can no longer meet its financial obligations (21)

wage survey a collection of data on prevailing wage rates within an industry or a geographic area (9)

warehouse store a minimal-service retail food outlet (13)

warehousing the set of activities that are involved in receiving and storing goods and preparing them for reshipment (13)

wheel of retailing a hypothesis that suggests that new retail operations usually begin at the bottom—in price, profits, and prestige—and gradually evolve up the cost/price scale, competing with newer business

whistle blowing informing the press or government officials about unethical practices within one's organization (2)

whole life insurance life insurance that provides both protection and savings (20)

wholesaler a middleman that sells products to other firms (13)

wildcat strike a strike that has not been approved by the strikers' union (10)

word processing program a software package that allows the user to store documents (letters, memos, reports) in the computer memory or on a disk (15)

worker's compensation insurance insurance that covers medical expenses and provides salary continuation for employees who are injured while they are at work (20)

working capital the difference between current assets and current liabilities (16)

workplace diversity see **cultural diversity**

zero-based budgeting a budgeting approach in which every expense must be justified in every budget (18)

Name Index

Subject Index

5 INFORMATION FOR BUSINESS

62 40% of Americans under 30 say they read a daily newspaper

63 65% of Americans over 50 say they read a daily newspaper

64 The Swiss Army maintains 20,000 carrier pigeons for emergency communications in wartime

65 There is a 1 in 39 chance that a tax return filed by a U.S. corporation will be audited

66 In 1991, 12 U.S. companies with assets of $1 billion or more filed for bankruptcy

67 It is estimated that the IRS loses approximately 2,000,000 documents each year

6 FINANCE AND INVESTMENT

68 Since 1989, net purchases of U.S. Treasury securities by U.S. banks have increased 35%

69 Since 1989, net purchases of U.S. Treasury securities by Japanese banks have decreased 34%

70 In 1990, Moody's downgraded 4 corporate bonds for every 1 that it upgraded

71 In 1984, the ratio of downgraded to upgraded corporate bonds was 1:1

72 In 1990, the stocks of the funeral industry earned the highest return

73 There is a 50% chance that an American's credit record contains errors

74 30% of the business loans made in 1990 in the U.S. were made by foreign-owned banks

75 There was an average of 12 business mergers every business day in the 1980s

76 An average of 173 companies per day filed for bankruptcy in 1989

77 The price of a seat on the New York Stock Exchange has dropped 38% since 1987

78 Since 1989, U.S. investments in foreign stocks and bonds have increased 68%

79 Since 1988, the number of American college students who have their own credit cards has increased 37%

7 THE BUSINESS ENVIRONMENT AND INTERNATIONAL ISSUES

80 Tupperware sales in Japan in 1991 were $100,000,000

81 Romania has launched 1,000 new periodicals since 1989

82 150,416 miles of fiber-optic cable were laid last year worldwide

83 Since 1990, U.S. tobacco sales to the countries that were in the former Soviet Union have increased 73%

84 In 1991, 6 shopping malls per month opened in Japan

85 During the war with Iraq, 9,905 businesses in the U.S. failed

86 Of the world's 5 largest record companies, only 1 is owned by Americans

87 In 1990, Germany's foreign trade surplus dropped 90%

88 In 1990, Japanese companies donated an estimated $300,000,000 to American charities

89 Japan has invested the same amount in Latin America as it has in Asia

90 The Gates Rubber Company of Dumfries, Scotland, sold 3,000 Wellington boots for cows in 1989

91 In the 6 months following the fall of the Berlin Wall, 7 dating service agencies opened up in Magdeburg, in formerly East Germany

92 There are 27 7-Eleven stores per 1,000 square miles in Japan

93 There are 2 7-Eleven stores per 1,000 square miles in the U.S.